West's Law School Advisory Board

PRINCIPLES OF LEGAL RESEARCH

Successor to
How to Find the Law, 9th Edition

By

Kent C. Olson
Director of Reference, Research and Instruction
University of Virginia Law Library

CONCISE HORNBOOK SERIES®

A Thomson Reuters business

Mat #13349932

Concise Hornbook Series and Westlaw are trademarks registered in the U.S. Patent and Trademark Office.

© 2009 Thomson Reuters

> 610 Opperman Drive
> St. Paul, MN 55123
> 1–800–313–9378

Printed in the United States of America

ISBN: 978–0–314–21192–7

For Morris

*

Preface

This text began life as a long-overdue revision of *How to Find the Law*, a venerable work that was first published in 1931 but had not been revised since 1989. It still bears some genetic imprint of that work, but the world of legal research has changed just a bit in the past twenty years. The primacy of printed materials in law libraries is long gone, microform has become a delivery vehicle of last resort, and even the dependence on subscription databases is fading as government and academic websites take more responsibility for disseminating the primary and secondary sources of the law.

Not everything, however, has been digitized or is available free online, and a thorough legal researcher needs to be familiar with both online and print materials as well as both free and subscription online resources. This book provides an overview of all of these resources. It includes a bit more historical background than some researchers may feel they need, but the footnotes may provide a sense of the continuum from printed to electronic research as well as leads to further reading.

This work is written as a guide for practicing researchers and covers some eight hundred resources (publications and websites), far more than a beginning student needs but fewer than experienced legal researchers encounter in their careers. It is arranged differently from many legal research texts and doesn't prescribe a single path for learning about legal information. The organization is based on the treatment of the branches of government in the Constitution. The legislature is discussed first, followed by the executive branch and then the judiciary. This is followed finally by treatment of secondary and reference sources. Secondary sources are often the easiest place to begin research, but to understand them you need to know something about the primary sources they discuss. The material is suitable for use in a legal research course, but assigned readings may swerve wildly from chapter to chapter.

The first twelve chapters focus on research in United States law. The final two chapters provide a brief treatment of international and foreign legal research, because no modern practice is untouched by globalization. The treatment of international and foreign resources is relatively cursory, providing basic information and leads to several of the more detailed resources available.

Even though most researchers do the overwhelming majority of their research online, most of the illustrations in this book are still based on printed sources or online PDF files rather than screenshots of websites. The simple reason is that a browser window makes a relatively poor book illustration. Its information is unlocked by scrolling and by clicking from one site to another. A printed page still conveys a lot more information in one image.

Any book is already becoming obsolete as soon as it is published, and this is certainly true of one with references to hundreds of websites. All links were current and active as of April 2009, but some will undoubtedly disappear or migrate. For this purpose, and to save the trouble of typing lengthy URLs, a regularly updated list of links to every site in this book is available through the University of Virginia Law Library website <www. law.virginia.edu/plr>.

In preparing this volume I benefited greatly from the help of numerous colleagues. Virginia Wise of the Harvard Law School began the revision project and then graciously turned her notes over to me. Leslie Ashbrook, Kristin Glover and Amy Wharton, my colleagues at the University of Virginia Law Library, read every chapter, found most of my typos, and made countless excellent suggestions. Ben Doherty did the same for the international and foreign law chapters, and also covered for me in class and at the reference desk so that I could finish the project. Pavani Reddy, UVA Law '06, helped me to think a bit more visually about information.

A number of librarians have also played major inspirational roles. Joan Jurale at Wesleyan University first shared with me the satisfactions of helping people find information, steering me towards my eventual career path. Tom Woxland at the University of Minnesota gave me a start in law librarianship, and Bob Berring at the University of California brought out my interest in writing about legal research. Larry Wenger and Taylor Fitchett, my library directors at the University of Virginia, have been wonderfully supportive of my focusing so much time and attention on this and earlier publications.

The greatest of these, though, is my good friend Morris Cohen, professor emeritus and retired librarian of the Yale Law School. Morris is truly the godfather of legal bibliography, and legal research is just one aspect of his wide-ranging interests. In his ninth decade he still approaches life with more joy and curiosity than just about anyone I've met. I was a law student in 1984 when I first had the chance to work with Morris, updating two chapters of his *Legal Research in a Nutshell*. A few years later he took me on as a coauthor, and it is my great honor to strive here to be a worthy successor.

KENT C. OLSON

Charlottesville, Virginia
April 2009

Summary of Contents

*

Table of Contents

PRINCIPLES OF LEGAL RESEARCH

Successor to
How to Find the Law, 9th Edition

*

Chapter 1

INTRODUCTION: CONTEXT AND PROCESS

Table of Sections

The modern world is awash in information. The millions of published books have been supplemented by billions of web pages, many of which provide access to copies of documents that would once have been inaccessible or nearly impossible to obtain. Navigating successfully through this sea of information is necessary for developing knowledge of a legal topic, and legal knowledge is a key component of competent representation.[1]

Legal research is the skill of successful navigation, the ability to craft searches that identify the necessary documents and ensure

---

1. Rule 1.1 of the Model Rules of Professional Conduct provides that a lawyer "shall provide competent representation to a client. Competent representation requires the legal knowledge, skill, thoroughness and preparation reasonably necessary for the representation." See Carol M. Bast & Susan W. Harrell, *Ethical Obligations: Performing Adequate Legal Research and Legal Writing*, 29 Nova L. Rev. 49 (2004). Ellie Margolis, *Surfin' Safari—Why Competent Researchers Should Research on the Web*, 10 Yale J.L. & Tech. 82 (2007), summarizes several cases on the problems of incompetent representation.

that significant information is not overlooked. It involves successful use of online and print resources, and a mastery of a variety of specialized procedures. Research identifies the rules that govern an activity and finds materials that explain, analyze or criticize those rules. These resources yield the knowledge necessary to provide accurate and insightful advice, to draft effective documents, or to defend a client's (or one's own) rights in court.

Finding relevant information is only the first step towards competent representation. Analyzing that information, understanding its significance, and applying it to a new situation are essential components of the research process.[2]

The way in which people find information has changed dramatically in recent years. Commentators have discussed a "sea change" or "paradigm shift" from subject-based research in books to keyword searching by computer.[3] But awareness of the range of available information is more important than ever for successful research. You have to know the landscape in order to understand what you've found, and to know whether other relevant materials may yet be undiscovered.

§ 1.1   The U.S. Legal System

Several aspects of the American legal system shape the process of legal research:

— The basic parameters are determined by the Constitution of the United States, which created a federal system with both national and state governments making laws.

— The federal and state constitutions all divide lawmaking power among legislative, executive, and judicial branches.

— The United States is part of the *common law* legal tradition, in which the law adapts and grows through the decisions of the courts.

— In both practice and scholarship, the law is divided into numerous doctrinal areas. The boundaries between these areas can overlap, but each has its own distinct rules and literature.

---

2.   Michael Lynch has explained the importance of legal research particularly well: " 'Legal research' is not merely a search for information; it is primarily a struggle for understanding. The need to think deeply about the information discovered is what makes legal research the task of a professional lawyer." Michael J. Lynch, *An Impossible Task but Everybody Has to Do It—Teaching Legal Re-* *search in Law Schools*, 89 LAW LIBR. J. 415, 415 (1997).

3.   See, e.g., Carol M. Bast & Ransford C. Pyle, *Legal Research in the Computer Age: A Paradigm Shift?*, 93 LAW LIBR. J. 285 (2001); Carrie W. Teitcher, *Rebooting the Approach to Teaching Research: Embracing the Computer Age*, 99 LAW LIBR. J. 555 (2007).

Federalism. Instead of having a single government creating the law to be enforced throughout the country, the United States is comprised of fifty states (and numerous tribal governments)[4] that create laws governing their citizens. The federal government has only the limited, specific powers granted to it under the Constitution, and the Tenth Amendment provides: "The powers not delegated to the United States by the Constitution, nor prohibited by it to the States, are reserved to the States respectively, or to the people." Many major areas of law, such as commercial law, criminal law, and family law, are governed primarily by state law and can differ dramatically between jurisdictions.

Federal law, of course, governs a wide range of activity under Article 1, Section 8 of the Constitution, such as the powers to collect taxes, to provide for the general welfare, and to regulate interstate commerce. Over the past century, federal legislation has come to encompass an ever wider area of activity. Article VI, the Supremacy Clause, declares that the Constitution and laws made in pursuance thereof are the supreme law of the land, and that federal law governs in case of conflict between federal and state laws.[5]

Three Branches of Government. Both federal and state governments are divided into legislative, executive, and judicial branches.

— The Legislature. As the elected voice of the citizens, the legislature is the primary lawmaking body of government. It raises and spends money, defines crimes, regulates commerce, and generally determines public policy by enacting statutes. Because statute drafters can rarely foresee all the situations to which their work may apply, it has usually been necessary for the courts to interpret, clarify and explain statutory language in the course of resolving legal controversies.

— The Executive. The executive branch consists of the president or governor, as well as most government agencies. The president's "executive power of the government" under Article II of the Constitution means that this branch is charged with enforcing the law. In order to do so fairly and predictably, it creates legally binding rules and standards in a variety of ways. The president and most governors issue executive orders, and administrative agencies provide detailed regulations governing activity within their areas of

4. Native Americans have sovereign rights of self-government, including the power to pass laws and have court systems. Native American tribes are generally subject to federal law but not to state law, except under limited circumstances. See *California v. Cabazon Band of Mission Indians*, 480 U.S. 202 (1987). Reference resources include AMERICAN IN-DIAN LAW DESKBOOK (Clay Smith ed., 3d ed. 2004–date) and ENCYCLOPEDIA OF UNITED STATES INDIAN LAW AND POLICY (Paul Finkelman & Tim Alan Garrison eds., 2009).

5. For more information, see, e.g., FEDERALISM IN AMERICA: AN ENCYCLOPEDIA (Joseph R. Marbach et al., 2006).

expertise. Agencies also act in a "quasi-judicial" capacity by conducting hearings and issuing decisions to resolve particular disputes. These *administrative law* sources are frequently less well publicized than statutes and court decisions, but they may be just as important in determining legal rights and responsibilities. Attorneys in heavily regulated areas such as securities law or telecommunications may work more frequently with agency pronouncements than with legislative enactments.

— The Judiciary. The judicial branch plays a complex role in this system. Judges apply the language of constitutions and statutes to court cases, which often involve circumstances that were not foreseen when the laws were enacted. These judicial interpretations can become as important as the text of the provisions they interpret. The courts have determined, for example, that sexual harassment is a form of employment discrimination under the Civil Rights Act of 1964 even though those words do not appear in the statute. Through the power of *judicial review*, asserted by Chief Justice John Marshall in the landmark case of *Marbury v. Madison*,[6] the courts also determine whether the acts of the legislative and executive branches are within the scope of their constitutional authority.

The Common Law. In the common law system that the American colonists brought from Great Britain, the law is expressed in an evolving body of doctrine determined by judges in specific cases, rather than through the *civil law* paradigm of a group of codified abstract principles. As established rules are adapted to meet new situations, the common law grows and changes over time.[7]

An essential element of the common law is the doctrine of precedent, or *stare decisis* ("let the decision stand"). Under this doctrine, courts are bound to follow earlier decisions. These provide guidance to later courts faced with similar cases, and aid in preventing further disputes. People can study earlier cases, evaluate the legal impact of planned conduct, and modify their behavior to conform to existing rules. Precedent is designed to provide both fairness and stability. People similarly situated are similarly dealt with, and judgments are consistent, rather than arbitrary, so that the consequences of contemplated conduct can be predicted by referring to the treatment afforded similar conduct in the past.

It is the importance of judicial decisions as precedent that gives them such a vital place in American legal research. The prece-

---

6. 5 U.S. (1 Cranch) 137 (1803).

7. On the various meanings of "the common law," see Morris L. Cohen, *The Common Law in the American Legal*

System: The Challenge of Conceptual Research, 81 LAW LIBR. J. 13 (1989), and works cited therein.

dential value of a decision is determined in large part by a court's place in the judicial hierarchy. Each court system, federal and state, has a system of trial and appellate courts, with a *court of last resort* that creates rules that are binding on the lower courts in the system. A central function of courts of last resort and other appellate courts is establishing rules of conduct for society, as well as simply determining the rights of the parties appearing before them.

Decisions from a higher court in a given jurisdiction are binding or *mandatory authority*, and must be followed by a lower court in the same jurisdiction. Decisions from courts in *other* jurisdictions are not binding, but may be very useful if a court in another state has considered a situation similar to that in issue. A decision that is not binding in a jurisdiction is called *persuasive authority*. A court may choose to follow its lead and reach a similar conclusion, or it may consider it inapplicable or poorly reasoned and arrive at a very different result.

Doctrinal Areas. Legal scholarship and the law school curriculum sort legal issues into distinct areas of doctrine such as contract, criminal law, property, and torts. Most legal problems also involve both *substance*, the rules governing the underlying activity, and *procedure*, the rules governing the ways in which legal proceedings are conducted. These classifications provide a framework for analyzing legal situations and applying a particular body of rules. Legal materials also follow this paradigm, and treatises and other resources focus on specific fields such as torts or federal civil procedure. Being able to analyze a problem's doctrinal areas is key to knowing where to look for answers.[8]

It is necessary, however, to learn how to classify an issue without pigeonholing it too narrowly. Analysis within a particular doctrinal field can clarify a specific issue, but most situations contain issues from a number of substantive and procedural areas. Analogous problems in other areas of law can also provide clarification and guidance in analyzing a novel or undecided legal issue.

§ 1.2   The Forms of Legal Information

Most research these days is conducted on the Internet, but law is unique in that many historical sources from decades or centuries ago continue to have just as much validity as the latest material available online. A medical text from the eighteenth century has

---

8. Works offering an introductory overview of the doctrinal areas of American law include FUNDAMENTALS OF AMERICAN LAW (Alan B. Morrison ed., 1996); INTRODUCTION TO THE LAW OF THE UNITED STATES (David S. Clark & Tuğrul Ansay eds., 2d ed. 2002); and PETER HAY, LAW OF THE UNITED STATES: AN OVERVIEW (2d ed. 2005). The latter works are written primarily as comparative works for foreign lawyers.

little current value, but a judicial decision or statute from that period can still be binding law today. In addition, law has a crucial dichotomy between primary and secondary sources that must be understood by the successful researcher.

(a) Current and Historical Information

The legal system is created over the course of time, and the law in force today is a combination of old and new enactments and decisions. The United States Constitution has been in force for more than 200 years, and many judicial doctrines can be traced back even farther. Other laws are just days or weeks old, as legislatures, courts, and executive agencies address issues of current concern.

These laws have been published as they were issued, whether in volumes of legislative acts or court reports, or through electronic dissemination. They retain their force and effect until they are expressly repealed or overruled. A large law library contains sets with hundreds of volumes of chronologically published statutes and decisions. The need for subject access to this vast body of information has led to the creation of several important resources. Today the most widely used approach is keyword searching in databases containing the full text of thousands of court decisions or other documents. Many of these databases also provide indexing and classification systems allowing for documents to be found by subject as well as keyword. More traditional means of access to court opinions include *digests* classifying summaries of points from cases; *encyclopedias* and *treatises* summarizing and comparing similar cases; and *citators* that can be used to trace doctrines forward in time.

Statutes and regulations in force are arranged by subject in codes, which are accessible online by keyword or in print through extensive indexes. Even laws that were repealed years ago, however, may still be important in resolving disputes. Interpreting a deed or will, for example, may require finding the statutes in force when it was drafted. To determine the law that governs a particular situation, you may need to examine a wide range of both current and historical sources. Older materials are increasingly being digitized, but thorough research may still require access to documents available only in print.

Lawyers and others interested in the legal system also need to keep up with new developments, and an extensive body of resources exists to provide current information. New statutes, regulations, and court decisions are issued by the government and by commercial publishers, both in print and electronically. Newsletters, looseleaf services, websites, and blogs provide notice of and analyze these new developments. In addition, the codes and texts lawyers use are updated regularly to reflect changes. New documents can be incorporated into databases within minutes of their release. Many print publications are updated through the use of *pocket parts*, supplements which fit inside the back covers of bound volumes, while others are issued in looseleaf binders and updated with supplementary inserts or replacement pages. No matter what type of resource is used, electronic or print, it is essential to verify that it provides current information.

(b) Primary and Secondary Sources

Legal research makes an important distinction between *primary* and *secondary sources*. Primary sources are the official pronouncements of the governmental lawmakers: the court decisions, legislation, and regulations that form the basis of legal doctrine. Secondary sources are works which are not themselves law, but which discuss or analyze legal doctrine.[9] Whether primary or secondary source, each document must be used with a sense of its place in the hierarchy of authority.

Not all primary sources have the same force for all purposes. A decision from a state supreme court is mandatory authority in its jurisdiction and must be followed by the lower state courts. A state statute also must be followed within the state. Other primary sources are only persuasive authority; a court in one state may be influenced by decisions in other states faced with similar issues, but it is free to make up its own mind. A statute or regulation from one state is not even persuasive authority in another state.

Secondary sources include treatises, hornbooks, *Restatements*, practice manuals, and the academic journals known as *law reviews*. Secondary sources serve a number of important functions in legal research. Scholarly commentaries can have a persuasive influence on the law-making process by pointing out problems in current legal doctrine and suggesting solutions. More often, they serve to clarify the bewildering array of statutes and court decisions, or they provide current awareness about developing legal doctrines. Finally, their footnotes provide extensive references to primary sources and to other secondary material.

A secondary source is not a primary authority and cannot be binding, but it may have more persuasive force than rulings of courts in other jurisdictions. Even primary and secondary sources that are not persuasive authority can be useful research resources, because their references can help analyze a problem and can

9. This sense of the terms "primary" and "secondary" is different from that found in history and other disciplines, where a "primary source" can be a letter or contemporary newspaper account while a "secondary source" is a later scholarly analysis.

provide fruitful research leads through references to both primary and other secondary sources.

Resources in disciplines other than law are also essential in legal research. In the 1800s and early 1900s, American judicial opinions typically cited only legal authorities in support of their conclusions. Many modern judicial opinions, however, articulate quite clearly the social, economic, political and even psychological consequences with which they are concerned. Law has become an interdisciplinary study, and research in materials considered "non-legal" is an inherent part of legal research.

§ 1.3   Research Methods

Legal research is different from scholarly research in other disciplines. Most legal research problems do not require a comprehensive review of the literature in an area, but instead seek to solve specific problems. The history or development of a rule of law is usually less important than what that rule says today in regard to a very specific question.

Applying rules of law to a specific fact situation is the process of legal analysis, and requires determining the scope and meaning of various rules and determining how they pertain in a given situation. Legal research is not simply gathering information, but being able to analyze that information and grasp its significance. It is a process that requires a significant commitment of time and focus.[10]

This section discusses research methods in both electronic and print materials. Electronic research has several obvious advantages over print resources. The computer can integrate a variety of tasks that were once conducted with separate print sources, such as finding cases, checking the current validity of their holdings, and tracking down secondary commentary. An online database can have much more current information than a print source, and can be updated much more frequently. The ability to search the full text of documents for specific combinations of words makes it easy to find documents which address a specific confluence of factual and legal topics. Hyperlinks between documents allow you to follow lines of authority and reasoning, from a case to a secondary source, for example, and from there to another secondary source or statute.

Yet researchers forced to work only with an uncontrolled mass of electronic data can quickly find themselves drowning in unsorted information. Secondary sources such as treatises and encyclopedias are still invaluable starting points to understand the terminology

---

10. See *Williams v. Leeke*, 584 F.2d 1336, 1340 (4th Cir. 1978), *cert. denied*, 442 U.S. 911 (1979) ("We believe that meaningful legal research on most legal problems cannot be done in forty-five minute intervals.").

and parameters of an area of law. An online keyword search finds only those documents that match its terms and misses related documents that use different terms or involve slightly different facts.

No single process will work for all research situations. With experience comes an understanding of which resources to consult first in each situation. Experienced researchers know which sources are authoritative or useful for what purposes, and how to use these sources most effectively. Versatility and flexibility are needed.

(a) Finding Legal Information on the Internet

A quest for legal information often begins with a general search on the Internet, in large part because it is free and readily available. Indeed, the Internet can provide a great deal of useful information, but it is important to know how to use it effectively and to understand its limitations. There are more focused ways to find information than using a general search engine's basic search screen, and much information is not available online in free databases. Just as a doctor must do more than a quick Google search before prescribing a course of treatment, a competent legal researcher needs to find the correct answers—not just some information. Legal literature has a complex structure, but it is designed to lead you to the answers you need.

Free Internet sites, particularly those provided by the federal and state governments, can be valuable sources of legal information. Statutes and regulations in force for most jurisdictions are available free online, as is a growing body of case law. Among the most useful sites are those providing access to previously hard-to-find resources such as legislative documents, administrative agency materials, and court documents. The Internet also provides an invaluable means of linking scholars and researchers through websites, blogs, and electronic mail.

When using information from free Internet sites, it is essential to evaluate the currency and accuracy of the resource. Even government sites can present obsolete information without indicating that it is no longer current, and other websites can be biased, selective in coverage, or dangerously out of date. Verifying that a website is current, accurate, and impartial leads to greater confidence in the information it contains.[11]

---

11. The University of California Berkeley Library provides an excellent and regularly updated online guide, *Evaluating Web Pages: Techniques to Apply & Questions to Ask* <www. lib.berkeley.edu/TeachingLib/Guides/ Internet/Evaluate.html>.

Another problem with free Internet sites is that material can be available one day but disappear the next.[12] URLs can change frequently, so be patient in trying to find cited information on a website. Hunting around the site or running a site-specific search can often locate material that has been moved and assigned a different URL, but sometimes material has been removed and is no longer accessible. The Internet Archive's Wayback Machine <www. archive.org> and repositories for dead websites such as CyberCemetery <govinfo.library.unt.edu> provide some access to "obsolete" information, but this remains an unsolved problem.

The Internet can be approached in several ways. Search engines, directories, and other resources all have their uses and advantages in legal research.

(1) Search Engines

Most people's first stop on the Internet is a search engine, a service with a box in which to type keywords.[13] This is often a very sensible approach, because a simple search can frequently lead directly to the necessary information. This is particularly true if you are looking for specific factual information or for the website of a particular institution or organization.

Simple Internet searches are a place to start, but they rarely provide thorough and reliable answers to most legal questions. Sources of the law are too diverse and complex for a search engine to pick out authoritative documents from the mass of information available online. A search is ideal for finding specific documents or answering factual questions, but familiarity with more specialized sites is necessary for most successful legal research.

A number of search engines are available, with features that are evolving over time. The market is currently dominated by Google <www.google.com>, although several other major search engines such as Yahoo! <search.yahoo.com>, Ask <ask.com>, and Live Search <live.com> are also available. Several sites provide comparisons of the scope and features of major search engines. A comparison of major search engines is available at Search Engine

---

12. A study in 2002 found that only 30% of URLs in law review citations still worked after four years. Mary Rumsey, *Runaway Train: Problems of Permanence, Accessibility, and Stability in the Use of Web Sources in Law Review Citations*, 94 LAW LIBR. J. 27 (2002). More recent studies in other disciplines have found similar problems with disappearing references. See, e.g., Edmund Russell & Jennifer Kane, *The Missing Link: Assessing the Reliability of Internet Citations in History Journals*, 49 TECH. & CULTURE 420 (2008); Carmine Sellitto,

The Impact of Impermanent Web–Located Citations: A Study of 123 Scholarly Conference Publications, 56 J. AM. SOC'Y INFO. SCI. & TECH. 695 (2005).

13. See Anthony Grafton, *Future Reading: Digitization and its Discontents*, NEW YORKER, Nov. 5, 2007, at 50, 52 ("Now even the most traditional-minded scholar generally begins by consulting a search engine. As a cheerful editor at Cambridge University Press recently told me, 'Conservatively, ninety-five per cent of all scholarly inquiries start at Google.' ")

Showdown <www.searchengineshowdown.com>, which includes a chart showing the features of each service.

Search engines focusing on legal materials are also available. Westlaw WebPlus, available only to Westlaw subscribers while logged in, is designed to focus more specifically on legal information. It can be reached through a "Search the Web" box in the corner of the database screen or by a link on the search results page, and provides options to search specifically for legal issues, government entities, persons, companies, or news. Search results are filtered so that government, educational and other legal information sites that complement Westlaw databases are listed first.

Lexis Web <www.lexisweb.com>, available in a beta version, also focuses on legal content, from sites validated by Lexis attorney editors. It offers options to narrow search results by legal topic, citation, legal terms, source, or file format. It can be used without logging in, but for subscribers it offers links to recommended content within Lexis databases in addition to free websites.

Search engines are designed to be simple, but you can achieve more professional results with just a small amount of sophistication. Being an advanced web searcher requires three simple attributes:

— **Know the search engine's syntax.** Each search engine has its own rules for how it combines terms and searches the web. Your results can be more focused if you can understand and manipulate how words are connected to reach a result. Simply typing a string of words into a box may not retrieve the same result as a search that combines terms in a specific way. Google, for example, assumes an "and" between search terms, but you can search for synonyms by using "OR" (capitalized), and you can exclude a term by putting a minus sign directly in front of it. Most search engines have "search tips" or help screens that provide examples.[14]

— **Use the "advanced search" screen.** Go beyond the basic search box and use the "advanced search" screen available from most search engines. Google's advanced search screen <www.google.com/advanced_search>, for example, provides very useful options such as specifying documents in a particular format, such as .pdf, or limiting retrieval to particular domains. Like using search syntax correctly, the advanced search screen allows you to be more specific about the types of material for which you are searching.

---

14. Search guidance tips are also available in books such as RANDOLPH HOCK, THE EXTREME SEARCHER'S INTERNET HANDBOOK (2d ed. 2007); MICHAEL MILLER, GOOGLEPEDIA: THE ULTIMATE GOOGLE RESOURCE (2006); or NIALL O'DOCHARTAIGH, INTERNET RESEARCH SKILLS (2007).

— **Use more than one search engine.** Despite the convenience of using a familiar search engine for most purposes, different search engines will reach different results—and a second search engine may find sites or documents that the first one missed. For most purposes, the familiar favorite is probably fine. But for extensive research or for those times when your favorite isn't turning up what you need, try another.

Metasearch engines such as Clusty <www.clusty.com> and Dogpile <www.dogpile.com> aggregate results from several search engines, but it is unclear whether results are more effective than those obtained from individual search engines. One way to compare search engines is to use GrabAll <www.graball.com>, which simultaneously displays results from two search engines of your choice in side-by-side frames.

It is important to recognize that search engines don't cover everything on the Internet, even everything available for free. Billions of pages of online information, known as the "deep web" or the "invisible web," are beyond the reach of even the most powerful search engine because they are inside databases and do not have fixed URLs. It is estimated that the "deep web" covers a trillion pages of information, while search engines can locate about 20 billion pages.[15] Reaching this information requires familiarity with and access to the databases or other repositories where it is held.

(2) Directories and Other Resources

It is also important to recognize that a search engine will not always find everything. Sometimes a web directory will provide leads to better sites than those that appear at the top of a list of search results. A directory is particularly valuable if you want to learn what resources are available. If you search, for example, for "Illinois Supreme Court," you may go to one site that has the court's decisions but never learn that another site may offer deeper coverage or more extensive search options. But a directory site listing Illinois legal resources will list these various alternatives and provide for easy comparison of the sites. Working just with a computer and your choice of keywords, you can often find useful and relevant information. But turning to experts in the area, whether through a web directory or a treatise or a digest, may turn up related information you didn't know to look for or didn't know was there.

Several general directories are available, including versions from the major search engines (e.g., <www.google.com/dirhp>, <dir.yahoo.com>), as well as more selective directories prepared by

---

15. Marcus P. Zillman, *Deep Web Research 2009*, LLRX.com (Dec. 28, 2008), <www.llrx.com/features/deepweb 2009.htm>.

librarians such as Infomine <infomine.ucr.edu> and the Librarians' Internet Index <lii.org>. Directories focusing on legal topics can do a better job of selecting quality law-related sites. Chief among these are FindLaw <www.findlaw.com> and Cornell Law School's Legal Information Institute <www.law.cornell.edu>. These sites provide links to primary sources, blogs, journals, and many other materials.

Other resources such as blogs and wikis can be useful in legal research, particularly early in the process when general information is needed. An article from Wikipedia <www.wikipedia.org> can quickly provide factual background information, although relying on such a source as authoritative may be problematic.[16]

(b) Using Subscription Databases

Two major commercial database systems, Westlaw <www.westlaw.com> and Lexis <www.lexis.com>, are widely used in law schools and in legal practice as comprehensive legal research tools. Westlaw and Lexis, however, are available only to subscribers and other paying customers. Law students generally have access through their schools' subscriptions, but for many researchers these resources can be prohibitively expensive.[17]

Other commercial online research systems may provide lower-cost alternatives to Westlaw and Lexis for access to primary sources. These systems generally provide reliable access to case law and statutes, but offer a smaller range of secondary sources and other features. Some of these, such as Loislaw <www.loislaw.com> and VersusLaw <www.versuslaw.com>, are available free to law

---

16. Wikipedia and other websites have been cited in numerous court opinions, but some judges have been withering in their criticism of such trends. See, e.g., *St. Clair v. Johnny's Oyster & Shrimp, Inc.*, 76 F. Supp. 2d 773, 774 (S.D. Tex. 1999) (emphasis in original) ("There is no way Plaintiff can overcome the presumption that the information he discovered on the Internet is inherently untrustworthy. Anyone can put anything on the Internet. No website is monitored for accuracy and *nothing* contained therein is under oath or even subject to independent verification absent underlying documentation. Moreover, the Court holds no illusions that hackers can adulterate the content on *any* web-site from *any* location at *any* time. For these reasons, any evidence procured off the Internet is adequate for almost nothing ... "); *Campbell v. Sec'y of Health and Human Servs.*, 69 Fed. Cl. 775, 781 (2006) ("A review of the Wik-

ipedia website reveals a pervasive and, for our purposes, disturbing series of disclaimers ... ").

See also R. Jason Richards, *Courting Wikipedia*, TRIAL, Apr. 2008, at 62, 62 ("Since when did a Web site that any Internet surfer can edit become an authoritative source by which law students could write passing papers, experts could provide credible testimony, lawyers could craft legal arguments, and judges could issue precedents? It is one thing to embrace technology and the convenience it offers; it is quite another to rely on an inherently unreliable source as grounds for shaping this country's law and policy for generations to come.").

17. Much of the information in these databases may be available to university faculty and students through LexisNexis Academic <web.lexis-nexis.com/universe/> or Westlaw Campus Research <campus.westlaw.com>.

students. Others, such as Fastcase <www.fastcase.com> and Case-maker <www.casemaker.us>, have contracts with state bar associations to provide low-cost access to their members.[18]

The use of subscription database systems requires different skills from those needed for finding information on the free Internet. These services provide much more comprehensive collections of resources and much more sophisticated methods for searching. Online databases such as Westlaw and Lexis permit very powerful and focused searches, allowing the use of features such as synonyms, truncation, proximity connectors, and field restrictions for searching specific parts of documents. They also accommodate natural language searching, provide hyperlinks between documents, and incorporate into their displays information on the validity of primary sources.

(1) Westlaw

The Westlaw research system was introduced in 1975 by West Publishing Company as a case research tool. It has since grown to cover billions of pages of content including not only cases and statutes but also journal articles, texts, news sources, and business information. Westlaw offers a vast array of resources and a sophisticated range of search approaches.

Database Selection. One of the first choices confronting a Westlaw user is the selection of an appropriate database. Westlaw has a wide selection of databases, some limited to particular jurisdictions or specific subject areas and others providing comprehensive access. In most instances, it is also possible to combine a number of databases into one search.

Westlaw provides several methods for choosing databases. The welcome screen for most users lists the most frequently used databases, but clicking "Directory" at the top of the screen reveals a much more extensive listing by type of material and topic. Each database identifier on the list and on the search screen is followed by an information icon (i) that provides an explanation of the contents and scope of coverage.

The list of databases is available for free <directory.westlaw.com>; you can do a search in the directory to find databases containing specific publications or with particular terms in their

---

18. Twenty-eight state bars are members of the Casemaker Consortium, providing access for their members. Access is limited to members of these participating organizations. Nine state bars provide access to Fastcase, which is also available to individuals, and a smaller number of state bars have subscription arrangements for their members with other vendors including Lexis, Loislaw, and VersusLaw. A few states have their own homegrown legal research systems for state bar members and other researchers.

descriptions, without logging in or incurring search charges. The same resource is available within Westlaw as the IDEN database.

The simplest way to choose a database is to type relevant keywords into the "Search these databases" box on the introductory Westlaw screen. Typing keywords such as "products liability" in the box will retrieve a list of suggested databases from which to choose; typing the exact name of a publication or database leads directly to a search screen.

Whether to limit research to a particular jurisdiction or topical area depends upon a variety of factors, including cost (searches in large databases are generally more expensive), the purpose of the research, and the value of information from other jurisdictions or in other subjects. A smaller database will retrieve more focused results, but it may miss materials that are relevant or analogous but not within a particular subject area or jurisdiction.

Searching. Westlaw offers two basic methods of searching: natural language, and terms and connectors (or Boolean). Each of these search methods has its strengths. A natural language search allows the researcher to enter a phrase, or a combination of words (e.g., *Can the FCC sanction broadcasters for indecency for airing fleeting expletives?* or simply *indecency fleeting expletive*). The system assigns relative weights to the terms in a query, depending on how often they appear in the database. It then retrieves a specified number of documents which appear most closely to match the query, giving greater weight to the less common terms. Not all terms will necessarily appear in every document retrieved, but you can specify "required terms" that *must* appear in all documents.[19]

A terms and connectors search can provide greater precision in retrieval, but it does require learning a structured search syntax. Specific terms or phrases are joined by logical connectors such as *and*, or by proximity connectors specifying the maximum number of words that can separate the search terms (e.g., */10*) or specifying that the words appear in the same sentence (*/s*) or the same paragraph (*/p*). In Westlaw, an *or* connector is understood between two adjacent terms. The search *expletive obscenity*, for example, searches for documents containing either the word *expletive* or the word *obscenity*.

To search for a phrase such as "fleeting expletive," it is necessary to place the phrase in quotation marks. Phrases should be used carefully, however, as they will often retrieve far fewer documents than individual words with proximity connectors. "Fleeting w/5 expletive" will retrieve a case referring to "fleeting

---

19. For more on how natural language searching works, see Elizabeth M. McKenzie, *Natural Language Searching:* *How WIN Works in Westlaw*, Legal Reference Services Q., Winter 2001, at 39.

use of an expletive," even if the phrase "fleeting expletive" does not appear.

Another aspect of terms and connectors searching is the use of the truncation symbols *!* and ***. An exclamation point is used to find any word beginning with the specified letters. *Obscen!*, for example, will find *obscene, obscenity*, and *obscenely*. Without a truncation symbol, only the search term itself and its plural form are retrieved. *Obscenity* will retrieve *obscenities*, but not *obscene* or any other variations. It is important not to truncate too early in a word; *obs!* would retrieve several irrelevant terms such as *observation, obsidian*, and *obsolete*.

The asterisk is less frequently used, but represents a particular character or a limited number of characters. *Legali*e* will retrieve either the American *legalize* or the British *legalise*, and *labo*** will retrieve *labor* or *labour* but not *laboratory* or *laborious*.

Term frequency is another valuable tool available with terms and connectors searching. Clicking on this link before running a search allows you to specify that a particular term appear a minimum number of times (up to fifty) in a document. This makes it more likely that a case or article will focus on the term rather than mentioning it in passing. Setting a high term frequency for *expletive* , for example, will limit a search to cases about the use of expletives rather than every case in which offending language is deleted.

A Westlaw terms and connectors search can be quite long and complicated, with several groups of terms in parentheses telling the system which terms to combine first. This is fine for the mathematically minded, but it requires spending a great deal of time drafting a complex search. Often it is more effective to draft a simple search and use its results as a springboard to find further documents.

Whether natural language or terms and connectors searching is used, the terms entered will determine what documents are retrieved. Since more than one term can usually be used to denote a particular concept, it is important to enter synonyms or related terms regardless of the search method chosen. One court decision may use the word *ambiguous*, another *vague*, and a third *unclear*. Westlaw provides help in identifying additional terms with an online thesaurus. For *expletive*, it provides such terms as *profanity, swearing*, and *vulgarity*. In a terms and connector search, these alternates are simply typed one after the other, as in *fleeting /p expletive profanity vulgarity*; in a natural language search, alternate terms are included in parentheses after the term to which they relate, as in *fleeting expletive (profanity vulgarity) indecency*.

One major difference between the two types of searching is that a natural language search always retrieves the same number of documents, unless it includes required terms that you indicate must appear in every document. (The number is something you determine on the Preferences–Search Method screen, and can be anywhere from 1 to 100.) The display shows the documents that best match the query, in order of relevance. A terms and connectors search, on the other hand, can retrieve anywhere from nothing to thousands of cases, depending on how well the search is crafted and how often the terms appear in the database. The number of retrieved documents can be a useful indication of whether an appropriate search was performed. In a natural language search, the first few documents may be right on point but the degree of relevance can drop off precipitously. It is important to recognize when relevance declines, and to be aware that reading every document retrieved will usually be a waste of time. The effectiveness of a search depends on the quality of the resulting documents, not their quantity.

Natural language and terms and connectors search methods are best suited for different purposes. Because natural language searching retrieves documents based on how frequently search terms appear, it is ideal for finding documents on issues revolving around frequently used terms such as "summary judgment." Many cases mention the standards for summary judgment, but the few decisions focusing on it in depth would be retrieved first as most relevant. Natural language is also useful for finding one highly relevant document as a starting point, and it can provide a place to begin if drafting an appropriate terms and connectors search seems too daunting a task.

Terms and connectors searches require documents to match a request exactly, so this approach is generally preferable when searching for a particular phrase or a precise combination of terms. It is often fruitful to perform similar searches using both methods.

Fields. An important feature of Westlaw searching is the use of document fields. These are specific parts of a documents, such as the title of an article or the name of the judge writing an opinion. Limiting a search to a particular field can produce a much more specific result. A search in a case database for *fox* retrieves any decisions mentioning a person named Fox or simply using the word "fox" anywhere in the opinion. A title search, *ti(fox)*, retrieves only those cases where "Fox" appears in one of the parties' names.

Some fields allow research that is virtually impossible by other means. It would be a lengthy and tedious process manually to find all opinions written by a particular judge, but online databases can easily retrieve a complete list of a judge's opinions with searches such as *ju(pooler)*. You can examine a judge's decisions on a particular topic by combining this request with other search terms.

A drop-down menu on the search screen shows the fields available for a particular database. Clicking on a field name enters its abbreviation into the search with parentheses symbols into which to insert the search terms.

Display. Once a search is entered, Westlaw displays either the first document or a list of retrieved documents showing the context in which the search terms appear (depending on the display preferences chosen by the user). Buttons at the bottom of the document display allow you to jump to that part of the document with terms matching the search query or to the next document. Natural language search results also include a *Best* button to focus on that part of the document that most closely matches the query.

Most documents on Westlaw include *star paging*, which indicates the page breaks in the original printed sources. This allows you to cite to a particular passage in a case, law review article, or other document without having to track down the printed version.

In addition to the documents retrieved by the search, most Westlaw results also display a "ResultsPlus" list suggesting secondary sources and finding tools based on the concepts in the search or the terms in a specific document retrieved. These references to legal encyclopedias and other sources may provide helpful background or lead to additional research resources.[20]

Locate. If a completed search retrieves too many cases, you can narrow the focus of inquiry by using the *Locate* feature. This allows you to examine the retrieved set of documents for specific terms, whether or not they were included in the initial request. Instead of identifying a new set of cases replacing the original search result, *Locate* searches for and highlights particular terms among the retrieved documents. This feature is particularly valuable if each new search costs money, because it does not incur an additional search charge. (Another time- and money-saving feature is Research Trail, which allows you to return to searches from earlier in the same day without additional charges and saves searches for two weeks.)

It is also possible, of course, to revise a search by adding new terms or to pursue new topics, perhaps in another database. Clicking on "Edit Search" provides a new search screen, including a "Change Database(s)" link to specify other resources to check.

WestClip. A valuable Westlaw feature that is often overlooked is the ability to save a search and have the system automatically run it to check for new material on a daily or weekly basis. This feature, WestClip, can be accessed by clicking on the "Add Search

---

20. See Thomas R. Keefe, *Results-Plus: The Perfect Marriage Between* *Technology and Tradition*, LEGAL INFO. ALERT, Mar. 2004, at 1.

to WestClip" link at the top of the full screen list of search results, and provides for notification by e-mail or when you sign onto Westlaw. WestClip provides a very convenient way to stay abreast of developments in a specific case or in an area of interest.

Locate and WestClip only work with terms and connectors searches, not natural language. Both services identify documents that match specific criteria, rather than finding the most relevant documents as a natural language search does. The ability to take advantage of these services is one good reason to become proficient in terms and connectors syntax and procedures instead of relying heavily on natural language.

Links and KeyCite. Most legal documents cite extensively to other documents, such as cases, statutes, and law review articles, and it is often important or helpful to examine these other sources. Westlaw's display includes hypertext links to these other sources if they are available online. Clicking on a hyperlink opens up a new "link viewer" window, making it easy to return to the original citing document.

Westlaw provides links not only from a document to the resources it cites, but also from a document to later sources that cite it. This is done through the KeyCite feature, which is an integral part of Westlaw's document display. If later citing documents are available, the display includes a small "C" (or other symbol) at the top of the document and a "Citing References" link to the left. Clicking on either of these links will lead to a list of cases, law review articles, court documents, and other sources that make some reference to the document being viewed. This is an invaluable way to find related materials and to bring your research forward in time.

If a document has been frequently cited, KeyCite provides several ways to focus retrieval. *Limit KeyCite Display* can be used to see only particular types of documents, references from specific jurisdictions, or (using the *Locate* feature) those documents containing specific keywords. In the same way that WestClip provides automatic notification of new documents matching a particular search, KeyCite Alert is a service that provides notice of any new citations to an important document. You can limit a KeyCite Alert to specific *Locate* terms, providing an easy way to learn of new citing documents meeting very specific criteria. KeyCite's important role in case research, where it is used to determine that a decision is still "good law," will be discussed more fully in Chapter 8.

(2) Lexis

Like Westlaw, Lexis is designed as a comprehensive resource for legal and business research, with cases, statutes, law review articles, treatises, news, and other sources. The search approaches of the two systems are similar, with just enough differences to make using one system a challenge for someone familiar only with the other.

Databases. The first step in using Lexis is to choose an appropriate database. You can browse through the databases listed on the screen, use the "Find a Source" tab to look for a database, or search the free directory <w3.nexis.com/sources/>. The Lexis database list includes "i" icons linking to information about the contents and scope of coverage of each database.

Searching. Lexis offers both natural language and terms and connectors searching. Natural language searching is similar to Westlaw's. You can specify the number of documents retrieved, from as few as ten to as many as 250. "Mandatory terms" that must appear in all documents can be added and may produce a smaller result.

Lexis syntax for terms and connectors searching is slightly different than Westlaw's. Most connectors are similar, although the word *or* must be included between synonyms or related terms. Because an *or* is not understood between adjacent words, phrases in Lexis do not have to be entered in quotations. Proximity connectors begin with *w/* (as in *w/10*, *w/s*, or *w/p*), although each system is forgiving enough to understand the other's format. Like Westlaw, Lexis uses the *!* and * characters to truncate terms and find word variations.

Lexis includes a "suggest terms for my search" feature that is broader than a thesaurus. It lists not only synonyms and related concepts but terms that regularly appear in close proximity to the term. *Handgun*, for example, leads to such terms as *arrest, possession, probable cause, search warrant,* and *victim*. These may suggest further search terms or other lines of inquiry.

You may find it useful to begin a research project by searching by topic or headnote. This provides a way to explore legal topics, such as Communications Law–Related Legal Issues–Indecency & Obscenity, and to search for cases within this specific subject area. Like choosing too narrow a database, however, this may cause documents on analogous issues to be missed. Using more than one approach and comparing the results can help ensure that your research is thorough enough.

Segments. The Lexis counterpart to Westlaw's *fields* are called *segments*. Segments are added to a terms and connectors search by clicking on "Restrict by Document Segment," and to a natural language search by using "Restrict using Mandatory Terms."

Display. Lexis has three basic display formats. *Cite* provides a list of citations, including the overview and core terms; you can choose *Show hits* to display the search terms as well. *Full* displays an entire document, and *KWIC*, short for "key words in context," shows an individual case with a window of twenty-five words around the occurrence of your search terms. Lexis includes star paging references for most documents, and provides hyperlinks between cases, statutes, law review articles, and other documents available in its databases.

Focus and More Like This. Like Westlaw's *Locate*, the *Focus* feature provides a way to examine a retrieved set of documents for specific terms without incurring additional charges. The *Focus* option is available in a search box at the top of the screen when examining a list or case display. This is in the same position as Westlaw's "Edit Search" option, so if you use both Westlaw and Lexis you need to be aware of whether you are focusing or editing when you enter terms in the search box.

Two other Lexis features providing ways to focus or expand research are *More Like This* and *More Like Selected Text*. *More Like This* finds either cases that cite the same authorities (*Core Cites*) or cases that use similar terms (*Core Terms*). Choosing this feature when viewing the *Fox Television Stations* case, for example, leads to options to retrieve documents citing the same cases that *Fox* cites or to find similar cases by selecting from a list of core terms in *Fox* (including *broadcaster*, *expletive*, *fleeting*, and *patently offensive*).

Alerts. Lexis offers a service, *Alerts*, that automatically runs a search on a daily or weekly basis to monitor new developments. Along with *Focus*, *More Like This*, and *More Like Selected Text*, *Save as Alert* is listed at the top of a document display. These searches can be retrieved by clicking on the *Alerts* tab at the top of the screen. To the right of the tabs, a *History* link allows you to return to any search performed within the past four weeks.

Shepard's. Lexis also provides a way to bring research forward by finding later citations to a given document. The Lexis feature, *Shepard's*, is represented at the top of a document display by a "Shepardize" link and (in some databases) by graphic symbols such as red or yellow signs. *Restrictions* on Shepard's can be used to see negative or positive citing references, or to run a *Focus* search within the text of the citing documents to find specific terms. You can set up *Shepard's Alerts* to receive automatic notice of new citing documents.

(3) Other Databases

Westlaw and Lexis are the major databases in the legal market, but they are by no means the only options. Several other companies offer databases of cases and statutes, with some providing selected secondary sources as well. In general these databases provide less comprehensive coverage than Westlaw or Lexis, but more extensive resources and more sophisticated search options than are freely available on the Internet. They have been called "tier two" legal research services—not as powerful as Westlaw or Lexis, but more reliable than free Internet sites that can be "incomplete, out-of-date, and of questionable quality."[21]

Searching in these other database systems is similar to Westlaw or Lexis, with proximity connectors and fields for particular information such as judges' names. Some offer natural language approaches as well. Display generally provides hyperlinks to other documents within the system.

Loislaw <www.loislaw.com>, the most substantial of these other systems, includes several major treatises as well as extensive case databases. It uses the Boolean search connectors AND, OR, and NOT; for proximity searches it uses the connector NEAR to find terms within twenty words of each other, or permits NEARn to specify that the terms appear no more than n words apart. It automatically searches for variants such as plurals and past tense, and the asterisk is used as a root expander to retrieve all possible forms of a word. Loislaw also provides a "Search within a Search" option, similar to "Locate" or "Focus," to narrow retrieval once an initial search is completed, and it offers a "LawWatch" feature that saves and runs a search to monitor for current developments.

VersusLaw <www.versuslaw.com> also uses Boolean searching with the connectors AND, OR, and w/n, as well as the asterisk as a root expander. Two words entered together are assumed to be a phrase.

Casemaker <www.casemaker.us> has its own distinctive syntax. Like Google (but unlike Westlaw), it reads a space between words as an "and" to search for documents with all terms. "Or" searches are performed by placing terms in parentheses, separated by commas without spaces. Phrases must be put in quotations, and the asterisk is used as a root expander.

Fastcase <www.fastcase.com> offers both Boolean and natural language searching. The Boolean search uses the standard AND, OR, and NOT connectors as well as "w/n" to find terms within n (up to fifty) words of each other. Phrases must be in quotes, as the AND connector is assumed if two terms are entered. The asterisk is

21. Thomas Keefe, *Fastcase: A Legal Research Tool Whose Time Has Come*, 95 ILL. B.J. 46, 46 (2007) ("A tier-two product is one whose breadth and capabilities lie somewhere between full-service systems like the big two and the hit or miss world of free Internet legal research.").

used as a root expander. A natural language search returns the 100 most relevant documents.

Searching free Internet sites is often the same as using Google, with simple search boxes and few advanced options. Some sites, however, provide more extensive approaches such as truncation and proximity searching. Public Library of Law <www.plol.org> supports *w/n* proximity searching as well as truncation using asterisks. PreCYdent <www.precydent.com> also uses asterisks to truncate words; its proximity searching takes the form of *"indecency fleeting"~10* to retrieve "indecency" and "fleeting" within ten words of each other. It also has a "More Like This" feature that finds other documents textually similar to the one displayed. Search capabilities are in development and can change rapidly, so it always pays to check a site's FAQ or Help documentation for updated information.

(c) Using Print Resources

Print materials are often considered a dying medium for research, but they have a place in any serious researcher's toolbox. Resources are rapidly being digitized, but there remains a great deal of legal information that is stored only in printed form. Superseded statutory codes and session laws provide information about the state of the law twenty or fifty years ago, and journal articles and treatises may provide insights even if they are not available through one of the major online services.

Even for material that is available online, the print format can offer advantages. It is easier to browse from section to section in a book than online, and therefore to see related topics and to develop a sense of how a field of law is organized. Searching online may find the specific terms in a search, but it will not reveal analogies that might be discussed in the same context.[22]

The computer plays a vital role in print-based research. The first step to researching in print material is usually to consult a library's online catalog, which tells you what the library has and where it is located.

---

22. Over-reliance on electronic research can lead to what one author has called a "loss of peripheral vision." John K. Hanft, *A Model for Legal Research in the Electronic Age*, 17(3) LEGAL REFERENCE SERVICES Q. 77, 79 (1999). See also Molly Warner Lien, *Technocentrism and the Soul of the Common Lawyer*, 48 AM. U. L. REV. 85, 89 (1998) ("While technology unquestionably gives lawyers the ability to marshal bits of information instantly from a host of cases, and to dispatch them into memoranda and briefs like well-drilled soldiers in a war of logic, the speed of deployment inevitably discourages lawyers from taking the time to analyze the wisdom, correctness and applicability of legal arguments.... Concomitantly, the methodology of researching in and working with electronic texts encourages work habits that prioritize speed and all too easily enable lawyers to find a kernel of phraseology that may support their often incorrect preconceived notions.")

The next step is generally to peruse a work's table of contents or index to find a specific discussion. Indexes in legal publications can be lengthy and full of cross-references. It can sometimes be frustrating trying to find a reference to the right topic. Even the most thorough index cannot list every possible approach to a legal or factual issue. You may need to rethink issues, reframe questions, check synonyms and alternate terms, and follow leads in cross-references. But the index provides related references that might be worth following, something a keyword search (limited to one specific set of terms) doesn't do.

Print-based research, of course, is not without limitations and problems. Sometimes keyword searching is essential in getting quickly to a precise point in a large work. And downloading material or requesting it by e-mail has several advantages over photocopying, in terms of both flexibility and environmental protection. But using printed resources is an important part of the skill set of any experienced researcher.

§ 1.4 Handling a Research Project

A research project generally involves answering a specific question, applying a general legal principle to a particular set of facts. It often requires two distinct steps: (1) coming up to speed in the law governing a situation, and (2) searching for the specific rules that apply. These are different tasks and require different approaches. It has been estimated that it takes eighty percent of a researcher's time to learn about an unfamiliar area, and just twenty percent to provide a specific answer.[23]

(a) First Steps

The first step in most research projects is to determine the legal issues in a factual situation. This is "thinking like a lawyer," as taught in law school, and it requires an understanding of basic doctrinal areas such as contract or tort law. The areas of law involved in a particular problem may determine the choice of resources.

Before looking anywhere, step back and study the problem. If possible, determine whether the jurisdictional focus is federal or state. Formulate tentative issues, but be prepared to revise your statement of the issues as research progresses and you learn more about the legal background.

The first step in most projects is to do some preliminary research to understand the context of a particular problem and to

---

23. Thomas Keefe, *The 80/20 Rule of Legal Research*, 93 ILL. B.J. 258 (2005).

get some sense of the terminology and rules of an area of law. It is essential for a researcher unfamiliar with an area to do some background reading in order to understand the significance of material found. Without knowing the parameters of a particular field, you cannot appreciate the nuances.

It is often best to begin research by going to a trustworthy secondary source, such as a legal treatise or a law review article. Primary sources such as statutes and cases can be confusing, ambiguously worded documents. Secondary materials, on the other hand, are usually more straightforward and try to explain the law. They summarize the basic rules and the leading authorities and place them in context, allowing you to select the most promising primary sources to pursue.

A treatise explains the major issues and terminology, and provides a context in which related matters are raised or considered. If no treatise is available, a legal encyclopedia such as *American Jurisprudence 2d* or *Corpus Juris Secundum* can be a useful first step. Like a treatise, an encyclopedia outlines basic legal rules and provides extensive references to court decisions. Even if it does not address a specific situation, a treatise or encyclopedia provides the general framework in which to place the situation.

Law review articles are particularly useful starting points when researching a new or developing area of law that may not be very well covered in treatises or encyclopedias. Sources such as legal newspapers, newsletters, and blogs are even more current than law reviews.

This early stage of the research process is also a good point at which to use free Internet sites such as Wikipedia. At this point you are looking for background information and not definitive answers or citable authority, so a free and readily accessible website can be a real boon. A general encyclopedic source such as Wikipedia can provide basic information and leads to more in-depth resources.

The most difficult part of many research projects is finding the first piece of relevant information. Once one document is found, it often lead to a number of other sources. Cases cite earlier cases as authority; a statute's notes provide useful leads to decisions, legislative history documents, and secondary sources; and law review articles cite a wide variety of sources.

(b) In–Depth Research

Once you gain background knowledge of an area, you then must apply that knowledge to a specific set of facts. In some cases this is simple and straightforward, but it is often a process that requires time and concentration.[24]

Several research tools are designed for in-depth research:

— Annotated codes not only provide the texts of current statutes, but also lead directly to most of the other relevant primary sources and may provide references to secondary sources as well. Specialized services in areas such as securities or taxation often combine the statutory text with editorial explanatory notes.

— Key-number digests, whether used in print or on Westlaw, expand on keyword searches by grouping cases together by topic whether or not they use the same terminology. They are a wonderful resource for finding analogous situations with different facts but similar legal issues.

— Once you know the contours of a legal issue, you have the background necessary to talk to experts in the area. The most current information is not always available in print or online. Sometimes an e-mail or telephone call can uncover information that couldn't be found through ordinary research methods. Government agencies and professional associations are staffed with experts who can answer questions, provide invaluable references, or send essential documents. Do your homework first, and make sure that the information isn't posted on the organization's website.

In-depth research may require several approaches. At first you may seem to be facing a blank wall, or think you have found everything there is to be found. Expect to be frustrated in a difficult research project. Try rephrasing the question and running searches for the new terminology. Taking a break from the project for a few hours or talking to colleagues may lead you to fresh insights.

Your in-depth research must be sufficient to give you confidence that your work is based on information that is complete and accurate. The surest way to achieve this confidence is to try several different approaches to the research problem. If a review of several secondary sources, case law research, and examination of the underlying statutes all lead to the same sources and a single conclusion, chances are good that you have found all of the key pieces of information. If they produce different conclusions, more research is necessary.

(c) Providing Current Information

An essential part of legal research is verifying that the information found is current, that new statutes have not been enacted

---

24. "[O]rdinarily, meaningful legal research cannot be performed in time periods of less than two hours." *Glover v. Johnson,* 931 F. Supp. 1360, 1369 (E.D. Mich. 1996), *aff'd in part, rev'd in part,* 138 F.3d 229 (6th Cir. 1998) (quoting a Michigan Department of Corrections policy directive).

and that cases relied upon have not been reversed or overruled. You must verify that sources to be relied upon are still in force and "good law." No research is complete unless you have checked the latest supplements, searched current-awareness sources for new developments, and determined the status of cases to be relied upon.

There are at least two distinct aspects to making sure that information is current. The major online systems provide KeyCite and Shepard's Citations, tools for checking the validity of precedent and for finding more current information. These systems provide signals indicating that the precedential value of cases might be affected by subsequent decisions or other developments, and they alert you to recent citing documents that might provide additional clarification or new perspectives.

The other aspect of having current information comes with experience in a particular subject area, and is a result of monitoring new developments on a regular basis. When researching in an unfamiliar area, you may only find out about the effect of a new case or regulation by finding it in a keyword search. But keeping up with newsletters, trade magazines, and blogs in a particular area ensures that you won't be blindsided by a new development.

(d) Completing a Project

Knowing when to stop researching can be just as difficult as knowing where to begin. In every research situation, however, there comes a time when it is necessary to synthesize the information found and produce the required memorandum, brief, or opinion letter.

Sometimes the limits to research are set by the nature of the project. An assignment may be limited to a specified number of hours or a certain amount of money. If so, the ability to find information quickly and accurately is essential.

If there is no preset limit to the amount of research to be done, it is up to you to determine when you are finished. The best gauge of this comes from having used several research approaches that lead to the same answers. Keyword searches, digests, and secondary sources may seem at first to provide distinct answers, but once they all fit together you can be more confident that you are not missing any key pieces of information.

––––––––––

Confidence in your research results is more likely when you have confidence generally in your research skills. Familiarity with legal resources and experience in their use will produce the assurance that your research is complete and accurate.

As we will see in the following chapters, the law has a voluminous literature and a wide range of highly developed research tools. Many of these are unfamiliar even to experienced scholars in other disciplines. Learning to use these tools requires patience and effort, but in time you should become aware of the different functions they serve, their strengths and weaknesses, and the ways they fit together.

Too many practitioners of legal research understand little about the tools they use. As a result, they spin their wheels and overlook aids and shortcuts designed to help them. If you learn how legal resources work as you encounter them, and hone your skills through practice, this mastery will save you valuable time and effort.

Chapter 2

CONSTITUTIONAL LAW

Table of Sections

———

Constitutions are the basic law of states and nations, detailing the powers of the government and protecting individual liberties. They can take a variety of forms, ranging from relatively brief and general statements to lengthy documents of considerable specificity. The original United States Constitution was written on just four pages,[1] and remains one of the shortest of such documents in the world. The Alabama constitution is more than forty times its length.

Only a small part of constitutional law research, however, relates to locating relevant constitutional provisions. Most research problems focus on historical background, judicial interpretations, legislative actions, and scholarly commentaries. They involve research in case law and secondary sources, using materials to be discussed in later chapters. To a substantial extent, though, consti-

---

1. The pages of the original parchment Constitution measured more than 23 by 28 inches. The U.S. Constitution has appeared in smaller formats as well. In 2004, A.B. Rajbansh, an engineer in northern India, spent more than 196 hours writing it in a 124–page book two centimeters high and weighing less than an ounce. *Indian Villager Pens Two-Centimeter Version of US Constitution*, AGENCE FRANCE PRESSE ENGLISH WIRE, July 1, 2004, *available in* Westlaw, All-newsplus Database.

tutional literature is a distinct research field with its own procedures and tools.

Most lawyers may not face constitutional law issues very often in their daily practice, but any time a client deals with the government there can be constitutional implications. Knowledge of the scope and meaning of the federal and state constitutions is also an asset to any informed citizen.

§ 2.1   The United States Constitution

The Constitution of the United States is usually considered the oldest constitutional document in continuous force in the world today. Drafted in the summer of 1787 and ratified by the required nine states within a year, it entered into force in March 1789 and has been amended just twenty-seven times in more than two centuries. Among the most important of these amendments are the Bill of Rights, guaranteeing personal liberties, and the Fourteenth Amendment, applying these protections to the states.

The following sections discuss sources for obtaining the text of the Constitution, interpreting its provisions, locating court decisions, and finding historical material on its framing and amendment.

(a) Text

The text of the Constitution can be found in a variety of sources. For most purposes, including citation form, any source will serve as well as another. Unlike references to statutes, court decisions or most other authorities, a citation to a current state or federal constitution does not need to provide either a source or a date.[2]

The Constitution appears in many pamphlet editions, at the beginning of the first volume of the *United States Code,* in standard reference works such as *Black's Law Dictionary,* and in almost all state annotated codes. It is available at dozens of Internet sites from the federal government and from various organizations. The Government Printing Office's GPO Access site provides easy access to an extensive annotated version (to be discussed below) and several shorter versions in PDF <www.gpoaccess.gov/constitution/>, and other sites can be found with a simple Internet search for "constitution."

---

2. THE BLUEBOOK: A UNIFORM SYSTEM OF CITATION R. 11, at 100 (18th ed. 2005); ALWD CITATION MANUAL: A PROFESSIONAL SYSTEM OF CITATION R. 13.2, at 107–08 (3d ed. 2006). Even obsolete provisions or outdated constitutions need only a date, not a source, which can sometimes make tracking them down a challenge.

(b) Reference Sources

The extensive literature of constitutional law in such secondary sources as encyclopedias, treatises, and periodicals approaches its subject from both historical and contemporary viewpoints. While later chapters of this text will deal in depth with secondary sources generally, a few specific sources can be of particular help to the constitutional researcher.

Of the many commentaries on the Constitution, one of the most extensive and accessible is *The Constitution of the United States of America: Analysis and Interpretation* (Johnny H. Killian et al. eds., 2002 ed.).[3] This work, prepared by the Congressional Research Service of the Library of Congress, is published as a Senate Document every ten years and is available free on the Internet from GPO Access <www.gpoaccess.gov/constitution/>.[4]

This edition of the Constitution is a useful starting point for constitutional research, with a thorough analysis of Supreme Court decisions applying each provision. The current edition covers cases through June 2002, with a supplement extending coverage to June 2006.[5] The constitutional text is accompanied by more than 2100 pages of commentary, historical background, legal analysis, and summaries of judicial interpretation of each clause and amendment. The major constitutional decisions of the Supreme Court are discussed in detail, and the footnotes include numerous citations to other relevant cases and scholarly interpretations. Illustration 2–1 on page 47 shows the opening page of the discussion of Article II, The Executive Department, with footnotes citing *The Federalist* and a pair of scholarly monographs.

Besides an index and a table listing all cases discussed or noted in the text, the main volume and supplement also include tables of Acts of Congress, state constitutional and statutory provisions, and municipal ordinances which have been held unconstitutional by the Supreme Court; and a list of Supreme Court decisions overruled by subsequent decisions.[6]

3. S. Doc. No. 108–17 (2004). This is the tenth annotated edition of the Constitution prepared under congressional direction. The first, in 1913, merely listed citations of Supreme Court cases after each provision. The work grew in scope with each edition, and adopted much of its present form with the 1952 edition, which was edited by the distinguished constitutional law scholar, Edward S. Corwin, and is available online in PDF in HeinOnline's Legal Classics Library <www.heinonline.org>.

4. FindLaw   <www.findlaw.com/casecode/constitution/> has the annotated Constitution with hypertext links to footnotes and to Supreme Court cases discussed, but as of 2009 it had not updated its version since the 2000 supplement to the 1992 edition.

5. S. Doc. No. 110–6 (2007).

6. As of 2006 the Supreme Court had invalidated 160 Acts of Congress and 1296 state and local provisions, and it had overruled more than 300 of its earlier decisions.

Although the Library of Congress volume is updated by a cumulative supplement, coverage is usually not very current. Finding current information generally requires the use of other, more frequently updated resources, but this version of the Constitution remains a useful and free online source for background information on constitutional jurisprudence.

Another helpful beginning point for analysis of constitutional issues is *Encyclopedia of the American Constitution* (Leonard W. Levy & Kenneth L. Karst eds., 2d ed. 2000). This six-volume work contains more than two thousand articles, many by leading legal scholars, historians and political scientists. More than half of the articles discuss doctrinal concepts of constitutional law, but others focus on specific people (including every Supreme Court justice), judicial decisions, statutes, and historical periods. Most articles include numerous cross-references and short bibliographies of further readings. The final volume has chronologies of the Constitution's birth and development, a brief glossary, and indexes by case, name and subject.

Coverage of constitutional issues is also provided by numerous other reference works, particularly those dealing with the Supreme Court. Several of these are one-volume encyclopedias and reference handbooks. *The Oxford Companion to the Supreme Court of the United States* (Kermit L. Hall ed., 2d ed. 2005) covers constitutional principles as well as Supreme Court history and the American judicial system, with entries for major cases and Supreme Court justices. Jethro K. Lieberman, *A Practical Companion to the Constitution* (1999) focuses specifically on constitutional doctrines as interpreted by the Court. Robert L. Maddex, *The U.S. Constitution A to Z* (2d ed. 2008) is a shorter reference work for a general audience, with about 250 brief articles and coverage of the most significant cases and Supreme Court justices.

A new extensive series of smaller reference works, *Reference Guides to the United States Constitution*, was launched in 2002. Each volume focuses on a specific aspect of constitutional law, such as double jeopardy or freedom of speech, and includes a brief history of the topic, before and since its inclusion in the Constitution; a lengthy analysis of the state of the law in the area; and a bibliographical essay with annotated references to further readings. Nineteen volumes have been published to date, and the series is projected for completion in thirty-seven volumes.[7]

---

7. Alphabetically by title, volumes published to date are:

MICHAEL L. WELLS & THOMAS A. EATON, CONSTITUTIONAL REMEDIES (2002)

DAVID S. RUDSTEIN, DOUBLE JEOPARDY (2004)

KEITH WERHAN, FREEDOM OF SPEECH (2004)

LYRISSA BARNETT LIDSKY & R. GEORGE WRIGHT, FREEDOM OF THE PRESS (2004)

Encyclopedias and other reference works provide a broad perspective of constitutional history and theory. Several major treatises focus on constitutional issues from a doctrinal perspective. Laurence H. Tribe, *American Constitutional Law* (2d & 3d eds. 1988–2000) is the most cited modern treatment of the subject, although the author suspended revision of the work midway through the third edition.[8] Ronald D. Rotunda & John E. Nowak, *Treatise on Constitutional Law: Substance and Procedure* (4th ed. 2007) is also an extensive and frequently cited analysis of constitutional issues, with less of a personal viewpoint than Tribe's work.[9] Abridged one-volume versions are published as *Constitutional Law* (7th ed. 2004) and *Principles of Constitutional Law* (3d ed. 2007), and the full treatise is available on Westlaw as the CONLAW database. The newest entry is a one-volume work by Erwin Chemerinsky, *Constitutional Law: Principles and Policies* (3d ed. 2006). Chemerinsky's work tends to have briefer footnote references than the other treatises. It has not yet been cited nearly as often as the other treatises but has been well received.[10]

Numerous scholarly monographs have been written on the U.S. Constitution. One of the most useful for researchers is Akhil Reed

William L. Reynolds & William M. Richman, The Full Faith and Credit Clause (2005)

Patrick Baude, Judicial Jurisdiction (2007)

James M. McGoldrick, Limits on States (2005)

Richard E. Levy, The Power to Legislate (2006)

Thomas B. McAffee, Jay S. Bybee & A. Christopher Bryant, Powers Reserved to the People and the States (2006)

David S. Bogen, Privileges and Immunities (2003)

Rhonda Wasserman, Procedural Due Process (2004)

Jack Stark, Prohibited Government Acts (2002)

Peter K. Rofes, The Religion Guarantees (2005)

Susan N. Herman, The Right to a Speedy and Public Trial (2006)

James J. Tomkovicz, The Right to the Assistance of Counsel (2002)

Robert M. Bloom, Searches, Seizures, and Warrants (2003)

Melvyn R. Durchslag, State Sovereign Immunity (2002)

Christopher R. Drahozal, The Supremacy Clause (2004)

Erik M. Jensen, The Taxing Power (2005)

8. The first and second editions were single-volume works. Tribe published one volume of a third edition in 2000, but announced five years later in an "open letter to interested readers of American constitutional law" that the subject was in such a state of flux that he had decided not to complete the work. Laurence H. Tribe, *The Treatise Power*, 8 Green Bag 2d 291 (2005). The volume published in 2000 covers issues such as federalism and separation of powers, but does not provide much discussion of individual rights and liberties.

9. According to coauthor Nowak, his philosophy differs from Rotunda's on many constitutional issues but their books do not advocate a particular point of view. Jan Crawford Greenburg, *Starr's Aide on Ethics, Constitution No Ivory–Tower Professor*, Chi. Trib., Mar. 25, 1998, at 6.

10. See Edward Rubin, *Casebook Review: Politics, Doctrinal Coherence, and the Art of Treatise Writing*, 21 Seattle U. L. Rev. 837, 851 (1998) ("Professor Chemerinsky's treatise is the best constitutional law treatise that has been produced to date.")

Amar's *America's Constitution: A Biography* (2005), which provides a clause-by-clause survey of the document, explaining the background and history of major provisions and accompanied by more than one hundred pages of endnotes.[11]

In addition to the numerous relevant articles in law reviews of general coverage, several periodicals specialize in constitutional issues. Student-edited law reviews include *Harvard Civil Rights–Civil Liberties Law Review*, *Hastings Constitutional Law Quarterly*, and *University of Pennsylvania Journal of Constitutional Law*. *Constitutional Commentary* is a faculty-edited journal from the University of Minnesota with a preference for "shorter, less ponderous articles" than those found in most traditional law reviews.[12] Journals focusing on the Supreme Court, such as the *Supreme Court Review* and the annual survey of the Court's term in the *Harvard Law Review*, also provide extensive coverage of constitutional topics.

(c) Court Decisions

The Constitution's provisions have been applied over the past two centuries to a wide array of situations which its drafters could not have foreseen. To interpret the language of the Constitution, it is essential to understand how it has been applied by the courts—particularly the Supreme Court, but also the lower federal courts and state courts. As Charles Evans Hughes said in a speech when he was governor of New York, "We are under a Constitution, but the Constitution is what the judges say it is."[13] The reference works discussed earlier highlight leading court decisions, but far more extensive coverage is available from two heavily annotated editions of the Constitution and other resources.

(1) Annotated codes

Two of the most useful versions of the Constitution are published as part of the unofficial editions of federal statutes, *United States Code Annotated* (*USCA*) (on Westlaw and in print from West) and *United States Code Service* (*USCS*) (on Lexis and in

---

11. Older books can be found using ROBERT J. JANOSIK, THE AMERICAN CONSTITUTION: AN ANNOTATED BIBLIOGRAPHY (1991), which is arranged by subject and includes helpful descriptive annotations of more than a thousand monographs. A wide range of books and articles are covered in SHELLEY L. DOWLING & MARY C. CUSTY, THE JURISPRUDENCE OF UNITED STATES CONSTITUTIONAL INTERPRETATION: AN ANNOTATED BIBLIOGRAPHY (1999).

12. *Preface*, 1 CONST. COMMENT. 181, 181 (1984).

13. *Speech before the Elmira Chamber of Commerce, May 3, 1907*, ADDRESSES OF CHARLES EVANS HUGHES, 1906–1916, at 179, 185 (2d ed. 1916). The modern reader may think that Hughes was warning about the danger of judges' unchecked power, but he went on, "and the judiciary is the safeguard of our liberty and of our property under the Constitution."

print from LexisNexis). Both are annotated with extensive notes of judicial decisions that have applied or interpreted each constitutional provision. For some heavily litigated provisions such as the First Amendment or the Equal Protection Clause of the Fourteenth Amendment, these notes cover thousands of cases. In the printed versions, the entire Constitution occupies twenty-eight volumes in *USCA* and ten volumes in *USCS*. The Due Process Clause of the Fourteenth Amendment alone covers more than six volumes of the *USCA* set.

Each constitutional provision follows a standard format in *USCA* and *USCS*. The text of a section or amendment is broken down into individual clauses, each of which is followed by references to encyclopedias, annotations, and formbooks; a list of law review articles; and then abstracts of cases arranged by subject. These abstracts may be divided into hundreds or even thousands of subject divisions. The Fourth Amendment in *USCA*, for example, has more than four thousand classifications of notes on various aspects of search and seizure law, covering broad topics such as probable cause, exigent circumstances, electronic surveillance, and the exclusionary rule. Illustrations 2–2 and 2–3 on pages 48–49 show the pages from the bound volume of *USCA* containing Article II, Section 1, concerning the executive power. Illustration 2–2 has the text of the provision, cross-references, and a list of law review articles, while Illustration 2–3 provides notes of decisions preceded by a topical index.

The online versions on Westlaw and Lexis provide the opportunity to search the references and annotations by keyword and thus to pinpoint very specific fact situations without having to browse through other unrelated issues. There are times, however, when the print volumes may be more productive to use than their online counterparts, especially early in the research process. Browsing through the annotations and establishing a broader context for a particular fact situation can provide a better research framework than simply pinpointing one or two specific cases by keyword.

Neither *USCA* nor *USCS* contains any explanatory text summarizing or linking the annotations, so they are not the places to find an overview of constitutional doctrine. Their exhaustive case abstracts, however, make them ideal for determining how the courts have applied the Constitution's broad principles to specific circumstances.

There are some differences between the two sets. *USCA* is limited to federal court decisions, but *USCS* provides coverage of both federal and state cases. The annotations in *USCA* include relevant key numbers so that a search can easily continue by subject in a case digest or on Westlaw. At the beginning of the annotations in *USCS* there is a complete topical outline of all the issues covered, while *USCA* lists only the major subdivisions into which annotations are grouped. At the beginning of each subdivision, it then provides an alphabetical index listing the issues within that particular area.

The printed *USCA* and *USCS* volumes are supplemented annually by pocket parts, and between pocket parts by quarterly pamphlets. On Westlaw and Lexis, new annotations are incorporated into the main listing—but coverage is no more current than the latest printed supplement. To find more recent decisions, you will need to search the case databases or use KeyCite or Shepard's (as discussed below).

As noted earlier, the text of the U.S. Constitution also appears in the annotated code for nearly every state. Only a few of these state code publications, however, provide case annotations for the federal constitution.[14] Those that do so provide a valuable service by allowing researchers to focus on how the Constitution's provisions have been interpreted in the context of a particular state's law. The annotations usually include abstracts of both state court decisions and federal cases arising in that state.

(2) KeyCite, Shepard's, and Other Resources

References to court decisions applying and construing the provisions of the Constitution can also be found using KeyCite (on Westlaw) and Shepard's Citations (on Lexis or in print). These services provide extensive lists of citing cases, law review articles, and other secondary sources. The citation form recognized by KeyCite and Shepard's includes the specific section and clause of a provision, as in "us const art 2 sec 1 cl 1."

KeyCite and Shepard's include references to far more documents than the selective coverage in *USCA* and *USCS*—well over 100,000 in the case of the Fourteenth Amendment, for example—so their most valuable feature is to narrow retrieval by using Locate (Westlaw) or Focus (Lexis). These allow you to use keywords to narrow your research to very specific fact situations or legal issues mentioned in conjunction with a constitutional provision. The Locate and Focus features only work, however, with a KeyCite or Shepard's result of 2000 documents or fewer. For major constitutional provisions with tens of thousands of citing cases, it is

---

14. Annotated codes for Delaware, Georgia, Hawaii (official), Indiana (LexisNexis), Kansas, Massachusetts (LexisNexis), Michigan (LexisNexis), Mississippi, New Mexico (both official and LexisNexis), New York (LexisNexis), Rhode Island, South Carolina, Tennessee, and Vermont contain annotated editions of the federal constitution. Even in these few states, the annotated U.S. Constitutions are not included in the online state code databases on Westlaw and Lexis.

necessary first to restrict retrieval in another way, such as by document type or jurisdiction.

One helpful feature Westlaw incorporates into its *USCA* display of constitutional provisions (as well as statutes) is a link in the left margin to "Cases—Last 60 Days," for any provision that has been cited in very recent cases. This provides convenient KeyCite access to recent citing decisions too new to be incorporated into the annotations, although there may still be a gap of several weeks or months between the annotations and the most recent sixty days.

Researchers without access to an online citator can Shepardize the U.S. Constitution in *Shepard's Federal Statute Citations* and in each of Shepard's state citators. *Shepard's Federal Statute Citations* provides references in citing federal court decisions, arranged by circuit, and the state citators list references to the U.S. Constitution in the particular state's courts. For many provisions these citators simply provide long, unannotated lists of citations, but they may be of use if one needs to know how a particular court has applied or interpreted the federal constitution.

Standard case-finding tools can also be of value in finding case law under the Constitution. A search in Westlaw or Lexis can combine the citation of a constitutional section or amendment with relevant factual or legal terms, such as "first amendment" within the same paragraph as "commercial speech." Westlaw retrieval can be even more focused if a search is limited to the synopsis (*sy*) and digest (*di*) fields, as will be discussed in Chapter 8 on case research.

Print resources such as digests, *ALR*, and encyclopedias can also be useful starting places in finding court decisions on constitutional issues. Digests arrange headnotes of cases by subject; the "Constitutional Law" topic is arranged not by provision but along general themes such as construction and interpretation of constitutions, governmental powers, and protection of individual liberties. Digests can thus be used to find cases with similar themes whether interpreting provisions of the U.S. Constitution or a state constitution. Many of the annotations in *ALR Federal* contain extensive discussion of federal constitutional issues, and the "Constitutional Law" articles in the general encyclopedias *American Jurisprudence 2d* and *Corpus Juris Secundum* occupy more than 1500 pages in each set. Like the digests, these encyclopedias cover both federal and state constitutional issues.

(d) Historical Background

The events and discussions leading to the adoption of the Constitution and its amendments are recorded in a variety of reports, journals and other documents. These materials continue to be important resources, as courts attempt to apply the terms of an eighteenth century document to evolving modern circumstances. The significance of the framers' intent in interpreting the Constitution is a subject of considerable debate,[15] but for any researcher these proceedings and documents can provide valuable historical information.

(1) Drafting and Ratification

The Constitutional Convention of 1787 met behind closed doors and kept no official record of its proceedings. The journal of proceedings was eventually published in 1819, more than thirty years later, pursuant to a congressional resolution,[16] but it contained only a simple record of questions presented and votes. For more extensive background on the substance of the proposals and the debates, researchers must look to notes taken by James Madison and other delegates. Madison's notes were not published until 1840, four years after his death, and other notes were also published posthumously.[17]

The standard modern source for documentation of the convention is Max Farrand, *The Records of the Federal Convention of 1787* (1911; suppl. 1987, James H. Hutson ed.). This four-volume set includes the notes by major participants, arranged chronologically, and the texts of various alternative plans presented. The Library of Congress website provides full-text access to the 1911 edition of Farrand's *Records* <lcweb2.loc.gov/ammem/amlaw/lwfr.html>, while Madison's notes, generally considered to be the most authoritative source, are available from Yale Law School's Avalon Project <avalon.law.yale.edu/subject_menus/debcont.asp> and in HeinOnline's Legal Classics Library <www.heinonline.org>.[18]

---

15. There is a voluminous literature on the role of original intent in constitutional interpretation. Opposing perspectives can be found in books by two Supreme Court justices: STEPHEN BREYER, ACTIVE LIBERTY: INTERPRETING OUR DEMOCRATIC CONSTITUTION (2005) and ANTONIN SCALIA, A MATTER OF INTERPRETATION: FEDERAL COURTS AND THE LAW (1997). INTERPRETING THE CONSTITUTION: THE DEBATE OVER ORIGINAL INTENT (Jack N. Rakove ed., 1990) is an older volume collecting several influential law review articles and other commentaries from both sides of the debate.

16. Res. 8, 3 Stat. 475 (1818).

17. On the background and reliability of these sources, see James H. Hutson, *The Creation of the Constitution: The Integrity of the Documentary Record*, 65 TEX. L. REV. 1 (1986). Madison

delayed publication of his notes until after his death because he felt they should not be an authoritative source of constitutional interpretation. See H. Jefferson Powell, *The Original Understanding of Original Intent*, 98 HARV. L. REV. 885, 936–38 (1985).

18. 1787: DRAFTING THE U.S. CONSTITUTION (Wilbourn E. Benton ed., 1986) reproduces excerpts from participants' notes, arranged by article and section. Two earlier officially published compilations of notes, letters and other documents that may be available in libraries are DOCUMENTARY HISTORY OF THE CONSTITUTION OF THE UNITED STATES OF AMERICA, 1786–1870 (1894–1905; reprinted 1965), and DOCUMENTS ILLUSTRATIVE OF THE FORMATION OF THE UNION OF THE AMERICAN STATES, H.R. DOC. NO. 69–398 (1927).

The cases for and against ratification were published at the time in the newspapers. The most famous series of articles in support of the Constitution, originally published under the pseudonym "Publius," was written by Alexander Hamilton, John Jay, and James Madison, and was published in collected form as *The Federalist: A Collection of Essays, Written in Favour of the New Constitution* (1788) (available on HeinOnline). These essays remain an indispensable work for the study of the Constitution, and have been published since in numerous editions. Full texts of *The Federalist* are also available at several free Internet sites, including the Library of Congress's THOMAS <thomas.loc.gov/home/histdox/fedpapers.html> and the Avalon Project <avalon.law.yale.edu/subject_menus/fed.asp>.

The opponents of ratification, known generally as the Anti–Federalists, also presented their arguments in various newspapers and pamphlets. The most comprehensive collection of these writings is *The Complete Anti–Federalist* (Herbert J. Storing ed., 1981).[19] The first volume provides an analysis of Anti–Federalist thought; this is followed by the objections of non-signers of the Constitution, major series of pseudonymous essays published in contemporary newspapers (by writers such as the "Federal Farmer," Brutus, and Cato), and materials from the state ratifying conventions.

The Founders' Constitution (Philip B. Kurland & Ralph Lerner eds., 1987), which is available free online <press-pubs.uchicago.edu/founders/>, takes a different approach. Arranged by constitutional provision, it collects excerpts from the debates and articles, as well as documents with which the founders would have been familiar (such as Blackstone's *Commentaries*, the Declaration of Independence, and early state constitutions) and early post-Constitution court decisions and commentaries. The first volume is devoted to major themes such as republican government and separation of powers, the next three volumes cover the seven original articles of the Constitution, and volume five deals with the first twelve amendments.

Some consider the state convention debates concerning ratification of the federal Constitution to be more important as interpretive sources than the proceedings in the Philadelphia convention.[20]

---

19. A one-volume abridgment of THE COMPLETE ANTI-FEDERALIST was published as THE ANTI-FEDERALIST (Murray Dry ed., 1985). Jon L. Wakelyn, BIRTH OF THE BILL OF RIGHTS: ENCYCLOPEDIA OF THE ANTIFEDERALISTS (2004) has one volume of biographies of 140 prominent Anti–Federalists, and another of major speeches and writings, arranged by state.

20. In James Madison's view, "whatever veneration might be entertained for the body of men who formed our Constitution, the sense of that body could never be regarded as the oracular guide in expounding the Constitution. As the instrument came from them it was nothing more than the draft of a plan, nothing but a dead letter, until life

Historically the standard source for these has been Jonathan Elliot, *The Debates in the Several State Conventions on the Adoption of the Federal Constitution* (2d ed. 1836–45). The Library of Congress website has the full text of Elliot's volumes <lcweb2.loc.gov/ ammem/amlaw/lwed.html>, searchable and in page images, as does HeinOnline.

Elliot's *Debates* was riddled with errors,[21] and a much more comprehensive modern set originally edited by Merrill Jensen and now by John P. Kaminski et al., *The Documentary History of the Ratification of the Constitution* (1976–date), is considered more accurate and authoritative. It contains debates, commentaries, and other documents on the ratification process, gathered from a variety of sources, including convention journals, personal papers, contemporary newspapers and pamphlets, and secondary sources. To date, it covers ratification debates in eight states and extensive commentaries in the contemporary press.[22]

A useful website providing free access to a number of major historical documents is that of the Constitution Society <www.constitution.org>. The society has strongly held views,[23] but researchers can benefit from the wide range of constitutional documents it has put online. Under the heading "Founding Documents" <www.constitution.org/cs_found.htm>, it provides several versions of the Constitution, Madison's *Debates in the Federal Convention of 1787*, *The Federalist*, and other texts. Its "Liberty Library of Constitutional Classics" <www.constitution.org/liberlib.htm> contains more than a hundred classical texts, from authors including Plato, Thomas Hobbes and John Stuart Mill.

(2) The Bill of Rights and Subsequent Amendments

Under the terms of Article V, amendments to the Constitution are proposed by Congress and presented to the states for ratifica-

and validity were breathed into it by the voice of the people, speaking through the several State Conventions. If we were to look, therefore, for the meaning of the instrument beyond the face of the instrument, we must look for it, not in the General Convention, which proposed, but in the State Conventions, which accepted and ratified the Constitution." 5 ANNALS OF CONG. 776 (1796).

21. See Hutson, supra note 17, at 13–21.

22. Excerpts are also available in a shorter modern collection, THE DEBATE ON THE CONSTITUTION: FEDERALIST AND ANTI-FEDERALIST SPEECHES, ARTICLES, AND LETTERS DURING THE STRUGGLE OVER RATIFICATION (Bernard Bailyn ed., 1993). Research in contemporary press coverage can now be done through extensive online databases such as America's Historical Newspapers <www.readex.com>, which includes full-text coverage of dozens of newspapers published at the time of the constitutional convention and ratification.

23. A reviewer noted that Constitution Society founder Jon Roland "sees violations of the Constitution of the United States everywhere. Because of his beliefs, he has mounted this full-text collection of classic books and other works on constitutional government for all to read. Take advantage of Roland's paranoia and peruse ... the seminal works of the U.S. government." Irene McDermott, *Great Books Online*, SEARCHER, Sept. 2001, at 71, 76.

tion. The Constitution as originally ratified had no provisions for individual rights, in part because the framers felt that protections in state constitutions would be sufficient, but it was soon recognized that protection of rights on the national level was needed. The first ten amendments, the Bill of Rights, were proposed in 1789 and ratified in 1791. Although many other amendments have been suggested over the years, the Constitution has so far been amended only twenty-seven times.[24]

These amendments are discussed in reference sources such as *The Constitution of the United States of America: Analysis and Interpretation* and *Encyclopedia of the American Constitution*. Two notable reference works focus specifically on the amendments. *Constitutional Amendments: 1789 to the Present* (Kris E. Palmer ed., 1999) addresses each amendment in order with a lengthy article on the original context and subsequent interpretation. John R. Vile, *Encyclopedia of Constitutional Amendments, Proposed Amendments, and Amending Issues, 1789–2002* (2d ed. 2003) covers a broader range of topics, with about 400 short articles on the amendments and related issues. Both works provide references for further research.

Documents on the Bill of Rights and other proposed or enacted amendments to the federal Constitution can be found in several sources. As noted above, *The Founders' Constitution* covers the first twelve amendments as well as the original seven articles. The texts of major documents relating to the Bill of Rights appear in Bernard Schwartz, *The Bill of Rights: A Documentary History* (1971) and *The Complete Bill of Rights: The Drafts, Debates, Sources, and Origins* (Neil H. Cogan ed., 1997). Schwartz's collection is arranged chronologically, while Cogan's work provides excerpts from source documents arranged by amendment. Both include texts of proposals in Congress and from the state conventions; earlier and contemporaneous provisions on related issues; and discussion of the amendments in Congress, conventions, newspapers, and letters.

The most important amendments since the Bill of Rights have been the Reconstruction amendments, in particular the Fourteenth Amendment's Due Process and Equal Protection Clauses. Because the Reconstruction amendments were proposed by Congress, the sources for deliberations are the House and Senate debates in the *Congressional Globe* and *Congressional Record*. These are reprinted in *The Reconstruction Amendments' Debates: The Legislative and Contemporary Debates in Congress on the 13th, 14th, and 15th*

---

24. PROPOSED AMENDMENTS TO THE U.S. CONSTITUTION, 1787–2001 (John R. Vile ed., 2003) reprints and updates several published reports analyzing and listing the more than 11,000 proposed amendments that have been introduced in Congress, and includes a comprehensive index of all amendments proposed through 2001.

Amendments (Alfred Avins ed., 1967), which includes a 30–page "Reader's Guide" explaining the context and significance of each document. Volume one of *Statutory History of the United States: Civil Rights* (Bernard Schwartz ed., 1970) also contains extensive excerpts from these debates.

Numerous books have been written on the drafting and interpretation of the Fourteenth Amendment and other constitutional provisions. These can generally be found by doing a subject search in a library catalog under the heading "United States–Constitution–___th Amendment." Works on the Bill of Rights are cataloged under "United States–Constitution–1st-10th Amendments," and more general works are listed under "Constitutional amendments–United States."

§ 2.2   State Constitutions

Each of the fifty states is governed by its own constitution, which establishes the structure of government and guarantees fundamental rights. These documents vary considerably in length and scope, and most address the day-to-day activities of government in a far more detailed manner than that of the U.S. Constitution. The federal Constitution deals only with a limited number of specified powers, but state constitutions must deal with a broader range of institutions and government activity. In general, states also amend their constitutions far more frequently, with an average of more than 100 amendments per state.[25]

State constitutions can be a vital tool in ensuring citizens' rights, and many state constitutions have bills of rights that are more extensive and detailed than their federal counterpart. Even where the words in a state document mirror those in the federal Constitution, the judiciary of each state can interpret the terms of its own fundamental law. A state constitution cannot deprive persons of federal constitutional rights, but it can guarantee additional protections not found in federal law. In an influential *Harvard Law Review* article in 1977, Justice William J. Brennan, Jr. urged the independent consideration and application of state constitutional rights.[26] This call for "judicial federalism" has been followed by numerous similar articles by state court jurists in the 1980s, a scholarly backlash during the 1990s, and a continuing discussion in the journal literature.[27]

25. Christopher W. Hammons, *State Constitutional Reform: Is It Necessary?*, 64 Alb. L. Rev. 1327, 1328–34 (2001).

26. William J. Brennan, *State Constitutions and the Protection of Individual Rights*, 90 Harv. L. Rev. 489 (1977).

27. Two recent articles summarizing these developments, with citations to many of the relevant articles, are Shirley S. Abrahamson, *State Constitutional Law, New Judicial Federalism, and the Rehnquist Court*, 51 Clev. St. L. Rev. 339 (2004), and Robert F. Williams, *The*

As with the federal constitution, a variety of online and print resources provide access to the constitutional texts as well as to notes of court decisions, commentary, and historical documents.

(a) Texts

The texts of state constitutions are easily located in several sources. Each state's statutory code contains the text of its current constitution, usually along with earlier constitutions and other fundamental documents, and almost every state provides online access to its constitution through its website. Several sites provide multistate access to these online constitutions, with FindLaw's list <www.findlaw.com/11stategov/indexconst.html> one of the most concise and convenient.

Another source for the texts of state constitutions is *Constitutions of the United States, National and State* (2d ed. 1974–date). This seven-volume set collects the current constitutions of all the states and territories in looseleaf binders, kept up to date by regular revisions of individual state pamphlets. The constitutions are not accompanied by either case annotations or commentary, but this may nonetheless provide a convenient way to compare provisions between states. Unfortunately, there is no general index to the set, as there had been for previous editions.[28] Instead just two separate subject indexes were published, both still useful but now quite dated: "Fundamental Liberties and Rights: A 50–State Index" (1980), and "Laws, Legislature, Legislative Procedure: A Fifty State Index" (1982).

(b) Cases and Secondary Sources

The most useful versions of state constitutions are those found in the annotated editions of the state codes, in which the text is accompanied by notes of court decisions and secondary sources. These are similar to the versions of the U.S. Constitution in *USCA* and *USCS*, and are the versions generally found on Westlaw or Lexis. Westlaw's constitutions are simply included within statutory databases, but in Lexis you can choose a file containing only the constitution or one containing both constitutions and statutes. Both Westlaw and Lexis also have databases with the constitutions of all fifty states for comparative research, called the ST–CONST database on Westlaw and "State Constitutions, Combined" on Lexis. Illustration 2–4 on page 50 shows the beginning of the article on

---

Third Stage of the New Judicial Federalism, 59 N.Y.U. ANN. SURV. AM. L. 211 (2003). Many of the major articles are reprinted in STATE EXPANSION OF FEDERAL CONSTITUTIONAL LIBERTIES: INDIVIDUAL RIGHTS IN A DUAL CONSTITUTIONAL SYSTEM (James A. Gardner ed., 1999).

28. The first (1915) and second (1959, with 1967 supplement) editions of INDEX DIGEST OF STATE CONSTITUTIONS may still be useful for historical coverage.

executive power in the Rhode Island Constitution, as it appears in *General Laws of Rhode Island.* The excerpt provides a cross-reference to a statutory provision, references to comparable provisions in the Connecticut and Massachusetts constitutions, and notes of state supreme court decisions.

Standard approaches to case-finding can also be used in researching state constitutional law. The state case law databases in Westlaw and Lexis allow you to search for documents by combining citations of constitutional provisions with specific keywords. The topic "Constitutional Law" is used in West's digests for issues arising under both federal and state constitutions, and many issues of state governmental powers are digested under the topic "States." Both KeyCite and Shepard's Citations cover state constitutions, and for many provisions they provide a more extensive list of citing sources than the annotated code.

For research into a particular state's constitution, one of the best places to start may be a volume in the series *Reference Guides to the State Constitutions of the United States* (1990–date), which now covers more than forty states. Each volume includes a summary of the state's constitutional history, a detailed section-by-section analysis of the constitution with background information and discussion of judicial interpretations, and a brief bibliographical essay providing references for further research.[29]

Robert L. Maddex, *State Constitutions of the United States* (2d ed. 2006) is a useful starting place for surveying constitutional provisions in several states. This volume has a brief summary of each state's constitutional history, followed by a summary and article-by-article explanation of its current constitution. It also includes tables providing a convenient comparison of such state constitutional issues as governmental structure, number of amendments, and rights protected.

The first chapter of the Council of State Governments' annual *Book of the States* also focuses on constitutions. It provides a narrative survey of current developments in state constitutional law, accompanied by tables on topics such as the length of each constitution, dates of adoption, and amendment procedures.

Two recent guides to the study of state constitutions are G. Alan Tarr, *Understanding State Constitutions* (1998), discussing the nature and history of state constitutions since independence; and James A. Gardner, *Interpreting State Constitutions: A Juris-*

---

29. Titles follow the standard format THE ___ STATE CONSTITUTION: A REFERENCE GUIDE. As of 2009, the only states not yet covered are Illinois, Massachusetts, Missouri, Oregon, Pennsylvania, and South Dakota. THE CONSTITUTIONAL- ISM OF AMERICAN STATES (George E. Connor & Christopher W. Hammons eds., 2008) is a single-volume work covering all fifty states, with a separate chapter on the constitutional history and theory of each state.

prudence of Function in a Federal System (2005), an analysis of their modern relationship to the national government. The three-volume set *State Constitutions for the Twenty–First Century* (G. Alan Tarr et al. eds., 2006) focuses on issues of constitutional reform and drafting. Law reviews feature symposia on state constitutions from time to time, and *Rutgers Law Journal* publishes an annual issue on state constitutional law.

The major treatise covering individual rights under state constitutions is Jennifer Friesen, *State Constitutional Law: Litigating Individual Rights, Claims, and Defenses* (4th ed. 2006–date). The first volume of this set discusses issues such as freedom of expression and civil actions for the violation of state constitutional rights; the second covers search and seizure, the rights of defendants, and punishment issues.

(c) Historical Research

Unlike the venerable and rarely amended United States Constitution, state constitutions are subject to frequent amendment and revision. Many states have had several constitutional conventions and a number of complete revisions; the most recent constitution in the country is Georgia's tenth, adopted in 1983. Louisiana has had eleven constitutions in its history. On the other hand, nineteen states still operate under amended versions of their original constitution, and the constitutions for Massachusetts, New Hampshire and Vermont date back to the eighteenth century.

Just as records from the 1787 federal convention may be useful in interpreting the U.S. Constitution, journals and proceedings of state constitutional conventions can provide insight into the meaning or intent of constitutional provisions. These can be found in online catalogs under headings such as "Constitutional conventions–[State]" and "[State]–Constitutional convention–[Year]." The most comprehensive source for such documents is the LexisNexis microfiche collection *State Constitutional Conventions, Commissions, and Amendments,* containing material published from 1776 to 1988 for all fifty states.[30] Information on resources for territorial and initial state constitutions can be found in *Prestatehood Legal Materials: A Fifty–State Research Guide* (Michael Chiorazzi & Marguerite Most eds., 2005).

The major constitutional documents of every state, including enabling acts, acts of admission, and all enacted constitutions, are

---

30. Access to the microfiche is provided by three guides: STATE CONSTITUTIONAL CONVENTIONS FROM INDEPENDENCE TO THE COMPLETION OF THE PRESENT UNION, 1776–1959: A BIBLIOGRAPHY (Cynthia E. Browne comp., 1973), STATE CONSTITU- TIONAL CONVENTIONS, 1959–1978: AN ANNOTATED BIBLIOGRAPHY (1981), and STATE CONSTITUTIONAL CONVENTIONS, COMMISSIONS & AMENDMENTS, 1979–1988: AN ANNOTATED BIBLIOGRAPHY (1989).

reprinted in *Sources and Documents of United States Constitutions* (William F. Swindler ed., 1973–79). Past constitutions and other documents are assembled in chronological order for each state, with background notes, editorial comments on provisions of succeeding constitutions, selected bibliographies on the constitutional history of each state, and indexes. The texts of the older documents in this set are mostly reprinted from two government compilations that may still be valuable for historical research: *The Federal and State Constitutions, Colonial Charters, and Other Organic Laws of the United States* (Benjamin Perley Poore ed., 2d ed. 1878); and *The Federal and State Constitutions, Colonial Charters, and Other Organic Laws of the States, Territories and Colonies Now or Heretofore Forming the United States of America,* H.R. Doc. No. 59–357 (Francis Newton Thorpe ed., 1909). Commentators have noted, however, that all three of these sets contain numerous errors and omissions.[31]

The NBER/Maryland State Constitutions Project <www.state constitutions.umd.edu> has put online most of the roughly 150 state constitutions adopted since 1776, based on the original sources and thus correcting errors in the earlier printed collections. The site's goal is to provide searchable and indexed text for every one of the roughly 150 state constitutions since 1776, as well as quantitative databases on the characteristics of state constitutions. Historical state constitutions are also included in two major collections of worldwide scope, *Constitutions of the World from the late 18th Century to the Middle of the 19th Century* (Horst Dippel ed., 2005–date) and the microfiche *Constitutions of the World 1850 to the Present* (Horst Dippel ed., 2002–date).

---

31. See, e.g., Horst Dippel, *Human Rights in America, 1776–1849: Rediscovering the States' Contribution*, 67 ALB. L. REV. 713, 716 n.15 (2004); W. F. Dodd, Book Review, 4 AM. POL. SCI. REV. 135, 137–38 (1910).

EXECUTIVE DEPARTMENT

ARTICLE II

SECTION 1. Clause 1. The executive Power shall be vested in a President of the United States of America. He shall hold his Office during the Term of four Years and, together with the Vice President, chosen for the same Term, be elected, as follows:

NATURE AND SCOPE OF PRESIDENTIAL POWER

Creation of the Presidency

Of all the issues confronting the members of the Philadelphia Convention, the nature of the presidency ranks among the most important and the resolution of the question one of the most significant steps taken.[1] The immediate source of Article II was the New York constitution, in which the governor was elected by the people and thus independent of the legislature, his term was three years and he was indefinitely re-eligible, his decisions except with regard to appointments and vetoes were unencumbered with a council, he was in charge of the militia, he possessed the pardoning power, and he was charged to take care that the laws were faithfully executed.[2] But when the Convention assembled and almost to its closing days, there was no assurance that the executive department would not be headed by plural administrators, would not be unalterably tied to the legislature, and would not be devoid of many of the powers normally associated with an executive.

Debate in the Convention proceeded against a background of many things, but most certainly uppermost in the delegates' minds was the experience of the States and of the national government under the Articles of Confederation. Reacting to the exercise of powers by the royal governors, the framers of the state constitu-

[1] The background and the action of the Convention is comprehensively examined in C. THACH, THE CREATION OF THE PRESIDENCY 1775-1789 (1923). A review of the Constitution's provisions being put into operation is J. HART, THE AMERICAN PRESIDENCY IN ACTION 1789 (1948).

[2] Hamilton observed the similarities and differences between the President and the New York Governor in THE FEDERALIST, No. 69 (J. Cooke ed. 1961), 462-470. On the text, see New York Constitution of 1777, Articles XVII-XIX, in 5 F. Thorpe, *The Federal and State Constitutions*, H. DOC. No. 357, 59th Congress, 2d sess. (1909), 2632-2633.

483

Illustration 2–1. THE CONSTITUTION OF THE UNITED STATES OF AMERICA: ANALYSIS AND INTERPRETATION 1273, S. DOC. No. 108–17 (Johnny H. Killian et al. eds., 2004).

For more information on using Westlaw to supplement your research, see the Westlaw Electronic Research Guide, which follows the Explanation.

Section 1, Clause 1. Executive Power, Term

Section 1. The executive Power shall be vested in a President of the United States of America. He shall hold his Office during the Term of four Years, and, together with the Vice President, chosen for the same Term, be elected, as follows:

CROSS REFERENCES

Delegation of functions of President, see 3 USCA § 301 et seq.
Judicial power vested in Supreme Court and inferior courts, see USCA Const. Art. III § 1.
Legislative power vested in Congress, see USCA Const. Art. I, § 1.
Limitation on terms served by President, see USCA Const. Amend. XXII.
Procedure for choosing President and Vice President, see USCA Const. Amend. XII.

LAW REVIEW AND JOURNAL COMMENTARIES

A national security workshop: separation of powers: Do we have an "Imperial Congress"? R. Friedman et seq., 11 Geo.Mason U.L.Rev. 61 (1988).
Checks and balances in an era of presidential lawmaking. Abner S. Greene, 61 U.Chi.L.Rev. 123 (1994).
Constitutional bait and switch: Executive reinterpretation of arms control treaties. David A. Koplow, 137 U.Pa.L.Rev. 1353 (1989).
Do we have an imperial Congress? John Norton Moore, 43 U.Miami L.Rev. 139 (1988).
Executive privilege. Archibald Cox, 122 U.Pa.L.Rev. 1383 (1974).
Executive privilege, congressional subpoena power, and judicial review: Three branches, three powers, and some relationships. Rex E. Lee, 1978 B.Y.U.L.Rev. 231.
Extradition of government agents as a municipal law remedy for state-sponsored kidnapping. Comment, 81 Cal.L.Rev. 1541 (1993).
Normalizing the separation of powers. Keith Werhan, 70 Tul.L.Rev. 2681 (1996).
Pendent party jurisdiction: Congress giveth what the Eighth Circuit taketh away. Thomas Jamison, 17 Wm.Mitchell L.Rev. 753 (1991)
President and the Administration. Lawrence Lessig and Cass R. Sunstein, 94 Colum.L.Rev. 1 (1994).
Presidential power to gather intelligence. Philip A. Lacovara, 40 Law & Contemp.Probs. 106 (1976).
Toward a state constitutional analysis of allocation of powers: legislators and legislative appointees performing administrative functions. John Devlin, 66 Temp.L.Rev. 1205 (1993).
What the constitution means by executive power. Charles J. Cooper, Orrin Hatch, Eugene v. Rostow, and Michael Tigar, 43 U.Miami L.Rev. 165 (1988).

WESTLAW ELECTRONIC RESEARCH

See WESTLAW guide following the Explanation pages of this volume.

Notes of Decisions

Generally 1   Administrative agencies 3

179

Illustration 2–2. U.S. CONST. art. II, § 1, cl. 1, in UNITED STATES CODE ANNOTATED.

Art. II § 1, cl. 1   **THE PRESIDENT**

Agents 4, 5
    Generally 4
    Presumption of authority 5
Aliens and nationality 6
Antitrust regulation 7
Balancing test, executive privilege 14
Bridges and tunnels 8
Compensation of government officers and employees 9
Emergencies 10
Eminent domain 11
Executive orders 12
Executive privilege 13-15
    Generally 13
    Balancing test 14
    Persons entitled to assert privilege 15

Express and implied powers generally 2
Foreign commerce and communications 16
Foreign relations 17
Immunity from suit 18
Impoundment of funds 20
Initiation of judicial proceedings 19
Persons entitled to assert privilege, executive privilege 15
Presidential papers and records 21
Presumption of authority, agents 5
Prisons and prisoners 22
Travel 23
Wiretapping 24

---

1. Generally

There can be no impairment of executive power, where actions pursuant to that power are impermissible under the Constitution. (Per Mr. Justice Brennan, with two Justices joining and two Justices concurring in result.) Elrod v. Burns, U.S.Ill.1976, 96 S.Ct. 2673, 427 U.S. 347, 49 L.Ed.2d 547. Constitutional Law ⬅ 72

Restrictions upon the President's power which are appropriate in cases of domestic security become artificial in the context of the international sphere. U. S. v. Brown, C.A.5 (La.) 1973, 484 F.2d 418, certiorari denied 94 S.Ct. 1490, 415 U.S. 960, 39 L.Ed.2d 575. United States ⬅ 28

The powers and duties of the executive inure to the office of the presidency and not to any individual officeholder; the president is but a transient holder of the public trust. Nixon v. Sampson, D.C.D.C.1975, 389 F.Supp. 107, stay granted 513 F.2d 430, 168 U.S.App.D.C. 172, action dismissed on other grounds 437 F.Supp. 654, reversed on other grounds 591 F.2d 944, 192 U.S.App.D.C. 335. United States ⬅ 26

Constitution's grant of executive power does not include power to nullify congressional actions. Sioux Val. Empire Elec. Ass'n, Inc. v. Butz, D.C.S.D.1973, 367 F.Supp. 686, affirmed 504 F.2d 168. Constitutional Law ⬅ 77

The theory that the President not only has the right but the duty to do anything that the needs of the Nation demand unless such action is forbidden by the Constitution or acts of Congress, is not in accord with our theory of government of laws rather than of men. Youngstown Sheet & Tube Co. v. Sawyer, D.C.D.C. 1952, 103 F.Supp. 569, 62 Ohio Law Abs. 405, 47 O.O. 307, order stayed 197 F.2d 582, 90 U.S.App.D.C. 416, certiorari granted 72 S.Ct. 775, 343 U.S. 937, 96 L.Ed. 1344, affirmed 72 S.Ct. 863, 343 U.S. 579, 96 L.Ed. 1153, 62 Ohio Law Abs. 417, 62 Ohio Law Abs. 473, 47 O.O. 430, 47 O.O. 460. United States ⬅ 28

2. Express and implied powers generally

Congress and the President, like the courts, possess no power not derived from the Constitution. Ex parte Quirin, U.S.Dist.Col.1942, 63 S.Ct. 2, 317 U.S. 1, 87 L.Ed. 3, 87 L.Ed. 7, modified 63 S.Ct. 22. Constitutional Law ⬅ 50; Constitutional Law ⬅ 76

Unless Congress grants executive branch authority by statute, authority of executive branch is limited to express and implied powers of this article, insofar as those powers are not inconsistent with express and implied legislative authority of Congress in article I. In re Grand Jury Investigation of Ven-Fuel, M.D.Fla. 1977, 441 F.Supp. 1299. See, also, Olegario v. U.S., C.A.2 (N.Y.) 1980, 629 F.2d 204, certiorari denied 101 S.Ct. 1513, 450 U.S. 980, 67 L.Ed.2d 814. Constitutional Law ⬅ 76

The President can exercise no power which cannot be fairly and reasonably traced to some specific grant of power, or justly implied and included within such express grant, as proper and necessary to its exercise and such specific grant must be either in Federal Constitution or in act of Congress passed in pursuance thereof, and there is no undefined residuum of power which President can exercise because it seems to him to be in the public interest. Youngstown Sheet & Tube Co.

Illustration 2–3. U.S. Const. art. II, § 1, cl. 1 notes, in United States Code Annotated.

ARTICLE IX

OF THE EXECUTIVE POWER

Section 1. Power vested in governor. — The chief executive power of this state shall be vested in a governor, who, together with a lieutenant governor, shall be elected by the people.

Cross References. Powers and duties of governor, § 42-7-1.
Comparative Provisions. Power of governor:

Conn. 1965 Const., art. Fourth, § 5.
Mass. Const. Pt. 2, C. 2, § 1, Art. 4.

NOTES TO DECISIONS

1. Power of Governor.
Under this provision the chief executive power of the state is vested in the governor, but the Constitution gives him expressly very little exeuctive power and gives the general

assembly in grand committee power to elect officers whose choice is not expressly provided for in the Constitution. Gorham v. Robinson, 57 R.I. 1, 186 A. 832 (1936).

Section 2. Faithful execution of laws. — The governor shall take care that the laws be faithfully executed.

Comparative Provisions. Execution of laws:

Conn. 1965 Const., art. Fourth, § 12.

NOTES TO DECISIONS

ANALYSIS

1. Advisory opinions.
2. Loss of federal funds.
3. Appointment of commission.

1. Advisory Opinions.
This provision requires the performance of a continuing obligation by the governor and the general assembly, and the effective performance of this obligation requires from time to time assistance from the judges of the supreme court, upon questions of law, as best provided through the device of the advisory opinion (R.I. Const., Art. X, Sec. 3). Opinion to Governor, 96 R.I. 358, 191 A.2d 611 (1963).

2. Loss of Federal Funds.
Under this provision the governor must strictly adhere to the provisions of a state statute, although to do so may result in the loss to the state of substantial federal welfare funds. Advisory Opinion to Governor, 109 R.I. 474, 287 A.2d 353 (1972).

3. Appointment of Commission.
The governor has the authority to appoint a commission to investigate in his behalf alleged malfeasance and nonfeasance in management of state penal institutions, but the members would not be entitled to administer oaths or enforce attendance of witnesses, and their report would be a privileged communi-

Illustration 2–4. R.I. CONST. art. 9, §§ 1–2.

Chapter 3

THE LEGISLATURE, PART 1: STATUTES

Table of Sections

The role of statutory law in legal research is often underemphasized, perhaps due to the focus on appellate decisions in American legal education, and on cases in the popular conception of the lawyer's work. In practice, however, statutes are central to most legal issues, and ascertaining whether there is a governing statute should usually precede searching for judicial precedents. Indeed, the vast majority of appellate decisions today involve the application or interpretation of statutes rather than the consideration of common law principles.[1]

---

1. Two influential series of lectures recognizing the importance of statutes in the judicial system are GUIDO CALABRESI, A COMMON LAW FOR THE AGE OF STATUTES (1982) and JAMES WILLARD HURST, DEALING WITH STATUTES (1982). The publication of these and other works led a leading scholar to refer to 1982 as the "annus mirabilis" for the renaissance of interest in statutes. WILLIAM N. ESKRIDGE, JR., DY-

Statutory research is shaped by the doctrine of judicial review established in Chief Justice John Marshall's opinion in *Marbury v. Madison*, holding that the judicial branch had the power to review actions of the legislature and executive and to rule on their constitutionality.[2] In considering statutes, therefore, it is important to find not only the relevant text but also court decisions that interpret this text and define its terms. The most common research sources are *annotated codes*, which provide the text of the statutes in force accompanied by notes of court decisions.

The forms of statutory publication and research vary somewhat from jurisdiction to jurisdiction, although they share similar features. This chapter begins with an overview of the way statutes are published online and in print, discusses common research approaches and concerns, and then examines sources for federal and state statutes more closely. The scope of the chapter is limited to the sources and use of enacted legislation. The legislative process and research in pending bills will be considered in Chapter 4.

§ 3.1   Patterns of Statutory Publication

The texts of enacted legislation for the various jurisdictions of the United States are issued successively in a series of forms which follow a common pattern. Each of these forms of publication, whether used online or in print, may be needed in the research process. Although you will begin most statutory research with an annotated code, an understanding of the earlier forms of the statute is essential background.

Slip Laws. A new statute is first available as a slip law, an individual sheet or pamphlet containing just the one act. Slip laws are usually individually paginated, designated by a chapter or law number, and issued officially by the government.

Slip laws are not widely distributed in paper, but this is the form of law that is most frequently available from legislative websites. Some sites have only the *enrolled bill*, or the final form of the bill that was passed by the legislature and presented to the executive for approval, but most states and the federal government provide access to the legislation as approved and enacted into law.

NAMIC STATUTORY INTERPRETATION 335 n.1 (1994).

2. "It is emphatically the province and duty of the judicial department to say what the law is. Those who apply the rule to particular cases, must of necessity expound and interpret that rule. If two laws conflict with each other, the courts must decide on the operation of each. So if a law be in opposition to the constitution; if both the law and the constitution apply to a particular case, so that the court must either decide that case conformably to the law, disregarding the constitution; or conformably to the constitution, disregarding the law; the court must determine which of these conflicting rules governs the case. This is of the very essence of judicial duty." *Marbury v. Madison*, 5 U.S. (1 Cranch) 137, 177–78 (1803),

(The text of these documents should be identical, but one is identified by a bill number and the other by a slip law or chapter number.)

Session Laws. At the end of a legislative session, the laws enacted during the session are gathered and published together in chronological order in a permanent format in bound volumes. The designation for these publications varies between jurisdiction, but they are known by such names as *Statutes at Large, Laws, Session Laws, Acts,* or *Acts and Resolves.*

The slip laws and session laws print exactly the same legislation, unless typographical errors in the slip laws were later corrected. The difference between these two sources is simply one of citation form: The session laws provide a page number by which the law can be cited. It is the session law source, with page numbers, that is generally required by *The Bluebook.*[3]

In most states, the session laws constitute the *positive law* form of legislation, *i.e.,* the authoritative, binding text of the laws, and the determinative language if discrepancies are found in subsequent printed versions such as codes. These other forms are only *prima facie* evidence of the statutory language, unless they have been specifically designated as positive law by the legislature.

The federal government and each of the fifty states publish their session laws following the end of each legislative session, and these publications generally include subject indexes and tables indicating which existing laws have been modified or repealed by newly enacted legislation. Most jurisdictions also have commercial services which provide more prompt access to new laws as they are enacted. These services, publishing the texts of new laws in pamphlet form, are known as *advance legislative services* or *advance session law services.* They are also available through Westlaw and Lexis, and mirror the coverage of the slip laws on most official websites. The advance services generally do *not* have the same page numbers as the final session laws volumes.

Codes. Although the chronologically arranged session laws contain the official text of legislation, their use as research tools is limited. Researchers usually need the laws currently in force, rather than the laws passed during a specific legislative term. They need to know about amendments and about other legislation on related topics. For this they turn to statutory compilations, known

---

3. The Bluebook: A Uniform System of Citation R. 12.4(b), at 106 (18th ed. 2005). The ALWD manual requires page references for thirty-two states, but for the other eighteen session laws may be cited by chapter, act or law number. ALWD Citation Manual: A Professional System of Citation 359–400 (3d ed. 2006).

generally as *codes*, which collect current statutes of general and permanent application and reprint them by subject.

In the strict sense of the word, a *code* is a broad, encompassing statement of general and systematic legal principles intended to cover all phases of human activity. This sort of comprehensive code is the basis of the legal system in civil law countries such as France and Germany. A *revision*, on the other hand, is a legislative redrafting and simplification of the various statutes previously enacted into law. A *compilation* is a subject arrangement without alteration of the statutes in force. A revision requires reenactment by the legislature, but a compilation can be unofficially published and does not require any legislative action.[4]

Only a few United States jurisdictions have codes in the civil law sense. The most well known are the civil codes in California and Louisiana.[5] Most states actually have revisions or compilations, but in practice the word "code" is used to encompass all three types of statutory collections.

The statutes in a code are grouped into broad subject topics, usually called *titles*, and within each title they are divided into chapters and then numbered sections. The parts of a single legislative act may be printed together or may be scattered by subject through several different titles. In the process of rearranging the codified statutes, amendments are incorporated, repealed laws are deleted, and minor technical adjustments are sometimes made in the text of the laws to fit them into a functional and coherent compilation. A detailed index for the entire code provides access to the sections dealing with particular problems or topics.

Almost every jurisdiction provides free online access to the text of its code, usually through the legislature's website. The free sites provide quick and convenient access to the statutes, but there are drawbacks. While all of the sites can be searched by keyword, only a few provide more sophisticated approaches such as natural language or proximity searching. Very few include notes of court decisions interpreting the statutes, and some do not even indicate the session law sources for code sections or amendments. A few online codes even include warnings that the online version is not

---

4. John Bell Sanborn, *The Problem of Statutory Revision*, 4 PROC. AM. POL. SCI. ASS'N 113, 113–14 (1907). Pennsylvania, for example, is in the process of its first official revision, *Pennsylvania Consolidated Statutes*, and those subjects that have not yet been revised are cited to the unofficial compilation *Purdon's Pennsylvania Statutes Annotated*.

5. For histories of these two major codifications, see VERNON VALENTINE PALMER, THE LOUISIANA CIVILIAN EXPERI-ENCE: CRITIQUES OF CODIFICATION IN A MIXED JURISDICTION (2005), and Lewis Grossman, *Codification and the California Mentality*, 45 HASTINGS L.J. 617 (1994). For a broader survey of American codification efforts beginning in the 17th century, see Gunther A. Weiss, *The Enchantment of Codification in the Common–Law World*, 25 YALE J. INT'L L. 435, 498–527 (2000).

official, and that the printed volumes must be consulted for the official text.

Some jurisdictions have official printed code publications containing the text of the statutes in force, usually without any notes of court decisions. In these jurisdictions, this is usually the authoritative text to which citation is expected in briefs and pleadings. It is also the preferred source specified by *The Bluebook* and the *ALWD Citation Manual.*[6] This can be somewhat problematic outside a jurisdiction, where very few libraries are likely to have copies of these official codes.

Whether online or in print, official editions of codes have two major shortcomings. They may not be very up to date and cannot be relied on for the most recent amendments. An outdated code may be good enough for a quick sense of the law, but serious research requires current information. Perhaps more significant for research purposes, the editorial additions in these codes are usually limited to a few notes about when a particular statute was enacted and amended. These are *unannotated* codes, which means that they do not provide citations to judicial decisions which have applied or construed the statutes. Finding relevant cases is such an important part of reading and interpreting statutes that official codes are simply not adequate for most statutory research.

Annotated Codes. An *annotated* code reproduces the text and arrangement of the official code. It incorporates new legislation, revisions and amendments, as does the official code, but an annotated code is not merely a record of legislative activity. After individual statutory sections, you will find references to a wealth of interpretive documents: relevant judicial or administrative decisions as well as regulations, attorney general opinions, legislative history materials, law reviews, legal encyclopedias, and treatises.

The case annotations are usually more than just lists of citations to relevant decisions, and most often take the form of short paragraphs summarizing specific points of law decided. These brief summaries allow researchers to browse the annotations to find relevant cases. Some statutory sections have been construed in thousands of court cases, and are accompanied by dozens or hundreds of pages of headnotes. These are usually divided into subject classifications, making it easier to find cases fitting a particular research problem. Other sections may have no annotations at all, if they are uncontroversial and have not led to litigation or are too new to have been considered in any published court decisions.

6. The Bluebook: A Uniform System of Citation R. 12.3, at 104 (18th ed. 2005); ALWD Citation Manual: A Profes-sional System of Citation R. 14.1(b), at 111 (3d ed. 2006).

Most annotated codes are commercial publications and thus are not available on free Internet sites. Westlaw and Lexis, however, have annotated codes for federal law and for all fifty states. These databases are among the most thorough and up-to-date resources for statutory research, incorporating new legislation within days of enactment and providing a variety of research links to lead from a code section to related cases and secondary sources.

In print, most annotated codes are supplemented by annual pocket parts and interim pamphlets over the course of the year. They are not as current as online sources but are usually much more up to date than official unannotated codes.

Other Sources. Session laws and annotated codes are the major comprehensive sources for statutes, but in specialized areas other resources may be even more useful. Looseleaf services provide the text of statutes in some specialized areas with updates on a weekly or biweekly basis. Tax services such as the *Standard Federal Tax Reporter* and the *United States Tax Reporter*, for example, provide the complete text of the Internal Revenue Code with each section accompanied by related regulations, extensive excerpts from legislative history sources, and notes of cases and administrative decisions. These services are in effect very thorough annotated codes for their specific field of law.

§ 3.2   Statutory Research Methods

Statutory research is one of the few areas of legal research where working with books may actually be easier than working online. To understand the scope of a specific section, it's usually necessary to see an entire code chapter or title. Scanning a few pages in a code volume can be easier than going from document to document in an online database. In addition, because the wording in statutes is often more vague or technical than the language used in other legal writing, the indexes that accompany annotated codes can often provide quicker and more convenient access to relevant provisions than an online keyword search.

(a) Online Research

Searching for statutes online presents problems different from those found in searching for sources such as case law or journal articles. Statutory provisions are often long, complicated documents with multiple subsections and sub-subsections, and it is necessary to be aware of how these different subsections relate to each other. An online source that doesn't indent subsections properly to indicate this hierarchy can make the task almost impossible. Reading a statute on the screen can also require extensive scrolling up and down to understand the scope of cross-references and provisos.

Despite these difficulties, of course, online resources are now the most common starting points for statutory research.

This discussion of research procedures focuses primarily on Westlaw and Lexis, which provide access to the highly useful annotated versions of codes and which have the same search procedures for statutes from all jurisdictions. Search approaches and features in other online resources for statutes may vary from state to state.

Using Fields and Segments. The statutory databases on Westlaw and Lexis are rich resources, but their comprehensive nature can make them difficult to search successfully. A full-text search finds words appearing in the statutes themselves as well as in the extensive annotations. The case summaries in these annotations often include legal terminology unrelated to the particular code section, and many searches return far too many irrelevant documents.

You can focus Westlaw and Lexis searches on the statutory language, rather than the notes of decisions, by using specific fields and segments. The *sd* (substantive document) field on Westlaw and the *unanno* segment on Lexis contain the headings, the text, and any official notes, but not the annotations. This is often the most effective way to search for language that is likely to appear in the statute itself.

Statutory language often includes cross-references and exceptions that may result in retrieval of irrelevant documents, so you may find it helpful to limit a search to just the headings to a statute, those words used to identify the title and the section. Westlaw uses the field *prelim* or *pr* for title, subtitle and chapter designations, and *caption* or *ca* for the section number and description. Lexis uses the segment *heading* for titles, subtitles and chapters, and *section* for individual sections. On Westlaw, you can combine two fields and do a search in all of the headings by using *pr,ca("search terms")* if unsure whether a term would appear in the heading for a chapter or for an individual section. These various fields and segments are listed on menus on the basic statutory search screens in Westlaw and Lexis.

Westlaw provides another way to search in the statutory text, by offering both annotated and unannotated versions of federal and state codes. This may be easier than using a field search, but it has its own inconveniences. The unannotated version includes links to KeyCite information, but there is no direct link to the annotated version's notes of decisions. To see these, you must run the search again in the annotated database or use *Find* to retrieve the section.

In some instances, searching just the text of the statute may be underinclusive. Sometimes the language used in court decisions does not even appear in the text of the law itself. A commonly cited example is federal employment discrimination law, which bars activities such as hostile work environment sexual harassment—without using any of those words in its text.[7] These words do, however, appear frequently in the annotations, so a full-text search will retrieve the relevant code section. The difficulty is that searching in the annotations is likely to retrieve dozens of unrelated provisions. A search for "sexual harassment" retrieves some two hundred sections in the *United States Code*, including provisions defining "maritime transactions" and "commerce" in arbitration proceedings, outlining the responsibilities of the Secretary of Defense, and establishing a minimum wage.

If terms and connectors searches retrieve too few or too many code sections, statutory research is an area where you may get better results with natural language searching. In a database of cases or journal articles, older, less important documents may rank abnormally high in a natural language search result. The documents in a code database, however, are all statutes currently in force, so a search will not retrieve obsolete or insignificant documents. The key terms in a statute are likely to appear over and over again in its annotations, causing it to rise to the top of a relevance-ranked listing. A terms and connectors search will usually retrieve more focused results, especially in finding precise statutory language. Natural language, which weighs terms unequally and retrieves a set number of documents even if they do not contain all of the search terms, should rarely be the default search method, but it may help you isolate a relevant code section when terms and connectors deliver too large a pile of tangential references.

Establishing Context. No matter how a search is performed, be aware that it retrieves only those specific *sections* that match the particular query. Westlaw and Lexis treat each code section as a separate document. The online display of a section indicates the title and chapter in which it belongs, but there is otherwise little perspective of its place in the statutory scheme. Because it is essential in statutory research to understand the context of a specific provision, it is usually necessary to examine nearby sections after finding one that is on point. There are several ways to do this.

Both Westlaw and Lexis allow you to browse the sections immediately preceding and following the document on your screen. Westlaw has "Previous Section" and "Next Section" links, and Lexis has a feature called "Book Browse." These allow you to move

---

7. 42 U.S.C. § 2000e–2(a)(1) (2000) prohibits discrimination "against any individual with respect to his compensation, terms, conditions, or privileges of employment, because of such individual's race, color, religion, sex, or national origin."

from one code section to the next, rather than between documents matching the search query. To go back to the original search results, you must then click on "Original Results" (Westlaw) or "Return to Search Results" (Lexis),

A more comprehensive way to grasp the context of a section is to see the table of contents for its chapter. In a Westlaw statutory display, this is done by clicking on "Table of Contents" in the left window. In Lexis, the same result is reached by clicking on the hyperlinked name of the chapter in the *TOC* heading at the top of the screen. By scanning the list of sections, you may find sections labeled "Definitions" or "Exclusions" that have a very direct impact on whether a particular statute is relevant to your research. A word does not necessarily have as broad a meaning in a statute as it may in everyday language.[8]

Westlaw offers an even more effective way to scan related sections. Clicking on the hyperlinked chapter number just above a code section opens a window with a display of the headings and text for all sections in the chapter. This is a stripped-down version, with no statutory notes or other annotations, but it may be the quickest way to scan a chapter to find relevant sections.

These browsing features are shown in the displays of code sections in Illustrations 3–1 and 3–2 on pages 93–94. Illustration 3–1, from Westlaw, includes the "Previous Section" and "Next Section" links at the top, as well as the links for "Table of Contents" at the left and the chapter number above the code section. Illustration 3–2, from Lexis, includes *Book Browse* at the top center and the "TOC" links to the lists of sections in this title, part, and chapter of the code.

Other Westlaw and Lexis Features. Both Westlaw and Lexis provide additional assistance with statutory research. Westlaw has an extensive menu of options on the left part of the screen, with links to KeyCite, notes of decisions, secondary sources, and legislative history resources. Some of this material is part of the full

---

8. In a case familiar to generations of law students, *Frigaliment Importing Co. v. B.N.S. Int'l Sales Corp.*, 190 F. Supp. 116, 117 (S.D.N.Y. 1960), Judge Henry Friendly posed the famous question "What is chicken?" The answer may depend on the jurisdiction and the context. A chicken is not an animal under the terms of the Nebraska Veterinary Medicine and Surgery Practice Act, which includes the following definition: "Animal means any animal other than man, and includes birds, fish, and reptiles, wild or domestic, living or dead, except domestic poultry." NEB. REV. STAT. § 38–3304 (LexisNexis Supp. 2007). Other definitions of "animal" are even more restrictive. IOWA CODE ANN. § 717B.1 (West 2003) excludes livestock, game, fur-bearing animals, fish, reptiles, and amphibians from its definition, and N.Y. GEN. BUS. L. § 752(1) (McKinney Supp. 2008) says simply, " 'Animal' means a dog or a cat." The New York definition is so narrow because it applies only to an article covering the sale of dogs and cats. It is essential to understand the context when reading a code section.

annotated version of the code section, available simply by scrolling down into the document, but some is provided by links through KeyCite. Lexis has a "Practitioner's Toolbox" for federal statutes and some states, linking to specific parts of the annotated code document (History; Interpretive Notes and Decisions; Commentary; Resources & Practice Tools). Some of these features are shown in the displays in Illustrations 3–1 and 3–2.

Other Free and Subscription Databases. Other statutory databases generally offer fewer options and research assistance than do Westlaw or Lexis. Most free websites have fairly simple keyword searching and may not provide ways to restrict a search to section headings, but this is less of an issue since most do not include any case annotations or other research references. No matter what source is used, however, it is vital to browse the nearby sections to make sure that important definitions or cross-references are not missed.

(b) KeyCite and Shepard's

Finding statutes is just the first step of statutory research. Before relying on a statute as authority, you must verify that it is still in force and ascertain how it has been affected by subsequent legislation and by judicial decisions. One reason that annotated codes are such effective research tools is that they provide regularly updated information on a statute's validity and treatment.

Even the annotated codes, whether online or in print, do not contain either the most recent legislative changes or references to *all* citing decisions. It may take weeks or months for amendments to be incorporated into the code database, and even longer for annotations to be written and assigned to specific code sections. Much more up-to-date and extensive research leads can be found by using KeyCite or Shepard's Citations.

KeyCite's coverage of statutes includes the cases summarized in code annotations, but it expands on these by listing other citing cases and articles as well as recent and pending legislation. The cases in the annotated code are listed first, followed by "Additional Citations" listed by jurisdiction in reverse chronological order. These have neither subject indexing nor abstracts, but they represent references that are not included in the annotated code. The older "Additional Citations" cases are not likely to be very significant, but this is also where the most recent court decisions can be found. Even a Supreme Court case may take several months to be incorporated into the annotations, but KeyCite lists it as soon as it is available in the database. A KeyCite display is shown in Illustration 3–3 on page 95, including eight cases from the annotated code and three "Additional Citations" cases.

Statutes on Westlaw include useful signals based on KeyCite information. A red flag appears at the top of the display if a code section has been found invalid or unconstitutional, or if it has been amended by recent legislation too new to be incorporated into the text. A yellow flag shows that a section's validity has been called into doubt, or that pending legislation would amend a section if enacted. As shown at the top of Illustrations 3–1 and 3–3, a small green C simply means that citing references are available.

Another valuable Westlaw feature, especially for people who work regularly with a statutory section, is a link to cases decided just in the most recent two months. This *Last 60 Days* link appears only if any recent decisions cite the statute, so it serves as an alert that there has been recent judicial activity. Because the time lag before a new decision is covered in the codes' annotations is often several months, however, it is important to remember that the "Last 60 Days" link does not necessarily include every case more recent than the notes of decisions.

The Lexis display of code sections does not include flags indicating unconstitutionality or recent amendments, but clicking on the "Shepardize" link (as shown at the top of Illustration 3–2) provides such information. As it does for cases, Shepard's uses signals to indicate judicial and legislative actions affecting a cited statute. Clicking on the "All Neg" link will limit a listing to documents such as cases that have found a statute unconstitutional. Clicking on "FOCUS–Restrict By" allows you to pick and choose particular treatments, specific jurisdictions, or certain types of citing documents. By clicking on "Index—*Shepard's* reports by court citation," you can also focus retrieval on documents citing a specific subsection. Illustration 3–4 on page 96 shows the Shepard's result for 18 U.S.C. § 879.

One of the most powerful uses of KeyCite or Shepard's is the ability to limit citing references to particular jurisdictions or to documents with specific keywords. The *Locate* and *Focus* features allow you to searching within a group of cases citing a specific code section, which can yield very effective and on-point results.

As with other sources, KeyCite and Shepard's provide references to any citing law review articles, encyclopedias, and other texts available through Westlaw or Lexis. In some instances these resources are also listed in the annotated code, but codes vary widely between jurisdictions in the scope of their secondary source references. For some states, KeyCite and Shepard's may provide far more extensive leads than the annotated code.

Shepard's, but not KeyCite, is available in print as well as online. In printed Shepard's volumes, the signals are in the form of abbreviations preceding the citing references. *C*, for example, indicates that a statute has been upheld as constitutional, and *U* that it has been held unconstitutional. These abbreviations are explained in a table at the beginning of each Shepard's statutory volume. One advantage of the printed versions of *Shepard's Citations* is that they include citations to session laws and to older codifications as well as current code provisions. The current code is the only statutory source that can be checked online in either KeyCite or Shepard's.

(c) Indexes and Tables

Even if you normally do all of your other work online, you might find it easier to begin statutory research with a printed code. Statutes can be long, complex documents, and it can be easier in print to flip back and forth within a section or between related sections. In addition, statutes are often written in a precise, sometimes obtuse language designed to eliminate ambiguities in interpretation, and the terms used in a code section may not be the ones that would occur to you in creating an online search. A subject index provides a more standard and straightforward vocabulary, and may lead more quickly to relevant provisions.

Indexes. The index to a federal or state annotated code is a complex and lengthy document, occupying as many as six volumes. Statutory indexes usually include numerous cross-references, between related headings as well as from terms that aren't used as subject headings. A researcher who looks in a code index under "Threats," for example, may find nothing but an entry saying "See Extortion" or "Extortion, this index." Illustration 3–5 on page 97 shows a page from the index to the *United States Code Annotated*, with several references to the statute shown in Illustrations 3–1 and 3–2.

Statutory indexes, unfortunately, can be sources of considerable frustration.[9] Indexers cannot foresee all possible terms a person might use, so it sometimes is necessary to rethink search terms and reformulate a query in order to find references. Even though they can be unwieldy and confusing, indexes may allow you to zero in on statutes that are directly on point more quickly than a full-text keyword search.[10]

---

9. We have come some distance from the reviewer who wrote of an early 19th-century state code: "The index is very elaborate, copious and accurate, and presents a beautiful analysis of the whole volume. It may be called, to use the language of Bayle, the *soul* of the statutes. One may read them all, by passing his eyes over its fine type, so completely and analytically is the whole

there displayed." *Revised Statutes of Massachusetts*, 15 AM. JURIST & L. MAG. 294, 319 (1836) (emphasis in original).

10. A few indexes are available online, although maneuvering between entries may still be easier in print. Westlaw has index databases for its United States Code Annotated (USCA–IDX) and for some forty state codes (___-ST–IDX), with links to listed code sections but not

Popular Name Tables. At times you may have a reference to a particular law by its name, without a citation, and need to find the text of the statute. How do you find the Americans with Disabilities Act? You could look in a subject index under "Disabilities," but a quicker way is to use a *popular name table*, which lists acts by name and provides references to citations in the session laws and code.

For older statutes, "popular name" often means a name with which a law has come to be associated over time, such as "Lanham Act" or "Mann Act." Most modern statutes, on the other hand, specify titles by which they may be cited. Some of these are short, some are technical, and some are rather tortured acronyms such as the Prosecutorial Remedies and Other Tools to End the Exploitation of Children Today Act of 2003 (PROTECT Act).[11] Both types of names are listed in popular name tables. Illustration 3–6 on page 98 shows an example of a popular name table in the *United States Code Annotated* listing the Presidential Threat Protection Act of 2000, which amended the section illustrated in this chapter.

While popular name tables include the names by which acts are designated by Congress and state legislatures, they don't always encompass the terms by which laws are known in the newspapers or on television. "Title VII" and "Title IX" are familiar terms for antidiscrimination laws, but neither appears in the table. In order to find citations from references such as these, the first step is to find more of the name (in these cases, Title VII of the Civil Rights Act of 1964 or Title IX of the Education Amendments of 1972). It may be simplest to do an online search for the phrase in order to identify the act. An Internet or newspaper search may turn up the full name of the act, and even better is a mention in a legal text or law review article that contains a footnote providing the statute's code citation.

Parallel Reference Tables and Parenthetical Notes. At times you may have a citation to a statute, but not the one that provides immediate access in a code. Some references are to session law citations, while others are to an outdated codification. In either instance you will need to determine whether a law is currently in force and, if so, where it is codified. For this, most codes include *parallel reference tables* providing cross-references to the code sections.

between cross-references. Lexis generally does not provide online indexes, and only half a dozen free state sites (Colorado, Iowa, Minnesota, Nevada, Oregon, and Wisconsin) include access by means of subject indexes.

11. Pub. L. No. 108–21, 117 Stat. 650 (2003) (codified in scattered sections of 18 U.S.C. and 28 U.S.C.).

The most extensive of the parallel reference tables are from the session laws to the code. For federal statutes and for some states, these can occupy several volumes spanning more than 200 years of enactments. In most instances, these tables also indicate which sections of session laws have been repealed or were of a temporary nature. They thus make it possible to track the fate of an act as it is moved around the code, amended, and perhaps repealed in part. Illustration 3–7 on page 99 shows an excerpt from a parallel reference table listing references from the federal session laws to the *United States Code*.

Not only are code sections sometimes assigned to new locations, but individual titles or entire codes can be reorganized under a revised numbering system. In such instances, tracking a statutory reference found in an older case or secondary source may require use of a parallel reference table providing cross-references from the older classification to the new one. These tables can be very handy if your reference to a code section from an older case or article finds either nothing at all or an unrelated provision. If a code doesn't have a table providing parallel references, it may be necessary to start from scratch in the subject index to identify comparable provisions under current law.

Just as parallel reference tables provide access to current code provisions from session laws or older code citations, the parenthetical references that follow the text of a code section allow you to reconstruct the language of a statute at any given point in the past. Obsolete statutes may be needed for any number of reasons, not just historical research. The terms of a repealed statute may still be of value in interpreting related provisions still in force, and older laws are needed to determine the law in effect and the meaning of terms when instruments such as wills or deeds were drafted.

The parenthetical references after a code section provide leads to earlier codifications and to all session laws that have amended the section. These references are the keys not only to determining earlier versions of a section but also to finding legislative history information for a particular enactment. They may appear as a hieroglyphic string of letters and numbers, but they have invaluable information.

Some codes make it easier to reconstruct past versions of a statute by including notes indicating the precise nature of each change. Others merely present a list of citations, making it necessary to check the session laws to determine the changes. Worse yet, some codes indicate only recent changes or (particularly in the case of many free Internet sites) have no notes at all.

As noted, the parenthetical references may indicate the location of the same or a comparable provision in an older codification.

Many jurisdictions have recodified their statutes several times, so to find a related provision from, say, thirty years ago, may require access to a completely different set of code volumes. These older sets are rarely available online but they can be found in many larger law libraries, and William S. Hein & Co. publishes a microfiche edition of superseded federal and state codes.

Westlaw and Lexis have statutes from most jurisdictions going back to the late 1980s or early 1990s, and reconstructing the law as of a date during that period may simply require a search in the appropriate archived database. For a few selected jurisdictions (federal law back to 1996, and eight states back to 1999 or 2000), Westlaw has a feature called PastStat Locator that indicates the effective dates of current and prior versions and includes an option to view the version in force on a specific date.

§ 3.3 Statutory Interpretation

In finding a statute and obtaining current information on its validity, you have taken only the first steps in applying it to a real-life situation. Even though statutes generally are written in a way that tries to leave no room for confusion, lawyers are constantly able to find ambiguities. Several tools and methods are used to determine the purpose and meaning of the terms of a statute.

One major approach to statutory interpretation, examining legislative materials in order to determine the purpose or meaning of a statute, has its own research procedures and will be a major focus of Chapter 4. Other methods include analyzing the plain meaning of a statute's words, examining the context in which a given provision was enacted, and applying canons of statutory construction.

These various methods of statutory interpretation are discussed in the treatise which dominates this field, Norman J. Singer, *Statutes and Statutory Construction* (6th & 7th eds. 2000–date).[12] Known as *Sutherland Statutory Construction* from its first author, J. G. Sutherland (1825–1902), this work covers the field in considerable depth and provides exhaustive references to federal and state cases. It is available on Westlaw as the SUTHERLAND database. William D. Popkin, *A Dictionary of Statutory Interpretation* (2007)

---

12. Justice Antonin Scalia has noted, "There is to my knowledge only one treatise on statutory interpretation that purports to treat the subject in a systematic and comprehensive fashion ... Despite the fact that statutory interpretation has increased enormously in importance, it is one of the few fields where we have a drought rather than a glut of treatises—fewer than we had fifty years ago, and many fewer than a century ago." ANTONIN SCALIA, A MATTER OF INTERPRETATION: FEDERAL COURTS AND THE LAW 15 (1997).

provides concise treatment of more than a hundred concepts in the field.[13]

The most authoritative interpretive guidelines are those mandated by the legislature, and every state code has provisions establishing the meaning of certain terms and clarifying topics such as the effect of amendments or repeals.[14] The National Conference of Commissioners on Uniform State Law promulgated a Uniform Statute and Rule Construction Act in 1993, but to date it has been adopted in only one jurisdiction.[15] Commentators have recently recommended that rules of statutory construction be adopted by Congress or drafted by the American Law Institute.[16]

§ 3.4 Sources for Federal Statutes

While annotated codes are the most useful resources in most statutory research, they are not the most authoritative sources of the text of statutes. Annotated codes are usually unofficial, commercial publications, and the official code is controlling if there is any discrepancy between it and an annotated code. Moreover, the language in the session laws generally controls over the official code in case of discrepancies between those two sources. In order to use the annotated codes effectively, it is necessary to understand the role of these other sources and the ways statutes are enacted and published.

The United States Congress meets in two-year terms, consisting of two annual sessions, and enacts several hundred statutes

13. Introductory overviews of statutory interpretation are available in several recent paperback texts, including WILLIAM N. ESKRIDGE, JR. ET AL., LEGISLATION AND STATUTORY INTERPRETATION (2d ed. 2006); KENT GREENAWALT, LEGISLATION: STATUTORY INTERPRETATION: 20 QUESTIONS (1999); ABNER J. MIKVA & ERIC LANE, AN INTRODUCTION TO STATUTORY INTERPRETATION AND THE LEGISLATIVE PROCESS (1997); and MICHAEL SINCLAIR, GUIDE TO STATUTORY INTERPRETATION (2000). YULE KIM, STATUTORY INTERPRETATION: GENERAL PRINCIPLES AND RECENT TRENDS (2008) is a Congressional Research Service report providing an overview similar to these other works, and has the advantage of being available free online <www.fas.org/sgp/crs/misc/97–589.pdf>.

WILLIAM N. ESKRIDGE, JR., DYNAMIC STATUTORY INTERPRETATION (1994) is one of the most frequently cited recent monographs in the field, and WILLIAM D. POPKIN, STATUTES IN COURT: THE HISTORY AND THEORY OF STATUTORY INTERPRETATION (1999) provides valuable historical background by surveying methods courts have used to interpret statutes over the past 200 years. Influential older works include REED DICKERSON, THE INTERPRETATION AND APPLICATION OF STATUTES (1975), and Karl N. Llewellyn, *Remarks on the Theory of Appellate Decision and the Rules or Canons About How Statutes Are To Be Construed*, 3 VAND. L. REV. 395 (1950).

14. Citations to these state provisions on statutory construction can be found in Nicholas Quinn Rosenkranz, *Federal Rules of Statutory Interpretation*, 115 HARV. L. REV. 2085, 2089 n. 10 (2002).

15. 14 U.L.A. 477 (2005); N.M. Stat. Ann. §§ 12–2A–1 to 12–2A–20 (West 2003). An earlier Model Statutory Construction Act (1965) was adopted in four states. 14 U.L.A. 709 (2005).

16. Rosenkranz, supra n. 14; Gary E. O'Connor, *Restatement (First) of Statutory Interpretation*, 7 N.Y.U. J. LEGIS. & PUB. POL'Y 333 (2004).

each term. These range from simple designations of commemorative days to complex trade bills or appropriations acts spanning hundreds of pages. Acts of Congress are introduced and passed as either *bills* or *joint resolutions*. There is no substantive distinction between these two forms, although joint resolutions are used primarily for limited or temporary matters. Other forms of congressional action, *simple resolutions* (adopted by only one chamber and either expressing its opinion or concerning internal procedures) and *concurrent resolutions* (adopted by both chambers but used to express "the sense of Congress"), do not become law.

Each act is designated as either a *public law* or a *private law*, and assigned a number indicating the order in which it was passed. The number, as in Public Law 106–544, identifies the Congress that enacted the law (in this case, the 106th Congress, which met in 1999–2000) and the chronological sequence of its enactment (the 544th public law enacted by that Congress).[17] Public laws are designed to be of general application, while private laws are passed for the benefit of a specific individual or small group.[18] Both types are passed in the same way and both appear in the session laws, but in separate numerical series. Only public laws, however, become part of the statutory code.

(a) Slip Laws and Advance Session Law Services

The first official form of publication of a federal law is the *slip law,* a separately paginated pamphlet. Beginning with the 104th Congress in 1995, the Government Printing Office's GPO Access website provides PDF files of public laws <www.gpoaccess.gov/plaws/>. For current legislation this is one of the quickest and most effective sources. New laws are generally online in PDF within a few weeks of enactment, although lengthier acts may not be available for two or three months. You can either browse public laws by number or search for specific words or phrases.

The most recent enactments may not yet be available from GPO Access, but the legislative site THOMAS <thomas.loc.gov> can provide the text of the *enrolled bill*, or the version that was passed by both houses and sent to the President. THOMAS also has links to GPO Access for the full text of laws since 1995, and lists of public laws (but not full text) back to the 93d Congress in 1973–74.

---

17. Acts and joint resolutions were numbered in separate series (Public Laws and Public Resolutions) before 1941, but now they are both included among Public Laws.

18. Most private laws in the modern era concern special relief for individuals under the immigration laws. For more on the history of private laws and the rules and procedures by which they are enacted, see BERNADETTE MAGUIRE, IMMIGRATION: PUBLIC LEGISLATION AND PRIVATE BILLS (1997); Matthew Mantel, *Private Bills and Private Laws,* 99 LAW LIBR. J. 87 (2007).

The form of the printing of slip laws is almost identical to that which appears in the bound session law publication, the *Statutes at Large,* and in fact the slip laws include *Statutes at Large* page references when they are first printed and posted on GPO Access. This makes it possible to cite to the official *Statutes at Large* as soon as a new public law is available.

Public laws are also available within days of enactment in the US–PL database on Westlaw and in the USCS Public Laws file on Lexis. Both have *Statutes at Large* citations for new acts, although neither immediately includes the internal Stat. page references needed for pinpoint citations. Westlaw's US–PL database has only laws from the current term of Congress, with older laws back to 1973 in a separate US–PL–OLD database. The USCS Public Laws file on Lexis has laws back to 1988.

In print, the next appearance of federal statutes after the slip laws is in two advance session law services, West's *United States Code Congressional and Administrative News* (*USCCAN*) and LexisNexis's *Advance* pamphlets to the *United States Code Service* (*USCS*). Both services issue monthly pamphlets, publishing new federal statutes within two or three months of enactment. Like the slip laws, each page of text in both *USCCAN* and *USCS Advance* indicates the location at which it will eventually appear in the official *Statutes at Large*.

Availability of new laws on GPO Access has greatly diminished the importance of *USCCAN* and *USCS Advance* for most research, but they include a variety of useful features. In addition to the text of newly enacted public laws, both services publish court rule amendments, presidential proclamations, and executive orders. Each pamphlet includes a cumulative index of the session's legislation and tables indicating the sections of the *United States Code* that have been affected by recent legislative, executive, or administrative actions. *USCCAN*, but not *USCS Advance*, also publishes selective legislative history materials such as House and Senate Reports. *Advance* pamphlets are designed only for temporary use until the new material is incorporated into *USCS*, but *USCCAN* pamphlets are cumulated at the end of each year into bound volumes to form a permanent record of session laws and legislative history. This contains the text of statutes since it began publication (as *United States Code Congressional Service*) in 1941, although it did not indicate the official *Statutes at Large* pagination until 1975.

(b) *U.S. Statutes at Large*

The official, permanent session law publication for federal laws is the *United States Statutes at Large* (cited as Stat.). At the end of each annual session of Congress, the public and private laws enacted are cumulated and published in chronological order, along with concurrent resolutions and Presidential proclamations. The *Statutes at Large* is the positive law form of statutes, and "legal evidence of laws ... in all the Courts of the United States."[19] The *United States Code* is only *prima facie* evidence of the laws, except for those of its titles which have been reenacted by Congress as positive law.[20] If there is a discrepancy between what is in the *Statutes at Large* and what is in the *United States Code*, the former controls.[21]

In recent years, each session's compilation has comprised three to six volumes, with overall indexes by popular name and subject at the back of each volume.[22] A federal session law is cited by its Public Law number and the volume and page in which it appears in *Statutes at Large*.[23] The Presidential Threat Protection Act of 2000, Pub. L. No. 106–544, 114 Stat. 2715, shown in Illustration 3–8 on page 100, begins on page 2715 of volume 114 of the *Statutes at Large*.

The *Statutes at Large* was first published in 1846 and provides retrospective coverage back to 1789.[24] It contains all laws passed by

19. 1 U.S.C. § 112 (2006).

20. 1 U.S.C. § 204 (2006).

21. In *United States National Bank of Oregon v. Independent Insurance Agents of America, Inc.*, 508 U.S. 439 (1993), the Supreme Court held that a statutory provision that had been omitted from the *U.S. Code* for more than forty years was still good law because it had never been repealed. As the leading treatise on statutory construction puts it, "[L]awyers still must rely upon the Statutes at Large as the primary source of federal law. In an important case no lawyer can afford to depend on the code as ultimate authority." 2 NORMAN J. SINGER, STATUTES AND STATUTORY CONSTRUCTION § 36A:10 (6th ed., rev. vol. 2001).

22. The *Statutes at Large* indexes can be used to find laws passed in a particular year, but separate year-by-year coverage is not particularly useful for most research. Two retrospective indexes to federal law prepared by the Library of Congress are also of occasional use in historical research: MIDDLETON G. BEAMAN & A. K. McNAMARA, INDEX ANALYSIS OF THE FEDERAL STATUTES, 1789–1873 (1911), and WALTER H. McCLENON & WILFRED C. GILBERT, INDEX TO THE FEDERAL STATUTES, 1874–1931 (1933).

23. Session laws before 1957 are designated by chapter numbers, not Public Law numbers. Public Law numbers have been assigned to Acts of Congress since 1901, but chapter numbers remained the primary means of identification until they were discontinued at the end of the 1956 session. *The Bluebook* continues to follow this rule for statutes before 1957. THE BLUEBOOK: A UNIFORM SYSTEM OF CITATION 196 (18th ed. 2005). The *ALWD Citation Manual* doesn't make this distinction and uses Public Law numbers for all federal session laws. ALWD CITATION MANUAL: A PROFESSIONAL SYSTEM OF CITATION R. 14.7, at 118–19 (3d ed. 2006).

24. The *Statutes at Large*, edited by former Supreme Court reporter Richard Peters, were published pursuant to the Resolution of March 3, 1845, no. 10, 5 Stat. 798, and they were declared to be competent evidence of the law by the Act of Aug. 8, 1846, ch. 100, § 2, 9 Stat. 75, 76. The new set had several predecessors. In its first session in 1789, Congress enacted a law ordering that the Secretary of State cause each of its acts "to be published in at least three of the public newspapers printed within the United States." Act of Sept. 15, 1789, ch. 14, § 2, 1 Stat. 68, 68. It did not take long to realize that a more permanent form of publication was necessary, and several chronological collections of federal laws with the title *Laws of the United*

Congress, including those that were already obsolete or had been repealed in 1846. The series was privately published by Little, Brown & Co. until 1873, after which the Government Printing Office was given the responsibility.[25] The first five volumes of the *Statutes at Large* contained public laws from the 1st to the 28th Congresses (1789–1845), and volumes 6–8 contained private laws, treaties with Indian tribes, and treaties with foreign countries respectively. The full texts of newly approved treaties were also included in each volume until a separate series, *U.S. Treaties and Other International Agreements,* was begun as of January 1, 1950. Publication of current volumes of the *Statutes at Large* lags a year or two behind the session covered.

The subscription site HeinOnline <www.heinonline.org> has complete retrospective coverage of the *Statutes at Large* in PDF, with the text of all acts and treaties back to 1789 searchable by keyword or title. Up to two hundred pages can be downloaded or printed at a time.

Westlaw and Lexis also provide retrospective coverage of the *Statutes at Large* back to 1789, but keyword searching is available only for recent decades. Earlier acts are available as image-based PDFs and only citations, dates, and summary information are searchable. On Westlaw, the US–STATLRG file covers 1789–1972 and the full-text searchable US–PL–OLD file begins coverage in 1973. On Lexis the full-text searchable USCS Public Laws begins in 1988, with the United States Statutes at Large file providing retrospective coverage. LoisLaw also has public laws, searchable by keyword or number, back to the 105th Congress (1997–98).

The Library of Congress provides free access to the first eighteen volumes of the *Statutes at Large*, through 1875, as part of its "A Century of Lawmaking for a New Nation: U.S. Congressional Documents and Debates, 1774–1875" collection <lcweb2.loc.gov/ammem/amlaw/lwsl.html>. Only the index is

States of America were soon issued by private publishers under congressional authorization. The first, authorized by the Resolution of Feb. 18, 1791, no. 1, 1 Stat. 224, was printed in 1791 by Andrew Brown and covered the three sessions of the First Congress. A more comprehensive set was authorized four years later by the Act of March 3, 1795, ch. 50, 1 Stat. 443, this time with the specification that it include an index. Known as the Folwell edition from its printer, Richard Folwell, this set was published in 1796–97 in three volumes and covered the first four Congresses. Coverage was extended by eight supplementary volumes through the thirteenth Congress (1813–15), at which point Congress passed the Act of April 18, 1814, ch. 69, 3 Stat. 129, authorizing a new edition to be published by John Bioren and W. John Duane. The Bioren and Duane edition then covered acts through the twenty-eighth Congress (1843–45). For background on the history of federal statutory publication, see Ralph H. Dwan & Ernest R. Feidler, *The Federal Statutes—Their History and Use,* 22 MINN. L. REV. 1008 (1938), and Erwin C. Surrency, *The Publication of Federal Laws: A Short History,* 79 LAW LIBR. J. 469 (1987).

25. Act of June 20, 1874, ch. 333, § 7, 18 Stat. 113, 114.

searchable, but specific acts with known citations can be retrieved by choosing a particular volume to browse and then entering the page number.

The easiest way to find court decisions citing acts in the *Statutes at Large* is to do a full-text search for the citation in a case law database. Neither KeyCite nor Shepard's online covers citations to session laws, but two other resources are available in print. The *United States Code Service* includes two volumes, "Annotations to Uncodified Laws and Treaties," one of which provides case summaries by *Statutes at Large* citation. This covers acts that have been repealed as well as those that were never codified. Even more citing references can be found using *Shepard's Citations* in print. *Shepard's Federal Statute Citations* covers citations in federal court decisions to acts in the *Statutes at Large* which have not been incorporated into the code. Finding other citations requires checking Shepard's individual state citators for state court decisions, and *Shepard's Federal Law Citations in Selected Law Reviews* for journal articles. References to *Statutes at Large* citations are among the few features in print Shepard's that are not available online.

The *Statutes at Large* is not the most convenient source for federal legislation, but it maintains a vital role in legal research. In most instances it is the official statement of the law, and it is a necessary source for determining when Congress enacted specific language in a code section. This is important for lawyers as well as historians. It is often necessary to determine when a particular provision took effect or was repealed, or to reconstruct the precise text as it was enacted. Sections of a public law may be scattered among several titles in the code, but the *Statutes at Large* provides each act of Congress in its entirety.

(c) **Codification of Federal Statutes**

The most useful publications of federal laws are not published chronologically but instead arranged by subject. The most important of these is the current *United States Code* in its various editions, but it was preceded by an earlier codification that remains a source of positive law.

(1) *Revised Statutes*

Because of the difficulty of research in the numerous volumes of the *Statutes at Large* with their separate noncumulating indexes, it became apparent by the 1860s that some form of codification or subject arrangement was needed. After much drafting and redrafting, the first and only complete revision of federal laws was enacted in 1874,[26] and published the following year as the *Revised Statutes*

---

26. Act of June 22, 1874, 18 Stat. 1. The *Revised Statutes* were prepared pur-   suant to the Act of June 27, 1866, ch. 140, 14 Stat. 74. They were preceded by

of the United States. The *Revised Statutes* were published as part one of 18 Stat., and contained the general and permanent statutes in force on December 1, 1873.

This first edition of the *Revised Statutes* confusingly goes by several titles: the "Revised Statutes of 1873" (for the cut-off date of the laws it includes), or "of 1874" (for the date of its enactment) or "of 1875" (for the date of its publication). In any case, the publication was more than just a topical arrangement of laws into seventy-four subject titles and 5,601 sections. (The numbering is continuous throughout the *Revised Statutes*, so a citation is simply to the section number, e.g. Rev. Stat. § 5601.) It was a reenactment as positive law of all the statutes it contained, and it expressly repealed their original *Statutes at Large* texts.[27] The *Revised Statutes* is the authoritative text for most laws predating its publication which remain in force, and it is still needed occasionally in modern research.

The discovery of several errors in the *Revised Statutes* led to the publication of a second edition in 1878, including several corrections and replacing the earlier version as 18 Stat. part 1.[28] The second edition did not replace the first edition as the positive law, but it is the edition most commonly found in sets of the *Statutes at Large*.

The *Revised Statutes* is online in PDF form from several sources, as part of their coverage of the *Statutes at Large*. The Library of Congress provides free access to the 1878 second edition <lcweb2.loc.gov/ammem/amlaw/lwsl.html>, and Lexis has the same edition in its Statutes at Large database. Westlaw, on the other hand, has the original, reenacted first edition. In Westlaw and Lexis, the *Revised Statutes* can be retrieved with a *Find* or *Get a Document* command for "18 Stat 1," but as with other *Statutes at Large* materials it is divided into smaller ten-or fifty-page PDF documents. HeinOnline has both the first and second editions, with up to two hundred pages downloadable at a time.

---

a few privately published subject collections of federal statutes, beginning with *A Digest of the Laws of the United States of America* (Thomas Herty ed., 1800–02).

27. The *Revised Statutes* repealed acts of Congress prior to December 1, 1873, but only if any portion of them was covered by a section of the revision. Any act in the *Statutes at Large* "no part of which [was] embraced in" the *Revised Statutes* was unaffected by its

enactment and publication. Rev. Stat. § 5596. *Millsaps v. Thompson*, 259 F.3d 535 (6th Cir. 2001), considered an 1872 enactment not included in the *Revised Statutes* or the *United States Code*, and held that it remained good law.

28. Errors in the first edition were corrected by the Act of Feb. 18, 1875, ch. 80, 18 Stat. 316, and the Act of Feb. 27, 1877, ch. 69, 19 Stat. 240; and the second edition was published pursuant to the Act of Mar. 2, 1877, ch. 82, 19 Stat. 268.

Almost fifty more years of publication of the *Statutes at Large* ensued before another effort at an official codification of federal laws was undertaken. The chaos and inconvenience in statutory research were somewhat alleviated by privately published subject compilations, but the need for a new official code was apparent.[29]

For the rare occasion when you have a reference to the *Revised Statutes* and need to determine whether a provision is still in force, all three versions of the *United States Code* have parallel reference tables listing Rev. Stat. sections and indicating where the modern counterpart appears in the current code or if a provision has been repealed. (This table is included in the Westlaw USCA–TABLES database, but not in its counterpart on Lexis.)

(2) *United States Code*

After years of legislative effort,[30] a new codification initiative was approved on June 30, 1926, and published as part 1 of 44 *Statutes at Large* under the title: *The Code of the Laws of the United States of America of a General and Permanent Nature, in Force December 7, 1925*. It has ever since been known as the *United States Code*.

Unlike the *Revised Statutes,* the new *U.S. Code* was not a positive law reenactment and did not repeal the prior *Statutes at Large*. It was *prima facie* evidence of the law, rebuttable by reference to the *Statutes at Large*. However, beginning in 1947 Congress has revised individual titles of the code and reenacted them into positive law as the revision is completed. More than forty per cent of the titles have been reenacted so far, and are now legal evidence; for the rest the *Statutes at Large* remains legal evidence and the *U.S. Code* is *prima facie* evidence. A note following 1 U.S.C. § 204 indicates the titles that have been enacted into positive law.[31]

---

29. Two supplements to the *Revised Statutes* were issued for the periods 1874–91 and 1892–1901, but these also did not have the status of positive law. They contained lists of *Revised Statutes* sections affected by subsequent legislation, but instead of title-by-title supplements these were just chronological arrangements of new laws. The first commercial subject compilation was *Compiled Statutes of the United States, 1901* (1902), and the first commercial version with extensive annotations similar to those used today was *Federal Statutes Annotated* (1903–06).

30. This history is recounted in William L. Burdick, *The Revision of the Federal Statutes*, 11 A.B.A. J. 178 (1925).

31. Although the standard wisdom is that if a title has "been enacted into positive law, the Code title itself is deemed to constitute conclusive evidence of the law; recourse to other sources is unnecessary and precluded," *United States v. Zuger*, 602 F. Supp. 889, 891 (D. Conn. 1984), the Supreme Court has held more than once that the *Statutes at Large* controls even if a title has been reenacted as positive law, if the meanings differ and no substantive change was intended in the reenactment. *Cass v. United States*, 417 U.S. 72, 82 (1974) ("[T]he revisers expressly stated that changes in language resulting from the codification were to have no substantive effect"); *Fourco Glass Co. v. Transmirra Products Corp.*, 353 U.S. 222, 227 (1957)

The *U.S. Code* is arranged in fifty subject titles, generally in alphabetical order.[32] Titles are divided into chapters and then into sections, with a continuous sequence of section numbers for each title. Citations to the *Code* indicate the title, section number, and year. 18 U.S.C. § 879 (2000), for example, is part of title 18 (Crimes and Criminal Procedure), chapter 41 (Extortion and Threats). The chapter number does not appear in the citation.

Following each statutory section in the *U.S. Code,* there is a parenthetical reference to its source in the *Statutes at Large,* including citations to any amendments. This reference enables you to locate the original text, which may be the positive law form, and from there to find legislative history documents relating to the law's enactment. The *Code* also includes historical notes and cross-references to related sections. Illustration 3–9 on page 101 shows the *U.S. Code* page with 18 U.S.C. § 879, the codified form of the session law shown in Illustration 3–8. The statute is followed by citations to the public laws in the *Statutes at Large* and by an explanation of the change made by each amendment.

Some titles of the *U.S. Code* have been revised and renumbered, but others retain the section numbering they were assigned in 1926. Because the basic structure is now some eighty years old, several titles have grown unwieldy as new sections are shoehorned into their appropriate subject locations. Section numbers such as 15 U.S.C. § 78aaa and 42 U.S.C. § 2000e–2 are used to squeeze new material between existing sections. This doesn't mean that 2000e–2 is a subsection of 2000 or 2000e. Subsections are indicated with parentheses; 15 U.S.C. § 78(a) is a subsection, but 15 U.S.C. § 78a is a discrete section of the *United States Code.*

It is important to be aware that not every federal law is published as a section of the *United States Code.* The Office of the Law Revision Counsel of the House of Representatives, which is responsible for preparing the code, includes what it deems to be

("[N]o changes in law or policy are to be presumed from changes of language in the revision unless an intent to make such changes is clearly expressed").

The distinction between positive law titles and *prima facie* titles is a matter of evidence, not substance, as litigants have learned if they attempt to argue that a title that has not been enacted into positive law has no legal force. See, e.g., *Ryan v. Bilby,* 764 F.2d 1325 (9th Cir. 1985) ("Congress's failure to enact a title into positive law has only evidentiary significance and does not render the underlying enactment invalid or unenforceable"); *United States v. Zuger,* supra, at 891–92 ("[T]he failure of Congress to enact a title as such and in such form into positive law ... in no way impugns the validity, effect, enforceability or constitutionality of the laws as contained and set forth in the title").

32. There are actually forty-nine titles at present. The newest title, Domestic Security, was added as Title 6 in 2002, and replaced Surety Bonds, which was repealed in 1982 and incorporated into Title 31, Money and Finance. Title 34, Navy, was repealed in 1956 and its provisions incorporated into Title 10, Armed Forces. A new Title 51, National and Commercial Space Programs, has been proposed for codification. H.R. 4780, 110th Cong. (2007).

"general and permanent laws of the United States,"[33] but its determination does not have the force of law. Some laws appear only in the *Statutes at Large*, and others are published as notes following sections of the code. The validity of a statute is unaffected by whether it is published as a code section or a note, or is omitted entirely from the *United States Code*.

The *United States Code* is published in a new edition every six years by the federal government, and updated between editions by annual bound supplements. Each year's supplement incorporates material in preceding supplements, so that only the latest one need be consulted for changes since the last revision. Although the original 1926 edition and its 1934 successor were one-volume works, subsequent editions have grown into ever larger multi-volume publications. The 2000 edition is a 35–volume set, and its 2005 supplement occupies seven volumes.

The official *U.S. Code* is not the most current of publications. The 2006 edition, containing laws enacted through the 109th Congress (2005–06), did not begin publication until April 2008. The annual supplements are usually published a year or more after their effective dates. Even though it is woefully out of date, the *U.S. Code* is the officially recognized source for federal statutes and is the authority that both *The Bluebook* and the *ALWD Manual* specify must be cited if it contains the relevant and current language.[34]

The U.S. Code is available free online from several sources. The most important of these sites are the House of Representatives Office of the Law Revision Counsel <uscode.house.gov> and Cornell Law School's Legal Information Institute <www.law.cornell.edu/uscode/>.

The Office of Law Revision Counsel site is the best online government source for the text, in that it is more current and easier to search than the version available from GPO Access <www.gpoaccess.gov/uscode/>. It provides search boxes for convenient access by title and section number, and allows several search options including keywords using proximity connectors and truncation. The site also provides an option to search prior versions of the code back to 1990, and access to large PDF files for entire code titles.[35]

---

33. 2 U.S.C. § 285b (2006). Although the code contains laws of a "permanent" nature, Congress is increasingly enacting provisions of limited duration, often with express "sunset" clauses that set expiration dates. See Jacob E. Gersen, *Temporary Legislation*, 74 U. CHI. L. REV. 247 (2007).

34. THE BLUEBOOK: A UNIFORM SYSTEM OF CITATION R. 12.3, at 104 (18th ed. 2005); ALWD CITATION MANUAL: A PROFESSIONAL SYSTEM OF CITATION R. 14.1(b), at 111 (3d ed. 2006).

35. These PDF files incorporate the material in the supplements to the

The Law Revision Counsel site has its drawbacks. Search results are displayed in a list that includes the heading of each section but not the names of its title or chapter, so the subject matter of retrieved documents is not always very clear, and code sections are presented in an unappealing and difficult-to-read AS-CII display. The sections displayed are only as current as the latest printed *U.S. Code* version, and updating a section to determine if it has been amended is a bit laborious. The simplest way is to run a search by title and section number. If a code section has been amended since the most recent published edition or supplement, this retrieves an "UPDATE" link as well as the code section itself. The update lists the sections of any public laws that have amended the code section, but it does not provide links to the amendments. It is then necessary to retrieve the public law using a site such as GPO Access or THOMAS. But if no "UPDATE" link appears, this is an easy way to verify that there have been no recent amendments. The information is very current, within two or three days of new enactments.[36]

Cornell's version of the *U.S. Code* is much more user-friendly. Like the official site, it provides a fill-in-the-blank form for citation searches and allows simple keyword searches with phrases and basic connectors (*and*, *or*, or *not*), in either the entire code or individual titles. Its display, however, is much more attractive than the official site, and hyperlinked cross-references between code sections are provided. The Statutes at Large citations for the source of enactments and amendments are available by clicking on a "Notes" link to the right.

One major advantage of using the Cornell site is that it provides "Update(s)" links as part of its display of a code section. These are based on the official site's information, but they include links to any new public laws amending the section. If a section has not been amended, a "No Update(s)" note makes this clear without requiring further investigation. The "Update(s)" and "No Update(s)" notes are current within just a few days of enactment. Illustration 3–10 on page 102 shows 18 U.S.C. § 879 as it appears

printed edition of the code rather than presenting the supplements separately. This makes them more convenient than the printed supplement, but it means that they do not mirror the published source required for citation purposes.

36. The Law Revision Counsel site also provides a "Classification Tables"

page <uscode.house.gov/classification/ tables.shtml> containing lists for each year of sections amended, enacted, omitted, repealed, or transferred. These are available sorted in public law order and in *U.S. Code* order. The lists do not cumulate or include hypertext links to the new public laws.

on the Cornell site, including the "Notes" link and a "No Update(s)" notation.

The *U.S. Code* in print features a number of useful research aids, including an extensive general index and several tables. An "Acts Cited by Popular Name" table lists laws alphabetically under either short titles assigned by Congress or popular names by which they have become known, and parallel conversion tables provide references from earlier revisions and between different forms of statutory publication. Table I covers *U.S. Code* titles that have been revised and renumbered since the original 1926 adoption of the code, showing where former sections of the title are incorporated into the current edition. Table II indicates the location and status of sections of the *Revised Statutes of 1878* within the code, and Table III lists the *Statutes at Large* in chronological order and indicates where each public law section is codified. Other tables cover executive orders, proclamations, reorganization plans, and internal cross-references within the code.

The subject index and tables can be useful resources online as well as in print, because keyword searches are not always the most effective way to find statutes. The Office of the Law Revision Counsel provides the tables in PDF, while Cornell includes only the popular name table. Neither of these sites includes the subject index.

Another online source for the *U.S. Code* is HeinOnline, which has every edition from 1926 in searchable PDF, including indexes, tables, and supplements. The older editions can be useful for tracking the history of a provision, and maybe be needed for a citation to a statute that is no longer in force.[37]

Although statutory provisions are often affected by court decisions, there is no indication or reflection of these decisions in the printed *U.S. Code* or in the versions available free on the Internet. A statute can even be declared unconstitutional, but it remains in the text until Congress repeals or amends it. Before relying on a *U.S. Code* provision, you should use resources such as the annotated editions of the code to ascertain what judicial treatment may have occurred.

(3) Annotated Codes

The *United States Code* has the text of federal laws, but two major shortcomings limit its value to legal researchers. It is not

---

37. "Cite statutes no longer in force to the current official or unofficial code if they still appear therein. Otherwise, cite the last edition of the official or unofficial code in which the statute appeared, the session laws, or a secondary source—in that order of preference." THE BLUEBOOK: A UNIFORM SYSTEM OF CITATION R. 12.2.1(b), at 102 (18th ed. 2005). The ALWD manual does not require a publication date for statutes no longer in force. ALWD CITATION MANUAL: A PROFESSIONAL SYSTEM OF CITATION R. 14.3, at 115(3d ed. 2006).

updated on a timely basis, and there is no information about court decisions applying or interpreting code sections. Instead, most researchers turn to one of two commercial annotated editions of the code, *United States Code Annotated* (cited as U.S.C.A.), published by West, or *United States Code Service* (cited as U.S.C.S.), published by LexisNexis.[38] Each is available in print, on CD–ROM, and on its publisher's online service. These annotated codes are updated on a more timely basis and provide much more extensive information than the official code. The print version of each of these sets occupies more than two hundred volumes.

The annotated codes provide the same research aids found in the official *U.S. Code,* such as authority references, historical notes, cross references, tables, and index. They add references to such sources as the *Code of Federal Regulations*, law review articles, legal encyclopedias, annotations, and major treatises. *USCA* also includes references to legislative history materials in *U.S. Code Congressional and Administrative News (USCCAN)* and citations to digest topics and key numbers.

Following each code section which has been interpreted or applied judicially, *USCA* and *USCS* provide "Notes of Decisions" or "Interpretive Notes and Decisions," consisting of abstracts of cases dealing with the particular section. Unless there have been only a few cases, the annotations are arranged by topic into numbered classifications. To assist in finding relevant cases, *USCA*'s annotations are preceded by an alphabetical subject index and *USCS*'s by a topical outline. *USCA* usually includes more case notes, but *USCS* covers administrative decisions from several dozen agencies as well as court decisions. Illustrations 3–11 and 3–12 on pages 103–104 show 18 U.S.C. § 879 as printed in *USCA,* followed by various research aids and notes of decisions. This volume was published *before* the amendment to this section enacted by Pub. L. No. 106–544.

One minor difference between *USCA* and *USCS* is that *USCA* mirrors the language of the official *United States Code* and uses cross-references to other *USCA* sections, while *USCS* preserves more closely the context and language of the original *Statutes at Large* text and uses parentheticals and notes for clarification. *USCA* may refer to "this chapter," while *USCS* uses the term "this Act" and prints cross-references as they appear in the original public law. There are sometimes differences in how the scope of a

---

38. *USCA* began publication in 1927, shortly after the 1926 creation of the *United States Code.* Its format is based on the publisher's earlier *United States Compiled Statutes Annotated* (1916–17). *USCS* succeeded an earlier compilation entitled *Federal Code Annotated*, first published in 1936.

definition or exception is expressed, but these are not substantive changes.[39]

The online code databases in Westlaw and Lexis are updated to include laws from the current session of Congress, with a note accompanying each section indicating the most recent public law to be included in code coverage. Westlaw goes further by adding a red flag for sections with amendments that have not yet been incorporated, so its database generally includes notice of new amendments within a day or two of their enactment.

Even in print *USCA* and *USCS* are far more current than the official edition, and are kept up to date by several forms of supplementation. The most basic of these is the annual pocket part, which is inserted in the back of each volume and indicates changes in the statutory text, as well as annotations to recent judicial decisions and other sources. Some volumes have so much new material that they are accompanied by separate pamphlets rather than pocket part supplements.

Replacement volumes are published when supplements get too unwieldy. Some volumes in each set are several years old,[40] but every volume has an up-to-date supplement. Any time a *USCA* or *USCS* volume is used, you *must* check its supplement for current amendments or judicial developments.

Between annual pocket parts, legislative and judicial developments are noted in quarterly pamphlets supplementing the entire set. Each pamphlet is arranged by code section, and contains the text of new laws and notes of recent decisions. These are further updated by the monthly advance pamphlets of *USCCAN* and *USCS Advance*, which contain the text of newly enacted statutes in chronological order and provide parallel tables indicating the code sections affected by recent legislation.

Thorough research involving a particular statute may require checking both *USCA* and *USCS*. Each provides selective annotations of court decisions, and cases may be included in one but not the other. *USCA*'s annotations are generally more extensive, but some court decisions appear only in *USCS*—which is also the only source for references to administrative decisions. A person with access to both *USCA* and *USCS* usually develops a preference for one or the other, but should become somewhat familiar with both.

---

39. Errors may also occasionally be found in one of the unofficial codes. In *United States v. Carroll*, 105 F.3d 740, 744 & n.4 (1st Cir. 1997), the decision turned on a comma that was printed in the *Statutes at Large* and in the *United States Code*, but was omitted from *USCA*.

40. Title 27, Intoxicating Liquors, is the last of the original 1927 volumes in the current *USCA* set. It is still updated by a pocket part more than eighty years after its publication.

One edition can be used on a regular basis for most research needs, but the other may occasionally be needed for its editorial features or to ensure comprehensive coverage.

§ 3.5 Sources for State Statutes

Research in state statutory law is quite similar to the federal paradigm already outlined. State statutes also appear as slip laws, session laws, codes, and annotated codes. Current session laws and codes are available from government Internet sites, and annotated codes are published online and on CD–ROM as well as in print.

(a) Slip Laws and Session Laws

State statutes are enacted and published in a manner that mirrors the federal pattern. Every state has a session law publication similar to the *U.S. Statutes at Large*, containing the laws enacted at each sitting of its legislature. The names of these publications vary from state to state (e.g., *Acts of Alabama*, *Statutes of California*, *Laws of Delaware*). In most states the session laws are the authoritative positive law text of the statutes, and they may be needed to examine legislative changes or to reconstruct the language in force at a particular date. These publications are listed in Table 1 of *The Bluebook* and Appendix 1 of the *ALWD Citation Manual*.[41]

Slip laws from every state legislature are available online in one form or another. Most legislative websites permit browsing of recent slip laws, but in some states new laws are available only as enrolled bills and may even be mixed in with bills that are still pending or that did not become law. Only a few state websites include page numbers that would facilitate citation to the official session laws publication.[42]

State legislative websites are easily accessible through web searches or online directories. One of the more useful sources is the National Conference of State Legislatures <www.ncsl.org/public/leglinks.cfm>, which provides specific links for each state to pages focusing on bills, statutes, or other website content. Selecting more than one state at a time creates a list of links with search tips for each site.

Slip laws and session laws from all fifty states are also available from Westlaw and Lexis. These are known on Westlaw as "Legisla-

---

41. THE BLUEBOOK: A UNIFORM SYSTEM OF CITATION 198–239 (18th ed. 2005); ALWD CITATION MANUAL: A PROFESSIONAL SYSTEM OF CITATION 359–400 (3d ed. 2006).

42. The discrepancies between states in the way session laws are pub-

lished and designated have caused complaints for more than a century. See *Uniformity in the Preparation and Publication of Session Laws*, 11 AM. LAW. 144 (1903).

tive Services" and on Lexis as "Advance Legislative Services." The major difference between the two systems is that Westlaw has two separate databases for each state, one for the current legislative sessions (___-LEGIS) and a "historical" database with the older session laws back to the late 1980s or early 1990s (___-LEGIS–OLD). Lexis has just one database for each state combining current and archived sessions. Both systems also have databases combining the session laws from all states, although Westlaw's multistate database is limited to the current sessions. LoisLaw also has state session laws, back to 1999 for most jurisdictions.

In 45 states (all but Kansas, Montana, Nebraska, South Carolina, and Wyoming), commercially published advance session law services or legislative services publish new acts before they are printed in the bound session laws. These monthly or bimonthly pamphlets are generally issued as supplements to a state's annotated code, and are similar to the *USCCAN* and *USCS Advance* pamphlets. These services generally do not provide the pagination that will appear in the bound session laws volumes, but they are the preferred *Bluebook* source for laws not yet printed in the official volumes.

HeinOnline's Session Laws Library has a growing collection of state session laws in PDF. For most states it has volumes from 1995 to date, with retrospective coverage being added. Most larger law libraries also have older state session laws in microform. William S. Hein & Co., Inc. publishes a comprehensive and regularly updated microfiche backfile of state and territorial session laws.[43]

(b) State Codes

Publication of colonial and state law began early in the 17th century, with *For the Colony in Virginea Britannia: Lavves Diuine, Morall and Martiall, & c.* (1612), a short pamphlet containing mostly martial law provisions. The first revision of Virginia law was in 1632, although it was issued only in manuscript form until 1809.[44] In 1648, the first printing press in the colonies published *The Book of the General Lawes and Libertyes*, a compilation of Massachusetts statutes arranged by subject.[45]

---

43. 2 Pimsleur's Checklists of Basic American Legal Publications (Marcia Singal Zubrow ed., 1962–date) provides a comprehensive listing of colonial, territorial and state session law volumes. For information on the availability of state slip and session laws generally, see William H. Manz, Guide to State Legislation, Legislative History, and Administrative Materials (7th ed. 2008).

44. *A Grand Assembly Holden at James Citty the 4th Day of September, 1632,* 1 The Statutes at Large, Being a Collection of All the Laws of Virginia, from the First Session of the Legislature, in the Year 1619, at 178 (William Waller Hening ed., 1809). Hening's source for this revision was a manuscript owned by Thomas Jefferson.

45. Only one of six hundred copies printed is known to exist, in the Hunt-

In the eighteenth and nineteenth centuries, the colonies and then the states issued a variety of compilations and codifications of their laws. The early publications were generally chronological collections of statutes in force, with subject-based collections becoming more prominent in the nineteenth century. Most publications were unofficial compilations, although from time to time most states had official revisions or codifications of their statutes akin to the federal *Revised Statutes of 1873*. Gradually compilations and codifications were published with increasingly extensive annotations of case law, leading by the early twentieth century to the now-familiar multi-volume annotated codes.[46]

All states now have subject compilations of their statutes similar to the *U.S. Code*, but the form and official status of these compilations vary widely from state to state. Some states have reenacted their codified statutes, while others rely on unofficial compilations.[47] Maryland, Pennsylvania and Texas have for several years been in the lengthy process of completing official codifications.

Every state makes its code available through its state website, although these free online codes vary widely in their currency, official status, and features. Only six state codes available free of charge (Colorado, Hawaii, Missouri, Nebraska, Oregon, and Wisconsin) include annotations of court decisions, which are essential in evaluating the meaning and validity of statutory provisions. Some

---

ington Library in San Marino, California. For more information on this collection of laws, see Mark D. Cahn, *Punishment, Discretion, and the Codification of Prescribed Penalties in Colonial Massachusetts*, 33 AM. J. LEGAL HIST. 107 (1989), and Thorp L. Wolford, *The Laws and Liberties of 1648: The First Code of Laws Enacted and Printed in English America*, 28 B.U. L. REV. 426 (1948).

46. Historical compilations and codifications for each state are listed in WILLIAM H. MANZ, GUIDE TO STATE LEGISLATION, LEGISLATIVE HISTORY, AND ADMINISTRATIVE MATERIALS (7th ed. 2008), and volume 1 of PIMSLEUR'S CHECKLISTS OF BASIC AMERICAN LEGAL PUBLICATIONS (Marcia Singal Zubrow ed., 1962–date). On colonial codifications, see Erwin C. Surrency, *Revision of Colonial Laws*, 9 AM. J. LEGAL HIST. 189 (1965). Histories of state codifications appear in most state legal research guides. More extensive surveys of particular states include Joel Fishman, *The History of Statutory Compilations in Pennsylvania*, 86 LAW LIBR. J.

559 (1994), and Kent C. Olson, *State Codes*, in VIRGINIA LAW BOOKS: ESSAYS AND BIBLIOGRAPHIES 1 (W. Hamilton Bryson ed., 2000).

47. "Some states such as Alaska and Missouri have not enacted their code into positive law. The entire text is merely prima facie evidence of the law. Other states such as Arkansas enact their codes but with a 'rabbit hole' that allows writers to cite the session law instead if the code text is wrong. Still other states, such as Arizona, enact their codes but do not enact codified forms of the subsequent, amending session laws. Others such as Louisiana and Texas are in the codification process, and have a combination of completed codes and compilations. Finally, other states such as Alabama and California have enacted their entire codes and also enact codified amendments." Lynn Foster, *The Universal Legal Citation Project: A Draft User Guide to the AALL Universal Statutory Citation: Introduction*, 90 LAW LIBR. J. 91, 92 (1998) (citations omitted).

online state codes bear prominent disclaimers that they are unofficial versions for convenience only, and that it is necessary to consult the printed version for any official purpose. All of the codes, however, can be searched by keyword and browsed through tables of contents. Several convenient compilations of links are available, including lists of state legal materials at Cornell's Legal Information Institute <www.law.cornell.edu/states/listing.html> and Find-Law <www.findlaw.com/11stategov/>.

Some states publish an official, unannotated code, regularly revised on an annual or biennial basis.[48] In states with regularly published official codes, these are usually the authoritative text to which citation is expected in briefs and pleadings, and according to the citation manuals.[49] This can be somewhat problematic outside a jurisdiction, where very few libraries are likely to have copies of other states' unannotated codes.

Most researchers rely on codes annotated with summaries of relevant court decisions and other references, in most cases commercially published or accessed through Westlaw or Lexis. The authority of unofficial codes varies from state to state, but they are usually accepted as at least *prima facie* evidence of the statutory law.[50]

Annotated states codes are not a homogeneous lot. Some are more thorough and comprehensive than others. Most codes are published by either West or LexisNexis, and some states have competing codes from both publishers. A few of the smaller states prepare and publish their own annotated codes. Others have ar-

---

48. Nine states have regularly published official revisions. These are published annually in Florida; biennially in Connecticut, Illinois, Iowa, Massachusetts, Minnesota, and Washington; every six years in Indiana; and every ten years in Oklahoma.

49. The Bluebook: A Uniform System of Citation R. 12.3, at 104 (18th ed. 2005); ALWD Citation Manual: A Professional System of Citation R. 14.1(b), at 111 (3d ed. 2006).

50. Researchers in states with unofficial compilations may face occasional difficulties if discrepancies occur. See R. Perry Sentell, Jr., *Codification and Consequences: The Georgian Motif*, 14 Ga. L. Rev. 737, 739 (1980) ("The ramifications of a jurisdiction's reliance upon private unofficial codification are diverse. The convenience of the source may be offset by the uncertainty of the results. There is the ever present potential for clerical conflict between the official statutory

law and the unofficial presentation of the law. There is the gnawing insecurity kindled by knowledge that no portion of the private presentation has received either the scrutiny or the stamp of public approval. In short, no matter how perfect the product in fact, the distracting nuances are inevitable. Indeed, on occasion the difficulties may transcend the sphere of mere nuances.").

This distinction has led to some problems for litigants relying on unofficial publications. In *In re Appeal of Tenet HealthSystems Bucks County*, 880 A.2d 721 (Pa. Commw. Ct. 2005), the court rejected as untimely an appeal filed in reliance on a deadline as published in *Purdon's Pennsylvania Statutes Annotated*. The court held that "while Purdon's has been the key to finding statutory law in Pennsylvania, it is not itself positive law." The law in question had not been codified by the legislature, so its only official source was the state session laws.

rangements with commercial publishers to prepare annotated codes, which are legislatively or administratively sanctioned as official. Most state codes are published in bound volumes supplemented by annual pocket parts, updated further in many states by quarterly interim pamphlets. A few state codes are published instead in binders or in annual softcover editions. *The Bluebook* and *ALWD Citation Manual* provide listings by state of the names and citations of current official and commercially published codes.[51]

In addition to noting state and federal cases applying or interpreting statutory provisions, the state codes provide various research aids including legal encyclopedias, law review articles, and *ALR* annotations. Features vary from state to state, depending in part on the publisher of the code. West and LexisNexis both publish codes for more than thirty-five states, so in many states there is a choice between codes with slightly different features. Illustrations 3–13 and 3–14 on pages 105–106 show pages from annotated codes for Florida (published by West) and Maryland (published by Lexis-Nexis).

The outline and arrangement of codes also vary from state to state. While most codes are divided into titles and sections, in a format similar to the *U.S. Code*, several states have individual codes designated by name rather than title number (e.g., commercial code, penal code, tax code). Louisiana has five subject codes (children's, civil, civil procedure, criminal procedure, evidence) combined with numbered revised statutes. Until recently, some states even had competing classification systems from different publishers.[52]

State codes usually provide references to the original session laws in parenthetical notes following each section, but only a few include notes indicating the changes made by each amendment—making access to the session laws essential for reconstructing the language of an earlier version. Most codes also include tables with cross references from session law citations and earlier codifications to the current code, and each has a substantial index of one or more volumes.

Westlaw and Lexis provide access to codes from all fifty states, as well as the District of Columbia, Guam, Puerto Rico, and the

---

51. THE BLUEBOOK: A UNIFORM SYSTEM OF CITATION 198–239 (18th ed. 2005); ALWD CITATION MANUAL: A PROFESSIONAL SYSTEM OF CITATION 359–400 (2d ed. 2003).

52. In both Georgia and Michigan, older annotated codes (*Georgia Code Annotated* and *Michigan Statutes Annotated*) that began publication in the 1930s continued to maintain their numbering systems for years after official codification with different systems were adopted (in 1982 and 1948 respectively). Until 2001, Michigan court rules even required citation of both systems. Admin. Order No. 1987–2, 428 Mich. cviii, cxxi (1987), *amended by* Admin. Order No. 2001–5, 464 Mich. lxxviii (2001).

Virgin Islands, including the case notes and other references from the annotated codes. Westlaw even offers two different publishers' versions of annotated codes in twenty-one states and the District of Columbia, and *three* different versions for Nevada. Westlaw users can choose between annotated and unannotated versions of codes, and Lexis users can search in the *unanno* segment to avoid documents where relevant terms appear only in the annotations. Both systems add notices to statutes that have been amended by slip laws not yet incorporated into the code database. Lexis has a "Legislative Alert" with links to new acts, and the Westlaw display has a red flag linking to legislative action.

Loislaw and VersusLaw also have state codes, although their versions are not annotated with notes of court decisions or reference materials (other than lists of the session law sources for each code section). In Loislaw, a "Currency" link on the search screen indicates the most recent acts covered in the database. Its code databases can be browsed or searched, and each section is conveniently linked to a display of its chapter contents and thus to nearby sections. VersusLaw indicates the currency at the top of each displayed section. Its code sections can only be retrieved by searching, and no method is offered to see tables of contents or nearby sections.

Every state's statutes are also available on CD–ROM, often in more than one version. The search engine, contents, and frequency of updating varies from state to state and publisher to publisher. Some discs provide annotated codes, while others don't include annotations but combine the statutes with case law and other sources.[53]

State code sections are also covered by KeyCite and Shepard's Citations, which may provide references to cases and articles not mentioned in the annotated code. Because codes publish selective annotations while KeyCite and Shepard's list every citing case found in the Westlaw or Lexis databases, the citators' coverage may well be more thorough than the code's. They are also updated continually, so their coverage is considerably more current than the annotations. Even if a code is supplemented quarterly, it is necessary to use a citator for the latest developments.

KeyCite also lists citations of statutes in attorney general opinions. The state attorneys general are often called upon to render opinions on statutory language of uncertain effect, and their opinions can be very influential in statutory interpretation. Only

---

53. Chapter 28, *State Legal Publications and Information Sources*, in KENDALL F. SVENGALIS, LEGAL INFORMATION BUYER'S GUIDE AND REFERENCE MANUAL (annual) provides regularly updated information on the contents and pricing of these CD–ROM products. They are also listed by title in DIRECTORY OF LAW-RELATED CD–ROMs (annual), and indexed under the heading "Statutes–[State]."

some annotated codes include references to attorney general opinions, and Shepard's covers these opinions for only a few states. Both Lexis and Westlaw have attorney general opinion databases for every state, however, and these can be searched for specific statutory citations.

(c) Multistate Research Sources

Most state statutory research situations require finding the law in one particular state, for which that state's code is the primary research tool. Sometimes, however, it is necessary to compare statutory provisions among states or to survey legislation throughout the country. Multistate surveys of state laws can be frustrating and time-consuming endeavors, in part because state codes do not always use the same terminology for similar issues. It is possible, and sometimes necessary, to search in each state code's index. If doing so, you will quickly learn that different indexes can treat similar subjects in very different ways and the same search won't work for every state.

Several resources can help to make multistate statutory research a bit easier. Both Westlaw and Lexis have databases containing the codes of all fifty states; Westlaw offers either annotated (STAT–ANN–ALL) or unannotated (STAT–ALL) versions. Even though statutory language differs from state to state, these are nonetheless powerful resources for someone doing comparative statutory research or interested in finding how a particular word or phrase has been applied in other states.

Westlaw and Lexis also provide compilations of state surveys on selected topics, listing citations with links to the full text databases. Westlaw's 50–State Surveys (SURVEYS) database is accessible as a link from any state code database search screen and is included as a KeyCite citing reference for sections included in a survey. The surveys cover about two hundred topics in twenty broad subject areas, providing state-by-state links to relevant statutes. Lexis provides a similar set of "50 State Comparative Legislation/Regulations," covering nearly four hundred topics in thirty subjects. Lexis has searchable one-line summaries of surveys, with the links to code sections provided in Excel spreadsheet format.

Some of the surveys available through Westlaw are drawn from the printed source by Richard A. Leiter, *National Survey of State Laws* (5th ed. 2005). This book is arranged by topic and has tables summarizing statutes in forty-five areas and providing citations to codes. It focuses in part on current social and political issues, with sections on topics such as capital punishment, prayer in public schools, right to die, and stalking. The tables highlight specific aspects of each state's law, allowing immediate comparisons of these provisions, and provide citations to the codes for fuller examination.

The Martindale–Hubbell Law Digests are another valuable source for comparing state laws. The Law Digests are arranged by state and cover more than a hundred legal topics, with a focus on commercial and procedural information most likely to be needed by lawyers in other states. Citations are provided to both code sections and court decisions. Formerly published in print as a companion to the *Martindale-Hubbell Law Directory*, the Law Digests are now available online in two formats. Martindale.com <www.martindale. com> provides access to each state's digest as a PDF document as part of the "Search Legal Topics" section. Access is free, but registration is required. The Law Digests are also available through Lexis, in the "Reference" folder with other Martindale–Hubbell material. The Lexis database is probably the more convenient source for multistate research, because each topic is a separate document and a search for a topic heading can retrieve the relevant section for every state. Illustration 3–15 on page 107 shows the Lexis version of the Wisconsin criminal law digest, one of 53 documents retrieved (50 states, the District of Columbia, Puerto Rico, and the Virgin Islands) with the search *section(criminal law)*. Links are provided to cases cited, while statute citations are provided but not linked.

Other Internet sites provide convenient multistate access to code provisions in some subject areas. One of the most comprehensive sites is Cornell Legal Information Institute's topical index to state statutes on the Internet <topics.law.cornell.edu/wex/ state_statutes>, with links to code databases in several dozen broad categories. As with printed sources, it is important that a site summarizing state laws is regularly updated and that it provides the code citations necessary for verification and further research.

Topical looseleaf services often collect state laws in their subject areas, providing a convenient way to compare state provisions in areas such as taxation or employment law. The *Blue Sky Law Reporter* (CCH) includes the text of state security acts, for example, while the *Labor Relations Reporter* (BNA) has state statutes on topics such as wages and hours, fair employment practices, and individual employment rights.

State laws on particular subjects are also collected or surveyed in a variety of other sources, such as treatises, websites, law review articles, and government publications. Some of these sources provide the texts of laws, but even those that list only code citations can save a considerable amount of research time.

These various collections and lists of state statutes are described in a valuable series of bibliographies, *Subject Compilations of State Laws* (1981–date), now compiled annually by Cheryl Rae Nyberg. This set does not itself summarize or cite the statutes, but it provides annotated descriptions of sources that do so. Entries in *Subject Compilations* indicate whether sources include the code citations that are essential for verifying and updating their information. Illustration 3–16 on page 108 shows a page from this publication, with entries for three law review articles, a National Conference of State Legislatures database, and a Westlaw fifty-state survey. *Subject Compilations of State Laws* is available by subscription through HeinOnline, cumulative and with links to law review articles in HeinOnline's database as well as to publicly available Internet sites.[54]

Shepard's Acts and Cases by Popular Names: Federal and State (5th ed. 1999, with bimonthly supplements) which lists statutes from throughout the country, may be useful if you are seeking similar acts from several states. Its listings can provide citations of acts from numerous states on related topics, such as blue sky laws or lemon laws. Entries under "Dental Practice Act," for example, include listings for statutes from 47 states, the District of Columbia, and Puerto Rico.

(d) Uniform Laws and Model Acts

Most multistate research requires finding a wide variety of legislative approaches to a particular topic. In a growing number of areas, however, states have adopted virtually identical acts in an attempt to reduce the confusion caused by conflicting state statutes.

For more than a century, one of the major aspects of the law reform movement in the United States has been a drive for state enactment of uniform laws in fields in which uniformity would be beneficial. The National Conference of Commissioners on Uniform State Laws was formed in 1892 for this purpose. The Conference, consisting of representatives of each state, meets annually to draft, promulgate and promote uniform laws, which the states can then adopt as proposed, modify, or ignore, as they see fit. More than 200 uniform laws have been approved by the Conference, of which more than 150 have been adopted by at least one state.[55]

The most widely known of the uniform laws is the Uniform Commercial Code, jointly sponsored by the Conference and the American Law Institute. The UCC was originally promulgated in

---

54. Another guide to subject compilations is JON S. SCHULTZ, STATUTES COMPARED: A U.S., CANADIAN, MULTINATIONAL RESEARCH GUIDE TO STATUTES BY SUBJECT (2d ed. 2001–date). This annotated work focuses on treatises and looseleaf services that reprint, summarize or cite state statutes by subject.

55. For a history of NCCUSL and its proposed legislation, see James J. White, *Ex Proprio Vigore*, 89 MICH. L. REV. 2096, 2097–2105 (1991).

1951, but it has changed considerably over the years as individual articles have been revised and reissued. The latest version is published annually in a large paperback volume familiar to many law students, *Uniform Commercial Code: Official Text with Comments*. The UCC has a substantial literature, including its own series of court reports, *Uniform Commercial Code Reporting Service* (1964–date), and numerous treatises and hornbooks. James J. White & Robert S. Summers, *Uniform Commercial Code* (5th ed. 2002–date), is widely considered to be the most authoritative of the treatises.

The UCC has been enacted by every state, but the law in force varies widely from state to state because individual articles are revised from time to time. A table listing the status of the UCC in each state requires eighteen different footnotes indicating which revised articles have been adopted in each jurisdiction.[56]

Other, less well-known acts have been almost as widely adopted, such as the Uniform Act to Secure the Attendance of Witnesses from Without a State in Criminal Proceedings, which has been enacted in every state but North Dakota.[57] On the other hand, more than thirty uniform acts have been adopted by just one or two states, including the Uniform Statute and Rule Construction Act mentioned earlier in this chapter.[58]

Uniform Laws Annotated, a multi-volume set published by West, contains every uniform law approved by the NCCUSL, tables of adopting states with code citations, commissioners' notes, and annotations to court decisions from any adopting jurisdiction. These annotations allow researchers in one state to study the case law developed in other states with the same uniform law. A decision from another state is not binding authority, but its interpretation of similar language may be quite persuasive. The set is supplemented annually by pocket parts and by a pamphlet, *Directory of Uniform Acts and Codes; Tables—Index*, which lists the acts alphabetically and includes a table of jurisdictions indicating the acts adopted in each state.

Uniform Laws Annotated is available on Westlaw as the ULA database, with material accessible by full-text search or through browsing the table of contents. Lexis has a Model Acts & Uniform Laws folder in its Secondary Legal collection, which has more than fifty unannotated acts including the UCC official text and comments.

---

56. *Uniform Commercial Code: Tables of Jurisdictions Wherein Code has been Adopted*, 1 U.L.A. 1, 2–3 (Supp. 2008). The *Uniform Commercial Code Reporting Service* includes a "State UCC Variations" volume indicating how each state varies from the official text.

57. 11 U.L.A. 1 (2003).

58. Supra n. 15.

Uniform acts are available on the Internet from the NCCUSL Archives at the University of Pennsylvania Law Library <www. law.upenn.edu/bll/ulc/ulc.htm>. The site provides more than 100 acts dating back to 1922, as well as extensive sets of drafts for recent and current projects.[59] The NCCUSL website <www.nccusl. org>, under the heading "Final Acts and Legislation," has summaries of its acts and explanations of why each should be adopted. The annual *Handbook of the National Conference of Commissioners on Uniform State Laws* contains minutes of proceedings, the text of uniform and model laws approved, and tables of state adoptions, but it is published after a delay of several years.

The text of a uniform law can also be found, of course, in the statutory code of each adopting state, accompanied by annotations from that state's courts. The state code contains the law as actually adopted and in force, rather than the text as proposed by the Commissioners. The NCCUSL version is merely a proposal, but the state code version is the law. For about fifty acts, Cornell's Legal Information Institute provides "Uniform Law Locators" <www. law.cornell.edu/uniform/> listing links to official sites where the text as adopted in particular states can be found.

"Model acts" are drafted for fields where individual states are expected to modify a proposed law to meet their needs, rather than adopt it *in toto*. Two of the most influential model acts are the Model Penal Code and the Model Business Corporation Act, both developed by the American Law Institute. Research resources for these acts include *Model Penal Code and Commentaries* (1980–85), and *Model Business Corporation Act Annotated* (4th ed. 2008–date).

The Council of State Governments (CSG) publishes an annual volume of *Suggested State Legislation*. This reproduces statutes recently enacted in one jurisdiction and recommended for consideration in others, with each preceded by a brief explanation. The acts in each volume are printed alphabetically, but a cumulative subject index in each volume provides access to suggested legislation from the preceding twenty years or so. Recent volumes are available on the CSG website <www.csg.org/programs/ssl/>.

(e) Interstate Compacts

An interstate compact is an agreement between two or more states, which under the Constitution requires approval by Con-

---

59. Early drafts of the UCC have been published in the multi-volume sets UNIFORM COMMERCIAL CODE: DRAFTS (Elizabeth Slusser Kelly comp., 1984), and UNIFORM COMMERCIAL CODE: CONFIDENTIAL DRAFTS (Elizabeth Slusser Kelly & Ann Puckett comps., 1995). On the background, drafting and early history of the UCC, see two articles by Allen R. Kamp, *Uptown Act: A History of the Uniform Commercial Code, 1940–1949*, 51 SMU L. REV. 275 (1998), and *Downtown Act: A History of the Uniform Commercial Code, 1949–1954*, 49 BUFF. L. REV. 359 (2001).

gress.[60] After the compact is agreed upon by the states, it goes to Congress for authorizing legislation. If enacted, each compact thus appears in the *U.S. Statutes at Large* and in the session laws of the states which are parties to it. Most interstate compacts also appear in the annotated statutory codes of the states enacting them, and can usually be found in the indexes under "Compacts" or "Interstate Compacts" as well as the underlying subject.

The website for National Center for Interstate Compacts, a branch of the Council of State Governments <www.csg.org/programs/ncic/>, provides a variety of useful resources on the subject, including an "Interstate Compacts Tool Kit" and numerous other documents and analyses in PDF format. It also has the text of nearly 200 compacts and a searchable database of more than 1,500 compacts in state codes. Citations, and in many instances links to state code websites, are provided.

Joseph F. Zimmerman, *Interstate Cooperation: Compacts and Administrative Agreements* (2002) discusses the compacting process, compact commissions, and formal and informal administrative agreements, and includes an extensive bibliography of books, documents, and articles. Caroline N. Broun et al., *The Evolving Use and the Changing Role of Interstate Compacts: A Practitioner's Guide* (2006) also provides background information as well as a survey of the current uses of compacts, and an appendix lists and describes compacts with citations to the enabling federal and state legislation.

———

Statutory law plays a pivotal role in the legal system and in legal research. Most court decisions involve the application or interpretation of statutes, and the scope of judicial authority and jurisdiction is largely determined by legislative enactments. Administrative regulations, court rules, and local laws are all based on statutory delegations of power created by statute. All legal research must therefore include the question: Is there a statute on point?

In some ways statutory research is easier than case research, because the major resources are more accessible and more regularly updated. In many situations an annotated code provides most of the necessary research leads. This convenience is undercut, however, by the opacity of statutory language. Judicial prose can be a model of clarity when compared to the texts of many federal and state statutes.

60. Article I, § 10 provides: "No state shall, without the Consent of Congress, ... enter into any Agreement or Compact with another State ..."

Some statutory ambiguities stem from poor draftsmanship, but many are the inevitable result of negotiation and compromise in the legislative process. Several approaches to interpretation of ambiguous statutes are available, including the study of legislative documents created during the drafting of the statutory text. This research in legislative history is the focus of the next chapter.

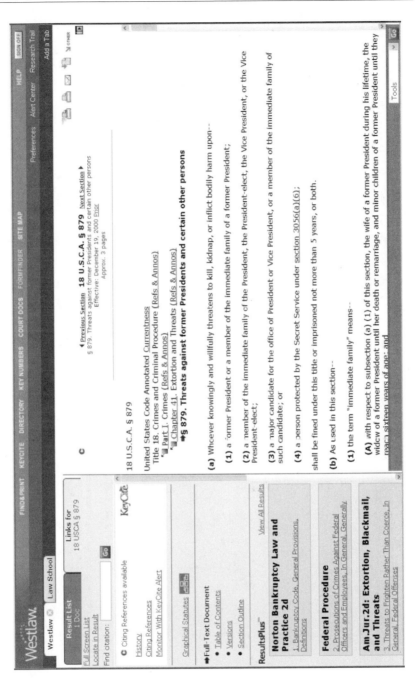

Illustration 3–1. 18 U.S.C.A. § 879 (Westlaw
through 2008 legislation).

LexisNexis® *Total Research System*

Search | Research Tasks | Get a Document | Shepard's® | Alerts | Total Litigator | Transactional Advisor | Counsel Selector

Custom ID ▼ | No Description | Switch Client | Preferences | Live Support | Sign Out | Help

History

FOCUS™ Terms

Search Within Original Results (1 - 2) | Go | Advanced...

View: TOC | Cite | Full | Custom

Book Browse | More Like This | More Like Selected Text | Shepardize®
18 USCS § 879 (Copy w/ Cite)

◇ 1 of 2 ◇

Pages: 7

18 USCS ◆ 879

Retrieve Legislative Impact◆

UNITED STATES CODE SERVICE
Copyright ◆ 2008 Matthew Bender & Company, Inc.
a member of the LexisNexis Group (TM)
All rights reserved.

*** CURRENT THROUGH PL 110-460, APPROVED 12/23/2008 ***

TITLE 18. CRIMES AND CRIMINAL PROCEDURE
PART I. CRIMES
CHAPTER 41. EXTORTION AND THREATS

Go to the United States Code Service Archive Directory

18 USCS ◆ 879

◆ 879. Threats against former Presidents and certain other persons

(a) Whoever knowingly and willfully threatens to kill, kidnap, or inflict bodily harm upon--
(1) a former President or a member of the immediate family of a former President;
(2) a member of the immediate family of the President, the President-elect, the Vice President, or the Vice President-elect;
(3) a major candidate for the office of President or Vice President, or a member of the immediate family of such candidate; or
(4) a person protected by the Secret Service under section 3056(a)(6) [18 USCS ◆ 3056(a)(6)];

Practitioner's Toolbox

⊕ History
⊕ Interpretive Notes and Decisions
⊕ History; Ancillary Laws and Directives

Resources & Practice Tools
⊕ Related Statutes & Rules
⊕ Research Guide

Criminal Law and Practice:
> 3 Criminal Defense Techniques (Matthew Bender), ch 55, Defense of a Kidnapping Case ◆ 55. 02.
⊕ More...

Doc 1 of 2 ▲ ▼

Term ▲ ▼

Outline

Illustration 3–2. 18 U.S.C.S. § 879 (Lexis
through 2008 legislation).

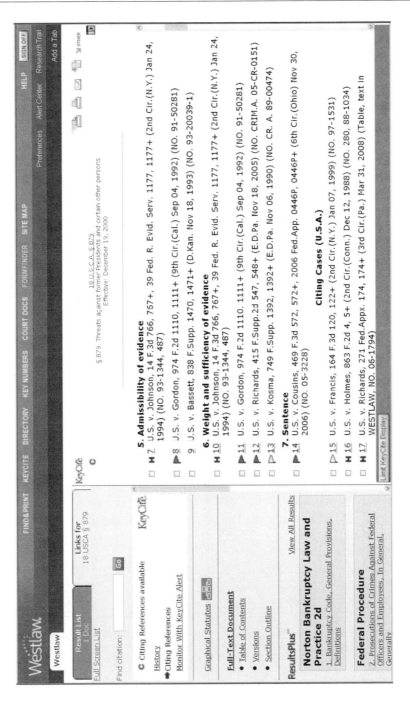

Illustration 3–3. KeyCite results for 18 U.S.C.A. § 879.

LexisNexis *Total Research System*   Custom ID ▼ No Description Switch Client | Preferences | Live Support | Sign Out | ⊡ Help   History ⏧

| Search | Research Tasks | Get a Document | Shepard's® | Alerts | Total Litigator | Transactional Advisor | Counsel Selector |

Shepardize:®

[Go →   ]

View: Index | KWIC | **Full**
▶ Display Options   Save As Shepard's Alert® | **Unrestricted** | All Neg | All Pos | FOCUS™ | Restrict By   ⟺ 1 - **50** of 51 Total Cites ⟺

Shepard's® **18 U.S.C. sec. 879**   📠 ⊞ 🖨 💾 🖫 ✎ 🖫 ⊞

⊟ **HIDE**   SHEPARD'S SUMMARY

⎯⎯

Unrestricted *Shepard's* Summary

Citing References:

◆ **Positive Analyses:**   Constitutional (1)

Neutral Analyses: Construes (1)   Interprets (1)

Other Sources: Law Reviews (3), Statutes (10), Treatises (8), Court Documents (1)

Index - Shepard's reports by court citation...

⎯⎯

⊟ **HIDE**   **HISTORY**

(Added Oct. 12, 1982, P.L. 97-297, § 1(a), 96 Stat. 1317; Oct. 30, 1984, P.L. 98-587, § 3(a), 98 Stat. 3111; Sept. 13, 1994, P.L. 103-322, Title XXXIII, § 330016(1)(H), 108 Stat. 2147; Dec. 19, 2000, P.L. 106-544, § 2(a), (b)(1), 114 Stat. 2715.)

⎯⎯

CITING DECISIONS (29 citing decisions)

2ND CIRCUIT - COURT OF APPEALS

⇗ Select for Delivery

☐ 1. Cited by:

United States v. Francis, 164 F.3d 120, 1999 U.S. App. LEXIS 154 (2d Cir. N.Y. 1999)

164 F.3d 120 p.122

☐ 2. Cited by:

United States v. Johnson, 14 F.3d 766, 1994 U.S. App. LEXIS 1240, 39 Fed. R. Evid. Serv. (CBC) 1177 (2d Cir. N.Y. 1994)

14 F.3d 766 p.762

Trail | Summary | Legend   Total (51) **Cites**   ⊼ | ▲ ▼ | [69] of 51 🔍 | ◀ | ▶

Illustration 3–4. Shepard's results for 18 U.S.C.S. § 879.

577　　　　　　　　　　　　　　　　　THREATS

THIRD PROTOCOL (RED CRYSTAL) EMBLEM
Generally, 18 § 706a

THIRD WORLD NATIONS
Less Developed Countries, generally, this index

THIRTY–PAYMENT LIFE INSURANCE
National service life insurance, 38 § 1904

THOMAS ALVA EDISON COMMEMORATIVE COIN ACT
Generally, 31 § 5112 nt

THOMAS COLE NATIONAL HISTORIC SITE
Generally, 16 § 461 nt

THOMAS CREASE HOUSE
Boston National Historical Park, 16 § 410z–1

THOMAS H. KUCHEL VISITOR CENTER
Redwood National Park, 16 § 79a nt

THOMAS JEFFERSON
Commemorative coins, 31 § 5112 nt
Congressional Gold Medal, authorization, 31 § 5111 nt
Flags, display, birthday, 36 § 141
Jefferson National Expansion Memorial, generally, this index
Jefferson National Forest, generally, this index
Proclamations, birthday, 36 § 141

THOMAS JEFFERSON NATIONAL MEMORIAL
Generally, 16 § 431 nt

THOMAS JEFFERSON STAR FOR FOREIGN SERVICE
Generally, 22 § 2708a

THOMAS STONE NATIONAL HISTORIC SITE
Generally, 16 § 461 nt

THORACENTESIS
Medicare, 42 § 1395u

THORACOTOMY
Medicare, 42 § 1395u

THORIUM
Development, 42 § 2011 et seq.

THOUSAND LAKES WILDERNESS
Generally, 16 § 1132 nt

THREAT REDUCTION WORKING GROUP
Russia, nuclear non-proliferation, 22 § 5951 nt

THREATENED SPECIES
Endangered Species, this index

THREATS
Generally, 18 § 871 et seq.
Aircraft, this index
Airports and Landing Fields, this index

THREATS—Cont'd
Armed Forces, elections, 18 § 593
Atomic Energy, this index
Bioterrorism, 42 § 247d–6b
　Assessments, 6 § 321j
Blackmail, 18 § 873
Buildings, 18 § 844
Business and commerce, interference, 18 §§ 1951, 2516
Chemical and biological warfare and weapons, 18 § 229
　Terrorists and terrorism, assessments, 6 § 321j
Civil Rights, this index
Comprehensive employment and training programs, 18 § 665
Computers, this index
Congress, reports, 18 § 351 nt
Cooperative Threat Reduction Programs, Independent States of the Former Soviet Union, 22 § 5951 et seq.; 50 § 2901 et seq.
Crime victims, 18 § 1512
Critical infrastructure, national security, 42 §§ 5195 nt, EON 13010, 5195c
Cyber threats, critical infrastructure, national security, 42 §§ 5195 nt, EON 13010, 5195c
Debt collection practices, 15 §§ 1692d, 1692e
Defense Production Act of 1950, foreign government controlled transactions, 50 App. § 2170
Definitions,
　Former Presidents, 18 § 879
　President elect, 18 § 871
　Presidential candidates, 18 § 879
　Social Security Administration, 42 § 1320a–8b
　Vice-President elect, 18 § 871
Dominican Republic-Central America-United States Free Trade Agreement, 19 § 4101
Explosives, mail and mailing, 18 § 844
Exports and Imports, this index
Extortion, generally, this index
Fair housing, 42 § 3631
Federal Officers and Employees, this index
Federally protected activities, 18 § 245
Food, this index
Foreign intelligence, 50 § 401 nt, EON 12333
Foreign officials, 18 §§ 878, 970
Former Presidents, 18 § 879
Independent States of the Former Soviet Union, Cooperative Threat Reduction Programs, 22 § 5951 et seq.; 50 § 2901 et seq.
Informers, this index
Infrastructure, critical infrastructure, national security, 42 §§ 5195 nt, EON 13010, 5195c
Interagency Threat Assessment and Coordination Group, 6 § 124k
Internal Revenue Service, this index
Internationally protected persons, 18 § 878
Job Training Partnership Programs, 18 § 665
Judges or Justices, this index
Kidnapping, this index

Illustration 3–5. United States Code Annotated, General Index S–Z 577 (2008).

POPULAR NAME TABLE 1044

Presidential Inaugural Ceremonies Act—Continued
Jan. 30, 1968, Pub.L. 90–251, 82 Stat. 4 (36 §§ 722, 723, 728, 730)
Aug. 12, 1998, Pub.L. 105–225, § 6(b), 112 Stat. 1505 (36 §§ 721 to 725, 727 to 730)

Presidential Libraries Act
Aug. 12, 1955, ch. 859, 69 Stat. 695 (See 44 §§ 2101, 2107, 2108)
Oct. 22, 1968, Pub.L. 90–620, § 3, 82 Stat. 1309 (44 § 397)

Presidential Libraries Act of 1986
Short title, see 44 USCA § 101 note
Pub.L. 99–323, May 27, 1986, 100 Stat. 495 (44 §§ 101 note, 2101, 2112, 2112 note)

Presidential Primary Matching Payment Account Act
Short title, see 26 USCA § 9031
Pub.L. 93–443, Title IV, § 408(c), Oct. 15, 1974, 88 Stat. 1297 (26 §§ 9031 to 9042)

Presidential Protection Assistance Act of 1976
Pub.L. 94–524, Oct. 17, 1976, 90 Stat. 2475 (18 § 3056 note)
Pub.L. 99–190, Title I, § 143, Dec. 19, 1985, 99 Stat. 1324 (18 § 3056 note)
Pub.L. 101–136, Title V, § 527, Nov. 30, 1989, 103 Stat. 815 (18 § 3056 note)
Pub.L. 101–509, Title V, § 531(a), Nov. 5, 1990, 104 Stat. 1469 (18 § 3056 note)
Pub.L. 102–141, § 533, Oct. 28, 1991, 105 Stat. 867 (18 § 3056 note)
Pub.L. 104–52, Title V, § 529, Nov. 19, 1995, 109 Stat. 496 (18 § 3056 note)
Pub.L. 104–316, Title I, § 109(a), Oct. 19, 1996, 110 Stat. 3832 (18 § 3056 note)

Presidential Recordings and Materials Preservation Act
Pub.L. 93–526, Dec. 19, 1974, 88 Stat. 1695 (44 §§ 2107 note, 3315 to 3324)
Pub.L. 98–497, Title I, § 107(c), Oct. 19, 1984, 98 Stat. 2291 (44 § 2111 note)
Pub.L. 108–199, Div. F, Title V, § 543(a), Jan. 23, 2004, 118 Stat. 346 (44 § 2111 note)

Presidential Records Act of 1978
Short title, see 44 USCA § 101 note
Pub.L. 95–591, Nov. 4, 1978, 92 Stat. 2523 (44 §§ 2201 to 2207)

Presidential Science and Technology Advisory Organization Act of 1976
Short title, see 42 USCA § 6601 note
Pub.L. 94–282, Title II, May 11, 1976, 90 Stat. 463 (42 §§ 6611 to 6618)

Presidential Succession Act
Jan. 19, 1886, ch. 4, 24 Stat. 1 (See 3 §§ 1, 19)
July 18, 1947, ch. 264, § 1(a) to (f), 61 Stat. 380 (3 § 17)

Presidential Threat Protection Act of 2000
Short title, see 18 USCA § 871 note
Pub.L. 106–544, Dec. 19, 2000, 114 Stat. 2715 (18 §§ 871 note, 879, 3056, 3486, 3486A; 28
§§ 509 note, 551 note, 566 note)
Pub.L. 110–177, Title V, § 507, Jan. 7, 2008, 121 Stat. 2543 (28 § 566 note)

Presidential Transition Act of 1963
Pub.L. 88–277, Mar. 7, 1964, 78 Stat. 153 (3 § 102 note)
Pub.L. 94–499, §§ 1 to 3, Oct. 14, 1976, 90 Stat. 2380 (3 § 102 note)
Pub.L. 100–398, §§ 2(a), 3, 4, Aug. 17, 1988, 102 Stat. 985, 986 (3 § 102 note)
Pub.L. 106–293, § 1, Oct. 12, 2000, 114 Stat. 1035 (3 § 102 note)
Pub.L. 108–458, Title VII, § 7601(a), Dec. 17, 2004, 118 Stat. 3856 (3 § 102 note)

Presidential Transition Act of 2000
Short title, see 3 USCA § 101 note
Pub.L. 106–293, Oct. 12, 2000, 114 Stat. 1035 (3 § 102 note)

Presidential Transitions Effectiveness Act
Short title, see 3 USCA § 1 note
Pub.L. 100–398, Aug. 17, 1988, 102 Stat. 985 (3 § 102 notes; 5 §§ 3345, 3348, 5723)

President's Emergency Food Assistance Act of 1984
Short title, see 7 USCA § 1728 note
Pub.L. 98–473, Title III, Oct. 12, 1984, 98 Stat. 2194 (7 §§ 1723, 1728, 1728a, 1728b)

President's Media Commission on Alcohol and Drug Abuse Prevention Act
Short title, see 21 USCA § 1301 note
Pub.L. 99–570, Title VIII, Oct. 27, 1986, 100 Stat. 3207–161 (21 §§ 1301, 1301 note, 1302 to
1308)

Illustration 3–6. UNITED STATES CODE ANNOTATED,
POPULAR NAME TABLE 1044 (2008).

Page 1075		TABLE III—STATUTES AT LARGE					
106th Cong.					U.S.C.		
114 Stat.	Pub. L.	Section	Page	Title	Section		Status
2000—Dec. 11 .... 106-541		224(a)	2597	33	2283		
		224(b)	2598	33	2283 nt		
		225	2598	33	2215		
		226	2598	10	2695 nt		
		227	2599	33	2232		
		342	2612	33	2263		
		343	2613	33	426o-1		
		344	2613	33	1268 nt		
		346	2614	33	59bb-1		
		347(a)(2)	2618	33	59ee-1		
		403	2634	33	652 nt		
		404	2635	33	652 nt		
		504(a), (b)	2644	42	1962d-20		
		505	2645	33	2326b		
		506	2645	42	1962d-22		
		518	2653	42	1962d-20 nt		
		554	2679	33	892a nt		
		801-810	2699-2706	16	668dd nt		
19 .... 106-544		1	2715	18	871 nt		
		2(a), (b)(1)	2715	18	879		
		2(b)(2)	2715	18	prec. 871		
		3	2716	18	3056		
		4	2716	18	3056 nt		
		5(a), (b)(1)	2716, 2718	18	3486		
		5(b)(2)	2718	18	prec. 3481		
		5(b)(3)	2718	18	3486A	Rep.
		5(b)(5)	2718	18	prec. 3481		
		5(c)	2718	18	3486		
		6	2718	28	506 nt		
		7	2719	5	551 nt		
	106-545	1	2721	42	201 nt		
		2	2721	42	285l-2		
		3	2721	42	285l-3		
		4	2723	42	285l-4		
		5	2724	42	285l-5		
	106-546	1	2726	42	13701 nt		
		2	2726	42	14135		
		3	2728	42	14135a		
		4	2730	42	14135b		
		5(a)(1)	2731	10	1565		
		5(a)(2)	2732	10	prec. 1561		
		5(b)	2733	10	1565 nt		
		5(c)	2733	10	1565 nt		
		6(a)	2733	28	531 nt		
		6(b)	2733	42	14132		
		7(a)	2734	18	3563		
		7(b)	2734	18	3583		
		7(c)	2734	18	4209		
		7(d)	2734	42	14135c		
		8(a)	2734	42	3753		
		8(b)	2735	42	3796kk-2		
		8(c)	2735	42	14133		
		9	2735	42	14135d		
		10	2735	42	14135e		

Illustration 3–7. Table III–Statutes at Large,
29 UNITED STATES CODE 1075 (2000).

PUBLIC LAW 106–544—DEC. 19, 2000   114 STAT. 2715

Public Law 106–544
106th Congress

An Act

To amend section 879 of title 18, United States Code, to provide clearer coverage over threats against former Presidents and members of their families, and for other purposes.

Dec. 19, 2000
[H.R. 3048]

Be it enacted by the Senate and House of Representatives of the United States of America in Congress assembled,

Presidential
Threat Protection
Act of 2000.
18 USC 871 note.

SECTION 1. SHORT TITLE.

This Act may be cited as the "Presidential Threat Protection Act of 2000".

SEC. 2. REVISION OF SECTION 879 OF TITLE 18, UNITED STATES CODE.

(a) IN GENERAL.—Section 879 of title 18, United States Code, is amended—
    (1) by striking "or" at the end of subsection (a)(2);
    (2) in subsection (a)(3)—
        (A) by striking "the spouse" and inserting "a member of the immediate family"; and
        (B) by inserting "or" after the semicolon at the end;
    (3) by inserting after subsection (a)(3) the following:
    "(4) a person protected by the Secret Service under section 3056(a)(6);";
    (4) in subsection (a)—
        (A) by striking "who is protected by the Secret Service as provided by law,"; and
        (B) by striking "three years" and inserting "5 years"; and
    (5) in subsection (b)(1)(B)—
        (A) by inserting "and (a)(3)" after "subsection (a)(2)"; and
        (B) by striking "or Vice President-elect" and inserting "Vice President-elect, or major candidate for the office of President or Vice President".
(b) CONFORMING AMENDMENTS.—
    (1) HEADING.—The heading for section 879 of title 18, United States Code, is amended by striking "protected by the Secret Service".
    (2) TABLE OF SECTIONS.—The item relating to section 879 in the table of sections at the beginning of chapter 41 of title 18, United States Code, is amended by striking "protected by the Secret Service".

Illustration 3–8. Presidential Threat Protection Act
of 2000, Pub. L. No. 106–544, 114 Stat. 2715.

§ 879 TITLE 18—CRIMES AND CRIMINAL PROCEDURE Page 190

for a threatened assault shall not exceed three years.

(b) Whoever in connection with any violation of subsection (a) or actual violation of section 112, 1116, or 1201 makes any extortionate demand shall be fined under this title or imprisoned not more than twenty years, or both.

(c) For the purpose of this section "foreign official", "internationally protected person", "national of the United States", and "official guest" shall have the same meanings as those provided in section 1116(a) of this title.

(d) If the victim of an offense under subsection (a) is an internationally protected person outside the United States, the United States may exercise jurisdiction over the offense if (1) the victim is a representative, officer, employee, or agent of the United States, (2) an offender is a national of the United States, or (3) an offender is afterwards found in the United States. As used in this subsection, the United States includes all areas under the jurisdiction of the United States including any of the places within the provisions of sections 5 and 7 of this title and section 46501(2) of title 49.

(Added Pub. L. 94–467, § 8, Oct. 8, 1976, 90 Stat. 2000; amended Pub. L. 95–163, § 17(b)(1), Nov. 9, 1977, 91 Stat. 1286; Pub. L. 95–504, § 2(b), Oct. 24, 1978, 92 Stat. 1705; Pub. L. 103–272, § 5(e)(2), July 5, 1994, 108 Stat. 1373; Pub. L. 103–322, title XXXIII, § 330016(1)(K), (N), Sept. 13, 1994, 108 Stat. 2147, 2148; Pub. L. 104–132, title VII, §§ 705(a)(4), 721(e), Apr. 24, 1996, 110 Stat. 1295, 1299.)

AMENDMENTS

1996—Subsec. (a). Pub. L. 104–132, § 705(a)(4), struck out "by killing, kidnapping, or assaulting a foreign official, official guest, or internationally protected person" before "shall be fined".

Subsec. (c). Pub. L. 104–132, § 721(e)(1), inserted "'national of the United States,'" before "and 'official guest'".

Subsec. (d). Pub. L. 104–132, § 721(e)(2), inserted first sentence and struck out former first sentence which read as follows: "If the victim of an offense under subsection (a) is an internationally protected person, the United States may exercise jurisdiction over the offense if the alleged offender is present within the United States, irrespective of the place where the offense was committed or the nationality of the victim or the alleged offender."

1994—Subsec. (a). Pub. L. 103–322, § 330016(1)(K), substituted "fined under this title" for "fined not more than $5,000".

Subsec. (b). Pub. L. 103–322, § 330016(1)(N), substituted "fined under this title" for "fined not more than $20,000".

Subsec. (d). Pub. L. 103–272 substituted "section 46501(2) of title 49" for "section 101(38) of the Federal Aviation Act of 1958, as amended (49 U.S.C. 1301(38))".

1978—Subsec. (d). Pub. L. 95–504 substituted reference to section 101(38) of the Federal Aviation Act of 1958 for reference to section 101(35) of such Act.

1977—Subsec. (d). Pub. L. 95–163 substituted reference to section 101(35) of the Federal Aviation Act of 1958 for reference to section 101(34) of such Act.

§ 879. Threats against former Presidents and certain other persons

(a) Whoever knowingly and willfully threatens to kill, kidnap, or inflict bodily harm upon—

(1) a former President or a member of the immediate family of a former President;

(2) a member of the immediate family of the President, the President-elect, the Vice President, or the Vice President-elect;

(3) a major candidate for the office of President or Vice President, or a member of the immediate family of such candidate; or

(4) a person protected by the Secret Service under section 3056(a)(6);

shall be fined under this title or imprisoned not more than 5 years, or both.

(b) As used in this section—

(1) the term "immediate family" means—

(A) with respect to subsection (a)(1) of this section, the wife of a former President during his lifetime, the widow of a former President until her death or remarriage, and minor children of a former President until they reach sixteen years of age; and

(B) with respect to subsection (a)(2) and (a)(3) of this section, a person to whom the President, President-elect, Vice President, Vice President-elect, or major candidate for the office of President or Vice President—

(i) is related by blood, marriage, or adoption; or

(ii) stands in loco parentis;

(2) the term "major candidate for the office of President or Vice President" means a candidate referred to in subsection (a)(7) of section 3056 of this title; and

(3) the terms "President-elect" and "Vice President-elect" have the meanings given those terms in section 871(b) of this title.

(Added Pub. L. 97–297, § 1(a), Oct. 12, 1982, 96 Stat. 1317; amended Pub. L. 98–587, § 3(a), Oct. 30, 1984, 98 Stat. 3111; Pub. L. 103–322, title XXXIII, § 330016(1)(H), Sept. 13, 1994, 108 Stat. 2147; Pub. L. 106–544, § 2(a), (b)(1), Dec. 19, 2000, 114 Stat. 2715.)

AMENDMENTS

2000—Pub. L. 106–544, § 2(b)(1), struck out "protected by the Secret Service" after "other persons" in section catchline.

Subsec. (a). Pub. L. 106–544, § 2(a)(1)–(4), in par. (3), substituted "a member of the immediate family" for "the spouse", added par. (4), and, in concluding provisions, struck out "who is protected by the Secret Service as provided by law," before "shall be fined" and substituted "5 years" for "three years".

Subsec. (b)(1)(B). Pub. L. 106–544, § 2(a)(5), in introductory provisions, inserted "and (a)(3)" after "subsection (a)(2)" and substituted "Vice President-elect, or major candidate for the office of President or Vice President" for "or Vice President-elect".

1994—Subsec. (a). Pub. L. 103–322 substituted "fined under this title" for "fined not more than $1,000" in concluding provisions.

1984—Subsec. (b)(2). Pub. L. 98–587 substituted "subsection (a)(7) of section 3056 of this title" for "the first section of the joint resolution entitled 'Joint resolution to authorize the United States Secret Service to furnish protection to major Presidential or Vice Presidential candidates', approved June 6, 1968 (18 U.S.C. 3056 note)".

TRANSFER OF FUNCTIONS

For transfer of the functions, personnel, assets, and obligations of the United States Secret Service, including the functions of the Secretary of the Treasury relating thereto, to the Secretary of Homeland Security, and for treatment of related references, see sections 381, 551(d), 552(d), and 557 of Title 6, Domestic Security,

Illustration 3–9. 18 U.S.C. § 879 (2006).

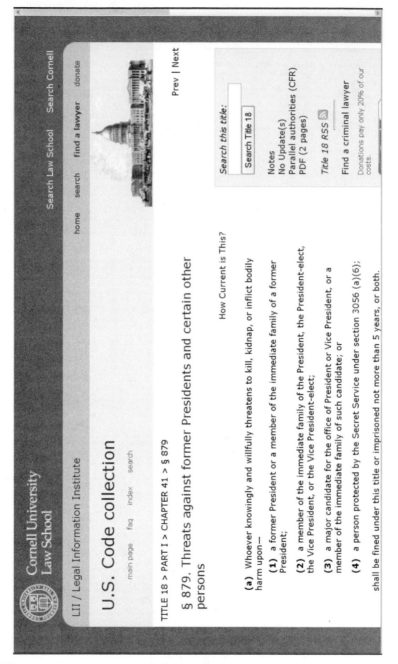

Illustration 3–10. 18 U.S.C. § 879, Legal Information Institute
U.S. Code collection <www.law.cornell.edu/uscode/>.

18 § 879　　　　　　　　　　　　　CRIMES　　Part 1

§ 879. Threats against former Presidents and certain other persons protected by the Secret Service

(a) Whoever knowingly and willfully threatens to kill, kidnap, or inflict bodily harm upon—

(1) a former President or a member of the immediate family of a former President;

(2) a member of the immediate family of the President, the President-elect, the Vice President, or the Vice President-elect; or

(3) a major candidate for the office of President or Vice President, or the spouse of such candidate;

who is protected by the Secret Service as provided by law, shall be fined under this title or imprisoned not more than three years, or both.

(b) As used in this section—

(1) the term "immediate family" means—

(A) with respect to subsection (a)(1) of this section, the wife of a former President during his lifetime, the widow of a former President until her death or remarriage, and minor children of a former President until they reach sixteen years of age; and

(B) with respect to subsection (a)(2) of this section, a person to whom the President, President-elect, Vice President, or Vice President-elect—

(i) is related by blood, marriage, or adoption; or

(ii) stands in loco parentis;

(2) the term "major candidate for the office of President or Vice President" means a candidate referred to in subsection (a)(7) of section 3056 of this title; and

(3) the terms "President-elect" and "Vice President-elect" have the meanings given those terms in section 871(b) of this title.

(Added Pub.L. 97–297, § 1(a), Oct. 12, 1982, 96 Stat. 1317, and amended Pub.L. 98–587, § 3(a), Oct. 30, 1984, 98 Stat. 3111; Pub.L. 103–322, Title XXXIII, § 330016(1)(H), Sept. 13, 1994, 108 Stat. 2147.)

HISTORICAL AND STATUTORY NOTES

Revision Notes and Legislative Reports
1982 Acts. House Report No. 97–725, see 1982 U.S. Code Cong. and Adm. News, p. 2624.
1984 Acts. House Report No. 98–1001, see 1984 U.S. Code Cong. and Adm. News, p. 5403.

1994 Acts. House Report Nos. 103–324 and 103–489, and House Conference Report No. 103–711, see 1994 U.S. Code Cong. and Adm. News, p. 1801.

72

Illustration 3–11. 18 U.S.C.A. § 879 (West 2000).

Ch. 41   EXTORTION AND THREATS   **18 § 879**
Note 5

Amendments

1994   **Amendments.** Subsec.   (a). Pub.L. 103–322, § 330016(1)(H), substituted "under this title" for "not more than $1,000".

1984   **Amendments.** Subsec.   (b)(2). Pub.L. 98–587 substituted "subsection (a)(7) of section 3056 of this title" for "the first section of the joint resolution entitled 'Joint resolution to authorize the United States Secret Service to furnish protection to major Presidential or Vice Presidential candidates', approved June 6, 1968 (18 U.S.C. 3056 note)".

CROSS REFERENCES

Secret Service—

     Authorization to detect and arrest persons violating this section, see 18 USCA § 3056.

     Investigative authority and protection of officers and employees of the United States, see 18 USCA § 115.

FEDERAL SENTENCING GUIDELINES

See Federal Sentencing Guidelines § 2A6.1, 18 USCA.

LIBRARY REFERENCES

American Digest System

     Extortion and Threats ⊜25.

Encyclopedias

     Threats and Unlawful Communications, see C.J.S. § 2–9.

WESTLAW ELECTRONIC RESEARCH

     Extortion and Threats cases: 165k[add key number].
     See WESTLAW guide following the Explanation pages of this volume.

Notes of Decisions

Admissibility of evidence   5
Constitutionality   1
Insanity   4
Intent   3
Threat   2
Weight and sufficiency of evidence   6

---

1. Constitutionality

     Congress had rational basis for prohibiting threats against former Presidents but not threats against other former federal officials, and therefore equal protection principles were not violated by criminal statute prohibiting threats against former President. U.S. v. Gordon, C.A.9 (Cal.) 1992, 974 F.2d 1110.

2. Threat

     To convict defendant of making threats against former President, government was required to prove beyond reasonable doubt that defendant made "true threat" against former President. U.S. v. Gordon, C.A.9 (Cal.) 1992, 974 F.2d 1110.

3. Intent

     Intent required to convict defendant of making threats against former President is intent to make a threat, as opposed to actual intent to inflict harm. U.S. v. Gordon, C.A.9 (Cal.) 1992, 974 F.2d 1110.

4. Insanity

     Although defendant understood meaning of words and concept of threat against former president, his paranoid schizophrenia and his incarceration at time he made threats precluded finding beyond reasonable doubt that defendant intended his statement to be threat against former president's life. U.S. v. Kosma, E.D.Pa.1990, 749 F.Supp. 1392, affirmed 951 F.2d 549.

5. Admissibility of evidence

     Offense of knowingly and willfully threatening to kill former President of the United States was general intent crime, and defendant thus was not entitled to admission of evidence of his alleged mental illness for purposes of showing whether he possessed subjective intent that his

73

Illustration 3–12. 18 U.S.C.A. § 879 notes (West 2000).

BRIBERY; MISUSE OF PUBLIC OFFICE   § 838.021
Ch. 838

838.02.   Repealed by Laws 1974, c. 74–383, § 66

Historical and Statutory Notes

The repealed § 838.02, which prohibited an officer from accepting a bribe, was derived from:

Laws 1971, c. 71–136, § 1002.
Laws 1953, c. 28052, § 1.

Comp.Gen.Laws 1927, § 7482.
Rev.Gen.St.1920, § 5347.
Gen.St.1906, § 3477.
Rev.St.1892, § 2565.
Laws 1868, c. 1637, subc. 6, § 8.

838.021.   Corruption by threat against public servant

(1) Whoever unlawfully harms or threatens unlawful harm to any public servant, to his or her immediate family, or to any other person with whose welfare the public servant is interested, with the intent or purpose:

(a) To influence the performance of any act or omission which the person believes to be, or the public servant represents as being, within the official discretion of the public servant, in violation of a public duty, or in performance of a public duty.

(b) To cause or induce the public servant to use or exert, or procure the use or exertion of, any influence upon or with any other public servant regarding any act or omission which the person believes to be, or the public servant represents as being, within the official discretion of the public servant, in violation of a public duty, or in performance of a public duty.

(2) Prosecution under this section shall not require any allegation or proof that the public servant ultimately sought to be unlawfully influenced was qualified to act in the desired way, that the public servant had assumed office, that the matter was properly pending before him or her or might by law properly be brought before him or her, that the public servant possessed jurisdiction over the matter, or that his or her official action was necessary to achieve the person's purpose.

(3)(a) Whoever unlawfully harms any public servant or any other person with whose welfare the public servant is interested shall be guilty of a felony of the second degree, punishable as provided in s. 775.082, s. 775.083, or s. 775.084.

(b) Whoever threatens unlawful harm to any public servant or to any other person with whose welfare the public servant is interested shall be guilty of a felony of the third degree, punishable as provided in s. 775.082, s. 775.083, or s. 775.084.

Amended by Laws 1997, c. 97–102, § 1316, eff. July 1, 1997.

Historical and Statutory Notes

Derivation:

Laws 1975, c. 75–298, § 37.
Laws 1974, c. 74–383, § 61.

Laws 1975, c. 75–298, substituted references to "§ 775.082, § 775.083, or § 775.084" for "chapter 775" in subsec. (3).

Laws 1997, c. 97–102, eff. July 1, 1997, removed gender-specific references applicable to human beings from volume 4 of the Florida Statutes without substantive changes in legal effect.

45

Illustration 3–13. FLA. STAT. ANN. § 838.021 (West 2000).

economic, or political association or organization." Ball v. UPS, Inc., 325 Md. 652, 602 A.2d 1176 (1992).

§ 3-708. Threat against State or local official.

(a) *Definitions.* — (1) In this section the following words have the meanings indicated.

(2) "Local official" means an individual serving in a publicly elected office of a local government unit, as defined in § 10-101 of the State Government Article.

(3) (i) "State official" has the meaning stated in § 15-102 of the State Government Article.

(ii) "State official" includes the Governor, Governor-elect, Lieutenant Governor, and Lieutenant Governor-elect.

(4) "Threat" includes:

(i) an oral threat; or

(ii) a threat in any written form, whether or not the writing is signed, or if the writing is signed, whether or not it is signed with a fictitious name or any other mark.

(b) *Prohibited — Making threat.* — A person may not knowingly and willfully make a threat to take the life of, kidnap, or cause physical injury to a State official or local official.

(c) *Same — Sending or delivering threat.* — A person may not knowingly send, deliver, part with, or make for the purpose of sending or delivering a threat prohibited under subsection (b) of this section.

(d) *Penalty.* — A person who violates this section is guilty of a misdemeanor and on conviction is subject to imprisonment not exceeding 3 years or a fine not exceeding $2,500 or both. (An. Code 1957, art. 27, § 561A; 2002, ch. 26, § 2.)

REVISOR'S NOTE

This section is new language derived without substantive change from former Art. 27, § 561A.

In subsection (b) of this section, the reference to "caus[ing] physical injury to" a State official or local official is substituted for the former reference to "inflict[ing] bodily harm upon" a State official or local official for consistency with similar language used in §§ 3-705(a)(2) and 3-706(b)(2) of this subtitle.

The Criminal Law Article Review Committee notes, for the consideration of the General Assembly, that subsection (b) of this section covers only threats involving killing, kidnapping, or causing physical injury, whereas §§ 3-705(a)(2) and 3-706(b)(2) of this subtitle cover oral and written threats of "injur[ing] the person or property of anyone". The Committee brings this distinction to the attention of the General Assembly.

Defined term:
"Person" § 1-101

This section similar to federal law. — The legislative history of former Art. 27, § 561A (see now this section), enacted in 1989, reveals that it was patterned on a substantially similar provision in 18 U.S.C. § 871 (a), which prohibits threats to take the life of or inflict bodily harm upon the President of the United States. Pendergast v. State, 99 Md. App. 141, 636 A.2d 18 (1994).

Section narrowly construed. — Because former Art. 27, § 561A (see now this section) makes criminal certain speech and thereby implicates the free protections of the First Amendment and of article 40 of the Maryland

205

Illustration 3–14. MD. CODE ANN., CRIM. LAW § 3–708 (LexisNexis 2002).

LexisNexis® Total Research System

Custom ID ▾ | No Description | Switch Client | Preferences | Live Support | Sign Out | Help

Search | Research Tasks | Get a Document | Shepard's® | Alerts | Total Litigator | Transactional Advisor | Counsel Selector

FOCUS™ Terms [section(criminal law)]   Search Within Original Results (1 - 53) ▾ | Go | Advanced...

View TOC | Cite | KWIC | Full | Custom

Book Browse | Save As Alert | More Like This | More Like Selected Text
1-1 WI - Martindale-Hubbell(R) Law Digest 7.01 (Copy w/ Cite)

◆ 52 of 53 ◆   Pages: 3

Source: Legal > Reference > Martindale-Hubbell(R) > Law Digests > Martindale-Hubbell(R) Law Digest ⃞
TOC: WI - Martindale-Hubbell(R) Law Digest > 1 WISCONSIN LAW DIGEST > 7 CRIMINAL LAW > 7.01 CRIMINAL LAW:
Terms: **section(criminal law)** (Edit Search | Suggest Terms for My Search)

⌲ Select for FOCUS™ or Delivery
⃞

1-1 WI - *Martindale-Hubbell(R) Law Digest 7.01*

WI - Martindale-Hubbell(R) Law Digest

Copyright 2008, Matthew Bender & Company, Inc., a member of the LexisNexis Group.

1 WISCONSIN LAW DIGEST
7 CRIMINAL LAW

1-1 WI - Martindale-Hubbell(R) Law Digest 7.01

7.01 CRIMINAL LAW:

Criminal Code is contained in cc. 939-951. Crimes are divided into nine classes of felonies and three classes of misdemeanors. (Wis. Stat. 939.50-.51). Maximum sentence is determined by class. C. 949 provides awards for victims of crimes. C. 950 outlines rights of victims and witnesses of crime. Restitution for victim generally required for sentencing including probationary sentence. (Wis. Stat. 973.09, 973.20). Procedure in criminal matters is governed generally by cc. 967, 968, 970, 971, 972, 974. Mandatory for trial court to ascertain defendant's understanding of nature of charge and any waiver of constitutional rights at plea hearing. (Wis. Stat. 971.08; 131 Wis. 2d 246, 389 N.W.2d 12).

Indictment or Information.

◄ Outline   Page [Enter a Page]   ◄ Doc | 52 of 53 | ► | ▼ Term

Illustration 3–15. Wisconsin Law Digest: Criminal Law,
MARTINDALE-HUBBELL LAW DIGEST on Lexis (2008).

Education

5473.01 Adams, Christopher E. "Is Economic Integration the Fourth Wave in School Finance Litigation?" *Emory Law Journal* 56 (2007):1613-59.

P. 1614, fn. 5. Citations only. Cites to constitutions. Covers the forty-nine states that have constitutional provisions on education.

5473.02 "Education Finance Database." *National Conference of State Legislatures* http://www.ncsl.org/programs/educ/ed_finance/intro.htm.

Summaries. Cites to constitutions and codes. Covers earmarked lottery and other revenue; funding for bilingual, gifted, special, and talented education; local taxing methods (property and sales taxes); tax and spending limits; tax credits and exemptions (including homesteads); teacher benefits and retirement; transportation; and related topics.

5473.03 Matthew, Dayna Bowen. "Disastrous Disasters: Restoring Civil Rights Protections for Victims of the State in National Disasters." *Journal of Health & Biomedical Law* 2 (2006):213-48.

P. 244, fn. 122. Citations only. Cites to constitutions. Covers the forty states that have constitutional provisions on public education.

5473.04 Saiger, Aaron Jay. "School Choice and States' Duty to Support 'Public' Schools." *Boston College Law Review* 48 (2007):909-69.

Pp. 909-10, fn. 1. Citations only. Cites to constitutions. Covers constitutional provisions on public education.

5473.05 "State Implementation of No Child Left Behind Law." Westlaw (State Stat. Surveys Implement NCLB).

Citations and table. Cites to codes. Covers public reporting, teaching, testing, standards, and related provisions. Includes thirty-five states, Guam, and U.S. Dated Jan. 2007.

5473.06 "State Laws Relating to Pre-K." *Starting at 3* http://www.startingat3.org/state_laws/index.html.

Illustration 3–16. Cheryl Rae Nyberg, Subject Compilations of State Laws 2006–2007: An Annotated Bibliography 91 (2008).

Chapter 4

THE LEGISLATURE, PART 2: LEGISLATIVE INFORMATION

Table of Sections

Legal researchers need legislative information in many contexts. The ambiguities so common in the language of statutes lead lawyers and scholars to use legislative documents in interpreting the intended purpose of an act or the meaning of particular statutory terms. Congressional hearings and reports also provide background information on a wide array of issues, from Supreme Court nominations to oversight of administrative agency actions. Because pending legislation may affect their clients' interests, lawyers also need to be able to determine the status of bills the legislature is considering.

The use of legislative history in statutory construction is highly controversial, with strong disagreement within the Supreme Court and among commentators. Judges have traditionally used congressional materials to interpret ambiguous statutory language, but textualist critics insist that meaning must be determined from the statutory language alone. Justice Antonin Scalia is well known for his opposition to the use of legislative history, while other justices rely on legislative history sources to correct drafting errors, to provide information on specialized meanings of terms, or to identify the purpose of a statutory phrase. In the words of Justice John Paul Stevens, they "see no reason why conscientious judges should not feel free to examine all public records that may shed light on the meaning of a statute."[1]

Legislative information is one area in which there can be striking differences between federal and state research. Federal legislative history is thoroughly documented with numerous sources, while availability of state legislative history varies widely from state to state. On both the federal and state level, however, this is an area in which the Internet has made a significant contribution to the dissemination of information. Government websites facilitate learning about the status of pending legislation and obtaining documents relating to recently passed acts. Research into the background of older acts of Congress, however, still requires access to printed sources, and resources on older state laws, if they exist at all, may be found only on tape recordings or in archives at the state capitol.

§ 4.1 The Federal Legislative Process

Consideration of legislative history begins with the legislative process itself—how a bill wends its way through Congress or a state legislature. The documents of legislative history must be understood in the context of the parliamentary practices which produce them. The legislative processes of the states vary considerably in their patterns and forms. The federal process is often long and complicated, beginning formally with the introduction of a bill and ending with passage by both houses of Congress of either an act or a joint resolution, and its approval by the President (or repassage over a presidential veto).[2]

Overviews of the federal legislative process can be found in two brief congressional guides prepared by the House and Senate parliamentarians and available from the Library of Congress's THOMAS

---

1. *Bank One Chicago, N.A. v. Midwest Bank & Trust Co.*, 516 U.S. 264, 278 (1996) (Stevens, J., concurring). The leading and representative statements of the two positions are Stephen Breyer, *On the Uses of Legislative History in Interpreting Statutes*, 65 S. Cal. L. Rev. 845 (1992), and Antonin Scalia, A Matter of Interpretation: Federal Courts and the Law (1997). Recent articles summarizing the debate and providing references to earlier works include Paul E.

McGreal, *A Constitutional Defense of Legislative History*, 13 Wm. & Mary Bill Rts. J. 1267 (2005); Lawrence M. Solan, *Private Language, Public Laws: The Central Role of Legislative Intent in Statutory Interpretation*, 93 Geo. L.J. 427 (2005); and Charles Tiefer, *The Reconceptualization of Legislative History in the Supreme Court*, 2000 Wis. L. Rev. 205.

2. U.S. Const., Art. I, § 7, cl. 2.

system <thomas.loc.gov>, under the heading "The Legislative Process."[3]

More extensive guides to congressional lawmaking procedures are also available. Charles Tiefer, *Congressional Practice and Procedure: A Reference, Research, and Legislative Guide* (1989) is a comprehensive treatise on congressional procedure, with extended explanations of committee organization and procedure, rules governing floor debates and consideration of bills, conference committee procedure, and other matters such as the budget and appropriations processes. Walter J. Oleszek, *Congressional Procedures and the Policy Process* (7th ed. 2007) is a more concise explanation of the lawmaking process, with a focus on the way floor consideration is scheduled and managed in each house. It includes several useful tables and a handy glossary of congressional terms. More in-depth coverage of legislative language is provided by Walter Kravitz, *Congressional Quarterly's American Congressional Dictionary* (3d ed. 2001), which defines hundreds of terms and phrases such as "continuing resolution" and "engrossed bill." Michael L. Koempel & Judy Schneider, *Congressional Deskbook* (biennial) is a regularly updated practical guide to congressional politics and procedures filled with illustrations, interesting facts, and research tips.

Background reference works for understanding Congress and its work in their historical and political contexts include Congressional Quarterly's *Guide to Congress* (6th ed. 2008). This two-volume set has a wide range of political, historical, and statistical information; Part III, Congressional Procedures, is particularly useful in understanding committee and floor action. One of the most thorough reference works is *Encyclopedia of the United States Congress* (Donald C. Bacon et al. eds., 1995), which provides a broad historical and political science perspective on the institution.

Because they work closely with Congress and with administrative agencies, law firms in Washington, D.C. are particularly well known for their expertise in legislative history research. Several of the larger firms and agencies have librarians who specialize in this particular field. The Law Librarians' Society of Washington, D.C. shares this expertise in its Internet-based *LLSDC's Legislative Source Book* <www.llsdc.org/sourcebook/>, which is regularly updated and includes insightful guides, historical information, and valuable lists and tables of printed and Internet resources.

---

3. CHARLES W. JOHNSON, HOW OUR LAWS ARE MADE, H.R. DOC. NO. 108–93 (2003), <thomas.loc.gov/home/lawsmade.toc.html>; ROBERT B. DOVE, ENACTMENT OF A LAW (1997), <thomas.loc.gov/home/enactment/enactlawtoc.html>. The Center on Congress at Indiana University provides a similar overview, *The Legislative Process*, with an emphasis on recent trends such as bills that bypass committee consideration and the increasing use of omnibus legislation <congress.indiana.edu/backgrounders/the_legislative_process.php>.

Of the many types of documents issued by Congress, a few are particularly important for legislative history research. *Bills* are the major source for the texts of pending or unenacted legislation. *Committee reports* analyze and describe bills and are usually considered the most authoritative sources of congressional intent. *Floor debates* may contain a sponsor's interpretation of a bill or the only explanation of last-minute amendments. *Hearings* can provide useful background on the purpose of an act.

This section introduces these various documents, with a brief explanation of how they are published and their availability in electronic sources. Several major resources will be mentioned again and again. Two of these are free government websites: the Library of Congress website for legislative information, THOMAS <thomas. loc.gov>, and the Government Printing Office's GPO Access <www.gpoaccess.gov/legislative.html>. Others are commercial sites, including Westlaw and Lexis. One of the most important providers of congressional documentation is a company called Congressional Information Service, Inc. (CIS), now a subsidiary of LexisNexis. CIS databases are available as part of regular Lexis subscriptions, but a separate system called LexisNexis Congressional <web.lexis-nexis.com/congcomp/> provides more extensive search templates focusing specifically on legislative information.

(a) Preliminary and Informal Consideration

Documents relating to particular enactments may exist even before a proposal is introduced as a bill. Hearings on a problem of legislative concern may be held prior to the introduction of specific bills to remedy that condition, even in an earlier session of Congress. Sometimes these hearings continue through several sessions. Research into the legislative history of a particular law limited only to the session of its enactment may overlook relevant and important debates, hearings or reports.

Many bills introduced in Congress stem from presidential recommendations and may be accompanied by presidential messages or executive agency memoranda describing the purpose of the proposed legislation. The President's annual State of the Union message proposes various laws in general terms, and other presidential messages describe individual measures in greater detail and urge their introduction and passage.[4] Official messages to Congress are available in several sources, including the *Congressional Rec-*

---

4. The President "shall from time to time give to the Congress Information of the State of the Union, and recommend to their Consideration such Measures as he shall judge necessary and expedient." U.S. CONST. art. II, § 3. For a discussion of the State of the Union and Recommendation Clauses, see Vasan Kesavan & J. Gregory Sidak, *The Legislator-in-Chief*, 44 WM. & MARY L. REV. 1 (2002).

ord, the *Daily* or *Weekly Compilation of Presidential Documents,* the *House* and *Senate Journals,* and separately as House and Senate Documents. Other presidential recommendations are published in a less formal manner, as press releases or fact sheets available on the White House website <www.whitehouse.gov>. Illustration 4–1 on page 148 shows President Bush's support for H.R. 1350, the bill which would eventually become the Individuals with Disabilities Education Improvement Act of 2004 (IDEIA), Pub. L. No. 108–446, 118 Stat. 2647.

Newspapers and services that cover Congress and politics are often good sources on topics of possible congressional action, providing information that may not be available from official documentation. Even if no bill has been introduced or a bill appears to be stalled in committee, news stories and documents such as letters between members of Congress, press releases, and government agency reports can provide leads to what is happening behind the scenes. Several newspapers focus on developments in the federal government. Most, such as *CQ Weekly* <www.cq.com>, *National Journal* <nationaljournal.com>, and *Roll Call* <www.rollcall. com> are available online only to subscribers. Others, such as *The Hill* <www.thehill.com>, are available on the Internet without charge. *National Journal* and its *CongressDaily* newsletter are both available through Westlaw and Lexis. Subscription websites such as GalleryWatch <www.gallerywatch.com>, designed for lobbyists and others needing access to very current congressional information, provide news as well as copies of both formal and informal documentation.

(b) Bills

An act of Congress begins its life as a bill. Researchers find texts of bills helpful in interpreting enacted laws and in understanding pending or failed legislation. The bill may be amended at any stage of its legislative progress, in committee or on the floor, and some bills are amended many times. Comparing the different versions of a bill may lead to useful conclusions about the scope or meaning of the provisions that were ultimately enacted.

Congressional bills are individually numbered in separate series for each chamber and retain their numbers through both of the annual sessions of each Congress. Each bill is assigned its number when it is introduced and referred to a committee of the chamber in which it was presented. Pending bills lapse at the end of the two-year term of Congress, and a new bill on the topic must be introduced the following term if it is to be considered.

A citation to a bill includes the number of the Congress and the year in which the particular version was published, such as S. 1248,

108th Cong. (2004) or H.R. 1350, 108th Cong. (2003). Illustration 4–2 on page   shows the first page of this House bill as introduced in March 2003.

Often bills with similar or identical language, known as *companion bills*, are introduced in both the House and Senate. If each chamber passes its own bill, however, there is no single *enrolled bill* that has passed both houses and can be presented to the President. Congress frequently employs a procedure known as an *amendment in the nature of a substitute*, which deletes everything after the enacting clause (i.e., "Be it enacted by the Senate and House of Representatives of the United States of America in Congress assembled")[5] and inserts new text in its place. Sometimes this is done simply because it is more convenient to replace an entire bill than to make specific changes, but it also permits the House and Senate to pass the same bill so that it can go to the President and become law. If the House passes H.R. 1350 while the Senate passes S. 1248, these are different bills even if their language is identical. Both must pass the same bill number. If the Senate amends H.R. 1350 by substituting its language for the House language, the bill can then go back to the House for it to consider the Senate amendments. Both houses are then working with the same document, and if both pass the bill it can be sent to the President.

The significance of this for researchers is that the number of the bill that becomes law may be different from the number of the version that was the subject of congressional hearings, committee reports, or perhaps even floor debates. The key language in an enacted law may have come from a bill with a different number and a different history. Sometimes you may need to compare the language in several similar bills. Tracing the development of particular statutory language can be like traveling up a river; you may need to determine which tributary to follow to get to a specific source.

Current and recent bills are available online from a number of sources. THOMAS <thomas.loc.gov> has the text of bills since the 101st Congress (1989–90). Starting with the 103rd Congress (1993–94), the THOMAS bill display also links to a PDF version available from GPO Access <www.gpoaccess.gov/bills/>. In both THOMAS and GPO Access, you can search for bills from a specific Congress or across the entire available time period. THOMAS also permits limiting a search to bills that have had floor action or those that have been passed and sent to the President.

5. This is the prescribed form for   § 101 (2006).
all congressional bills under 1 U.S.C.

Subscription databases, including Westlaw and Lexis, also provide extensive coverage of congressional bills. Lexis has bills back to the 101st Congress (1989–90), and Westlaw coverage begins in the 104th (1995–96). In both instances, bills from the current Congress are in a separate file than those from earlier terms. For researchers in general academic libraries, LexisNexis Congressional provides access to the text of bills from 1989 to date, with options to search the entire range or a specific Congress.

Older bills preceding these dates of online coverage may be harder to locate. Many libraries have microfiche collections of older bills, from the Government Printing Office (96th–106th Congress, 1979–2000) and LexisNexis Congressional (73rd–107th Congresses, 1933–2002). Early bills are available on the Library of Congress's American Memory site <memory.loc.gov/ammem/amlaw/lwhbsb. html> (House bills from the 6th to 42nd Congresses, 1799–1873, and Senate bills from the 16th to 42nd Congresses, 1819–73). Finding a bill text from a period not covered by these resources may require contacting the Law Library of Congress <www.loc.gov/ law/> or the National Archives' Center for Legislative Archives <www.archives.gov/legislative/>. The Center for Research Libraries in Chicago has bills on microfilm from 1789 to 1933 <www.crl. edu/content.asp?l1=5&l2=22&l3=39&top=19>.

(c) Hearings

Hearings are held by standing and special committees of the House and Senate to investigate various issues of concern, and also to elicit views on proposed legislation from interested persons or groups, executive branch personnel, or other legislators. Hearings may be designed to examine a controversial situation, to determine the need for new legislation, or to present information helpful to Congress's consideration of a pending bill. Hearings are not required for every bill, and legislation is frequently enacted without hearings in one or both houses.

A hearing, as published, consists of prepared statements from government officials, scholars, interest group representatives, and other witnesses; the transcript of questions by the legislators and answers by witnesses; exhibits submitted by interested individuals or organizations; and sometimes a copy of the bill under consideration. Hearings are generally identified by the title that appears on the cover, the bill number, the name of the subcommittee and committee, the term of Congress, and the year. Illustration 4–3 on page 150, for example, shows the first page of *Special Education: Is IDEA Working as Congress Intended?: Hearing before the H. Comm. on Gov't Reform*, 107th Cong. (2001). This hearing was held three years before IDEIA was passed in 2004 during the 108th Congress.

Hearings provide useful background information, but they are not generally considered persuasive sources of legislative history on the meaning of an enacted bill. Their importance as evidence of statutory purpose is limited because they focus more on the views of interest groups than on those of the lawmakers themselves. Testimony by agency officials who will be responsible for implementing legislation may, however, be helpful in determining the purpose and scope of a proposed statute.

Unlike other congressional materials such as bills and committee reports, published hearings are not generally numbered in one series for each house of Congress. Not every hearing is published, and they are also not as widely or systematically available on the Internet. Most committee websites provide access to material from recent hearings. Some only provide the texts of prepared statements from legislators and witnesses, but others have the transcripts of the committee members' questions and witnesses' answers. The Senate <www.senate.gov> and House <www.house.gov> sites provide links to committee pages, and *LLSDC's Legislative Source Book* has an annotated guide of "Quick Links to House and Senate Committee Hearings and Other Publications" <www.llsdc.org/quick-links/>, which indicates the material available from each committee. Prepared testimony by government officials may also be available on their agencies' websites.

THOMAS doesn't include hearings, but GPO Access has selected coverage beginning in 1995 <www.gpoaccess.gov/chearings/>. You can perform full-text keyword searches in Senate and/or House hearings from one or more Congresses, or browse a list of hearings from each Congress.

The major retrospective online source for hearings is the LexisNexis Congressional Hearings Digital Collection, with approximately 120,000 hearings back to 1824. This collection, a component of the LexisNexis Congressional system, contains documents previously available on microfiche from LexisNexis (formerly CIS) and indexed in several of its publications: *CIS/Index* (1970–date, covering contemporary hearings); *CIS US Congressional Committee Hearings Index* (1981–85, covering published hearings 1833–1969); *CIS Index to Unpublished US Senate Committee Hearings* (1986–2001, covering 1823–1980), and *CIS Index to Unpublished US House of Representatives Committee Hearings* (1988–2003, covering 1833–1972).[6] These sources provide abstracts of testimony, with indexing by subject, witness name, bill number, and hearing title. These various CIS indexes are available online through LexisNexis

---

6. The Library of the United States Senate publishes another series of indexes to the hearings of both houses, CUMULATIVE INDEX OF CONGRESSIONAL COMMITTEE HEARINGS (1935–84, covering the 41st–96th Congresses, 1869–1980), but these provide less detail and fewer points of access than the CIS indexes.

Congressional and Lexis (even in many libraries that do not own the Hearings Digital Collection), "Historical Indexes," with advantages such as the ability to combine keyword terms, to search across a specified range of years, and to search at one time in published and unpublished hearings as well as in other sources such as committee reports.

In libraries with hearings in print, they are usually organized by committee under the Superintendent of Documents classification system. The classification for the hearing shown in Illustration 4–3, for example, is Y 4.G 74/7:ED 8/14. The "G 74/7" indicates that this is a hearing of the House Committee on Government Reform. In many libraries hearings are available on microfiche, filed under a CIS number that includes the year in which the hearing was indexed (not necessarily the year it was held); a designation indicating the house, committee, and type of document; and a number for the hearing. The CIS number for the hearing in Illustration 4–3 in the CIS system is 2002–H401–26.[7]

Lexis has transcripts of hearings prepared by two commercial services, CQ Transcriptions and Federal News Service. Their coverage overlaps, but neither is comprehensive. These are in separate files within the "Legislation and Politics/U.S. Congress/Committee Hearing Transcripts" folder, but Lexis's "Combine Sources" feature allows a search to be run in both files at once.

Other services such as CQ.com and GalleryWatch.com also provide hearing transcripts. Even if a hearing has not been transcribed, an audio or video recording may be available from C–SPAN <www.c-span.org>.

Westlaw provides prepared statements rather than the full transcripts of hearings, also in two separate files: USTESTIMONY, with selective coverage beginning in 1993 and full coverage from 1996, and CONGTMY, with coverage beginning in late 2004. Each has some statements not found in the other. Prepared witness statements provide an incomplete view of what happens in hearings, but they are usually available long before the full hearing transcript is published.

(d) Committee Reports

The most important documents of legislative history are generally considered to be the reports of the committees of each house, and those of conference committees held jointly by the two houses.

---

7. In "2002–H401–26," "2002" indicates the year that the document was indexed by CIS (even though the hearing was actually held in 2001); "H40" shows the committee from which the document was issued, the House (H) Committee on Government Reform (40); "1" indicates the type of document (hearing); and "26" is part of a sequential arrangement of the committee's hearings for the year.

The House and Senate committees generally issue a report on each bill that is sent to the whole house for consideration, or "reported out of committee." These reports reflect the committee's proposal after a bill has been studied, hearings held, and amendments made.[8] They usually contain the revised text of the bill, an analysis of its content and purpose, and the committee's rationale for its recommendations. One of the most informative portions of a committee report is the section-by-section analysis of the bill, explaining the purpose and meaning of each provision. Sometimes the report also includes minority views, if there was disagreement among the committee members.

If different versions of a proposed enactment have been passed by each house, a conference committee is convened, including members from each house. The conference committee reconciles the differences and produces an agreed compromise for submission to both houses for final passage, as explained in its report. Conference committee reports are considered a very persuasive source for interpretation.[9]

Committee reports and conference committee reports are generally given more weight than other legislative history documents because they are produced by those members of Congress who have worked most closely with the proposed legislation. In Justice John M. Harlan's words, they are the "considered and collective understanding of those Congressmen involved in drafting and studying proposed legislation."[10]

The committee reports of each house are published as pamphlets in separate numerical series for each session of Congress,

---

8. Committee reports may also be issued on investigations and issues not related to the consideration of a specific bill. Reports are issued, for example, on nominations to the executive and judicial branches.

9. The politics and procedures of the conference process are discussed in LAWRENCE D. LONGLEY & WALTER J. OLESZEK, BICAMERAL POLITICS: CONFERENCE COMMITTEES IN CONGRESS (1989). For an explanation of the content and use of conference committee reports, see George A. Costello, *Average Voting Members and Other 'Benign Fictions': The Relative Reliability of Committee Reports, Floor Debates, and Other Sources of Legislative History*, 1990 DUKE L.J. 39, 47–50. For historical information on committee reports more generally, see Thomas F. Broden, *Congressional Committee Reports: Their Role and History*, 33 NOTRE DAME LAW. 209, 216–238 (1958).

10. *Zuber v. Allen*, 396 U.S. 168, 186 (1969). Justice Antonin Scalia has repeatedly challenged the position that committee reports are the most reliable sources of legislative history, in part because they are prepared by staff members rather than members of Congress themselves. See, e.g., *Blanchard v. Bergeron*, 489 U.S. 87, 99 (1989) (Scalia, J., concurring) ("What a heady feeling it must be for a young staffer, to know that his or her citation of obscure district court cases can transform them into the law of the land. . . ."). Others have argued that separation of powers principles demand that courts respect the way Congress chooses to organize its work and communicate its findings. E.g., Patricia M. Wald, *The Sizzling Sleeper: The Use of Legislative History in Construing Statutes in the 1988–89 Term of the United States Supreme Court*, 39 AM. U. L. REV. 277, 306–07 (1990).

with conference committee reports included in the series of House reports. Their citations include the numbers of the Congress and the year. Illustration 4–4 on page 151 shows the first page of S. Rep. No. 108–185 (2003), reporting the Senate Committee on Health, Education, Labor, and Pensions' views on S. 1248, the Senate version of what became the Individuals with Disabilities Education Improvement Act of 2004. The contents include at page 64 a section-by-section analysis of the bill.

Committee reports are published by the Government Printing Office and are available online through GPO Access <www.gpoaccess.gov/serialset/creports/> and THOMAS, going back to the 104th Congress (1995–96). The full text of all committee reports since 1990 are found on both Westlaw and Lexis; Westlaw's LH database also has selected committee reports from 1948 to 1990. *CIS/Index* and LexisNexis Congressional provide full coverage of committee reports, with the full text of the reports available on microfiche from CIS and (since 1990) online through LexisNexis Congressional. One or more committee reports on major enactments are reprinted in *U.S. Code Congressional and Administrative News,* and a few (usually just conference committee reports) appear also in the *Congressional Record.*

Committee reports are also published as part of a bound series of volumes known as the *Serial Set.* The Serial Set includes such other publications as House and Senate documents, annual reports, and manuals of procedural rules and precedents.[11] Bound Serial Set volumes are not widely distributed after the 104th Congress (1995–96), but many libraries now bind their own sets of individual reports.

The Serial Set began with the 15th Congress in 1817, when Congress enacted legislation specifying standards for publishing and collecting its reports and documents.[12] Earlier publications were collected and published under congressional authority in a set known as the *American State Papers* (1832–61).[13]

---

11. For more information on the history and contents of the Serial Set, see Richard J. McKinney, *An Overview of the U.S. Congressional Serial Set* <www.llsdc.org/sch-v/#Overview>.

12. Resolution of Mar. 3, 1817, no. 3, 3 Stat. 400.

13. The most comprehensive bibliography of early congressional documents was published more than a century ago. A. W. Greely, Public Documents of the First Fourteen Congresses, 1789–1817: Papers Relating to Early Congressional Documents, S. Doc. No. 56–428 (1900). Greely noted that the publica-

tions of the early Congresses "were issued as the occasion required in all sorts of shapes and sizes, with separate or no pagination and without any serial numbering," and that "there exists neither a complete collection nor detailed list of the documents of the First to the Fourteenth Congresses, inclusive, 1789 to 1817." Id. at 5. General Greely was Chief Signal Officer of the U.S. Army, and devoted his leisure hours for five years to this project. Id. at 3.

As with other materials, CIS and LexisNexis Congressional provide comprehensive retrospective coverage of the Serial Set. *CIS U.S. Serial Set Index* (1975–97) covers the period from 1789 to 1969 (including the *American State Papers*). The set is divided into twelve chronological parts, providing access by subjects, keywords, and proper names, while Part XIII is a four-volume index by bill number.

This index is also available online through Lexis and LexisNexis Congressional, with links to the documents themselves through the LexisNexis U.S. Serial Set Digital Collection (available as part of LexisNexis Congressional). Its coverage spans the entire period from 1789 to date, with full text searching as well as access by subject or numerical designation (including report number, bill number or public law number).

LexisNexis is not the only source for retrospective online coverage of the Serial Set and American State Papers. Readex, a division of NewsBank, has produced U.S. Congressional Serial Set (1817–1980) with American State Papers (1789–1838), with full text searching as well as searches by bill number, Congress, committee, and other criteria.[14]

Other committee materials can be even more helpful than reports in interpreting statutory language. The process by which committees or subcommittees examine proposed legislation in detail and reach consensus is through *markup sessions*, but the proceedings of these sessions are only rarely published.[15] Markup transcripts and related documents are occasionally available through committee websites, but in most instances the transcripts can only be examined in the committee's offices. Newspapers and wire services reporting on Capitol Hill matters frequently publish stories on markup sessions, and the subscription site GalleryWatch.com often has PDF copies of markup amendments and other unpublished documents from committee consideration.[16]

---

14. For comparative reviews of the LexisNexis and Readex versions of the Serial Set, see Ann E. Miller, *Digital U.S. Congressional Serial Set Collections—Reviews of the Readex and Lexis-Nexis Products*, DttP: DOCUMENTS TO THE PEOPLE, Summer 2005, at 37, and Jian Anna Xiong, *Readex U.S. Congressional Serial Set, Digital Edition and Lexis-Nexis U.S. Serial Set Collection*, CHARLESTON ADVISOR, Apr. 2004, at 5. The Library of Congress's "A Century of Lawmaking for a New Nation" site <memory.loc.gov/ammem/amlaw/lwss. html> includes the *American State Pa-*

pers and very selective coverage of the Serial Set from 1833 to 1917. This collection is free, but it includes very few reports for legislative history research purposes.

15. See Patricia M. Wald, *Some Observations on the Use of Legislative History in the 1981 Supreme Court Term*, 68 IOWA L. REV. 195, 200–203 (1983).

16. For more on markup sessions, see Paul Jenks, *CongressLine: The Committee Markup*, LLRX.com (Dec. 23, 2007)   <www.llrx.com/congress/ committeemarkup.htm>.

(e) Floor Debates

Floor debate in Congress on a pending bill can occur at almost any stage of its progress, but typically it takes place after the bill has been reported out by committee. During consideration of the bill, amendments may be proposed, discussed, and accepted or defeated. Arguments for and against passage are made, and explanations of unclear or controversial provisions are offered.

Debates in the House and Senate are generally not as influential as committee reports as sources of statutory purpose. While reports represent the considered opinion of those legislators who have studied the bill most closely, floor statements are often political hyperbole and may even represent the calculated use of prepared colloquies designed to manufacture evidence of legislative intent. Nonetheless, floor debates can be of value. The most influential statements are those from a bill's sponsor or its floor managers (the committee members responsible for steering the bill through consideration).[17] These statements may even explain aspects of a bill not discussed in a committee report or correct errors in a report.

In a few instances, floor debates are the best available legislative history source. If a bill is amended on the floor with language that was not considered in committee and thus was not discussed in a committee report, the record of floor debate may be the only explanation available of the intended purpose of the amendment.[18]

---

17. "Within the category of floor debate, some Members are more equal than others. Statements by sponsors and floor managers carry the most weight, statements by Members not associated with either formulation or committee consideration of the bill warrant little weight, and statements by bill opponents usually are not taken at face value." Costello, supra note 9, at 51. This paradigm is not always followed. Former representative (and judge) Abner Mikva has described railing in hyperbolic terms against the excesses of Racketeer Influenced Corrupt Organizations (RICO) provisions, only to find his remarks cited later cited as evidence of the broad scope of RICO. Abner J. Mikva, *Reading and Writing Statutes*, 28 S. Tex. L. Rev. 181, 185 (1986).

18. The authoritative explanation of the Bankruptcy Reform Act of 1994, Pub. L. No. 103–394, 108 Stat. 4106, is considered to be a section-by-section review inserted in the *Congressional Record*, 140 Cong. Rec. 27,691 (1994). The act "had an unusual history. It was

passed by the Senate first, then the House waited until close to congressional recess to act on the bill. Since there was not enough time to pass a different bill and work out the differences with the Senate in conference, Senators and staffers interested in passage of the bill met with House members to work out differences before the bill passed the House. This was done. Thus, there is no conference report. This section-by-section review of the legislation was written after the compromise bill was agreed upon." Janet A. Flaccus, *A Potpourri of Bankruptcy Changes: 1994 Bankruptcy Amendments*, 47 Ark. L. Rev. 817, 821 n. 30 (1994). This section-by-section review has been cited in dozens of court decisions.

The most famous example of a significant change made on the floor with no supporting legislative history is the inclusion of sex discrimination in Title VII of the Civil Rights Act of 1964, Pub. L. No. 88–352, tit. VII, § 703, 78 Stat. 241, 255 (current version at 42 U.S.C. § 2000e-2 (2000)). The traditional story

The essential source for the text of floor debates is the *Congressional Record,* which is published daily while either house is in session. The *Congressional Record* provides a more or less verbatim transcript of the legislative debates and proceedings, but legislators have the opportunity to revise their remarks and to insert material that was not actually spoken. Material that was not spoken is generally indicated in the Senate proceedings by the use of bullets, and in the House proceedings by a sans serif typeface.[19] Each daily issue has separately paginated sections for Senate and House proceedings, with page number prefixed with either S or H. In addition, the *Record* includes an Extensions of Remarks section containing additional statements from members of the House of Representatives, tributes to constituents, reprints of newspaper articles, and whatever other material House members wish to have printed.

The *Congressional Record* never contains hearings and only rarely includes committee reports—although it does include the text of conference committee reports. Bills are sometimes read into the *Record,* particularly if they have been amended on the floor or in conference committee. The *Congressional Record*'s primary role, however, is as a report of debates and actions taken. An excerpt from the *Record,* showing Senate consideration of S. 1248, is shown in Illustration 4–5 on page 152. The illustrated page shows the introduction and passage of a technical amendment to the bill.

Each issue of the *Congressional Record* contains a Daily Digest, which summarizes the day's proceedings, lists actions taken and

is that "sex" was added at the last minute as a strategy to defeat the bill, although this version of events has been disputed. See Robert C. Bird, *More than a Congressional Joke: A Fresh Look at the Legislative History of Sex Discrimination of the 1964 Civil Rights Act,* 3 WM. & MARY J. WOMEN & L. 137 (1997). What is undisputed is that "[v]irtually no legislative history provides guidance to courts interpreting the prohibition of sex discrimination." *Ellison v. Brady,* 924 F.2d 872, 875 (9th Cir. 1991).

19. 44 U.S.C.§ 901 (2000) provides that the Record "shall be substantially a verbatim report of proceedings." This language is unchanged since it was first enacted in 1895. Act of Jan. 12, 1895, c. 23, § 13, 28 Stat. 601, 603. On the history and practice of allowing legislators to revise their remarks and the use of symbols and typefaces, see MILDRED L. AMER, THE *CONGRESSIONAL RECORD*: CONTENT, HISTORY AND ISSUES 14–21 (1993) (CRS Report 93–60 GOV) <www.llsdc.org/sourcebook/docs/CRS-93-60.pdf>; Howard N. Mantel, *The Congressional Record: Fact or Fiction of the Legislative Process,* 12 W. POL. Q. 981 (1959), and Michelle M. Springer, *The* Congressional Record: "*Substantially a Verbatim Report?*", 13 GOV'T PUBLICATIONS REV. 371 (1986).

These typeface conventions are not always honored, particularly in the Senate, and some speeches that never occurred appear in the *Record* as if they had. In 2006, the Supreme Court rejected reliance on a colloquy between two senators that was inserted into the *Congressional Record* after the debate. *Hamdan v. Rumsfeld,* 548 U.S. 557, 580 n.10 (2006). For background on this colloquy, see Emily Bazelon, *Invisible Men,* SLATE, Mar. 27, 2006 <www.slate.com/id/2138750/>; Emily Bazelon, *Not Live from Capitol Hill,* SLATE, June 29, 2006 <www.slate.com/id/2144780/>.

enactments signed by the President that day, and provides useful committee information. Page references are included, making the Daily Digest a good starting place if only the date of congressional action is known. The Daily Digests are cumulated and indexed in one volume of the bound edition. Illustration 4–6 on page 153 shows the first page of the Daily Digest for May 13, 2004, showing under "IDEA Reauthorization" that the Senate passed H.R. 1350 after substituting the language from its own version, S. 1248.

An index to the proceedings, by subjects, names of legislators, and titles of legislation, is included in the *Record* every two weeks. The printed indexes do not cumulate during a session, but an online version on GPO Access <www.gpoaccess.gov/cri/> does cumulate. The indexes include a useful History of Bills and Resolutions listing references to bills that have been acted on during the two-week period. This too is available online <www.gpoaccess.gov/hob/> with cumulated information for the entire session.

The daily edition of the *Congressional Record* can be searched electronically through several online sources. Coverage begins in 1989 on THOMAS, and in 1994 on GPO Access <www.gpoaccess.gov/crecord/> (which also has the index back to 1983 and History of Bills and Resolutions tables with page references beginning in 1993). THOMAS's version has links from the index and Daily Digest to *Record* pages and to bill texts, while GPO Access offers the *Record* in PDF format replicating the printed version. Westlaw and Lexis coverage extends back to 1985. Each offers a file for searching the entire run of *Record* holdings, but Lexis also has separate files for each Congress and for each section of the *Record*. You can search in the Daily Digest file (or add *pr(digest)* to a Westlaw search) to focus in on a particular issue.

A bound permanent edition of the *Congressional Record,* in recent years comprising over twenty-five volumes, is published after the end of each session. There is generally a five or six year lag between a session and its coverage in bound volumes, but once the permanent edition is published it becomes the standard source to be cited for congressional debates.[20] The daily and permanent editions have the same volume numbers, but their page numbers are completely different. The separate S and H sections in the daily edition are merged in the permanent edition into one numerical sequence. The bound edition also includes a comprehensive index to the session, including a cumulative History of Bills and Resolutions table, and, since the 80th Congress (1947–48), a bound version of

---

20. The Bluebook: A Uniform System of Citation R. 13.5, at 118 (18th ed. 2005); ALWD Citation Manual: A Profes- sional System of Citation R. 15.12, at 135 (3d ed. 2006).

the Daily Digest. These versions of the indexes and Daily Digest provide page numbers for the permanent edition.

Neither Westlaw nor Lexis has the permanent edition of the *Congressional Record*, but it is available electronically from three other sources. GPO Access is adding the permanent edition to its database <www.gpoaccess.gov/crecordbound/>, but thus far only three volumes are available (volume 145–147, 1999–2001). Two commercial databases, HeinOnline and the LexisNexis Congressional Record Permanent Digital Collection, have retrospective coverage back to the first volume in 1873. Both systems are in the process of providing date-matching tools to convert a daily edition citation to a permanent edition citation, easing what has in the past been an onerous process. To find the permanent edition citation without these databases, you will usually need to start over in the index or the Daily Digest looking for references to the topic or speaker, or to skim through the specific day's section looking for a specific passage.

The *Congressional Record* has been published by the government since the 43rd Congress (1873–74), and is the successor to three earlier series reporting debates of Congress.[21] The earliest sessions of Congress were not reported very thoroughly; the Senate even met behind closed doors until 1794. Decades later, newspaper accounts and other early sources covering the 1st Congress through the 18th Congress, 1st Session (1789–1824) were compiled and published as the *Annals of Congress* (also known as *The Debates and Proceedings in the Congress of the United States*) (1834–56).[22]

The period from 1824 to 1873 is covered by two overlapping private publications, the *Register of Debates* (1824–37) (18th Congress, 2d Session to 25th Congress, 1st Session) and the *Congressional Globe* (1833–73) (23rd to 42nd Congress). The *Register of Debates* and the early *Congressional Globe* volumes were summaries of statements rather than transcripts, but verbatim reporting became possible with improved shorthand techniques and by mid-century the *Globe*'s debates had taken on a form quite similar to the modern *Congressional Record*.

All of these earlier publications, as well as the *Congressional Record* for 1873–77, are available free online through the Library of

---

21. The standard source on the early sources is Elizabeth G. McPherson, *Reporting the Debates of Congress*, 28 Q.J. SPEECH 141 (1942), an article based on her 305–page 1940 doctoral dissertation, THE HISTORY OF REPORTING THE DEBATES AND PROCEEDINGS OF CONGRESS. An excellent modern summary is provided by Richard J. McKinney, *An Overview of the Congressional Record and Its Prede-*cessor Publications <www.llsdc.org/cong-record/>.

22. Two volumes were published in 1834, pursuant to the Act of Mar. 2, 1831, ch. 65, 4 Stat. 471, but then nothing more appeared until congressional authorization of further funding fifteen years later. Res. of Mar. 3, 1849, no. 16, 9 Stat. 419.

Congress "A Century of Lawmaking for a New Nation" site <memory.loc.gov/ammem/amlaw/lawhome.html>. The full text is not searchable, but indexes for each volume can be searched and the debates themselves browsed in image files. The *Record's* predecessors are also included, and searchable, in the HeinOnline and LexisNexis digital *Congressional Record* collections.

House and *Senate Journals* are also published, but unlike the *Congressional Record*, they do not include the verbatim debates. The journals merely record the proceedings, indicate whether there was debate, and report the resulting action and votes taken. The *House Journal* is more voluminous and includes the texts of bills and amendments considered; both journals also include "History of Bills and Resolutions" tables.[23]

(f) Presidential Approval or Veto

After a bill is passed by both houses of Congress, it goes to the President for approval. If the President approves a bill, it becomes law and generally goes into effect on the day of enactment, unless some other effective date is specified.[24] If the President vetoes a bill, to become law it must be repassed by both houses by a two-thirds majority. The messages or statements issued when the President signs or vetoes particular enactments can shed light on legislative history. Like other Presidential messages to Congress, these documents appear in several places, including the *Congressional Record* and the *Daily* or *Weekly Compilation of Presidential Documents*.

While most presidential signing statements just make general statements about a statute's purposes, presidents sometimes use signing statements to convey interpretations of ambiguous provisions. These statements have been included in *USCCAN's* legislative history section beginning in 1986, although their importance in interpreting statutory language has been subject to dispute. The controversy heated up during the George W. Bush administration, following reports that Bush's signing statements had "quietly claimed the authority to disobey more than 750 laws enacted since he took office, asserting that he has the power to set aside any statute passed by Congress when it conflicts with his interpretation of the Constitution."[25] Congress held hearings on the topic, and

---

23. The journals are the only publications required by Art. I, § 5 of the Constitution: "Each House shall keep a Journal of its Proceedings, and from time to time publish the same, excepting such Parts as may in their Judgment require Secrecy; and the Yeas and Nays of the Members of either House on any question shall, at the Desire of one fifth of those Present, be entered on the Journal."

24. *Gozlon-Peretz v. United States,* 498 U.S. 395, 404 (1991).

25. Charlie Savage, *Bush Challenges Hundreds of Laws*, BOSTON GLOBE, Apr. 30, 2006, at A1.

legislation was introduced in an effort to bar judicial use of signing statements.[26]

Illustration 4–7 on page ___ shows President Bush's statement on signing the Individuals with Disabilities Education Improvement Act of 2004, as it appeared in the *Weekly Compilation of Presidential Documents*. In the statement he explains how the executive branch will interpret specific provisions in the act.

§ 4.2　Other Congressional Publications

Congress also produces a variety of other publications that are less frequently consulted in legislative history research. These can be important sources of information, however, on statutes, legislative policies, and the workings of the federal government.

House and Senate Documents. Congress publishes many documents as required by law or by special request. These House and Senate Documents contain material such as the *Budget of the United States Government*, special studies and reports, reprints of presidential messages, executive agency reports and memoranda, reports of nongovernmental organizations, and a variety of papers ordered to be printed by either house of Congress. The value of House and Senate Documents for legislative history is usually negligible, but occasionally a document will have some relevance to a pending bill.

Documents are issued in numbered series for each Congress, similar to the way committee reports are published. They are published, along with committee reports, in the Serial Set. Documents are available online back to the 104th Congress (1995–96) through GPO Access <www.gpoaccess.gov/serialset/cdocuments/> and Lexis, and before 1970 through the LexisNexis U.S. Serial Set Digital Collection and the Readex U.S. Congressional Serial Set (1817–1980) with American State Papers (1789–1838). Comprehensive index coverage is provided by LexisNexis Congressional (in print, since 1970 in the *CIS/Index* and before that date in the *CIS U.S. Serial Set Index*).

Senate Executive Reports and Treaty Documents. The Senate also issues two confidential series of publications in connection with its responsibility for treaty ratification. Senate Treaty

---

26. See, e.g., *Presidential Signing Statements under the Bush Administration: A Threat to Checks and Balances and the Rule of Law?: Hearing before the H. Comm. on the Judiciary*, 110th Cong. (2007); Presidential Signing Statements Act of 2007, H.R. 3045, 110th Cong. (2007). See also T.J. HALSTEAD, PRESIDENTIAL SIGNING STATEMENTS: CONSTITUTIONAL AND INSTITUTIONAL IMPLICATIONS (2007)

(CRS Report RL33667) <ftp.fas.org/sgp/crs/natsec/RL33667.pdf>. President Obama announced in a memorandum for the heads of executive departments and agencies that he would continue using signing statements to raise constitutional concerns but "with caution and restraint." Memorandum of Mar. 9, 2009, 74 Fed. Reg. 10,669, 10,669 (Mar. 11, 2009).

Documents contain the text of treaties sent to the Senate for its advice and consent, together with related messages or correspondence from the President and Secretary of State. Senate Executive Reports are issued by the Senate Foreign Relations Committee after its consideration of the treaty. These materials are discussed more fully in Chapter 13.

Committee Prints. Many congressional committees publish material prepared at their request, such as staff studies or compilations of legislative history documents. These contents of committee prints vary; some have statements by committee members on pending bills, and others can be useful analyses and compilations of laws under the jurisdiction of a committee. The House's *Green Book: Background Material and Data on Major Programs Within the Jurisdiction of the Committee on Ways and Means* is an example of a committee print with a wide range of useful information.

Committee prints are distributed by the Government Printing Office, but they are not as widely available online as are reports or hearings. Selective coverage through Lexis begins in 1994, and GPO Access has a limited number of prints beginning in 1997 <www.gpoaccess.gov/cprints/>. Westlaw has no separate files for committee prints, but some are included in its compiled legislative histories.

The most comprehensive subscription source for committee prints is the LexisNexis Congressional Research Digital Collection, available as part of the LexisNexis Congressional system. "Congressional Research" in the title means research performed for Congress, an apt description of the purpose of committee reports. This online collection includes thousands of committee prints dating back to 1830, with PDF images of the original documents and search options including full text and indexed fields.

CIS also publishes prints from 1830 to 1969 on microfiche, with a comprehensive retrospective index covering this period, the *CIS US Congressional Committee Prints Index* (1980), included in the online LexisNexis Congressional. Like other congressional documents, committee prints since 1970 are also indexed and abstracted in *CIS/Index* and in LexisNexis Congressional.

Legislative Agencies. In addition to its own lawmaking and investigative functions, Congress also supervises three major investigative and research agencies that produce a range of important analyses and reports. Two of these (Congressional Budget Office and Government Accountability Office) provide convenient access to their documentation, while information from the third (Congressional Research Service) is only available indirectly.

The Congressional Budget Office <www.cbo.gov> was created in 1974[27] and produces cost estimates for bills reported out of committee as well as a variety of budget reports, analytical studies, and background papers. The CBO website provides options to search its publications by subject area and by document type.

The Government Accountability Office <www.gao.gov> was created in 1921 as the General Accounting Office and given its present name in 2004.[28] It is charged with studying the programs and expenditures of the federal government. The GAO issues more than a thousand reports each year, and frequently recommends specific congressional actions. If legislation is enacted, these reports can provide valuable background information on its purpose.

Like the CBO, the GAO provides extensive access to its reports through its website. PDF copies of reports are available as far back as the 1960s, and reports not available online can be ordered for free. The site also offers daily and monthly e-mail notification of new reports and other documents. GPO Access also has GAO reports, back to 1995 <www.gpoaccess.gov/gaoreports/>, and Westlaw (GAO–RPTS database) and Lexis provide coverage back to 1994.

The head of the GAO is the Comptroller General of the United States, who also issues decisions regarding contract claims by or against the United States and other matters involving federal agencies. These adjudicative decisions are available from 1995 to date on GPO Access <www.gpoaccess.gov/gaodecisions/>, and back to 1921 in Westlaw (CG database) and Lexis. Decisions before GPO Access coverage were published in print as *Decisions of the Comptroller General of the United States* (1921–94).

The third and most wide-ranging research arm of Congress is the Congressional Research Service, created in 1915 as the Legislative Drafting Bureau and Reference Division.[29] It issues reports like

---

27. Congressional Budget Act of 1974, Pub. L. No. 93–344, tit. 2, 88 Stat. 297, 302–05 (codified as amended at 2 U.S.C. §§ 601–611 (2006)).

28. The General Accounting Office was established by the Budget and Accounting Act of 1921, ch. 20, tit. 3, 42 Stat. 20, 23–27 (current version at 31 U.S.C.A. §§ 701–783 (West 2003 & Supp. 2008)). It was renamed the Government Accountability Office pursuant to the GAO Human Capital Reform Act of 2004, Pub. L. No. 108–271, § 8, 118 Stat. 811, 814. For the early history of the GAO, including its precursors, see ROGER R. TRASK, DEFENDER OF THE PUBLIC INTEREST: THE GENERAL ACCOUNTING OFFICE, 1921–1966 (1996).

29. Act of Mar. 4, 1915, ch. 141, 38 Stat. 997, 1005. Thirty-one years later, the agency's mandate was expanded and it was named the Legislative Reference Service. Legislative Reorganization Act of 1946, ch. 753, § 203, 60 Stat. 812, 836. The present name was adopted and the Service's wide range of functions specified under the Legislative Reorganization Act of 1970, Pub. L. No. 91–510, § 321, 84 Stat. 1140, 1181–85 (codified as amended at 2 U.S.C. § 166 (2000)). For more information, see Deborah A. Liptak, *Congressional Research Service Reports Revealed*, ONLINE, Nov./Dec. 2005, at 23; Stephen Young, *Guide to CRS Reports on the Web*, LLRX.com

the other offices, but the CRS has no publicly accessible website and does not regularly publish its reports. Each year it produces several thousand new or updated reports, including legal and policy analyses, economic studies, bibliographies, statistical reviews, and issue briefs that provide background information on major legislative issues. These reports are written exclusively for members of Congress and their staff, however, and cannot generally be found online or requested by members of the public.[30]

While the CRS itself does not release its reports, many have been made available by others. Several sites provide links to thousands of CRS reports available free at various websites. Among the most extensive are the University of North Texas Libraries' Congressional Research Service Reports site <digital.library.unt.edu/govdocs/crs/index.tkl>, which provides subject indexing and keyword searching, and Open CRS <www.opencrs.com>.[31]

CRS reports back to 1916 are available online through the subscription-based LexisNexis Congressional Research Digital Collection. As it does with committee prints, this service provides PDF images of the original documents and full-text searching. LexisNexis publishes a microform edition of reports since 1916 called *Major Studies and Issue Briefs of the Congressional Research Service*, accompanied by a two-volume cumulative index covering 1916–89 and annual indexes for subsequent years. CRS reports are also available from other private suppliers, including Gallery Watch <www.gallerywatch.com> and Penny Hill Press <www.pennyhill.com>.

§ 4.3   Congressional Research Resources

Researchers are interested in Congress for numerous reasons, such as policy formation, voting patterns, and the influence of lobbyists on legislative behavior. This discussion, however, focuses on tools useful for two basic legal research tasks: investigating the meaning of enacted laws and tracking the status of pending legislation. A number of approaches can be used for these purposes. For recently enacted laws and pending legislation, a range of online

(Sept. 17, 2006) <www.llrx.com/features/crsreports.htm>.

30. There has been a move, thus far unsuccessful, to make CRS materials available to the public. See, e.g., Congressional Research Accessibility Act, H.R. 2545, 110th Cong. (2007); Elizabeth Williamson, *Information, Please: Watchdog Groups, Some Lawmakers Say Congressional Reports Should Be Made Public*, WASH. POST, Feb. 19, 2007, at A17. The CRS Director issued a memo

to his staff explaining the purposes for limiting public dissemination. Memorandum from Daniel P. Mulhollan to All CRS Staff, Access to CRS Reports (Apr. 18, 2007) <ftp.fas.org/sgp/crs/crs041807.pdf>.

31. *LLSDC's Legislative Source Book* includes a CRS page <www.llsdc.org/crs-congress/>, with selected reports on Congress and its procedures, and links to several other websites with CRS reports.

resources provides current and thorough coverage. For older bills, the choices dwindle to a few tools that provide retrospective coverage.

The bill number is usually the key to finding congressional documents or tracing legislative action. It appears on an enacted law both in its slip form and in the *Statutes at Large*. Illustration 4–8 on page 155 shows the first page of Pub. L. No. 108–446, the Individuals with Disabilities Education Improvement Act of 2004. The bill number (H.R. 1350) is included in brackets in the right margin. Bill numbers have been included in *Statutes at Large* since 1903, but they unfortunately do not appear in the *United States Code* or in either of its annotated editions.[32]

Bill numbers lead easily to printed or electronic *status tables*, which indicate actions taken and provide references to relevant documents. These tables can be used both for pending bill searches and for retrospective research on enacted laws.

A quick head start in legislative history research can come from the public law itself. At the end of each act, in either slip law or *Statutes at Large*, there appears a brief legislative history summary with citations of committee reports, dates of consideration and passage in each house, and references to presidential statements. Summaries have appeared at the end of each law passed since 1975, and *Statutes at Large* volumes from 1963 to 1974 include separate "Guide to Legislative History" tables. The legislative history summaries in *Statutes at Large* are by no means complete, but they are conveniently published with the text of an act.

Compiling legislative histories is an important skill, but it can also be a very frustrating endeavor. Even after finding all the relevant legislative materials on a statute, you may learn that the legislature never explained or discussed the particular language at issue. This is one reason that legislative history is just one of several tools used in statutory interpretation.

Another frustration comes from the increasing use of omnibus legislation and unorthodox procedures. Especially towards the end of a legislative session, numerous bills may be combined into mammoth enactments of several hundred pages. These can complicate the research process enormously, as materials addressing a provision within a huge omnibus bill are much more difficult to locate than those on a bill with one discrete subject. Online keyword searches in lengthy committee reports and debates can pin-

---

32. For laws before 1903, bill numbers can be found in EUGENE NABORS, LEGISLATIVE REFERENCE CHECKLIST: THE KEY TO LEGISLATIVE HISTORIES FROM 1789–1903 (1982). Tables for each Congress provide references from public law numbers and *Statutes at Large* citations to bill numbers.

point particular issues, but working with complex legislative histories is still an onerous task. In other instances a bill may bypass the committee process and go directly to the floor for consideration, meaning that there are no relevant committee reports to be found.[33]

Several guides to legislative history are available on the Internet. A particularly thorough and useful resource is part of *LLSDC's Legislative Source Book*: Richard J. McKinney & Ellen A. Sweet, *Federal Legislative History Research: A Practitioner's Guide to Compiling the Documents and Sifting for Legislative Intent* <www.llsdc.org/Fed–Leg–Hist/>. It even includes links to dozens of the other Internet guides on the topic.

The following sections describe several major legislative history research resources. Which of these to use in any particular circumstance depends on the date of the law and the scope of information needed. The handiest way to access the text of relevant committee reports may be to scan those reprinted in *USCCAN*. The most up-to-date information on current legislation is found in THOMAS or one of the other online bill-tracking services. The most comprehensive coverage of documents relating to laws enacted within the past two decades is usually found in CIS materials. For legislative history information on older laws, the only resource available may be the "History of Bills and Resolutions" in the *Congressional Record* index, which dates back to the nineteenth century.

(a) Compiled Legislative Histories

Gathering a complete legislative history can be a very time-consuming process, as the necessary documents are scattered among many publications and may be difficult to obtain. For some enactments, however, convenient access is provided by publications or databases that compile the relevant documents. Compiled legislative histories have been issued by government agencies charged with the enforcement of particular acts, by commercial publishers, and by trade associations and other private interest groups. At their best, these compilations include bills, hearings, committee reports, committee prints, and debates, with detailed indexing. A comprehensive compiled history can save many hours of time identifying and retrieving these documents. It is important to be aware, though, that a compiled legislative history may not necessarily have *every* relevant document. Sometimes only some of the essential documents are included, and indexing may be omitted or inadequate.

---

33. For more information on omnibus bills and other changes in lawmaking procedures, see GLEN S. KRUTZ, HITCHING A RIDE: OMNIBUS LEGISLATING IN THE U.S. CONGRESS (2001), and BARBARA SINCLAIR, UNORTHODOX LAWMAKING: NEW LEGISLATIVE PROCESSES IN THE U.S. CONGRESS (3d ed. 2007). The authors of both works are political scientists, and they focus on institutional and public policy impacts rather than the effects of these changes on legislative history research.

Online compiled legislative histories, including bills and committee reports, are available on Lexis and Westlaw for several dozen major acts in areas such as bankruptcy, tax, and environmental law. To make sure that necessary documents are included, you can retrieve a list by searching for "ci(contents)" in Westlaw or clicking on "Review List of Documents" in Lexis. You can search for references to a particular section of an act, but you will probably want to double-check these results by searching as well for the specific language you need to interpret.

Westlaw also has a database, FED–LH, of several thousand legislative history compilations prepared by the Government Accountability Office. When completed, coverage will span from 1915 to 1995. These compilations list relevant congressional documents for each act, including reports, *Congressional Record* excerpts, and hearings, with links to PDF versions of most documents. You can search by keyword or retrieve legislative histories with the public law number, bill number, or name of act.

HeinOnline's Legislative History Library provides searchable PDFs of documents for dozens of acts, including major legislation in areas such as environmental law, immigration, intellectual property, labor law, and taxation. This collection is based on William S. Hein & Company's publications of compiled legislative histories, which has volumes or sets covering individual acts as well as more extensive sets such as *Congress and the Courts: A Legislative History 1787–1998* and *Internal Revenue Acts of the United States, 1909–1950*.

You can quickly determine what legislative histories are available on Westlaw, Lexis, and HeinOnline through the "Legislative Histories of Selected U.S. Laws on the Internet" page <www.llsdc. org/leg-hist> of *LLSDC's Legislative Source Book*. This lists acts alphabetically and by public law number, with links to the legislative histories, and also provides links to legislative history compilations available from free Internet sites.

A basic tool for identifying and locating published and online compiled legislative histories is Nancy P. Johnson, *Sources of Compiled Legislative Histories* (1979–date), which is available electronically as part of HeinOnline's Legislative History Library. Arranged chronologically by Congress and public law number, it provides a checklist of all available compiled legislative histories for acts as far back as 1789, and includes an index by name of act. It covers not only compilations which reprint the legislative history documents in full, but also law review articles and other sources that provide references to the relevant documents.

Another source listing compilations is Bernard D. Reams, Jr., *Federal Legislative Histories: An Annotated Bibliography and Index to Officially Published Sources* (1994). As the subtitle indicates, this volume covers only sources published by the federal government, such as a congressional committee or an agency. Coverage is thus not as broad as the Johnson work, but the detailed annotations are helpful.

A compiled legislative history is an invaluable time-saver, so checking to see whether one is available is an important first step in researching an act. To determine whether a local library has any printed compilations on a particular act, one approach is to search the online catalog for keywords from the act in question and the words "legislative history." For many acts, unfortunately, you will need to start fresh and to gather the materials from a variety of sources.[34]

(b) THOMAS and Other Congressional Websites

For current legislation or laws enacted since 1973, one of the easiest places to begin research is with Congress itself. THOMAS <thomas.loc.gov>, named for Thomas Jefferson, is the website introduced in 1995 by the Library of Congress to make legislative information freely available to the public. The scope of THOMAS has grown considerably since its debut, and it now provides access to a wide range of information and documents.

With THOMAS, you can find documents relevant to a particular act by searching either the full text of bills or summary and status information. A summary and status search retrieves an overview of the bill's provisions, a list of all committee and floor actions on the bill with links to the full text of committee reports and *Congressional Record* pages, and lists of sponsors, committees, related bills, and amendments. Searches can be conducted by bill number, word or phrase, but the search mechanism is relatively unsophisticated and you cannot use synonyms or proximity connectors. You can search for bill text across multiple terms of Congress, but status searches must be run in one individual term. Documents are displayed in HTML format, with links to the PDF versions available from GPO Access.

Legislative history summaries are available in THOMAS for laws enacted since 1973, but summaries for older laws lack some of

---

34. A useful guide for researchers in the Washington, D.C. area is the Law Librarians' Society of Washington, D.C.'s Union List of Legislative Histories (7th ed., 2000–date), which lists legislative histories held by more than 120 libraries in the area, including law firms and government agencies. It covers thousands of acts all the way back to 1790. Most of these histories were compiled in-house, and some can contain many volumes of bill versions, reports, debates, hearings, committee prints, and other documents. A list of participating libraries indicates whether the compilations can be borrowed by other libraries or used by appointment. A similar but much shorter guide is available for Chicago: Kevin P. Gray, Legislative History Union List of the Chicago Association of Law Libraries (2001).

the features included for more recent legislation. Links to the text of bills, for example, are available beginning in 1989, and *Congressional Record* page references and links have been added beginning with 1993. A portion of the THOMAS summary for H.R. 1350 is shown in Illustration 4–9 on page 156. This screen shows the "Major Actions" status section, with links to the *Congressional Record* and references to the House report and the conference report.

As noted above, THOMAS includes links to the Government Printing Office's GPO Access <www.gpoaccess.gov/legislative.html>, which provides the text of bills, reports, and other congressional materials as PDF files.[35] The legislative branch resources on GPO Access include bills back to 1993, the *Congressional Record* beginning with 1994, committee reports and hearings from 1995, and selected committee prints from 1997. GPO Access is the more comprehensive source for documents, but it is less user-friendly and informative than THOMAS. It has no links between its congressional documents, and does not provide bill summaries or status information.

THOMAS and GPO Access are the major comprehensive websites for congressional information, but each chamber also maintains a website (<www.senate.gov> and <www.house.gov>) with information on its procedures as well as links to pages for individual members and committees. Most committee homepages have summaries of major pending legislation, background information, hearing statements, and schedules of upcoming meetings. In some instances, a "legislation" link provides status tables for bills within the committee's jurisdiction. *LLSDC's Legislative Source Book's* "Quick Links to House and Senate Committee Hearings and Other Publications" <www.llsdc.org/quick-links/> lists each House, Senate, and joint committee, with direct links to features such as hearing lists, news, schedules, testimony, and transcripts if available. Helpful comments provide further guidance to the scope of available resources on each committee's site.

(c) LexisNexis Congressional and CIS

In 1970, a company called Congressional Information Service (CIS) began publishing a monthly service, *CIS/Index*, that provided

---

35. GPO Access was authorized by the Government Printing Office Electronic Information Access Enhancement Act of 1993, Pub. L. No. 103–40, § 2, 107 Stat. 112, 112 (codified at 44 U.S.C. § 4101–04 (2000)). This requires the Superintendent of Documents to "provide a system of online access to the Congressional Record, the Federal Register, and ... other appropriate publications distributed by the Superintendent of Documents." 44 U.S.C. § 4101(a)(2) (2000). See Peggy Garvin, *GPO Access and THOMAS for Legislative Research*, LLRX.com (June 23, 2005) <www.llrx.com/columns/govdomain6.htm>, for a good comparison of the two systems with several tips for effective use.

indexing and abstracts of congressional publications. Its coverage was far more extensive and detailed than anything else then available.[36] For the first time, for example, one could track every appearance by a witness in published committee hearings. CIS, now a subsidiary of LexisNexis, is still the most comprehensive resource on Congress, covering virtually all congressional publications except the *Congressional Record*. Its information is now available online through LexisNexis Congressional <web.lexis-nexis.com/congcomp/> (for academic users) and Lexis (for others), as well as in print in three annual volume (*Abstracts*, *Legislative Histories*, and *Index*).

CIS indexes reports, hearings, prints, and documents by subject, title, and bill number, with abstracts summarizing the contents of these documents, the names and affiliations of witnesses, and the focus of their testimony. Abstracts provide both the the the Superintendent of Documents classification (e.g., Y 4.G 74/7:ED 8/14) used in most libraries for locating government publications and the CIS numbers (e.g., 2002–H401–26) used to find documents in CIS's online and microfiche collections.

In addition to abstracting individual congressional publications, CIS also provides legislative histories for each enacted law, listing relevant bills, hearings, reports, debates, presidential documents and any other legislative actions. Rather than limiting coverage to a single term of Congress, these summaries include references to earlier hearings and other documents on related bills from prior Congressional sessions. A summary for a complex and lengthy act can span several years and list hundreds of items.[37] CIS legislative histories are generally considered the most complete and descriptive summaries available for federal enactments.

Illustration 4–10 on page 157 shows the first page of the CIS legislative history of the Individuals with Disabilities Education Improvement Act of 2004, summarizing the law and two committee reports (including the Senate report shown earlier in this chapter's illustrations). The legislative history goes on to provide references to other reports, related bills, *Congressional Record* debates, and sixteen hearings going back to 1998. Some of these are only indirectly related to the bill passed in 2004 but may nonetheless be relevant in interpreting its provisions.

---

36. For background on the situation before 1970 and the beginnings of CIS, see Sandra Peterson & Susan Tulis, *An Interview with James B. Adler and Esthy Adler, Founders, Congressional Information Service, Inc.*, 15 GOV'T PUBLICATIONS REV. 411 (1988).

37. For example, the summary for the Bipartisan Campaign Reform Act of 2002, Pub. L. No. 107–155, 116 Stat. 81, lists more than 140 separate bills and more than 100 *Congressional Record* references, going back to the 100th Congress in 1987.

CIS legislative histories cover laws enacted since 1970, but its summaries before 1984 are far less convenient to use because they simply list the CIS numbers for the reports, hearings, and other materials. (In print, these are included in the *Abstracts* volumes rather than in separate *Legislative Histories* volumes.) No links are provided, and it is necessary to retrieve each individual abstract for more information. These earlier summaries, nonetheless, are among the most thorough sources available for their period.

LexisNexis Congressional's online legislative histories are unfortunately no more up-to-date than the original printed versions; if a document was listed as "unavailable" when the volume was published, the information on the website is the same. The links to reports, hearings, and *Congressional Record* pages, of course, make the online version a substantial improvement over the printed summaries.

The search screen for legislative histories, bills and laws includes a "Get a Document" tab that can be used to find legislative histories by public law number. Other features of LexisNexis Congressional include bill-tracking summaries; full-text access to bills, reports, the *Congressional Record*, and other congressional documents beginning in the 1980s; transcripts of hearing testimony; and information on committees and legislators.

For the period before 1970, CIS provides retrospective coverage of reports, documents, hearings, and committee prints online and in a series of printed indexes, most of which have been mentioned earlier in the sections on the specific types of materials they cover. The various pre–1970 printed indexes are cumulated online as LexisNexis Congressional's "Congressional Publications" and as the CIS/Historical Index file on Lexis.[38] LexisNexis Congressional's digital collections of reports, hearings, and committee prints provide online full-text access to much of the material it indexes, and CIS also publishes microfiche reproductions of all published bills and other congressional documents covered in its indexes.

Besides its CIS files, Lexis has other materials useful for legislative history research including text of bills since 1989, committee reports since 1990, selected committee prints since 1995, and the *Congressional Record* since 1985. Bill-tracking databases since the 101st Congress (1989–90) include extensive links to the *Congressional Record*, but less thorough coverage of reports and very little treatment of hearings.

38. Some libraries may have this information in a CIS CD–ROM product known as *Congressional Masterfile I*, which covers the same time period but is no longer being published.

(d) *USCCAN* and Westlaw

United States Code Congressional and Administrative News (*USCCAN*) was discussed in Chapter 3 as a source for the texts of enacted laws. For major acts it also reprints one or more committee reports, making it a convenient compilation for basic legislative research. The scope of coverage varies, but *USCCAN* generally prints either a House or Senate report and the conference committee report, if one was issued. It has been printing committee reports since it began in 1941, and may be one of the most convenient sources for reports predating online coverage. The major benefit of *USCCAN* in legislative history research is its ready availability; it is found in many smaller libraries that do not have very extensive collections of congressional materials.

The public laws and committee reports are published in separate "Laws" and "Legislative History" sections of *USCCAN*. Each section prints material in order by public law number, and cross-references are provided between the laws and reports. Illustration 4–11 on page 158 shows the beginning of the conference report on the IDEIA, as set out in *USCCAN*. The report is preceded by references to dates of consideration and passage in each house and to the House report, but that there is no mention of the companion Senate bill or the Senate report. The conference report is reprinted in full, except for the portion reprinting the text of the act.[39]

The LH database on Westlaw includes the reports reprinted in USCCAN beginning in 1948, and from 1990 on it contains all congressional committee reports, including reports on bills that did not become law.

One reason that *USCCAN* legislative histories are easy to find is that references to them are provided in the notes in the *United States Code Annotated*. Westlaw's online version of *USCA* includes links from the statutory notes to the *USCCAN* summary and reports, making it easy to get to the reports from a code section. Note, however, that a reference after a specific section means only that legislative history on the act as a whole is available, not that pertinent material on that specific section will be found.

USCCAN provides only selective coverage of committee reports, and further research is often required. There are no references to hearings, prints, documents, or materials on related bills in previous Congresses, so anyone preparing a complete legislative history will need to use other resources. But it does provide a handy

---

39. *USCCAN* also includes tables with basic legislative history information, listing each public law's date of approval, *Statutes at Large* citation, bill and report numbers, committees, and dates of passage in each house. Monthly issues also include a "Major Bills Pending" table, arranged by subject and showing the progress of current legislation.

starting point, and the material printed in USCCAN may be sufficient if all you need is general background or a quick section-by-section analysis.

As noted earlier, Westlaw also has databases with congressional bills, the *Congressional Record*, hearing testimony, and compiled legislative histories. One means of access to these resources is through the Westlaw Tab for "Legislative History—Fed," which shows the congressional lawmaking process in graphical format. Clicking on any of the twelve steps in the diagram leads to a menu of possible databases to search for information. This may suggest some useful leads, particularly to news sources in the early "Preliminary Congressional Inquiry" section. Westlaw also has bill-tracking databases (US–BILLTRK for the current Congress, and BILLTRK–OLD for coverage back to 1991), but the summaries are not as complete as those available free from THOMAS and they have no links to the relevant documents.

(e) CQ Resources

Congressional Quarterly Inc. (CQ) <www.cq.com>, a news service focusing on political issues, publishes several sources of information on congressional activity. Its flagship publication is *CQ Weekly* (formerly *Congressional Quarterly Weekly Report*), which provides background information on pending legislation and news of current developments. *CQ Weekly* does not include the texts of documents or comprehensive bill-tracking, but it does provide valuable analysis and background discussion of laws and legislative issues.

CQ Weekly contains tables of House and Senate votes, a status table for major legislation, and a legislative history table for new public laws. An annual *Congressional Quarterly Almanac* cumulates much of the information in the *Weekly Report* into a useful summary of the congressional session. More frequent publications for people needing current information on legislative activity include *CQ Today* and *CQ Midday Update*, which is available free by e-mail.

Congressional Quarterly's online service CQ.com <www.cq.com> provides many of the same documents available from other online sources, as well as customized bill tracking information, committee markup summaries, and other less widely available materials. It includes the full text of CQ's weekly and daily news publications, as well as a Bill Comparison feature useful in identifying changes between two versions of proposed legislation. For academic and public libraries, CQ Electronic Library <library.cqpress.com> provides a subscription-based Web version of *CQ Weekly* and free access to its index.

CQ Weekly and *CQ Today* are available in Westlaw as the CQWEEK and CQTODAY databases, with coverage beginning in 2005. CQ publications are also available through Lexis, but only in the legal, government and business markets (not in law schools). CQ also publishes a wide range of texts and reference books relating to Congress. Several of these, including *Guide to Congress*, have already been mentioned earlier in this chapter.

Other online subscription services, such as GalleryWatch.com <www.gallerywatch.com>, also provide information on Congress, including bill tracking and committee markup reports. Designed for specialists needing current congressional information, these services may offer a range of sophisticated tracking and notification services unavailable from free government sites and more general database systems.

(f) Printed Status Tables

For the purpose of tracking current legislation and researching laws enacted since the mid–1990s, online resources provide advantages of convenience and speed that are unmatched by printed resources. For earlier bills and laws, however, printed resources may still be the best available sources of information. There are several publications in which a researcher may find useful leads.

Congressional Index **(CCH) (1937–date).** A commercial looseleaf service published by CCH (formerly Commerce Clearing House), *Congressional Index* is issued in two looseleaf volumes for each Congress, with weekly updates. It is one of the most convenient and current printed sources of congressional information, with extensive coverage of pending legislation including an index of bills by subject and author, a digest of each bill, and a status table of actions taken on each bill. This status table contains references to hearings, a feature lacking in many of the online resources.

The *Congressional Index* status table has references to report numbers and public law numbers but not to *Congressional Record* pages. Unlike the CIS legislative history, there are no references to related bills in earlier terms of Congress. This table might not be the first choice for information on recent enactments, but older *Congressional Index* volumes back to the 75th Congress (1937–38) can be valuable sources of information on bills predating the coverage of electronic bill-tracking services.

Congressional Index does not contain the actual text of bills, debates, reports, or laws. It is only a finding tool, but a useful one with weekly supplementation and generally good indexing. It also provides a wide range of other information on Congress, including lists of members and committee assignments, an index of enactments and vetoes, lists of pending treaties and nominations, and a table of voting records.

Congressional Record and Earlier Status Tables (1789–date). As noted earlier, the *Congressional Record* includes status tables that can be useful for both current and retrospective research. A History of Bills and Resolutions table is published in the biweekly index and cumulated for each session in the bound index volume. This table includes a brief summary of each measure, the name of the sponsor, the committee to which it has been referred, and references to debates, legislative actions, committee reports, amendments and passage. Each entry also provides reference to the page number in the *Congressional Record* at which action is reported. This is one of the best sources of page citations for debates within the *Record*. It includes report and public law numbers, but no references to committee hearings or companion bills.

The biweekly table lists only those bills and resolutions acted upon during the two-week period covered by the index, but for bills that are listed the information is cumulative from the beginning of the session. The History of Bills is also available online through GPO Access <www.gpoaccess.gov/hob/>, and this version (unlike the printed version) cumulates all entries for the session. GPO Access has the History of Bills back to 1983, but page references are only available beginning in 1993. Entries provide dates and page references, but do not have hypertext links from these references to the documents.

The final cumulative History of Bills and Resolutions, published in the Index volume of the bound *Congressional Record* set, is a valuable resource because it uses the final pagination of the bound volumes instead of the separate "S" and "H" pages in the daily edition. This makes it an easy way to locate the bound volume pagination if needed for a citation.

Although the History of Bills and Resolutions is less comprehensive than some commercial sources such as *CIS/Index*, it remains one of the best sources available for older laws. These tables have been published annually since the 1867 volume of the *Congressional Globe*, long before the earliest coverage of most commercial publications.

For even earlier acts, the House and Senate Journals all the way back to the First Congress (1789–91) include tables or lists of bills indicating when they were reported, passed, or received other floor action. Most of these lists, usually found in the subject index under "Bills," are arranged by bill number, but some early volumes list bills without numbers by subject or by date of introduction. These early journals are all available online through the Library of

Congress's "A Century of Lawmaking for a New Nation" site <memory.loc.gov/ammem/amlaw/lwss.html>.

***Digest of Public General Bills and Resolutions* (1936–90).** The *Digest of Public General Bills and Resolutions* was published for more than fifty years by the Congressional Research Service and may still be useful for retrospective research. The *Digest* provided extensive summaries of all bills and resolutions introduced. For enacted bills, listed by public law number, and for all other measures reported out of committee, listed by bill number, it also indicated major steps in their consideration. These include citations to committee reports but not to hearings. There are indexes by sponsor and by subject.

Legislative Calendars (1919–date). Both houses and most committees issue calendars of pending business for the use of their members. These provide current information on the status of pending bills and are particularly useful for information on hearings.

Perhaps the most valuable of these is *Calendars of the United States House of Representatives and History of Legislation*, which is issued daily. This includes a table, "History of Bills and Resolutions: Numerical Order of Bills and Resolutions Which Have Been Reported to or Considered by Either or Both Houses," which is updated each day and cumulates legislative information for bills on which action has been taken. The table in the final *Calendars* issue at the end of each Congress cumulates both sessions and is useful for retrospective reference. It provides report numbers and dates of consideration, but not *Congressional Record* page numbers. GPO Access has the current House and Senate calendars, and final calendars beginning with the 104th Congress (1995–96) <www.gpoaccess.gov/calendars/>.

(g) Directories

One of the fastest ways to find out about the status of pending legislation is to contact congressional staff members responsible for drafting or monitoring the bill. They may be able to provide information or insights that would never appear in published status tables or reports. The best sources for detailed information on staff members are two competing commercial directories, *Congressional Staff Directory* (three times per year) and *Congressional Yellow Book* (quarterly). They have addresses, telephone numbers, and (for some staff members) brief biographical information. Internet versions of both directories (<library.cqpress.com/csd/>, <www.leadershipdirectories.com/products/cyb.htm>) are updated daily but are available to subscribers only.

The *Official Congressional Directory* (biennial) is not updated as frequently or published as rapidly as the commercial directories, but it too provides information about individuals, offices and the organizational structure of Congress. It includes listings of committee assignments, staff for representatives and committees, and statistical data, as well as other information useful to representatives such as directories of the executive branch, foreign diplomatic offices in the United States, and the press galleries. The *Congressional Directory* is available free online through GPO Access <www.gpoaccess.gov/cdirectory/>; the Internet version, unlike its print counterpart, is modified during the term to reflect changes.

The *Official Congressional Directory* began publication with the 50th Congress (1887–88), and older volumes provide valuable information on members and committees in previous Congresses. Volumes since the 105th Congress (1997–98) are included on GPO Access. Committees and committee assignments in previous Congresses can also be found in *USCCAN*, which has lists back to 1947, as well as in two sets of reference books, *Committees in the U.S. Congress, 1789–1946* (Charles Stewart III et al. eds., 2002), and *Committees in the U.S. Congress, 1947–1992* (Garrison Nelson ed., 1993–94). Both include listings of committee rosters and indexes by representatives' names of committee assignments.

A retrospective *Biographical Directory of the United States Congress, 1774–Present* (including coverage of the Continental Congress) is available online <bioguide.congress.gov>, and provides basic information on the more than 13,000 persons who have served in Congress. It is searchable by name, position, state, party, and year or Congress. Once a biography is displayed, clicking on "Research Collections" or "Bibliography" provides leads, if available, to manuscript collections and a list of books and articles by and about the person.

A printed version of the same resource, under the title *Biographical Directory of the American Congress, 1774–1996* (1997), covers the 1st through 104th Congresses. Although it is not as up to date as the online version, it includes valuable Congress-by-Congress directories of congressional leaders and state delegations. These lists fill more than 500 pages, with extensive footnotes indicating deaths, resignations, and other changes.

Two useful sources for background information on members of Congress, both published biennially, are National Journal's *Almanac of American Politics* and *CQ's Politics in America*. These provide in-depth biographical portraits with information on voting records and ratings from interest groups, as well as a brief narrative and statistical overview of each congressional district.

§ 4.4　State Legislative Information

Legislative history on the state level is a research area of sharp contrasts. Information on current legislation is widely available on the Internet, but documents that might aid in the interpretation of enacted laws can be difficult or impossible to find.

First the good news: Most state legislatures do excellent jobs of providing Internet access to current status information and to the text of pending bills. The better websites have several means of searching for bills, and some offer e-mail notification services when particular bills are acted upon. Some states have other features such as bill summaries, committee minutes, and staff analyses. Illustration 4–12 on page 159 shows a printout from the Arizona State Legislature website <www.azleg.gov>, providing a bill summary explaining the history and purpose of a bill relating to an extended school year for students with disabilities.

Legislative websites can be found by using a search engine to find "[state] legislature," from state homepages, or from one of many general starting points. The National Conference of State Legislatures maintains a convenient "State Legislatures Internet Links" site <www.ncsl.org/public/leglinks.cfm>, which allows you to go directly to a specific site or to create a customized list of links for specific content (such as bill information or legislator biographies) from all states or a selected list of states. *LLSDC's Legislative Source Book* includes a "State Legislatures, State Laws, and State Regulations: Website Links and Telephone Numbers" page <www.llsdc.org/state-leg/>, useful for quick links.

Many legislative websites include an introductory guide to the state's lawmaking procedures, a useful starting point in state legislative history research. Even though state legislatures generally follow the federal paradigm, there can be significant differences from state to state and an important first step in studying legislative action in a particular state is to learn about its procedures and terminology. It may not be immediately apparent in Illustration 4–12 that "COW" (in the heading "Caucus and COW") means "Committee of the Whole," or that a "truly agreed" version of a Missouri bill means one that has been passed by both houses of the legislature. Guides and other resources, such as charts showing how bills become law, can save considerable time and confusion.

The commercial databases also provide text and status information for pending legislation. Both Westlaw and Lexis have databases for each state, as well as multistate databases useful for monitoring developments in legislatures throughout the country.

Historical bill text and tracking databases extend on both systems back to the early 1990s.[40]

For thirty-six states Westlaw also provides legislative history databases containing documents such as reports, bill analyses, legislative journals, and committee reports. Contents vary from state to state depending on the materials available. These documents are in searchable databases, and are also tied to the display of specific state code sections. If a code section is derived from an act for which legislative history documents are available, "Reports and Related Materials" appears as one of the links on the left of the screen. As with federal statutes, however, a link does not necessarily mean that there is relevant information on the particular section. Dates of coverage vary between states but generally begin in the late 1990s or early 2000s. This can be a very useful resource for legislation that has been recently enacted or amended.

Researchers needing to interpret statutes enacted before the late 1990s face a more difficult task.[41] Bills from older sessions can be hard to locate. Almost every state has a legislative journal, but very few of these actually include transcripts of the debates. Only a few states publish committee reports, and even fewer publish hearings.

The materials that are available vary widely from state to state.[42] Often they are not published in either print or electronic form, and are available only at the state capitol. Some states have "bill jackets" with legislative information, and some have micro-form records or tape recordings of sessions. In many instances, contemporary newspaper accounts may be the best available source of information about a sponsor's statements or proceedings. A few states have legislative history websites providing some retrospective coverage.[43]

---

40. Researchers in university and public libraries may have access to LexisNexis's bill-tracking and other legislative information through its State Capital website <web.lexis-nexis.com/stcapuniv/>.

41. Here is the perspective from the early 1990s: "As those who seek to determine the 'policy' informing significant state statutes continue to find, it is frequently impossible to determine the pertinent subjective intent of a state legislature from any source. Indifference to the documentation of legislative history at the state level has been, and continues to be to this day, a basic feature of American legal culture." Hans W. Baade, *"Original Intent" in Historical Perspective: Some Critical Glosses*, 69 TEX. L. REV. 1001, 1085 (1991) (citation omitted).

42. Chapter three of *The Book of the States* (annual), "State Legislative Branch," has more than two dozen tables summarizing and comparing procedures in the fifty states.

43. Pennsylvania <www.legis.state.pa.us>, for example, has a "Legislation Enacted Since 1975" link to summaries for more than 30 years of acts, with copies of bill versions and references to remarks in the House and Senate Journal if any. The Jenkins Law Library <www.jenkinslaw.org>, a private library in Philadelphia, has a legislative history collection of more than 800 Pennsylvania acts back as far as 1836, and sells copies of these compiled histories (ranging from 1 to 176 pages) electronically or by mail.

Two useful books identify the resources available for each state. Lynn Hellebust, *State Legislative Sourcebook: A Resource Guide to Legislative Information in the Fifty States* (annual) contains eight to ten pages of detailed information on the legislature and legislative process of each state, with references to available published and online sources. For each state there is a "best initial contact," as well as information on websites, introductory guides, telephone numbers for ascertaining bill status, bill tracking services, and legislative documents such as session laws and summaries of legislation. Also included are references to newspapers and services that cover political and legal developments in the state. William H. Manz, *Guide to State Legislation, Legislative History, and Administrative Materials* (7th ed. 2008) lists printed and online sources for bills and for legislative history materials, if available, such as hearings, reports, floor debates, and journals.

A guide to legislative research processes in a specific state can be invaluable. Most of the state legal research guides listed on pages 392–398 include discussion of available legislative history resources for their states. Law libraries in the jurisdiction you are researching, particularly the state legislative library, may have posted legislative history research guides on their websites. The Indiana University School of Law's "State Legislative History Research Guides on the Web" <www.law.indiana.edu/lawlibrary/research/guides/statelegislative/> provides links to more than a hundred online guides, and state bar journals frequently publish articles describing legislative history research in the state.[44]

Many states have official or quasi-official agencies devoted to the research and recommendation of new legislation. These include independent law revision commissions, legislative councils, and academic bodies devoted to legislative study and drafting. These

---

44. E.g., Susan Adamczak, *Researching Online Sources for Michigan Legislative History*, MICH. B.J., Jan. 2006, at 46; Mari Cheney, *Utah Legislative History Research Tips*, UTAH B.J., Nov./Dec. 2008, at 31; James E. Duggan, *Illinois Legislative History*, 88 ILL. B.J. 665 (2000); Kristin Ford, *Researching Legislative Histories in Idaho: Why, Where, How*, ADVOCATE, Jan. 2002, at 21; Tom Gaylord, *Illinois Statutory and Legislative Resources—Beyond the Basics*, ILL. B.J., Jan. 2009, at 48; Tom Gaylord, *New Legislative History Resources at the Illinois General Assembly's Web Site*, 95 ILL B.J. 268 (2007); Andrea L. Hamilton, *Conducting Colorado Legislative History Research*, COLO. LAW., Aug. 2008, at 113; Betty Karweick, *Researching Legislative History*, BENCH & B. MINN., Nov. 1994, at 22; Richard E. Levy & Robert Mead, *Using Legislative History as a Tool of Statutory Construction in Kansas*, J. KAN. B.A., May 2002, at 35; William H. Manz, *If It's Out There: Researching Legislative Intent in New York*, N.Y. ST. B.A.J., Mar. 2005, at 43; Kristen McKeaney, *Compiling a Pennsylvania Legislative History: Making a Daunting Task Seem Easy*, PA. L. WKLY., Jan. 3, 2000, at 12; Steven R. Thorpe, *Uncovering Legislative History Sources in Tennessee*, TENN. B.J., May–June 1995, at 18; *Uncovering Legislative History in Colorado*, COLO. LAW., Feb. 2003, at 47. Older articles are listed in José R. Torres & Steve Windsor, *State Legislative Histories: A Select, Annotated Bibliography*, 85 LAW LIBR. J. 545 (1993).

organizations often publish annual or topical reports summarizing their work. For studies and proposals enacted into law, such publications may shed considerable light on the interpretation of the resulting enactment.

Contacting legislative staff members may be the quickest way to get information on current legislative activity, but state legislature websites vary in the extent of directory information they provide. Official state manuals (sometimes called *blue books*), published annually or biennially by most states, generally provide information on state legislatures such as organization, members, committees, and staffs. These directories are listed in the *State Legislative Sourcebook* with other reference sources for each state, and can usually be found in online catalogs with the subject search "[State]–Registers."

The directory for a specific state is likely to provide the most detailed information, but several multistate directories are also published. The Council of State Governments publishes an annual *CSG State Directory*, comprised of three parts. *Directory I: Elective Officials* includes legislators, with telephone numbers and e-mail addresses, along with other statewide officials, and *Directory II: Legislative Leadership, Committees and Staff* lists principal officers and staff for each chamber. General multistate government directories such as *State Yellow Book* (quarterly) also include extensive coverage of the legislative branches, with information on members and committee assignments.

In twenty-four states, statutes or constitutional amendments can be not only introduced by the legislature but submitted directly to voters through the initiative process. (Twenty-four states also permit popular referendums, or ballot measures to reject measures enacted by the legislature). Information on the enactment and intent of these measures may not appear in the standard legislative history sources. The Initiative & Referendum Institute at the University of Southern California <www.iandrinstitute.org> provides state-by-state information on the history and procedures of popular ballot measures, with links to state-specific sites. M. Dane Waters, *Initiative and Referendum Almanac* (2003) provides a comprehensive history as well as lists and charts tracking the use of these processes. *Exploring Initiative and Referendum Law: Selected State Research Guides* (Beth Williams ed., 2007) explains research the initiative processes and research procedures in twenty-three states.[45]

---

45. *Exploring Initiative and Referendum Law* was also published as 26 *Legal Reference Services Q.*, nos. 3/4. The state omitted from its coverage is

Legislative materials are essential tools both in interpreting statutes and in monitoring current legal developments, but legislative history documents are hardly the only resources of value in understanding statutes. Court decisions may provide authoritative judicial interpretations, and even secondary sources may be persuasive in determining the scope and meaning of an act. Many statutes are implemented by more detailed regulations and decisions from administrative agencies. These administrative materials, to be discussed in the next chapter, are key elements in understanding of the scope and meaning of the underlying statutes.

California, which was covered separately in Tobe Liebert, *Researching California* *Ballot Measures*, 90 LAW LIBR. J. 27 (1998).

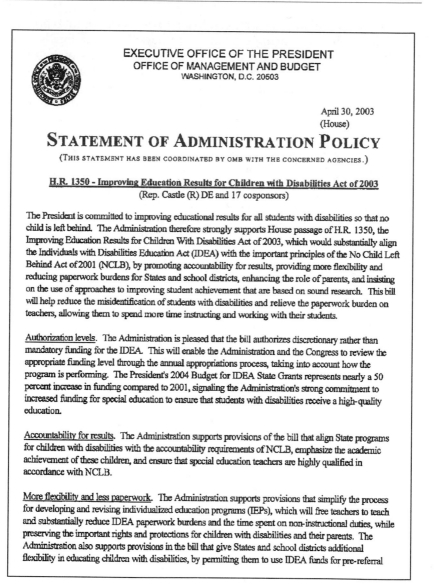

EXECUTIVE OFFICE OF THE PRESIDENT
OFFICE OF MANAGEMENT AND BUDGET
WASHINGTON, D.C. 20503

April 30, 2003
(House)

STATEMENT OF ADMINISTRATION POLICY

(THIS STATEMENT HAS BEEN COORDINATED BY OMB WITH THE CONCERNED AGENCIES.)

H.R. 1350 - Improving Education Results for Children with Disabilities Act of 2003
(Rep. Castle (R) DE and 17 cosponsors)

The President is committed to improving educational results for all students with disabilities so that no child is left behind. The Administration therefore strongly supports House passage of H.R. 1350, the Improving Education Results for Children With Disabilities Act of 2003, which would substantially align the Individuals with Disabilities Education Act (IDEA) with the important principles of the No Child Left Behind Act of 2001 (NCLB), by promoting accountability for results, providing more flexibility and reducing paperwork burdens for States and school districts, enhancing the role of parents, and insisting on the use of approaches to improving student achievement that are based on sound research. This bill will help reduce the misidentification of students with disabilities and relieve the paperwork burden on teachers, allowing them to spend more time instructing and working with their students.

Authorization levels. The Administration is pleased that the bill authorizes discretionary rather than mandatory funding for the IDEA. This will enable the Administration and the Congress to review the appropriate funding level through the annual appropriations process, taking into account how the program is performing. The President's 2004 Budget for IDEA State Grants represents nearly a 50 percent increase in funding compared to 2001, signaling the Administration's strong commitment to increased funding for special education to ensure that students with disabilities receive a high-quality education.

Accountability for results. The Administration supports provisions of the bill that align State programs for children with disabilities with the accountability requirements of NCLB, emphasize the academic achievement of these children, and ensure that special education teachers are highly qualified in accordance with NCLB.

More flexibility and less paperwork. The Administration supports provisions that simplify the process for developing and revising individualized education programs (IEPs), which will free teachers to teach and substantially reduce IDEA paperwork burdens and the time spent on non-instructional duties, while preserving the important rights and protections for children with disabilities and their parents. The Administration also supports provisions in the bill that give States and school districts additional flexibility in educating children with disabilities, by permitting them to use IDEA funds for pre-referral

Illustration 4–1. Executive Office of the President, Statement of Administration Policy (Apr. 30, 2003).

108TH CONGRESS
1ST SESSION

H. R. 1350

To reauthorize the Individuals with Disabilities Education Act, and for other purposes.

IN THE HOUSE OF REPRESENTATIVES

MARCH 19, 2003

Mr. CASTLE (for himself, Mr. BOEHNER, Mr. BALLENGER, Mr. MCKEON, Mr. SAM JOHNSON of Texas, Mr. GREENWOOD, Mr. DEMINT, Mrs. BIGGERT, Mr. TIBERI, Mr. KELLER, Mr. WILSON of South Carolina, and Mr. COLE) introduced the following bill; which was referred to the Committee on Education and the Workforce

---

A BILL

To reauthorize the Individuals with Disabilities Education Act, and for other purposes.

1   *Be it enacted by the Senate and House of Representa-*

2 *tives of the United States of America in Congress assembled,*

3 **SECTION 1. SHORT TITLE.**

4   This Act may be cited as the "Improving Education

5 Results for Children With Disabilities Act of 2003".

Illustration 4–2. H.R. 1350, 108th Cong. (2003).

SPECIAL EDUCATION: IS IDEA WORKING AS CONGRESS INTENDED?

WEDNESDAY, FEBRUARY 28, 2001

HOUSE OF REPRESENTATIVES,
COMMITTEE ON GOVERNMENT REFORM,
Washington, DC.

The committee met, pursuant to notice, at 1:45 p.m., in room 2154, Rayburn House Office Building, Hon. Dan Burton (chairman of the committee) presiding.

Present: Representatives Burton, Morella, Shays, Horn, Barr, Davis, Platts, Weldon, Putnam, Schrock, Waxman, Owens, Maloney, Norton, Kucinich, Tierney, and Schakowsky.

Also present: Representatives Cunningham, Pence, and Sununu.

Staff present: Kevin Binger, staff director; Daniel R. Moll, deputy staff director; S. Elizabeth Clay, Nicole Petrosino, and Jen Klute, professional staff members; Marc Chretien, senior investigative counsel; Sarah Anderson, staff assistant; Robert A. Briggs, chief clerk; Robin Butler, office manager; Michael Canty and Toni Lightle, legislative assistants; John Sare, deputy chief clerk; Corinne Zaccagnini, systems administrator; Sarah Despres, minority counsel; Ellen Rayner, minority chief clerk; and Earley Green, minority assistant clerk.

Mr. BURTON. Good afternoon. A quorum being present, the Committee on Government Reform will come to order and I ask unanimous consent that all Members' and witnesses' written and opening statements be included in the record, and, without objection, so ordered.

I ask unanimous consent that all articles, exhibits and extraneous or tabular material referred to be included in the record, and, without objection, so ordered.

During the 106th Congress we began looking at the increased rates of autism. As we did that, we repeatedly heard from families that they were facing serious challenges obtaining services from their schools. Any family that is raising a child with a developmental delay or a learning disability or a physical disability faces tremendous challenges on a daily basis.

Through this investigation, we have already learned that families are physically, emotionally and financially exhausted. Why is it that when we have a Federal law that requires that every child receive a free and appropriate public education, many families are having to go to court to receive these services? And it's very costly.

The committee received thousands of e-mails, telephone calls, and letters and faxes from families, teachers, administrators and organizations about the implementation of the Individuals with

(1)

Illustration 4–3. *Special Education: Is IDEA Working as Congress Intended?: Hearing before the H. Comm. on Gov't Reform*, 107th Cong. 1 (2001).

Calendar No. 362

108TH CONGRESS *1st Session*	SENATE	REPORT 108–185

INDIVIDUALS WITH DISABILITIES EDUCATION ACT

NOVEMBER 3, 2003.—Ordered to be printed

Mr. GREGG, from the Committee on Health, Education, Labor, and
Pensions, submitted the following

R E P O R T

[To accompany S. 1248]

The Committee on Health, Education, Labor, and Pensions, to
which was referred the bill (S. 1248) to reauthorize the Individuals
with Disabilities Education Act, and for other purposes, having
considered the same, reports favorably thereon with an amendment
and recommends that the bill (as amended) do pass.

CONTENTS

I. INTRODUCTION

S. 1248 is the product of an extensive bipartisan effort among
Senators on the committee, as well as significant input from parents of children with disabilities, children with disabilities, edu-
cators, the U.S. Department of Education, and other individuals interested in improving the quality of education for children with disabilities. What makes this legislation unique is that it was bipartisan in its inception.

90–210

Illustration 4–4. S. Rep. No. 108–185 (2003).

S5394   CONGRESSIONAL RECORD — SENATE   *May 13, 2004*

INDIVIDUALS WITH DISABILITIES EDUCATION IMPROVEMENT ACT OF 2003

The PRESIDING OFFICER. Under the previous order, the Senate will resume consideration of S. 1248, which the clerk will report.

The assistant legislative clerk read as follows:

A bill (S. 1248) to reauthorize the Individuals with Disabilities Education Act, and for other purposes.

Pending:

Gregg (for Santorum) amendment No. 3149, to provide for a paperwork reduction demonstration.

AMENDMENT NO. 3150

Mr. GREGG. Senator KENNEDY and I have a number of technical and conforming amendments that have been cleared on both sides of the aisle and put into a managers' package. Therefore, I send an amendment to the desk and ask for its immediate consideration.

The PRESIDING OFFICER. Without objection, the pending amendment is set aside.

The clerk will report.

The legislative clerk read as follows:

The Senator from New Hampshire [Mr. GREGG], for himself and Mr. KENNEDY, proposes an amendment numbered 3150.

Mr. GREGG. I ask unanimous consent that the reading of the amendment be dispensed with.

The PRESIDING OFFICER. Without objection, it is so ordered.

The amendment is as follows:

(Purpose: To provide a manager's amendment)

On page 382, line 21, strike "or the postsurgical" and all that follows through page 383, line 2, and insert "or the replacement of such device.".

On page 398, line 21, strike "or the postsurgical" and all that follows through page 399, line 2, and insert "or the replacement of such device.".

On page 406, between lines 11 and 12, insert the following:

"SEC. 610. FREELY ASSOCIATED STATES.

"The Republic of the Marshall Islands, the Federated States of Micronesia, and the Republic of Palau shall continue to be eligible for competitive grants administered by the Secretary under this Act to the extent that such grants continue to be available to States and local educational agencies under this Act.

On page 451, line 19, strike the comma after "consult".

On page 453, line 25, strike "affirmations" and insert "affirmation".

On page 503, line 2, strike "educational".

On page 503, line 11, strike "educational".

On page 504, line 9, strike "educational".

On page 504, line 21, strike "educational".

On page 509, line 24, strike "preferral".

On page 515, strike lines 10 through 15, and insert the following:

"(ii) are provided and administered in the language and form most likely to yield accurate information on what the child knows and can do academically, developmentally, and functionally, unless it is not feasible to so provide or administer;".

On page 553, lines 13 and 14, strike *"statute of limitations"* and insert *"timeline"*.

On page 553, line 14, strike "statute of limitations" and insert "timeline".

On page 615, line 13, insert "and supervised" after "appropriately trained".

On page 664, lines 11 and 12, strike "administrators, principals, and teachers" and insert "personnel".

On page 669, line 10, strike "and" after the semicolon.

On page 669, line 17, strike the period and insert "; and".

On page 669, between lines 17 and 18, insert the following:

"(C) encourage collaborative and consultative models of providing early intervention, special education, and related services.

On page 671, line 8, strike "and administrators" and insert ", administrators, and, in appropriate cases, related services personnel".

On page 672, line 11, strike "providing" and insert "provide".

On page 672, line 14, strike "and" after the semicolon.

On page 672, line 17, strike the period and insert "; and".

On page 672, between lines 17 and 18, insert the following:

"(D) Train early intervention, preschool, and related services providers, and other relevant school personnel, in conducting effective individualized family service plan (IFSP) meetings.

On page 702, line 24, insert "early childhood providers," after "ability of".

On page 702, line 25, insert "related services personnel," after "administrators,".

On page 720, lines 5 and 6, strike "alternate" and insert "alternative".

On page 720, lines 22 and 23, strike *"Students With Significant Disabilities"* and insert *"Students Who Are Held to Alternate Achievement Standards"*.

On page 721, strike lines 1 through 3, and insert the following:

"(1) the criteria that States use to determine—

"(A) eligibility for alternate assessments; and

"(B) the number and type of children who take those assessments and are held accountable to alternate achievement standards;

On page 721, strike lines 6 through 8, and insert the following:

"(3) the alignment of alternate assessments and alternative achievement standards to State academic content standards in reading, mathematics, and science; and

On page 753, line 16, insert "(as appropriate when vocational goals are discussed)" after "participation".

On page 756, line 6, insert "vocational" after "school".

On page 756, line 7, insert "vocational" after "school".

On page 764, line 13, strike "(C)" and insert "(A)".

On page 766, after line 20, insert the following:

SEC. 302. NATIONAL BOARD FOR EDUCATION SCIENCES.

Section 116(c)(9) of the Education Sciences Reform Act of 2002 (20 U.S.C. 9516(c)(9)) is amended by striking the third sentence and inserting the following: "Meetings of the Board are subject to section 552b of title 5, United States Code (commonly referred to as the Government in the Sunshine Act).".

SEC. 303. REGIONAL ADVISORY COMMITTEES.

Section 206(d)(3) of the Education Sciences Reform Act of 2002 (20 U.S.C. 9605(d)(3)) is amended by striking "Academy" and inserting "Institute".

On page 777, after line 15, insert the following:

TITLE   —MISCELLANEOUS

SEC.   01. GAO REVIEW OF CHILD MEDICATION USAGE.

(a) REVIEW.—The Comptroller General shall conduct a review of—

(1) the extent to which personnel in schools actively influence parents in pursuing a diagnosis of attention deficit disorder and attention deficit hyperactivity disorder;

(2) the policies and procedures among public schools in allowing school personnel to distribute controlled substances; and

(3) the extent to which school personnel have required a child to obtain a prescription for substances covered by section 202(c) of the Controlled Substances Act (21 U.S.C. 812(c)) to treat attention deficit disorder, attention deficit hyperactivity disorder, or other attention deficit-related illnesses or disorders, in order to attend school or be evaluated for services under the Individuals with Disabilities Education Act.

(b) REPORT.—Not later than 1 year after the date of enactment of this Act, the Comptroller General shall prepare and submit to Congress a report that contains the results of the review under subsection (a).

Mr. GREGG. I ask unanimous consent that the Senate consider and agree to amendment No. 3150.

The PRESIDING OFFICER. The question is on agreeing to the amendment.

The amendment (No. 3150) was agreed to.

The PRESIDING OFFICER. The Senator from Massachusetts.

Mr. KENNEDY. A very brief word on the technical amendment, the managers' amendment. We give assurance to all of our colleagues that it is a technical amendment. All the matters that are in that managers' amendment are directly related to provisions in the legislation. I give the assurance to our colleagues that is the nature and description of the managers' amendment, and we appreciate their willingness to accept it.

We have several of our colleagues on their way over who wish to address the Senate on this issue. Then we will hopefully move along to final passage somewhere in the noon area.

Mr. GREGG. Mr. President, for Members' information, we expect to have a vote on final passage around 12:10. In fact, we may have a unanimous consent, although I will withhold that for a moment.

I ask unanimous consent that the time between now and 12:10 be equally divided between the sides.

The PRESIDING OFFICER. Without objection, it is so ordered.

Mr. GREGG. I suggest the absence of a quorum.

The PRESIDING OFFICER. The clerk will call the roll.

The legislative clerk proceeded to call the roll.

Mr. GREGG. Mr. President, I ask unanimous consent that the order for the quorum call be rescinded.

The PRESIDING OFFICER. Without objection, it is so ordered.

Mr. GREGG. Mr. President, I ask unanimous consent that once Senator SANTORUM's amendment is modified and we agree to it, at 12:10 today the Senate proceed to a vote on passage of H.R. 1350, with all provisions of the original agreement in place, and I ask for the yeas and nays.

The PRESIDING OFFICER. Without objection, it is so ordered.

Illustration 4–5. 150 CONG. REC. S9087 (daily ed. May 13, 2004).

Thursday, May 13, 2004

Daily Digest

HIGHLIGHTS

Senate passed H.R. 1350, Individuals with Disabilities Act.

The House passed H.R. 4275, to amend the Internal Revenue Code of 1986 to permanently extend the 10-percent individual income tax rate bracket.

The House passed H.R. 4281, Small Business Health Fairness Act of 2004.

Senate

Chamber Action

Routine Proceedings, pages S5383–S5486

Measures Introduced: Nine bills and three resolutions were introduced, as follows: S. 2415–2423, and S. Res. 360–362.   **Page S5472**

Measures Reported:

S. 2238, to amend the National Flood Insurance Act of 1968 to reduce losses to properties for which repetitive flood insurance claim payments have been made, with amendments. (S. Rept. No. 108–262)

S. 1164, to provide for the development and coordination of a comprehensive and integrated United States research program that assists the people of the United States and the world to understand, assess, and predict human-induced and natural processes of abrupt climate change. (S. Rept. No. 108–263)

S. 1721, to amend the Indian Land Consolidation Act to improve provisions relating to probate of trust and restricted land, with an amendment in the nature of a substitute. (S. Rept. No. 108–264)

S. Res. 331, designating June 2004 as "National Safety Month".

S. 1609, to make aliens ineligible to receive visas and exclude aliens from admission into the United States for nonpayment of child support, with an amendment in the nature of a substitute. **Page S5472**

Measures Passed:

IDEA Reauthorization: Committee on Health, Education, Labor and Pensions was discharged from further consideration of H.R. 1350, to reauthorize the Individuals with Disabilities Education Act, and by 95 yeas to 3 nays (Vote No. 94), Senate passed the bill, after striking all after the enacting clause and inserting in lieu thereof, the text of S. 1248, Senate companion measure, and after taking action on the following amendments proposed thereto:

     Pages S5394–S5411

Adopted:

Gregg/Kennedy Amendment No. 3150, to provide a manager's amendment. **Page S5394**

Gregg (for Santorum) Modified Amendment No. 3149, to provide for a paperwork reduction demonstration. **Pages S5406–10**

Subsequently, S. 1248 was returned to the calendar. **Page S5411**

Department of Defense Authorization Act—Agreement: A unanimous-consent agreement was reached providing for the consideration of S. 2400, to authorize appropriations for fiscal year 2005 for military activities of the Department of Defense, for military construction, and for defense activities of the Department of Energy, to prescribe personnel strengths for such fiscal year for the Armed Services, at 2:30 p.m., on Monday, May 17, 2004. **Page S5485**

Service Medals Act—Agreement: A unanimous-consent agreement was reached providing that, at a time determined by the Majority Leader, after consultation with the Democratic Leader, Senate begin consideration of H.R. 3104, to provide for the establishment of separate campaign medals to be awarded to members of the uniformed services who participate in Operation Enduring Freedom and to members of the uniformed services who participate in Operation Iraqi Freedom, on Tuesday, May 18, 2004, and that there be 20 minutes for debate and Senate then vote on final passage of the bill.

     Page S5485

D497

Illustration 4–6. Daily Digest, 150 CONG. REC. D497 (daily ed. May 13, 2004).

like their fellow classmates. Children with disabilities deserve high hopes, high expectations, and extra help.

In the bill I sign today, we're raising expectations for the students. We're giving schools and parents the tools they need to meet them. We're applying the reforms of the No Child Left Behind Act to the Individuals with Disabilities Education Improvement Act so schools are accountable for teaching every single child. All our students deserve excellent teachers, so this law ensures that students with disabilities will have special education teachers with the skills and training to teach special education and their subject area.

Some students with disabilities will need intensive, individualized help. So this law, for the first time, will support tutoring programs to help children in schools that need improvement. When schools are so busy trying to deal with unnecessary and costly lawsuits, they have less time to spend with students. So we're creating opportunities for parents and teachers to resolve problems early. We're making the system less litigious so it can focus on the children and their parents.

The people who care most about the students are, of course, the teachers and especially the parents, who know their needs and know their names. So we're giving more flexibility and control over the students' education to parents and teachers and principals. We'll make sure that parents and schools can change a student's educational program to better meet their needs, without having to attend unnecessary meetings or complete unnecessary paperwork. We trust the local folks to meet high standards for all our kids, and this bill gives them the freedom and flexibility to meet our goals.

All students in America can learn. That's what all of us up here believe. All of us understand we have an obligation to make sure no child is left behind in America. So I'm honored to sign the Individuals with Disabilities Education Improvement Act of 2004, and once again thank the Members for being here.

NOTE: The President spoke at 10:20 a.m. in Room 350 of the Dwight D. Eisenhower Executive Office Building. In his remarks, he referred to Eunice Kennedy Shriver, founder, Special Olympics.

At the time of publication, H.R. 1350, approved December 3, had not been received by the Office of the Federal Register for assignment of a Public Law number.

Statement on Signing the Individuals with Disabilities Education Improvement Act of 2004

December 3, 2004

Today, I have signed into law H.R. 1350, the "Individuals with Disabilities Education Improvement Act of 2004." The Act strengthens the ability of the Federal Government to assist States in the education of children with disabilities.

The executive branch shall construe provisions of the Act that require taking account of race, culture, gender, age, region, socioeconomics, ideology, secularity, and partisan politics, including sections 612, 616, 618, 637, 663, 664, and 681 of the Individuals with Disabilities Education Act, as enacted by section 101 of the Act, and section 177(b)(3) of the Education Sciences Reform Act of 2002, as enacted by section 201(a)(2) of the Act, in a manner consistent with the First Amendment and the requirement of the Due Process Clause of the Fifth Amendment to the Constitution to afford equal protection of the laws.

The executive branch shall construe section 615(e)(2)(G) of the Individuals with Disabilities Education Act, as enacted by section 101 of the Act, as establishing a duty for a State to follow the specified statutory exclusionary rule only when that duty is a condition of a Federal grant or contract accepted by or under the authority of that State, as is consistent with the principles governing Federal-State relations enunciated by the Supreme Court of the United States in *Printz* v. *United States.*

George W. Bush

The White House,
December 3, 2004.

NOTE: At the time of publication, H.R. 1350, approved December 3, had not been received by the Office of the Federal Register for assignment of a Public Law number.

Illustration 4–7. 40 WEEKLY COMP. PRES. DOC. 2898 (Dec. 3, 2004).

PUBLIC LAW 108–446—DEC. 3, 2004   118 STAT. 2647

Public Law 108–446
108th Congress

An Act

To reauthorize the Individuals with Disabilities Education Act, and for other purposes.

Dec. 3, 2004
[H.R. 1350]

Individuals with
Disabilities
Education
Improvement Act
of 2004.
20 USC 1400
note.

Be it enacted by the Senate and House of Representatives of the United States of America in Congress assembled,

SECTION 1. SHORT TITLE.

This Act may be cited as the "Individuals with Disabilities Education Improvement Act of 2004".

SEC. 2. ORGANIZATION OF THE ACT.

This Act is organized into the following titles:
Title I—Amendments to the Individuals With Disabilities Education Act.
Title II—National Center for Special Education Research.
Title III—Miscellaneous Provisions.

TITLE I—AMENDMENTS TO THE INDIVIDUALS WITH DISABILITIES EDUCATION ACT

SEC. 101. AMENDMENTS TO THE INDIVIDUALS WITH DISABILITIES EDUCATION ACT.

Parts A through D of the Individuals with Disabilities Education Act (20 U.S.C. 1400 et seq.) are amended to read as follows:

"PART A—GENERAL PROVISIONS

"SEC. 601. SHORT TITLE; TABLE OF CONTENTS; FINDINGS; PURPOSES.   20 USC 1400.

"(a) SHORT TITLE.—This title may be cited as the 'Individuals with Disabilities Education Act'.
"(b) TABLE OF CONTENTS.—The table of contents for this title is as follows:

Illustration 4–8. Individuals with Disabilities Education Improvement Act of 2004, Pub. L. No. 108–446, 118 Stat. 2647.

MAJOR ACTIONS: o⁰☰

3/19/2003	Introduced in House
4/29/2003	Reported (Amended) by the Committee on Education and the Workforce. H. Rept. 108-77.
4/30/2003	Passed/agreed to in House: On passage Passed by the Yeas and Nays: 251 - 171 (Roll no. 154).
5/13/2004	Senate Committee on Health, Education, Labor, and Pensions discharged by Unanimous Consent.
5/13/2004	Passed/agreed to in Senate: Passed Senate H.R. 1350 in lieu of S. 1248 with an amendment by Yea-Nay Vote. 95 - 3. Record Vote Number: 94.
11/17/2004	Conference report H. Rept. 108-779 filed.
11/19/2004	Conference report agreed to in House: On agreeing to the conference report Agreed to by the Yeas and Nays: 397 - 3 (Roll no. 537).
11/19/2004	Conference report agreed to in Senate: Senate agreed to conference report by Unanimous Consent Vote.
11/19/2004	Cleared for White House.
11/30/2004	Presented to President.
12/3/2004	Signed by President.
12/3/2004	Became Public Law No: 108-446 [Text, PDF]

ALL ACTIONS:

3/19/2003:
Referred to the House Committee on Education and the Workforce.
3/24/2003:
Referred to the Subcommittee on Education Reform.
4/2/2003:
Subcommittee Consideration and Mark-up Session Held.
4/2/2003:
Forwarded by Subcommittee to Full Committee (Amended) by Voice Vote.
4/10/2003:
Committee Consideration and Mark-up Session Held.
4/10/2003:
Ordered to be Reported (Amended) by the Yeas and Nays: 29 - 19.
3/20/2003:
Sponsor introductory remarks on measure. (CR E527)
4/29/2003 3:23pm:
Reported (Amended) by the Committee on Education and the Workforce. H. Rept. 108-77.
4/29/2003 3:23pm:

Illustration 4–9. THOMAS Bill Summary and Status, H.R. 1350, 108th Cong. (2004) <thomas.loc.gov>.

Public Law 108-446　　　　　　　　　　　　　　　　　**118 Stat. 2647**

Individuals with Disabilities Education Improvement Act of 2004

December 3, 2004

Public Law

1.1　Public Law 108-446, approved Dec. 3, 2004. (H.R. 1350)

(CIS04:PL108-446　162 p.)

"To reauthorize the Individuals with Disabilities Education Act, and for other purposes."

Amends the Individuals with Disabilities Education Act (IDEA) and other acts to authorize FY2005-FY2010 appropriations for and revise IDEA programs, under which the Department of Education provides grants to State and local agencies for the education of children with disabilities.

Authorizes the Department of Education to create a pilot program in fifteen States to reduce the individualized education plans (IEP) paperwork burden on teachers in order to increase instructional time and resources and improve results for students with disabilities.

Authorizes States to establish risk pool funds to assist school districts in serving high-need children with disabilities or meeting unanticipated special education costs.

Revises requirements for IEP for disabled children to specifically address each child's academic achievement.

Clarifies responsibilities of local educational agencies to ensure that services to handicapped children placed in private schools are provided equitably.

Revises procedures regarding administrative review of IDEA-related complaints, and modifies requirements governing disciplinary actions against disabled students.

Establishes a National Center for Special Education Research within the Department of Education Institute of Education Sciences, and authorizes creation of a Commissioner for Special Education Research.

P.L. 108-446 Reports

108th Congress

2.1　H. Rpt. 108-77 on H.R. 1350, "Improving Education Results for Children with Disabilities Act of 2003," Apr. 29, 2003.

(CIS03:H343-6　384 p.)
(Y1.1/8:108-77.)

Recommends passage, with an amendment in the nature of a substitute, of H.R. 1350, the Improving Education Results for Children with Disabilities Act of 2003, to amend the Individuals with Disabilities Education Act (IDEA) to extend through FY2009 and revise programs authorized under IDEA, under which the Department of Education provides grants to State and local agencies for the education of children with disabilities.

Includes provisions to:

a.　Require that States align their accountability systems for students with disabilities to the accountability system included in the No Child Left Behind Act.

b.　Require that each child's Individualized Education Plan (IEP) specifically address that child's academic achievement.

c.　Establish a National Center for Special Education Research within the Department of Education Institute of Education Sciences and authorize creation of a Commissioner for Special Education Research.

d.　Consolidate all education research at the Department of Education under the Institute of Education Sciences.

e.　Authorize the Department of Education to create a pilot program in ten States to reduce the IEP paperwork burden on teachers in order to increase instructional time and resources and improve results for students with disabilities.

f.　Allow local educational agencies to use up to 15% of their funds for prereferral services for students before they are identified as needing special education.

g.　Require local educational agencies with significant overidentification of minority students to operate prereferral programs that work to reduce overidentification.

h.　Allow parents and the local educational agencies to support their charter schools equitably.

Includes minority views (p. 377-384).

2.2　S. Rpt. 108-185 on S. 1248, "Individuals with Disabilities Education Act," Nov. 3, 2003.

(CIS03:S433-13　357 p.)
(Y1.1/5:108-185.)

Recommends passage with an amendment of S. 1248, the Individuals with Disabilities Education Improvement Act of 2003, to amend the Individuals with Disabilities Education Act (IDEA) and three other acts to extend and revise programs authorized under IDEA, under which the Department of Education provides grants to State and local agencies for the education of children with disabilities.

Includes provisions to:

a.　Require States to establish risk pool funds to assist school districts in serving high-need children with disabilities or meeting unanticipated special education costs.

b.　Clarify responsibilities of local educational agencies to ensure that services to handicapped children placed in private schools are provided equitably.

c.　Align the accountability system for students with disabilities with the accountability system included in the No Child Left Behind Act.

d.　Ensure that public charter schools are treated equitably by local educational agencies in the provision of IDEA funds and services.

e.　Allow local educational agencies to use up to 15% of their funds for prereferral services for students before they are identified as needing special education.

f.　Revise requirements for individualized education programs (IEPs) for disabled children, and streamline IEP paperwork.

g.　Revise procedures regarding administrative review of IDEA-related complaints, and modify requirements governing disciplinary actions against disabled students.

h.　Improve and expand vocational rehabilitation services to students with disabilities during their transition to postsecondary education and employment.

i.　Establish a National Center for Special Education Research within the Department of Education Institute of Education Sciences, and authorize creation of a Commissioner for Special Education Research.

Illustration 4-10. 2004 CIS/INDEX ANNUAL: LEGISLATIVE
HISTORIES OF US PUBLIC LAWS 507 (2005).

INDIVIDUALS WITH DISABILITIES EDUCATION IMPROVEMENT ACT OF 2004

PUBLIC LAW 108–446, see page 118 Stat. 2647

DATES OF CONSIDERATION AND PASSAGE

House: April 30, 2003

Senate: May 13, 2004

Cong. Record Vol. 150 (2004)

**House Report (Education and the Workforce Committee)
No. 108–77, April 29, 2003
[To accompany H.R. 1350]**

**House Conference Report
No. 108–779, November 17, 2004
[To accompany H.R. 1350]**

The House Conference Report is set out below.

HOUSE CONFERENCE REPORT 108–779

[page 1]

* * * * * * * * * *

[page 167]

JOINT EXPLANATORY STATEMENT OF THE COMMITTEE
OF CONFERENCE

The managers on the part of the House and the Senate at the conference on the disagreeing votes of the two Houses on the amendment of the Senate to the bill (H.R. 1350), an Act to reauthorize the Individuals with Disabilities Education Act, and for other purposes, submit the following joint statement to the House and the Senate in explanation of the effect of the action agreed upon by managers and recommended in the accompanying conference report:

RECOMMENDATIONS

Enacting Clause, Short Title, and Organization

(1) The House bill and Senate amendment have different titles and different organization systems.

2480

Illustration 4–11. H. Conf. Rep. No. 108–77, *as reprinted in* 2004 U.S.C.C.A.N. 2480.

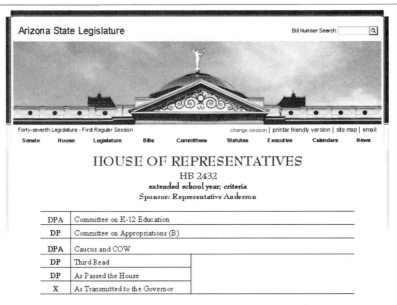

Arizona State Legislature

Bill Number Search:

Forty-seventh Legislature - First Regular Session　　　change session | printer friendly version | site map | email

Senate　　House　　Legislature　　Bills　　Committees　　Statutes　　Executive　　Calendars　　News

HOUSE OF REPRESENTATIVES
HB 2432
extended school year; criteria
Sponsor: Representative Anderson

DPA	Committee on K-12 Education
DP	Committee on Appropriations (B)
DPA	Caucus and COW
DP	Third Read
DP	As Passed the House
X	As Transmitted to the Governor

HB 2432 changes the criteria for determining the need and eligibility of a pupil with disabilities for extended school year services.

History

Currently, A.R.S. Section 15-881 requires a school district to provide a pupil with disabilities an extended school year program in order prevent harm to the pupil's ability to maintain skills or behavior and to accommodate critical learning periods for pupils who may not receive another opportunity to learn targeted skills or behavior.

Arizona Administrative Code, R7-2-408, allows for the Individualized Education Program Team to determine the eligibility of a pupil for an extended school year program using the criteria set by A.R.S. Section 15-881. This includes taking into account regression and recoupment factors, critical learning stages, least restrictive environment considerations, teacher and parent interviews and recommendations, data-based observations of the pupil, considerations of the pupil's previous history and parental skills and abilities. The decision to be placed into an extended school year program should not be based on a need or desire for a day care service, a program to maximize the pupil's academic potential or a summer recreation program for pupils with a disability. Eligibility for an extended school year program must be determined no later than 45 days before the last day of the school year.

Provisions

　Requires a school district to provide a pupil with disabilities extended school year services if the benefits the pupil gained during the regular school year would be significantly jeopardize or the pupil would experience significant regression that would seriously impede the pupil's progress towards educational goals.

　Changes extended school year programs to extended school year services.

　Changes the criteria for determining the eligibility of a pupil for extended school year services to consist of least restrictive environment considerations and retrospective and predictive data, by an expert and empirical data is not

Illustration 4–12. House Summary, HB 2432, 47th leg., 1st sess. (Mar. 31, 2005), Arizona State Legislature <www.azleg.gov>.

Chapter 5

THE EXECUTIVE BRANCH

Table of Sections

The executive is one of the three coordinate branches of government, but historically its lawmaking role was limited to orders and regulations needed to carry out the legislature's mandates. With the modern growth of government bureaucracy, however, the rules created by executive agencies can be legal sources with pervasive impact. In many aspects of modern society, administrative law plays a powerful role and can be more immediately relevant to day-to-day legal practice than either statutory or judge-made law.[1]

Several major treatises are published on administrative law. They focus primarily on judicial review of agency decisionmaking,

---

1. Recognizing this, some law schools have started making administrative law a required component of the first-year law school curriculum. Richard B. Stewart, *On the "Administrative and Regulatory State" Course at N.Y.U. Law*, 7 N.Y.U. J. Legis. & Pub. Pol'y 39 (2003).

but most also cover topics such as historical developments, rule-making and adjudication procedures, and access to government information. The most frequently cited work in the field is Richard J. Pierce, Jr., *Administrative Law Treatise* (4th ed. 2002–date) and its earlier editions. The treatise's original author, Kenneth Culp Davis (1908–2003), is generally considered the founding father of administrative law.[2]

Two other multi-volume treatises are Charles H. Koch, Jr., *Administrative Law and Practice* (2d ed. 1997–date), and Jacob A. Stein, Glenn A. Mitchell & Basil J. Mezines, *Administrative Law* (1977–date). The Koch treatise is available on Westlaw (ADMLP database), and the Stein, Mitchell & Mezines treatise on Lexis. Single-volume texts written specifically for student use include Alfred C. Aman, Jr. & William T. Mayton, *Administrative Law* (2d ed. 2001) (Westlaw ADMINLAW–HB) and Richard J. Pierce, Jr., Sidney A. Shapiro & Paul R. Verkuil, *Administrative Law and Process* (4th ed. 2004).

Two sets focus on procedural aspects of administrative practice. *West's Federal Administrative Practice* (3d & 4th eds. 1996–date) is arranged by subject, with chapters devoted to practice before specific federal agencies, and includes forms as well as explanatory text. The voluminous *Federal Procedure, Lawyers Edition* (1981–date) provides guidance on practice before agencies and in court, and its accompanying set *Federal Procedural Forms, Lawyers Edition* (1975–date) includes numerous examples of official agency forms in addition to court documents. All three of these works are available on Westlaw, as the WEST–FDADM, FEDPROC, and FEDPROF databases respectively.

The leading specialized journal in the field is *Administrative Law Review*, published by American University in conjunction with the American Bar Association's Section of Administrative Law and Regulatory Practice. The ABA also publishes an annual *Developments in Administrative Law and Regulatory Practice*; the first part of each volume provides a general survey of recent developments in areas such as government information, judicial review, and regulatory policy, while the second part focuses on specific areas such as antitrust, energy, and homeland security.

Federal Administrative Procedure Sourcebook (4th ed. 2008), another ABA publication, is a thick paperback containing the texts of major statutes in the area, accompanied by related materials such as the *Attorney General's Manual on the Administrative Proce-*

---

2. On Davis's death, the chairman of the ABA administrative law section, William Funk, said that his "shadow falls over virtually all that administrative lawyers do. To say he was a giant in his field is like saying Mount Everest is a big mountain." Jack Williams, *Kenneth Culp Davis, 94; Pioneer in Administrative Law*, SAN DIEGO UNION-TRIBUNE, Sept. 19, 2003, at B–5.

dure Act (originally published in 1947), executive orders, and major guidance documents. Each of its twenty chapters begins with a brief overview, notes on legislative history, and a bibliography of government documents, books and articles.

Like these reference texts, most of this chapter focuses on the work of the federal government. States have executive offices and administrative agencies that operate much like their federal counterparts, but variations from state to state make generalizations difficult. States also delegate lawmaking responsibilities to counties and cities, which enact ordinances and have their own local agencies. While federal administrative law is relatively easy to research, state and local sources can be difficult to locate and even harder to update.

§ 5.1   The Presidency

Article II, section 1 of the Constitution begins simply: "The executive Power shall be vested in a President of the United States of America." The president has the power to veto legislation passed by Congress and the duty to enforce enacted laws, and supervises the workings of the departments and administrative agencies. The president also has a wide-ranging lawmaking authority in his or her own right, as the nation's agent of foreign relations and its military commander. In fulfilling these roles and functions, the president issues executive orders, proclamations, and other documents of legal effect.

Background information on the presidency is available in numerous sources. Two of the more comprehensive and focused reference works are *Encyclopedia of the American Presidency* (Leonard W. Levy & Louis Fisher eds., 1993) and *Guide to the Presidency* (Michael Nelson ed., 4th ed. 2008). Both of these works cover a wide range of political and historical aspects of the presidency. *Encyclopedia of the American Presidency* is arranged alphabetically, with more than 1,000 articles by leading scholars, while *Guide to the Presidency* is arranged topically into seven broad parts covering issues such as presidential powers (Part III) and relations with Congress, the Supreme Court, and the federal bureaucracy (Part VI). Both works include reference materials such as tables listing cabinet members and other presidential appointees.

Presidential lawmaking power more specifically is discussed in several recent works, many of which focus on perceived excesses of the second Bush administration. Harold J. Krent, *Presidential Powers* (2005) provides an overview of the executive's various powers and authorities, and Steven G. Calabresi & Christopher S. Yoo, *The Unitary Executive: Presidential Power from Washington to*

Bush (2008) surveys the practices of each of the first forty-three presidents.

(a) Executive Orders and Proclamations

Two basic forms of executive fiat are used to perform presidential functions pursuant to statutory authority or inherent powers. These are *executive orders* and *proclamations*. Executive orders are generally issued to government officials and cover a wide range of topics, while proclamations are general announcements of policy issued to the nation as a whole. Proclamations are commonly associated with ceremonial occasions such as observance of National School Lunch Week,[3] but a few substantive proclamations deal with trade policy or tariff issues. The two types of document have substantially the same legal effect.[4]

Executive orders and proclamations are published in the *Federal Register*, the U.S. government's official daily publication. They are numbered sequentially as they are issued, in separate series, and these numbers are the official and permanent means of identifying the documents.[5]

Presidential documents in the *Federal Register* since 1994 are available online from GPO Access <www.gpoaccess.gov/fr/>, and Westlaw and Lexis include them in their *Federal Register* databases back to the early 1980s. Westlaw also has a separate PRES database with executive orders since 1936 and other presidential documents since 1984, and Lexis has executive orders since 1980.

At the end of each year executive orders and proclamations are compiled and published as Title 3 of the *Code of Federal Regulations* (*CFR*), the annual codification of agency rules in force. This becomes the standard source for these documents.[6] Documents

---

3. See, e.g., Proclamation No. 8304, 73 Fed. Reg. 61,649 (Oct. 10, 2008).

4. Presidential use of executive orders has been the focus of several recent books, including KENNETH R. MAYER, WITH THE STROKE OF A PEN: EXECUTIVE ORDERS AND PRESIDENTIAL POWER (2001) and ADAM L. WARBER, EXECUTIVE ORDERS AND THE MODERN PRESIDENCY: LEGISLATING FROM THE OVAL OFFICE (2006). PHILLIP J. COOPER, BY ORDER OF THE PRESIDENT: THE USE AND ABUSE OF EXECUTIVE DIRECT ACTION (2002) discusses executive orders as well as other lawmaking procedures such as proclamations, presidential memoranda, national security directives, and signing statements. Two Congressional Research Service publications also provide background information. JOHN CONTRUBIS, EXECUTIVE ORDERS AND PROCLAMATIONS (1999)

(CRS Report 95–772 A) <www.llsdc.org/sourcebook/docs/CRS-95–772.pdf> focuses on the two major types of documents, and HAROLD C. RELYEA, PRESIDENTIAL DIRECTIVES: BACKGROUND AND OVERVIEW (2008) (CRS Report 98–611 GOV) <www.fas.org/sgp/crs/misc/98–611.pdf> provides a broader overview of several presidential lawmaking instruments.

5. Executive orders and proclamations by the current president are also posted on the White House website <www.whitehouse.gov/briefing_room/PresidentialActions/>, but these are issued as press releases and do not have the document numbers or *Federal Register* citations necessary for citation.

6. Both *The Bluebook* and the *ALWD Citation Manual* require citation to *CFR* if a document appears there, or

from the years 1936 to 1975 have been recompiled into multiyear hardcover editions, and all volumes from 1936 through 2001 are available online as part of HeinOnline's U.S. Presidential Library <www.heinonline.org>.

The American Presidency Project at the University of California, Santa Barbara <www.presidency.ucsb.edu> provides free online access to executive orders dating back to 1826 and proclamations back to 1789, as well as a wide range of other documents such as public papers, signing statements, inaugural addresses, and State of the Union messages. The Project's homepage provides a range of options for searching or browsing these materials.[7]

The Office of the Federal Register website has a disposition table of all executive orders since 1937 <www.archives.gov/federal-register/executive-orders/>, with information on their amendment, revocation, and current status. For executive orders since 1993, the site also includes subject indexes and links to the full text of documents.

Many executive orders are also reprinted in the notes following related sections of the *United States Code*. This is an important source, if only because *The Bluebook* requires a parallel U.S.C. citation "whenever possible."[8] Tables in each version of the code list presidential documents by number and indicate where they can be found.[9]

Coverage of proclamations and executive orders is included in KeyCite and Shepard's (in print in *Shepard's Code of Federal*

to the *Federal Register* if not. THE BLUE-BOOK: A UNIFORM SYSTEM OF CITATION R. 14.7, at 127 (18th ed. 2005); ALWD CITATION MANUAL: A PROFESSIONAL SYSTEM OF CITATION R. 19.9(c), at 176 (3d ed. 2006).

7. Older documents can also be found in the *CIS Index to Presidential Executive Orders and Proclamations* (covering 1787–1983, and accompanied by a microfiche set of all documents indexed) and *CIS Federal Register Index* (1984–98). HeinOnline provides access to two earlier guides, *Presidential Executive Orders* (1944) and *List and Index of Presidential Executive Orders: Unnumbered Series (1789–1941)* (1943).

8. THE BLUEBOOK: A UNIFORM SYSTEM OF CITATION R. 14.7, at 127 (18th ed. 2005). The *ALWD Citation Manual* says you "may include" a parallel citation. ALWD CITATION MANUAL: A PROFESSIONAL SYSTEM OF CITATION R. 19.9(g), at 173 (2d ed. 2003).

9. Executive orders and proclamations are also reprinted in numerical order in *U.S. Code Congressional and Administrative News* and *USCS Advance*. USCCAN bound volumes have reprinted all orders and proclamations since 1943. Proclamations, but not executive orders, are also printed in *Statutes at Large* (with retrospective coverage back to 1791 in an appendix in volume eleven).

In 1990 the Office of the Federal Register published a *Codification of Presidential Proclamations and Executive Orders,* which arranged proclamations and orders into fifty titles by subject. It contained executive orders and proclamations of general applicability and continuing effect issued from January 20, 1961 to January 20, 1989, with amendments incorporated into the texts of documents. A searchable version of this publication is available online <www.archives.gov/federal-register/codification/>.

Regulations Citations). Shepard's provides references to citing court decisions and law review articles, while KeyCite's more extensive coverage adds amendments and citations in administrative materials and court documents.

(b) Other Presidential Documents

While executive orders and proclamations are the most usual forms of presidential directives, a variety of other presidential documents have legal effect. The president issues administrative orders, transmits messages to Congress, and makes executive agreements with other countries.

Memoranda and Directives. A variety of other documents are printed in the *Federal Register* along with executive orders and proclamations, but not included in either numbered series. Presidential determinations pursuant to specific statutory mandates are issued in a numbered series, and unnumbered documents include various memoranda and notices. Many of these documents deal with foreign affairs. They are reprinted in the annual cumulation of 3 C.F.R. in a separate section following executive orders.

Some presidential directives relating to national security issues are not published in the *Federal Register* or *CFR*. The Federal Register Act requires only that proclamations and executive orders be published,[10] so other documents can be used to advance presidential goals without being published. These range in name from Homeland Security Presidential Directives to Presidential Decision Directives.[11]

Reorganization Plans. A reorganization plan consisting of a presidential proposal to transfer or abolish agency functions was a mechanism used from 1946 to 1979. Several major agencies, including the Environmental Protection Agency and the Department of Health, Education and Welfare, were initially created by reorganization plans.

A reorganization plan became law automatically unless either chamber of Congress passed a resolution disapproving it, but in 1983 the Supreme Court found such one-house legislative vetoes to

---

10. 44 U.S.C. § 1505(a) (2000).

11. "Presidents have learned since at least the Truman administration that, by using labels other than those specified in the Federal Register Act, they can avoid publication of statements issued with the formal authority of the presidency behind them." Phillip J. Cooper, *Power Tools for an Effective and Responsible Presidency*, 29 ADMIN. & SOC'Y 529, 544 (1997). The Federation of American Scientists Intelligence Resource Program has a website <www. fas.org/irp/offdocs/direct.htm> focusing on presidential directives on foreign affairs and intelligence, listing the designations and directives used by presidents since Truman and providing links to many of the documents. Some of President George W. Bush's directives have been printed in H. COMM. ON HOMELAND SECURITY, 110TH CONG., COMPILATION OF HOMELAND SECURITY PRESIDENTIAL DIRECTIVES (HPSD) (Comm. Print 2008).

be unconstitutional.[12] The following year Congress enacted a law ratifying and affirming each reorganization plan implemented to that date, and providing that reorganization plans could only take effect if transmitted to Congress by the end of 1984.[13] Older reorganization plans, however, remain relevant in interpreting the scope of agency authority.

Reorganization plans were designated by year and plan number within that year, and were published in the *Federal Register,* in Title 3 of *CFR,* and in the *Statutes at Large.*[14] Many are reprinted in all three versions of the *United States Code* (in appendices to title 5 in the *U.S. Code* and *USCA,* and following 5 U.S.C.S. § 903). *USCA* and *USCS* include notes, presidential messages, and executive orders relating to the plans, and are therefore often the most useful research sources.

Messages to Congress. Communications to Congress by the president are typically made in the form of presidential messages. These may propose new legislation, explain vetoes, transmit reports or other documents, or convey information about the state of national affairs or some matter of concern. Messages are published in the *Congressional Record* and as House Documents. Messages proposing legislation may have some value in determining the intent of laws that are enacted as a result.

Presidential statements upon signing legislation into law have been discussed in the preceding chapter, at pages 125–126. These often provide the president's interpretation of ambiguous or disputed provisions. Their relevance in legislative history research is controversial, but they certainly provide guidance to executive agencies in how to carry out their duties under newly enacted legislation.

Executive Agreements. The president makes agreements with other countries, under the authority to conduct foreign affairs. Unlike treaties, they do not require the advice and consent of the Senate. In recent years, more and more diplomatic arrangements have been made through these convenient methods. Because their purposes and publication methods are basically the same as trea-

---

12. *Immigration and Naturalization Service v. Chadha,* 462 U.S. 919 (1983).

13. Reorganization Act Amendments of 1984, Pub. L. No. 98–614, § 2(a), 98 Stat. 3192, 3193 (codified at 5 U.S.C. § 905(b) (2006)). A lone exception since 1984 is Reorganization Plan for the Department of Homeland Security, H.R. Doc. No. 108–16 (2003), which was mandated by the Homeland Securi-

ty Act of 2002, Pub. L. No. 107–296, § 1502, 116 Stat. 2135, 2308. Congress expressly exempted this plan from § 905(b)'s prohibition.

14. When submitted to Congress, reorganization plans were printed in the *Congressional Record* and in the House and Senate Documents series. These are the best sources for plans rejected by Congress.

ties, the two forms of international agreement will be discussed together in Chapter 13.

(c) Compilations of Presidential Papers

The most comprehensive source for current presidential material is the *Daily Compilation of Presidential Documents* <www. gpoaccess.gov/presdocs/>, which succeeded the *Weekly Compilation of Presidential Documents* in January 2009.[15] The *Daily Compilation* includes nominations, announcements, and transcripts of speeches and press conferences, as well as orders, proclamations, signing statements, and other legally significant documents. *Daily Compilation* and *Weekly Compilation* issues are available in PDF on GPO Access back to 1993, and HeinOnline has comprehensive coverage back to the first *Weekly Compilation* volume in 1965. Westlaw's WCPD database goes back to 2000.

Public Papers of the Presidents is an official publication cumulating the contents of the daily or weekly *Compilation of Presidential Documents.* Series of annual volumes have been published for Herbert Hoover and for all presidents after Franklin D. Roosevelt.[16] The official set contains only annual indexes, but the commercially published *Cumulated Indexes to the Public Papers of the Presidents of the United States* (1977–date) provides single-volume coverage of each administration. GPO Access provides online access to the *Public Papers* since 1991 <www.gpoaccess.gov/pubpapers/>, and Lexis coverage goes back to 1979. The American Presidency Project at UC Santa Barbara and HeinOnline's U.S. Presidential Library both have the complete retrospective collection since 1929, as well as materials from Roosevelt and earlier presidents.

§ 5.2   Federal Agencies

Fifteen cabinet departments and dozens of independent agencies, boards, commissions, and advisory committees report to the president.[17] Although executive agencies have existed in this coun-

---

15. Availability and Official Status of Presidential Documents, 74 Fed. Reg. 3950 (Jan. 21, 2009) (codified in various sections of 1 C.F.R.).

16. While Franklin D. Roosevelt's papers have not been included in the official series, they were commercially published as *The Public Papers and Addresses of Franklin D. Roosevelt* (Samuel I. Rosenman ed., 1938–50). The papers of earlier presidents are available in various forms. A comprehensive official collection was published at the end of the nineteenth century, *A Compilation of the Messages and Papers of the Presi-*

dents, 1789–1897 (James D. Richardson ed., 1896–99); several later editions under the same title were commercially published, updating the set into the 1920s.

17. Cabinet departments and independent agencies operate under similar legal principles and create law in similar ways. The main distinction between the forms of organization is the degree of insulation from direct presidential supervision. See Dominique Custos, *The Rulemaking Power of Independent Regulatory Agencies*, 54 Am. J. Comp. L. 615 (2006).

try since its creation,[18] the real growth of administrative law began in the late nineteenth century as the government sought to deal with the increasingly complex problems of industrialized society. The existing executive offices were not equipped to handle the administration of new social and economic legislation; Congress could not legislate the detailed requirements of complex industrial activities; and the courts could not cope with the mass of adjudication required to enforce the legislative and regulatory standards. The creation of new independent regulatory commissions and the expansion of existing agencies provided the expertise and specialization necessary for these tasks. The first of these new agencies was the Interstate Commerce Commission, created in 1887 to administer the Interstate Commerce Act.[19]

Other regulatory agencies, such as the Federal Reserve Board and the Federal Trade Commission, joined the ICC in the early 20th century. The real growth in administrative law, however, came in the 1930s as Congress created new entities to administer its New Deal programs. Major New Deal agencies included the Federal Deposit Insurance Corporation, Federal Communications Commission, Securities and Exchange Commission, and National Labor Relations Board.

A third boom in administrative law occurred around 1970, as agencies such as the Environmental Protection Agency and the Consumer Product Safety Commission were created to address growing environmental and health concerns. The regulatory landscape is still evolving, as the Homeland Security Act of 2002 created a new cabinet department and several new agencies. Administrative regulations and decisions continue to proliferate.

In researching administrative law, it is important to determine what agency has jurisdiction and to develop a preliminary understanding of its structure and functions. In some situations the relevant agency is obvious, but in others it may require background analysis or a close reading of statutory and judicial sources to determine an agency's role. It is then important to develop an understanding of the agency's organizational structure, legal mandates and information sources in order to understand more fully the scope and purpose of the documents it produces.

18. The first cabinet departments were created by Congress in 1789. The Department of Foreign Affairs was created by the Act of July 27, 1789, ch. 4, 1 Stat. 28 (and renamed the Department of State less than three months later by the Act of Sept. 15, 1789, ch. 14, 1 Stat. 68); the Department of War by the Act of Aug. 5, 1789, ch. 7, 1 Stat. 49; and the Department of Treasury by the Act of Sept. 2, 1789, ch. 12, 1 Stat. 65. The position of Attorney General was also created that year, as part of the Judiciary Act of 1789, § 35, 1 Stat. 73, 93.

19. Act of Feb. 4, 1887, ch. 104, § 11, 24 Stat. 379, 383. The ICC was abolished by the ICC Termination Act of 1995, Pub. L. No. 104–88, § 101, 109 Stat. 803, 804.

(a) Websites

An agency's website often provides a convenient source of information on its history and current activities. Here, depending on the agency, it is usually possible to find introductory overviews, organization charts, speeches, policy documents, directories, and other useful resources often unavailable in print.

One reason agency websites are putting regulatory information online is that they were ordered to do so by Congress. The Electronic Freedom of Information Act Amendments of 1996 mandated that records available for inspection and copying under the Freedom of Information Act (FOIA) must be made accessible electronically.[20] Records to be available online include "statements of policy and interpretations that have been adopted by the agency and are not published in the *Federal Register*" as well as "administrative staff manuals and instructions to staff that affect a member of the public."[21]

Congress further defined the scope of agency websites in the E–Government Act of 2002.[22] This act mandates that each agency "ensure that a publicly accessible Federal Government website includes all information about that agency required to be published in the Federal Register," as well as information about the agency's organizational structure and descriptions of its mission and statutory authority.[23]

In part as a result of this legislation, agency websites are increasingly the first place to look for information on an agency's history and current activities as well as documents such as regulations, decisions, and forms. Website organization and ease of access, however, vary considerably from agency to agency.[24] U.S. Citizen and Immigration Services <www.uscis.gov>, for example, has a "Laws & Regulations" link at the top of its homepage, with direct links to relevant statutes, regulations, administrative decisions, and

---

20. Pub. L. No. 104–231, 110 Stat. 3048 (codified as amended at 5 U.S.C.A. § 552 (West 2007 & Supp. 2008)).

21. 5 U.S.C. § 552(a)(2) (2006).

22. Pub. L. No. 107–347, tit. II, 116 Stat. 2899, 2910 (codified at 44 U.S.C. § 3501 note (Supp. V 2005)).

23. Id. at §§ 206(b), 207(f)(1), 116 Stat. at 2916, 2918.

24. A 2002 General Accounting Office report, *Update on Implementation of the 1996 Electronic Freedom of Information Act Amendments*, GAO–02–493, found that much of the material required by e-FOIA to be online was not there. Even if material was online, it was often difficult to find or unavailable

due to links that did not function properly. A more recent study found that only one in five agencies was complying with e-FOIA requirements. National Security Archive, George Washington University, *File Not Found: 10 Years After E–FOIA, Most Federal Agencies Are Delinquent* (2007) <www.gwu.edu/~nsarchiv/NSAEBB/NSAEBB216/>. The Federal Communications Commission's site has been singled out as one of the least user-friendly sites. See Jerry Brito, *Hack, Mash, & Peer: Crowdsourcing Government Transparency*, 9 Colum. Sci. & Tech. L. Rev. 119, 123 (2008) ("In practice, the site seems to be an exercise in obscurantism.").

other documents. The Department of State <www.state.gov>, on the other hand, has documents in an "Electronic Reading Room" accessible only by clicking on a "FOIA" link at the bottom of the page.

Policies established under the E–Government Act of 2002 mandate that an agency's principal public website include a search function.[25] Some agency search engines work well, but others are rather rudimentary. Better results can often be achieved by using a general search engine such as Google, limited to a particular agency's site.

Most agency websites can be easily found through web searches or by using an acronym and the domain *.gov* as a URL. Several lists of government websites are also available. One of the most thorough is Louisiana State University's Federal Agency Directory <www.lib.lsu.edu/gov/>, which lists agencies both alphabetically and by departmental hierarchy with links to more than 1000 sites. Washburn School of Law's WashLaw site has an "Agency Index" page <www.washlaw.edu/doclaw/executive5m.html> which covers only about seventy major agencies, but for each it provides direct links (if available) to publications, organization charts, forms, opinions, manuals, libraries, and directories. USA.gov <www.usa.gov>, the federal government's public portal, also provides an A–Z Agency Index with links to websites.

(b) Guides and Directories

Federal government guides and directories can be valuable resources for several purposes. They can point you to which agency has jurisdiction over a particular subject area. Once an appropriate agency is identified, these reference works can provide background on its history and organization. Some of these works also contain information that is unavailable from the agency's website or publications is needed, such as contact information for specific personnel.

Statutes or cases found during the research process may identify the relevant agency and lead to its regulations or decisions, but it is also possible to identify agencies by using a resource such as CQ Press's annual *Washington Information Directory*. This subject guide is organized into about twenty chapters in areas such as education, energy, and international affairs, and provides brief descriptions, website addresses, and access information for federal agencies as well as congressional committees and nongovernmental organizations. Illustration 5–1 on page 205 shows an excerpt from

---

25. Office of Management and Budget, Policies for Federal Agency Public Websites (Dec. 17, 2004) <www.usa.gov/ webcontent/reqs_bestpractices/omb_ policies.shtml>.

this directory for the topic Pharmaceuticals, within the broader Health division. It includes several federal agencies, including four offices within the Food and Drug Administration (FDA), as well as several professional organizations of pharmacists and scientists. The *Washington Information Directory* is also available in a sub-scription-based online edition <library.cqpress.com>.

One of the most convenient sources for general information about agencies' structures, authority, and functions is the *United States Government Manual*. The *Government Manual* was first published in 1935 by the National Emergency Council and is now published annually by the Office of the Federal Register. Available both in print and on the Internet <www.gpoaccess.gov/gmanual/>, it provides descriptive entries for each executive department and more than fifty independent agencies and commissions. Listings include references to statutes under which the agencies operate and explain their functions and major operating units. Organization charts are provided for most major agencies, and sources of infor-mation (including publications, telephone numbers, and websites) are listed. An appendix lists executive agencies and functions that have been abolished, transferred or terminated since 1933.

The *United States Government Manual* provides an overview of the entire federal government, with a relatively terse treatment of every department and agency. As a division of the Department of Health and Human Services, for example, the FDA merits just one short paragraph. Another guide with a more specific focus on major regulatory agencies is CQ Press's *Federal Regulatory Directory* (13th ed. 2007). Most of this directory focuses on twelve major agencies such as the Environmental Protection Agency, Federal Trade Commission, and Securities and Exchange Commission, with more summary treatment of nearly one hundred other regulatory boards and agencies. For the FDA, one of the agencies treated in depth, the directory provides historical background, a description of recent controversies such as efforts to regulate tobacco, and a discussion of current issues facing the agency. This is followed by several pages listing specific offices and contact persons, an exten-sive annotated list of acts that the FDA enforces, and three pages describing libraries and other information sources.[26]

To learn about the status of a particular regulation or enforce-ment activity, you will often need to contact an agency directly by phone or e-mail. You should direct your inquiries as specifically as possible to the responsible division and official. Agency websites and resources such as the *U.S. Government Manual* and *Federal*

---

26. Background information can also be found in *A Historical Guide to the U.S. Government* (George T. Kurian ed., 1998), with alphabetically arranged entries on departments and agencies, as well as major concepts and issues in administrative law.

Regulatory Directory provide general information and the names of senior officials, but they do not have very extensive listings of other personnel. Several directories have detailed information about specific offices and staff members, including telephone numbers and e-mail addresses. Three with comparable coverage are *Carroll's Federal Directory* (quarterly), CQ Press's *Federal Staff Directory* (three times a year) and Leadership Directories' *Federal Yellow Book* (quarterly). Carroll Publishing and Leadership Directories also produce companion volumes covering federal regional offices outside the Washington, D.C. area, *Carroll's Federal Regional Directory* and *Federal Regional Yellow Book* (both semiannual). All of these directories are also available through their publishers' subscription websites (<www.govsearch.com>, <library.cqpress.com/fsd/>, and <www.leadershipdirectories.com>).

(c) Regulations

The major forms of agency lawmaking are regulations and adjudicative decisions. The Supreme Court has held that agencies have discretion to create policies through either of these methods.[27] The powers of early regulatory agencies were considered *quasi-judicial*, and they acted much like courts with lengthy trial-type procedures. Gradually, however, rulemaking became the predominant form by which agency law was created. By the time the new agencies of the late 1960s and early 1970s were created, they were expressly charged by Congress to promulgate regulations in their subject areas.[28]

The *Federal Register* and the *Code of Federal Regulations* (*CFR*) are the two major resources in most federal administrative law research. Regulations are first published in a daily gazette, the *Federal Register*. The rules in force are arranged by agency and subject in the *CFR*. This publication of regulations, first chronologically and then by topic, mirrors the way statutes are published in the *Statutes at Large* and the *United States Code*.

Texts on rulemaking may help provide background and perspective. Jeffrey S. Lubbers, *A Guide to Federal Agency Rulemaking* (4th ed. 2006) provides a concise overview of the rulemaking process, including chapters on the statutory framework of rulemaking and judicial review. Cornelius M. Kerwin, *Rulemaking: How*

---

27. *SEC v. Chenery Corp.*, 332 U.S. 194 (1947). The extensive literature on the choice between adjudication and rulemaking is summarized in M. Elizabeth Magill, *Agency Choice of Policymaking Form*, 71 U. CHI. L. REV. 1383, 1403 n. 69 (2004).

28. The terms "rule" and "regulation" are used interchangeably in administrative law and have the same

meaning, according to the Administrative Committee of the Federal Register. 1 C.F.R. § 1.1 (2008). The change from adjudication to rulemaking is discussed in Reuel E. Schiller, *Rulemaking's Promise: Administrative Law and Legal Culture in the 1960s and 1970s*, 53 AD-MIN. L. REV. 1139, 1145–55 (2001).

Government Agencies Write Law and Make Policy (3d ed. 2003) provides a more political perspective on the substance and process of agency regulations, with chapters on topics such as public participation and congressional oversight. James T. O'Reilly, *Administrative Rulemaking: Structuring, Opposing, and Defending Federal Agency Regulations* (2d ed. 2007) focuses more on the procedures governing legal challenges to rulemaking.

(1) *Federal Register*

The executive branch has been issuing regulations since the beginning of the federal government. One of the acts passed during the first session of Congress in 1789 provided that pensions would be paid "under such regulations as the President of the United States may direct."[29] For almost 150 years, however, there was no standard procedure for publishing administrative regulations.[30]

The new agencies created to deal with the effects of industrialization in the late 19th century and the extension of government control during World War I caused an increase in agency regulation, and demonstrated the need for a centralized system of publication. During the war a newly created Committee on Public Information published a daily *Official U.S. Bulletin* that included the texts of regulations and orders as well as war news and general government information, but publication ceased a few months after the Armistice.[31]

---

29. Act of Sept. 29, 1789, ch. 24, 1 Stat. 95, 95.

30. The validity of unpublished administrative orders did not go unquestioned by courts and commentators. In 1872 the Supreme Court upheld the validity of an unpublished presidential proclamation, over Justice Ward Hunt's vigorous dissent. He wrote: "A proclamation may be published in the newspapers, or scattered by writing, or in any demonstrative manner, but it cannot be published by a deposit in a place to which the public have no access.... In the case before us no publicity was given to the paper. It was in no gazette, in no market-place, nor in the street. It was signed by the President and the Acting Secretary of State, and deposited in the Secretary's office. It does not appear that a single person besides the President and Secretary was aware of its existence. A deposit in the office of state is not notice or publicity." *Lapeyre v. United States*, 84 U.S. (17 Wall.) 191, 201–03 (1873) (Hunt, J., dissenting).

Decades passed, but little changed. A federal appellate court in 1906 revealed

its frustrations: "No department ever sends its compilation of regulations to the judges. They are frequently amended, and, without special information from the department, no one can tell whether a particular regulation in some printed compilation was in force a year later.... It is a hopeless task for an appellate court to determine what such regulations were at any particular time. It must either accept counsel's statement, or itself make inquiry of the particular department; neither of which practices is to be commended." *Nagle v. United States*, 145 F. 302, 306 (2d Cir. 1906).

31. See STEPHEN VAUGHN, HOLDING FAST THE INNER LINES: DEMOCRACY, NATIONALISM, AND THE COMMITTEE ON PUBLIC INFORMATION 197–200 (1980), and John Walters, *The* Official Bulletin of the United States: *America's First Official Gazette*, 19 GOV'T PUB. REV. 243 (1992). A year after the *Official Bulletin* ceased, the status quo had resumed and a scholar wrote: "In the matter of publication there is a maximum of variety and con-

No further action was taken even when the depression and the New Deal brought about a tremendous increase in the number of agencies and the scope of their business. Thousands of regulations were issued with no regular method of publication, in many instances without even an attempt at public notice.

In 1934 an American Bar Association committee advocated that regulations "should be made easily and readily available in some central office, and . . . should be subjected to certain requirements by way of registration and publication as prerequisite to their going into force and effect."[32] This "government in ignorance of the law" was also the focus of an influential *Harvard Law Review* article later that year by Professor Erwin Griswold.[33]

Public pressure for reform finally came to a head when two cases on New Deal regulation of the oil industry reached the Supreme Court, even though they were based on a provision that had been revoked before the lawsuits were filed. The cases proceeded through the courts with no one aware of the regulatory change, until finally the Solicitor General's office discovered the revocation and informed the parties and the Court. In a criminal case, four Texas oil producers had been indicted and jailed for conspiracy to violate the nonexistent regulation, which the lower court then found unconstitutional. The government's appeal was dismissed on its own motion.[34] A civil suit proceeded to oral argument, where the Justices had several questions about the accessibility of regulations and asked the government for a supplemental memorandum on the issue within two days.[35] The resulting furor provided the final impetus for the enactment of remedial legislation in 1935.

fusion. Not only is there no general system, but no department has developed a system for itself. Each bureau, and often each local office, has its own methods, or more often lack of method." John A. Fairlie, *Administrative Legislation*, 18 MICH. L. REV. 181, 199 (1920). The article concluded with a recommendation that "there should be an official publication which will record all regulations and instructions issued by all branches of the government service." Id. at 200.

32. *Report of the Special Committee on Administrative Law*, 59 A.B.A. REP. 539, 540 (1934). The committee noted that "the total volume of administrative legislation now in force greatly exceeds the total legislative output of Congress since 1789." Id. at 555.

33. Erwin N. Griswold, *Government in Ignorance of the Law–A Plea for Better Publication of Executive Legislation*, 48 HARV. L. REV. 198 (1934).

34. *United States v. Smith*, 293 U.S. 633 (1934) (appeal dismissed); see *Oil Suit Dismissed in Supreme Court*, N.Y. TIMES, Oct. 2, 1934, at 6.

35. *Panama Refining Co. v. Ryan*, 293 U.S. 388 (1935). Newspapers reported on the "[c]austic criticism from the Supreme Court of the way in which the New Deal keeps its records" and "the tremendous eruption of administrative law." *NRA Made 10,269 Laws in Year, or 200 a Week*, N.Y. TIMES, Dec. 14, 1934, at 26. The justices asked the government to explain why criminal indictments had been obtained under a provision no longer in effect. "Smiles appeared on the usually solemn faces of the justices and the crowd of lawyers that filled the room" when it was admitted that the error was not discovered until a few days before the case was to be argued. Theodore C. Wallen, *Complete File of New Deal Laws Lacking*,

The Federal Register Act[36] was designed to end this chaotic uncertainty by initiating a new daily gazette, the *Federal Register,* for the publication of regulations, notices and other documents. The first *Federal Register* issue was published on Saturday, March 14, 1936.[37]

The *Register*'s statutory mandate is to publish "documents having general applicability and legal effect."[38] Publication in the *Federal Register* is deemed to provide any parties affected by a regulation with constructive notice of its contents.[39]

The *Federal Register* substantially improved access to regulations, but agencies were still free to use unclear or arbitrary decision-making procedures. In 1946, Congress passed the Administrative Procedure Act (APA) to create standards for agency actions.[40] The APA provides procedures for both formal and informal rulemaking, but formal rulemaking requiring trial-type hearings has been little used. For informal rulemaking, the APA requires that agencies publish notices in the *Federal Register* with "either the terms or substance of the proposed rule or a description of the subjects and issues involved," that individuals have the opportunity to comment on the proposed rules, and that the agency give a concise explanation of its basis for adopting the rule.[41]

N.Y. HERALD TRIB., Dec. 12, 1934, at 1, 6. For more on this background, see Lotte E. Feinberg, *Mr. Justice Brandeis and the Creation of the Federal Register,* 61 PUB. ADMIN. REV. 359 (2001). The Office of the Federal Register has published a pamphlet surveying its work since the 1930s, A BRIEF HISTORY COMMEMORATING THE 70TH ANNIVERSARY OF THE PUBLICATION OF THE FIRST ISSUE OF THE FEDERAL REGISTER, MARCH 14, 1936 (2006) <www.archives.gov/federal-register/the-federal-register/history.pdf>.

36. Ch. 417, 49 Stat. 500 (1935) (codified at 44 U.S.C. §§ 1501–1511 (2000)). Decades later Rep. Emanuel Celler, who introduced the bill, would claim that he conceived the idea for the *Federal Register* when Interior Secretary Harold Ickes appeared before his committee and pulled from his pocket an envelope on which a new departmental regulation had been scrawled. Richard L. Madden, *What Harding (and 8 Other Presidents) Told Manny Celler,* N.Y. TIMES, Oct. 5, 1972, at 49.

37. See Lawrence Sullivan, *Uncle Sam Issues Daily Newspaper,* N.Y. TIMES, Mar. 15, 1936, at E10.

38. 44 U.S.C. § 1505(a) (2000). The Administrative Committee of the Federal Register has further defined "document having general applicability and legal effect" as "any document issued

under proper authority prescribing a penalty or course of conduct, conferring a right, privilege, authority, or immunity, or imposing an obligation, and relevant or applicable to the general public, members of a class, or persons in a locality, as distinguished from named individuals or organizations." 1 C.F.R. § 1.1 (2008).

39. 44 U.S.C. § 1507 (2000). Justice Jackson sharply criticized the effects of this constructive notice provision:

To my mind, it is an absurdity to hold that every farmer who insures his crops knows what the Federal Register contains or even knows that there is such a publication. If he were to peruse this voluminous and dull publication as it is issued from time to time in order to make sure whether anything has been promulgated that affects his rights, he would never need crop insurance, for he would never get time to plant any crops. Nor am I convinced that a reading of technically-worded regulations would enlighten him much in any event.

Federal Crop Ins. Corp. v. Merrill, 332 U.S. 380, 387 (1947) (Jackson, J., dissenting).

40. Ch. 324, 60 Stat. 237 (codified as amended at 5 U.S.C.A. § 551–59, 701–06 (West 2007 & Supp. 2008)).

41. 5 U.S.C. § 553 (2006). The APA does not provide the only rulemaking

The publication of proposed rules significantly expanded the scope of the *Federal Register*. In its first 1947 issue, the *Federal Register* inaugurated a new "Proposed Rule Making" section with proposed standards for grades of canned tangerine juice.[42] For years the agency explanations were cursory at best. Judicial decisions in the 1960s and 1970s, however, began taking a "hard look" at agency regulations and overturning those seen as arbitrary or capricious.[43] This soon led agencies to supply fuller explanations of their actions and greater evidence of public involvement in the decisionmaking process. Within five years the number of pages in the *Federal Register* had tripled.[44]

Through 1972 explanations generally accompanied proposed rules but not final rules. Since 1973 agencies have been required to preface final rules with an explanatory preamble.[45] In 1976 the preamble to final rules was expanded to include summaries of the comments submitted and the agency's responses to these comments.[46]

standards. Some rules are created under the Negotiated Rulemaking Act of 1990, Pub. L. No. 101–648, 104 Stat. 4969 (codified as amended at 5 U.S.C. §§ 561–570a (2006)), which permits private interest groups to participate directly in rulemaking by meeting with agency personnel and negotiating the contents of rules under which they are affected. The Administrative Conference of the United States publishes *Negotiated Rulemaking Sourcebook* (1995), which explains the process and reprints statutes, regulations, and other documents including several law review articles.

42. 12 Fed. Reg. 32 (Jan. 1, 1947).

43. This development is generally attributed to Judges David Bazelon and Harold Leventhal of the U.S. Court of Appeals for the District of Columbia Circuit. On this and other developments in judicial approaches to regulations, see Susan Low Bloch & Ruth Bader Ginsburg, *Celebrating the 200th Anniversary of the Federal Courts of the District of Columbia*, 90 GEO. L.J. 549, 575–77 (2002); Patricia M. Wald, *Judicial Review in Midpassage: The Uneasy Partnership between Courts and Agencies Plays On*, 32 TULSA L.J. 221, 221–28 (1996); Matthew Warren, Note, *Active Judging: Judicial Philosophy and the Hard Look Doctrine in the D.C. Circuit*, 90 GEO. L.J. 2599 (2002).

44. The Law Librarians' Society of Washington, D.C. (LLSDC) maintains a "Federal Register Pages Published Annually" table <www.llsdc.org/attachments/wysiwyg/544/fed-reg-pages.pdf>. The first volume in 1936 contained 2,400 pages, while most recent years have 70,000 pages or more. Each year's output comprises a new volume of the *Federal Register*, with continuous pagination throughout the year.

The LLSDC website also provides an informative and regularly updated guide to regulatory research. Richard J. McKinney, *A Research Guide to the Federal Register and the Code of Federal Regulations* <www.llsdc.org/fed-reg-cfr/>.

45. The change was made by the Administrative Committee of the Federal Register in order to make the *Register* "a more meaningful and more useful publication." 37 Fed. Reg. 23,602, 23,602 (Nov. 4, 1972). The current version provides that the agency "prepare a preamble which will inform the reader, who is not an expert in the subject area, of the basis and purpose for the rule or proposal." 1 C.F.R. § 18.12(a) (2008).

46. 41 Fed. Reg. 56,624 (Dec. 29, 1976) (codified as amended at 1 C.F.R. § 18.12(c) (2008)).

As a result of these judicial and administrative developments, proposed and final rules in the *Federal Register* now include extensive preambles describing the need for the regulatory changes and providing the required "concise general statement of ... basis and purpose" of the rules.[47] These "concise" statements can be quite lengthy and detailed, with extensive scientific and technical background information as well as responses to comments offered by interested parties.[48]

The introductory preambles appear only in the *Federal Register* and are not reprinted with the text of regulations in the *Code of Federal Regulations*. A *Federal Register* preamble may be invaluable in interpreting the scope and meaning of a regulation in the same way that committee reports and other legislative materials help explain the purpose of a statute.[49]

Additions to the contents of the *Federal Register* were also made in 1966 by the Freedom of Information Act (FOIA), mandating that agencies publish organizational descriptions and policy statements,[50] and in 1976 by the Government in the Sunshine Act, requiring agencies to publish notices of most meetings.[51]

The *Federal Register* has permanent reference value because it contains material which never appears in the *Code of Federal Regulations*. Not only does it provide the agency preambles explaining regulatory actions, but it may also be the only available source for short-lived changes occurring between annual *CFR* revisions. It is also the only published source for proposed rules, agency policy statements, discussion of comments received, descriptive statements on agency organization, and notices.

Access. The *Federal Register* is published in print, and most large academic and law libraries also have complete runs of the *Federal Register* back to 1936 in microform. These days, however, most access to the *Federal Register* is through the Internet. Issues since volume 59 (1994) are available free from GPO Access <www.

---

47. 5 U.S.C. § 553(c) (2006).

48. The FDA's final rule governing the marketing of cigarettes and tobacco products included a 220–page preamble, as well as a 700–page "annex" explaining the agency's basis for assuming jurisdiction over tobacco products. 61 Fed. Reg. 44,396 (Aug. 28, 1996). As one scholar has noted, "the modern statement of basis and purpose is often a monstrously long and complex document." GARY LAWSON, FEDERAL ADMINISTRATIVE LAW 280 (4th ed. 2007).

49. The D.C. Circuit has written: "Although the preamble does not 'control' the meaning of the regulation, it may serve as a source of evidence concerning contemporaneous agency intent." *Wyoming Outdoor Council v. U.S. Forest Serv.*, 165 F.3d 43, 53 (D.C. Cir. 1999). For more on the use of preambles and other pre-promulgation sources in interpreting regulations, see Lars Noah, *Divining Regulatory Intent: The Place for a 'Legislative History' of Agency Rules*, 51 HASTINGS L.J. 255 (2000).

50. Act of July 4, 1966, Pub. L. No. 89–487, 80 Stat. 250 (codified as amended at 5 U.S.C. § 552(a)(1) (2006)).

51. Pub. L. No. 94–409, § 3, 90 Stat. 1241, 1244 (1976) (codified at 5 U.S.C. § 552b(e)(3) (2006)).

gpoaccess.gov/fr/>, with each new issue added the morning of its publication. You can browse tables of contents or search by keyword or page number, and documents can be viewed in HTML or as PDF files replicating the printed *Federal Register*. Skimming the *Register*'s table of contents is part of many lawyers' daily routine, and from the GPO Access search page you can sign up to have it delivered each morning by e-mail.[52]

The *Federal Register* is also available online through several commercial services. Westlaw has current issues the day they are published, with coverage extending all the way back to the first Federal Register issue in 1936. Documents from 1936 to 1980 are available only in PDF, while documents since 1981 are displayed on the screen in the standard Westlaw format (and are not available in PDF). There are three databases to choose from. The FR database has documents 1981–date, FR–ALL database provides complete retrospective coverage, and FR–OLD covers only 1936–1980.

HeinOnline <www.heinonline.org> is another retrospective source for all *Federal Register* issues back to 1936. Its PDF collection extends all the way from 1936 to issues published within the past two to three months. HeinOnline's searching is less sophisticated than Westlaw's, with simpler options of searching for a combination of words or phrases anywhere in an entire daily *Federal Register* issue. A search result retrieves an entire issue rather than a specific document, so it may take a few moments to determine the scope of a document and how many pages need to be printed or downloaded.

Other services lack full retrospective coverage, but have the recent issues needed in most research. Lexis coverage begins in July 1980, CQ.com in 1990, and Loislaw.com in 1999. Lexis and CQ.com generally have new issues online the day they are published, and Loislaw coverage lags only two or three days behind.

Format. The daily *Federal Register* begins with a table of contents and a list of the *Code of Federal Regulations* citations for new or proposed regulations in the issue. The table of contents is organized alphabetically by agency. This makes it easy to monitor a particular agency's activity, but it also means that anyone looking for regulations on a specific topic needs to know which agency or agencies have jurisdiction in that area.

Each issue of the *Federal Register* contains, in order, presidential documents (such as proclamations and executive orders), new rules and regulations, proposed rules, and notices. Illustrations 5–2

---

52. The Office of the Federal Register also has a Public Inspection Desk <www.federalregister.gov/inspection. aspx> providing advance access to documents that are scheduled for publication in the next day's *Federal Register*.

and 5–3 on pages 206–207 show a Food and Drug Administration rule governing the marketing of ingrown toenail relief drug products, as published in the *Federal Register*. This rule was proposed in October 2002 and published as a final rule in May 2003, after two comments were received. Illustration 5–2 shows the preamble containing background information, including the citations of previous *Federal Register* documents. Illustration 5–3 shows part of the text of the new rule as it appeared in the *Federal Register*.

Readers' aids in the back of each issue include a table of pages and dates for each *Federal Register* issue published during the month, which can be helpful in tracking down a citation; and a cumulative list of *CFR* parts affected during the current month. Illustration 5–4 on page 208 shows these features for the *Federal Register* issue the day of the final regulation in Illustrations 5–2 and 5–3.

A monthly index to the *Federal Register* is arranged like the daily table of contents, with entries by agency rather than by subject. Each month's index cumulates those earlier in the year, so the January–February index replaces the January index, and the January–December index serves as the final annual index. The index is available back to 1994 from the Office of the Federal Register <www.archives.gov/federal-register/the-federal-register/indexes.html>, and back to 1936 on HeinOnline.[53]

Pending Regulations. Lawyers whose clients are subject to federal regulation need to know more than the rules currently in force. They also need to anticipate rule changes and to track developments in pending regulations. Several tools are available for monitoring the development of regulations that have not yet come into force.

The Unified Agenda is a useful feature published twice a year in the *Federal Register*.[54] It lists and summarizes regulatory actions under development and provides information on their status and projected dates of completion, although those dates are subject to revision. Most online sources, including Westlaw and Lexis, include the Unified Agenda in their *Federal Register* files, but GPO Access maintains the Agenda on a separate page <www.gpoaccess.gov/ua/>.

---

53. A much more detailed *CIS Federal Register Index* was published from 1984 to 1998 in bound semiannual volumes. It provided access by numerous methods, including general policy area, specific subject matter, agency name, authorizing legislation, and affected industries, organizations, corporations, individuals, or geographic areas.

54. The Unified Agenda is published pursuant to the Regulatory Flexibility Act, Pub. L. No. 96–354, § 3, 94 Stat. 1164, 1166 (1980) (codified as amended at 5 U.S.C. § 602 (2006)), and Executive Order 12,866, § 4, 3 C.F.R. 638, 642–43 (1993), *reprinted as amended in* 5 U.S.C. § 601 note (2006).

Further information on pending regulations is available from RegInfo.gov, the General Services Administration's regulatory information website <www.reginfo.gov>. which includes an extensive subject index to entries in the Unified Agenda. Westlaw also has a regulatory tracking database, US–REGTRK, with information on the status of proposed and recently adopted regulations.

Dockets of regulatory decisionmaking are becoming available online, providing access to agency analyses, public comments, and other documents involved in the rulemaking process. Regulations.gov <www.regulations.gov> is a centralized site for commenting on proposed regulations and viewing submitted comments.[55]

(2) *Code of Federal Regulations*

In 1935, when Congress finally sought to control the tremendous mass of federal regulations, it understood the need for subject access to regulations in force. The Federal Register Act required each agency to compile and publish in the *Register* its then current body of regulations.[56] An amendment in 1937 established a regular form of codification, the *Code of Federal Regulations (CFR)*.[57] The first edition was published in 1939, and contained regulations in force as of June 1, 1938.

The first edition of the *CFR* consisted of seventeen volumes kept up-to-date through cumbersome bound supplements. For the second edition, delayed by World War II until 1949, a different method of supplementation was instituted: pocket parts, with republication of volumes as necessary. Gradually this approach became unworkable, as an increasing number of volumes required annual republication. In 1967 the code changed to paperbound volumes published annually. The colors of the volume covers change each year, so annual editions can be readily distinguished from each other.

The *CFR* contains "documents of each agency of the Government having general applicability and legal effect, . . . relied upon by the agency as authority for, or . . . invoked or used by it in the

---

55. For more information on electronic rulemaking initiatives, see Cary Coglianese, *E–Rulemaking: Information Technology and the Regulatory Process*, 56 ADMIN. L. REV. 353 (2004). Regulations.gov has been criticized for its inadequate search options and lack of uniformity, but a committee under the auspices of the American Bar Association has recommended numerous changes in the site to enhance public access. Committee on the Status and Future of Federal e-Rulemaking, *Achieving the Potential: The Future of Federal E–Rulemaking* (2008) <ceri.law.cornell.edu/erm-comm.php>.

56. Ch. 417, § 11, 49 Stat. 500, 503 (1935). The only pre-*CFR* compilation of rules was a one-volume collection, *Federal Rules and Regulations*, privately published in 1918 and never supplemented. See Nicholas Triffin & Penny Hazelton, *Questions and Answers*, 76 LAW LIBR. J. 684, 685 (1983).

57. Act of June 19, 1937, ch. 369, 50 Stat. 304 (codified as amended at 44 U.S.C. § 1510 (2000)).

discharge of, its activities or functions."[58] The regulations are codified in a subject arrangement of fifty titles somewhat similar to those used for federal statutes in the *United States Code.* Some of the titles in the two codes cover the same subject. Title 7 of each code is concerned with agriculture, for example, and Title 26 with taxation. The titles do not always match, however. Education statutes are in 20 U.S.C., but corresponding regulations are in 34 C.F.R.; and there is no direct statutory counterpart for 40 C.F.R., Protection of the Environment.

CFR titles are divided into chapters, each of which is devoted to the regulations of a particular agency. In the back of every *CFR* volume there is an alphabetical list of federal agencies indicating the *CFR* title and chapter (or chapters) of each agency's regulations. The regulations in a chapter are divided into parts, each of which consists of a body of regulations on a particular topic or agency function. Parts are further divided into sections, the basic unit of the code. The citation identifying a *CFR* section shows the title, the part and the section (but not the chapter), so that 21 C.F.R. § 358.301 is title 21, part 358, section 301. Illustration 5–5 on page 209 shows this *CFR* section, codifying the ingrown toenail relief drug product regulation seen in the earlier *Federal Register* illustrations.

At the beginning of each *CFR* part is an *authority note* showing the statutory or executive authority under which the regulations have been issued. Some of these are statutes directly related to the topic of the regulation, while others are more general grants of rulemaking authority to the agency. After this note is a *source note* providing the citation and date of the *Federal Register* in which the regulations were most recently published. This reference is the key to finding the preamble with background information explaining the regulations. If an individual section has been added or amended more recently than the other sections in a part, it is followed by a separate source note. In Illustration 5–5, the source of "68 FR 24348, May 7, 2003, unless otherwise noted" is indicated at the beginning of Subpart D.

The current *CFR* consists of more than 220 volumes, which are revised and reissued on a quarterly basis. Titles 1–16 contain regulations in force as of January 1 of the cover year; titles 17–27 as of April 1; titles 28–41 as of July 1; and titles 42–50 as of October 1. The date of the latest annual edition can be an important detail to note, because it is the source that must be cited in most *CFR* references.[59] One year's edition gradually supplants the

---

58. 44 U.S.C. § 1510(a) (2000).

59. *The Bluebook* mandates citation to the official, annually revised edition of the *CFR*. THE BLUEBOOK: A UNIFORM SYSTEM OF CITATION R. 14.2, at 121 (18th ed. 2005). The *ALWD Citation Manual*

previous year's, and a current *CFR* set almost always consists of volumes of two or more colors. The *CFR* page shown in Illustration 5–5 is current as of April 1, 2008, and appears in a volume published three months later in July 2008.

The *CFR* is available in several electronic formats. GPO Access provides two versions. One is a PDF mirroring the official printed edition and updated on the same basis <www.gpoaccess.gov/cfr/>, and provides the official text needed for citations. A *CFR* section can be retrieved by citation, and specific titles can be browsed by clicking on specific chapters, parts, and then sections. Either individual titles or the entire *CFR* can be searched, using simple Boolean (and, or, not) and proximity (near, followed by).

GPO Access also has a much more current *Electronic Code of Federal Regulations*, or *e-CFR* <ecfr.gpoaccess.gov>, that incorporates new amendments from the *Federal Register* within two business days. The *e-CFR* has been available for several years, but it remains an "unofficial" version of the code subject to correction in the annual revision. It nonetheless represents a significant improvement over the annual edition and is one of the handiest available sources for up-to-date regulatory information. Like the annual *CFR*, the *e-CFR* can be accessed by browsing or through keyword searches.

Current versions of the *CFR* are also available online from several subscription databases, including Westlaw and Lexis. Like the *e-CFR*, these files are updated on an ongoing basis to reflect changes published in the *Federal Register* and incorporate amendments within a week or two after they appear in the *Register*. Westlaw's *CFR* provides notice of even newer developments, because it includes red flags indicating "Regulatory Action" and linking to *Federal Register* documents the same day they are published.

Older editions of the *CFR* are sometimes needed to trace a regulation's history and to determine the regulations in force on a specific date. GPO Access retains older editions as new versions are added, with coverage starting in mid–1996. Westlaw and Lexis provide more extensive historical access, with retrospective coverage extending back to 1984 (Westlaw) and 1981 (Lexis). The most comprehensive online historical collection is at HeinOnline, which has older versions back to the original 1938 edition. Older editions are also available in retrospective microform collections in most large law libraries.[60]

appears to permit citation to an online database, if the source is noted parenthetically. ALWD CITATION MANUAL: A

PROFESSIONAL SYSTEM OF CITATION R. 19.1(d), at 168 (3d ed. 2006).

60. Erwin C. Surrency & Robert E. Surrency, *The Code of Federal Regula-*

(3) Finding and Updating Regulations

You can find federal regulations through several methods. The *Federal Register* and the *Code of Federal Regulations* have indexes, and both publications can be searched through GPO Access or other databases including Westlaw and Lexis.

Most research into the regulations of a federal agency begins with the *Code of Federal Regulations*, rather than the daily *Federal Register*. The *CFR* includes an annually revised *Index and Finding Aids* volume providing access by agency name and subject. This index is far less detailed than most statutory indexes, listing parts rather than specific sections.[61]

Much more detailed subject access is provided in the annual four-volume *West's Code of Federal Regulations General Index*, which indexes specific *CFR* sections rather than entire parts. This index is available on Westlaw as the *RegulationsPlus Index*, accessible as a link from the *CFR* search page.

Online keyword searches can also be an effective way to find regulations, although the *CFR* is so voluminous and wide-ranging that you should search within a particular title or a topical file when possible. GPO Access offers options of searching the entire *CFR* or specific titles or volumes, while Westlaw and Lexis have files for regulations in topical areas such as banking, environmental law, and securities. On the subscription databases, you can also narrow retrieval by limiting a search to words appearing in the part and section headings. Westlaw uses the prelim field (*pr*) for all headings, while Lexis has separate *part* and *section* segments.

If you have a statute and need to find related regulations promulgated under its authority, the simplest method is to check the *U.S. Code Annotated* (in print or on Westlaw) or *U.S. Code Service* (in print or on Lexis). Cross-references to relevant *CFR* parts or sections follow individual sections in both codes. The online versions have hypertext links from the statutes to the regulations.[62]

---

tions: Bibliography and Guide to Its Use, 1939–1982 (2d ed. 1986) includes a list of volumes and an alphabetical list of all current and former agencies represented in the *CFR*.

61. The *Index and Finding Aids* volume was first published in 1979, after an attorney had brought suit to compel the government to publish an analytical subject index to the set. *Cervase v. Office of the Federal Register*, 580 F.2d 1166 (3d Cir. 1978). It was a marked improvement over earlier indexes, and the plaintiff agreed to dismissal of his suit upon

its publication. Howard A. Hood, *Indexing and the Law*, 8 INT'L J.L. LIBR. 61 (1980).

62. The *CFR's Index and Finding Aids* volume also has a "Parallel Table of Authorities and Rules" that lists every statute and presidential document cited by an agency as authority for its rules, taken from the rulemaking authority citation in *CFR*. The table is available with the GPO Access version of the *CFR*, as a link at the top of the "Browse and/or search the CFR" screen.

For some agencies, regulations are reprinted in treatises and looseleaf services covering their topical area. Looseleaf services focusing on the work of particular agencies (such as the Internal Revenue Service or the Securities and Exchange Commission) provide regularly updated and well-annotated texts of both statutes and regulations. These services are discussed more fully in § 5–3 on pages 194–198.

Finding relevant regulations is only the first step of research. It is also necessary to verify that those regulations remain current, and to find cases and other documents that apply and interpret the regulations.

The first part is a relatively simple task for users of the *e-CFR*, commercial databases, or looseleaf services, because the versions of *CFR* available through these sources are regularly updated. For researchers using the *CFR* in its print format or in its official version on GPO Access, it is necessary to update a regulation from the most recent annual *CFR* edition. Obviously the simplest course is to check a section in the *e-CFR* or a commercial database to see if it lists among its sources any *Federal Register* issues more recent than the latest annual *CFR* revision. Unlike the commercial databases, unfortunately, the *e-CFR* does not link directly to the changes in the *Federal Register*.

Another tool for updating regulations is a monthly pamphlet accompanying the *CFR* entitled *LSA: List of CFR Sections Affected* (also available through GPO Access <www.gpoaccess.gov/lsa/>), which lists the *Federal Register* pages of any rule changes affecting *CFR* sections since the most recent annual revision. *LSA* usually brings a search for current regulations up to date within a month or so, and more recent changes can then be found by using the cumulative "List of CFR Parts Affected" in the latest *Federal Register* issue (as well as in the last issue of any month not yet covered by *LSA*). Until recently, this somewhat cumbersome process was the standard *CFR* updating procedure. *LSA* can still be a convenient resource for scanning an entire *CFR* chapter or part to identify any recent regulatory changes.

While *LSA*'s value in current regulatory research has diminished, older issues remain important resources in tracking regulatory history. Because regulations change frequently, you may occasionally hit a dead end when trying to find a *CFR* reference cited in a case or article. The regulation may have been repealed or transferred to another *CFR* location. Tables tracing regulatory changes since 2001 are published in the back of each *CFR* volume, listing all sections in that volume that have been repealed, transferred, revised, or otherwise affected. Earlier changes from 1949 to 2000 are listed in a separate series of *List of CFR Sections Affected* volumes for the entire *CFR*. GPO Access's *LSA* page provides coverage from 1986, and HeinOnline's *Federal Register* collection provides *LSA* coverage from 1949 to 1980.

The official *CFR*, whether used in print or online (including the *e-CFR*), contains no annotations of court decisions like those in the *United States Code Annotated* or *United States Code Service*. Yet a court may invalidate a regulation or provide an important interpretation of key provisions, and identifying relevant cases is an essential part of regulatory research.

The most convenient way to find court decisions is to use Westlaw's version of the *CFR*, which includes notes of decisions similar to those in *United States Code Annotated*, as well as references to agency decisions, statutes, and secondary sources. Westlaw gives regulations basically the same treatment as statutes, providing a springboard from the text to a wide range of research references.[63] The Westlaw display also includes KeyCite symbols such as red flags for sections that have been amended, repealed, or adversely affected by a court decision. Illustration 5–6 on page 210 shows the Westlaw version of 21 C.F.R. § 358.301, including links to the *Federal Register* sources of the regulation and the authority citations in the *United States Code* as well as a KeyCite "C" symbol indicating that this section has citing references.

Lexis provides an unannotated *CFR* and does not use Shepard's symbols with regulations. A "Shepardize" link at the top of the display, however, allows you to find citing cases and law review articles. Comparable coverage in print is provided by *Shepard's Code of Federal Regulations Citations*. As it does in its coverage of statutes, Shepard's lists citing references under the exact provision cited. This can make it more difficult to do comprehensive research on an entire section, but it can also be a great time-saver if you are looking for references to a specific subsection of a long, detailed *CFR* section.

Research in federal regulations has simplified dramatically in recent years, and users of *e-CFR*, Westlaw or Lexis no longer need to find updates using the cumbersome *LSA* and "List of CFR Parts Affected" process. No matter what approach is used, however, you should always verify that the regulation is current and to search for any court decisions that may affect its scope or validity.

(d) Guidance Documents

Regulations published in the *Federal Register* and *CFR* are the most authoritative sources of agency law, but over the years the

---

63. West also publishes selected *CFR* titles in printed, annotated editions. These include Titles 8 (Aliens and Nationality), 12 (Banks and Banking), 20 (Employees' Benefits), 29 (Labor), 37 (Patents, Trademarks and Copyrights), 48 (Federal Acquisition Regulations System), and 49 (Transportation), as well as chapter IV of title 42 (Medicare/Medicaid).

creation of regulations has become increasingly time-consuming and complicated. As a result of this "ossification" of the rulemaking process, agencies now are just as likely to create new rules through documents that do not require the notice-and-comment procedures mandated by the Administrative Procedure Act. These "guidance documents" include a wide range of agency pronouncements and publications, including handbooks, policy statements, interpretive rules, and private advice letters. Guidance documents do not have the same binding force as regulations, but they can be important indications of how an agency perceives its mandate and how it will respond in a specific situation.[64]

Most guidance documents do not appear in the *Federal Register*, the *CFR*, or any other widely available published source, but many are available through agency websites. The Electronic Freedom of Information Act Amendments of 1996 (e-FOIA) mandates that agencies make policy statements, manuals, and frequently requested information available to the public electronically.[65] In 2007, an Office of Management and Budget bulletin required that agency websites maintain current lists of significant guidance documents in effect, with links to each document listed.[66]

Some agencies have issued regulations articulating their perspectives on guidance documents. The Food and Drug Administration, for example, has stated that guidance documents "do not establish legally enforceable rights or responsibilities" and "do not legally bind the public or the FDA," but that "they represent the agency's current thinking. Therefore, FDA employees may depart from guidance documents only with appropriate justification and supervisory concurrence."[67]

---

64. See, e.g., Todd D. Rakoff, *The Choice Between Formal and Informal Modes of Administrative Regulation*, 52 ADMIN. L. REV. 159 (2000); Barbie Selby, *Administrative Decisions and Other Actions*, VA. LAW., Dec. 2002, at 28. The leading article on the ossification of rulemaking is Thomas O. McGarity, *Some Thoughts on "Deossifying" the Rulemaking Process*, 41 DUKE L.J. 1385 (1992).

On the difference between legislative rules and interpretive rules, see, e.g., William Funk, *A Primer on Nonlegislative Rules*, 53 ADMIN. L. REV. 1321 (2001); Stephen M. Johnson, *Good Guidance, Good Grief!*, 72 MO. L. REV. 695, 698–713 (2007). It is not always clear whether a rule is legislative (and must follow APA requirements) or interpretive (and need not). See Kristin E. Hickman, *Coloring*

Outside the Lines: Examining Treasury's (Lack of) Compliance with Administrative Procedure Act Rulemaking Requirements, 82 NOTRE DAME L. REV. 1727 (2007).

65. Pub. L. No. 104–231, § 4, 110 Stat. 3048, 3049 (codified at 5 U.S.C. § 552(a)(2) (2006)).

66. Final Bulletin for Agency Good Guidance Practices, 72 Fed. Reg. 3432, 3440 (Jan. 25, 2007). The bulletin's preamble explains that the lists should be maintained "in a quickly and easily identifiable manner (e.g., as part of or in close visual proximity to the agency's list of regulations and proposed regulations)." Id. at 3437.

67. 21 C.F.R. § 10.115(d)(1)–(3) (2008).

The use of guidance documents to formulate policy instead of notice-and-comment rulemaking has drawn some criticism from the courts.[68] Their growing importance was recognized by the Bush administration in 2007, when it ordered that proposed "significant guidance documents" be submitted to the Office of Management and Budget for review.[69]

For the legal researcher, guidance documents are essential statements of agency policy. What sets guidance documents apart from regulations is that there is little consistency in their form and function between agencies. Regulations take basically the same form from all agencies and are published in the *Federal Register* and *CFR*, but an understanding of guidance documents requires a familiarity with an agency's website and the ways in which the agency informs interested parties of its policies and interpretations.

(e) Decisions and Rulings

While regulations and guidance documents are the primary means by which most agencies create legal rules within their areas of expertise, administrative agencies also have quasi-judicial functions in which they hold hearings and issue decisions involving specific parties. These adjudications usually involve a fact-finding process and the application of agency regulations to particular situations or problems. The procedures and precedential value of these decisions vary among agencies.

Formal Adjudications. In most agencies, adjudicatory hearings are only used when imposing a sanction on a specific person or

---

68. In *Appalachian Power Co. v. E.P.A.*, 208 F.3d 1015 (D.C. Cir. 2000), the court set aside a guidance document in its entirety as improperly promulgated without complying with rulemaking procedures. Its opinion explained:

The phenomenon we see in this case is familiar. Congress passes a broadly worded statute. The agency follows with regulations containing broad language, open-ended phrases, ambiguous standards and the like. Then as years pass, the agency issues circulars or guidance or memoranda, explaining, interpreting, defining and often expanding the commands in the regulations. One guidance document may yield another and then another and so on. Several words in a regulation may spawn hundreds of pages of text as the agency offers more and more detail regarding what its regulations demand of regulated entities. Law is made, without notice and comment, without public participation, and with-

out publication in the Federal Register or the Code of Federal Regulations. With the advent of the Internet, the agency does not need these official publications to ensure widespread circulation; it can inform those affected simply by posting its new guidance or memoranda or policy statement on its web site.

Id. at 1020. For discussion of the judicial treatment of guidance documents, see, e.g., Robert Anthony, *Interpretive Rules, Policy Statements, Guidances, Manuals, and the Like—Should Federal Agencies Use Them to Bind the Public*, 41 DUKE L.J. 1311 (1992); Peter L. Strauss, *Publication Rules in the Rulemaking Spectrum: Assuring Proper Respect for an Essential Element*, 53 ADMIN. L. REV. 803 (2001).

69. Exec. Order No. 13,422, 3 C.F.R. 191 (2007).

organization.[70] In many instances they are not binding on other parties or on the agency in future adjudications. Some agencies, such as the Federal Trade Commission and National Labor Relations Board, rely on adjudication to establish legal rules.[71] In effect they use the case-by-case adjudication process to create a common law in their subject fields.[72]

Agency hearings are usually conducted by an administrative law judge, who has a role very similar to that of a trial judge and issues the initial decision of the agency.[73] That decision can be appealed to a higher authority within the agency, such as the secretary of the department or the commission, and review of a final agency decision can generally be sought in federal court. The statutes governing judicial review of decisions by most major agencies provide that actions be brought in the U.S. Court of Appeals rather than at the U.S. District Court level.

Most federal agencies write formal opinions to justify or explain their decisions. An agency decision can be an important document in interpreting a regulation or statute, or in applying regulations to particular facts. Although most agencies do not consider themselves strictly bound by their prior decisions under the doctrine of *stare decisis*, the decisions do have considerable precedential value for attorneys practicing before an agency or appealing an agency decision.

Agency decisions have traditionally been published in both official and unofficial sources. They are now available from a variety of print and online sources, both officially from the agency itself and commercially through online databases, looseleaf services, and topical reporters.

About fifteen federal agencies and regulatory commissions publish official reports of their decisions, in a form very similar to official court reports. According to *The Bluebook*, these reports are the source to which decisions should be cited if they appear therein.[74] Official reports usually contain tables and indexes to provide

70. See Richard B. Stewart, *Administrative Law in the Twenty–First Century*, 78 N.Y.U. L. Rev. 437, 444 (2003).

71. The NLRB's historical reliance on adjudication is the subject of several critical articles over the years. See Mark H. Grunewald, *The NLRB's First Rulemaking: An Exercise in Pragmatism*, 41 Duke L.J. 274, 274 n.3 (1991).

72. See Charles H. Koch, Jr., *Policymaking by the Administrative Judiciary*, 56 Ala. L. Rev. 693 (2005).

73. Agency adjudications are subject to procedural requirements mandated by §§ 5–8 of the Administrative Procedure Act, 5 U.S.C. § 554–57 (2006). For an overview of hearing procedures, see Morell E. Mullins, *Manual for Administrative Law Judges*, 23 J. Nat'l Ass'n Admin. L. Judges (Special Issue 2004); 2001 interim Internet ed. available online <ualr.edu/malj/malj.pdf>.

74. The Bluebook: A Uniform System of Citation R. 14.3.2(a), at 123 (18th ed. 2005). The *ALWD Citation Manual* appears to permit citation to either official or unofficial reporters. ALWD Citation Manual: A Professional System of Citation R. 19.5(c)(1), at 172 (3d ed. 2006).

access to their contents, but these are of limited research value if they apply only to the decisions in one volume. For some agencies, cumulative tables or indexes are published and may be useful as ways to find decisions or to double-check online search results.

Recent decisions are also available from agency websites, but there is little consistency in how agencies provide access to these documents. Because they can be hard to find, a directory of websites with agency decisions can be a valuable resource. One of the most extensive and current listings of these websites is available from the University of Virginia Library <www2.lib.virginia.edu/govtinfo/fed_decisions_agency.html>. Even once a site with decisions is found, its search engine may be ineffective and it may lack retrospective coverage.

Extensive collections of federal agency reports are available from the online databases. The decisions of more than seventy agencies and offices are available through both Westlaw and Lexis. Both database systems provide decisions of specific agencies as individual databases, and also include these decisions in topical files containing both judicial and administrative decisions in specific subject areas. In many instances, coverage is retrospective to the first published decisions. Westlaw and Lexis coverage includes many administrative decisions not published in official reports, and generally extends much earlier than official websites.

Retrospective collections of published reports are also offered by both HeinOnline <www.heinonline.org> and LLMC Digital <www.llmcdigital.org>. Each covers decisions from several dozen administrative agencies, with PDF copies of the original printed reports.

Many administrative decisions are also published, along with other documents such as statutes, regulations, and court decisions, in topical looseleaf services. These services, which combine access to primary sources with commentary and current information, are discussed below in § 5.3.

A researcher specializing in a particular area must be familiar with decisions of relevant agencies. The easiest way for nonspecialists to learn of administrative decisions is through the annotations in *United States Code Service*, which includes notes of decisions from more than fifty commissions and boards. *United States Code Annotated* does not include references to administrative decisions but does cite opinions of the Attorney General and Office of Legal Counsel.

Major series of agency reports are listed in both citation guides. THE BLUEBOOK, T.1 at 196–197; ALWD CITATION MANUAL, app. 8 at 539–540.

KeyCite and Shepard's both have coverage of selected administrative decisions. They list these decisions among other citing references to court decisions, statutes, and other sources, and they also provide references to later documents that affect or cite administrative decisions. In print, Shepard's coverage is split among *Shepard's United States Administrative Citations*, which lists citations to the decisions and orders of more than a dozen major administrative tribunals, and topical citators such as *Shepard's Federal Tax Citations*, and *Labor Law Citations*.

Advice Letters and Other Rulings. Agencies also provide advice to individuals or businesses seeking clarification of their policies or regulations as applied to particular factual situations. This advice is usually accompanied by a disclaimer that the reply has no precedential value in future instances, but it is nonetheless a strong indication of how an agency interprets its mandate.

Internal Revenue Service private letter rulings and Securities and Exchange Commission no-action letters are leading examples of this sort of decision. These documents were originally sent only to the recipients and not made public, but changing views of the value of informal rulings led to their availability in print and online.[75]

Materials like private letter rulings and no-action letters are generally available from agency websites and commercial databases, as well as in printed looseleaf services. Systems such as Westlaw and Lexis often offer more sophisticated search options, and combine these materials in databases with other relevant materials from the agencies and courts.

The difficult first step is identifying what informal documentation is available from a particular agency. This can be done by

---

75. The SEC decided in 1970 to release its no-action letters for public availability. Procedures Regarding Public Availability of Requests for No–Action and Interpretative Letters and Responses, Release Nos. 33–5098, 34–9006, 35–16875, 39–281, IC–6220, IAA–274, 35 Fed. Reg. 17779 (Oct. 29, 1970) (codified as amended at 17 C.F.R. § 200.81 (2008)). A lawsuit was required, however, for the IRS to begin releasing its private letter rulings. *Tax Analysts and Advocates v. IRS*, 362 F. Supp. 1298 (D.D.C. 1973), *modified*, 505 F.2d 350 (D.C. Cir. 1974). The dispute was finally settled in 1976. *Protagonists Reach Agreement on IRS Rulings Disclosure*, TAX NOTES, Mar. 15, 1976, at 3.

SEC regulations explain its official perspective on informal advice by its staff:

While opinions expressed by members of the staff do not constitute an offi-

cial expression of the Commission's views, they represent the views of persons who are continuously working with the provisions of the statute involved. And any statement by the director, associate director, assistant director, chief accountant, chief counsel, or chief financial analyst of a division can be relied upon as representing the views of that division.

17 C.F.R. § 202.1(d) (2008). On the reception by the courts of no-action letters and private letter rulings, see Donna M. Nagy, *Judicial Reliance on Regulatory Interpretations in SEC No–Action Letters: Current Problems and a Proposed Framework*, 83 CORNELL L. REV. 921 (1998); Dale F. Rubin, *Private Letter and Revenue Rulings: Remedy or Ruse?*, 28 N. KY. L. REV. 50 (2001).

perusing its website, by noting the sources cited in the case law and secondary literature, or by studying a guide to the resources in a particular area of law.[76] This process may take some time, as agencies are notorious for having unique and idiosyncratic processes and unwritten "lore."[77]

Attorney General Opinions. Somewhat different from other agency decisions are the opinions of the Attorneys General of the United States and the Department of Justice's Office of Legal Counsel (OLC). As the federal government's law firm, the Department of Justice provides legal advice to the president and to other departments.[78] These are advisory opinions and are not binding, but they are nonetheless usually given some persuasive authority.

Between 1791 and 1982, these opinions were signed by the U.S. Attorney General and published in a series entitled *Opinions of the Attorneys General of the United States*. The opinion function has now been delegated to the OLC.[79] The opinions of this office were published from 1977 to 1996 in a 20–volume series *Opinions of the Office of Legal Counsel*, and are available on the DOJ website back to 1992 <www.usdoj.gov/olc/>. Opinions of the Attorney General and OLC are also available online through Westlaw, Lexis, and HeinOnline, with coverage back to 1791.

(f) Other Publications

Presidential documents, regulations, guidance documents, and agency decisions are among the most legally significant of federal government publications, but they constitute only a small fraction

---

76. *Specialized Legal Research* (Penny A. Hazelton ed., 1987–date) covers administrative and other resources in several major areas including securities regulation, federal income taxation, copyright law, federal labor and employment law, environmental law, immigration law, banking law, patent and trademark law, government contracts, and customs law.

77. See, e.g., GARY M. BROWN, SODERQUIST ON THE SECURITIES LAWS § 1:3, at 1–12 (5th ed. 2006) ("There is one other item that must be considered—what securities lawyers sometimes call 'lore.' Much of the knowledge it takes to deal with the Commission, and otherwise practice in the field, is not the subject of an official pronouncement. If, for example, a lawyer were to prepare and file a Securities Act registration statement following only the statute, rules, and registration statement form, the Commission would likely reject it on the basis that it is so far afield that the staff does not know how to deal with it."); Stanley M.

Gorinson et al., *Competition Advocacy before Regulatory Agencies*, ANTITRUST, Summer 1991, at 24, 24 ("Regulatory agencies have their own unique law and lore. Lawyers acclimated to the courtroom can be astounded by the 'oddities' that are the heart of regulatory practice.")

78. 28 U.S.C. §§ 511–12 (2006). This responsibility of the Attorney General dates back to the Judiciary Act of 1789, ch. 20, § 35, 1 Stat. 73, 93.

79. 28 C.F.R. § 0.25(a) (2008). See generally Symposium, *Attorney General's Opinion Function and the Office of Legal Counsel*, 15 CARDOZO L. REV. 337 (1993). The OLC was relatively little known until the early 2000s, when some of its memoranda on the treatment of terrorism suspects gave it greater notoriety. See, e.g., JACK GOLDSMITH, THE TERROR PRESIDENCY: LAW AND JUDGMENT INSIDE THE BUSH ADMINISTRATION (2007).

of the information available. Agencies also issue other materials containing a great deal of information relating to their legal business. These may include annual reports, monographs, and various pamphlets providing information for the public or regulated industries.

Annual reports can be important information sources about the work of an agency. They may describe important litigation and include statistics concerning cases handled, prosecutions, settlements and dispositions. They often discuss enforcement policies and interpret agency statutes or proposed amendments. Almost every agency also produces pamphlets and monographs explaining its structure and operation, varying from short, popular descriptions to detailed administrative handbooks. Many agencies publish periodicals of general interest in their field of activity, such as the *Federal Reserve Bulletin* and *Monthly Labor Review,* as well as technical journals and newsletters. Agencies and commissions have also issued special studies, reports, and monographs on major problems.[80]

Recently published reports and documents are generally available on agency websites, but finding older material may require some hunting in a government depository library. The Government Printing Office, the central publishing arm of the federal government, distributes materials at no cost to libraries around the country. A selected number of libraries, no more than two per state, are known as "regional depositories" and receive everything GPO publishes for distribution.[81]

Material distributed by the GPO can be found through its online and print catalogs. The online catalog <catalog.gpo.gov> lists publications since 1976, and older material can be found using the printed *Monthly Catalog of United States Government Publications,* which began publication in 1895.[82] These resources are useful not only in determining what the government publishes, but they also provide the Superintendent of Documents (SuDocs) classification numbers used to shelve documents in most large libraries.[83]

80. *Popular Names of U.S. Government Reports* (4th ed. 1984) provides help in identifying older reports known by short or unofficial titles, such as the subject or the name of a commission chairperson.

81. 44 U.S.C. § 1912 (2000). GPO Access provides a map with information about each federal depository library <catalog.gpo.gov/fdlpdir/FDLPdir.jsp>.

82. Older material is described and indexed in *CIS Index to Executive Branch Documents 1789–1909* (1990–97)

and *CIS Index to Executive Branch Documents 1910–1932* (1996–2002), both accompanied by microfiche collections of the materials listed. Together these cover several hundred thousand publications from the executive departments and independent agencies. The earlier set is based on *Checklist of United States Public Documents: 1789–1909* (1911), which is available free online <govdocs.evergreen.edu/tools/1909checklist/>.

83. For more information on SuDocs, see *An Explanation of the Superin-*

This is particularly important information, since many libraries' online catalogs do not include their extensive holdings of older federal documents.

The SuDocs system is also the basis of *Guide to U.S. Government Publications* (Donna Batten ed., annual), which lists the published series and periodicals for all agencies, both current and defunct. The book includes extensive indexes by agency, title, and subject keyword, and is a good first place to learn what reports and documents a particular agency has published over the years.[84]

Not all documents produced by the federal government are published by GPO and made available to depository libraries. Thousands of "fugitive documents" are published internally by agencies or made available temporarily online, with no system for permanent archiving or preservation.[85] GPO's Federal Digital System (FDsys) <fdsys.gpo.gov> is a new site designed to provide access to these materials and other government publications.

Some government information was once available on agency websites, but has disappeared when policies have changed or agencies have terminated or been eliminated.[86] Several sites are attempting to archive Internet sites that are no longer available from the government. CyberCemetery <govinfo.library.unt.edu> provides access to material from several dozen defunct commissions, boards, and other entities. Missing documents may also be available from sites such as the Wayback Machine <www.archive.org> and the Memory Hole <www.thememoryhole.org>.

(g) Unpublished Information

Even though agency websites have greatly increased access to government information, the government also has a vast store of additional documentation that it does not publish, such as internal records, data collected on individuals, and staff studies. The Freedom of Information Act (FOIA) dramatically expands the public's access to government files by enabling individuals to request copies of most documents, although it may take weeks or months to receive a reply. There are broad exceptions of material that agen-

---

tendent of Documents Classification System, FDLP Desktop <www.access.gpo.gov/su_docs/fdlp/pubs/explain.html>.

84. PETER HERNON ET AL., UNITED STATES GOVERNMENT INFORMATION: POLICIES AND SOURCES (2002) and JOE MOREHEAD, INTRODUCTION TO UNITED STATES GOVERNMENT INFORMATION SOURCES (6th ed. 1999) provide further information on the SuDocs system and access to federal government information generally.

85. Aliya Sternstein, *Fugitive Documents Elude Preservationists: GPO, Library of Congress Turn to Web Harvesting*, FCW.com, May 9, 2005 <tinyurl.com/cc87u5>; see also *Fugitive Documents: Scope and Solutions*, 143 CONG. REC. 9489 (1997) (extension of remarks of Rep. Hoyer).

86. See Robert Pear, *In Digital Age, Federal Files Blip Into Oblivion*, N.Y. TIMES, Sept. 13, 2008, at 1.

cies need not disclose, such as classified documents, internal personnel material, trade secrets, and law enforcement information.[87]

The first place to check for information request policies and procedures is the specific department or agency's website, which should have a Freedom of Information or FOIA link somewhere on the front page. This link leads to frequently requested documents made available online under e-FOIA and to instructions for filing requests with the agency.

More general resources are also available for assistance in filing FOIA requests. The Reporters Committee for Freedom of the Press <rcfp.org/foia/> has a useful guide, *How to Use the Federal FOI Act*, and a fill-in-the-blank FOI Letter Generator. The House Committee on Government Reform has published a handbook with sample request forms, *A Citizen's Guide on Using the Freedom of Information Act and the Privacy Act of 1974 to Request Government Records,* H.R. Rep. 109–226 (2005) (available online from GPO Access and through the Federation of American Scientists <www.fas.org/sgp/foia/citizen.pdf>), and the Department of Justice website also has an extensive *Freedom of Information Act Guide* <www.usdoj.gov/oip/foi-act.htm>.

Several books provide more extensive treatment of the history and interpretation of FOIA, including procedures and sample forms for filing requests and suing to compel disclosure. An American Bar Association publication by Stephen P. Gidiere, *The Federal Information Manual: How the Government Collects, Manages, and Discloses Information Under FOIA and Other Statutes* (2006), includes a chapter on "The Elements of a Successful FOIA Request" and is available on Westlaw as the ABA–FIM database).[88]

§ 5.3   Looseleaf Services

A looseleaf service is a frequently updated resource that compiles the statutes, regulations, administrative decisions, court decisions, and other materials in a particular area of law, and presents them in a cohesive manner accompanied by commentary or analysis. The term "looseleaf" comes from the traditional manner of publication and supplementation in binders, but most modern looseleaf services are available online as well as in print.

---

87. 5 U.S.C.A. § 552(b) (West 2007 & Supp. 2008). But see Lotte E. Feinberg, *FOIA, Federal Information Policy, and Information Availability in a Post–9/11 World,* 21 Gov't Info. Q. 439 (2004) (noting that access to government records "is increasingly shifting to a nether world" of new categories of records protected from disclosure but not governed by FOIA exemptions).

88. Two more comprehensive treatises are Justin D. Franklin & Robert F. Bouchard, Guidebook to the Freedom of Information and Privacy Acts (2d ed. 1986–date); and James T. O'Reilly, Federal Information Disclosure: Procedures, Forms and the Law (3d ed. 2000–date) (Westlaw FEDINFO database).

Not all looseleaf services cover topics with extensive administrative law sources, but those services that provide convenient access to regulations and administrative decisions are particularly valuable. They are often more organized and thorough than official sources, appearing more promptly and with better indexing than official reports.

The first looseleaf services were issued shortly before World War I to facilitate research in the new federal income tax law. By the 1930s other services had developed in public law areas where government regulation was the central focus of legal development, such as antitrust, labor law, and securities regulation. Services are now also published in numerous other areas such as banking, environmental protection, health care, and product safety.[89]

There are several ways to determine whether there is a looseleaf service for a particular area of law. Lawyers or professors specializing in a field can provide helpful advice, and references to looseleaf services may appear in law review articles and cases. The annual directory *Legal Looseleafs in Print* includes regularly supplemented services, although it also lists numerous other publications that are not updated very frequently. In this volume, the Appendix on topical resources at pages 449–479 includes a selected list of looseleaf and electronic services in fields of major interest.

Printed services are more likely to be available to most law library patrons, but many lawyers and other researchers rely on the electronic versions of looseleaf services. Keyword searching provides more flexibility than indexes, and hypertext links allow you to move conveniently back and forth between various documents. The looseleaf publishers BNA <www.bna.com>, CCH Internet Research Network <www.cch.com>, and RIA Checkpoint <ria.thomson reuters.com> all have platforms for Internet research.[90] Illustration 5–7 on page 211 shows the basic search screen for Food & Drug

---

89. For a history of the looseleaf form of publication, see Howard T. Senzel, *Looseleafing the Flow: An Anecdotal History of One Technology for Updating*, 44 AM. J. LEGAL HIST. 115 (2000). While this section focuses on looseleaf services that provide the text of primary sources such as administrative regulations and decisions, the looseleaf-binder format is also used for many weekly or monthly newsletters that provide summaries of current developments but generally do not reprint texts. BNA publishes several newsletters of this sort, such as *Antitrust & Trade Regulation Report*, *Criminal Law Reporter*, *Family Law Reporter*, and *Securities Regulation & Law Report*.

90. The content and functionality of major electronic services in taxation are compared in Katherine Pratt, Jennifer Kowal & Daniel Martin, *The Virtual Tax Library: A Comparison of Five Electronic Tax Research Platforms*, 8 FLA. TAX REV. 935 (2008).

Services are also available on CD-ROM. This format eliminates the need for laborious filing of replacement pages, but it is not updated as frequently as either online services or printed looseleaf supplements. The annual *Directory of Law–Related CD–ROMs* provides an extensive listing of more than 1,600 electronic products, and indicates which are also available on the Internet.

materials available through the CCH Internet Research Network, including daily updates, legislation, regulations, and court decisions.

Looseleaf services cover a wide range of subjects, and the methods of access and organization vary according to the nature of the primary sources and the characteristics of the legal field. In areas where a major set of statutes dominates the legal order, services are usually arranged by code section. Most federal tax services, for example, are structured according to the sections of the Internal Revenue Code. The statutory text is followed by excerpts from legislative history documents, regulations, and references to court decisions and Internal Revenue Service documents. Other services are organized more broadly by subject.

Many looseleaf services cover complex, technical areas and are quite extensive. The major taxation services *Standard Federal Tax Reporter* (CCH) and *United States Tax Reporter* (RIA), for example, both occupy more than twenty volumes. Looseleaf binders can rapidly fill up as the rulings and other material multiply, so older material is often moved from the binder for permanent retention. Some services publish permanent bound volumes of court and agency decisions, while others issue transfer binders for storage of older material.

Most looseleaf services are updated by replacing individual pages throughout the set, so that the text is kept current without the need for separate supplements. Page numbering is designed to facilitate filing of new material and can be rather convoluted; pages 603–1 to 603–24 may be inserted, for example, between pages 603 and 604. To help identify specific references as page numbers change, many services assign *paragraph numbers* to each section of material. A "paragraph" in this sense can vary in length from a few sentences to several pages. Each administrative decision, for example, is assigned one paragraph number and retains this number no matter how many new pages are added to the service. Paragraph numbers and page numbers can be easily confused, but it is paragraph numbers that are generally used in indexes and cross-references. They are also the designations by which most looseleaf services are cited.[91] Illustration 5–8 on page 212 shows ingrown toenail relief regulations as reprinted in CCH's *Food Drug Cosmetic Law Reports*. The page includes both a page number at the top right (72,837) and a paragraph number at the bottom right (¶ 72,-617).

---

91. THE BLUEBOOK: A UNIFORM SYSTEM OF CITATION R. 19.1, at 162–63 (18th ed. 2005); ALWD CITATION MANUAL: A PROFES-SIONAL SYSTEM OF CITATION R. 28.1(e), at 248 (3d ed. 2006).

Services not only provide convenient access to relevant primary authorities but also summarize and analyze the way these authorities fit together. In this way, they function much like frequently updated legal treatises. Illustration 5–9 on page 213 shows a page from the *Food Drug Cosmetic Law Reports* explaining the provisions of the Federal Anti–Tampering Act, with footnote references to a *Federal Register* preamble and to cases in the service's transfer binders.

Another important feature of most services is that they classify and index the case law in their subject areas, often with better and more systematic access than official government sources available online or in print. Unlike West's key-number digest system, which is used only for judicial case law, most looseleaf classification systems cover both judicial and administrative decisions. Because they are designed for specific areas, these specialized systems may also offer a more sophisticated and detailed analysis of topics within their expertise.

Regularly updated indexes are designed to provide fast and convenient access to looseleaf services. A typical service includes several types of indexes. The general or *topical index* provides detailed subject access. In many services, an additional index known as a "Current Topical Index" or "Latest Additions to Topical Index" covers new material between the periodic recompilations of the main index. Illustration 5–10 on page 214 shows a page from the topical index for the *Food Drug Cosmetic Law Reports*, with references under "Tampering" to the discussion in ¶ 4235 shown in the previous illustration.

Finding lists provide direct references to particular statutes, regulations, or cases by their citations. These can be particularly useful in searching for numerically designated agency materials, such as IRS rulings or SEC releases. Some of these lists also provide information on the current validity of materials listed.

Another device used in some services is the *cumulative index*. This is not a subject index but a tool providing cross-references from the main body of the service to current material. Under listings by paragraph number, cumulative indexes update each topic with leads to new materials that have not yet been incorporated into the main discussion.

Detailed instructions, often entitled "How to Use This Reporter" or "About This Publication," are frequently provided at the beginning of the first volume of a looseleaf service. A particular service may include features that appear confusing at first but are very useful to the experienced researcher. These instructions are often neglected by new users, but a few moments of orientation can save you considerable time and frustration.

Some agency decisions are also published with court decisions in topical reporters. Pike & Fischer's *Administrative Law* consists primarily of judicial decisions reviewing agency action, but each volume contains a number of agency decisions on issues relating to administrative procedure. Other reporters, such as *Public Utilities Reports,* also contain a mixture of court and agency decisions.

§ 5.4   State Administrative Materials

The executive branches of the states affect their citizens no less profoundly than does the federal bureaucracy. State agencies set and enforce public health and housing standards, fix and regulate utility rates and practices, and govern labor and business activities. In most states, however, publication of agency rules and decisions is far less systematic than it is on the federal level.

(a) Websites and Directories

State websites are often the best starting point to determine the jurisdiction of relevant agencies and their publications, and many have directories with contact information for government officials. If a search engine does not quickly lead you to the state homepage, the Library of Congress's State Government Information page <www.loc.gov/rr/news/stategov/> provides links for each state.

Nearly all states publish official manuals, or "blue books," paralleling the *United States Government Manual* and providing basic information about government agencies and officials. Some of these manuals describe state agency functions and publications, while others simply serve as government phone directories. The Bradley University Library has a State Blue Books page <wiki.bradley.edu/library_reference/index.php/State_Blue_Books> that lists most of these resources and links to versions available online. A more extensive listing, describing each source, can be found in the annual *State Legislative Sourcebook*. Directories and manuals are listed in the General State Government Information section for each state, along with information about Internet sites, statistical abstracts, and other reference sources.

In addition to single-state resources, a number of websites and directories provide multistate access to officials' names and numbers. National organizations of government officials generally provide links and contact information for members in each state. Besides the Council of State Governments <www.csg.org>, which studies policy trends in a broad range of areas, more specific organizations include:

> *Agriculture:* National Association of State Departments of Agriculture <www.nasda.org>

Budgeting: National Association of State Budget Officers <www.nasbo.org>

Corporations and elections: National Association of Secretaries of State <www.nass.org>

Corrections: Association of State Correctional Administrators <www.asca.net>

Energy: National Association of State Energy Officials <www.naseo.org>

Environment: Environmental Council of the States <www.ecos.org>

Financial management: National Association of State Auditors, Comptrollers and Treasurers <www.nasact.org>

Fish & wildlife: Association of Fish & Wildlife Agencies <www.fishwildlife.org>

Governors: National Governors Association <www.nga.org>

Insurance: National Association of Insurance Commissioners <www.naic.org>

Justice: National Association of Attorneys General <www.naag.org>

Motor vehicles: American Association of Motor Vehicle Administrators <www.aamva.org>

Securities: North American Securities Administrators Association <www.nasaa.org>

Social services: American Public Human Services Association <www.aphsa.org>

Taxation: Federation of Tax Administrators <www.taxadmin.org>

Transportation: American Association of State Highway and Transportation Officials <www.transportation.org>

Utilities: National Association of Regulatory Utility Commissioners <www.naruc.org>

Commercial multistate directories include *Carroll's State Directory* (three times a year) and Leadership Directories' *State Yellow Book* (quarterly); these generally provide more extensive listings than the state or multistate websites, and they are also available as subscription-based Internet services (<www.govsearch.com>, <www.leadershipdirectories.com>). The Council of State Governments' annual *CSG State Directory III: Administrative Officials* has listings by function, rather than by state, and may be the most convenient source for someone needing to contact similar officials in several states.

The Council of State Governments also publishes the annual *Book of the States*, which supplements these directories with more than 170 tables presenting a broad range of legal, political and statistical information on government operations in each of the fifty states. Chapter five focuses on state executive branches, with tables summarizing the powers and duties of governors, lieutenant governors, secretaries of state, attorney generals, and other officials.

(b) Regulations and Executive Orders

Almost every state issues a subject compilation of its administrative regulations, and most supplement these with weekly, biweekly or monthly registers. While the states generally follow the paradigm established by the *CFR* and *Federal Register*, few state administrative codes and registers are as organized and accessible as their federal counterparts. Some simply compile a variety of material submitted by individual agencies, and some have incomplete coverage. Indexing is often inadequate, sometimes even nonexistent.

The Bluebook and *ALWD Citation Manual* identify administrative codes and registers in their lists of the major primary sources for each state. More detailed information is available in William H. Manz, *Guide to State Legislation, Legislative History, and Administrative Materials* (7th ed. 2008), which lists print and online sources for each state's administrative code and register. The annual two-volume *CAL INFO Guide to the Administrative Regulations of the States & Territories* provides the tables of contents for each administrative code, making it easier to identify relevant regulations in order to know which title or code volume is needed.

Although a few states still do not provide Internet access to their regulations, the vast majority make their codes and registers available online. An easy way to find available sites is through the National Association of Secretaries of State's listing, Administrative Rules Online by State <www.administrativerules.org>, which provides links to both codes and registers. The University of Michigan Library's State Legal Sources on the Web <www.lib.umich.edu/govdocs/statelaw.html> also has links to regulatory codes and registers, as well as attorney general opinions and a range of other major legal sources.

Westlaw and Lexis also have administrative codes from every state (__-ADC databases on Westlaw) and the District of Columbia, although a few states may not be available through academic accounts. Westlaw also covers Puerto Rico, while Lexis has codes for Guam and the Virgin Islands. Both systems also have nationwide databases combining all state regulations, archives of earlier versions of administrative codes back generally to the early 2000s, and tracking databases for information on proposed and recently adopted regulations. Lexis has administrative registers from forty-four states and territories, while Westlaw has just nine registers. Westlaw also has a "50 State Regulatory Surveys" database (REG–SURVEYS) providing citations and links for each state's administrative code provisions on about three hundred topics.

Some of the administrative codes and registers include executive orders or similar legal pronouncements from governors. Several governors include the text of executive orders on their websites, which can be accessed through state government homepages or by links from the National Governors Association <www.nga.org>. Sources for executive orders are also listed in *Guide to State Legislation, Legislative History, and Administrative Materials*.

(c) Decisions, Rulings, and Other Documents

Some state agencies hold adjudicative hearings, like their federal counterparts, and publish official reports of their decisions. The most common are the reports of commissions governing banking, insurance, taxation, and utilities. A few looseleaf services and topical reporters also include state administrative decisions, and a growing number of state agency decisions are included in the online databases and on agency websites. Manz's *Guide to State Legislation, Legislative History, and Administrative Materials* lists publications and online sources for agency rulings, decisions, and orders. For retrospective research, Cheryl Rae Nyberg, *State Administrative Law Bibliography: Print and Electronic Sources* (2000) may also be useful.

The opinions of state attorneys general, written in response to questions from government officials, can have considerable significance in legal research. Although attorney general opinions are advisory in nature and do not have binding authority, courts generally give them considerable weight in interpreting statutes and regulations. Most states publish attorney general opinions in slip opinions and bound volumes, and recent opinions are available on the attorneys general's websites, which can be found through links at the National Association of Attorneys General website <www.naag.org>. Opinions are also available online in Lexis and Westlaw, with coverage in most states beginning in 1977 or earlier. Some attorney general opinions are included in the annotations in state codes, but coverage varies from state to state. KeyCite (but not Shepard's) includes attorney general opinions as citing sources in its coverage of cases, statutes, and other sources.

As with federal agencies, guidance documents and other publications from agencies can also be important in interpreting state law. Materials such as guidelines and manuals are increasingly available from agency websites.[92]

Like the federal government, each state has open records laws under which unpublished information can be obtained upon request. Information on each state's laws and procedures is available from the National Freedom of Information Coalition <www.nfoic.org/state-foi-laws> and the Reporters Committee for Freedom of the Press's Open Government Guide <rcfp.org/ogg/>.

§ 5.5 Local Law

Legal problems and issues are governed not only by federal and state law, but also by the laws of counties, cities, and other local units. Housing, transportation, social welfare, education, municipal services, zoning, and environmental conditions are all heavily regulated at the local level of government.

Counties and cities are administrative units of the states, with lawmaking powers determined by state constitution or by legislative delegation of authority. The scope of their authority varies considerably from state to state.[93] They create a variety of legal documents which can be important in legal research. A city's *charter* is its organic law, similar in purpose to a federal or state constitution. An *ordinance* is a measure passed by its council or governing body to regulate municipal matters, and is the local equivalent of a federal or state statute. In addition many localities have administrative agencies which issue rules or decisions.

Local law sources can often be quite difficult to locate. Most large cities and counties publish collections of their charters and ordinances, with some attempt at regular supplementation. For many smaller cities and counties, however, there is still no accessible, up-to-date compilation, and individual ordinances must be obtained from the local clerk's office.

---

92. The role of guidance documents in state administrative law is examined in Michael Asimow, *Guidance Documents in the States: Toward a Safe Harbor*, 54 ADMIN. L. REV. 631 (2002), and in a more specific context in Samuel J. McKim, III, *The Sometimes Dubious Efficacy of Michigan Department of Treasury "Rules," "Revenue Administrative Bulletins," "Letter Rulings," "Questions and Answers," and Other Publications*, 60 TAX LAW. 1019 (2007).

One way to identify available documents, online or in print, is to check a state's monthly or annual list of publications. Links to these lists are available through Statelist: The Electronic Source for State Publication Lists <www.library.uiuc.edu/doc/researchtools/guides/state/statelist.html>. Older state documents in print can be hard to identify and even harder to locate, but the *Monthly Checklist of State Publications,* published by the Library of Congress from 1910 to 1994, may provide leads.

93. DALE KRANE ET AL., HOME RULE IN AMERICA: A FIFTY-STATE HANDBOOK (2000) provides a state-by-state survey of the relationship between state governments and their counties and cities.

A growing number of county and city codes are available on the Internet. State and Local Government on the Net <www. statelocalgov.net> provides convenient links to county and city homepages, which usually provide background and contact information, as well as the text of ordinances and regulations in some instances.

The Municipal Code Corporation <www.municode.com> and the Seattle Public Library <www.spl.org/default.asp?pageID= collection_municodes> have the most extensive sets of links to collections of local ordinances. Together they cover cities from almost every state; the Seattle site also includes links to several other publishers with online county and city codes. Other major sources include American Legal Publishing Corp. <www.amlegal. com/library/>, which covers more than 1,800 counties and municipalities nationwide, and the LexisNexis Municipal Codes Library <municipalcodes.lexisnexis.com> with some 270 localities, more than half of which are in California.

State and local law often incorporates industry codes on areas such as construction and fire safety. The International Code Council <www.iccsafe.org> publishes a series of fourteen codes on building and related codes, available through subscription sites such as MADCAD.com <www.madcad.com>. The Building Code Reference Library <www.reedconstructiondata.com/building-codes/> provides a database to identify the codes in force in specific states and major cities, and PDF versions of many state and local codes are available free from Public.Resource.org <bulk.re-source.org/codes.gov/>.

Works of national scope that might be of help in working on a local law problem include *Ordinance Law Annotations* (1969–date), which provides abstracts of court decisions on local law issues, arranged by subject; and the leading treatise in the area, Eugene McQuillin, *The Law of Municipal Corporations* (3d ed. 1949–date).[94] These are both available on Westlaw, as the ORDLAWANNO and MUNICORP databases respectively.

Because much local law information is not available in print or on the Internet, direct contact by telephone or e-mail may be essential. Directories with information on local governments throughout the country include *Carroll's County Directory*, *Carroll's Municipal Directory*, and *Municipal Yellow Book*. These directories are all updated twice a year and are available to subscribers through their publishers' websites (<www.govsearch.com> and <www.leadershipdirectories.com>). The annual *Municipal Year*

---

94. Other treatises include SANDRA M. STEVENSON, ANTIEAU ON LOCAL GOVERNMENT LAW (2d ed. 1997–date) (available on Lexis) and JOHN C. MARTINEZ ET AL., LOCAL GOVERNMENT LAW (1981–date) (available on Westlaw, LOCGOVTLAW database).

Book provides a directory of city and county officials, as well as articles and table summarizing trends and current developments.

Index to Current Urban Documents (in print, 1972–2007; online by subscription <www.urbdocs.com>) provides access to documents issued by cities, counties, and regional agencies. Each year it indexes more than 2,400 items from more than 500 cities in the United States and Canada, with the documents available as PDF files.

Further guidance on finding local government resources, by type of information and by subject, is available in *Local and Regional Government Information: How to Find It, How to Use It* (Mary Martin ed., 2005).

(202) 326-3090. Fax, (202) 326-3259. Mary Engle, Associate Director.

Web, www.ftc.gov

Protects consumers from deceptive and unsubstantiated advertising through law enforcement, public reports, and industry outreach. Evaluates the nutritional and health benefits of foods and the safety and effectiveness of dietary supplements, drugs, and medical devices, particularly as they relate to weight loss.

Food and Drug Administration (FDA), *(Health and Human Services Dept.), Center for Drug Evaluation and Research, 10903 New Hampshire Ave., Silver Spring, MD 20993; (301) 796-5400. Fax, (301) 847-8752. Dr. Steven K. Galson, Director. Information, (301) 827-4570. Press, (301) 827-6242.*

Web, www.fda.gov/cder

Reviews and approves applications to investigate and market new drugs; monitors prescription drug advertising; works to harmonize drug approval internationally.

Food and Drug Administration (FDA), *(Health and Human Services Dept.), Center for Drug Evaluation and Research: Generic Drugs, 7519 Standish Pl., Rockville, MD 20855; (240) 276-9310. Fax, (240) 276-9327. Gary Buehler, Director.*

Web, www.fda.gov/cder/ogd

Oversees generic drug review process to ensure the safety and effectiveness of approved drugs.

Food and Drug Administration (FDA), *(Health and Human Services Dept.), Center for Drug Evaluation and Research: New Drug Quality Assessment, 10903 New Hampshire Ave., Silver Spring, MD 20993; (301) 796-1900. Fax, (301) 796-9748. Moheb Nasr, Director.*

Web, www.fda.gov/cder/ondc

Reviews the critical quality attributes and manufacturing processes of new drugs, establishes quality standards to ensure safety and efficacy, and facilitates new drug development.

Food and Drug Administration (FDA), *(Health and Human Services Dept.), Drug Marketing, Advertising, and Communications, 10903 New Hampshire Ave., Bldg. 22, #1400, Silver Spring, MD 20903-0002; (301) 796-1200. Fax, (301) 796-2877. Thomas Abrams, Director.*

Web, www.fda.gov/cder

Monitors prescription drug advertising and labeling; investigates complaints; conducts market research on health care communications and drug issues.

National Institutes of Health (NIH), *(Health and Human Services Dept.), Dietary Supplements, 6100 Executive Blvd., #3B01, MSC-7517, Bethesda, MD 20892-7517; (301) 435-2920. Fax, (301) 480-1845. Paul M. Coates, Director.*

General e-mail, ods@nih.gov

Web, http://ods.od.nih.gov

Provides accurate, up-to-date information on dietary supplements. Reviews the current scientific evidence on the safety and efficacy of dietary supplements on the market to evaluate the need for further research. Conducts and coordinates scientific research within the NIH relating to dietary supplements. Plans, organizes, and supports conferences, workshops, and symposia on scientific topics related to dietary supplements.

Public Health Service *(Health and Human Services Dept.), Orphan Products Development, 5600 Fishers Lane, #6A55, Rockville, MD 20857; (301) 827-3666. Fax, (301) 827-0017. Timothy Coté, Director.*

Web, www.fda.gov/orphan

Promotes the development of drugs, devices, and alternative medical food therapies for rare diseases or conditions. Coordinates activities on the development of orphan drugs among federal agencies, manufacturers, and organizations representing patients.

▶ **NONGOVERNMENTAL**

American Assn. of Colleges of Pharmacy, *1426 Prince St., Alexandria, VA 22314-2841; (703) 739-2330. Fax, (703) 836-8982. Lucinda L. Maine, Executive Vice President.*

Web, www.aacp.org

Represents and advocates for pharmacists in the academic community. Conducts programs and activities in cooperation with other national health and higher education associations.

American Assn. of Pharmaceutical Scientists, *2107 Wilson Blvd., #700, Arlington, VA 22201-3042; (703) 243-2800. Fax, (703) 243-9650. John Lisack Jr., Executive Director. Public Relations, (703) 248-4744.*

General e-mail, aaps@aaps.org

Web, www.aapspharmaceutica.com

Membership: pharmaceutical scientists from biomedical, biotechnological, and health care fields. Promotes pharmaceutical sciences as an industry. Represents scientific interests within academia and public and private institutions. Monitors legislation and regulations.

American Pharmacists Assn., *1100 15th St. N.W., #400 20005; (202) 628-4410. Fax, (202) 783-2351. Dr. John A. Gans, Chief Executive Officer. Information, (800) 237-2742. Library, (202) 429-7524.*

Web, www.aphanet.org

Membership: practicing pharmacists, pharmaceutical scientists, and pharmacy students. Promotes professional education and training; publishes scientific journals and handbooks on nonprescription drugs; monitors international research. Library open to the public by appointment.

American Society for Pharmacology and Experimental Therapeutics, *9650 Rockville Pike, Bethesda, MD 20814-3995; (301) 634-7060. Fax, (301) 634-7061. Dr. Christine K. Carrico, Executive Officer.*

Illustration 5–1. WASHINGTON INFORMATION DIRECTORY 2008–2009, at 339 (2008).

Federal Register / Vol. 68, No. 88 / Wednesday, May 7, 2003 / Rules and Regulations   **24347**

Office of the Federal Register, 800 North Capitol Street, NW., Suite 700, Washington, DC.

By the Commission.

Dated: April 30, 2003.

Margaret H. McFarland,

Deputy Secretary.

[FR Doc. 03–11208 Filed 5–6–03; 8:45 am]

BILLING CODE 8010-01-P

DEPARTMENT OF HEALTH AND HUMAN SERVICES

Food and Drug Administration

21 CFR Parts 310 and 358

[Docket No. 02N–0359]

RIN 0910–AA01

Ingrown Toenail Relief Drug Products for Over-the-Counter Human Use

AGENCY: Food and Drug Administration, HHS.

ACTION: Final rule.

SUMMARY: The Food and Drug Administration (FDA) is issuing a final rule establishing conditions under which over-the-counter (OTC) ingrown toenail relief drug products containing sodium sulfide 1 percent in a gel vehicle are generally recognized as safe and effective and not misbranded. This rule also amends the regulation that lists nonmonograph active ingredients in OTC drug products for ingrown toenail relief by removing sodium sulfide from that list. This final rule is part of FDA's ongoing review of OTC drug products.

DATES: This rule is effective June 6, 2003.

FOR FURTHER INFORMATION CONTACT: Gerald M. Rachanow, Center for Drug Evaluation and Research (HFD–560), Food and Drug Administration, 5600 Fishers Lane, Rockville, MD 20857, 301–827–2307.

SUPPLEMENTARY INFORMATION:

I. Background

In the **Federal Register** of September 9, 1993 (58 FR 47602), FDA published a final rule establishing that any ingrown toenail relief drug product for OTC human use is not generally recognized as safe and effective and is misbranded. (See 21 CFR 310.538.) In that final rule, sodium sulfide 1 percent was considered effective but not safe for the temporary relief of pain associated with ingrown toenails because of its potential for causing adverse reactions, particularly burning sensations and skin irritation.

In the **Federal Register** of October 4, 2002 (67 FR 62218), after reviewing new data that had been submitted, FDA proposed to establish conditions under which OTC ingrown toenail relief drug products containing sodium sulfide 1 percent in a gel vehicle are generally recognized as safe and effective and not misbranded. The product is used with a retainer ring to keep the product at the area of application. The agency also proposed to amend the regulation (21 CFR 310.538) that lists nonmonograph active ingredients in OTC drug products for ingrown toenail relief by removing sodium sulfide from that list.

II. Comments Received in Response to the Proposal

In response to the proposal, the agency received two comments, which are on public display in the Dockets Management Branch (HFA–305), Food and Drug Administration, 5630 Fishers Lane, rm. 1061, Rockville, MD 20852. One comment, from a drug manufacturer, supported the agency's proposals and requested that the agency's review of the comments and publication of the final rule be completed as expeditiously as possible. The second comment, from a consumer, stated that the use of the product with a "restraining" ring as indicated should have a "green light." The comment added that there are many people who experience the pain of an ingrown toenail, and that these products will help.

III. The Agency's Final Conclusions

The agency concludes that the data support OTC drug monograph status for 1 percent sodium sulfide in a gel vehicle applied topically for the relief of discomfort (pain) of ingrown toenail. The product is used with a retainer ring to keep the product at the area of application. Accordingly, the agency is proposing a new monograph in part 358, subpart D (21 CFR part 358, subpart D) for ingrown toenail relief drug products that includes 1 percent sodium sulfide gel. The agency is also amending § 310.538 to state that it no longer applies to sodium sulfide.

Mandating warnings in an OTC drug monograph does not require a finding that any or all of the OTC drug products covered by the monograph actually caused an adverse event, and FDA does not so find. Nor does FDA's requirement of warnings repudiate the prior OTC drug monographs and monograph rulemakings under which the affected drug products have been lawfully marketed. Rather, as a consumer protection agency, FDA has determined that warnings are necessary to ensure

that these OTC drug products continue to be safe and effective for their labeled indications under ordinary conditions of use as those terms are defined in the Federal Food, Drug, and Cosmetic Act. This judgment balances the benefits of these drug products against their potential risks (see 21 CFR 330.10(a)).

FDA's decision to act in this instance need not meet the standard of proof required to prevail in a private tort action (*Glastetter* v. *Novartis Pharmaceuticals, Corp.,* 252 F.3d 986, 991 (8th Cir. 2001)). To mandate warnings, or take similar regulatory action, FDA need not show, nor do we allege, actual causation. For an expanded discussion of case law supporting FDA's authority to require such warnings, see Labeling of Diphenhydramine-Containing Drug Products for Over-the-Counter Human Use, Final Rule (67 FR 72555, December 6, 2002).

IV. Analysis of Impacts

FDA has examined the impacts of this final rule under Executive Order 12866, the Regulatory Flexibility Act (5 U.S.C. 601–612), and the Unfunded Mandates Reform Act of 1995 (2 U.S.C. 1501 *et seq.*). Executive Order 12866 directs agencies to assess all costs and benefits of available regulatory alternatives and, when regulation is necessary, to select regulatory approaches that maximize net benefits (including potential economic, environmental, public health and safety, and other advantages; distributive impacts; and equity). Under the Regulatory Flexibility Act, if a rule has a significant economic impact on a substantial number of small entities, an agency must analyze regulatory options that would minimize any significant impact of the rule on small entities. Section 202(a) of the Unfunded Mandates Reform Act of 1995 requires that agencies prepare a written statement of anticipated costs and benefits before proposing any rule that may result in an expenditure in any one year by State, local, and tribal governments, in the aggregate, or by the private sector, of $100 million (adjusted annually for inflation).

The agency believes that this final rule is consistent with the principles set out in Executive Order 12866 and in these two statutes. FDA has determined that the final rule is not a significant regulatory action as defined by the Executive order and so is not subject to review under the Executive order. As explained later in this section, FDA concludes that the final rule will not have a significant economic impact on a substantial number of small entities. The Unfunded Mandates Reform Act

---

Illustration 5–2. Ingrown Toenail Relief Drug Products for Over-the-Counter Human Use, 68 Fed. Reg. 24,347 (May 7, 2003) (codified at 21 C.F.R. pts. 310 and 358).

24348　　　**Federal Register** / Vol. 68, No. 88 / Wednesday, May 7, 2003 / Rules and Regulations

does not require FDA to prepare a statement of costs and benefits for this final rule, because the rule is not expected to result in any 1-year expenditure that would exceed $100 million adjusted for inflation. The current inflation adjusted statutory threshold is about $110 million.

The purpose of this final rule is to establish a monograph for ingrown toenail relief drug products for OTC human use and include sodium sulfide 1 percent in a gel vehicle in the monograph. This final rule provides for OTC availability of this type of product.

Manufacturers who wish to market this type of product have the standard costs associated with the introduction of any new product. These include preparation of labeling, stability testing, and implementing manufacturing procedures. Any cost incurred will be voluntary if manufacturers elect to market this type of product. This cost may vary from manufacturer to manufacturer; however, the burden on small manufacturers is not greater than that for large manufacturers. Manufacturers will not incur any costs related to proving safety and effectiveness of the active ingredient for this intended use.

Under the Regulatory Flexibility Act, if a rule has a significant impact on a substantial number of small entities, an agency must analyze regulatory options that would minimize any significant impact of a rule on small entities. This final rule allows manufacturers to market OTC ingrown toenail relief drug products containing sodium sulfide 1 percent in a gel vehicle without having to obtain an approved new drug application, as is currently required, and is beneficial to small entities. Thus, this final rule will not impose a significant economic burden on affected entities. Therefore, under the Regulatory Flexibility Act, the agency certifies that the final rule will not have a significant economic impact on a substantial number of small entities. No further analysis is required.

V. Paperwork Reduction Act of 1995

FDA concludes that the labeling requirements in this document are not subject to review by the Office of Management and Budget because they do not constitute a "collection of information" under the Paperwork Reduction Act of 1995 (44 U.S.C. 3501 *et seq.*). Rather, the labeling statements are a "public disclosure of information originally supplied by the Federal Government to the recipient for the purpose of disclosure to the public" (5 CFR 1320.3(c)(2)).

VI. Environmental Impact

The agency has determined under 21 CFR 25.31(a) that this action is of a type that does not individually or cumulatively have a significant effect on the human environment. Therefore, neither an environmental assessment nor an environmental impact statement is required.

VII. Federalism

FDA has analyzed this final rule in accordance with the principles set forth in Executive Order 13132. FDA has determined that the rule does not contain policies that have substantial direct effects on the States, on the relationship between the National Government and the States, or on the distribution of power and responsibilities among the various levels of government. Accordingly, the agency has concluded that the rule does not contain policies that have federalism implications as defined in the Executive order and, consequently, a federalism summary impact statement is not required.

List of Subjects

21 CFR Part 310

Administrative practice and procedure, Drugs, Labeling, Medical devices, Reporting and recordkeeping requirements.

21 CFR Part 358

Labeling, Over-the-counter drugs.

■ Therefore, under the Federal Food, Drug, and Cosmetic Act and under authority delegated to the Commissioner of Food and Drugs, 21 CFR parts 310 and 358 are amended as follows:

PART 310—NEW DRUGS

■ 1. The authority citation for 21 CFR part 310 continues to read as follows:

Authority: 21 U.S.C. 321, 331, 351, 352, 353, 355, 360b–360f, 360j, 361(a), 371, 374, 375, 379e; 42 U.S.C. 216, 241, 242(a), 262, 263b–263n.

■ 2. Section 310.538 is amended by removing the ingredient sodium sulfide in paragraph (a) and by adding paragraph (e) to read as follows:

§ 310.538　Drug products containing active ingredients offered over-the-counter (OTC) for use for ingrown toenail relief.

*　　*　　*　　*　　*

(e) This section does not apply to sodium sulfide labeled, represented, or promoted for OTC topical use for ingrown toenail relief in accordance with part 358, subpart D of this chapter, after June 6, 2003.

PART 358—MISCELLANEOUS EXTERNAL DRUG PRODUCTS FOR OVER-THE-COUNTER HUMAN USE

3. The authority citation for 21 CFR part 358 continues to read as follows:

Authority: 21 U.S.C. 321, 351, 352, 353, 355, 360, 371.

■ 4. Part 358 is amended by adding new subpart D, consisting of §§ 358.301 to 358.350, to read as follows:

Subpart D—Ingrown Toenail Relief Drug Products

Sec.

358.301　Scope.
358.303　Definitions.
358.310　Ingrown toenail relief active ingredient.
358.350　Labeling of ingrown toenail relief drug products.

Subpart D—Ingrown Toenail Relief Drug Products

§ 358.301　Scope.

(a) An over-the-counter ingrown toenail relief drug product in a form suitable for topical administration is generally recognized as safe and effective and is not misbranded if it meets each condition in this subpart and each general condition established in § 330.1 of this chapter.

(b) References in this subpart to regulatory sections of the Code of Federal Regulations are to chapter 1 of title 21 unless otherwise noted.

§ 358.303　Definitions.

As used in this subpart:

(a) *Ingrown toenail relief drug product.* A drug product applied to an ingrown toenail that relieves pain or discomfort either by softening the nail or by hardening the nail bed.

(b) *Retainer ring.* A die cut polyethylene foam pad coated on one side with medical grade acrylic pressure-sensitive adhesive. The retainer ring has slots, center-cut completely through the foam with the cut of sufficient size to allow for localization of an active ingredient in a gel vehicle to a specific target area. The retainer ring is used with adhesive bandage strips to place over the retainer ring to hold it in place.

§ 358.310　Ingrown toenail relief active ingredient.

The active ingredient of the product is sodium sulfide 1 percent in a gel vehicle. The gel vehicle is an aqueous, semisolid system with large organic molecules interpenetrated with a liquid.

§ 358.350　Labeling of ingrown toenail relief drug products.

(a) *Statement of identity.* The labeling of the product contains the established

Illustration 5–3. 68 Fed. Reg. at 24,348.

i

Reader Aids

Federal Register

Vol. 68, No. 88

Wednesday, May 7, 2003

CUSTOMER SERVICE AND INFORMATION

Federal Register/Code of Federal Regulations

General Information, indexes and other finding aids	202-741-6000
Laws	741-6000

Presidential Documents

Executive orders and proclamations	741-6000
The United States Government Manual	741-6000

Other Services

Electronic and on-line services (voice)	741-6020
Privacy Act Compilation	741-6064
Public Laws Update Service (numbers, dates, etc.)	741-6043
TTY for the deaf-and-hard-of-hearing	741-6086

ELECTRONIC RESEARCH

World Wide Web

Full text of the daily Federal Register, CFR and other publications is located at: **http://www.access.gpo.gov/nara**

Federal Register information and research tools, including Public Inspection List, indexes, and links to GPO Access are located at: **http://www.archives.gov/federal_register/**

E-mail

FEDREGTOC-L (Federal Register Table of Contents LISTSERV) is an open e-mail service that provides subscribers with a digital form of the Federal Register Table of Contents. The digital form of the Federal Register Table of Contents includes HTML and PDF links to the full text of each document.

To join or leave, go to **http://listserv.access.gpo.gov** and select *Online mailing list archives, FEDREGTOC-L, Join or leave the list (or change settings);* then follow the instructions.

PENS (Public Law Electronic Notification Service) is an e-mail service that notifies subscribers of recently enacted laws.

To subscribe, go to **http://listserv.gsa.gov/archives/publaws-l.html** and select *Join or leave the list* (or change settings); then follow the instructions.

FEDREGTOC-L and **PENS** are mailing lists only. We cannot respond to specific inquiries.

Reference questions. Send questions and comments about the Federal Register system to: **info@fedreg.nara.gov**

The Federal Register staff cannot interpret specific documents or regulations.

FEDERAL REGISTER PAGES AND DATE, MAY

23183–23376	1
23377–23568	2
23569–23884	5
23885–24332	6
24333–24604	7

CFR PARTS AFFECTED DURING MAY

At the end of each month, the Office of the Federal Register publishes separately a List of CFR Sections Affected (LSA), which lists parts and sections affected by documents published since the revision date of each title.

3 CFR

Proclamations:

7668	23821
7669	23823
7670	23825
7671	23827
7672	23829
7673	24333

5 CFR

Ch. XIV	23885
2424	23885
2429	23885
2471	23885
2472	23885

Proposed Rules:

2601	23876

7 CFR

46	23377
932	23378
985	23569
1424	24596
1710	24335

Proposed Rules:

274	23927
276	23927
278	23927
279	23927
280	23927
360	23425
1530	23230

9 CFR

Proposed Rules:

2	24052

10 CFR

70	23574
71	23574
72	23183
73	23574

Proposed Rules:

20	23618
490	23620

12 CFR

740	23381

Proposed Rules:

613	23425, 23426

14 CFR

25	24336, 24338
39	23183, 23186, 23190, 23384, 23387, 23575, 23886
71	23577, 23579, 23580, 23581, 23682, 24340, 24341, 24342
77	23583
97	23888, 23889

Proposed Rules:

3	23808

39 23231, 23235, 23427, 23620, 24383

71	23622, 23624, 23625, 23626
330	23627

15 CFR

270	24343

16 CFR

305	23584

17 CFR

232	24345

19 CFR

178	24052

20 CFR

404	23192
416	23192

21 CFR

310	24347
358	24347
1300	23195
1310	23195

Proposed Rules:

1	23630
101	23930

22 CFR

228	23891

23 CFR

Proposed Rules:

630	23239, 24384

24 CFR

203	23370

25 CFR

Proposed Rules:

170	23631

26 CFR

1	23586, 24349, 24351

Proposed Rules:

1	23632, 23931, 24404, 24405, 24406
54	24406
602	24406

29 CFR

Proposed Rules:

1480	23634
1910	23528

30 CFR

36	23892
948	24355

Illustration 5–4. Reader Aids, FEDERAL REGISTER, May 7, 2003, at i.

Food and Drug Administration, HHS   **§ 358.303**

(1) *For products containing any ingredient identified in § 358.110.* (i) "For external use only."

(ii) "Do not use this product on irritated skin, on any area that is infected or reddened, if you are a diabetic, or if you have poor blood circulation."

(iii) "If discomfort persists, see your doctor."

(iv) "Do not use on moles, birthmarks, warts with hair growing from them, genital warts, or warts on the face or mucous membranes."

(2) *For any product formulated in a flammable vehicle.* (i) The labeling should contain an appropriate flammability signal word, e.g. "extremely flammable," "flammable," "combustible," consistent with 16 CFR 1500.3(b)(10).

(ii) "Keep away from fire or flame."

(3) *For any product formulated in a volatile vehicle.* "Cap bottle tightly and store at room temperature away from heat."

(4) *For any product formulated in a collodion-like vehicle.* (i) "If product gets into the eye, flush with water for 15 minutes."

(ii) "Avoid inhaling vapors."

(d) *Directions.* The labeling of the product contains the following information under the heading "Directions":

(1) *For products containing salicylic acid identified in § 358.110(a).* "Wash affected area." (Optional: "May soak wart in warm water for 5 minutes.") "Dry area thoroughly." (If appropriate: "Cut plaster to fit wart.") "Apply medicated plaster. Repeat procedure every 48 hours as needed (until wart is removed) for up to 12 weeks."

(2) *For products containing salicylic acid identified in § 358.110(b).* "Wash affected area." (Optional: "May soak wart in warm water for 5 minutes.") "Dry area thoroughly. Apply" (select one of the following, as appropriate: "one drop" or "small amount") "at a time with" (select one of the following, as appropriate: "applicator" or "brush") "to sufficiently cover each wart. Let dry. Repeat this procedure once or twice daily as needed (until wart is removed) for up to 12 weeks."

(3) *For products containing salicylic acid identified in § 358.110(c).* "Wash affected area." (Optional: "May soak

wart in warm water for 5 minutes.") "Dry area thoroughly. Gently smooth wart surface with emery file supplied." (If appropriate: "Cut plaster to fit wart.") "Apply a drop of warm water to the wart, keeping the surrounding skin dry. Apply medicated plaster at bedtime and leave in place for at least 8 hours. In the morning, remove plaster and discard. Repeat procedure every 24 hours as needed (until wart is removed) for up to 12 weeks."

(e) The word "physician" may be substituted for the word "doctor" in any of the labeling statements in this section.

(f) The phrase "or podiatrist" may be used in addition to the word "doctor" in any of the labeling statements in this section when a product is labeled with the indication identified in § 358.150(b)(2).

[55 FR 33255, Aug. 14, 1990; 55 FR 37403, Sept. 11, 1990, as amended at 57 FR 44495, Sept. 28, 1992; 59 FR 60317, Nov. 23, 1994]

Subpart C [Reserved]

Subpart D—Ingrown Toenail Relief Drug Products

SOURCE: 68 FR 24348, May 7, 2003, unless otherwise noted.

§ 358.301   Scope.

(a) An over-the-counter ingrown toenail relief drug product in a form suitable for topical administration is generally recognized as safe and effective and is not misbranded if it meets each condition in this subpart and each general condition established in § 330.1 of this chapter.

(b) References in this subpart to regulatory sections of the Code of Federal Regulations are to chapter 1 of title 21 unless otherwise noted.

§ 358.303   Definitions.

As used in this subpart:

(a) *Ingrown toenail relief drug product.* A drug product applied to an ingrown toenail that relieves pain or discomfort either by softening the nail or by hardening the nail bed.

(b) *Retainer ring.* A die cut polyethylene foam pad coated on one side with medical grade acrylic pressure-

311

Illustration 5–5. 21 C.F.R. § 358.301 (2008).

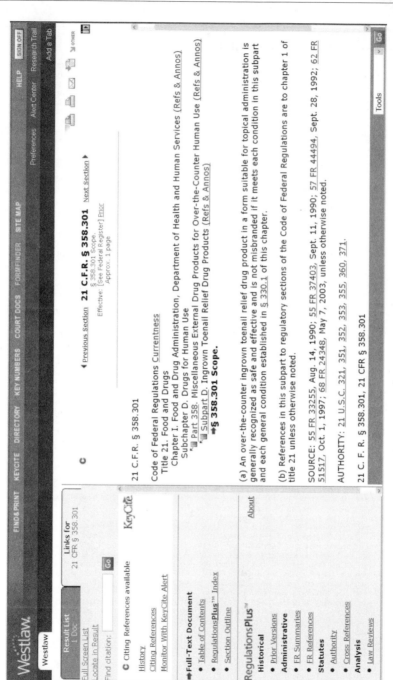

Illustration 5–6. 21 C.F.R. § 358.301 (2008), on Westlaw.

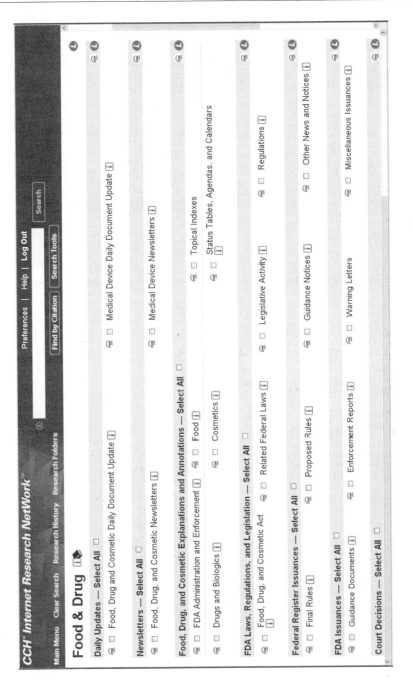

Illustration 5–7. Food & Drug, CCH Internet
Research NetWork <hr.cch.com>.

;;;→ *Caution: Subpart D of Part 358 is added, effective June 6, 2003.—CCH*

Subpart D—Ingrown Toenail Relief Drug Products

[As added, 68 FR 24347, May 7, 2003.]

[¶ 72,607]

§358.301 Scope.

(a) An over-the-counter ingrown toenail relief drug product in a form suitable for topical administration is generally recognized as safe and effective and is not misbranded if it meets each condition in this subpart and each general condition established in §330.1 of this chapter.

(b) References in this subpart to regulatory sections of the Code of Federal Regulations are to chapter 1 of title 21 unless otherwise noted.

[As added, 68 FR 24347, May 7, 2003.]

[¶ 72,609]

§358.303 Definitions.

As used in this subpart:

(a) *Ingrown toenail relief drug product.* A drug product applied to an ingrown toenail that relieves pain or discomfort either by softening the nail or by hardening the nail bed.

(b) *Retainer ring.* A die cut polyethylene foam pad coated on one side with medical grade acrylic pressure-sensitive adhesive. The retainer ring has slots, center-cut completely through the foam with the cut of sufficient size to allow for localization of an active ingredient in a gel vehicle to a specific target area. The retainer ring is used with adhesive bandage strips to place over the retainer ring to hold it in place.

[As added, 68 FR 24347, May 7, 2003.]

[¶ 72,615]

§358.310 Ingrown toenail relief active ingredient.

The active ingredient of the product is sodium sulfide 1 percent in a gel vehicle. The gel vehicle is an aqueous, semisolid system with large organic molecules interpenetrated with a liquid.

[As added, 68 FR 24347, May 7, 2003.]

[¶ 72,617]

§358.350 Labeling of ingrown toenail relief drug products.

(a) *Statement of identity.* The labeling of the product contains the established name of the product, if any, and identifies the product as an "ingrown toenail relief product" or as an "ingrown toenail discomfort reliever."

(b) *Indications.* The labeling of the product states, under the heading "Use," the following:

"for temporary relief of" [select one or both of the following: 'pain' or 'discomfort'] "from ingrown toenails". Other truthful and nonmis leading statements, describing only the use that has been established and listed in this paragraph (b), may also be used, as provided in Sec. 330.1(c)(2) of this chapter, subject to the provisions of section 502 of the Federal Food, Drug, and Cosmetic Act (the act) relating to misbranding and the prohibition in section 301(d) of the act against the introduction or delivery for introduction into interstate commerce of unapproved new drugs in violation of section 505(a) of the act.

(c) *Warnings.* The labeling of the product contains the following warnings under the heading "Warnings":

(1) "For external use only" in accord with Sec. 201.66(c)(5)(i) of this chapter.

(2) "Do not use [bullet][1] on open sores".

(3) "Ask a doctor before use if you have [bullet] diabetes [bullet] poor circulation [bullet] gout".

(4) "When using this product [bullet] use with a retainer ring".

(5) "Stop use and ask a doctor if [bullet] redness or swelling of your toe increases [bullet] discharge is present around the nail [bullet] symptoms last more than 7 days or clear up and occur again within a few days".

(d) *Directions.* The labeling of the product contains the following statements under the heading "Directions":

(1) "[Bullet] adults and children 12 years and over:"

(i) "[Bullet] wash the affected area and dry thoroughly [bullet] place retainer ring on toe with slot over the area where the ingrown nail and the skin meet. Smooth ring down firmly. [bullet] apply enough gel product to fill the slot in the ring [bullet] place round center section of bandage strip directly over the gel-filled ring to seal the gel in place. Smooth ends of bandage strip around toes."

(ii) "[Bullet] repeat twice daily (morning and night) for up to 7 days until discomfort is relieved or until the nail can be lifted out of the nail groove and easily trimmed".

(2) "[Bullet] children under 12 years: ask a doctor".

[As added, 68 FR 24347, May 7, 2003.]

[The next page is 72,839.]

---

[1] See §201.66(b)(4) of this chapter for definition of bullet.

Illustration 5–8. 21 C.F.R. pt. 358, subpt. D, Food Drug Cosmetic Law Reports (CCH) ¶ ¶ 72–607–72–617 (2006).

Federal Anti-Tampering Act Provisions

¶ **4235   Tamper-Resistant Packaging, Penalties for Tampering**

A rash of drug-tampering incidents in 1982 prompted the Food and Drug Administration to issue regulations mandating tamper-resistant packaging for most over-the-counter (OTC) drugs and some cosmetics. The regulations were issued under the same authority to prevent misbranding and adulteration that the agency has used to establish good manufacturing practice requirements (.01). The requirements for tamper-resistant packaging for OTC drugs and cosmetics are discussed in the Drugs Cosmetics Volumes at ¶ 70,219 and ¶ 78,109, respectively.

In 1983, the Congress acted to make tampering with consumer products a federal crime, and the Federal Anti-Tampering Act was signed into law on October 13, 1983. Tampering committed with "reckless disregard for the risk that another person will be placed in danger of death or bodily injury" is subject to penalties of up to a $100,000 fine, 20 years imprisonment, or both, depending on the consequences of the tampering. The penalties for tampering with a consumer product, including a food, drug, or cosmetic product, with the intent to cause serious injury to a business are the same as the penalties authorized under the FDC Act for fraudulent adulteration.

The Federal Anti-Tampering Act also penalizes the knowing communication of false information that a consumer product has been tainted. Threatening to or conspiring to tamper can result in penalties of five-years imprisonment, $25,000 fines, or both. The Act empowers the Food and Drug Administration to investigate violations of the Federal Anti-Tampering Act concerning products regulated by the FDA under other acts (.02).

.01 Preamble to Final Order, 47 FR 50442, November 5, 1982, 21 CFR § 211.132 and 21 CFR § 700.25.

.02 October 13, 1983, P.L. 98-127; 18 U.S.C. 1365.

False Claims

.15 The jury was presented sufficient evidence to support its verdict convicting a man of falsely claiming that a product was tainted. The government alleged that the man placed syringe in a soft drink can and then informed an employee of the diner where he received the beverage, a state trooper, and agents of the Federal Bureau of Investigation that he found the syringe in the can. Although there was no direct evidence to support the government's allegation, the government presented strong circumstantial evidence that the defendant was the only person who had the opportunity of placing the syringe in the can. Testimony presented by the defendant that attempted to refute the government's case did not alter the fact that a rational jury could have found the defendant guilty beyond a reasonable doubt. *U.S. v. Claypool* (3rd Cir. 1996) unpub op, 1996 FDC LRept Dev Trans Bind ¶ 38,443.

Product Substitution

.25 By removing hydrocodone tablets from their bottles and replacing them with other medications, a physician's assistant was guilty of consumer product tampering. Contrary to the assistant's assertion, it was not necessary that he tamper with the hydrocodone tablets. Substituting other medicines for the labeled product is tampering within the meaning of the federal antitampering provision, which was enacted because penalties under the Federal Food, Drug, and Cosmetic Act were too lenient. In light of the purposes of the FDC Act,

which defines substitution as a form of adulteration, replacing one drug with another constituted tampering with the first drug. *U.S. v. Garnett* (11th Cir.) 122 F3d 1016.

Interstate Commerce

.35 A man was properly convicted of falsely claiming that a can of soft drink contained a syringe, even though he made the claim after he purchased the beverage. Contrary to the defendant's argument, his false tampering claim affected interstate commerce within the meaning of the antitampering statute. His accusation about the manufacturer's beverage added to the concern that was already created by earlier reports that the cans contained syringes. The interstate commerce element of the statute was satisfied when the government proved that the defendant's can of soft drink previously traveled in interstate commerce. It was not necessary to prove that the defendant knew that the can traveled in interstate commerce. *U.S. v. Botello* (9th Cir. 1995) 1996 FDC LRept Dev Trans Bind ¶ 38,445.

.36 The removal of morphine from cassettes before administering it to hospital patients sufficiently affected interstate commerce for the application of the federal product tampering statute. A woman found guilty of product tampering contended that the cassettes had reached the end consumer and were not in the stream of commerce at the time the tampering occurred. Because some portion of the morphine prescribed for the patients never reached them because of removal from the cassettes, it was reasonable to conclude that the morphine was still in

Illustration 5–9. Federal Anti–Tampering Act Provisions, Food Drug Cosmetic Law Reports (CCH) ¶ 4235 (2005).

2352 2-18-2008 **Topical Index** **3155**

References are to paragraph (¶) numbers.

State laws—continued
. Pennsylvania . . . 30,000
. Rhode Island . . . 31,500
. South Carolina . . . 32,003
. South Dakota . . . 32,500
. Tennessee . . . 33,000
. Texas . . . 33,500
. Utah . . . 34,000
. Vermont . . . 34,500
. Virginia . . . 35,000
. Washington . . . 35,500
. West Virginia . . . 36,000
. Wisconsin . . . 36,500
. Wyoming . . . 36,700

Subpoenas
. FDC Act suits
. . nationwide . . . 104

Substances
. generally recognized as safe—see Food
. Index... page 25

Sunscreen drug products, over-the-counter
. regulations
. . promulgation . . . 1193Q

Sweeteners, nonnutritive—see Nonnutritive substances

T

Tableting machines
. Controlled Substances Act prohibition . . . 1484

Tampering—see also Packaging
. false claims
. . soft drink can . . . 4235.15
. interstate commerce element . . . 4235.35
. penalties . . . 4235
. product substitution
. . medications . . . 4235.25

Tea Importation Act
. repeal . . . 700

Tennessee
. basic food, drug, and cosmetic laws
. . text . . . 33,010
. court decisions . . . 33,200
. officials, FDA-related functions . . . 33,009

Territory, U.S.
. definition
. . FDC Act . . . 32
. manufacture of adulterated or misbranded article . . . 67

Tests
. clinical—see Clinical investigations
. nonclinical—see Good laboratory practices, nonclinical

Texas
. basic food, drug, and cosmetic laws
. . text . . . 33,510

Texas—continued
. court decisions . . . 33,850
. officials, FDA-related functions . . . 33,509

Tobacco products
. regulation
. . authority . . . 1195F; 2010.35

Tolerances
. pesticides
. . agricultural commodities, raw . . . 176
. . establishment, confidential nature of data submitted . . . 181
. . establishment, procedure . . . 179
. . initiation by HHS . . . 180

Tort liability, federal
. FDA as defendant . . . 2011
. imports, detained
. . recovery . . . 4175.91

Tort liability, state—see Products liability

Trade correspondence
. finding list... page 2109

Trade regulation
. Federal Trade Commission Act . . . 890

Trade secrets
. disclosure
. . protective orders . . . 4040.20

Trade secrets—see also Information disclosure
. definition . . . 1240; 2153; 4205
. disclosure
. . allowance . . . 4040
. . condemnation proceeding . . . 4147.70
. . congressional committees . . . 2153.20
. . FOI Act, exemption . . . 2147.27
. . FPL Act, exemption . . . 4205
. . protection . . . 2153; 4040
. discoverability
. . effect . . . 4205.37
. product formula or ingredients
. . labeling, authority to require, Texas . . . 33,850.35
. property interest . . . 4205.35
. release to contractors . . . 398; 2153
. revelation . . . 70

Tropical disease treatments
. generally . . . 4195

U

Uniform State Food, Drug, and Cosmetic Bill
. text . . . 10,100

Unwholesome
. definition . . . 804

User fees—see Drugs, prescription

Utah
. basic food and animal drug laws
. . text . . . 34,030
. court decisions . . . 34,200
. officials, FDA-related functions . . . 34,009

Food Drug Cosmetic Law Reports **UTA**

Illustration 5–10. Topical Index, Food Drug Cosmetic Law Reports (CCH) (2008).

Chapter 6

THE JUDICIARY, PART 1: INTRODUCTION

Table of Sections

The legislative branch makes the laws by enacting statutes, and the executive branch enforces these laws through regulations and other administrative action. The judicial branch decides disputes, but in doing so it creates law and determines how these statutes and regulations will be interpreted. The judiciary's place in the American legal system is vitally important, and reports of judicial decisions are among the most important sources of legal authority in the common law system.

The next four chapters concentrate on the judicial branch. This chapter introduces judicial decisions and provides historical background on case publication. Chapters 7 and 8 explain where to find these decisions and several of the major methods used for case law research. Chapter 9 discusses several other aspects of judicial and case information, such as court rules and briefs, that are important resources in legal research.

§ 6.1 The Nature of Case Law

"Case law" generally refers to the written opinions of appellate courts on specific issues raised in litigated disputes. Understanding case law's role in the common law system requires a familiarity with the hierarchical structure of court systems and the nature of judicial decisions.

(a) Court Systems

Each court system, federal and state, has a system of trial and appellate courts, with a *court of last resort* that creates rules that are binding on the lower courts in the system. A central function of courts of last resort and other appellate courts is to establish rules of conduct for society, as well as simply determining the rights of the parties appearing before them.[1]

Trial Courts. The *trial court* is where litigation usually begins. The jurisdiction of these courts may be based on geography (the U.S. District Courts in the federal system, or county courts in many states) or subject (the U.S. Tax Court, or state family courts and probate courts). In the trial court, *issues of fact* (such as which of two cars entered an intersection first) are decided by the fact finder, either the judge or a jury. These findings are binding on the parties and cannot be appealed. *Issues of law* (such as whether a witness's statement is admissible at trial) are decided by the judge, and a party who disagrees with these rulings can appeal them to a higher court.

Appellate Courts. Appeals from trial court decisions are generally taken to an intermediate appellate court (the U.S. Courts of Appeals and similar state tribunals). An appellate court usually consists of a panel of three or more judges, who typically confer and vote on the issues after considering written briefs and oral argument for each side. One of the judges writes an opinion summarizing the question and stating the court's holding. Dissenting judges may write separate opinions outlining their views.

Courts of Last Resort. The court of last resort in each jurisdiction (called the Supreme Court in the federal system and in most states) usually reviews cases from the intermediate appellate courts, but may take appeals directly from trial courts. Unlike other appellate courts, most courts of last resort have discretion in deciding which cases they will hear.[2] Their role in the judicial system is not to resolve every individual dispute, but rather to establish rules, review legislative and administrative acts, and resolve differences among intermediate appellate courts. A court of last resort's decisions on issues of law are binding on all courts within its jurisdiction.

---

1. Numerous works discuss the role of judges in deciding cases and creating legal doctrine. Useful introductory works include LAWRENCE BAUM, AMERICAN COURTS: PROCESS AND POLICY (6th ed. 2008), ROBERT A. CARP ET AL., JUDICIAL PROCESS IN AMERICA (7th ed. 2007), and DANIEL JOHN MEADOR, AMERICAN COURTS (2d ed. 2000).

2. Most courts of last resort can simply reject an appeal from a lower court. When the Supreme Court of the United States refuses to hear a case, its action is known as *denying a petition for writ of certiorari,* or "denying cert." A court of last resort may determine the outcome of a case by refusing to hear an appeal and thereby letting a lower court decision stand. The Supreme Court has repeatedly stressed that a denial of certiorari has no precedential value. See, e.g., *Brown v. Allen,* 344 U.S. 443, 488–97 (1953) (opinion of Frankfurter, J.).

(b) The Doctrine of Precedent

An essential element of the common law is the doctrine of precedent, or *stare decisis* ("let the decision stand"), under which courts are bound to follow earlier decisions. These provide guidance to later courts faced with similar cases, and aid in preventing further disputes. Although the law changes with time, precedent is designed to provide both fairness and stability. People similarly situated are similarly dealt with, and judgments are consistent rather than arbitrary, so that the consequences of contemplated conduct can be predicted.

The precedential value of a decision is determined in large part by a court's place in the judicial hierarchy. Decisions from a higher court in a jurisdiction are binding or *mandatory authority*, and must be followed by a lower court in the same jurisdiction. Decisions from courts in other jurisdictions are not binding, but a court in another state may have considered a situation similar to that in issue and may provide *persuasive authority*. A court may be persuaded to follow its lead and reach a similar conclusion, or may consider it poorly reasoned or inapplicable and arrive at a very different result.

Under the doctrine of *stare decisis,* a case's holding will govern other cases in its jurisdiction presenting the same or substantially similar facts and issues. The holding, or *ratio decidendi,* of a case can usually be summed up in a single declaratory sentence. Everything else in the court's opinion is *dictum,* or *obiter dicta,* something "said by the way."

Only the holding of the court is authoritative and binding under the doctrine of precedent. A court is considered competent to decide only those issues which were in dispute and therefore argued before it. The holding is limited to the decision and the significant or material facts upon which the court necessarily relied in arriving at its determination.

A judge may comment in an opinion on extraneous issues or speculate about possibilities not at issue in the immediate controversy. These portions of an opinion are dicta and therefore not binding. Dictum in an opinion can explain a decision and signal the court's intention regarding the narrowness or breadth of its holding, so the entire opinion is important and none of it can be ignored. A later court, however, is free to disagree with dictum, which cannot be relied upon as precedent and should be identified as dictum if cited.[3]

---

3. THE BLUEBOOK: A UNIFORM SYSTEM OF CITATION R. 10.6.1(a), at 91 (18th ed. 2005) ("When a case is cited for a proposition that is not the single, clear holding of a majority of the court (e.g., alternative holding; by implication; dictum; dissenting opinion; plurality opinion; holding unclear), indicate that fact par-

§ 6.2   Forms of Court Decisions

Most court reports, both online and in print, consist of the decisions of courts of last resort and intermediate appellate courts on issues of law. Very few trial court decisions are published. Trial court decisions on issues of fact have no precedential effect and usually do not even result in written judicial opinions. A jury verdict at the end of a trial, for example, produces no published decision unless the judge rules on a motion challenging the verdict on legal grounds. Trial court decisions on issues of law are sometimes published, but these are generally less important than appellate court decisions.

Whether online or in print, most judicial decisions are published in two formats. Their first appearance contains only the text of the court's opinion, but editorial material is then added to help readers understand the case and to use it as a vehicle for finding other documents. These editorial enhancements are found in the versions of cases in most reporter volumes and in major online services such as Westlaw and Lexis.

Slip Opinions. A new decision first appears as the official *slip opinion* issued by the court itself and usually available in PDF from the court's website. Slip opinions are individually paginated documents containing the full text of the court's decision, but they have two major drawbacks for research purposes. They rarely provide material that would facilitate research, such as a summary of the court's decision, and because their page numbering is not final they are cited by docket number and date rather than to a permanent published source.

The case shown in Illustration 6–1 on page 229, for example, would be cited as a slip opinion as *Goree v. State*, No. F–2005–1088 (Okla. Crim. App. May 23, 2007). Westlaw and Lexis provide access to slip opinions as soon as they are available, and add their own online citations, as in 2007 WL 31213 or 2007 Okla. Crim. App. LEXIS 21. If a case is then published in a reporter volume, its online citation is generally replaced by a citation to the reporter volume and page number: *Goree v. State*, 163 P.3d 583 (Okla. Crim. App. 2007).

Court Reports. The next form of court reports provides the editorial summaries and page citations lacking in slip opinions. On Westlaw and in West's National Reporter System series, each case is prefaced with a brief summary of its holding, called a *synopsis*, and with numbered editorial abstracts, or *headnotes*, of the specific legal issues. Each headnote is assigned a legal topic and a number

enthetically"). The ALWD manual says only that "[y]ou may parenthetically provide information about the weight of the case." ALWD CITATION MANUAL: A PROFESSIONAL SYSTEM OF CITATION R. 12.11(b), at 94 (3d ed. 2006).

indicating a particular section within that topic. This classification plan, known as the *key number system*, consists of over four hundred broad topics with tens of thousands of sections. The headnotes are reprinted by subject in *digests*, case-finding resources that will be discussed in Chapter 8. *Goree v. State* in Illustration 6–1 has three numbered headnotes, all in the Assault and Battery topic.

Lexis also replaces the initial slip opinion with a version that adds editorial material, including a case summary, a list of computer-generated "core terms," and headnotes. Illustration 6–2 on page 230 shows the Lexis version of *Goree v. State*, including the beginning of the case summary.

In print, several cases are issued together in weekly or biweekly pamphlets known as *advance sheets*. The cases in advance sheets are published with volume and page numbers, and are eventually reissued with revisions and corrections in permanent bound volumes that consolidate the contents of several advance sheets. These volumes are numbered consecutively, often in more than one successive series.

Public Domain Citations. In recent years, there has been a movement for jurisdictions to provide *public domain citations* to new decisions. This gives the decisions a permanent citation as soon as they are announced, and it allows researchers to cite decisions without having to use printed volumes or a commercial database. Public domain citations have been endorsed by the American Bar Association,[4] and if a public domain citation is available its use is required by *The Bluebook*.[5] Only a few jurisdictions, however, have adopted rules requiring paragraph numbers or other public domain citation features.[6] The public domain citation for the case in Illustration 6–1, *Goree v. State*, is 2007 OK CR 21, indicating that this is the 21st decision delivered in 2007 by the Court of Criminal Appeals of Oklahoma. The page shown includes the first numbered paragraph of the court's opinion.

In most instances and for most jurisdictions, cases are still identified by citations to the published volumes. Even though many

---

4. 121 no. 2 REP. A.B.A. 16–19, 427–52 (1996).

5. THE BLUEBOOK: A UNIFORM SYSTEM OF CITATION R. 10.3.3 (18th ed. 2005). The ALWD manual permits, but does not require, use of public-domain citations. ALWD CITATION MANUAL: A PROFESSIONAL SYSTEM OF CITATION R. 12.16 (3d ed. 2006).

6. The ABA Universal Citation page <www.abanet.org/tech/ltrc/research/citation/> and American Association of

Law Libraries (AALL) Citation Formats Committee <www.aallnet.org/committee/citation/> both provide background information and links for adopting jurisdictions. The AALL has issued a *Universal Citation Guide* (2d ed. 2004) providing rules for a uniform public domain format. See also Peter W. Martin, *Neutral Citation, Court Web Sites, and Access to Authoritative Case Law*, 99 LAW LIBR. J. 329 (2007) for a history of the public domain citation movement.

researchers find and read cases online instead of in printed reports, both *The Bluebook* and the *ALWD Citation Manual* specify that cases generally be cited to printed reports if they are published in that form.[7] Indeed, the published version in most jurisdictions is the official text in case of any discrepancies between it and an online version.[8]

§ 6.3 Features of Published Cases

A published decision has several distinct features, some available as soon as the slip opinion is first released and others added later to the final printed or online version. Several of these standard features are shown in Illustration 6–1 on page 229.

Case Name. The name (or *caption* or *style*) of a case identifies the parties involved. The normal form is *X v. Y*. The party named first is usually the plaintiff, or the party bringing suit, and the second party the defendant. In appellate cases the first party is often the appellant or petitioner (i.e., the party that filed the appeal) and the second party the appellee or respondent, no matter which was the original plaintiff. In Illustration 6–1, *Goree v. State*, Goree is the appellant and the state of Oklahoma is the appellee. In some cases a procedural phrase such as *Ex parte* or *In re* is used instead, followed by the name of one party or a description of the property that is the subject of the action.

Docket Number. The docket number, or record number, is assigned by the court clerk to the case when it is filed initially for the court's consideration. It is the number the court uses to keep track of the documents and briefs filed in the case. As noted earlier, the docket number in the case shown in Illustration 6–1 is No. F–2005–1088. Cases are generally cited by docket number only if they are not available in a published reporter. As will be discussed in Chapter 9, the docket number is useful in following the status of a case on the court's calendar and for finding the briefs and appendices filed by the parties.

Citation. While slip opinions are generally cited by docket number, published opinions are cited by the reporter volume in

---

7. THE BLUEBOOK: A UNIFORM SYSTEM OF CITATION R. 10.3.1, at 86–87 (18th ed. 2005); ALWD CITATION MANUAL: A PROFESSIONAL SYSTEM OF CITATION R. 12.4, at 76 (3d ed. 2006).

8. For several years the Westlaw version of *Diffenderfer v. Diffenderfer*, 491 So.2d 265 (Fla. 1986), contained a typographical error changing the phrase "her interest in the pension" to "his interest in the pension," causing some citing courts to misapply its holding. Sixteen years later, *Acker v. Acker*, 821 So.2d 1088, 1091 (Fla. Dist. Ct. App. 2002), *aff'd*, 904 So. 2d 384 (Fla. 2005), held that the version of the case published in the bound reporter was authoritative. See Mary M. McCormick, *Differences between Electronic and Paper West Reporters*, Posting to Law–Lib@ucdavis.edu (Sept. 5, 2003) <listproc.ucdavis.edu/archives/law-lib/law-lib.log0309/0102.html>.

which they appear and the page number on which the caption appears (and by public domain citation in those jurisdictions which have adopted such systems). In Illustration 6–1, the citation for *State v. Goree* is indicated at the top of the page. A full case citation also identifies the deciding court, if not obvious from the reporter abbreviation, and includes the year of decision. These are both essential pieces of information for determining the importance of a case and its weight as precedent.

Many cases have more than one reporter citation, particularly if they are published in both official and commercial sources. Two citations to the same case are known as *parallel citations*. Which citation, or citations, to use is determined by the rules being followed—such as local court rules, *The Bluebook*, or the *ALWD Citation Manual*. Westlaw, Lexis, and most other online sources provide all available citations for cases. Many printed reporters also include the parallel citation if it is available when the volume is issued. Note in Illustration 6–1 that the public domain citation is provided just above the name of the case.

Official Syllabus and Headnotes. Below the docket number in Illustration 6–1 is the *syllabus,* a summary of the case's facts and the court's holding. Many actions contain more than one question of law, and a court may dispose of several individual legal questions in a single opinion. Some official reports provide separate *headnotes* describing the various points decided by the court.

In the official reports of some jurisdictions, the syllabus is written by the court itself. Generally, however, the syllabus and headnotes are prepared by a reporter and are not an official statement of the holding.[9] The syllabus and headnotes serve as useful guides to what is discussed in the case, but the holding is found in the words of the opinion itself. If a syllabus or headnote is inconsistent with the court's opinion, the opinion governs.[10] Not all

---

9. The syllabus is prepared by the court in three states. KAN. STAT. ANN. § 20–111 (2007); OHIO REV. CODE § 2503.20 (LexisNexis 2008 Supp.); W. VA. CONST., Art. 8, § 4. In other jurisdictions, justices may review syllabi prepared by the reporter. Justice Ruth Bader Ginsburg described Supreme Court practices in a published speech: "The syllabus is drafted by the Reporter of Decisions, but the justice who wrote the opinion may edit it closely and sometimes rewrite passages, as I more than occasionally do, mindful that busy lawyers and judges may not read more." Ruth Bader Ginsburg, *Informing the Public About the U.S. Supreme Court's Work*, 29 LOYOLA U. CHI. L.J. 275, 275–76

(1998). For the story of an extended dispute among Supreme Court justices and their reporter about the wording of a headnote, see Alan F. Westin, *Stephen J. Field and the Headnote to* O'Neil v. Vermont: *A Snapshot of the Fuller Court at Work*, 67 YALE L.J. 363 (1958).

10. Ohio is an exception, in providing that the syllabus is the official statement of the law of the case and governs if there is any inconsistency between it and the opinion. Ohio S. Ct. R. Rep. Op. 1(B)(2). Every U.S. Supreme Court slip opinion carries a warning that the syllabus "constitutes no part of the opinion of the Court and has been prepared by the Reporter of Decisions for the con-

cases include official syllabi or headnotes; there are none, for example, for decisions of the lower federal courts.

Commercial Summaries and Headnotes. The official syllabus and headnotes are preceded or followed in some sources, such as Westlaw, Lexis, and West reporters, by summaries and headnotes prepared by the publisher's editorial staff.

Westlaw and West reporters include a *synopsis*, similar to but generally more concise than an official syllabus. The synopsis for recent cases (beginning in late 2003) is divided into separate sections for "Background," explaining the facts and procedure of the case, and "Holdings," itemizing the matters decided by the court. Older cases have a simpler one-paragraph synopsis.

The West synopsis is followed by numbered headnotes, which are usually more extensive than those of the official reporter and are assigned topics and key numbers to identify the subject matter. The online headnotes are hyperlinked to the portion of the opinion from which they are drawn, and bracketed bold numbers in the text of the opinion (online and in print) indicate the corresponding headnote.

Lexis cases generally begin with a case summary divided into three sections: outline of the procedural posture, overview of the issues, and outcome. Lexis also provides headnotes, drawn directly from the language of the opinion. As in Westlaw, the headnotes are hyperlinked to the corresponding location in the text.

It is important to remember that the synopsis and headnotes are not prepared by the court but by an editor working for a commercial publisher, and that they are merely finding aids and should not be cited or relied upon as authoritative. Many headnotes cover topics discussed in dictum, sometimes even in footnotes, rather than the case's holding. It is necessary to read the opinion to determine the court's holding, and then to rely on and cite the text in the opinion rather than a synopsis or headnote.

Names of Counsel. In commercial databases and in most reporters, the names of the lawyers who represented the parties usually appear after the headnotes and before the opinion of the court. Identifying the attorneys can be helpful because they may be able to provide further information about the litigation or copies of briefs they submitted. In online databases, searching for the names of lawyers can lead you to other cases on which they've worked. At one time reports regularly carried excerpts or summaries of the

venience of the reader," citing *United States v. Detroit Timber & Lumber Co.,* 200 U.S. 321, 337 (1906). But see Gil Grantmore, *The Headnote*, 5 GREEN BAG 2D 157, 158 (2002) (encouraging "reliance upon the syllabus, rather than on the Court's increasingly long-winded, turgid opinions. Ideally, anything not found in the syllabus should be presumptively classified as dictum.")

arguments of counsel. These summaries are no longer provided in most reports, but Westlaw and Lexis increasingly provide links to the full texts of the briefs themselves.

Names of Judges. The final element before the opinion itself is usually the names of the judges, identifying the members of the panel who heard the case and the author of the opinion. Most appellate cases are heard by panels of three or more judges, and in courts of last resort there is usually a bench of five, seven or nine judges. The names of any judges writing concurring or dissenting opinions are also usually indicated at this point.

Opinion(s). Finally we get to the work of the court, the opinion. A *majority opinion*, representing the opinion of the court, almost always appears first. It is usually signed by an individual judge, but in some cases a *per curiam* opinion is issued, one which represents the court without authorship attributed to any individual judge. *Per curiam* opinions are generally short, and either cover points of law the court feels are too obvious to merit elaboration or represent sensitive issues the court does not want to treat at length. They do, however, carry the weight of precedent. It can be assumed that all other judges subscribe to the first opinion, unless they have written or expressly joined in either a concurring or dissenting opinion.

Occasionally there is no line of reasoning agreed upon by a majority, and a *plurality opinion* is printed first. This announces the judgment of the court, but its views are not binding authority in subsequent cases.

A concurring opinion is written when a judge agrees with the result reached by the majority of the court, but either does not fully agree with the reasoning used to reach that result or feels the need to add something further. In some decisions, there is more than one concurring opinion.

Following the majority opinion and any concurrences, there may be one or more dissenting opinions. These reflect the views of judges who do not agree with the result reached by the majority of the court. Some cases, particularly from the Supreme Court of the United States, feature a dizzying array of concurrences and dissents, with some judges concurring in part and dissenting in part and others joining an opinion except for a particular section or even a footnote.[11]

---

11. A great variety of permutations is possible. *Planned Parenthood of Southeastern Pa. v. Casey*, 505 U.S. 833 (1992), featured a joint opinion of Justices O'Connor, Kennedy and Souter, which "announced the judgment of the Court and delivered the opinion of the Court with respect to Parts I, II, III, V–A, V–C, and VI, an opinion with respect to Part V–E, in which Justice Stevens joins, and an opinion with respect to Parts IV, V–B, and V–D." This was fol-

Although dissenting opinions carry no force as precedent, they may have persuasive authority and can be cited if clearly labeled as dissents. A well-reasoned dissent may eventually lead to changes in the law. Dissents by justices such as John Marshall Harlan and Oliver Wendell Holmes are among the most influential opinions in the Supreme Court's history.[12]

§ 6.4   A Brief History of Case Publication

A knowledge of the history of court reports can help in understanding case law. Most decisions are now retrieved electronically, but they are usually still cited to printed sources. A case citation communicates information about the scope and nature of a decision's precedential value. A familiarity with cited sources and their background can place a decision in context and provide a quicker understanding of a decision's importance.

From its earliest beginnings in antiquity, the reporting of cases helped to achieve certainty in the law by providing written records for later tribunals faced with similar issues and thereby reducing further disputes. The earliest evidence of recorded judicial decisions in England dates from the 11th century. Two hundred years later a series known as the Year Books began providing notes of debates between judges and counsel on the points in issue in cases. While not containing the texts of decisions, the Year Books were used as guidance in subsequent cases. Manuscripts of reported cases exist from as early as the 13th century, the first printed versions appeared in about 1481, and the Year Books continued until 1535.[13]

The Year Books were followed by *nominative* reports, that is, reports named for the person who recorded or edited them. The first volume of nominative reports was prepared by Edmund Plowden and published in 1571. It was followed by numerous series by dozens of jurists and lawyers, of varying accuracy and authority.[14]

lowed by opinions by four other justices: one concurring in part and dissenting in part; one concurring in part, concurring in the judgment in part, and dissenting in part; and two concurring in the judgment in part and dissenting in part.

12. See, e.g., *Lochner v. New York*, 198 U.S. 45, 74 (1905) (Holmes, J., dissenting); *Plessy v. Ferguson*, 163 U.S. 537, 552 (1896) (Harlan, J., dissenting).

13. See Paul Brand, *The Beginnings of English Law Reporting*, in Law Reporting in Britain 1 (Chantal Stebbings ed., 1995) (on the period before the Year Books); Percy H. Winfield, The Chief Sources of English Legal History 158–83 (1925) (on the Year Books).

Many of the Year Books have been translated into English and published by the Selden Society, and they have been indexed and summarized by David J. Seipp, *Legal History: The Year Books* <www.bu.edu/law/seipp/>. For a growing bibliography of published and online sources, see the University of Southern California's English Medieval Legal Document Wiki <emld.usc.edu>. Anyone interested in deciphering the original texts should probably start with J.H. Baker, Manual of Law French (2d ed. 1990).

14. L. W. Abbott, Law Reporting in England 1485–1585 (1973) provides an excellent history of early English re-

The development of printed reports changed the nature of legal practice dramatically, from a reliance on general principles to an increasing use of case citations as authority.[15]

More than 270 series of nominative reports were cumulated into *The English Reports* (1900–32), covering cases from 1220 to 1865 in 176 volumes. This is now the standard source for older English cases, many of which have been incorporated as part of American common law.[16] *The English Reports* is available from several subscription online sources, including Westlaw (ENG–RPTS), HeinOnline, and Justis <www.justis.com>. The Commonwealth Legal Information Institute has free access to the set <www.commonlii.org/int/cases/EngR/>.[17]

The American colonies inherited the English legal system and its common law tradition. The decisions of American courts were not published at all during the colonial period and the early years of independence, and American lawyers and judges relied for precedent on the decisions of the English courts. The first volumes of American court decisions were not published until thirteen years after independence, in 1789 when Ephraim Kirby's *Reports of Cases Adjudged in the Superior Court of the State of Connecticut* and Francis Hopkinson's *Judgements in the Admiralty of Pennsylvania*

---

ports, and JOHN WILLIAM WALLACE, THE REPORTERS, ARRANGED AND CHARACTERIZED WITH INCIDENTAL REMARKS (4th ed. 1882), has a more extensive survey of the nominative reporters. Among the less reliable reporters Wallace discusses were Joseph Keble (1632–1710) ("Mr. Justice Park burned his copy, thinking it not worth while to lumber his library with trash") and Thomas Barnardiston (1706–1752) (quoting the nineteenth century jurist Lord Lyndhurst telling a lawyer that it was said "that he was accustomed to slumber over his note-book, and the wags in the rear took the opportunity of scribbling nonsense in it"). Id. at 315, 424 (footnote omitted).

15. By 1600 lawyers could already complain about "such an ocean of reportes, and such a perplexed confusion of opinions. WILLIAM FULBECK, A DIRECTION, OR PREPARATIVE TO THE STUDY OF THE LAWE 5b (London: T. Wight 1600). On the changing nature of precedent, see Richard J. Ross, *The Memorial Culture of Early Modern English Lawyers: Memory as Keyword, Shelter, and Identity, 1560–1640*, 10 YALE J. L. & HUMAN. 229, 267–70 (1998).

16. The "reception" statutes passed by many early state legislatures accepted English common law limited to cases

that were not repugnant to the law of the newly independent state, and often further limited to cases decided before the date of independence or the founding of the first English colony. These statutes are conveniently listed and summarized in Joseph Fred Benson, *Reception of the Common Law in Missouri: Section 1.010 as Interpreted by the Supreme Court of Missouri*, 67 MO. L. REV. 595, 607–611 (2002).

17. Two other compilations of older English cases, including some not found in *The English Reports*, are the *Revised Reports* (1891–1917) and the *All England Law Reports Reprint, 1558–1935* (1957–68). Decisions in some criminal cases appear in the nominative reports and *The English Reports*, but the source for accounts of major trials for treason and related offenses is *A Complete Collection of State Trials* (William Cobbett & Thomas Bayly Howell eds., 1809–28). Less lofty criminal proceedings are represented in The Proceedings of the Old Bailey, 1674–1913 <www.oldbailey online.org>, which has searchable access to synopses of nearly 200,000 trials at London's central criminal court.

were published.[18] In a preface Kirby discusses the concerns which led to the publication of his reports, including the inapplicability of English law in the new country and the need to create a permanent body of American common law.

Reports from other states and from the new federal courts soon followed, although the courts of some states operated for decades without published decisions. *Official* series of court reports (published pursuant to statutory direction or court authorization) began in several states in the early 1800s. Many of these early publications were nominative reports, cited, like their English predecessors, by the names of their reporters.

Gradually the nominative reports gave way to officially published sets of sequentially numbered reports. Some states subsequently renumbered their reports, incorporating the nominative volumes as the first numbered volumes in the official set, but other states have early nominative volumes without an overall numbering sequence. If the reporter abbreviation doesn't identify the deciding court, you need to include this information in parentheses as part of the citation.

As the country grew in the 19th century, the number of reported decisions increased dramatically and official reporting systems began to lag further and further behind.[19] The need for timely access to cases was met by commercial publishers. In 1876, John B. West began publishing selected decisions of the Minnesota Supreme Court in a weekly leaflet, the *Syllabi*. Three years later he launched the *North Western Reporter*, covering five surrounding states as well as Minnesota.

Other publishers also began their own series of regional reporters, with the result that some states were covered by two or three rival publications.[20] West, however, established a national system,

---

18. Kirby followed a 1784 Connecticut statute that judges provide written opinions and that they be kept on file in order that "a Foundation be laid for a more perfect and permanent System of common Law in this State." An Act establishing the Wages of the Judges of the Superior Court, 1784, Conn. Acts & Laws 268. For more on Kirby, see Alan V. Briceland, *Ephraim Kirby: Pioneer of American Law Reporting, 1789*, 16 AM. J. LEGAL HIST. 297 (1972). Although Kirby and Hopkinson's reports were the first to be published, some later reports provide coverage of cases decided earlier. Thomas Jefferson, for example, compiled a collection of Virginia General Court cases dating back to 1730, but these

weren't published until 1829, three years after his death.

19. As a journal article in the 1870s noted, "Seventy-five years ago, in this country, there were but eight volumes of indigenous reports; to-day there are about 2,700, and the number is increasing about ninety volumes yearly." *Reports, Reporters, and Reporting*, 5 S. L. REV. (N.S.) 53, 53 (1879).

20. "This rivalry is really to be regretted. These enterprising houses have started out to do a very important work for the legal profession, and each of them ought to reap the reward of its enterprise in reasonable profits. But this competition will have the effect of dividing up the patronage among them, so

publishing all the states' decisions in seven regional reporters as well as reporters covering the Supreme Court and the lower federal courts. By 1887 the competitors had folded and West's National Reporter System had become the dominant commercial source for court opinions.[21] One of the most significant aspects of West's reporters as they developed over the following decades was that each case was accompanied by the classified key number headnotes that allowed comprehensive and uniform subject access to the cases of different jurisdictions.

The next major development in American case reporting was electronic access, as exemplified initially by the competing commercial services Lexis and Westlaw. The Ohio State Bar Association began work in 1966 on the system that became Lexis and was introduced in 1973, providing access to the decisions of all fifty states and the federal system. The West Publishing Company's Westlaw began in 1975, initially with only the headnotes to its published decisions, but full-text retrieval was added in 1979.[22] At first coverage in some states extended back a few decades, but both systems now have comprehensive retrospective coverage back to the earliest reported decisions.

Westlaw and Lexis dominated electronic case publishing until the rise of the Internet in the 1990s. Both systems adapted to web-based interfaces and continue to be the most comprehensive sources for opinions, but they have been joined by a number of other commercial case systems and by free court websites. Other commercial systems, such as Loislaw and VersusLaw, generally provide thorough coverage of modern opinions but lack the editorial summaries and headnotes found in Westlaw and Lexis. The scope of coverage on free Internet sites varies widely by court. Federal appellate decisions are now available online back to 1950, but only a few state court sites provide retrospective coverage before the 1990s and some are limited to only the most recent slip opinions.

With an increasing volume of cases available on the Internet, one of the leading issues of case publication in this century has been how and whether to limit the significance of some of those cases. For several decades, many courts have followed policies of selective publication in order to shape precedent and to cut down on the glut of reported cases. The online databases and the Inter-

---

that it will prove a losing enterprise for all." *The New "Reporters"*, 19 Am. L. Rev. 930, 932 (1885). It turned out, of course, to be a losing enterprise for all but one.

21. For more on the history of West, see Thomas A. Woxland, *"Forever Associated with the Practice of Law":*

The Early Years of the West Publishing Company, Legal Reference Services Q., Spring 1985, at 115.

22. For a survey of these early developments, see William G. Harrington, *A Brief History of Computer–Assisted Legal Research*, 77 Law Libr. J. 543 (1985).

net, however, have made the "unpublished" cases more widely accessible. As we will see in the next chapter, courts and judges are still debating how to deal with this increased access to their decisions.

GOREE v. STATE   Okl. 583
<small>Cite as 163 P.3d 583 (Okla.Crim.App. 2007)</small>

2007 OK CR 21

Wesley Darrell GOREE, Appellant

v.

STATE of Oklahoma, Appellee.

No. F–2005–1088.

Court of Criminal Appeals of Oklahoma.

May 23, 2007.

Background: Defendant was convicted in the District Court, Kay County, Leslie D. Paige, J., of assault and battery with a deadly weapon and intentional discharge of a weapon into a dwelling. Defendant appealed.

Holdings: The Court of Criminal Appeals, Chapel, J., held that:

(1) intent to kill is not an element of assault and battery with a deadly weapon;

(2) evidence was sufficient to support convictions; and

(3) sentence of 25 years imprisonment on each of two counts of assault and battery with a deadly weapon, and 20 years for intentional discharge of a weapon into a dwelling was not excessive.

Affirmed.

Lumpkin, P.J. concurred in the results and filed an opinion.

Lewis, J., concurred in part and dissented in part and filed an opinion.

1. Assault and Battery ⟜56

    Intent to kill is not an element of the crime of assault and battery with a deadly weapon. 21 Okl.St.Ann. § 652(C).

2. Assault and Battery ⟜91.6(3), 91.13(5)

    Evidence was sufficient to support convictions for assault and battery with a deadly weapon and intentional discharge of a weapon into a dwelling, although State failed to prove that defendant intended to kill his

victims; defendant shot at a house and into a crowd of people, injuring two victims, and defendant fired the first shots, such that the trial court rejected claim of self-defense at trial and the jury was not instructed on it. 21 Okl.St.Ann. §§ 652(C), 1289.17A.

3. Assault and Battery ⟜100

    Sentence of 25 years imprisonment on each of two counts of assault and battery with a deadly weapon, and 20 years imprisonment on conviction for intentional discharge of a weapon into a dwelling was not excessive, where defendant shot at a house and into a crowd of people, injuring two victims, and defendant fired the first shots. 21 Okl. St.Ann. §§ 652(C), 1289.17A.

Royce Hobbs, Stillwater, OK, Attorney for defendant at trial.

Ed Goodman, Assistant District Attorney, Newkirk, OK, attorney for State at trial.

Bill Zuhdi, Oklahoma City, OK, attorney for petitioner on appeal.

W.A. Drew Edmondson, Attorney General of Oklahoma, Thomas Lee Tucker, Assistant Attorney General, Oklahoma City, OK, attorneys for respondent on appeal.

OPINION

CHAPEL, Judge.

¶ 1 Wesley Darrell Goree was convicted in a non-jury trial of Counts I and II, Assault and Battery with a Deadly Weapon in violation of 21 O.S.2001, § 652(C), and Count III, Intentional Discharge of a Weapon into a Dwelling in violation of 21 O.S.2001, § 1289.17A, all after two or more former felony convictions, in the District Court of Kay County, Case No. CF–2004–191.[1] The Honorable Leslie D. Paige sentenced Goree to twenty-five (25) years imprisonment on each of Counts I and II, and twenty (20) years imprisonment on Count III. Goree appeals from these convictions and sentences and raises three propositions of error in support of his appeal.

---

1. Judge Paige also revoked Goree's five (5) year suspended sentence in Kay County District Court

Case No. CF–1997–307.

Illustration 6–1. *Goree v. State*, 163 P.3d
583 (Okla. Crim. App. 2007)

LexisNexis® *Total Research System*

Search | Research Tasks | Get a Document | Shepard's® | Alerts | Total Litigator | Transactional Advisor | Counsel Selector

Custom ID ▾ : No Description : Switch Client : Preferences : Live Support : Sign Out : Help : History

FOCUS™ Terms   Search Within : Original Results (1 - 1) ▾ Go ⇨ Advanced...

View : Case Brief | **Full** | Custom   ⇦ 1 of 1 ⇨

More Like This | More Like Selected Text | Shepardize® | TOA

ⓘ **Goree v. State, 2007 OK CR 21** (Copy w/ Cite)   Pages: 10

*2007 OK CR 21, *; 163 P.3d 583, **;*
*2007 Okla. Crim. App. LEXIS 21, ***

WESLEY DARRELL GOREE, Appellant -vs- STATE OF OKLAHOMA, Appellee

Case Number: F-2005-1088

COURT OF CRIMINAL APPEALS OF OKLAHOMA

2007 OK CR 21; 163 P.3d 583; 2007 Okla. Crim. App. LEXIS 21

May 23, 2007, Decided
May 23, 2007, Filed

CASE SUMMARY

PROCEDURAL POSTURE: Defendant was convicted in a non-jury trial, before the District Court of Kay County, Oklahoma, of assault and battery with a deadly weapon in violation of Okla. Stat. tit. 21, ◆ 652(C), and intentional discharge of a weapon into a dwelling in violation of Okla. Stat. tit. 21 ◆ 1289.17A. Defendant appealed.

OVERVIEW: Defendant fired several shots into a crowd of partygoers in front of a house. Two other people were shot and injured. At least one bullet entered the house. Defendant claimed, however, that he began shooting after other shots were fired. The appellate court found that the trial court did not err in removing the element of intent to take a human life from the charges of assault and battery with a deadly weapon under Okla. Stat. tit. 21, ◆ 652(C) (2001). The latest revision of ◆ 652(C) did not explicitly require an intent to injure or kill if the weapon or force used was likely to produce death. Given the current statutory language, requiring the State to prove intent to kill for this crime would amount to adding an element not present in the statute. The jury instruction on this crime should have reflected the change in the law. In conjunction with this case, the appellate court referred the matter to remove the fourth element,

Page ◀ Select a Reporter ▾

◀ Outline

Illustration 6–2. *Goree v. State*, 163 P.3d 583
(Okla. Crim. App. 2007), on Lexis.

Chapter 7

THE JUDICIARY, PART 2: CASE LAW SOURCES

Table of Sections

This chapter describes the sources the researcher encounters in working with case law from courts in United States jurisdictions. It covers both online and printed sources. Even if most research is done electronically, it is still important to know what the numbers in citations mean and it may even be necessary to refer to an official printed source.

Because of the preeminent role of the United States Supreme Court, in both practical and jurisprudential terms, its decisions are discussed first and in some detail. Explanation of sources covering lower federal courts, state courts, and other jurisdictions follow in subsequent sections.

§ 7.1   Supreme Court of the United States

The Supreme Court of the United States stands at the head of the judicial branch of the federal government, and provides the definitive interpretation of the U.S. Constitution and federal statutes. Its decisions are studied not only by lawyers but also by political scientists, historians, and citizens interested in the development of social and legal policy.

The Supreme Court is the court of last resort in the federal court system. It also has the final word on federal issues raised in state courts, and it hears cases arising between states. The Court exercises tight control over its docket and has wide discretion to decline review, or to *deny a writ of certiorari* as it is called in almost all cases. The Supreme Court usually accepts for consideration only those cases that raise significant policy issues. In recent years it has issued opinions in fewer than ninety cases during its annual term, which begins on the first Monday of October and ends in late June or early July.[1]

(a) Reference Sources

Numerous reference works explain the history and role of the Supreme Court in the American political and legal system. Two of the more highly esteemed are *Encyclopedia of the American Constitution* (Leonard W. Levy et al. eds., 2d ed. 2000), and *The Oxford Companion to the Supreme Court of the United States* (Kermit L. Hall ed., 2d ed. 2005), which both include articles on historical developments, doctrinal areas, and individual justices. Each also includes articles on several hundred cases, providing quick synopses of the background and impact of major decisions. The latter work's articles on cases are also available in *The Oxford Guide to United States Supreme Court Decisions* (Kermit L. Hall & James W. Ely, Jr. eds., 2d ed. 2009).

Encyclopedia of the Supreme Court of the United States (David S. Tanenhaus ed. 2008) is a new five-volume encyclopedia that rivals these more established works in scope. It has more than 1,000 articles by law professors and other contributors on all aspects of the Court and its history, including articles on specific cases and each of the justices. Overview essays on topics as citizenship and due process emphasize the social context of the Court's decisions in each of these areas.

David G. Savage, *Guide to the U.S. Supreme Court* (4th ed. 2004) is arranged thematically rather than alphabetically, but it too explains major doctrines and provides historical background as well as discussing the politics and procedures of the Court. An appendix provides a chronology of major decisions, with concise summaries of more than five hundred cases from 1793 to 2003.

---

1. On the size of the Court's docket, see, e.g., Kenneth W. Starr, *The Supreme Court and Its Shrinking Docket: The Ghost of William Howard Taft*, 90 Minn. L. Rev. 1363 (2006); Linda Greenhouse, *Case of the Dwindling Docket Mystifies the Supreme Court*, N.Y. Times, Dec. 7, 2006, at A1.

Perhaps the most practical reference work about the Supreme Court is Eugene Gressman et al., *Supreme Court Practice* (9th ed. 2007), a guide for lawyers bringing cases before the Court. In addition to procedural matters and case-preparation tips, it also provides an extensive analysis of the Supreme Court's jurisdiction, discusses factors affecting the decision whether to grant review, and covers specialized topics such as Court's original jurisdiction, extraordinary writs, and capital cases.

Several websites provide background information on the Court. The Supreme Court Historical Society site <www.supremecourt history.org> includes sections on the Court's history and how it works, as well as a guide to researching various Supreme Court topics. The Court's own website <www.supremecourtus.gov> also provides a bit of information in its "About the Supreme Court" section. The leading website for the most current information is SCOTUSblog <www.scotusblog.com>, which often has the first reports of new decisions and developments in pending cases.

Numerous texts have been devoted to the history and decisions of the Supreme Court. Among the many historical treatments of the Court, the most ambitious is the Oliver Wendell Holmes Devise *History of the Supreme Court of the United States* (1971–date), under the general editorship first of Paul A. Freund and then of Stanley N. Katz. This multi-volume, detailed history is still incomplete, with only ten of thirteen projected volumes issued so far.[2]

Among the many law review articles covering the Supreme Court, two sources merit special mention. The *Supreme Court Review*, a faculty-edited journal published by the University of Chicago, is an annual volume of articles by leading scholars on important, recent U.S. Supreme Court decisions. The first issue of

2. Each volume covers the major constitutional issues and decisions in its respective period:

JULIUS GOEBEL, ANTECEDENTS AND BEGINNINGS TO 1801 (1971)

GEORGE LEE HASKINS & HERBERT A. JOHNSON, FOUNDATIONS OF POWER: JOHN MARSHALL, 1801–15 (1981)

G. EDWARD WHITE, THE MARSHALL COURT AND CULTURAL CHANGE, 1815–35 (1988)

CARL B. SWISHER, THE TANEY PERIOD, 1836–64 (1974)

CHARLES FAIRMAN, RECONSTRUCTION AND REUNION 1864–88 (1971–87); FIVE JUSTICES AND THE ELECTORAL COMMISSION OF 1877 (1988)

OWEN M. FISS, TROUBLED BEGINNINGS OF THE MODERN STATE, 1888–1910 (1993)

ALEXANDER M. BICKEL & BENNO C. SCHMIDT, THE JUDICIARY AND RESPONSIBLE GOVERNMENT, 1910–21 (1984)

WILLIAM WIECEK, THE BIRTH OF THE MODERN CONSTITUTION: THE UNITED STATES SUPREME COURT, 1941–1953 (2006)

Three volumes are yet to be published: ROBERT C. POST, CONSTITUTIONAL RIGHTS AND THE REGULATORY STATE, 1921–1930; RICHARD D. FRIEDMAN, THE CRUCIBLE OF THE MODERN CONSTITUTION, 1930–1941; and MORTON J. HORWITZ, THE WARREN COURT AND AMERICAN DEMOCRACY, 1953–1976. For a brief history of the series, see Stanley N. Katz, *Official History: The Holmes Devise History of the Supreme Court*, 141 PROC. AM. PHIL. SOC'Y 297 (1997).

each *Harvard Law Review* volume contains an extensive analysis by its student editors of the activity of the Supreme Court in the preceding term. The survey is prefaced each year by two introductory articles written by noted scholars (a lengthy "Foreword" and a somewhat briefer "Comment"), and is accompanied by statistics on the term.[3]

The Supreme Court Compendium: Data, Decisions, and Developments (Lee Epstein et al. eds., 4th ed. 2007) provides a wide range of statistical and historical information, including information on the Court's caseload, voting alignments, litigants, and public opinion. Other sources for statistics on recent terms include *The United States Law Week*, the annual Supreme Court issue of the *Harvard Law Review*, and "StatPacks" on SCOTUSblog.

(b) Sources for Current Opinions

Reference sources are useful for historical and general background, but they are no substitute for reading the opinions of the Supreme Court. The Court makes law through its decisions in individual cases. These decisions can be retrieved through several free Internet sites and commercial databases, and they are published in a weekly newsletter and three permanent bound reporters. Maintaining current awareness of new decisions is essential.

The Supreme Court announces its decisions on an irregular basis at its 10 a.m. sessions, beginning in October or November and reaching a peak when the most contentious cases of the term are decided in late June. The first official appearance of a new decision is as a *bench opinion*, a pamphlet version available at the Court and distributed electronically to several publishers including FindLaw, Lexis, Loislaw, VersusLaw, and Westlaw. These publishers generally make the opinion available online within minutes. Cornell Law School's Legal Information Institute (LII) <www.law.cornell.edu/supct/> provides a PDF copy of the printed bench opinion, and also has a free e-mail notification service that delivers the syllabi of new opinions with links to the full text.

The bench opinion is superseded, usually within an hour, by the official *slip opinion*, which is posted in PDF on the Supreme Court website <www.supremecourtus.gov>. The bench opinion and slip opinion are usually identical, but it is possible that the slip opinion may contain corrections not found in the bench opinion.

---

3. Amid all the serious scholarship on the Supreme Court, it is worth noting a pair of landmark articles in which University of Chicago law professors attempted to identify the most forgettable justice in the Court's history. David P. Currie, *The Most Insignificant Justice: A Preliminary Inquiry*, 50 U. CHI. L. REV. 466 (1983); Frank H. Easterbrook, *The Most Insignificant Justice: Further Evidence*, 50 U. CHI. L. REV. 481 (1983).

The slip opinion text controls if there is any discrepancy between the two.

The quickest source for new slip opinions is usually SCOTUS-blog <www.scotusblog.com>, which also provides some of the earliest commentary and analysis of new decisions. SCOTUSblog often has a link to the slip opinion even before the bench opinion is available from LII and other sources.

Slip opinions contain the text of the Supreme Court's opinions, in a format very similar to the final published version, but they are individual paginated pamphlets and lack the volume and page references necessary for citation. For that purpose, and also because the final published version may contain corrections to the slip opinion, you should rely instead on the permanent official reports of the Court's opinions.

(c) *United States Reports*

Begun in 1790 as a private venture, the *United States Reports* (cited as U.S.) became official in 1817[4] and continues today as the official edition of United States Supreme Court decisions. Three to five volumes of the *U.S. Reports* are published each year. The slip decisions are cumulated after more than a year in an official advance sheet (called the "preliminary print"), which contains the pagination that will appear in the final bound volume. The bound volume is published after another year or more and is the authoritative text of the Court's decisions.[5]

The early volumes of Supreme Court decisions are now numbered sequentially as part of the *U.S. Reports* series, but for many years they were cited only by the names of the individual reporters. *Bluebook* citations to these early cases include a parenthetical reference to the nominative reporter volume, as in *Marbury v. Madison*, 5 U.S. (1 Cranch) 137 (1803), while *ALWD* rules use the *U.S. Reports* citation only.[6] Older cases and articles, however, tended to cite only the nominative reports, so a familiarity with the early reporters' names and their periods of coverage makes it easier to read and understand these citations:

---

4. Act of March 3, 1817, ch. 63, 3 Stat. 376. The act was limited to three years, but it was renewed periodically until finally made permanent in 1842. Act of Aug. 29, 1842, ch. 264, 5 Stat. 545.

5. The Court's website warns: "Only the bound volumes of the United States Reports contain the final, official text of the opinions of the Supreme Court of the United States. In case of discrepancies between the bound volume and any other version of a case—whether print or electronic, official or unofficial—the bound volume controls." Supreme Court of the United States, Information about Opinions <www.supremecourtus.gov/opinions/info_opinions.html>.

6. THE BLUEBOOK: A UNIFORM SYSTEM OF CITATION R. 10.3.2, at 88 (18th ed. 2005); ALWD CITATION MANUAL: A PROFESSIONAL SYSTEM OF CITATION R. 12.4(c)(3), at 79 (3d ed. 2006).

1–4 Dall. (Alexander Dallas)	1–4 U.S. (1790–1800)
1–9 Cranch (William Cranch)	5–13 U.S. (1801–15)
1–12 Wheat. (Henry Wheaton)	14–25 U.S. (1816–27)
1–16 Pet. (Richard Peters)	26–41 U.S. (1828–42)
1–24 How. (Benjamin C. Howard)	42–65 U.S. (1843–61)
1–2 Black (Jeremiah S. Black)	66–67 U.S. (1861–63)
1–23 Wall. (John W. Wallace)	68–90 U.S. (1863–75)

The earliest volumes were somewhat haphazard. Alexander Dallas's first volume of the *United States Reports* contains only Pennsylvania decisions, and none from the U.S. Supreme Court. His second and third volumes contain cases from both Pennsylvania and the U.S. Supreme Court, and his fourth volume adds decisions from Delaware and New Hampshire.[7] His reports contained numerous errors and did not even include all of the Court's cases from the

7. The presence of these cases in the *United States Reports* volumes explains why Westlaw and Lexis both include in their Supreme Court databases cases from courts other than the Supreme Court, leading to occasional errors in law reviews where pre-Constitution cases are attributed to the Court even though it had not yet been formed. See, e.g., Note, *Looking It Up: Dictionaries and Statutory Interpretation*, 107 HARV. L. REV. 1437, 1437 n. 2 (1994) ("At the time of this writing, LEXIS listed 664 Supreme Court cases that mention the words 'dictionary' or 'dictionaries.' ... The first such case was Respublica v. Steele, 2 U.S. (2 Dall.) 92 (1785), in which the Court noted counsel's use of a dictionary. See id. at 92. These computer searches are admittedly imperfect, but they suffice to confirm significant trends and patterns in the Court's practice.")

Dallas and his successors, though immortalized through nominative citations, were not all highly esteemed. "Delay, expense, omission and inaccuracy ... were among the hallmarks of Dallas' work." Craig Joyce, *The Rise of the Supreme Court Reporter: An Institutional Perspective on Marshall Court Ascendancy*, 83 MICH. L. REV. 1291, 1305 (1985). Justice Joseph Story complained that William Cranch's work was "partic-

ularly & painfully erroneous." Id. at 1309–10 (quoting a letter from Joseph Story to Richard Peters, Jr., Dec. 10, 1829). Henry Wheaton was an exception, and "brought to his duties a scholarly aptitude and zeal unique in the history of the reportership." Id. at 1388. He was succeeded, however, by Richard Peters, who was "apparently not burdened by the weight of an overpowering intellect." Id. at 1389.

A commentator many years later wrote: "We should expect to find models of reportorial work in the decisions of the Federal Court of last resort; but unfortunately as much bad work has probably been done in reporting the decisions of that court, as in reporting those of any respectable court in the Union. Not to speak of his predecessors, the head-notes of the sixteen volumes of Peters were abominable.... It is hard to understand how a court of that dignity, sensitive of its reputation, could have kept such a stick in such an office for so many years." Seymour D. Thompson, *The Reporter's Head–Note*, 2 GREEN BAG 215, 218 (1890). An unnamed reviewer (probably Thompson again, based on his choice of epithets) wrote of Peters' successor, Benjamin Howard: "Howard was not a good reporter.... It remains a wonder to the profession how the court

period.[8] Fortunately for researchers interested in the early Supreme Court, the recently completed *Documentary History of the Supreme Court of the United States, 1789–1800* (Maeva Marcus ed., 1985–2007) includes three volumes focusing on the early cases, containing notes, opinion drafts, correspondence, and other documents. (Other volumes in the series cover the early appointments and proceedings, the circuit court duties of the justices, the legislation creating and organizing the federal judiciary, and suits against states.)

Beginning with volume 91 (October Term 1875), *U.S. Reports* volumes are cited only by number and not by the name of the reporter. Thus the official citation of the Supreme Court's decision in *United States v. Olson* is 546 U.S. 43 (2005), meaning the case beginning on page 43 of volume 546 of the *U.S. Reports*. The opening pages of the official report of *Olson* appear in Illustrations 7–1 and 7–2 on pages 261–262. The Court's reporter of decisions prefaces the text of each decision with a syllabus summarizing the case and the Court's holding. Following the syllabus, Illustration 7–2 indicates that the opinion was unanimous, identifies the attorneys in the case, and shows the beginning of the opinion of the Court by Justice Stephen Breyer.

The official *U.S. Reports* versions of Supreme Court decisions are available online in PDF from two sources. The Supreme Court website, under the heading "Opinions—Bound Volumes" <www.supremecourtus.gov/opinions/boundvolumes.html> has files containing the bound volumes of *U.S. Reports* beginning with volume 502 (October Term 1991). These provide free access to the official text, but they are large and rather cumbersome files of more than a

could get along for so many years with such a stick for a reporter of its decisions." *Book Review*, 18 AM. L. REV. 708, 708 (1884).

MORRIS L. COHEN & SHARON HAMBY O'CONNOR, A GUIDE TO THE EARLY REPORTS OF THE SUPREME COURT OF THE UNITED STATES (1995) contains biographical sketches of the first seven reporters. Their most significant contribution to American jurisprudence began when Richard Peters, the fourth reporter, decided to publish a new condensed edition of his three predecessors' volumes. He was sued by Henry Wheaton, who asserted copyright in his reports, and the resulting Supreme Court decision held that United States copyright was governed by federal statute, not common law, and that the reporter had no copyright in the text of the decisions. *Wheaton v. Peters,* 33 U.S. (8 Pet.) 591 (1834).

8. All of the early reporters omitted some cases. Henry Wheaton noted in a preface to his first volume that "discretion has been exercised in omitting to report cases turning on mere questions of fact, and from which no important principle, or general rule, could be extracted." 14 U.S. (1 Wheat.) iv (1816). A number of omitted cases from earlier reports were collected and printed by J. C. Bancroft Davis, the second of the Court's "post-nominative" reporters. Appendix, 131 U.S. lxiv (1889).

Even the modern reports omit opinions of individual justices on emergency applications from the lower federal courts. These opinions from 1926 to 1998 have been collected and printed in A COLLECTION OF IN CHAMBERS OPINIONS BY THE JUSTICES OF THE SUPREME COURT OF THE UNITED STATES (Cynthia Rapp comp., 2004).

thousand pages each. They can be a bit difficult to use because the page numbers of the PDF documents include the prefatory matter in the volume and therefore do not match the printed page numbers. Page 1 of a volume, for example, could be page 95 or page 203 of the PDF file. The files are searchable, however, so the quickest way to find a particular known case may be to retrieve its volume and search for its name.

The subscription site HeinOnline <www.heinonline.org> provides more thorough and convenient coverage, with page images of the *U.S. Reports* all the way from volume one through the preliminary prints to the most recent slip opinions. Individual decisions can be easily retrieved by citation, and the entire collection is keyword-searchable. HeinOnline searching allows for the use of the Boolean connectors AND and OR, as well as proximity searching, but it uses a syntax quite different from that used by Westlaw and Lexis. A review of the "Searching in HeinOnline" brochure <heinonline.org/HeinDocs/SearchinginHOL.pdf> may help, although many researchers opt to search on Westlaw or Lexis and then turn to HeinOnline to retrieve the official text. HeinOnline's Supreme Court Library also includes more than thirty texts on the history and decisions of the Court.

(d) *Supreme Court Reporter* (Westlaw) and *Lawyers' Edition* (Lexis)

Supreme Court opinions are also printed in two commercially published series, West's *Supreme Court Reporter* (cited as S. Ct.) and LexisNexis's *United States Supreme Court Reports, Lawyers' Edition* (known simply as *Lawyers' Edition*, and cited as L. Ed.). These reporters contain editorial features not available in the official *U.S. Reports*, and they are the versions found in Westlaw and Lexis respectively.

Because the *U.S. Reports* are published so slowly, *The Bluebook* and the *ALWD Citation Manual* specify that a recent opinion that does not yet have a *U.S.* citation should be cited to the *Supreme Court Reporter* or *Lawyers' Edition*, in that order of preference.[9] Cases are published in both of these sources in paperback advance sheets within a few weeks of decision, and the citations are available online through Westlaw and Lexis even before publication. The permanent bound volumes are not published until the cases appear in the *U.S. Reports* volumes, so that the commercial editions can incorporate any corrections and include *star paging* with references to where each page in the official *U.S. Reports* begins. Both West-

---

9. The Bluebook: A Uniform System of Citation 193 (18th ed. 2005); ALWD Citation Manual: A Professional System of Citation 404 (3d ed. 2006).

law and Lexis use asterisks to indicate the beginnings of new pages in the printed reporters.

The *Supreme Court Reporter* began in 1882, with cases from volume 106 of the *U.S. Reports*. As a component of West's National Reporter System encompassing federal courts and state appellate courts, it includes the publisher's editorial synopses and headnotes. The opening page of *United States v. Olson* as it appears in the *Supreme Court Reporter* at 126 S. Ct. 510 is shown in Illustration 7–3 on page 263, including the synopsis, the West headnotes, and the beginning of the syllabus.

Westlaw provides the text of cases as they appear in the *Supreme Court Reporter*, but its SCT database of Supreme Court cases extends beyond the published reporter's coverage in both directions. The database has complete historical coverage of the Court's decisions since 1790, and new decisions are available within minutes of their release. For cases since 1882 that have been published in bound *Supreme Court Reporter* volumes, Westlaw provides the option to view and print a PDF file of the printed version. Illustration 7–4 on page 264 shows the beginning of *United States v. Olson*, as it appears on Westlaw.

Lawyers' Edition also began publication in 1882, but it contains all Supreme Court decisions since the Court's inception in 1790. For the earlier cases, its editors worked from the opinions on file in the clerk's office, correcting errors in the official reports and even printing some opinions that had been omitted.[10] For some cases *Lawyers' Edition* includes information not found in the official reports, such as the exact date of decisions. In 1956 *Lawyers' Edition* began a second series after reaching one hundred volumes, and its version of *Olson* is cited as 163 L. Ed. 2d 306 (2005). The first page of the decision is shown in Illustration 7–5 on page 265.

Like the *Supreme Court Reporter*, *Lawyers' Edition* contains editorial summaries and headnotes for each case. The headnotes are assigned subject classifications similar to West's headnotes, but the *Lawyers' Edition* digest system does not appear in other reports and is useful only for Supreme Court research. The headnotes are followed by "Research References," providing citations to relevant coverage in legal encyclopedias, digests, annotations, and the *United States Code*. The bound *Lawyers' Edition* volumes also contain annotations on a few of the more important cases in each volume, summarizing the Supreme Court's decisions on a specific topic. Note at the bottom of Illustration 7–5 that the *Olson* case is accompanied by an annotation on the Federal Tort Claims Act.

---

10. Book Review, 18 AM. L. REV. 1067, 1068 (1884); Book Review, 29 AM. L. REV. 477, 477 (1895).

Lawyers' Edition 2d also includes a "Citator Service" providing summaries of later Supreme Court cases citing each decision and is accompanied by a *Quick Case Table with Annotation References*, a convenient source for computerless researchers looking for a case citation.[11]

Like Westlaw, Lexis has Supreme Court cases since the Court's inception in 1790, as well as the most recent decisions the morning they are announced (and links to Lawyers' Edition PDFs back to December 1996). The online cases have an array of editorial additions; they include the *Lawyers' Edition* summaries and headnotes and the official synopsis, but these are preceded by a separate case summary and Lexis headnotes in the same style as other Lexis cases. For many cases, Lexis also provides "Case in Brief," an expanded case summary and guide to related cases and secondary sources. Illustration 7–6 on page 266 shows the beginning of *United States v. Olson* in Lexis, with links to the PDF version and the Case in Brief.

(e) *The United States Law Week*

As noted earlier, new Supreme Court decisions are available online within minutes or hours of their announcement. *The Bluebook* and the *ALWD Citation Manual*, however, specify that decisions not yet in the permanent reporters be cited to the weekly newsletter *The United States Law Week* (cited as U.S.L.W.).[12]

Beyond merely reporting Supreme Court decisions, *U.S. Law Week* is an excellent current awareness tool. A separate weekly section on Supreme Court Proceedings lists and summarizes new cases docketed, provides news of developments in cases on the calendar, and reports on oral arguments. A table of cases by name, a Case Status Report, and a subject index all cover cases pending on the Supreme Court docket or denied review as well as decided cases. In each list, however, the entries for opinions are preceded by black typographical triangles to make them a bit easier to pick out from the mass of other cases.

Another volume of *U.S. Law Week,* labeled "General Law Sections," contains news and abstracts of important opinions from other federal courts and state courts, and brief reports on legislative and administrative developments.

(f) Other Electronic Sources

Researchers without Westlaw or Lexis access can find Supreme Court opinions at several free Internet sites, in addition to the

11. The "Citator Service" is found in annual pocket parts for each volume since 32 L. Ed. 2d (1972), and in a separate *Citator Service* pamphlet covering 1 to 31 L. Ed. 2d (1956–72).

12. THE BLUEBOOK: A UNIFORM SYSTEM OF CITATION 193 (18th ed. 2005); ALWD CITATION MANUAL: A PROFESSIONAL SYSTEM OF CITATION 404 (3d ed. 2006).

Court's own website and Cornell's Legal Information Institute. Several sites provide free access to the entire retrospective Supreme Court collection back to 1790, including AltLaw <www.altlaw.org>, Justia <supreme.justia.com>, lexisONE <www.lexisone.com>, PreCYdent <www.precydent.com>, and Public Library of Law <www.plol.org>. FindLaw <www.findlaw.com/casecode/supreme. html> has all opinions since 1893. These sites offer a variety of search approaches, and several provide hypertext links in opinions to other Supreme Court cases cited. Some, such as PreCYdent, even include star paging indicating the *U.S. Reports* citation of specific language from an opinion.

Subscription sites such as Fastcase <www.fastcase.com> and Loislaw <www.loislaw.com> also have complete retrospective coverage, and VersusLaw <www.versuslaw.com> provides cases back to 1886. A number of publishers offer CD–ROM versions of Supreme Court opinions; some of these include only modern cases, while others provide complete coverage since 1790.

§ 7.2   The Lower Federal Courts

Congress has power to create the lower federal courts under Article III of the Constitution, which vests the judicial power of the United States "in one supreme Court, and in such inferior Courts as the Congress may from time to time ordain and establish." The Judiciary Act of 1789, which established the federal court system, created thirteen District Courts, one for each of the eleven states that had ratified the Constitution as well as for the Districts of Kentucky and Maine, and three Circuit Courts.[13] Both District and Circuit Courts served as trial courts, with the Circuit Courts having appellate jurisdiction in limited areas. The federal court system has grown extensively from its original structure, with one of the most significant changes occurring in 1891 when Congress created the Circuit Courts of Appeals to serve as intermediate appellate courts.[14] Twenty years later it abolished the old Circuit Courts,[15] and the Circuit Courts of Appeals were renamed the United States Courts of Appeals in 1948.[16]

The 1891 act created nine numbered circuits, each covering several states. The Tenth Circuit was added in 1929, and the Fifth Circuit was divided to create the Eleventh Circuit in 1980. As part

---

13. Judiciary Act of 1789, ch. 20, §§ 2 to 4, 1 Stat. 73.

14. Act of March 3, 1891, ch. 517, 26 Stat. 826.

15. Act of March 3, 1911, ch. 231, § 289, 36 Stat. 1087, 1167.

16. Act of June 25, 1948, ch. 646, § 2(b), 62 Stat. 869, 985. The growth

and development of the federal court system are detailed in ERWIN C. SURRENCY, HISTORY OF THE FEDERAL COURTS (2d ed. 2002) and RUSSELL R. WHEELER & CYNTHIA HARRISON, CREATING THE FEDERAL JUDICIAL SYSTEM (3d ed. 2005) <www.fjc.gov/ public/pdf.nsf/lookup/creat3rd.pdf/$file/ creat3rd.pdf>.

of the 1948 codification of the Judiciary Act, the U.S. Court of Appeals for the District of Columbia was formally given circuit status as the U.S. Court of Appeals for the District of Columbia Circuit. Each of these twelve Court of Appeals hears cases from the trial courts within its circuit, and its decisions have binding authority over those trial courts. Cases are generally decided by three-judge panels, but litigants can petition for a rehearing en banc by all of the circuit judges (or a panel of fifteen judges in the Ninth Circuit, by far the largest circuit).[17]

Every Court of Appeals has its own website, usually with recent opinions, information on pending cases, rules, forms, and other information. These sites have the format www.ca[circuit]. uscourts.gov, as in www.ca2.uscourts.gov, www.ca9.uscourts.gov, or www.cadc.uscourts.gov, or they can be reached through links from the general U.S. Courts website <www.uscourts.gov/courtlinks/>.

A thirteenth circuit, the Federal Circuit <www.cafc.uscourts. gov>, was created in 1982 with specialized subject jurisdiction to hear appeals from throughout the country on such matters as patents, trademarks, international trade, and government contracts.[18] It is the successor to the U.S. Court of Customs and Patent Appeals (1910–82) and the appellate division of the U.S. Court of Claims (1855–1982).

The federal court system also includes two other appellate courts with specialized jurisdictions:

— The U.S. Court of Appeals for the Armed Forces <www. armfor.uscourts.gov> hears cases from the Courts of Criminal Appeals for individual branches of the service, and its decisions are reviewable by the Supreme Court.

— The U.S. Court of Appeals for Veterans Claims <www. vetapp.uscourts.gov> reviews decisions of the Board of Veterans Appeals, and its decisions can in turn be appealed to the Court of Appeals for the Federal Circuit.

The general trial courts, the United States District Courts, are divided into ninety-four districts, with one or more in each state. California, New York and Texas are each divided into four districts, while twenty-six of the states have just one district apiece. Each district has a specified number of judges, from two in several districts to twenty-eight in the Southern District of New York.[19] The map in Illustration 7–7 on page 267 shows the boundaries of

---

17. 9th Cir. R. 35–3.

18. Federal Court Improvement Act of 1982, Pub. L. No. 97–164, 96 Stat. 25. The jurisdiction of the Federal Circuit is determined by 28 U.S.C. § 1295 (2000). For an account of the court's history and practice, see BRUCE D. ABRAMSON, THE

SECRET CIRCUIT: THE LITTLE-KNOWN COURT WHERE THE RULES OF THE INFORMATION AGE UNFOLD (2007).

19. 28 U.S.C. § 133 (Supp. V 2005). The districts with two judges are Idaho, the Northern District of Iowa, North

the circuits and districts. The U.S. Courts website has a color version of this map with links to individual court sites <www. uscourts.gov/courtlinks/>.

Each District Court has a website providing case information, local rules, forms, contact information, and other documents for attorneys, litigants, and jurors. The format is www.[state][district]. uscourts.gov, with the two-letter state abbreviation and a one-or two-letter indication of the district, as in www.casd.uscourts.gov for the Southern District of California or www.mnd.uscourts.gov for the District of Minnesota.

In addition, the federal court system has several trial courts with specialized jurisdictions:

— United States Bankruptcy Courts are located in each district as adjuncts to the District Courts, with specialized jurisdiction over bankruptcy matters. The system of separate bankruptcy courts was created in the 1978 revision of the Bankruptcy Code.[20] The courts' website URLs are similar to those for the District Courts, substituting "b" for "d" in the address, as in www.mnb.uscourts.gov for the U.S. Bankruptcy Court, District of Minnesota.

— The United States Court of Federal Claims <www.uscfc. uscourts.gov> has jurisdiction over federal contract disputes and most other claims for money damages against the United States. It was created at the same time as the Federal Circuit and is the successor to the U.S. Court of Claims (1855–1982). The new court was originally called the U.S. Claims Court but was renamed in 1992.[21]

— The United States Court of International Trade <www.cit. uscourts.gov> hears cases involving customs law and other aspects of international trade. Its decisions are appealed to the Federal Circuit. The Court of International Trade was created in 1980 to replace the U.S. Customs Court (1890–1980).[22]

— The United States Tax Court <www.ustaxcourt.gov> shares jurisdiction with the District Courts in disputes about federal income taxation. A decision is reviewable by the U.S. Court of Appeals for the circuit in which the petitioner resides or has its

Dakota, the Eastern District of Oklahoma, Vermont, and the Western District of Wisconsin. The history of each state's federal courts is recounted in *Sketches of the Establishment of the Federal Courts by States [Jurisdiction] and Their Judges*, 212 F.R.D. 611 (2003).

20. Bankruptcy Reform Act of 1978, Pub. L. No. 95–598, § 201, 92 Stat. 2549, 2657 (current version at 28 U.S.C. §§ 151–159 (2000 & Supp. V 2005)).

21. Federal Court Administration Act of 1992, Pub. L. No. 102–572, tit. IX, 106 Stat. 4506, 4516.

22. Customs Court Act of 1980, Pub. L. 96–417, 94 Stat. 1727 (current version at 28 U.S.C. §§ 251–258 (2000)).

principal office. The Tax Court was created in 1942 as the successor to the Board of Tax Appeals (1924–42).[23]

(a) Online Resources

There is no counterpart to the *U.S. Reports* for the decisions of the U.S. Courts of Appeals and District Courts. The only officially published sources are the individual slip decisions that the courts issue and post on their websites.[24] The Court of Appeals sites generally only include cases since the mid–1990s and provide rudimentary searching options. District Court sites are even more widely varied; some require login to the PACER case management system and have no full-text search capabilities.[25] PACER charges a per-page fee for pleadings and other documents, but provides free access to opinions.

Many federal court decisions are available, however, in commercially published reports and electronic sources. The most comprehensive sources for federal court opinions are the databases of Westlaw and Lexis, which have complete coverage from the beginning of the court system in 1789 and generally have new decisions within hours or days of their issuance. The systems have databases with all federal court opinions (ALLFEDS in Westlaw) as well as databases limited to the Courts of Appeals (CTA), District Courts (DCT), and specialized courts as well. Databases in both services include thousands of decisions not available in any other form, except as slip opinions.

Other databases have extensive collections, if not quite as comprehensive. For Courts of Appeals cases, Loislaw generally begins in 1924. Both VersusLaw and Casemaker have coverage from 1930, and Fastcase picks up in 1950. In most instances District Court coverage is slightly less extensive. These databases, while not as useful for exhaustive historical research, are sufficient for almost any modern legal inquiry.

---

23. Revenue Act of 1942, § 504, ch. 619, 56 Stat. 798, 957. The provisions governing the Tax Court are at 26 U.S.C.A. §§ 7441–7487 (West 2002 & Supp. 2008).

24. The Court of Appeals for the Federal Circuit does have an official reporter for the customs cases it decides, continuing the official reports of the former U.S. Court of Customs and Patent Appeals, but no volumes have been published for nearly a decade. Official reports are also published for specialized federal tribunals such as the U.S. Court of International Trade and the U.S. Tax Court.

25. Since December 2004, federal law has required that each court maintain a website with "[a]ccess to the substance of all written opinions issued by the court, regardless of whether such opinions are to be published in the official court reporter, in a text searchable format." E–Government Act of 2002, § 205(a)(5), Pub. L. No. 107–347, 116 Stat. 2899, 2913 (codified at 44 U.S.C. § 3501 note (Supp. V 2005)). Compliance with this provision has been slow and spotty. See Andrew T. Solomon, *Making Unpublished Opinions Precedential: A Recipe for Ethical Problems & Legal Malpractice?*, 26 MISS. C. L. REV. 185, 208–210 (2007).

Until quite recently, the options at free Internet sites were limited to cases from the most recent decade or so. In February 2008, however, published U.S. Court of Appeals cases since 1950 became available in the public domain and can now be searched through several websites including AltLaw <www.altlaw.org>, Justia <www.justia.com>, Public Library of Law <www.plol.org>, and PreCYdent <www.precydent.com>. As with Supreme Court cases, these sites provide free searching and the full text of opinions, and some have the internal page references needed to provide pinpoint citation. In some instances, however, they may lack reporter citations for recent cases. Most of these sites also include recent opinions from U.S. District Courts. LexisONE <www.lexisone.com> has five years of free coverage for the Courts of Appeals, but no District Court opinions.

(b) West Reporters

Despite the widespread online availability of lower federal court decisions, *The Bluebook* and the *ALWD Citation Manual* require that cases be cited to published reporters if available in print.[26] The most comprehensive printed sources for lower federal court decisions are reporters published by West. Like the *Supreme Court Reporter*, these reporters contain editorial synopses and headnotes with key numbers, allowing researchers to find cases through West's series of digest publications.

United States Courts of Appeals. In 1880 West's *Federal Reporter* began covering decisions of both the district and circuit courts, as well as the new Circuit Courts of Appeals following the reorganization of the federal judiciary system in 1891.[27] Since 1932 it has covered only the Courts of Appeals, and after more than 1,800 volumes it is now in its third series (cited as F.3d).[28]

---

26. THE BLUEBOOK: A UNIFORM SYSTEM OF CITATION R. 18, at 151 (18th ed. 2005) ("*The Bluebook requires the use and citation of traditional printed sources* unless (1) the information cited is unavailable in a traditional printed source; or (2) a copy of the source cannot be located because it is so obscure that it is practically unavailable."); ALWD CITATION MANUAL: A PROFESSIONAL SYSTEM OF CITATION R. 38.1(a), at 291 (3d ed. 2006) ("If a source is available in print and electronic formats, typically cite *only* the print source if it is readily available to most readers.") (emphases in originals).

27. The creation of the Circuit Courts of Appeals prompted the publication of two relatively short-lived commercial reporters limited, unlike the

Federal Reporter, to the appellate decisions, *Blatchford's United States Courts of Appeals Reports* (U.S. App.) (1893–99), and *United States Circuit Courts of Appeals Reports* (C.C.A.) (1892–1920).

28. The *Federal Reporter* has also contained decisions of various specialized courts created by Congress, including the U.S. Commerce Court (1910–13); the Court of Customs and Patent Appeals (1929–82), the U.S. Court of Claims (1930–32, 1960–82) (Court of Claims coverage was moved to the *Federal Supplement* from 1932 to 1960), the Emergency Court of Appeals (1942–61), and the Temporary Emergency Court of Appeals (1972–92).

As it does in the *Supreme Court Reporter*, West prefaces each court decision with a concise syllabus summarizing the issues and the holding, and with headnotes paraphrasing specific points of law in the case. The headnotes are arranged by topic and key number in West's series of digests, and the synopses and headnotes are included and searchable in Westlaw's version of the case. Westlaw also provides page images of the *Federal Reporter* version, from the first cases in the late 1870s through the most recently published bound volume.

Because the *Federal Reporter* covers many different courts (unlike the *U.S. Reports*), citations must identify the specific circuit in parentheses. The lower court's ruling in the *Olson* case (the Supreme Court decision shown in Illustrations 7–1 to 7–6), for example, is cited as *Olson v. United States*, 362 F.3d 1236 (9th Cir. 2004). Knowing the jurisdiction is vital in evaluating the scope and precedential value of a decision, but beginning researchers often omit this information.

Despite publishing more than thirty volumes each year, the *Federal Reporter* contains only a small portion of the decisions of the U.S. Courts of Appeals. It is limited to those opinions that the courts have designated as "published" and therefore as precedential. Since the 1970s, each circuit has had rules limiting publication to decisions meeting specific criteria. Generally a decision is published if it lays down a new rule of law or alters an existing rule, criticizes existing law, resolves an apparent conflict of authority, or involves a legal issue of continuing public interest.[29] As a result less than sixteen percent of Court of Appeals cases are terminated with a published opinion.[30]

From the beginning of the "nonpublication" era, commentators argued that the development of an unpublished body of decisions reduced judicial accountability, hindered the operation of stare decisis, and exacerbated inequities between frequent litigants such as government agencies (who would see numerous unpublished decisions and could predict how a court would rule) and infrequent litigants such as social security claimants.[31]

29. For a summary of these rules, see Michael Hannon, *Developments and Practice Notes: A Closer Look at Unpublished Opinions in the United States Courts of Appeals*, 3 J. App. Prac. & Process 199, 209 n.48 (2001).

30. Administrative Office of the United States Courts, Judicial Business of the United States Courts 52 tbl. S–3 (2007).

31. See, e.g., William L. Reynolds & William M. Richman, *An Evaluation of Limited Publication in the United States Courts of Appeals: The Price of Reform*, 48 U. Chi. L. Rev. 573 (1981); William L. Reynolds & William M. Richman, *The Non–Precedential Precedent—Limited Publication and No–Citation Rules in the United States Courts of Appeals*, 78 Colum. L. Rev. 1167 (1978); Lauren K. Robel, *The Myth of the Disposable Opinion: Unpublished Opinions and Government Litigants in the United States Courts of Appeals*, 87 Mich. L. Rev. 940 (1989).

Until recently, unpublished decisions could not even be cited as persuasive authority under most circuits' rules. These rules, however, did not quell the demand for unpublished cases. Even if they could not be cited as precedent, these cases could provide useful guidance of how a court would treat a similar subsequent claim. Although unpublished decisions were not generally available in print, Westlaw and Lexis provided access to thousands of decisions not otherwise accessible. Unpublished decisions became even more widely available with the growth of the Internet in the 1990s, and the controversy grew about whether they should be considered as precedent. The issue reached a crisis point in 2000, when a panel of the Eight Circuit ruled in *Anastasoff v. United States* that the ban on citing unpublished opinions was an unconstitutional violation of Article III.[32] This decision was vacated on other grounds within a few months, but the battle had been joined and the early 2000s saw a flurry of commentary on the issue.[33]

In the wake of the *Anastasoff* decision, West began publishing *Federal Appendix* in 2001, a series limited to Court of Appeals decisions "not selected for publication in the *Federal Reporter*." These decisions are published with synopses and headnotes and are indexed in West's digests, but it remains necessary to determine for each circuit to what extent they can be cited as precedent.

A new Federal Rule of Appellate Procedure was adopted in 2006 that permits "unpublished" or "non-precedential" decisions to be cited as persuasive authority. This new Rule 32.1 provides that courts cannot prohibit or restrict the citation of such opinions, but it is limited to decisions issued after January 1, 2007. The rule takes no position on how earlier decisions should be handled, and policies vary from circuit to circuit. Some circuits have declared by rule that unpublished opinions are not precedent, while others say that unpublished cases are not binding but can be cited for persuasive value.[34]

The nature of unpublished Court of Appeals opinions as precedent remains an open question, even after the adoption of Rule

---

32. 223 F.3d 898 (8th Cir.), *vacated as moot*, 235 F.3d 1054 (8th Cir. 2000) (en banc).

33. See, e.g., Stephen R. Barnett, *No-Citation Rules under Siege: A Battlefield Report and Analysis*, 5 J. App. Prac. & Process 473 (2003); Penelope Pether, *Inequitable Injunctions: The Scandal of Private Judging in the U.S. Courts*, 56 Stan. L. Rev. 1435 (2004); Lauren Robel, *The Practice of Precedent*: Anastasoff, *Noncitation Rules, and the Meaning of Precedent in an Interpretive Community*, 35 Ind. L. Rev. 399 (2002). Symposium, *Have We Ceased to Be a Common Law*

Country?: A Conversation on Unpublished, Depublished, Withdrawn and Per Curiam Opinions, 62 Wash. & Lee L. Rev. 1429 (2005), provides nearly a dozen articles on the topic.

34. The circuits' approaches are summarized in Sarah E. Ricks, *A Modest Proposal for Regulating Unpublished, Non–Precedential Federal Appellate Opinions While Courts and Litigants Adapt to Federal Rule of Appellate Procedure 32.1*, 9 J. App. Prac. & Process 17, 22–24 (2007).

32.1. As the law develops in this area, the only certainty is that familiarity with a circuit's local rules and decisions before filing a brief is essential.

United States District Courts. In 1932, with the increasing volume of litigation in the federal courts, West began another series called *Federal Supplement* (F. Supp.) for selected U.S. District Court decisions (leaving the *Federal Reporter* to cover the U.S. Courts of Appeals). *Federal Supplement* is now in its second series (F. Supp. 2d), and also includes decisions of the U.S. Court of International Trade and rulings from the Judicial Panel on Multi-district Litigation.[35]

Only a small fraction of U.S. District Court cases are represented by opinions published in the *Federal Supplement*. More decisions are available from the online databases or through court websites, but many District Court cases do not even result in written opinions. Unlike appellate cases which turn on the resolution by judges of disputed legal issues, trial court litigation can be tried to a jury verdict or settled before trial with no resulting court opinion. District Court cases may have a number of rulings on issues such as the exclusion of evidence or the qualification of expert witnesses, and some of these are published or available online, but only a few cases have a final "decision" in the same sense as an appellate proceeding.

Another West series, *Federal Rules Decisions* (F.R.D.), began publication in 1940 and contains a limited number of U.S. District Court decisions dealing with procedural issues under the Federal Rules of Civil Procedure and the Federal Rules of Criminal Procedure. *Federal Rules Decisions* does not contain *all* District Court procedural decisions; some cases involving interpretation of court rules continue to appear in *Federal Supplement,* and many others are available only online. *Federal Rules Decisions* also includes judicial conference proceedings and occasional speeches or articles dealing with procedural law in the federal courts; these materials are included in Westlaw's FRD database. (The ALLFEDS and DCT databases include the decisions in F.R.D., but not its articles and other materials.)

Specialized Courts. As Congress has periodically restructured the federal judiciary to create specialized courts over the years, West has at times added their coverage to the *Federal Reporter* or *Federal Supplement*. It has also created several new topical reporters to cover some of these courts. Each of these reporters includes West's syllabi and headnotes so that cases can be

---

35. The *Federal Supplement* has also included decisions of the U.S. Court of Claims (1932–60), the U.S. Customs Court (1956–80), and the Special Court under the Regional Rail Reorganization Act of 1973 (1974–97).

found through key number searches in West's digests or on West-law.

West's Bankruptcy Reporter (1980–date) covers decisions of the Bankruptcy Courts, as well as some District Court opinions on bankruptcy issues. The reporter also includes bankruptcy opinions from the Supreme Court and Courts of Appeals, but these are simply reprinted from the *Supreme Court Reporter* and *Federal Reporter* with their original page numbers.

Similarly, when Congress created the United States Claims Court in 1982, West began publication of the *United States Claims Court Reporter*. This became the *Federal Claims Reporter* when the court was renamed the Court of Federal Claims in 1992. The reporter includes appellate decisions from the Court of Appeals for the Federal Circuit and the Supreme Court, but these are merely reprints like those in the *Bankruptcy Reporter*.

Since 1978 West has also published the decisions of the U.S. Court of Appeals for the Armed Forces (formerly the U.S. Court of Military Appeals), and selected decisions of the Courts of Criminal Appeals for each military branch, in *West's Military Justice Report-er*. Decisions of the U.S. Court of Veteran Appeals are published in *Veterans Appeals Reporter* (1991–date).

West's National Reporter System does not include decisions from the U.S. Tax Court. These are published by the government in *Reports of the United States Tax Court* (1942–date), and by the major commercial tax publishers. The Tax Court also issues memo-randum opinions in cases that do not involve novel legal issues. These are not published in the official reports, but they can be cited as precedent. Memorandum opinions are available online and are published in *TC Memorandum Decisions* (RIA, 1942–date) and *Tax Court Memorandum Decisions* (CCH, 1942–date).

(c) Specialized Reporters

Federal court decisions are also available in print and online from a variety of other sources, including commercial topical re-porters published for practitioners in specialized subject areas. Some cases appearing in these sources are not printed in the *Federal Reporter* or *Federal Supplement*, but most are generally available on Westlaw and Lexis.

In addition to *Federal Rules Decisions*, West publishes two other series of cases on procedural issues. These are *not* part of its National Reporter System but are preferred over online sources in citations. These series, *Federal Rules Service* (1939–date) and *Fed-eral Rules of Evidence Service* (1979–date), duplicate some coverage with the National Reporter System volumes but contain many cases not found there. Each series is accompanied by a digest set arranging its cases' headnotes by Federal Rules of Civil Procedure, Federal Rules of Appellate Procedure, or Federal Rules of Evidence rule number.

Cases also appear in several dozen specialized reporters, usually published first in weekly or biweekly updates and then in some instances in permanent bound volumes. Most of these series also include reports of agency adjudications and state court decisions as well. Major specialized reporters, by subject, are:

Administrative law

Administrative Law (Pike & Fischer)

Admiralty and maritime law

American Maritime Cases (AMC, Inc.)

Bankruptcy

Bankruptcy Court Decisions (LRP Publications)

Bankruptcy Law Reports (CCH)

Collier Bankruptcy Cases (LexisNexis)

Commercial law

International Trade Reporter Decisions (BNA)

RICO Business Disputes Guide (CCH)

Trade Cases (CCH)

Uniform Commercial Code Reporting Service (West)

Communications and media

Communications Regulation (Pike & Fischer)

Media Law Reporter (BNA)

Environmental law

Environment Reporter Cases (BNA)

Environmental Law Reporter (Environmental Law Institute)

Insurance

Fire and Casualty Cases (CCH)

Life, Health and Accident Insurance Cases (CCH)

Intellectual property

Copyright Law Decisions (CCH)

United States Patent Quarterly (BNA)

Labor and employment law

Americans with Disabilities Cases (BNA)

Employee Benefits Cases (BNA)

Employment Practices Decisions (CCH)

Fair Employment Practice Cases (BNA)

Individual Employment Rights Cases (BNA)

Labor Cases (CCH)

Labor Relations Reference Manual (BNA)

National Disability Law Reporter (LRP Publications)

Occupational Safety & Health Cases (BNA)

Occupational Safety & Health Decisions (CCH)

Unemployment Insurance Reports (CCH)

Wage and Hour Cases (BNA)

Products liability

Products Liability Reports (CCH)

Securities

Blue Sky Law Reports (CCH)

Commodity Futures Law Reports (CCH)

Federal Securities Law Reports (CCH)

Taxation

American Federal Tax Reports (RIA)

U.S. Tax Cases (CCH)

Transportation

Aviation Cases (CCH)

Federal Carriers Cases (CCH)

Shipping Regulation (Pike & Fischer)

Utilities

Public Utilities Reports (PUR, Inc.)

Utilities Law Reporter (CCH)

(d) Historical Sources

During the 19th century, a number of individual nominative reporters published decisions of the lower federal courts. Over sixty separate reporters, most covering just a single court, published cases of the circuit and district courts, and scattered decisions appeared in more than a hundred other publications.

In the 1890s, the West Publishing Company collected the decisions from these various reporters and compiled them in a set entitled *Federal Cases* (and cited as F. Cas.). More than 18,000 cases are arranged in alphabetical order by case name and numbered. The thirty-volume set contains all available lower federal court case law up to 1880. These are cited by name, citation, and case number, e.g. *In re Zug*, 30 F. Cas. 947 (C.C.W.D. Pa. 1877) (No. 18,222). The first volume includes lists of the nominative reporters and other publications from which cases were drawn, as well as lists of all federal judges up to 1894, and the final volume reprints judicial tributes from the original reporters and provides brief biographical notes on the judges.

Westlaw and Lexis have complete retrospective coverage of the early federal cases, with citations to both the original nominative sources and *Federal Cases*. Unlike later cases in the *Federal Reporter* and *Federal Supplement*, however, Westlaw does not provide PDF images of these early decisions.

§ 7.3   State Courts

Although federal law governs an increasing range of activities, state courts have a vital lawmaking role on many issues, including important areas such as family law, contracts, insurance, and substantive criminal law. A state's court of last resort has the final say in interpreting the state's constitution and statutes.

The structure of most state court systems roughly follows the federal paradigm, with various trial courts, intermediate appellate courts, and a court of last resort. There are, however, wide variations. A few states have no intermediate appellate courts, with appeals going directly from the trial court to the state supreme court. Other states have more complicated systems, with more than one appellate court for different subject areas. Oklahoma and Texas even have separate courts of last resort for civil and criminal matters.

The U.S. Bureau of Justice Statistics (BJS) publishes charts showing the structure of each state's court system, indicating the jurisdiction of the various courts and the routes of appeal within the court hierarchy, in *State Court Organization 2004* (and subsequent editions as they are published), available on its website in PDF <www.ojp.usdoj.gov/bjs/abstract/sco04.htm>. This volume also includes a bevy of tables on all aspects of state judicial systems, from selection of judges and sources of rulemaking authority to collateral consequences of felony convictions.

The National Center for State Courts (NCSC) website provides a clickable map <www.ncsconline.org/D_Research/Ct_Struct/> linking to the court structure chart for each individual state. The NCSC's Court Statistics Project <www.ncsconline.org/D_Research/csp/CSP_Main_Page.html> provides access to a broad range of other information on the caseloads and work of state courts. The annual publication *State Court Caseload Statistics* contains both statistical tables and the State Court Structure Charts.

The court structure charts are reprinted in several other sources, including the annual editions of *BNA's Directory of State and Federal Courts, Judges, and Clerks* and CQ Press's *Federal-State Court Directory*, and the biennial *Legal Researcher's Desk Reference*. Any of these sources can provide the basic knowledge required to understand, for example, that the New York Supreme Court is a trial court rather than the state's court of last resort.

More detailed information, if needed, can then be found on the state court system's website. The National Center for State Courts maintains a comprehensive listing of court websites <www.ncsconline.org/d_kis/info_court_web_sites.html>, including for most states a link to the judicial branch site as well as links for specific courts. This list provides access as well to the state court structure charts.

Decisions from state courts are available in sources similar to those from the federal courts, with comprehensive access to appellate decisions on Westlaw and Lexis, extensive coverage from other commercial databases, some coverage on the free Internet, and published reporter volumes. Generally appellate decisions are widely available but very few state trial court decisions are available either in print or in online case databases.

(a) Online Resources

The computer systems of Westlaw and Lexis are virtually comprehensive sources for state appellate court decisions, lacking only a very few early reports from some states. In Westlaw, the database for a particular state's decisions is __-CS (using the state postal abbreviation), while __-CS–ALL combines the state court cases with those from the federal courts with jurisdiction in the state (and thus including the U.S. Supreme Court and the relevant U.S. Court of Appeals). Both systems also have databases combining all state cases (ALLSTATES in Westlaw) as well as all state and federal cases (ALLCASES).

For some states, the databases include numerous opinions which are not published in the official reports. Decisions of courts of last resort are generally published in full, but publication of decisions by intermediate appellate courts may be sharply limited. As in the federal system, many states limit the citation or precedential value of unpublished opinions.[36]

Coverage of state trial court decisions on Westlaw and Lexis has until recently been sparse, with the case databases generally

---

36. On state rules on unpublished opinions, see Melissa M. Serfass & Jessie L. Cranford, *Federal and State Court Rules Governing Publication and Citation of Opinions*, 3 J. APP. PRAC. & PROCESS 251, 253–85 (2001). Jason B. Binimow, Annotation, *Precedential Effect of Unpublished Opinions*, 105 A.L.R.5th 499 (2003), summarizes cases on this topic from some three dozen states.

including decisions from only a handful of states.[37] Westlaw has broadened its coverage of rulings by trial court judges, but these are found in separate "Trial Court Orders" databases. Coverage generally begins in 2001. A TRIALORDERS–ALL database covers the entire country.

In addition to Westlaw and Lexis, other commercial online databases also provide access to state court decisions; Loislaw, for example, has more than eighty years of case law for most states. VersusLaw coverage begins anywhere from 1910 to 1980. Fastcase generally covers back to 1950, and Casemaker has decisions back to 1930 in most jurisdictions. Although these databases may not be sufficient for comprehensive historical research, any of them would provide more than adequate coverage for most contemporary case law research.

Free Internet sites generally provide access to court decisions beginning in the mid- to late-1990s, although some states maintain only the most recent three months of decisions on their official websites. A few states lead the way with much more extensive databases; the Oklahoma State Courts Network <www.oscn.net> has all the decisions of the state's appellate courts, back to 1890, and the North Dakota Supreme Court <www.ndcourts.gov> has cases back to 1965.

Three commercial sites also provide coverage of recent state court opinions, and permit combined searches of all state jurisdictions. PreCYdent <www.precydent.com> has coverage mirroring that available on official court sites, Public Library of Law <www. plol.org> has cases back to 1997, and lexisONE <www.lexisone. com> provides a five-year collection of state appellate decisions.

Websites for state court decisions can be found through a search engine or by starting with a directory of online legal resources. FindLaw's State Resources page <www.findlaw.com/ 11stategov/> provides links to official and commercial sites for each state under "Primary Materials." One advantage of using a directory rather than a search is that for many states there are two or more sites with opinions, and these may have different dates of coverage or search capabilities.[38]

---

37. Selected decisions are included from general-jurisdiction trial courts in Connecticut, Delaware, Massachusetts, New Jersey, New York, Ohio, Pennsylvania, Rhode Island, and Virginia. The databases also cover tax courts and other courts with specialized jurisdictions in eight states.

38. New York Court of Appeals decisions, for example, are available from the New York Official Reports Service <government.westlaw.com/nyofficial/> back to 1995, with full Westlaw search capabilities. FindLaw <www.findlaw. com/11stategov/ny/nyca.html> and the Legal Information Institute <www.law. cornell.edu/nyctap/> have more cases, back to 1992, but with less powerful search options.

(b) West's National Reporter System

Just as Supreme Court decisions are published both in the official *U.S. Reports* and in commercial reporters, so decisions from state appellate courts are traditionally published both in official reports, issued by or under the auspices of the courts themselves, and in West's series of National Reporter System volumes.

West's National Reporter System includes a series of *regional reporters* publishing the decisions of the appellate courts of the fifty states and the District of Columbia. The National Reporter System divides the country into seven regions, and publishes the decisions of the appellate courts of the states in each region together in one series of volumes.

The regions were assigned in the 1880s and make little sense from a modern geographical perspective:

Atlantic Reporter: Connecticut, Delaware, the District of Columbia, Maine, Maryland, New Hampshire, New Jersey, Pennsylvania, Rhode Island, Vermont

North Eastern Reporter: Illinois, Indiana, Massachusetts, New York, Ohio

North Western Reporter: Iowa, Michigan, Minnesota, Nebraska, North Dakota, South Dakota, Wisconsin

Pacific Reporter: Alaska, Arizona, California, Colorado, Hawai'i, Idaho, Kansas, Montana, Nevada, New Mexico, Oklahoma, Oregon, Utah, Washington, Wyoming

South Eastern Reporter: Georgia, North Carolina, South Carolina, Virginia, West Virginia

South Western Reporter: Arkansas, Kentucky, Missouri, Tennessee, Texas

Southern Reporter: Alabama, Florida, Louisiana, Mississippi

Five of these sets are now in their second series (*Atlantic* (A.2d), *North Eastern* (N.E.2d), *North Western* (N.W.2d), *South Eastern* (S.E.2d), *Southern* (So. 2d)); and two have started their third series (*Pacific* (P.3d) and *South Western* (S.W.3d).[39]

These sets are supplemented by separate reporters for the two most populous states, *California Reporter* (Cal. Rptr. 3d) and *New York Supplement* (N.Y.S.2d). Cases from the highest courts of California and New York appear in both the regional and the state reporter, while lower court cases are not published in the *Pacific* or *North Eastern Reporter*.[40] These nine reporters, together with

---

39. Information on which states are included in each region of the reporter system is also available in an online map <lawschool.westlaw.com/federalcourt/ NationalReporterPage.asp>.

40. West also publishes individual reporters for more than thirty additional

West's federal court reporters, are all tied together by the key number headnote and digest system.

Illustration 7–8 on page 268 shows the first page of *In re Moe*, an opinion of the Appeals Court of Massachusetts, as printed in West's *North Eastern Reporter*. The opinion is prefaced, as in other West reporters, by an introductory synopsis and numbered headnotes. The *North Eastern Reporter* version includes star paging indicating the exact page breaks in the official *Massachusetts Reports*, as shown before the first paragraph of the opinion, and bracketed numbers indicating where headnoted topics are discussed in the opinion.

Regional reporter citations are the sources used in most law review references to state court decisions, especially in states that have not instituted public domain citation systems.[41] A regional reporter citation does not identify the deciding court, so remember to include this information in parentheses with the date: *In re Moe*, 855 N.E.2d 1136 (Mass. App. Ct. 2006).

Citations, including pinpoint cites to quoted material from opinions, can generally be found through Westlaw and Lexis without consulting the printed volumes. Both services indicate page breaks in their online versions of cases, and Westlaw also has PDFs back to the beginning of the National Reporter System.

(c) Official Reports

Like the *U.S. Reports*, state official reports are the authoritative version of a court's decisions and must be cited in briefs before that court. They are generally less widely available than commercial reporters, which are usually published more quickly and are more useful in research. As lawyers came to rely increasingly on National Reporter System volumes in the 20th century, twenty states decided to discontinue their official reports and to designate

states. Unlike the *California Reporter* and *New York Supplement*, however, most of these other series simply reprint a state's cases from its regional reporter, including the original regional reporter pagination. These "offprint" reporters are published so that practitioners can have their own state courts' decisions without cases from other states they don't need.

41. THE BLUEBOOK: A UNIFORM SYSTEM OF CITATION R. 10.3.1(b), at 87 (18th ed. 2005); ALWD CITATION MANUAL: A PROFESSIONAL SYSTEM OF CITATION R. 12.4(b)(2), at 78 (3d ed. 2006). But see Gil Grantmore, *True Blue*, 20 CONST. COMMENT. 5, 8–9 (2003) (discussing THE BLUEBOOK 17th ed. 2000):

Rule 10.3.1 directs law review authors to "cite the relevant regional reporter" for state court decisions, but not the official reporter (p. 62). This is a supremely arrogant rule that befits student editors at Ivy League law schools. We will not follow it. If a state goes to the trouble of paying for its own official reporter and requiring its lawyers and judges to cite that reporter, law journals should respect that choice (however frivolous it may seem in an age of electronic publishing and public domain citations). It is obnoxious for second-year law students to second-guess state courts.

the West reporter as the authoritative source of state case law. Florida was the first to make this move, in 1948.[42] In most states, however, cases appear in both official and unofficial editions. Tables in both *The Bluebook* and the *ALWD Citation Manual* provide information on the current status of the published reports in each state.

Forms of publication vary from state to state. Some states publish just one series of reports, containing decisions of the state supreme court and in some instances of intermediate appellate courts as well. More than a dozen states issue two or more series of reports, with separate series for the court of last resort, for intermediate appellate courts, and in a few states for selected decisions of trial courts. New York, for example, has three official series: *New York Reports*, covering the Court of Appeals, the state's court of last resort; *Appellate Division Reports*, covering the Appellate Divisions of the Supreme Court; and *Miscellaneous Reports*, with decisions of various lower courts. Some states, but not all, publish official slip decisions and advance sheets as well as bound volumes. Illustration 7–9 on page 269 shows the first page of *In re Moe* as it appears in *Massachusetts Appeals Court Reports*. Instead of numbered headnotes, it simply has an introductory paragraph summarizing the decision.

Even though official reports do not generally include links to a comprehensive digest system like West's, they can still provide a valuable perspective on a state's appellate court decisions. Summaries or headnotes written by court staff or by lawyers practicing in that state may be more attuned to local judicial developments than headnotes written by commercial editors.[43] Some official reports include research leads not found in the West reporters, and others provide their own classification and digest systems. Although official reports are less widely used than West's, in some states they maintain a valuable research role.[44]

42. See George A. Dietz, Legislative Note, *Sketch of the Evolution of Florida Law*, 3 U. FLA. L. REV. 74, 80–81 (1950) ("Gone at last are the tedious waiting for the official reports, the inevitable discrepancies between the earlier unofficial reports and the much later official ones, the needless duplication in printing resulting in higher cost per copy, the tremendous waste [of] time involved in checking what should be—but all too frequently is not—the same phraseology in two sets of books, and the squandering of space for citations on two references when one serves the purpose equally as well.")

43. See Richard F. Jones, *The Role of Official Headnotes in Legal Research*, 59 LAW LIBR. J. 277, 279 (1966) ("[T]he official reporter is not only an expert on the law of his jurisdiction, but he is also a specialist in dealing with the opinions of one particular court. He is personally acquainted with the authors of the opinions he headnotes, and familiar with their methods of expressing themselves.")

44. In most states, however, any local perspective of official reports has been abandoned. Besides the states without official reports at all, another dozen states have continued the state's numbered report series but simply pro-

As with the early *U.S. Reports* volumes, the early reports of several states were once cited as nominative reports (identified by the names of their reporters). Many of these volumes have now been incorporated into the numbered series, but it may still be necessary to use an abbreviations dictionary or other reference work to understand some older case citations. Westlaw and Lexis generally recognize the nominative reporter citations, so there may be no need to decipher the citation before retrieving a case online.

In states with official reports, those reports are the authoritative source for the decisions and must be cited in briefs and other court papers. As noted earlier, however, *Bluebook* and *ALWD* rules dictate that the more widely available regional reporter is the preferred source in most citations. Despite these rules, many sources provide both unofficial and official parallel citations so that readers can easily find a case no matter which source they have available.

If you have a citation to only one report of a case, there are several ways to find its parallel citation. The simplest is usually to retrieve the case in a commercial online database, which will generally provide both citations. In printed reporters, the parallel citation is sometimes, but not always, provided at the beginning of the case, as it is in Illustration 7–8. Another approach is to use a series of volumes called the *National Reporter Blue Book*, which is updated annually and lists the starting page of each case in the official reports and provides cross-references to National Reporter System citations.

Not all cases have parallel citations. Only the official citations exist for very early cases, before West created the National Reporter System in the 1880s. On the other hand, in those states that have discontinued their official reports and have not instituted public domain citation systems, only West reporter citations are available for cases in recent decades. Even if official reports are published, they are generally issued more slowly than the regional reporters and the unofficial citation is frequently the only one available for very recent cases.

(d) Topical Reporters and Other Sources

Almost all of the looseleaf services and topical reporters described in the "Lower Federal Courts" section contain state court decisions. Some areas, such as insurance or utilities regulation, are determined largely by state law, so reporters in these areas have predominantly state court decisions. Reporters in areas such as

vide the same editorial synopsis and headnotes that appear in the West regional reporter or on Westlaw.

commercial law or employment rights have a mix of federal and state cases. Even legal issues that are distinctly federal can arise in state court, so some state cases appear in admiralty, federal tax, or patent services.

A few of the legal newspapers published in large cities report lower court decisions which do not appear in the standard state court reports or the regional reporters. These elusive opinions can be hard to find, even online, because they may be located in newspaper databases rather than case databases.

Older decisions, particularly from the colonial period, can also be found in a variety of other sources. Many early court cases were preserved in manuscript collections but were never published as court reports, and some of these have been printed during the modern era in historical collections or journal articles. *Prestatehood Legal Materials: A Fifty–State Research Guide* (Michael Chiorazzi & Marguerite Most eds., 2005) provides a state-by-state overview of available resources from colonial and territorial courts. Other early decisions may be collected in topical compilations such as *Judicial Cases Concerning American Slavery and the Negro* (Helen Tunnicliff Catterall ed., 1926–37). These cases may not be very significant as modern-day precedent, but they are still of great historical value.

§ 7.4   Tribal and Territorial Courts

The United States has a number of appellate courts that are not represented at all in West's National Reporter System, and may even be hard to find in online sources. These are the courts of the territories and the Indian nations.

The District of Columbia Court of Appeals is included in the *Atlantic Reporter* with state court cases, but the supreme courts of Guam, Northern Mariana Islands, Puerto Rico, and the Virgin Islands can only be found in official reports (in some instances) or online through the databases or court websites. These territories also have U.S. District Courts, with decisions included in the federal case databases (and selectively in the *Federal Supplement*) and appealed to the First (Puerto Rico), Third (Virgin Islands), and Ninth (Guam and Northern Mariana Islands) Circuits.

Tribal court decisions have traditionally been even harder to find, with very few cases available in reporters or from the major database systems. The most extensive coverage of tribal courts is provided by VersusLaw, with free searchable access to its databases available through the National Tribal Justice Resource Center <www.ntjrc.org> and the Tribal Court Clearinghouse <www. tribal-institute.org>. The Resource Center also has a list of nearly six hundred federal recognized tribes, most with links to tribal websites that may provide more extensive access to court decisions. In 2009 *West's American Tribal Law Reporter* began publication, with coverage back to 1997 of decisions from about a dozen tribal courts. These decisions are also available on Westlaw as the AMTRIB-CS database.[45]

This chapter has focused on sources for case law, both in print and through a variety of electronic means. Using these sources to finding case law relevant to a particular research problem is the topic of the next chapter.

45. On tribal courts generally, see, e.g., Frank Pommersheim, *Tribal Court Jurisprudence: A Snapshot from the Field*, 21 VT. L. REV. 7 (1996); Michael Taylor, *Modern Practice in the Indian Courts,* 10 U. PUGET SOUND L. REV. 231 (1987).

OCTOBER TERM, 2005   43

Syllabus

UNITED STATES *v.* OLSON ET AL.

CERTIORARI TO THE UNITED STATES COURT OF APPEALS FOR THE NINTH CIRCUIT

No. 04–759.   Argued October 12, 2005—Decided November 8, 2005

Claiming that federal mine inspectors' negligence helped cause a mine accident, two injured workers (and a spouse) sued the United States under the Federal Tort Claims Act (Act), which authorizes private tort actions against the Government "under circumstances where the United States, if a private person, would be liable to the claimant in accordance with the law of the place where the act or omission occurred," 28 U. S. C. § 1346(b)(1). The District Court dismissed in part on the ground that the allegations did not show that Arizona law would impose liability upon a private person in similar circumstances. The Ninth Circuit reversed, reasoning from two premises: (1) Where unique governmental functions are at issue, the Act waives sovereign immunity if a state or municipal entity would be held liable under the law where the activity occurred, and (2) federal mine inspections are such unique governmental functions since there is no private-sector analogue for mine inspections. Because Arizona law would make a state or municipal entity liable in the circumstances alleged, the Circuit concluded that the United States' sovereign immunity was waived.

Held: Under § 1346(b)(1), the United States waives sovereign immunity only where local law would make a "private person" liable in tort, not where local law would make "a state or municipal entity" liable. Pp. 45–48.

  (a) The Ninth Circuit's first premise is too broad, reading into the Act something that is not there. Section 1346(b)(1) says that it waives sovereign immunity "under circumstances where the United States, if a *private person,*" not "the United States, if a state or municipal entity," would be liable. (Emphasis added.) This Court has consistently adhered to this "private person" standard, even when uniquely governmental functions are at issue. *Indian Towing Co.* v. *United States,* 350 U. S. 61, 64; *Rayonier Inc.* v. *United States,* 352 U. S. 315, 318. Even though both these cases involved Government efforts to *escape* liability by pointing to the *absence* of municipal entity liability, there is no reason for treating differently a plaintiff's effort to *base* liability solely upon the fact that a State would impose liability upon a state governmental entity. Nothing in the Act's context, history, or objectives or in this Court's opinions suggests otherwise. Pp. 45–46.

Illustration 7–1. *United States v. Olson,* 546 U.S. 43 (2005).

44 UNITED STATES *v.* OLSON

Opinion of the Court

(b) The Ninth Circuit's second premise reads the Act too narrowly. Section 2674 makes the United States liable "in the same manner and to the same extent as a private individual under *like circumstances.*" (Emphasis added.) The words "like circumstances" do not restrict a court's inquiry to the *same circumstances,* but require it to look further afield. See, *e. g., Indian Towing, supra,* at 64. The Government in effect concedes, and other Courts of Appeals' decisions applying *Indian Towing's* logic suggest, that private person analogies exist for the federal mine inspectors' conduct at issue. The Ninth Circuit should have looked for such an analogy. Pp. 46–47.

(c) The lower courts should decide in the first instance precisely which Arizona tort law doctrine applies here. P. 48.

362 F. 3d 1236, vacated and remanded.

BREYER, J., delivered the opinion for a unanimous Court.

Deanne E. Maynard argued the cause for the United States. With her on the briefs were *Solicitor General Clement, Assistant Attorney General Keisler, Deputy Solicitor General Kneedler, Mark B. Stern,* and *Dana J. Martin.*

Thomas G. Cotter argued the cause and filed a brief for respondents.

JUSTICE BREYER delivered the opinion of the Court.

The Federal Tort Claims Act (FTCA or Act) authorizes private tort actions against the United States "under circumstances where the United States, if a private person, would be liable to the claimant in accordance with the law of the place where the act or omission occurred." 28 U. S. C. § 1346(b)(1). We here interpret these words to mean what they say, namely, that the United States waives sovereign immunity "under circumstances" where local law would make a *"private person"* liable in tort. (Emphasis added.) And we reverse a line of Ninth Circuit precedent permitting courts in certain circumstances to base a waiver simply upon a finding that local law would make a "state or municipal entit[y]" liable. See, *e. g., Hines* v. *United States,* 60 F. 3d 1442, 1448 (1995); *Cimo* v. *INS,* 16 F. 3d 1039, 1041 (1994); *Cameron* v. *Janssen Bros. Nurseries, Ltd.,* 7 F. 3d 821, 825

Illustration 7–2. *Olson,* 546 U.S. at 44.

510　　　　**126 SUPREME COURT REPORTER**　　　　**546 U.S. 43**

546 U.S. 43, 163 L.Ed.2d 306

UNITED STATES, Petitioner,

v.

Joseph OLSON, et al.

No. 04–759.

Argued Oct. 12, 2005.

Decided Nov. 8, 2005.

Background: Injured miners sued the Mine Safety and Health Administration (MSHA) pursuant to the Federal Tort Claims Act (FTCA), alleging negligence by federal mine inspectors. The United States District Court for the District of Arizona, William D. Browning, J., granted MSHA's motion to dismiss, and miners appealed. The United States Court of Appeals for the Ninth Circuit, 362 F.3d 1236, reversed and remanded. Certiorari was granted.

Holding: The Supreme Court, Justice Breyer, held that FTCA waives federal government's sovereign immunity only where local law would make private person liable in tort, not where local law would make state or municipal entity liable, even where uniquely governmental functions are at issue; abrogating *Hines v. United States*, 60 F.3d 1442; *Cimo v. INS*, 16 F.3d 1039; *Cameron v. Janssen Bros. Nurseries, Ltd.*, 7 F.3d 821; *Aguilar v. United States*, 920 F.2d 1475; *Doggett v. United States*, 875 F.2d 684.

Vacated and remanded.

1. United States ⬤⟞78(3, 14)

Federal Tort Claims Act (FTCA) waives federal government's sovereign immunity only where local law would make private person liable in tort, not where local law would make state or municipal entity liable, even where uniquely governmental functions are at issue; abrogating

Hines v. United States, 60 F.3d 1442; *Cimo v. INS*, 16 F.3d 1039; *Cameron v. Janssen Bros. Nurseries, Ltd.*, 7 F.3d 821; *Aguilar v. United States*, 920 F.2d 1475; *Doggett v. United States*, 875 F.2d 684. 28 U.S.C.A. § 1346(b)(1).

2. United States ⬤⟞78(3)

Provision of Federal Tort Claims Act imposing liability in same manner and to same extent as private individual under "like circumstances" does not restrict court's inquiry to same circumstances; rather, it is required to look further afield. 28 U.S.C.A. § 2674.

_{₄₃}*Syllabus* *

Claiming that federal mine inspectors' negligence helped cause a mine accident, two injured workers (and a spouse) sued the United States under the Federal Tort Claims Act (Act), which authorizes private tort actions against the Government "under circumstances where the United States, if a private person, would be liable to the claimant in accordance with the law of the place where the act or omission occurred," 28 U.S.C. § 1346(b)(1). The District Court dismissed in part on the ground that the allegations did not show that Arizona law would impose liability upon a private person in similar circumstances. The Ninth Circuit reversed, reasoning from two premises: (1) Where unique governmental functions are at issue, the Act waives sovereign immunity if a state or municipal entity would be held liable under the law where the activity occurred, and (2) federal mine inspections are such unique governmental functions since there is no private-sector analogue for mine inspections. Because Arizona law would make a state or municipal entity

* The syllabus constitutes no part of the opinion of the Court but has been prepared by the Reporter of Decisions for the convenience of the reader. See *United States v. Detroit Timber & Lumber Co.*, 200 U.S. 321, 337, 26 S.Ct. 282, 50 L.Ed. 499.

Illustration 7–3. *United States v. Olson*, 126 S. Ct. 510 (2005).

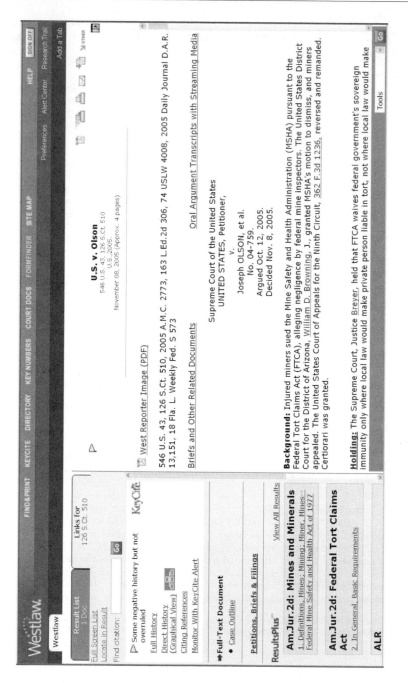

Illustration 7–4. *United States v. Olson,*
546 U.S. 43 (2005), on Westlaw.

[546 U.S. 43]

UNITED STATES, Petitioner

v

JOSEPH OLSON, et al.

546 U.S. 43, 126 S. Ct. 510, 163 L. Ed. 2d 306

[No. 04-759]

Argued October 12, 2005. Decided November 8, 2005.

Decision: United States held to waive sovereign immunity under Federal Tort Claims Act provision (28 U.S.C.S. § 1346(b)(1)) only where local law would make "private person" liable in tort.

SUMMARY

Workers who had been injured in a mine accident in Arizona brought, against the United States on the basis of federal mine inspectors' alleged negligence, a suit under the Federal Tort Claims Act (FTCA) (28 U.S.C.S. §§ 1346, 2671 et seq.), which in 28 U.S.C.S. § 1346(b)(1), authorized private tort actions against the United States "under circumstances where the United States, if a private person, would be liable to the claimant in accordance with the law of the place where the act or omission occurred."

The United States District Court for the District of Arizona dismissed the lawsuit in part on the ground that the allegations were insufficient to show that Arizona law would impose liability on a private person in similar circumstances.

The United States Court of Appeals reversed, as the Court of Appeals (1) reasoned that (a) where unique governmental functions were at issue, the FTCA waived sovereign immunity if a state or municipal entity would have been subject to liability under the law where the activity occurred, (b) federal mine inspections were unique governmental functions, since they had no private-sector analogue; and (2) held that the FTCA waived sovereign immunity in the instant case, since Arizona law would have made state or municipal entities liable in the circumstances alleged (362 F. 3d 1236).

SUBJECT OF ANNOTATION

Beginning on page 1223, infra

Supreme Court's construction and application of Federal Tort Claims Act (FTCA) provisions (in 28 U.S.C.S. §§ 1346(b)(1) and 2674, and similar predecessors) concerning "private person" and "private individual under like circumstances" standards for liability of United States

Summaries of Briefs; Names of Participating Attorneys, p 1154, infra.

306

Illustration 7–5. *United States v. Olson*, 163 L. Ed. 2d 306 (2005).

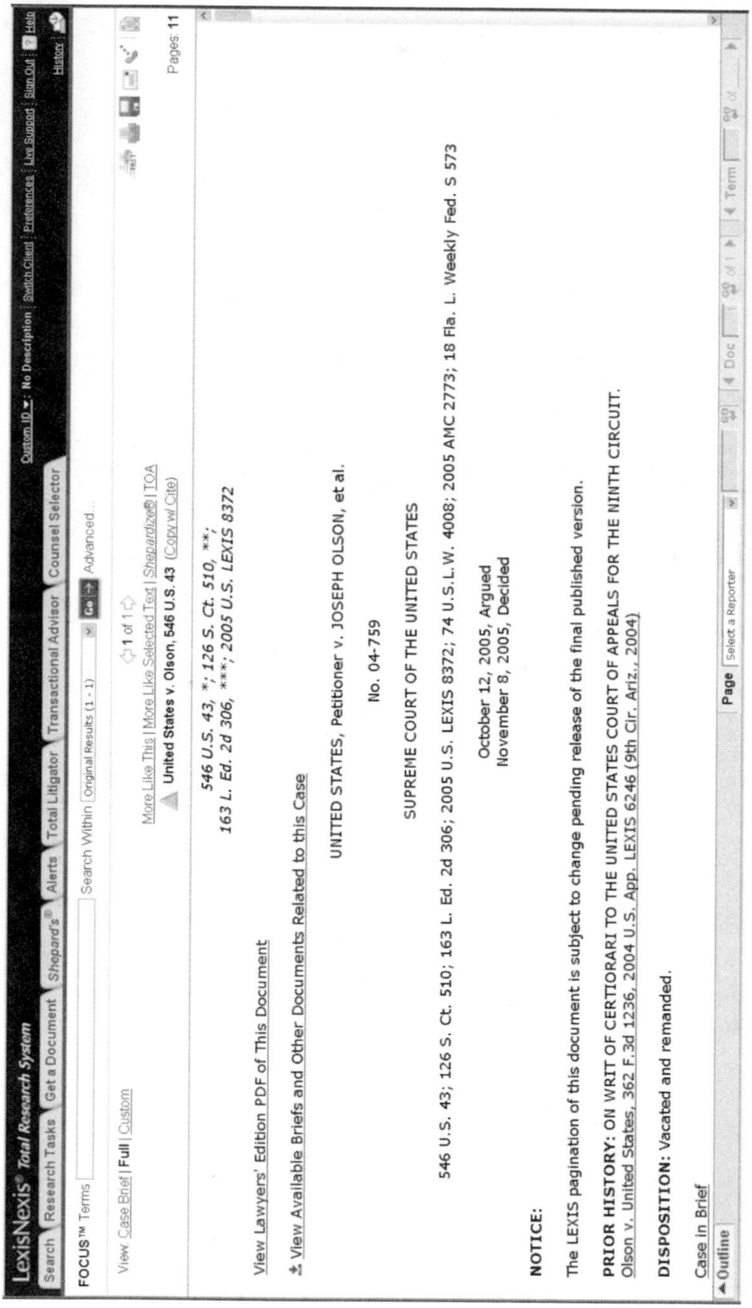

Illustration 7–6. *United States v. Olson,*
546 U.S. 43 (2005), on Lexis.

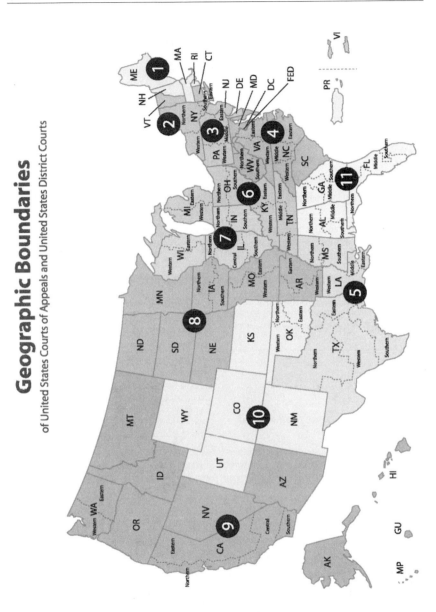

Illustration 7–7. Geographic Boundaries of United States
Courts of Appeals and United States District Courts
<www.uscourts.gov/images/CircuitMap.pdf>.

1136   Mass.   855 NORTH EASTERN REPORTER, 2d SERIES

67 Mass.App.Ct. 651

In the Matter of Mary MOE.

No. 06–P–924.

Appeals Court of Massachusetts,
Bristol.

Argued June 12, 2006.

Decided Oct. 30, 2006.

Background: Nonresident minor filed petition to have abortion performed in Massachusetts without parental consent. The Superior Court Department, Bristol County, Richard J. Chin, J., reported question to Appeals Court as to whether Massachusetts had jurisdiction to grant petition.

Holding: The Appeals Court, Kantrowitz, J., held that Massachusetts had jurisdiction to grant nonresident minor's petition for permission to have abortion performed without parental consent.

Reported question answered.

1. Abortion and Birth Control �119

Massachusetts had jurisdiction to grant nonresident minor's petition for permission to have abortion performed without parental consent; statute governing

---

24. By their amended complaints, the plaintiffs also alleged claims of: Title IX violation; § 1983 (substantive due process based) violation; breach of contract; and fraudulent inducement, as against the school, its board, Gurnon, Roy A. Fulgeras (school's director of admissions), the board of trustees of the State colleges and the Board of Higher Education. Certain of these claims remain pending in the trial court, but none, however, are the subject of or otherwise involved in the present appeal.

---

performance of abortions on minors did not contain residency requirement. M.G.L.A. c. 112, § 12S.

2. Statutes ⟧⟩203

The omission of terms in a statute may be deemed to be one of deliberate Legislature design.

Marisa A. Campagna, Boston (Karen D. Lane with her) for the petitioner.

Present: KANTROWITZ, DREBEN, & GRAHAM, JJ.

KANTROWITZ, J.

[₆₅₁]On June 12, 2006, the following question was reported, see Mass.R.Civ.P. 64(a), as amended, 423 Mass. 1403 (1996), to our court by a judge of the Superior Court:

"Does a Massachusetts Court have jurisdiction and authority pursuant to G.L. c. 112, § 12S, to grant a nonresident minor's petition seeking permission to have an abortion performed in Massachusetts without parental consent?" [1]

[1] We conclude that a plain reading of the statute in question does not impose a residency requirement.[2] As such, we answer the question in the affirmative.

---

1. Mary Moe, a seventeen year old minor, and a resident of the State of Rhode Island, was seeking to have an abortion performed, without parental consent, in Massachusetts. According to the brief filed in our court, Mary Moe, with counsel, filed a petition, pursuant to G.L. c. 112, § 12S, in Superior Court in Bristol County.

2. Our decision was made and recorded shortly after the hearing, allowing the petitioner the relief she sought in a timely manner. The

---

Illustration 7–8. *In re Moe,* 855 N.E.2d
1136 (Mass. App. Ct. 2006).

---

67 Mass. App. Ct. 651 (2006)   651

In the Matter of Moe.

In the Matter of Mary Moe.

No. 06-P-924.

Bristol. June 12, 2006. - October 30, 2006.

Present: Kantrowitz, Dreben, & Graham, JJ.

Abortion. Minor, Abortion. *Consent. Jurisdiction,* Juvenile, Nonresident.

This court concluded that a Massachusetts court had jurisdiction and authority, pursuant to G. L. c. 112, § 12S, to grant a nonresident minor's petition seeking permission to have an abortion performed in Massachusetts without parental consent. [651-653]

Civil action commenced in the Superior Court Department on June 9, 2006.

A question of law was reported by *Richard J. Chin,* J.

Marisa A. Campagna (*Karen D. Lane* with her) for the petitioner.

Kantrowitz, J. On June 12, 2006, the following question was reported, see Mass.R.Civ.P. 64(a), as amended, 423 Mass. 1403 (1996), to our court by a judge of the Superior Court:

> "Does a Massachusetts Court have jurisdiction and authority pursuant to G. L. c. 112, § 12S, to grant a nonresident minor's petition seeking permission to have an abortion performed in Massachusetts without parental consent?"[1]

We conclude that a plain reading of the statute in question does not impose a residency requirement.[2] As such, we answer the question in the affirmative.

---

[1] Mary Moe, a seventeen year old minor, and a resident of the State of Rhode Island, was seeking to have an abortion performed, without parental consent, in Massachusetts. According to the brief filed in our court, Mary Moe, with counsel, filed a petition, pursuant to G. L. c. 112, § 12S, in Superior Court in Bristol County.

[2] Our decision was made and recorded shortly after the hearing, allowing the petitioner the relief she sought in a timely manner. The purpose of this opinion is to explain the reasons for our decision.

Illustration 7–9. *In re Moe,* 67 Mass. App. Ct. 651 (2006).

Chapter 8

THE JUDICIARY, PART 3: CASE RESEARCH

Table of Sections

For the doctrine of precedent to operate effectively, lawyers must be able to find cases which control or influence a court's decisionmaking. This requires locating "cases on point," earlier decisions with factual and legal issues similar to a dispute at hand. It is then necessary to determine that these decisions are valid law and have not been reversed, overruled, or otherwise discredited.

This chapter discusses several major tools which perform these functions, but it is not exhaustive. Several resources discussed in other chapters—such as annotated codes (Chapter 3), legal encyclopedias and treatises (Chapter 10), and law review articles (Chapter 11)—are also valuable in case research.

Generally in case research you are looking for decisions from courts that have binding or persuasive precedent in your jurisdiction, on topics related to the issues in your case. A case could be relevant because it involves similar:

(1) parties (e.g., physicians, children, or government agencies)

(2) objects or places (e.g., surgical knives, swimming pools, or airports)

(3) acts or omissions giving rise to the cause of action (e.g., malpractice, attractive nuisance, or discrimination)

(4) relief sought (e.g., money damages or injunctive relief)

(5) defenses (e.g., statute of limitations, assumption of risk, or sovereign immunity), or

(6) procedures (e.g., motion to exclude evidence, summary judgment)

Which of these issues are significant in a specific situation depends on a variety of factors such as the nature of the case, the procedural status, and the purpose of the research. Generally you are searching for cases addressing similar or analogous factual or legal issues in order to determine how their holdings apply to the specific facts of your case.

This discussion of research processes starts with an overview of electronic case research, the approach most widely used in legal practice today. It then introduces printed tools such as West digests and *ALR* annotations. Digests are complex resources that at first may seem more confusing than helpful, but skill in their use can yield more thorough, accurate results than online searching alone.

Many law students tend to rely very heavily on keyword searching, and only when they enter practice do they learn that computerized research can be very expensive. Yet financial constraints are only one reason not to rely exclusively on methods that depend on your ability to phrase an effective search request. If the language of a decision does not precisely match the request, it will remain undiscovered unless other research methods are also used. Full-text keyword searches are most effective as part of a research strategy that integrates a number of different approaches.

§ 8.1 Electronic Case Research

Chapter 1 provided a brief overview of basic online research techniques. This section focuses more specifically on ways to use case databases effectively. It begins with the major commercial systems, Westlaw and Lexis, but also touches upon case-searching resources and methods in other systems and on the free Internet.

No matter which database or website you use, case research can be a complicated business requiring multiple searches. With luck an initial search will find one or two relevant cases, which will provide additional terms or citations that can be used in refining and expanding a search.

(a) Westlaw

As discussed in the preceding chapter, Westlaw is a comprehensive source for federal and state case law back to the earliest reported decisions. This means that it offers more than four million searchable cases. Finding one's way effectively through such a mass of documents requires considerable skill.

Database Selection. Westlaw has a wide selection of case law databases, some limited to particular jurisdictions or specific subject areas and others combining cases from the entire federal court system, from every state, or from all available federal and state courts. Whether to limit research to a particular jurisdiction or topical area depends upon a variety of factors, including cost (searches in large databases are generally more expensive), the purpose of the research, and the value of precedent from other jurisdictions or in other subjects. On some issues the only relevant cases for a research issue are those from a particular state or within a narrow doctrinal area. For many research questions, however, other cases may be persuasive authority or may provide useful analogies.

Westlaw's most extensive case databases cover the entire country (ALLCASES for federal and state cases, ALLFEDS for just federal cases, and ALLSTATES for just state cases). For research questions on issues of state law, it is usually most productive to begin in a database limited to the specific state (__-CS, using the postal abbreviation for the state). Because federal courts often interpret state laws, Westlaw also offers a database, __-CS–ALL, that combines those state cases with the relevant federal jurisdictions (the U.S. Supreme Court, the appropriate U.S. Court of Appeals, and the U.S. District Courts within the state). Searching this database may yield too many results, however, as it includes *all* Supreme Court cases and *all* cases from the Court of Appeals, whether or not they arose in that state. Most of these cases have no relevance on issues of state law, so it is usually best to start with just state courts and then expand to check federal case law later in the process, once the issues have been clarified. Finding a small number of cases directly on point is better than finding a large number of vaguely relevant cases.

Basic Searching. Simple keyword searches can be used to find cases, but it is important to take advantage of features such as proximity connectors, truncation, synonyms, and term frequency. Remember that you are searching through thousands (or millions) of documents. A search may retrieve a case containing the search terms, but those terms do not necessarily reflect its holding. The keywords may be unconnected to each other, or they may appear in a peripheral discussion unrelated to the holding. Using proximity connectors and term frequency increases the chances that a case is indeed relevant. In any event, the full text of retrieved cases must be read to understand their holdings and their relevance to the research.

Natural language searching can provide a starting point in case research because it finds the documents in which the search terms appear most frequently. This is especially useful if looking for terms such as "summary judgment" that appear over and over again in thousands of cases. There are two major problems, however, with natural language searching. First, because results are ranked by relevance rather than date, older, obsolete cases may well appear before more current precedent. (You can limit a search by date to retrieve only recent cases, but that would risk missing significant older cases.) Second, you determine in advance how many cases your search retrieves; the default is one hundred cases, but you can set a lower number. The number of cases retrieved can provide valuable feedback about the body of relevant case law and the accuracy of the search, but if every search retrieves exactly one hundred cases there are no clues that a search might need to be redrafted. Natural language is a place to begin, but important cases can easily be missed so it should not be relied upon for comprehensive searching.

Synopses and Headnotes. While searching the full text of opinions can usually find some relevant cases, the most effective and reliable Westlaw searches take advantage of the editorial synopsis and headnotes that precede each case. This focuses retrieval on cases that turn on the specific research issues, rather than any and all cases that may mention the terms in passing.

One way to use the synopses and headnotes in Westlaw is to limit a search to specific fields, or portions of the case document. Most fields can be entered into a search by using a two-letter abbreviation, followed by the search terms in parentheses. The *synopsis (sy)* field contains the introductory summary of the case's facts and holdings. A search for keywords in the synopsis field usually retrieves only the most relevant cases.[1]

Following the synopsis are the numbered headnotes, which make up the *digest (di)* field. The digest field combines the *topic (to)* field, consisting of the subject heading and key number, and the *headnote (he)* field, containing the text of the note itself. While each of these fields can be searched separately, often the strongest search is one that encompasses the synopsis and digest by using

---

1. In cases added to Westlaw since December 2003, the synopsis is divided into *background (bg)* and *holding (hg)* fields, as shown in Illustrations 7–3 and 7–8 on pages 263 and 268. In earlier cases, the synopsis is just one paragraph. The background and holding can also be searched separately, but the synopsis field combines the two and searches earlier cases as well.

both fields at once. A search for *sy,di(animal /s cruelty)* will retrieve a smaller body of cases more precisely on point than a simple full-text search for *animal /s cruelty*.[2]

Key Numbers. The other way to search the headnotes on Westlaw is to use the digest topics and key numbers assigned to each headnote. The West digest system consists of over 400 topics, arranged alphabetically from Abandoned and Lost Property to Zoning and Planning. Each topic is then divided into numbered sections, called *key numbers*, designating specific points of law for that topic. This classification system serves the same purpose for legal topics that call numbers do for library books, in that it allows related items to be classed together whether or not they use the same keywords. Similar legal issues may arise, for example, in cases involving cars and trucks, but it may not occur to you to include both types of motor vehicle in your search. The key numbers provide a way to find related cases that might otherwise be missed.

A separate numbering sequence is used for each of the topics, so a particular point of law is known by its topic name and its key number within that topic. Some of the larger and more complex topics have thousands of key numbers, while smaller topics have only a few. West uses the same topics and key numbers in every jurisdiction, so the same key number search can be used to find similar decisions from throughout the federal and state courts.

As an example, *People v. Garcia*, 812 N.Y.S.2d 66 (App. Div. 2006), the beginning of which is shown in Illustration 8–1 on page 296, has eight headnotes assigned to various key numbers in the topics Animals, Assault and Battery, Malicious Mischief, and Criminal Law and Weapons. The first headnote, on the issue of whether goldfish are "companion animals" within the meaning of a statute prohibiting aggravated cruelty to animals, is assigned to the Animals topic, ☞ 3.5(5), Protective and Anti–Cruelty Regulation in General. Other key numbers within the Animals topic cover a range of issues such as livestock, breeding, trespassing, and injuries by animals.

For use in Westlaw, each of the topics has been assigned a number between 1 and 450. Animals is topic 28, for example, and a search for Animals ☞ 3.5(5) is *28k3.5(5)*. This key number can be used in combination with other terms to create a very precise and effective search.

Obviously you are not going to begin a research project with a search like *28k3.5(5)*. You can, however, assess the headnotes in the cases you retrieve through a keyword search or a synopsis and digest search; if a retrieved headnote is particularly relevant, then

---

2. The *sy,di* search has been called the "Queen of Case Law searches." Rod Borlase, *Westlaw's "Field Searching" Capability* (1999) <tinyurl.com/cvlfsv>.

you can use its key number to find other cases. One way to do this is to click on the hyperlinked headnote topic number or key number. This brings up a Custom Digest search screen, on which you specify the courts to search and add keyword search terms if desired. The subsequent search finds similar headnotes, with links to the full text of the cases.[3]

Other Fields. In addition to the synopsis and digest, other fields can be used to search particular parts of case documents. Thus searches can be limited to the names of the parties (*ti* or *title*), the judge writing the opinion (*ju* or *judge*), or a particular court (*co* or *court*).

The entire list of available fields is shown in a drop-down box on the terms and connectors search screen. In natural language searching, the search screen includes boxes in which to specify a particular court, attorney, or judge.

Case Display. Once a search is entered, Westlaw displays either the first case or a list of cases (depending on the option selected by the user) accompanied by a "ResultsPlus" list of links to other relevant resources such as treatises and encyclopedias. The links in the Garcia case display in Illustration 8–1, for example, include sections on animal cruelty in the encyclopedias *American Jurisprudence 2d* and *Corpus Juris Secundum*.

Westlaw's KeyCite feature is an integral part of its case display, with flags and other symbols at the top of the screen providing clues to whether a case is still good law. KeyCite performs several other valuable functions in the research process, and will be discussed later in the chapter with other citators, in § 8.5 beginning on page 288.

(b) Lexis

For many years, a major difference between case research on Westlaw and Lexis was that Westlaw included editorial summaries of cases while Lexis had only the court opinions. Lexis, however,

---

3. Key numbers can also be incorporated into searches through the "Key Numbers" link at the top of the Westlaw screen. This brings up a "Search for Key Numbers" screen through which you can find relevant key numbers. The terms for which you search may appear in the key number heading or as factual terms in the text of headnotes. A search for "goldfish," for example, retrieves key numbers on both animal cruelty and trademarks (finding headnotes dealing with goldfish-shaped snack crackers). Selecting one of these key numbers retrieves a list of relevant headnotes (but does not provide an option for entering additional search terms).

Westlaw's "Key Numbers" link also has a feature called Keysearch, which allows you to browse through a list of broad topics and more detailed subtopics until you reach the specific focus of your inquiry. Clicking on this term leads to a search screen on which you can specify a jurisdiction and add additional search terms if you wish. Westlaw automatically creates a search to match the legal topic.

now has Case Summaries and headnotes for cases back into the nineteenth century, so its databases can be searched in several ways similar to those used in Westlaw. The Case Summaries and headnotes are accompanied by computer-generated "core terms" listing several of the major keywords found in the opinion. Illustration 8–2 on page 297 shows these features as part of its display of *People v. Garcia*.

Segments. The Lexis counterparts to Westlaw's *fields* are called *segments*. Among the most useful segments in case research are *name* for a particular party and *opinionby* for a particular judge. (Although they accept each other's proximity connectors, Lexis and Westlaw generally do *not* recognize searches using the other system's field or segment names.) Each of Lexis's introductory editorial features can be used as a document segment, making it possible to search for terms appearing only in the overview or the headnotes.

A Lexis Case Summary consists of three parts, Procedural Posture explaining the nature and status of the litigation, Overview summarizing the facts of the case, and Outcome providing a brief description of the court's decision. These can be searched as separate segments, but the most effective approach is to use the LN–Summary segment combining the three.

Headnotes. Lexis headnotes do not employ a numerical classification system like West's key numbers, but they can also be useful in case research. The terms in headnotes can be searched as a distinct segment. Once a relevant case is found, its headnotes can be incorporated into further searching in several ways. Clicking on "More Like This Headnote" runs a natural language search using the terminology of the headnote.

Search by Topic or Headnote. A feature that you may find useful when beginning a research project is *Search by Topic or Headnote*. You can browse through subject areas or search for particular terms. A search for "animal cruelty" leads to a list of topics, including Criminal Law & Procedure–Criminal Offenses–Miscellaneous Offenses–Cruelty to Animals and Governments–Agriculture & Food–Animal Welfare Act. Selecting a topic leads to a screen in which you can enter specific terms and then search for cases within that subject area.

Another way to use *Search by Topic or Headnote* is to click on a case headnote's hyperlinked topic heading. This opens up a window displaying a topical outline of the subject area, from which you can click on a specific topic within the subject area and run a search for cases and other documents assigned to this topic.

Shepard's. The Lexis case display often includes a symbol providing information about the precedential status of the case.

Clicking on this symbol, or on the *Shepardize* link at the top of the display, leads to the Shepard's Citations analysis for the case. Shepard's will be discussed later in the chapter, in § 8.5 beginning on page 288.

(c) Other Resources

This section has focused on Westlaw and Lexis procedures, but for researchers without access to these databases other alternatives are available. Several lower-cost databases include extensive coverage of case law, and many college and university libraries subscribe to LexisNexis Academic, which incorporates many of Lexis's features (including natural language searching and hyperlinks to cited cases). Some researchers may have access to their state's case law on CD–ROM rather than online. These services and products provide access to most of the same cases as Westlaw and Lexis, but usually without the extensive editorial materials those systems provide.

Subscription-based databases are providing increasingly sophisticated approaches to searching case law. Most allow truncation, Boolean connectors, and searching particular document fields; some even have natural language search options. What most databases lack are editorial features similar to those offered by Westlaw and Lexis. They provide the full text of court opinions, but these have no introductory synopses or summaries and they have no headnotes to provide research springboards to other cases.

Loislaw <www.loislaw.com> has the most extensive holdings after Westlaw and Lexis. Its basic search screen is organized into fields, with separate boxes for date range, citation, case name, docket number, or court, as well as a "Search Entire Document" box. In VersusLaw <www.versuslaw.com>, searches can be limited to specific fields such as cites, parties, court, date, or author by using a search phrase in parentheses such as *(author contains catterson)*. Casemaker <www.casemaker.us> has an "Advanced Search" tab that provides separate boxes for searching by citation or for a specific court, judge, or attorney, as well as means to limit a search by date.

Free Internet sites may also be a starting point in case research, but they rarely provide a comprehensive result. They may offer a searchable database of a particular court's opinions, but most are limited in coverage to the past few years (or months), and opportunities to search multiple jurisdictions are limited. The major exception is that federal appellate cases back to 1950 are now available from several free sites with powerful search capabilities supporting proximity searching and truncation. Perhaps the best of these is PreCYdent <www.precydent.com>, which also allows field searching and date restrictions, and has a "More Like This" feature that finds other documents textually similar to the one displayed.

LexisONE <www.lexisone.com> provides free access to the most recent five years of cases from all federal and state appellate courts, and permits the use of the extensive Boolean connectors and segments offered by Lexis. You can search individual jurisdictions, combined state cases, or combined federal cases. Registration is required to view the full text of cases.

Websites for individual courts or jurisdictions vary widely in value; some are much more accessible and more extensive than others. The Oklahoma State Courts Network <www.oscn.net> provides fully searchable retrospective coverage of appellate court decisions back to 1890, with hyperlinks to cited and citing cases. Some state court sites simply provide chronological access to opinions with no full-text searching. The Georgia Supreme Court has less than two years of opinions, and the Alabama judicial system has no free cases. Dramatic differences can be found even among the United States Courts of Appeals. Some have useful sites, while others have primitive search engines or do not even allow keyword searching.[4]

Court websites are most useful for obtaining copies of new decisions and monitoring recent developments, but they may provide one or two cases that can lead to other documents. When using a free resource for case research, it is essential to recognize its limitations and not to overlook important precedent just because it is beyond the scope of coverage.

§ 8.2 West Key–Number Digests

We have already seen in the discussion of Westlaw the importance of headnote classifications in finding relevant cases. West's key number system covers every case in the publisher's National Reporter System, and subject access can frequently find relevant cases that a keyword or natural language search would miss. Editorial analysis and classification can identify analogous cases that use different words from those that might occur to a researcher.[5]

4. The difficulties in searching official court websites are discussed in Andrew T. Solomon, *Making Unpublished Opinions Precedential: a Recipe for Ethical Problems & Legal Malpractice?*, 26 Miss. C. L. Rev. 185, 208–210 (2007).

5. "By skimming scores (or hundreds) of case digests, you will develop a sense for this area of the law.... Only then, after you know the location, size, and shape of the haystack, are you able to search intelligently for the needle." Mark Herrmann, The Curmudgeon's Guide to Practicing Law 19–20 (2006).

Although online research has become the primary case-finding method for most researchers, the *digest*, a tool which reprints in a subject arrangement the headnote summaries of each case's points of law, continues to be a valuable resource for finding cases by topic. A digest functions in a manner similar to an index; instead of simple one-line entries, however, it consists of paragraphs describing the legal principles decided in cases, with citations to the full text of the cases.

Printed digests are now used far less frequently than online databases,[6] but not all researchers have ready access to expensive online databases. Even if electronic resources are available, browsing through a collection of headnotes on related topics can at times be more cost-effective and productive than searching online.

English precursors to modern American digests began with *Statham's Abridgment,* published about 1490, which consisted of summaries of case law grouped under alphabetically arranged subject headings. This, and its many successors, employed relatively few subjects, broad in scope and lacking the detailed subdivisions of modern digests. The first comprehensive American digest, covering both federal and state courts, began publication in 1848 as the *United States Digest.*

The West Publishing Company acquired the property rights to this work and its classification scheme in 1887, and began publication of a new annual *American Digest.* West began assigning numbered headnotes to the cases in its reporters, adding section numbers in 1908 and designating these as "key numbers" in 1915. For many decades, the West digest system was the preeminent case-finding method, and it exercised an enormous intellectual impact on American jurisprudence.[7]

The first appearance of a new case in a printed digest is in the front of each West advance sheet, where the headnotes for the advance sheet's cases are arranged by topic and key number. These headnotes are cumulated in the back of each bound reporter volume, and then reprinted in multi-volume digest series to provide subject access to the cases in hundreds of reporter volumes. Illustration 8–3 on page 298 shows a page from a West digest with several headnotes under Animals ☞ 3.5(3), including one of the headnotes from *People v. Garcia.*

Whether online or in print, digests are valuable case-finders but have several shortcomings. They consist simply of case head-

---

6. See, e.g., Lee F. Peoples, *The Death of the Digest and the Pitfalls of Electronic Research: What Is the Modern Legal Researcher to Do?*, 97 LAW LIBR. J. 661 (2005).

7. For a discussion of the impact of West's digest system on legal thinking, see Robert C. Berring, *Legal Research and Legal Concepts: Where Form Molds Substance*, 75 CAL. L. REV. 15 (1987).

notes, with no text to explain which decisions are more important or how they fit together. Often a textual discussion of an area of law, such as in a treatise encyclopedia or a law review article, offers a clearer and more selective introduction to relevant case law.

Finding a case depends on an editor's subjective decision in assigning a key number to a headnote, and different editors can read cases differently.[8] Headnotes may reflect dicta, rather than holdings, and may even misstate points of law in the cases they abstract. Not every point of law in every case is headnoted, and if there is no headnote then there is no digest entry for that point.[9]

The same key number system covers all federal and state jurisdictions, so it can be used to find cases from throughout the country. This means, however, that the classification system sometimes fails to recognize significant differences between states in approaches to jurisprudential issues.

Digests also generally don't indicate that a case may no longer be good law, unless it was directly reversed or modified on appeal. An overruled case continues to be listed in the digest, with no notes on its validity. It is essential to locate and read the cases themselves in order to find those which are actually pertinent, and then to verify their status using KeyCite or Shepard's Citations.

(a) Finding Cases in Digests

Using a digest requires identifying the topic and key number relevant to a specific issue. The simplest way to do this is to use the headnotes of a case already known to be on point. If you know of one relevant case, you can find it in a West reporter volume or on Westlaw, scan its headnotes for relevant issues, and then use the key numbers accompanying those headnotes to search the digest. This approach, of course, requires that at least one initial case be

---

8. This was made apparent when a U.S. District Court case, *McGinnis v. United Screw & Bolt Corp.*, was somehow published in both *Federal Supplement* and *Federal Rules Decisions*. The two versions, at 637 F. Supp. 9 and 109 F.R.D. 532 (E.D. Pa. 1985), received different treatment by West editors; even though the text was the same, the F. Supp. version has four headnotes in the Workers' Compensation topic while the F.R.D. version has two headnotes under Federal Civil Procedure. (The F.R.D. version also corrected three minor errors not caught by the F. Supp. editors.)

9. See Carol M. Bast & Ransford C. Pyle, *Legal Research in the Computer Age: A Paradigm Shift?*, 93 Law Libr. J.

285, 290–91 (2001). As early as 1945, it was recognized that digests were "not usually the best starting point in research. The reason is obvious. In the digests there is neither fusion nor assimilation. . . . Each 'pin-point' is an isolated speck of light; its relationship, if any, to the specks around it is of no concern of the digester." Paul M. Dwyer, *Approach to Legal Research: A Study in Sources and Methods*, 21 Notre Dame Law. 92, 95 (1945). Dwyer also noted that "digesters are quite human, and what Digester A regards today as the proper pigeon-hole may not at all be the same as what Digester B will choose ten years later." Id. at 96.

found through other means, such as a full-text search or a reference in a treatise or journal article.

Without a case already in hand, the basic entry point into a printed digest is the Descriptive–Word Index shelved at the beginning or end of a digest set. This multi-volume index lists thousands of factual and legal terms, and provides references to key numbers. You can look up legal issues, such as causes of action, defenses, or relief sought, or factual elements in an action, such as parties, places, or objects involved. It is generally more productive to search for specific relevant facts rather than general legal theories, but success may require rethinking issues and checking synonyms and cross-references. Illustration 8–4 on page 299 shows a page from a Descriptive–Word Index, including references under the "Cruelty to Animals" heading to Animals ☞ 3.5(5).[10]

When turning from the index to the volume of digest abstracts, it is often helpful to look first at the outline of the topic to verify that the legal context is indeed appropriate. You may be looking for cases on substantive negligence issues, for example, but find that a key number that appeared relevant actually deals with some other issue such as the standard of review for summary judgment. Illustration 8–5 on page 300 contains the outline for the Animals topic, showing how ☞ 3.5(5) fits with other related issues.

(b) Jurisdictional and Regional Digests

West digests are available for the entire country, for some of the regional reporters, for individual states, and for a few specific subjects. Choosing the right digest depends on the scope of the inquiry. For most research you want to find cases from a specific jurisdiction, but for some projects you may be interested in developments throughout the country. A more focused digest obviously covers fewer cases but is usually easier to use.

West publishes digests for every state but Delaware, Nevada and Utah, as well as for the decisions in four of the regional reporter series (*Atlantic*, *North Western*, *Pacific*, and *South Eastern*). (Cases from Delaware, Nevada and Utah are covered in the *Atlantic* and *Pacific Digest.*) The state digests include references to all the cases West publishes from the state's courts, as well as federal cases arising from the U.S. District Courts in that state. Federal courts often interpret and apply state law, sometimes addressing issues with which the state courts have not yet dealt. (Unlike the __-CS–ALL databases on Westlaw, the state digests do

---

10. Digests also include Tables of Cases which can be used to find decisions by name. Most of these tables list cases under both plaintiffs' and defendants' names. In addition to reporter citations, they provide a list of key numbers under which the case's headnotes are digested.

not include *all* cases from the Supreme Court and the U.S. Court of Appeals.)

State digests are kept up to date by annual pocket parts in the back of each volume, by quarterly pamphlets between annual supplements, and by occasional replacement volumes incorporating the newer material. A single volume can thus contain headnotes of decisions from the earliest nominative reporters through a few months ago. For about a dozen states, the current digest only provides coverage of cases from recent decades. An earlier digest set must be consulted for complete retrospective coverage of the older court decisions, but most research requires consulting only the current set for modern cases on point.

The key number system has been in use for more than a century, but the law of course has not remained static in that time. Old doctrines have faded in significance and new areas of law have developed. West attempts to reflect new developments by revising and expanding old topics and by establishing new topics. The first sex discrimination cases, for example, were classified under "Rights protected by civil rights laws in general" because there were not yet any key numbers dealing with a more specific topic. Over the years, however, the Civil Rights topic has been revised several times, and there are now more than thirty key numbers covering various aspects of sex discrimination and sexual harassment.

When new or revised topics are introduced, West editors reclassify the headnotes in thousands of older relevant cases. On Westlaw, the numbers assigned to older cases are updated when the key number system is revised, and the current classification can be used to find relevant cases of any age. The new classifications are also used when state digest volumes are recompiled. Until the recompilation, new or revised topics are accompanied by tables converting older topics and key numbers to those newly adopted and vice versa.

The digest changes slowly, however, and it may take several years for new areas of legal doctrine to be recognized and to receive adequate coverage. Because cases in newly developing areas of the law are often assigned to general key numbers, digest research may not be the best way to find cases in these areas.

West also publishes a separate series of digests for federal court decisions, containing headnotes reprinted from the *Supreme Court Reporter, Federal Reporter, Federal Appendix, Federal Supplement, Federal Rules Decisions*, and the reporters for specialized federal courts. The current set is the *Federal Practice Digest 4th*. Its volumes are supplemented by annual pocket parts, and the entire set is further updated with bimonthly pamphlets. Earlier cases are covered by four previous sets.[11]

The decisions of the Supreme Court of the United States are also covered by a West digest devoted solely to its decisions, the *United States Supreme Court Digest*. Other digests for specialized federal courts include *West's Bankruptcy Digest*, *West's Military Justice Digest*, *United States Federal Claims Digest*, and *West's Veterans Appeals Digest*. References to these cases all appear as well in the *Federal Practice Digest* series.

(c) *Decennial* and *General Digests*

The most comprehensive series of digests is known as the American Digest System. This covers cases in all of West's federal and state reporters, and is therefore a massive and rather unwieldy finding tool. Its most current component, the *General Digest*, compiles headnotes from the advance sheets for about twenty West reporter volumes. A *General Digest* volume is published about every three weeks and covers the entire range of more than 400 digest topics.

The entries in the *General Digest* do not cumulate, so you may have to look through several dozen volumes to search for recent cases. This search is eased somewhat by tables listing the key numbers found in each volume. These tables cumulate every tenth volume. If twenty-seven *General Digest* volumes have been published, for example, you would need to check the tables in volumes 10, 20, and 27 to see which volumes contain cases classified under a specific key number. Even with this short cut, checking the *General Digest* can be a rather time-consuming process.

Every few years, West recompiles the headnotes from the *General Digest* and publishes them in a multi-volume set called a *Decennial Digest*. The name *Decennial* comes from the fact that these sets used to be published every ten years, but West now compiles these digests after every sixty volumes of the *General Digest*. The *Eleventh Decennial Digest, Part 3* is the most recent set, covering 2004–07.

One problem in using *Decennial Digests* is that older volumes are not revised to reflect changes in topics and classifications. Cases on Westlaw are updated with new key numbers and jurisdictional digest volumes are revised and reissued, but *Decennial Digest* users must use conversion tables indicating corresponding key numbers in older and newer classifications.

---

11. The earlier federal digests are *Federal Digest* (1754–1939), *Modern Federal Practice Digest* (1939–61), *Fed-* *eral Practice Digest 2d* (1961–75), and *Federal Practice Digest 3d* (1975 to mid–1980s).

The first unit of the American Digest System, called the *Century Digest*, covers early cases from 1658 to 1896. It was followed by a *First Decennial Digest* for 1897 to 1906, and subsequent *Decennials* for each decade since. *Decennial Digests* are little used these days, but they can be found in most large law libraries. For researchers without Westlaw access, they remain the most comprehensive collection of case headnotes available.

(d) *Words and Phrases*

West reprints some headnote abstracts in a separate multi-volume set, *Words and Phrases*. Headnotes are included in *Words and Phrases* if a court defines or interprets a legally significant term. *Words and Phrases* is arranged alphabetically rather than by key number, and it can be a useful tool when the meaning of a specific term is at issue. Illustration 8–6 on page 301 shows a page from *Words and Phrases* including the first headnote from *State v. Garcia*, interpreting the meaning of the phrase "companion animals."

The *Words and Phrases* set covers the entire National Reporter System. Shorter "Words and Phrases" lists also appear in many West digests and in West reporter volumes and advance sheets. Judicial definitions from *Words and Phrases* can also be found on Westlaw by searching the *wp* field. For example, a search for *wp(animal)* will retrieve *Garcia* and other cases defining terms such as "domestic animal," "service animal," and "wild animal."

§ 8.3 Other Digests

The West key number system is not the only digest classification system used in legal research. Other systems are available for a few jurisdictions and for several specialized areas of law.

United States Supreme Court Reports, Lawyers' Edition is accompanied by a digest arranging its cases' headnotes by subject, but the *Lawyers' Edition* classification system does not appear in other reports and is therefore of use only in Supreme Court research. The *Lawyers' Edition* digest set does, however, include other useful features, such as a table of Supreme Court cases (volumes 15–15D), a subject index to decisions and annotations (volumes 16–16D), and sets of federal court rules annotated with summaries of Supreme Court decisions (volumes 17–22).

Almost all specialized looseleaf and topical reporters provide subject access to their cases through digests of some sort. Some publish series of digest volumes, each covering cases in a particular range of years or reporter volumes, and others have cumulative digest sets for all of the reported cases.

Lawyers specializing in particular fields often swear by these topical digests. Because they focus on one specific area of law, they are often more finely tuned to developments in that area and can be quicker to adjust to changes in the law than the much more general key number system. In many instances, they include references to administrative agency decisions as well as court decisions.

These topical digests are of three basic types. Some are organized on an alphabetical basis similar to West's system, but with topics designed for a specialized area of law. Digests for *American Maritime Cases, Public Utilities Reports,* or the *United States Patents Quarterly* work in this way. Others have one classified numerical framework for the entire body of legal doctrine. The Bureau of National Affairs uses this approach in its digests covering cases in the *Environment Reporter* and *Labor Relations Reference Manual.* The third group are for reporters that focus on specific laws or court rules, and are arranged by code or rule section (similar to the way that casenotes are organized in annotated codes). This approach is used in the *Uniform Commercial Code Case Digest,* as well as in major looseleaf services such as CCH's *Federal Securities Law Reporter* and *Standard Federal Tax Reporter.*

§ 8.4 *American Law Reports* Annotations

At the same time that West was developing its National Reporter System in the late 19th century, other publishers were attempting a different approach to case reporting. They selected "leading cases" for full-text publication, and provided commentaries, or *annotations*, which surveyed other decisions on the subject of the selected case. Selective publication was not a successful alternative to comprehensive reporting, but the annotations have proved to be valuable case research tools.

Among the early sets of annotated reporters were *American Reports* (1871–88), *American Decisions* (1878–88), *American State Reports* (1888–1911), *Lawyers Reports Annotated* (*LRA*) (1888–1918), and *American and English Annotated Cases* (1901–18). These were succeeded in 1919 by *American Law Reports* (*ALR*), which is now published in two current series: *ALR6th* for general and state legal issues, and *ALR Federal 2d* for issues of federal law.

An *ALR* annotation provides a comprehensive summary of the case law on a specific topic. *ALR* does not cover all research issues, but an annotation directly on point can save considerable research time. It does the initial time-consuming work of finding relevant cases, and arranges them according to specific fact patterns and holdings. Because it synthesizes the cases into a narrative discussion and compares decisions that have reached conflicting results, rather than simply offering a collection of headnotes, an annotation is usually easier to understand than a digest.

Annotations differ significantly from other narrative resources such as treatises and law review articles. Their purpose is to present in a systematic way the varied judicial decisions from around the country. They generally do not criticize these decisions or analyze legal problems, nor do they attempt to integrate case law into a broader societal perspective. Annotations are occasionally cited, but as convenient compilations of prevailing judicial doctrine rather than as a secondary source with its own persuasive authority.

ALR annotations are available on Westlaw (ALR database), where coverage goes all the way back to the earliest annotations from 1919 and is updated weekly. Westlaw includes new annotations that have not yet been released for publication in the print *ALR*. (Lexis does not cover *ALR*, but it does have *Lawyers' Edition* annotations focusing on Supreme Court cases.)

(a) Format and Content

Each *ALR* annotation begins with a table of contents, a detailed subject index, and a table listing the jurisdictions of the cases discussed. In annotations since 1992 (the beginning of *ALR5th*), this introductory material has also included a Research References section providing leads to encyclopedias, practice aids, digests, and other sources, as well as West digest key numbers and sample electronic search queries. Research References on Westlaw and in *ALR6th* and *ALR Federal 2d* also include lists of related *ALR* annotations; in earlier printed volumes, these are listed in § 1[b] of the annotation itself. Illustrations 8–7 and 8–8 on pages 302–303 show pages from the beginning of an *ALR5th* annotation on what constitutes the offense of cruelty to animals. Illustration 8–7 shows part of the table of contents, organizing the annotation's sections according to particular acts and whether or not prosecution was warranted. Illustration 8–8 shows part of the index, listing specific animals, factual scenarios and legal issues arising in the cases discussed.

The first two sections of an annotation are an introduction describing its scope and a summary providing a general overview and giving practice pointers. The annotation then goes on to summarize case law from around the country, arranged according to their facts and holdings. Illustration 8–9 on page 304 shows the discussion of *People v. Garcia*, as it appears in the Westlaw version of the annotation.

The annotation in Illustrations 8–7 through 8–9 was originally published in 1992, but its pocket part or online supplement provides references to more recent developments. On Westlaw, annotations are updated with "Cumulative Supplement" notes after each section. In print, *ALR3d–6th*, *ALR Fed*, and *ALR Fed 2d* are updated with annual pocket parts in each volume. Many of the annotations in *ALR1st* and *ALR2d* remain current and continue to be updated, but these older series use other methods instead of pocket parts in each volume. *ALR2d* has a separate set of blue *Later Case Service* volumes, which have their own annual pocket parts; and *ALR1st* has an accompanying set, *ALR1st Blue Book of Supplemental Decisions*, that lists relevant new case citations and is updated annually.

If later cases substantially change the law on a subject covered by an annotation, a new annotation may either supplement or completely supersede the older annotation. Online, a notice with a link to the newer annotation simply replaces the older work. In print, the older volume's pocket part or other supplement alerts you to the existence of the newer treatment (another good reason to *always* check the pocket part for new developments). Superseded and supplemented annotations are also listed in an "Annotation History Table" in the back of each volume of the *ALR Index*.

(b) Finding Annotations

ALR annotations on Westlaw are searchable by keyword, just like cases or other documents. Because annotations describe the facts of the cases discussed, including aspects unrelated to the topic under discussion, a full-text search may turn up numerous annotations on irrelevant topics. This can be remedied by limiting a search to the *title* (*ti*) and/or *summary* (*su*) fields, where each annotation's subject is succinctly described. A natural language search, which automatically ranks documents by relevance, can also focus in on the most useful annotations.

The basic tool for subject access to the printed version of *ALR* is the nine-volume *ALR Index*, which is kept current by quarterly pocket parts. A less comprehensive *ALR Quick Index* covering only *ALR3d–6th* is published as an annual softcover volume; and a separate *ALR Federal Quick Index* is limited to *ALR Fed* and *ALR Fed 2d* annotations. Illustration 8–10 on page 305 shows a page from the *ALR Index*, including references under "Animals" to the annotation shown and to other annotations on topics such as the evidentiary use or evaluation of animals.

Remember that in almost all *ALR* annotations, either the Research References section or § 1[b] provides a list of other annotations on related topics. If an online search or a check of the index does not turn up an annotation directly on point but does lead to one on a related issue, the most productive next step may be to read through that annotation's list of related annotations. This could bring up analogies or concepts you may not have thought to check in the index. The list for the annotation on animal cruelty, for example, includes references to annotations on topics such as the liability of dog owners and veterinarians' liability for malpractice.

Another means of access to annotations is through the *ALR Digest*, a multi-volume set classifying *ALR*'s annotations and cases in West's key number system. Older digests using a different classification system may be found in some libraries, but these are no longer being updated.[12]

You can also find leads to relevant annotations from particular cases or statutes. KeyCite, which will be discussed in the next section, includes citing annotations in its coverage of cases and statutes. Westlaw's ResultsPlus display accompanying search results often includes links to relevant annotations. In print, the *ALR Index* is accompanied by volumes listing the cases, statutes, rules and regulations cited in annotations. Online or in print, many annotated codes and encyclopedias also provide references to relevant *ALR* annotations.

Annotations can be very useful research tools for many legal problems. If an annotation has been written on a point being researched, that means someone has already examined the issue and collected almost every relevant case. Because each annotation is written about a specific topic, however, coverage in the series is not comprehensive or encyclopedic. There are many issues for which no annotation can be found. Remember that annotations are only case finders, and are not generally regarded as persuasive authority. Unlike scholarly law review articles, the purpose of annotations is not to persuade but to gather and synthesize the cases from every jurisdiction, and to provide a comprehensive survey of court decisions on a particular point of law.

§ 8.5 Citators

Under the doctrine of precedent, the holdings of governing cases determine the resolution of issues in subsequent controversies. A precedential decision continues to have binding effect regardless of its age, but its authority can be affected by either sudden change or gradual erosion. A decision might be reversed on appeal to a higher court or overruled years later by a decision of the same court. Later cases may also criticize or question the reasoning of a decision, or limit its holding to a specific factual situation. Any

---

12. For the last word on these *ALR* digests, see Mary Whisner, *West's ALR Digest*, Posting to Law–Lib@ucdavis.edu (Oct. 25, 2004) <listproc.ucdavis.edu/ archives/law-lib/law-lib.log0410/0424. html>.

of these circumstances can diminish or negate the authority of a case.

Before relying on any case, it is necessary to verify its current validity. The need for such information was first met by an 1821 publication by Simon Greenleaf, *A Collection of Cases, Overruled, Denied, Doubted, or Limited in Their Application*, and a variety of successor publications in the 19th century. In 1875 Frank Shepard began printing lists of citations to Illinois Supreme Court cases on gummed paper for attorneys to stick in the margins of their bound reporters. Before long he began publishing his citation lists in book form, and coverage expanded gradually to include every state and the federal courts.[13]

As a result of the importance of these *Shepard's Citations* volumes, this process of updating cases became known as *Shepardizing*. Shepard's information is now available electronically on Lexis as well as in print, and Westlaw has a competing electronic resource, KeyCite, that provides a similar service.

Citators perform three major functions:

— They provide parallel citations and references to other proceedings in the same case, allowing you to trace a case's judicial history;

— They indicate if subsequent cases have overruled, limited, or otherwise diminished a case's precedent, enabling you to determine whether it is still good law; and

— They list citing cases, as well as treatises, law review articles, and other resources, providing research leads needed to trace the development of a legal doctrine forward in time.

KeyCite and Shepard's are invaluable resources not only because they validate research already done and ensure that cases are still "good law." They also serve as powerful links from one case to others addressing similar issues, providing one of the most effective ways to find sources for further research. You can use citators to shape your research and to focus in on specific aspects of relevant cases. Even the absence of citing references can provide important information about a case; if a decision has remained uncited for decades, it may indicate that it is a neglected backwater that need not be accorded great weight.[14]

---

13. For a history of Shepard's and its predecessors, see Patti Ogden, *"Mastering the Lawless Science of Our Law": A Story of Legal Citation Indexes*, 85 LAW LIBR. J. 1 (1993). For the more recent history of online citators, see Laura C. Dabney, *Citators: Past, Present, and* *Future*, 27 LEGAL REFERENCE SERVICES Q. 165 (2008).

14. A recent citation study of more than four million published federal and state cases found that about 400,000 cases have never been cited and another 773,000 have been cited only once.

KeyCite and Shepard's are not the only citators available. Loislaw has a GlobalCite service that provides a notice when viewing a case of the number of citing documents. The full Global-Cite display includes highlighted case treatment terms such as "Agree," "Disagree," or "Overrule" to indicate how a later decision treats a cited case. Other services such as Casemaker's "Case-check" or Fastcase's "Authority Check" provide links to subsequent citing cases, but neither has codes or flags indicating the nature of the citations. It is also possible, of course, to find citing references by including a case's name or citation in a full-text search.

(a) KeyCite

A case display on Westlaw provides several links to KeyCite information. Links on the left side of the screen include *Full History* (decisions which may bear a direct impact on a case's validity) and *Citing References* (the full list of citing documents). In addition, a small symbol at the top of the case display indicates what citator information is available. A red flag generally indicates that a case is not good law on some point, and a yellow flag that there is some negative history. If neither of these flags is applicable, a blue "H" indicates that there is some case history information available or a green "C" shows that there are citing references. Clicking on the displayed symbol links to the case's KeyCite references. KeyCite information can also be accessed by typing a citation into a form on Westlaw's welcome screen, or by clicking on the KeyCite link at the top of any Westlaw screen.

Full History includes prior and subsequent decisions in the same litigation, so that the case can be traced through the appellate process, and "negative citing references," decisions that may have an adverse impact on the precedential value of the cited case. Be aware, however, that the term "negative" is broadly defined. A lower court decision that declines to extend a Supreme Court precedent beyond its intended scope is listed as "distinguishing" its holding. This is considered a negative citation, even though it has no impact on the Supreme Court decision's precedent.[15]

Citing References lists negative cases first, and then other cases are ranked by the extent to which they discuss the cited case, from four stars (an extended discussion) to one star (mentioned in a list with other citations). KeyCite also indicates which cases quote

Thomas A. Smith, *The Web of Law*, 44 SAN DIEGO L. REV. 309, 324–28 (2007).

15. One study found that more than half of one term's Supreme Court cases were assigned "negative history" symbols in both KeyCite and Shepard's before the start of the next term. They were still good law, but lower courts had distinguished or declined to extend their holdings. Kent C. Olson, *Waiving a Red Flag: Teaching Counterintuitiveness in Citator Use*, 9 PERSPECTIVES 58, 60 (2001).

directly from the cited case by including quotation marks in the display. Secondary sources such as law review articles and *ALR* annotations are listed after citing cases, followed by briefs and other appellate and trial court documents. The court documents, but not the secondary sources, include star rankings and quotation marks. Links provide access to the full text of any of these citing documents.

KeyCite provides several ways to focus your retrieval. Limits can be used to see only those references from specific jurisdictions, or those that cite the point of law in particular headnotes. KeyCite can also limit by depth of treatment (number of stars) or by type of citing document (e.g., law review articles or court documents). One of the most powerful KeyCite tools is the *Locate* feature, which allows you to run a keyword search within the citing documents. This can often focus immediately on those documents applying a precedent to a particular set of facts.

Another way to move directly from a displayed case to a KeyCite result is to use the *KeyCite Citing References for this Headnote* link preceding each headnote. This takes you directly to a screen on which you choose what type of citing documents you wish to see (or to a notice that there are not yet any citing references for the headnote), and then to a list of KeyCite references limited to those discussing this particular legal issue.

Illustration 8–11 on page 306 shows KeyCite results for *People v. Garcia*, the text of which has already been shown in Illustration 8–1. *Garcia* has been cited in thirty-three documents, mostly secondary sources. The citing cases have been assigned different treatment levels from "Discussed" (three stars) to "Mentioned" (one star).

In the same way that WestClip provides automatic notification of new cases matching a particular search, KeyCite has an alert service that monitors developments in a case's history or citing references. KeyCite Alert can be set up to send notices for any case history developments, for just negative history, or for any and all citing references. It can also limit citing references by headnote, jurisdiction, KeyCite locate terms, or depth of treatment, providing an easy way to learn of new cases meeting very specific citing criteria. One could, for example, receive KeyCite Alert notifications of any New York cases affecting *Garcia*'s value as precedent on the specific issue summarized in its first headnote.

(b) Shepard's Citations Online

Shepard's Citations is an integral part of Lexis case research. One of the choices at the top of a case display is "Shepardize," and in most instances a signal to the left of the case name indicates the nature of citing documents. A red stop sign indicates strong negative treatment (e.g., the case has been reversed or overruled) and a gold "Q" indicates that a case's validity has been questioned, while a yellow caution sign indicates possible negative treatment (e.g., its holding has been criticized or limited). A green plus sign indicates positive history or treatment, and a blue circle indicates other citing references. Like KeyCite, Shepard's has a broad definition of "negative" treatment.[16]

You can also choose *Shepard's* from the menu at the top of the Lexis screen, and then type in a citation. When using this approach, you have the option of retrieving a list of decisions which may have a direct impact on a case's validity ("Shepard's for Validation," limited to proceedings in the same litigation and any negative citing cases) or the full list of citing documents ("Shepard's for Research").

Shepard's does not rank documents as Westlaw does, but instead provides a broader range of treatment codes. Some, but not all, positive cases are given treatment codes such as "followed" or "explained" to indicate the nature of their citations. Citing cases are displayed by jurisdiction, beginning with cases from the home jurisdiction of the cited case. *Restrictions* in Shepard's can be used to see only those references with particular treatments (negative only, positive only, or your choice of specific codes), as well as cases from specific jurisdictions or those that cite the point of law in particular headnotes. It is also possible to run a *Focus* search within the text of the citing cases to find specific fact patterns or terminology.

Illustration 8–12 on page 307 shows the Shepard's screen for *People v. Garcia*. The display begins with a Summary listing the number of citing cases, with links to those using specific treatment codes, and to citing secondary sources as well. This is followed by the case's prior history and then by the citing decisions and other documents.

---

16. The two systems do not always agree on the effect of citing decisions. In *Andreshak v. Service Heat Treating, Inc.*, 439 F. Supp. 2d 898, 900 n.2 (E.D. Wis. 2006), one of the parties relied on a case, *Roe v. O'Donohue*, 38 F.3d 298 (7th Cir. 1994), that was no longer good law because it had been abrogated on the cited point by *Murphy Bros., Inc. v. Michetti Pipe Stringing, Inc.*, 526 U.S. 344 (1999). The court noted this but declined to sanction the attorney: "A simple Westlaw keycite of *Roe* brings up a red flag next to the case name plus notations that *Murphy Bros.* abrogated *Roe* and that several other cases recognize *Roe's* overruling. However, a Lexis Shepard's summary states only that *Roe* was 'questioned' by *Murphy Bros.* and other cases. This court will give Andreshak's attorneys the benefit of the doubt and assume they either used Lexis or were careless in their research rather than intending to mislead the court by citing to *Roe's* receipt rule. The court will also contact Lexis to suggest that its Shepard's summary clearly reflect that *Roe* was overruled." *Roe* does indeed now have a red stop sign in Shepard's.

Although their editorial treatment and arrangement differ, KeyCite and Shepard's generally provide coverage of the same citing cases. Both include cases that are designated as unpublished but are available through the online databases, as well as cases published in the official reports, West reporters, and other topical reporters. Occasionally one service includes a reference to an unpublished decision available through its database but not the other, but the differences in case coverage are slight. Both provide thorough coverage and timely notice of new developments.

Coverage of secondary sources in the two services does differ. Both have references to law reviews available online, but otherwise each focuses on materials available on its system. This means that Westlaw has *ALR* annotations and West treatises, while Lexis has treatises and encyclopedias published by LexisNexis or Matthew Bender. Westlaw also includes citations in its growing collection of appellate and trial court documents.

The signals and editorial signposts in KeyCite and Shepard's are just tools for the researcher, not authoritative statements of the law. Relying on a red flag or a stop sign is no substitute for reading a citing document and determining for yourself its scope and effect. A case that has been overruled on one point may still be good law on other issues, but learning this requires reading the overruling case itself and perhaps examining *its* subsequent history.

(c) *Shepard's Citations* in Print

While the electronic versions of KeyCite and Shepard's compete for online customers, *Shepard's Citations* is the only choice for researchers using print resources. There is no print version of KeyCite, but sets of *Shepard's Citations* are published for the Supreme Court, the lower federal courts, every state, the District of Columbia, Puerto Rico, and each region of the National Reporter System.

In order to convey a large amount of information in a small space, the print versions of *Shepard's* use a system of one-letter symbols to indicate the treatment of citing cases. The letter *c*, for example, stands for *criticized*; *d* for *distinguished*, and *j* for *citing in dissenting opinion*. In addition, the abbreviations that identify citing sources are usually shorter than the citations commonly used in *The Bluebook* and other sources. *California Reporter 2d* becomes *CaR2d* in a *Shepard's* volume. These symbols and abbreviations are listed in tables at the front of each volume.

Printed *Shepard's Citations* can never be quite as current as the electronic resources, but most sets are supplemented biweekly or monthly. Each contains one or more maroon bound volumes, and supplementary pamphlets of varying colors. To help you know which volumes or supplements you need to use, the cover of each supplement includes a list, "What Your Library Should Contain," of the current volumes and pamphlets for the set.

Illustration 8–13 on page 308 shows a page from *Shepard's United States Citations* including references to *United States v. Olson*. After the page number (the large bold "43") and the name and date of the case, the rest of the column lists citations to *Olson*, including a Supreme Court case at the beginning of the list, several federal cases, and one state court case. Several of the citing cases follow (*f*) the *Olson* holding.

Some recent citing cases in supplementary *Shepard's* pamphlets are listed by their Lexis citations if reporter citations are not yet available. Lexis subscribers can use these citations to find the cases online, while other *Shepard's* users can learn the names of the cases by entering the citations in lexisONE <www.lexisone. com> or calling a toll-free customer service number.

Shepardizing state cases in print adds a complication not found online. References in law review articles are noted in the state *Shepard's* set, but not in the regional *Shepard's*. On the other hand, citing cases from other states appear only in the regional series and not in the state *Shepard's*. Both state citators and regional citators list citing cases from the home jurisdiction and in federal courts, but neither provides a complete list of all citing documents.

Electronic citators have numerous advantages over printed *Shepard's Citations*. New cases are added within hours or days. Coverage online is not divided into separate state and regional citators, with each displaying only some of the citing documents. Citing entries are compiled into a single listing, eliminating the need to search through multiple volumes and pamphlets. Because page space is not a concern, case treatments and names of publications are spelled out rather than abbreviated. One can easily narrow retrieval to specific treatments or headnote numbers without scanning a lengthy list of citations. Finally, hypertext links make it possible to go directly from the online citator to the text of citing cases. For some researchers, however, the printed version of *Shepard's Citations* remains the primary means to verify the validity of decisions and to find research leads.

This chapter has concentrated on materials such as online databases, digests and annotations which are designed expressly for the purpose of case finding. Because finding judicial decisions is a central part of most legal research, however, almost every resource discussed in this book can serve as a case-finding tool to some extent. Annotated statutory codes, for example, include notes of relevant cases applying or interpreting the terms of each code section, and secondary sources such as treatises, encyclopedias, and law review articles provide extensive footnote citations to cases. Each of these approaches may well lead you to cases that other methods might not find, and using a combination of approaches provides greater confidence that you have not missed any significant precedent.

years, that the certificate of occupancy did not permit the use of the demised premises as an automobile repair shop and that prior to executing the renewal lease, he had hired an architect for this very reason. Since plaintiff is unable to establish a material, false representation upon which he relied to his detriment, the fraud claim should also have been dismissed.

[4, 5] Finally, plaintiff's cause of action for breach of warranty of habitability must be dismissed since such a claim applies only to residential lease space, which is not at issue herein (Real Property Law § 235-b; *Fourth Fed. Sav. Bank v. 32–22 Owners Corp.*, 236 A.D.2d 300, 301, 653 N.Y.S.2d 588 [1997]; *Polak v. Bush Lumber Co.*, 170 A.D.2d 932, 933, 566 N.Y.S.2d 757 [1991]), and plaintiff's cause of action for breach of the warranty of quiet enjoyment is not viable as plaintiff has remained in full possession of the leased premises at all relevant times (*127 Rest. Corp. v. Rose Rlty. Group, LLC*, 19 A.D.3d 172, 173, 798 N.Y.S.2d 387 [2005]; *see also Barash v. Pennsylvania Term. Real Estate Corp.*, 26 N.Y.2d 77, 308 N.Y.S.2d 649, 256 N.E.2d 707 [1970]).

KEY NUMBER SYSTEM

29 A.D.3d 255

The PEOPLE of the State of
New York, Respondent,

v.

Michael GARCIA, Defendant–
Appellant.

Supreme Court, Appellate Division,
First Department.

March 28, 2006.

Background: Defendant was convicted, in a nonjury trial in the Supreme Court, New York County, Marcy L. Kahn, J., of second-degree attempted assault, third-degree criminal possession of a weapon, third-degree criminal mischief, three counts of third-degree assault, three counts of endangering the welfare of a child, and aggravated cruelty to animals. He appealed.

Holdings: The Supreme Court, Appellate Division, Catterson, J., held that:

(1) as a matter of first impression for the Appellate Division, pet goldfish were "companion animals" within the meaning of statute prohibiting aggravated cruelty to animals;

(2) trial court improperly exercised its discretion by considering, on its own motion, second-degree attempted assault as a lesser included offense of first-degree attempted assault;

(3) evidence of costs to repair fish tank, wall unit, and television set broken by defendant was sufficient to support conviction for third-degree criminal mischief; and

(4) resentencing was not required even though defendant's adjudication as a second violent felony offender had to be vacated since he was not convicted of a violent felony.

Affirmed as modified.

1. Animals ⚖3.5(5)

Pet goldfish were "companion animals" within the meaning of statute prohibiting aggravated cruelty to animals, and therefore defendant who stomped on a boy's pet goldfish was guilty of violating that statute; goldfish were domesticated inasmuch as they had been adapted to live in close association with humans, and they were being kept as part of boy's house-

Illustration 8–1. *People v. Garcia*, 812
N.Y.S.2d 66 (App. Div. 2006).

OVERVIEW: Defendant claimed his "stomping" on a pet goldfish was a misdemeanor (N.Y. Agric. & Mkts. Law § 353) and not a felony under N.Y. Agric. & Mkts. Law § 353-a(1) because a fish was not a "companion animal" and his actions did not constitute aggravated cruelty. The appeals court found the Legislature did not require a reciprocity of affection in the definition of "companion animal." "The statute's language was consistent with the People's claim that "domesticated" was commonly understood to mean "to adapt (an animal or plant) to life in intimate association with and to the advantage of humans." Thus, a goldfish was a domesticated rather than a wild animal under the common meaning. Section 353-a was sufficiently clear to apprise a person of ordinary intelligence that the sort of conduct in which defendant engaged came within its prohibition. The trial court improperly exercised discretion in considering attempted assault in the second degree as a lesser-included offense of first-degree attempted assault. It was not until after summations that the court indicated it would consider attempted second-degree assault, a significant departure from the prosecution's theory of the case.

OUTCOME: The judgment was modified, on the law, to the extent of vacating the conviction for attempted assault in the second degree, and replacing the second violent felony offender adjudication with a second felony offender adjudication, reducing the aggregate sentence to 5 1/2 to 11 years, and otherwise affirmed.

CORE TERMS: animal, repair, companion, assault, goldfish, fish's, pet', domesticated, cruelty, knife, physical injury, aggravated, felony offender, sentence, lesser, lv denied, mischief, violent, weapon, dog, documentation, television, convicted, apartment, cat, intentionally, girlfriend's, household, altercation, photographs

LEXISNEXIS ◆ HEADNOTES   ⊟ Hide

Criminal Law & Procedure > Criminal Offenses > Miscellaneous Offenses > Cruelty to Animals > Elements

HN1 ⬥ See N.Y. Agric. & Mkts. Law § 353-a(1). Shepardize: Restrict By Headnote

☞3.5(3) ANIMALS   2A N Y D 4th—20

For later cases, see same Topic and Key Number in Pocket Part

might escape and form feral populations. U.S.C.A. Const.Amend. 14; N.Y. Comp. Codes R. & Regs. title 10, § 2.14; title 24, §§ 11.65, 161.01.

> New York City Friends of Ferrets v. City of New York, 876 F.Supp. 529, affirmed 71 F.3d 405.

City's decision to regulate ferrets but not to also regulate pit bull terriers, which had been shown to be dangerous, did not violate equal protection clause, since, to satisfy equal protection, city was not required to address all potential threats from all breeds of pets, but was entitled to address phase of problem of particular concern. U.S.C.A. Const.Amend. 14; N.Y. Comp. Codes R. & Regs. title 10, § 2.14; title 24, §§ 11.65, 161.01.

> New York City Friends of Ferrets v. City of New York, 876 F.Supp. 529, affirmed 71 F.3d 405.

N.Y.A.D. 1 Dept. 2006. Statute defining "companion animals," for purposes of the application of statute prohibiting aggravated cruelty to animals, was not unconstitutionally vague as applied to defendant found to have intentionally stomped on a boy's pet goldfish; statute was sufficiently clear to apprise a person of ordinary intelligence that the sort of conduct in which defendant engaged came within the statute's prohibition. McKinney's Agriculture and Markets Law §§ 350(5), 353–a(1).

> People v. Garcia, 812 N.Y.S.2d 66, 29 A.D.3d 255, leave to appeal denied 821 N.Y.S.2d 818, 7 N.Y.3d 789, 854 N.E.2d 1282.

N.Y.A.D. 3 Dept. 1997. State statute specifically prohibiting owning, possessing or keeping of any animal under circumstances evincing intent that such animal engage in animal fighting was not unconstitutionally vague; statute was sufficiently definite to provide person of ordinary intelligence with fair notice of any prohibited conduct, and defendant's admissions to providing shelter for fighting animals, coupled with further objective physical evidence, demonstrated that he engaged in precisely type of activity that statute was designed to prohibit. McKinney's Agriculture and Markets Law § 351, subd. 3(b).

> People v. Mink, 655 N.Y.S.2d 115, 237 A.D.2d 664.

N.Y.Sup. 2004. Statute prohibiting intentionally killing or seriously injuring a companion animal, with no justifiable purpose and with aggravated cruelty, was not unconstitutionally vague as applied to defendant accused of killing a boy's pet goldfish by deliberately crushing it under his heel; any person of ordinary intelligence would know that a goldfish, as a household pet, was a companion animal intended to be protected under the statute. McKinney's Agriculture and Markets Law § 353-a.

> People v. Garcia, 777 N.Y.S.2d 846, 3 Misc.3d 699.

N.Y.Sup. 1979. Limited application of "Pooper Scooper Law," which required an owner's removal of canine wastes in any public area, to cities with a population in excess of 400,000 did not constitute a denial of equal protection of the law. Public Health Law § 1310; U.S.C.A.Const. Amend. 14.

> Schnapp v. Lefkowitz, 422 N.Y.S.2d 798, 101 Misc.2d 1075.

N.Y.Co.Ct. 2000. Absence from aggravated cruelty to animals statute of definitions for terms "extreme physical pain" and "especially depraved or sadistic manner" did not render statute void for vagueness, as meaning of such terms was matter of common usage and understanding and expressed clear legislative intent to punish only the most serious and egregious conduct. McKinney's Agriculture and Markets Law § 353-a.

> People v. Knowles, 709 N.Y.S.2d 916, 184 Misc.2d 474.

Statutory definition of "cruelty" arguably at odds with statutory definition of "aggravated cruelty" did not render aggravated cruelty to animals statute confusing or unconstitutionally vague, as definitions of cruelty and aggravated cruelty were separate and distinct. McKinney's Agriculture and Markets Law §§ 350, subd. 2, 353-a.

> People v. Knowles, 709 N.Y.S.2d 916, 184 Misc.2d 474.

Aggravated cruelty to animals statute was not unconstitutionally vague as applied to conduct of defendant who kicked eight-month-old dog down a walkway, then picked it up and threw it against a brick wall; person of ordinary intelligence

† This Case was not selected for publication in the National Reporter System
For legislative history of cited statutes, see McKinney's Consolidated Laws of New York

Illustration 8–3. Animals 3.5(3), 2A WEST'S
NEW YORK DIGEST 4TH 20 (2008).

47 N Y D 4th–81   **CURRICULUM**

References are to Digest Topics and Key Numbers

**CRUEL AND UNUSUAL
PUNISHMENT**—Cont'd
CONDITIONS of confinement—Cont'd

Treatment,
   Deliberate indifference, **Sent & Pun** ⟜ 1546

SENTENCE, length of,
   Illegal reentry after deportation, **Sent & Pun**
    ⟜ 1507

CRUELTY

MURDER, first degree murder, weight and sufficiency of evidence, **Homic** ⟜ 1144

CRUELTY TO ANIMALS

Generally, **Anim** ⟜ 3.5(5)

ANIMAL welfare acts in general, **Anim** ⟜ 3.5(5)

APPEAL and error, **Anim** ⟜ 3.5(9)

COCKFIGHTING, **Anim** ⟜ 3.5(7)

CONSTITUTIONAL law, **Anim** ⟜ 3.5(3)

CONTESTS, **Anim** ⟜ 3.5(7)

COSTS, **Anim** ⟜ 3.5(10)

CRIMINAL proceedings, **Anim** ⟜ 3.5(9)

DOGFIGHTING, **Anim** ⟜ 3.5(7)

FEDERAL preemption, **Anim** ⟜ 3.5(2)

FIGHTING, **Anim** ⟜ 3.5(7)

FINES and penalties, **Anim** ⟜ 3.5(10)

FORFEITURES, **Anim** ⟜ 3.5(8)

HUMANE societies, **Anim** ⟜ 3.5(11)

INSPECTION, **Anim** ⟜ 3.5(8)

JURY questions, **Anim** ⟜ 3.5(9)

LABORATORY animals, **Anim** ⟜ 3.5(6)

ORDINANCES, **Anim** ⟜ 3.5(3)

PENALTIES, **Anim** ⟜ 3.5(10)

POWER to regulate, **Anim** ⟜ 3.5(2)

PROCEEDINGS, **Anim** ⟜ 3.5(9)

PROSECUTIONS, **Anim** ⟜ 3.5(9)

PUNISHMENT, **Anim** ⟜ 3.5(10)

REGULATION in general, **Anim** ⟜ 3.5(5)

RESEARCH animals, **Anim** ⟜ 3.5(6)

REVIEW, **Anim** ⟜ 3.5(9)

SEARCHES and seizures, **Anim** ⟜ 3.5(8)

SOCIETIES for prevention, **Anim** ⟜ 3.5(11)

STATUTES, **Anim** ⟜ 3.5(3)

CRUTCHES

See heading **MEDICINE, MEDICAL DEVICES
AND INSTRUMENTS,** generally.

CULVERTS

FLOODS and flowage, highways, **High** ⟜ 120

**CUMULATIVE OR EXCLUSIVE
REMEDIES**

EMPLOYMENT law,
   Adverse employment decisions, **Labor & Emp**
    ⟜ 852

PRICE regulation, **Antitrust** ⟜ 481

PRIMARY jurisdiction doctrine,
   Unfair trade practices, **Antitrust** ⟜ 283

TORTIOUS interference,
   Inheritances, wills, trusts and gifts, **Torts** ⟜ 291

UNFAIR competition, **Antitrust** ⟜ 62

UNFAIR trade practices,
   Generally, **Antitrust** ⟜ 282
   Judicial remedies prior to or pending administra-
    tive proceedings, **Antitrust** ⟜ 283
   Primary jurisdiction doctrine, **Antitrust** ⟜ 283

CURATIVE ACTS

RETROACTIVITY, **Statut** ⟜ 278.11

TAX deeds, **Tax** ⟜ 3115

TAX sales, **Tax** ⟜ 2988

CURFEW

CHILDREN and minors,
   Equal protection,
    Age classifications, **Const Law** ⟜ 3088

EQUAL protection,
   Age classifications, **Const Law** ⟜ 3088

RELIGION, freedom of, **Const Law** ⟜ 1310

SPEECH, freedom of, **Const Law** ⟜ 1582

CURRICULUM

DUE process,
   Colleges and universities, **Const Law** ⟜ 4224(2)
   Schools and school districts, **Const Law** ⟜ 4207

RELIGION, freedom of. See heading **RELIGION,
FREEDOM OF, CURRICULUM.**

SCHOOLS and school districts,
   Due process, **Const Law** ⟜ 4207
   Speech, freedom of,
    Generally, **Const Law** ⟜ 1974
    Employees, **Const Law** ⟜ 1999

Illustration 8–4. Descriptive–Word Index, 47 WEST'S
NEW YORK DIGEST 4TH 81 (Supp. 2008).

ANIMALS

SUBJECTS INCLUDED

Animals as the subjects of property or of legal protection or regulation, other than game and fish

Nature and incidents of rights of property in animals, and liabilities for injuries by them; injuries to animals in general

Regulations for the protection of animals from disease, ill treatment, etc., and relating to estrays

Contracts for feeding, care, and use or hire

Offense of cruelty to animals

Livery Stable Keepers

SUBJECTS EXCLUDED AND COVERED BY OTHER TOPICS

Conveyances and contracts relating to animals, see SALES, CHATTEL MORTGAGES, BAILMENT, CARRIERS, INSURANCE, and other specific topics

Fence laws, see FENCES

Game, rights of taking and protection of, see GAME

Particular types of negligence causing injuries to animals, see AUTOMOBILES, NEGLIGENCE, RAILROADS, HIGHWAYS, and other specific topics

Protection of wildlife, particularly endangered or threatened species, see ENVIRONMENTAL LAW

For detailed references to other topics, see Descriptive-Word Index

---

Analysis

⟨⟩1.5. Animals as property; status.
   (1). In general.
   (2). Wild animals in unconfined state, in general.
   (3). Captured, confined or domesticated animals, in general.
   (4). Dogs.
   (5). Horses, cattle, sheep and other livestock.
   (6). Birds and fowl.
   (7). Bees.
   (8). Other particular animals.
   (9). Evidence of ownership.
2.5. Licensing.
   (1). In general.
   (2). Constitutional provisions, statutes and ordinances.
   (3). Licenses, permits and tags.
   (4). Taxes and fees.
3.5. Regulation in general.
   (1). In general.
   (2). Power to regulate in general; preemption.
   (3). Constitutional provisions, statutes and ordinances.
   (4). Particular regulations.
   (5). Protective and anti-cruelty regulation in general.
   (6). Laboratory and research animals.
   (7). Fighting and contests.
   (8). Searches, seizures, inspections and forfeitures.
   (9). Prosecutions and proceedings; review.
   (10). Penalties, punishments and costs.
   (11). Animal welfare societies and agencies.
5. Marks and brands.
5.1. —— In general.
6. —— Adoption and use in general.
7. —— Statutory regulations.
8. —— Recording.
9. —— Transfer.
10. —— Evidence of ownership.
11. —— Destroying or altering.
12. —— False marking or branding.
13. —— Criminal prosecutions.
14. Driving from range or pasture, and herding or confining young animals apart from their mothers.
15. Regulation of slaughtering.
16. Breeding and registration.
16.1. —— In general.
17. —— Statutory regulations.
18. —— Contracts.
19. —— Lien.
20. —— Right to offspring.
21. Agistment, keeping, and care.
21.1. —— In general.
22. —— Rights and duties in general.
23. —— Loss of or injuries to animals.
   (1). In general.
   (2). Actions.
24. —— Injuries by animals.
25. —— Compensation.

Illustration 8–5. Animals, 3 Eleventh
Decennial Digest 266 (2008).

COMPANION ANIMALS   8 W&P— 22

COMPANION ANIMALS

N.Y.A.D. 1 Dept. 2006. Pet goldfish were "companion animals" within the meaning of statute prohibiting aggravated cruelty to animals, and therefore defendant who stomped on a boy's pet goldfish was guilty of violating that statute; goldfish were domesticated inasmuch as they had been adapted to live in close association with humans, and they were being kept as part of boy's household. McKinney's Agriculture and Markets Law §§ 350(5), 353–a(1).—People v. Garcia, 812 N.Y.S.2d 66, 29 A.D.3d 255, leave to appeal denied 821 N.Y.S.2d 818, 7 N.Y.3d 789, 854 N.E.2d 1282.—Anim 3.5(5).

COMPANION CASE

C.A.6 (Mich.) 2006. Case of Michigan police officer who was allegedly retaliated against for testifying in fellow officer's discrimination suit was not "companion case" to the discrimination suit under applicable Michigan local rule governing reassignment of cases; though many of the same people would be involved in both suits, focus of their testimony would be different because one officer would present witnesses in support of fact he had been retaliated against and fellow officer would present witnesses in support of fact he was discriminated against, and though related parties were present, cases did not arise out of the same transaction or occurrence. U.S.Dist.Ct.Rules E.D. Mich., Rule 83.11(b)(7); M.C.L.A. § 15.362. —Jones v. City of Allen Park, 167 Fed.Appx. 398, 2006 Fed.App. 0001N, rehearing denied.—Courts 70.

COMPANIONSHIP

Ind.App. 2007. "Companionship," for purposes of Child Wrongful Death Statute (CWDS), which allows parent to recover damages for loss of child's companionship, refers to a type of love, care, and affection, and does not refer to solatium or recompense for grief or wounded feelings. West's A.I.C. 34-23-2-1.—Randles v. Indiana Patient's Compensation Fund, 860 N.E.2d 1212, rehearing denied, transfer denied 878 N.E.2d 205.—Death 88.

COMPANIONSHIP SERVICES

N.D.Okla. 2006. "Companionship services" and "domestic service employment" components are two separate elements of FLSA overtime exemption; employee "must both provide companionship services and be employed in domestic service employment". Fair Labor Standards Act of 1938, § 13(a)(15), 29 U.S.C.A. § 213(a)(15).— Zachary v. Rescare Oklahoma, Inc., 471 F.Supp.2d 1183.—Labor & Emp 2284.

COMPANY

Wash.App. Div. 3 2007. Husband and wife doing business together as sole proprietorship were not a "company" that could be served with process by serving office assistant, but rather individual defendants, and thus they had to be served with process personally or by abode service, not by serving an employee at their place of business. West's RCWA 4.28.080.—Dolby v. Worthy, 173 P.3d 946, 141 Wash.App. 813.—Proc 72, 78.

COMPANY DOCUMENT

Wis. 2007. For purposes of operating agreement, which permitted members of limited liability company (LLC) to inspect "Company documents," information that was stored as e-mail could be a "Company document," and thus operating agreement did not categorically deny inspection of information that was stored as e-mail.— Kasten v. Doral Dental USA, LLC, 733 N.W.2d 300, 301 Wis.2d 598, 2007 WI 76.—Ltd Liab Cos 25.

Wis. 2007. For purposes of operating agreement, which permitted members of limited liability company (LLC) to inspect "Company documents," stored information of a strictly personal or social nature, such as personal e-mails that did not touch upon business matters, was not a "Company document."—Kasten v. Doral Dental USA, LLC, 733 N.W.2d 300, 301 Wis.2d 598, 2007 WI 76.—Ltd Liab Cos 25.

COMPANY DOCUMENTS

Wis. 2007. For purposes of operating agreement, which permitted members of limited liability company (LLC) to inspect "Company documents," document drafts were "Company documents."—Kasten v. Doral Dental USA, LLC, 733 N.W.2d 300, 301 Wis.2d 598, 2007 WI 76.—Ltd Liab Cos 25.

COMPANY REFUSES TO PAY THE FULL AMOUNT OF A LOSS

Wyo. 2005. An insurer's unreasonable delay in claim settlement is within the ambit of statute permitting court in which judgment is rendered for claimant to award attorney fees, if it is determined in any action or proceeding that the insurer refused to pay the full amount of a covered loss and the refusal was unreasonable or without cause, even if the insurer can settle the claim by means other than payment of an amount for a monetary loss suffered by the insured; the phrase that "company refuses to pay the full amount of a loss" covered by the policy broadly means that the insurer refuses to fulfill its contractual obligations with regard to settling a loss covered by the policy. Wyo.Stat.Ann. § 26–15–124(c).—Stewart Title Guar. Co. v. Tilden, 110 P.3d 865, 2005 WY 53, appeal after remand 181 P.3d 94, 2008 WY 46. —Insurance 3335.

COMPARABLE

C.A.10 (Okla.) 2005. In order for state law to be "comparable" to Clean Water Act (CWA), and thus for state's enforcement action to bar

Illustration 8–6. "Companion Animals," 8
WORDS AND PHRASES 22 (Supp. 2008).

CRUELTY TO ANIMALS   6 ALR5th
6 ALR5th 733

Table of Contents

Research References
Index
Jurisdictional Table of Cited Statutes and Cases

ARTICLE OUTLINE

734

Illustration 8–7. Sonja A. Soehnel, Annotation, *What Constitutes Offense of Cruelty to Animals—Modern Cases*, 6 A.L.R.5th 733, 734 (1992).

CRUELTY TO ANIMALS   6 ALR5th
6 ALR5th 733

INDEX

Illustration 8–8. 6 A.L.R.5th at 738.

Westlaw. FIND&PRINT KEYCITE DIRECTORY KEY NUMBERS COURT DOCS FORMFINDER SITE MAP HELP SIGN OFF
Preferences Alert Center Research Trail
Add a Tab

Result List 1 Doc

Full Screen List
Locate in Result
Find citation: [Go]

H Annotation has some history

History
Citing References
Monitor With KeyCite Alert

→ Full-Text Document

ResultsPlus™ View All Results

Am.Jur. Trials
1. Solving Statutes of Limitation Problems

Am.Jur.2d: Animals
2. Prevention of Cruelty to Animals, What Constitutes Cruelty to Animals, Use of Animals Engaged in Fighting for Amusement or Sport

Am.Jur. Trials
3. Wrongful Death Actions

View All Results

Find: garcia   Next Previous Highlight all Match case

Links for 6 A.L.R.5th 733   KeyCite

6 A.L.R.5th 733
What constitutes offense of cruelty to animals—modern cases
Approx. 163 pages

Pet goldfish were "companion animals" within the meaning of statute prohibiting aggravated cruelty to animals, and therefore defendant who stomped on a boy's pet goldfish was guilty of violating that statute; goldfish were domesticated inasmuch as they had been adapted to live in close association with humans, and they were being kept as part of boy's household. McKinney's Agriculture and Markets Law §§ 350(5), 353–a(1). People v. Garcia, 812 N.Y.S.2d 66 (App. Div. 1st Dep't 2006).

Statute prohibiting intentionally killing or seriously injuring a companion animal, with no justifiable purpose and with aggravated cruelty, was not unconstitutionally vague as applied to defendant accused of killing a boy's pet goldfish by deliberately crushing it under his heel; any person of ordinary intelligence would know that a goldfish, as a household pet, was a companion animal intended to be protected under the statute. McKinney's Agriculture and Markets Law § 353–a. People v. Garcia, 3 Misc. 3d 699, 777 N.Y.S.2d 846 (Sup 2004).

Aggravated cruelty to animals statute was not unconstitutionally vague as applied to conduct of defendant who kicked eight-month-old dog down a walkway, then picked it up and threw it against a brick wall; person of ordinary intelligence would realize that such activity was precisely the sort of activity intended to be covered by statute. McKinney's Agriculture and Markets Law § 353–a. People v. Knowles, 184 Misc. 2d 474, 709 N.Y.S.2d 916 (County Ct. 2000).

Evidence was sufficient to support finding that defendant had custody of puppy, in cruelty to animals prosecution; animal cruelty inspector testified that he believed that defendant found the puppy earlier in the day and intentionally drove to the trail to abandon the puppy because it did not belong to him, and defendant offered conflicting stories regarding whether he found the puppy at his house or later in the back of his van. V.T.C.A., Penal Code § 42.09(a)(3). McDonald v. State, 64 S.W.3d 86 (Tex. App. Austin 2001), petition for discretionary review ref (Feb 7, 1996) § 13.

See Celinski v State (1995, Tex App Houston (1st Dist)) 911 SW2d 177, petition for discretionary review ref (Feb 7, 1996) § 13.

Tools Go

Illustration 8–9. 6 A.L.R.5th at 64 (Supp. 2008), on Westlaw.

ALR INDEX

ANIMALS—Cont'd

Contributory negligence or assumption of risk—Cont'd
- or injury to person riding therein resulting from collision with domestic animal at large in street or highway, **29 ALR4th 431**
- statutory violation contributory negligence as a defense to a cause of action based upon violation of statute imposing duty upon keeper of animals, **10 ALR2d 853**

Conversion
- emotional distress, recovery of damages for emotional distress due to treatment of pets and animals, **91 ALR5th 545, § 14**
- identification of animals involved in conversion, **51 ALR2d 1154**
- livestock, measure and elements of damages, in action other than one against a carrier, for conversion, injury, loss, or destruction of livestock, **79 ALR2d 677**

Covenants
- cats, restrictive covenant as to keeping cats on premises, **73 ALR2d 1040**
- grazing or pasturage agreement as violation of covenant in lease or provision of statute against assigning or subletting without lessor's consent, **71 ALR3d 780**
- livestock, construction and effect of restrictive covenant in deed or conveyance specifically prohibiting or limiting the keeping of animals, such as livestock, fowl, etc., on the premises, **89 ALR2d 990**

Criminal law. Cruelty, in this topic

Crossing and crossings, deer crossing warning signs, governmental liability for failure to post, **59 ALR4th 1217**

Cruelty
- constitutionality of statute to prevent cruelty in trapping animals, **79 ALR 1308**
- defamation, liability for statement or publication charging plaintiff with killing of, cruelty to, or inhumane treatment of animals, **69 ALR5th 645**

ANIMALS—Cont'd

Cruelty—Cont'd
- horses, construction and application of Horse Protection Act of 1970, 15 U.S.C.A. § 1821 et seq., **131 ALR Fed 363**
- indefiniteness of penal statute or ordinance relating to cruelty, or similar offenses, against animals, **144 ALR 1041**
- libel and slander, liability for statement or publication charging plaintiff with killing of, cruelty to, or inhumane treatment of animals, **69 ALR5th 645, § 3, 4(a, c), 6(b), 7, 9, 10**
- what constitutes offense of cruelty to animals, **6 ALR5th 733**

Customs duties and import regulations, state taxation of livestock as affected by Federal constitutional or statutory provisions relating to imports, exports, or interstate commerce, **130 ALR 969**

Damages
- **Cats** (this index)
- communicable disease, sale of livestock inflicted with, **14 ALR4th 1096**
- conversion, injury, loss or destruction of livestock, other than carriers, **79 ALR2d 677**
- **Dogs** (this index)
- emotional distress, recovery of damages for emotional distress due to treatment of pets and animals, **91 ALR5th 545**
- measure and elements of recovery of buyer rescinding sale of domestic animal for seller's breach of warranty, **35 ALR2d 1273**

Dead bodies, validity, construction, and application of statutes, ordinances, and other regulations relating to transportation or disposal of carcasses of dead animals not slaughtered for food, **121 ALR 732**

Death and death actions
- destruction of animals, in this topic

Consult POCKET PART for Later Annotations

339

Illustration 8–10. Animals, A–B ALR INDEX 339 (2008).

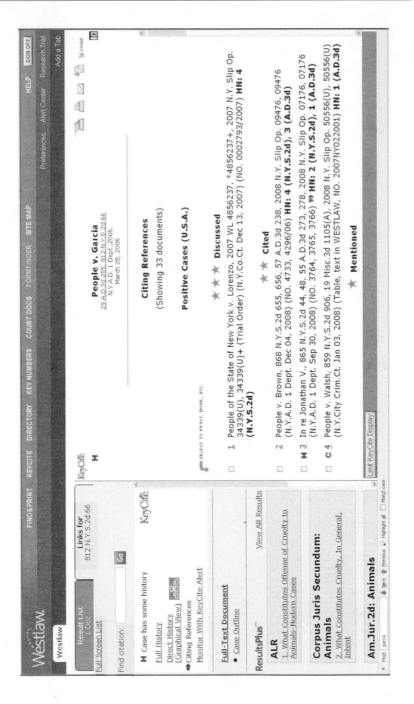

Illustration 8–11. KeyCite results for *People v. Garcia*, 812 N.Y.S.2d 66 (App. Div. 2006).

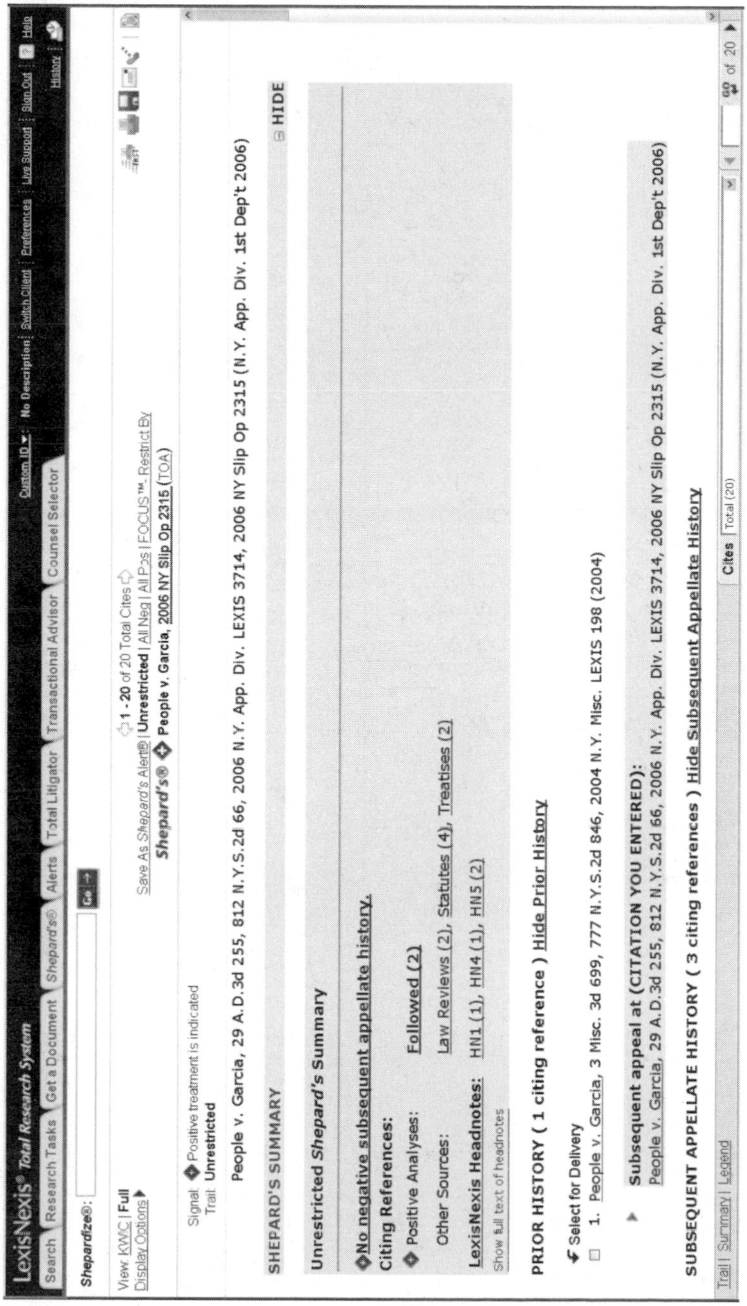

Illustration 8–12. Shepard's results for *People v. Garcia*, 812 N.Y.S. 66 (App. Div. 2006).

| Vol. 546 | | UNITED STATES REPORTS | | | |

~) 496F3d481	D C	Cir. 10	**—49—**	Cir. 10	253Fed Appx
f) 496F3d542	953A2d1044	534F3d1327	Schaffer v	478F3d1269	[525
f) 540FS2d921	Mont	Cir. 11	Weast	520F3d1124	Cir. 8
555FS2d845	344Mt304	568FS2d1311	2005	f) 540F3d1148	2008US Dist
Cir. 7	j) 344Mt310	571FS2d1241	~) 548US18	Cir. 11	[LX87249
f) 434F3d532	345Mt26	Cir. Fed.	548US295	518F3d1286	Cir. 9
535F3d636	~) 346Mt87	521F3d1378	j) 548US313	f) 525F3d1110	j) 503F3d824
2008US Dist	~f) 346Mt91	ClCt	~) 165LE316	f) 255Fed Appx	190Fed Appx
[LX91576	187P3d656	d) 83FedCl 239	165LE533	[366	[552
Cir. 8	j) 187P3d660	96Geo1083	j) 165LE544	2008US Dist	254Fed Appx
518F3d1007	192P3d198	96Geo1487	171LE290	[LX89359	[599
f) 518F3d1008	Tex	83NYL769	~) 126SC2448	Cir. DC	257Fed Appx
525F3d616	240SW415	**—43—**	126SC2458	f) 492F3d434	[33
f) 525F3d618	96Geo805	United States v	j) 126SC2469	f) 377ADC135	259Fed Appx2
d) 525F3d619	96Geo1987	Olson	128SC2400	433FS2d76	2008US Dist
Cir. 9	122HLR145	2005	Cir. 2	e) 435FS2d22	[LX86123
496F3d953	102NwL55	546US485	485F3d732	Cir. Fed.	2008US Dist
513F3d1099	157PaL279	163LE1087	j) 2008US Dist	519F3d1365	[LX86825
e) 156Fed Appx	61StnL1	126SC1256	[LX88163	N J	f) 2008US Dist
[932	117YLJ1225	Cir. 1	2008US Dist	196NJ21	[LX89991
282Fed Appx	**—21—**	f) 497FS2d205	[LX91448	951A2d999	2008US Dist
[587	IBP, Inc. v Al-	555FS2d324	2008US Dist	Wis	[LX90340
Cir. 10	varez	Cir. 3	[LX93528	289Wis2d144	f) 2008US Dist
2008US App	2005	j) 432F3d182	f) 531FS2d267	710NW182	[LX91182
[LX23564	547US86	479F3d283	550FS2d429	55CLA1041	2008US Dist
456F3d1190	164LE192	567FS2d750	554FS2d221	96Geo1083	[LX92809
469F3d948	~) 167LE313	Cir. 4	558FS2d439	117YLJ1802	2008US Dist
d) 469F3d952	168LE121	555FS2d587	559FS2d433	**—72—**	[LX93427
518F3d744	126SC1513	f) 555FS2d588	569FS2d380	Md	Cir. 10
e) 518F3d745	~) 127SC1437	Cir. 5	Cir. 3	405Md601	f) 2008US App
d) 518F3d745	127SC2417	2008US App	282Fed Appx	179MdA26	[LX23441
j) 518F3d753	Cir. 2	[LX18587	[990	943A2d701	Cir. 11
217Fed Appx	488F3d591	Cir. 7	j) 536FS2d571	954A2d1128	f) 527F3d1153
[835	514F3d285	541F3d694	h) 536FS2d572	**—74—**	**—81—**
Cir. 11	524F3d367	Cir. 8	f) 540FS2d615	Bradshaw v	Lincoln Prop.
459F3d1153	Cir. 3	534F3d962	544FS2d440	Richey	Co. v Roche
505F3d1272	e) 524F3d372	513FS2d1087	e) 557FS2d652	2005	2005
d) 194Fed Appx	f) 2008US Dist	Cir. 9	571FS2d660	j) 548US788	Cir. 3
[734	[LX87199	f) 511F3d851	Cir. 4	j) 165LE883	f) 540F3d182
f) 220Fed Appx	Cir. 4	~) 511F3d856	484F3d679	j) 126SC2742	2008US Dist
[967	508F3d187	275Fed Appx	261Fed Appx	Cir. 3	[LX87940
Cir. DC	Cir. 5	[681	[608	2008US Dist	Cir. 4
j) 475F3d1333	554FS2d702	2008US Dist	556FS2d550	[LX90726	2008US Dist
e) 480F3d1145	f) 568FS2d722	[LX86231	Cir. 5	Cir. 4	[LX91977
f) 480F3d1146	569FS2d692	f) 535FS2d1101	561FS2d601	f) 531FS2d708	531FS2d755
j) 480F3d1152	Cir. 6	Cir. 11	567FS2d927	Cir. 5	535FS2d558
j) 374ADC462	542FS2d800	530FS2d1318	Cir. 7	2008US App	Cir. 5
e) 375ADC262	f) 542FS2d801	Cir. DC	434F3d532	[LX20644	2008US Dist
f) 375ADC263	Cir. 7	f) 563FS2d214	Cir. 9	489FS2d657	[LX87351
j) 375ADC269	534F3d594	f) 570FS2d149	496F3d939	526FS2d687	2008US Dist
Cir. Fed.	542F3d208	h) 570FS2d150	513F3d928	Cir. 6	[LX88964
d) 457F3d1354	f) 2008US Dist	ClCt	2008US Dist	2008US App	2008US Dist
j) 457F3d1363	[LX87371	d) 71FedCl 779	[LX91298	[LX19013	[LX89482
479F3d842	e) 527FS2d865	So C	545FS2d997	2008US App	551FS2d572
j) 479F3d872	Cir. 9	379SoC322	f) 545FS2d998	[LX22943	Cir. 7
ClCt	523FS2d1162	665SE198	e) 545FS2d1005	f) 450F3d235	384BRW816
qop) 80FedCl	538FS2d1203		567FS2d1210	501F3d474	Cir. 9
[605	d) 538FS2d1209		250FRD460	f) 540F3d398	443F3d680
65MJ383				j) 540F3d421	
j) 126TCt172					

Illustration 8–13. Shepard's United States Citations, United States Reports 1092 (Supp. Jan. 1, 2009).

Chapter 9

THE JUDICIARY, PART 4:
OTHER COURT INFORMATION

Table of Sections

While much legal literature focuses on substantive rights, the processes under which parties come before courts to settle disputes play a vital role in determining the scope and exercise of these rights. A lawyer must be familiar with governing rules and procedures in order to avoid compromising clients' interests. As Justice Hugo Black complained more than fifty years ago: "Judicial statistics would show, I fear, an unfortunately large number of meritorious cases lost due to inadvertent failure of lawyers to conform to procedural prescriptions having little if any relevancy to substantial justice."[1]

For centuries the rules governing court proceedings developed piecemeal through case law, eventually creating the arcane and formalistic pleading rituals of the Court of Chancery in Dickens's *Bleak House*. Reforms within the past century have made court procedures simpler and more flexible, but there are still unforeseen complexities and differences of interpretation. Rules that seem straightforward must be applied in light of the large body of case law that has developed. Annotated sets of rules and an extensive secondary literature help to guide litigants through the intricate maze of court proceedings.

This chapter also covers a number of other resources dealing with court proceedings and legal practice. Briefs and docket sheets

---

1. Order Adopting Revised Rules of the Supreme Court of the United States, 346 U.S. 945, 946 (1954) (Black, J., dissenting).

contain background information on decided cases or pending lawsuits. Directories and formbooks provide practical assistance for anyone who needs to contact courts, draft documents, or transact other legal business.

These materials' value extends beyond litigation to other legal research situations. Rules of professional conduct are applicable to all lawyers, and sources such as briefs and model jury instructions may contain important information about substantive legal issues.

§ 9.1   Court Rules

Court rules are designed to guide and regulate the conduct of judicial business. They range from procedural details, such as the format to be followed in preparing a brief, to matters of substantial importance, such as the grounds for appeal, time limitations, or the types of motions and appeals that a court will hear. Court rules may specify or limit available remedies and thus can affect rights in significant ways. Rules regulating court proceedings have the force of law, but they generally cannot supersede or conflict with statutes.

Most jurisdictions have sets of rules governing trial and appellate procedure, as well as rules for specialized tribunals or for particular actions such as admiralty or habeas corpus. Each jurisdiction has its own requirements and procedures for creating these rules. Some involve action by special conferences of judges, and others require approval by the jurisdiction's highest court. Some court rules are statutory and are created by legislatures, while others require a combination of judicial action and legislative approval. Courts are traditionally considered to have inherent power to control the conduct of their affairs, but court rules are generally promulgated under authority granted by the legislature.

(a) Federal Rules

In 1789 the first Congress expressly gave the federal courts the power to make rules governing their procedures.[2] In 1822 the Supreme Court promulgated its first set of rules for procedures in equity,[3] but it did not issue general rules for actions at law for more than another century.

---

2. Congress gave the new federal courts the power "to make and establish all necessary rules for the orderly conducting business in the said courts, provided such rules are not repugnant to the laws of the United States." Judiciary Act of 1789, ch. 20, § 17, 1 Stat. 73, 83. An act three years later vested rulemaking power more specifically to the Supreme Court, providing that courts follow state procedures "subject ... to such regulations as the supreme court of the United States shall think proper from time to time by rule to prescribe to any circuit or district court." Act of May 8, 1792, ch. 36, § 2, 1 Stat. 275, 276.

3. 20 U.S. (7 Wheat.) v (1822).

A 1934 Act of Congress gave the Court authority to combine equity and law into one federal civil procedure and to make and publish rules governing federal actions as long as they did not "abridge, enlarge, nor modify the substantive rights of any litigant."[4] The resulting Federal Rules of Civil Procedure were prepared by a judicial Advisory Committee, adopted by the Supreme Court in December 1937, and became effective September 16, 1938.

The new rules were a widely acclaimed success in modernizing federal civil practice. One enthusiastic lawyer wrote that the rules were "one of the greatest contributions to the free and unhampered administration of law and justice ever struck off by any group of men since the dawn of civilized law."[5] Attorney General Robert H. Jackson noted in his 1940 report to Congress that the rules had created "probably the simplest form of civil procedure yet devised in any jurisdiction in which Anglo–Saxon jurisprudence prevails."[6]

Congress had given the Supreme Court authority to promulgate rules governing criminal appeals in 1933, and in 1940 the Court was also empowered to make rules with respect to criminal trial court proceedings.[7] In his 1940 report, Attorney General Jackson stressed the need for reform, writing that criminal procedure "still remains largely in a chaotic and archaic state. Many technicalities dating back a century or two are still in full vigor in the Federal courts."[8] The Federal Rules of Criminal Procedure went through several drafts before finally becoming effective March 21, 1946.

The criminal rules governed proceedings both before and after the verdict, but appeals in civil cases continued to be handled differently in each circuit. In 1966 Congress finally empowered the Supreme Court to prescribe rules for the Courts of Appeals in civil actions.[9] The Federal Rules of Appellate Procedure, governing both civil and criminal proceedings, took effect July 1, 1968.

The last of the four major sets of rules governing federal court proceedings had a rather different origin. In 1972 the Supreme Court submitted proposed Federal Rules of Evidence to Congress,

4. Rules Enabling Act, ch. 651, § 1, 48 Stat. 1064, 1064 (1934) (current version at 28 U.S.C. § 2072 (2000)). On the history and interpretation of the act, see, e.g., Stephen B. Burbank, *The Rules Enabling Act of 1934*, 130 U. Pa. L. Rev. 1015 (1982); Martin H. Redish & Uma M. Amuluru, *The Supreme Court, the Rules Enabling Act, and the Politicization of the Federal Rules: Constitutional and Statutory Implications*, 90 Minn. L. Rev. 1303 (2006).

5. B. H. Carey, *In Favor of Uniformity*, 18 Temp. U. L.Q. 146, 146 (1943).

6. *Annual Report of the Attorney General of the United States,* H.R. Doc. No. 77–9, at 5 (1940).

7. Act of Feb. 24, 1933, ch. 119, 47 Stat. 904, as amended by Act of Mar. 8, 1934, ch. 49, 48 Stat. 399; Act of June 29, 1940, ch. 445, 54 Stat. 688.

8. *Annual Report*, supra note 6.

9. Act of Nov. 6, 1966, Pub. L. No. 89–773, 80 Stat. 1323.

which passed a law preventing the rules from taking effect until expressly approved.[10] To some critics, the proposed rules covering evidentiary privileges were seen as substantive rather than procedural in nature, and were thus beyond the scope of the Court's rulemaking authority. Congress enacted its own amended version of the rules, which became law on July 1, 1975, and gave the Supreme Court authority to make amendments other than those creating, abolishing or modifying privileges.[11]

In addition to the sets of rules applying to the federal courts in general, there are also rules governing specialized procedures and particular courts. Rules governing bankruptcy proceedings were first promulgated in 1898,[12] and the current rules were adopted in 1983 for proceedings in the new Bankruptcy Courts created in the 1978 revision of the Bankruptcy Code.[13]

These various sets of federal procedural rules have all been amended numerous times in the years since their initial adoption. Under the current procedure established by Congress in 1988,[14] standing Advisory Committees for each set of rules recommend changes to the Judicial Conference, the principal policy-making body for administration of the federal court system. If the Judicial Conference approves the changes, it submits them to the Supreme Court for its approval. The Court in turn transmits the proposed amendments to Congress, which has at least seven months to enact legislation to reject, modify, or defer the changes. The rule amendments take effect if Congress declines to act. Congress has also directly amended federal rules on several occasions.

The major source for information on pending and recent amendments to federal rules is the "Federal Rulemaking" section of the U.S. Courts website <www.uscourts.gov/rules/>. This site provides the text of pending rule changes, as well as Advisory Committee reports, minutes of committee meetings, and background information on the rulemaking process. Rule amendments are also printed as House Documents, and reprinted in advance sheets for West's federal case reporters, as well as in *U.S. Code*

---

10. Act of Mar. 30, 1973, Pub. L. No. 93–12, 87 Stat. 9.

11. Act of Jan. 2, 1975, § 2(a)(1), Pub.L. No. 93–595, 88 Stat. 1926, 1948 (current version at 28 U.S.C. § 2074(b) (2000)). For a history of the proposed rules, their rejection in Congress, and references to criticism, see Kenneth S. Broun, *Giving Codification a Second Chance—Testimonial Privileges and the Federal Rules of Evidence*, 53 HASTINGS L.J. 769, 772–78 (2002).

12. General Orders and Forms in Bankruptcy, 172 U.S. 653 (1898), promulgated pursuant to the Bankruptcy Act of 1898, § 30, ch. 541, 30 Stat. 544, 554.

13. See Lawrence P. King, *The History and Development of the Bankruptcy Rules*, 70 AM. BANKR. L.J. 217 (1996).

14. Judicial Improvements and Access to Justice Act, § 401, Pub. L. No. 100–702, 102 Stat. 4642, 4648–50 (1988) (codified as amended at 28 U.S.C. §§ 2072–74 (2000)).

Congressional and Administrative News and *United States Code Service Advance.*

The commentary by the Advisory Committee that drafted the original rules or any later committee that drafted and proposed amendments is often an invaluable starting point in interpreting rule provisions.[15] These notes usually consist of a few paragraphs for each rule, discussing procedure under prior law and the purpose of the new rule or amendment, and provide a sort of "legislative history" analogous to congressional committee reports.

Sources. The various rules governing federal court proceedings can be found in a wide array of online and print sources, some unannotated and some accompanied by Advisory Committee Notes, summaries of judicial decisions, and extensive commentaries.

Most court rules are available at free Internet sites, but usually without annotations or commentary. The House Committee on the Judiciary publishes regularly updated versions of the Federal Rules of Appellate Procedure, Civil Procedure, Criminal Procedure, and Evidence as committee prints, with PDF versions of these documents available on the Committee website <judiciary.house. gov/about/procedural.html>. The Legal Information Institute at Cornell Law School provides searchable versions of these sets, as well as the Federal Rules of Bankruptcy Procedure <www.law. cornell.edu/rules/>.

Federal court rules are also available from subscription databases and in a variety of pamphlets and reference publications. The major sets of rules are printed in the *U.S. Code* with Advisory Committee comments after each section. An appendix to Title 28, Judiciary and Judicial Procedure, contains the Federal Rules of Civil Procedure, Appellate Procedure, and Evidence, as well as rules governing proceedings in the Supreme Court and specialized courts. The Federal Rules of Criminal Procedure appear in an appendix to Title 18, Crimes and Criminal Procedure; and Bankruptcy Rules and Official Forms are in an appendix to Title 11, Bankruptcy. The official *U.S. Code,* however, is always at least two or three years out of date when it is published, so it cannot be relied upon for coverage of current amendments.

---

15. "In interpreting the federal rules, the Advisory Committee Notes are a very important source of information and direction and should be given considerable weight. Although these Notes are not conclusive, they provide something akin to a 'legislative history' of the rules, and carry, in addition, the great prestige that the individual members of the successive Advisory Committees, and the Committees themselves, have enjoyed as authorities on procedure." 4 CHARLES ALAN WRIGHT & ARTHUR R. MILLER, FEDERAL PRACTICE AND PROCEDURE § 1029, at 160–61 (3d ed. 2002) (footnotes omitted). *But see* Laurens Walker, *Writings on the Margin of American Law: Committee Notes, Comments, and Commentary,* 29 GA. L. REV. 993 (1995) (arguing that courts should give little, if any, weight to committee notes).

United States Code Annotated (in print and on Westlaw) and *United States Code Service* (in print and on Lexis) contain not only Advisory Committee notes but also headnotes of cases applying and interpreting the rules, as well as other research aids such as references to treatises, law review articles, and legal encyclopedias. These annotations can be quite extensive; the Federal Rules of Civil Procedure, for example, occupy eighteen volumes in *USCA*.

USCA includes the rules at the same place they appear in the *U.S. Code,* following the code titles to which they are most closely related. *USCS* publishes several unnumbered "Court Rules" volumes, which are generally shelved at the end of the set. The one exception is the Federal Rules of Evidence; because they were enacted by Congress, *USCS* prints them as an appendix to Title 28. Both *USCA* and *USCS* also include annotated editions of the rules of the Supreme Court, of the thirteen individual circuits, and of specialized federal courts.

A somewhat less overwhelming source of annotated federal rules is the *United States Supreme Court Digest, Lawyers' Edition.* Volumes 17 to 22 of this set include the text of the major sets of rules, as well as rules for specialized federal courts, accompanied by Advisory Committee comments, commentaries by National Institute for Trial Advocacy professors, and annotations of Supreme Court cases. While this is a less comprehensive source, it may be a useful starting point for someone seeking significant judicial interpretations of the rules.[16]

Treatises. The technical nature of the rules and their importance in legal practice have led to the development of a number of excellent commentaries on federal practice. Two comprehensive treatises by distinguished scholars in the fields of federal courts and procedure are published, *Federal Practice and Procedure* and *Moore's Federal Practice.*

Federal Practice and Procedure (1st–4th eds. 1969–date) is an extensive treatment of federal procedural and jurisdictional issues, and is available on Westlaw as the FPP database. The five-part set covers the Federal Rules of Criminal Procedure, the Federal Rules of Civil Procedure, jurisdiction and related matters, the Federal Rules of Evidence, and judicial review of administrative action. The entire set is commonly referred to as "Wright & Miller," after its original authors, the late Charles Alan Wright (1927–2000) and Arthur R. Miller, although they have been joined on specific vol-

---

16. Several other commercially published sources also contain the texts of the major rules, in paperback desktop editions. The *National Volume of Federal Procedure Rules Service* (annual) contains the text and Advisory Committee notes for all of the major rules except the Federal Rules of Bankruptcy Procedure, and a variety of other annual pamphlet editions are published for practitioners or as casebook supplements.

umes by more than a dozen coauthors. *Federal Practice and Procedure* provides extensive discussion of each rule's history, purpose, and application, with copious footnotes to cases and other materials.

Moore's Federal Practice (3d ed. 1997–date), the other major treatise, is named after its initial author, the late James William Moore (1905–1994), and is available in print and on Lexis. The current edition is written by a team of more than forty authors. Like *Federal Practice and Procedure, Moore's* devotes several volumes to a rule-by-rule analysis of the Federal Rules of Civil Procedure, with other volumes focusing on matters such as jurisdiction, the Federal Rules of Criminal Procedure, the Federal Rules of Appellate Procedure, admiralty, Supreme Court practice, and the federal law of attorney conduct.

Another multi-volume treatment of federal practice, the encyclopedic *Federal Procedure, Lawyers' Edition* (1982–date), is organized by subject rather than by specific rule. It consists of eighty alphabetically arranged chapters, some of which focus on procedural issues (Access to District Courts, New Trial) and some on topical areas of federal law (Atomic Energy, Job Discrimination). The chapters deal with civil, criminal and administrative practice, and include checklists, synopses of law review articles, and texts of relevant statutes. It is available on Westlaw (FEDPROC database).

Other secondary sources cover specific subject areas and may be more helpful for detailed research. For example, Mark S. Rhodes, *Orfield's Criminal Procedure Under the Federal Rules* (2d ed. 1985–date) (Westlaw ORFIELDS database), is an extensive treatise limited to federal criminal practice. The text discusses the history of each rule's drafting, the law prior to its adoption, and judicial developments.

A number of works focus on the Federal Rules of Evidence, explaining the intent and application of each provision. The most frequently cited treatise is *Weinstein's Federal Evidence* (2d ed. 1997–date), available in print and on Lexis. It was originally written by Judge Jack B. Weinstein, one of the principal drafters of the rules, and Margaret A. Berger, and is now edited by Judge Joseph M. McLaughlin.

Other multi-volume rule-by-rule analyses available in print and online include Michael H. Graham, *Handbook of Federal Evidence* (6th ed. 2006–date) (Westlaw FEDEDIV database); Christopher B. Mueller & Laird C. Kirkpatrick, *Federal Evidence* (3d ed. 2007–date) (Westlaw FEDEV database); and Stephen A. Saltzburg et al., *Federal Rules of Evidence Manual* (9th ed. 2006–date) (available on Lexis).

Local Rules. Individual courts also have local rules to supplement the national sets of rules. The Supreme Court and specialized tribunals such as the Court of Federal Claims and the Court of International Trade have their own sets of rules, and individual Courts of Appeals and District Courts promulgate supplementary rules for local practice.

The Federal Rules of Civil Procedure and each of the other sets of national rules (except the Federal Rules of Evidence) provide that any federal court can establish rules for the conduct of its business, as long as they are not inconsistent with Acts of Congress or rules prescribed by the Supreme Court.[17]

Local court rules often detail procedural matters such as the time allowed to file papers, the format of documents, and the fees for filing various documents. Over the years, however, they have proliferated into an extensive array of local requirements that commentators have called "byzantine" and a "balkanization" of federal procedure.[18] In addition to rules for specific districts, some individual judges also promulgate guidelines for the cases they hear. What this means in practical terms is that lawyers must be every bit as aware of local and judge-specific rules as they are of more general rules.

Federal law requires that each court's website provide access to local court rules and individual judges' rules.[19] Many court websites also include answers to frequently asked questions about filing requirements and trial procedures. Links to local court homepages are available through the U.S. Courts website <www.uscourts.gov/courtlinks/>, and the LLRX (Law Library Resources Xchange) "Court Rules, Forms and Dockets" page <www.llrx.com/courtrules> provides links to the rules for each jurisdiction.

The Supreme Court's rules, in addition to being available online <www.supremecourtus.gov/ctrules/ctrules.html>, are also included in the *U.S. Code, USCA*, and *USCS*. The rules for each of the Courts of Appeals are also published in *USCA, USCS*, and several other sources including *Federal Procedure Rules Service* (which publishes a separate volume for each circuit, also containing the rules for each district court within the circuit).

---

17. FED. R. CIV. P. 83; FED. R. CRIM. P. 57; FED. R. APP. P. 47; FED. R. BANKR. P. 9029.

18. See, e.g., Carl Tobias, *Local Federal Civil Procedure for the Twenty-First Century*, 77 NOTRE DAME L. REV. 533, 535–56 (2002). Local rules in the Courts of Appeals are no less diverse. See Gregory C. Sisk, *The Balkanization*

of Appellate Justice: The Proliferation of Local Rules in the Federal Circuits, 68 U. COLO. L. REV. 1 (1997).

19. E-Government Act of 2002, § 205(a)(2)–(3), Pub. L. No. 107–347, 116 Stat. 2899, 2913 (codified at 44 U.S.C. § 3501 note (Supp. V 2005)).

Local U.S. District Court rules are usually available in court rules pamphlets published for individual states. Some of these state pamphlets, but not all, include annotations of court decisions applying the rules. District Court and Court of Appeals rules from the entire country are published, unannotated, in a seven-volume looseleaf set, *Federal Local Court Rules* (3d ed. 2001–date).

Local court rules are also available on Westlaw and Lexis. It may be easier to focus research on a specific federal court in Lexis, which has separate databases for the U.S. District and Bankruptcy Courts in each state. Westlaw provides local federal rules as part of its state court rules databases (__-RULES and RULES–ALL).

KeyCite and Shepard's coverage of federal court rules is similar to that for statutes. KeyCite begins with the annotations from *USCA*, but expands this to include additional cases and secondary sources. Shepard's treatment can be accessed online or in *Shepard's Federal Statute Citations* or *Shepard's Federal Rules Citations*. Both KeyCite and Shepard's cover local rules as well as the national sets.

Sentencing Guidelines. The Federal Sentencing Guidelines are not court rules, but they occupy a similar position in the hierarchy of legal authorities. They were originally promulgated in 1987 by the U.S. Sentencing Commission, which was created by Congress as an independent agency within the judicial branch. Like court rules, guidelines take effect unless Congress expressly disapproves them. The sentencing guidelines are not published with the official *U.S. Code*, but the Commission publishes an annual *Guidelines Manual* in print and on the Internet <www.ussc.gov/guidelin. htm>.

Both *USCA* and *USCS* include annotated versions of the sentencing guidelines, accompanied by notes of court decisions and other references. Westlaw has the guidelines as part of the USCA database, annotated and covered by KeyCite, and in a stripped-down Federal Criminal Justice—Federal Sentencing Guidelines (FCJ–FSG) database without notes of decisions or KeyCite references. The Lexis version includes annotations and Shepard's links. In print, *Shepard's Federal Statute Citations* includes coverage of sentencing guidelines.

Federal Practice and Procedure and *Moore's Federal Practice* do not cover sentencing guidelines, but shorter works such as David J. Gottlieb & Phyllis Skloot Bamberger, *Practice Under the Federal Sentencing Guidelines* (4th ed. 2001–date), and Thomas W. Hutchison et al., *Federal Sentencing Law and Practice* (annual), provide similar treatment, with extensive commentary and notes of court decisions applying the guidelines. Both of these are available on Westlaw, as the PRFSG and FSLP databases respectively.

(b) State Rules

There are significant differences in rules and procedures from state to state. These distinctions have decreased in recent decades as many states have adopted provisions modeled on the federal rules, particularly the Federal Rules of Evidence. If you know the relevant rules provision in federal court, you can often check the comparable provision in another state.[20] Federal procedural rules are less likely than evidence rules to be mirrored in state court practice.[21]

Procedures are generally governed by a combination of statutory provisions and court rules. The rules governing proceedings in state courts are usually included in the annotated state codes, accompanied by notes of relevant cases, as well as on Westlaw and Lexis. For many state codes, the rules volumes are published annually in a softcover format. Coverage of state court rules in KeyCite and Shepard's is similar to that for statutes, with references to citations in federal and state court decisions, law reviews, and other sources.

Most states also have annual paperback volumes providing convenient access to rules and procedural statutes. Many of these publications are unannotated, but some contain useful case notes and comments by scholars or drafting committees. More elaborate practice sets in many jurisdictions include all of these features, often accompanied by procedural forms. Like *Federal Practice and Procedure* or *Moore's Federal Practice*, the best of these provide a scholarly commentary on the rules and extensive analysis of relevant case law.

Most state court websites provide convenient access to rules and other procedural information. The National Center for State Courts' "Court Web Sites" <www.ncsconline.org/D_KIS/info_court_web_sites.html> is a leading source for finding both trial and appellate state courts on the Web. LLRX Court Rules, Forms and Dockets <www.llrx.com/courtrules> includes links to general and local rules for each state.

---

20. Rule-by-rule comparisons of federal and state evidence provisions are available in "Table of State and Military Adaptations of Federal Rules of Evidence," 6 WEINSTEIN'S FEDERAL EVIDENCE T–1.

21. John B. Oakley, *A Fresh Look at the Federal Rules in State Courts*, 3 NEV. L.J. 354 (2003). The author had surveyed the impact of the Federal Rules of Civil Procedure on state court procedures in the 1980s, in John B. Oakley & Arthur F. Coon, *The Federal Rules in State Courts: A Survey of State Court Systems of Civil Procedure*, 61 WASH. L. REV. 1367 (1986). Upon revisiting the issue, he found that the Federal Rules were "less influential in state courts than at anytime in the past quarter-century." 3 NEV. L.J. at 355.

§ 9.2　Legal Ethics

Researching questions of legal ethics is somewhat different from other doctrinal areas because it has its own distinct body of primary sources. In many jurisdictions, courts have delegated the responsibility for governing the professional activities of lawyers to state bar associations or oversight boards. The law of legal ethics is found in a distinct body of literature consisting of codified rules of conduct, ethics opinions, and disciplinary decisions. An ethics opinion is an advisory document, usually issued by a bar association, analyzing how lawyers or judges should handle a particular or hypothetical problem, while disciplinary decisions punish specific acts of misconduct.[22]

For more than a century, the American Bar Association has played a leading role in developing the rules of legal ethics. The ABA first adopted a set of Canons of Professional Ethics in 1908, and in 1969 it promulgated a more extensive Model Code of Professional Responsibility consisting of a series of Canons, Ethical Considerations, and Disciplinary Rules. The Model Code was in turn superseded in 1983 by the Model Rules of Professional Conduct, which contains about sixty rules divided into eight discrete areas based on lawyers' roles and relationships. The Model Rules have been amended several times since their initial adoption.[23] The ABA Center for Professional Responsibility <www.abanet.org/cpr/> has the text of both Code and Rules, as well as a directory of lawyer disciplinary agencies and a wide range of other information and documents on legal ethics.

Although provisions and amendments vary from state to state, almost all jurisdictions have adopted some form of the Model Rules of Professional Conduct. The only exceptions are California and Maine, which developed their own sets of rules, and New York, which continues to follow the older Model Code of Professional Responsibility.

Each state's rules of professional conduct are available online, from either the state court system or the state bar. Links to these sites are available from the ABA Center for Professional Responsibility <www.abanet.org/cpr/links.html> and the American Legal Ethics Library at Cornell's Legal Information Institute <www.law.cornell.edu/ethics/listing.html>.

The rules are usually included in the volumes containing a state's court rules, although in some states they are part of larger rule documents and can be a bit difficult to find. The rules can be

---

22. For a much more extensive treatment of the issues and resources in this section, see Lee F. Peoples, Legal Ethics: A Legal Research Guide (2d ed. 2006).

23. The ABA has published A Legislative History: The Development of the ABA Model Rules of Professional Conduct, 1982–2005 (2006), a compilation of the various amendments and comments.

even harder to find online in Westlaw or Lexis: Westlaw includes professional conduct rules in its more general court rules databases for each state, and Lexis includes them in the state code databases. Some of these sources are annotated with notes of decisions under the rules. The looseleaf set *National Reporter on Legal Ethics and Professional Responsibility* (1982–date) reprints the unannotated rules for every state as well as the District of Columbia and Puerto Rico.

Annotated Model Rules of Professional Conduct (6th ed. 2007) provides the text of the ABA rules with comments, legal background, and notes of decisions from various jurisdictions. Although it contains the ABA's rules rather than those adopted in any specific state, this is a useful source for comparative analysis and commentary. The annotated Model Rules are available online from Westlaw (ABA–AMRPC); Lexis has the Model Rules with official comments but no background notes or annotations.

The American Law Institute has also formulated basic rules of legal ethics in its *Restatement of the Law: The Law Governing Lawyers* (2000), employing the standard Restatement format of black-letter provisions, comments, and illustrations. The Model Rules and the *Restatement* have been compared in an ABA publication by Thomas D. Morgan, *Lawyer Law: Comparing the ABA Model Rules of Professional Conduct with the ALI Restatement (Third) of the Law Governing Lawyers* (2005). The *Restatement* is available on both Westlaw (REST–LGOVL) and Lexis, and *Lawyer Law* is on Westlaw (ABA–LAWYL).

Ethics Opinions. Ethics opinions, generally prepared in response to inquiries from attorneys, are issued by the American Bar Association and by state and local bar associations. ABA opinions are available on Westlaw and Lexis, as are opinions from selected state and local bars. Ethics opinions can also be found in the *National Reporter on Legal Ethics and Professional Responsibility*, and most state bars have publications either summarizing their opinions or reprinting them in full text. Links to ethics opinions on state bar websites are available in the American Legal Ethics Library's listing by jurisdiction <www.law.cornell.edu/ethics/listing. html>.

Secondary Sources. The leading modern treatise on legal ethics practice under the Model Rules is probably Geoffrey C. Hazard, Jr. & W. William Hodes, *The Law of Lawyering* (3d ed. 2000–date), a two-volume set designed as a workbook "for lawyers faced with immediate practical dilemmas." A slightly less extensive work by Ronald D. Rotunda & John S. Dzienkowski, *Legal Ethics: The Lawyer's Deskbook on Professional Responsibility* (annual) also provides commentary on the Model Rules, and is available on Westlaw as the LEGETH database.

The *ABA/BNA Lawyers' Manual on Professional Conduct* (1984–date) is often a good place to begin research. This looseleaf service includes an extensive commentary with background and practical tips, as well as news of developments and abstracts of new decisions. It consists of three parts: a looseleaf manual of basic doctrine, several volumes providing summaries or full text of ethics opinions, and a biweekly newsletter of current developments.

Judicial Conduct. Judges are governed by a separate set of rules, based in almost every jurisdiction on the ABA's Model Code of Judicial Conduct. The latest edition was promulgated by the ABA in 2007, but most states' rules are based on its 1990 predecessor. The ABA Center for Professional Responsibility <www.abanet.org/ cpr/judicial/> provides access to both versions of the Model Code, as well as background documents and state judicial ethics resources.

Links to state judicial conduct codes and related materials are also provided by Cornell's American Legal Ethics Library, and judicial conduct rules are generally published in state court rules pamphlets and available in the court rules databases on Westlaw and Lexis. The ABA has published an *Annotated Model Code of Judicial Conduct* (2004), and James J. Alfini et al., *Judicial Conduct and Ethics* (4th ed. 2007), provides extensive analysis of issues in this area.

§ 9.3 Records and Briefs

The materials submitted by the parties in appellate court cases are often available for research use. Briefs are the written arguments and authorities cited by the attorneys for the parties on appeal. Records are documents from the lower court proceeding, including pleadings, motions, trial transcripts, and judgments, usually reprinted as an appendix to the briefs. Records and briefs are usually filed by the docket number of the case in which they were submitted. These documents enable researchers to study in detail the arguments and facts of significant decisions.

Supreme Court Briefs. As might be expected, briefs from United States Supreme Court cases are the most widely available. They are often the most voluminous as well. In addition to petitions for certiorari, oppositions to petitions, and the parties' briefs on the merits, many cases also have numerous filings by *amici curiae* ("friends of the court") supporting one side or the other.

In its first decade the Supreme Court adopted a rule requiring that counsel submit "a statement of the material points of the

Case."[24] Very few briefs survive from the Court's early cases, even after the rule was strengthened in 1821 to require "a printed brief or abstract of the cause, containing ... the points of law and fact intended to be presented at the argument."[25] Some briefs before 1832 are available in the Court's case files at the National Archives, but for most cases none are available.[26]

After 1831 a new Supreme Court rule required the records of its cases be printed.[27] Although collections from the early years remain incomplete, the availability of briefs gradually increases. Most large law libraries have records and briefs back to 1832 in microform, and a few libraries around the country even have printed collections.[28]

Retrospective electronic coverage is offered by Gale's The Making of Modern Law: U.S. Supreme Court Records and Briefs, 1832–1978 <www.gale.cengage.com/SupremeCourt/>. This searchable collection contains more than 200,000 documents, including appendices and other filings as well as petitions and briefs.

One of the most convenient printed sources for briefs in major cases is *Landmark Briefs and Arguments of the Supreme Court of the United States: Constitutional Law* (1975–date), which covers hundreds of significant decisions dating back to the 19th century. Cases through the 1973 term are covered in the first eighty volumes of this set, and about a dozen new cases are added each year.

24. "Ordered, That the Gentlemen of the Bar be notified, that the Court will hereafter expect to be furnished with a statement of the material points of the Case, from the Counsel on each side of a Cause." Rules, Supreme Court of the United States, February Term, 1795, 3 U.S. (3 Dall.) 120, 120 (1795).

25. Rule XXX, General Rules, February Term, 1821, 19 U.S. (6 Wheat.) v, v (1821).

26. Michael McReynolds, *Documentary Sources for the Study of U.S. Supreme Court Litigation: Part III—Materials in the National Archives*, 69 Law Libr. J. 448, 449 (1976). Another problem with early Supreme Court records is that its clerk's office had five fires in the 19th century, culminating in an 1898 gas explosion that destroyed many of the Court's original documents. James R. Browning & Bess Glenn, *The Supreme Court Collection at the National Ar-*

chives, 4 Am. J. Legal Hist. 241, 243 (1960).

For more information on the use of briefs in the early Supreme Court, see R. Kirkland Cozine, *The Emergence of Written Appellate Briefs in the Nineteenth-Century United States*, 38 Am. J. Legal Hist. 482 (1994).

27. Rules and Orders of the Supreme Court of the United States, 30 U.S. (5 Pet.) [vii] (1831).

28. Libraries with Supreme Court records and briefs in paper or microform are listed geographically in Michael Whiteman & Peter Scott Campbell, A Union List of Appellate Court Records and Briefs: Federal and State (1999). The libraries that receive printed briefs are listed in a document on the Court's website, "Where to Find Briefs of the Supreme Court of the U.S." <www.supremecourtus.gov/oral_arguments/briefsource.pdf>.

Briefs in recent Supreme Court cases are widely available from free and subscription websites. Free sources for cases that have been decided on the merits or are scheduled for oral argument include FindLaw <supreme.lp.findlaw.com>, which has certiorari petitions, the parties' merits briefs, and amicus briefs back to 1999 in PDF, and the American Bar Association <www.abanet.org/publiced/preview/>, with merits and amicus briefs for the current term and merits briefs for earlier terms back to 2003.

Westlaw's SCT–BRIEF–ALL database includes full coverage of merits briefs back to 1990 and amicus briefs since 1995, as well as certiorari petitions since 1990 in cases granted review and since 1995 in cases denied review. The database also includes briefs from selected historical cases back as far as 1870. Lexis has briefs for cases granted review since 1979, as well as selected petitions for writs of certiorari.

Supreme Court Oral Arguments. Transcripts of Supreme Court oral arguments are also available in various formats. Microform collections begin with the 1953 term, and online coverage starts in 1979 (Lexis) or 1990 (Westlaw, SCT–ORALARG). The Supreme Court website <www.supremecourtus.gov> provides PDF transcripts of arguments the same day that cases are heard, with older arguments beginning with the 2000 term.

Transcripts have been officially prepared on a regular basis since 1968. Earlier transcripts for some cases back to 1935 were prepared privately by shorthand reporters, and more than 100 pre–1953 transcripts are held by the Supreme Court Library.[29] Arguments in major cases, if transcribed, are available in *Landmark Briefs and Arguments of the Supreme Court of the United States: Constitutional Law*.

One frustration with older oral argument transcripts is that until 2004, justices were not identified by name but only by the word "Question." Some lawyers who frequently argued before the Court made a point of prefacing their answer with the name of the justice, but in many instances the identity of the speaker is unclear from the transcript. This changed in September 2004 when the Court announced that transcripts would begin finally to identify justices by name.[30]

---

29. Alice I. Youmans et al., *Questions and Answers*, 78 Law Libr. J. 203, 206 (1986).

30. Oral Argument Transcripts, press release, Supreme Court of the United States, Sept. 28, 2004 <www.supremecourtus.gov/publicinfo/press/pr_09–28–04.html>.

The National Archives has audio records of oral arguments back to 1955, although some of its tapes have deteriorated and are not available to the public.[31] Oyez: U.S. Supreme Court Media <www.oyez.org> provides access to these recorded arguments in several hundred cases, in most instances accompanied by a copy of the transcript.

In Supreme Court cases in which full argument transcripts are unavailable, excerpts can often be found in contemporary newspaper accounts. One of the most thorough sources for information on arguments since the 1930s is *The United States Law Week*, BNA's weekly newsletter on the Court's activities, which provides extensive coverage of about two dozen arguments each term.

Other Appellate Courts. Records and briefs of the U.S. Courts of Appeals and state appellate courts are not as widely available as those from the U.S. Supreme Court. The most extensive source is Westlaw (BRIEF–ALL, and separate files for individual jurisdictions), with nationwide coverage of federal and state appellate courts. Briefs as far back as the 1970s for some federal circuits are available, while for state courts the starting date can be as late as 2007. Clicking on the *i* icon to check the scope of coverage, a good idea with any database, is particularly important with new and developing resources such as these.

Lexis also provides brief databases as part of its "Briefs, Motions, Pleadings & Verdicts" folder. It has a combined file of all available federal and state briefs and motions, as well as files for specific jurisdictions and practice areas. Coverage generally begins in 2000 but is not comprehensive.

Some court websites also provide access to recent briefs. For federal courts, the fee-based information system PACER (Public Access to Court Electronic Records) provides some briefs and other documents as well as docket information. Each court has its own PACER site, but the system has a central site <pacer.psc.uscourts.gov> for registration and links to the individual courts' sites.

Access to briefs on state appellate court websites is less advanced and systematic than it is for federal court briefs.[32] Only about a dozen state court websites provide access to briefs, but the list is growing. Sites for state briefs are listed, with links and tips on finding the briefs, in Michael Whiteman's regularly updated LLRX.com feature "Free and Fee Based Appellate Court Briefs Online" <www.llrx.com/features/briefsonline.htm>.[33]

---

31. "Audio at the National Archives," <www.oyez.org/about/>.

32. See Michael Whiteman, *Appellate Court Briefs on the Web: Electronic*

Dynamos or Legal Quagmire?, 97 LAW LIBR. J. 467 (2005).

33. Some briefs are available on the Internet on non-court websites. Parties or *amici curiae* may post their briefs in

For most courts, appellate records and briefs can also be found in local law libraries within the circuit or state. In some instances, however, it may be necessary to contact the court or a judicial records center to obtain copies. Michael Whiteman & Peter Scott Campbell, *A Union List of Appellate Court Records and Briefs: Federal and State* (1999) provides contact information for libraries and court clerks, with notes indicating the scope and format of each library's holdings and its lending policy.

§ 9.4   Other Case Information

Appellate cases generally follow a standard path and produce documentation consisting of the parties' briefs, the lower court record, and the court's opinion. Material from trial court litigation can be much harder to identify and find. Some cases result in judges' opinions, such as a decision granting a motion for summary judgment, but many matters are decided without a written opinion. Cases can be decided by jury verdict, summary disposition, or settlement agreement. Some cases produce dozens of memoranda or briefs submitted to support or oppose motions before, during and after trial, while others go to trial without any written submissions on points of law. A trial transcript, if available, can be an essential source of information.

The initial access point for information about trial documents is a case's docket sheet, which lists the proceedings and documents filed in chronological order. Docket sheets increasingly are available online, particularly for federal courts, and a growing number of courts provide online access to trial documents as well. Even if docket sheets and trial documents are not available directly from court websites, many are available from fee-based online services.

If electronic access is unavailable, you may need to contact the court directly to obtain a copy of a transcript or other documents. Determining the docket number or case number is usually the first step in obtaining documents. This number may be mentioned in a published decision or secondary source, but you may have to ask the court clerk to consult an index by party name.

Information on trial verdicts and damage awards, primarily for various types of tort litigation, is available in services known as *verdict reporters*. These generally provide a brief summary of the case's facts and claims, list attorneys and expert witnesses for each

major cases, and high profile documents are often available from sites such as FindLaw <www.findlaw.com> or CNN <www.cnn.com>. Several organizations and government agencies provide access to briefs they have filed in the Supreme Court and in other appellate courts. One of the most extensive collections is briefs filed by Solicitor General, with selected coverage back to 1982 <www.usdoj.gov/osg/briefs/search.html>. Whiteman's "Free and Fee Based Appellate Court Briefs Online" on LLRX.com provides links to a number of potential brief sites.

side, and report the resulting verdict. The account of a case rarely provides much detail, but in the absence of any published opinions it may be the best available record of a case's background and outcome. The best known of these reporters include several publications from Jury Verdict Research <www.juryverdictreseach.com> and the monthly newsletter *Verdicts, Settlements & Tactics*. Westlaw and Lexis both have several verdict databases, including some limited to individual states or specialized areas of law as well as the comprehensive JV–NAT (Jury Verdicts–National) on Westlaw and "Jury Verdicts and Settlements, Combined" on Lexis.

Supreme Court. Docket information for current Supreme Court cases is available online for free from the Court's website <www.supremecourtus.gov/docket/docket.html>. For each case, the docket provides a chronological listing of documents filed and actions taken as well as contact information for the parties' attorneys. There are no links to briefs or other documents, however, except for pages providing the questions presented in cases granted review.

Information on the Supreme Court's docket is also available through *The United States Law Week*, which publishes a record of proceedings and provides reports on arguments and other developments. *Law Week*'s Supreme Court binder includes a Topical Index and Table of Cases, which lists docket numbers for cases before the Court, and a Case Status Report table listing cases by docket number and providing references to developments. *U.S. Law Week* is also available online as a subscription-based Internet service <www.bna.com/products/lit/uslw.htm>. The *Supreme Court Today* section of the site provides several ways to track Supreme Court cases and is regularly updated with new decisions, filings, and other developments.

Other Federal Courts. For recent cases in federal court, access to docket sheet information is generally available electronically. The federal courts' PACER system (Public Access to Court Electronic Records) covers each of the U.S. District Courts and Bankruptcy Courts, as well as the Courts of Appeals. Each court in the federal system has its own PACER or CM/ECF (Case Management/Electronic Case Files) site. As electronic filing of case documents becomes the norm, pleadings, motions, and orders are increasingly available through PACER or CM/ECF sites along with docket information. Cases can be found by docket number or by parties' or attorneys' names. Registration is required, and there is a per-page charge to view docket sheets or documents other than opinions. The system has a central registration site <pacer.psc.uscourts.gov>, and a nationwide U.S. Party/Case Index <pacer.

uspci.uscourts.gov> that links directly to the docket sheets on individual courts' sites.[34]

For cases since 2000, Westlaw has an extensive collection of pleadings, memoranda, and trial motions from both federal and state courts. The FILING–ALL file combines pleadings, motions and other filings from all available courts, and more specific files are available for individual courts, specific types of filings, and particular subject areas.

Westlaw also has docket databases monitoring information in the federal courts and in some state courts. These databases, including DOCK–ALL combining federal and state dockets, provide a broader range of search options than official sites, and individual dockets can be tracked for e-mail notification of new developments.

Westlaw also has a separate service, CourtExpress, that enhances the online coverage with the option to order documents directly from the courts. Lexis has a similar service, CourtLink <courtlink.lexisnexis.com>, that also provides convenient and current access to docket information and documents. Both of these products provide several features unavailable through the official PACER system.[35]

State Courts. While docket sheets and court filings for some state courts are available online, for others this information may be more difficult to obtain. Most states have electronic docket systems, but means of access vary.[36] Dockets and filings for most states are now available through Westlaw, and this coverage continues to expand.

Courtport <www.courtport.com> is a subscription-based portal (free to academic users) with thousands of links to official court sites for case information and public records. The National Center for State Courts maintains a Public Access to Court Records: State Links site <www.ncsconline.org/WC/CourTopics/statelinks.asp?id= 62>, a shorter state-by-state list with brief annotations of contents. Both online and traditional access methods are explained in *The Sourcebook to Public Record Information: The Comprehensive Guide to County, State, & Federal Public Records Sources* (annual).

---

34. Open-government activists have been working to make the federal court records in PACER available online for free. See John Schwartz, *An Effort to Upgrade a Court Archive System to Free and Easy*, N.Y. Times, Feb. 13, 2009, at A16.

35. Warner J. Miller, *Trial Court Docket Research Tools*, Legal Info. Alert, July/Aug. 2007, at 1, provides an extensive analysis of available resources, particularly CourtExpress and CourtLink.

36. For a discussion of problems in access to state court docket information, see Peter W. Martin, *Online Access to Court Records—From Documents to Data, Particulars to Patterns* 15–25 (Cornell Law School research paper No. 08–003), *available at* http://papers.ssrn. com/abstract=1107412.

§ 9.5   Directories of Courts and Judges

Court directories serve a number of purposes. They provide contact information for clerks' offices, and some include judges' biographical data. This can be useful information for litigants appearing before a particular judge or panel, and for law students applying for clerkships after graduation.[37]

Court websites, which usually include judges' names and contact data as well as some brief biographical information, are accessible through portals such as the "Court Locator" section of the federal judiciary homepage <www.uscourts.gov/courtlinks/> or the National Center for State Courts list of court websites <www.ncsconline.org/D_KIS/info_court_web_sites.html>.

Court sites, however, often provide less information than is available through unofficial directories. *Judicial Staff Directory* and *Judicial Yellow Book* (both semiannual) have basic biographical information for judges, as well as extensive listings of court personnel such as clerks and staff attorneys. Like other volumes in the Staff Directories and Yellow Books series, these are available electronically by subscription (<library.cqpress.com/jsd/> and <www.leadershipdirectories.com>) as well as in print. CQ Press's *Federal-State Court Directory* (annual) provides a more concise listing of contact information for federal judges, clerks, and other court personnel.

Almanac of the Federal Judiciary is a two-volume looseleaf publication with detailed biographical information on federal judges, including annotated listings of noteworthy rulings, summaries of media coverage, and anonymous quotations by lawyers evaluating judges' abilities and temperaments. Volume 1 of this set covers district, magistrate, and bankruptcy judges, and volume 2 covers circuit judges. The *Almanac* is available on Westlaw as the AFJ database.

Several directories cover both federal and state courts. *BNA's Directory of State and Federal Courts, Judges, and Clerks* (annual) provides contact information (including e-mail addresses for some judges and clerks), and has other useful features such as a list of court websites and a personal name index. *The American Bench* (annual) is the most comprehensive biographical source, covering almost every judge in the United States. It includes an alphabetical index of all judges listed.

Judicial Staff Directory and *Judicial Yellow Book* include coverage of state appellate courts but not trial courts, and *Federal-*

---

37. For students seeking clerkships with new judges, and for others monitoring the judicial appointment process, the Department of Justice provides a page listing nominations and confirmations <www.usdoj.gov/olp/nominations.htm> with links to biographical information on each nominee.

State Court Directory has just one page per state listing a few key officials. CQ Press provides more thorough coverage of state courts in its *Directory of State Court Clerks & County Courthouses* (annual).

Contact information for tribal courts is available in April Schwartz & Mary Jo B. Hunter, *United States Tribal Courts Directory* (2d ed. 2006), and online through the National Tribal Justice Resource Center <www.ntjrc.org/tribalcourts/>. Tribal judges are also listed in the American Bar Association's *Directory of Minority Judges of the United States* (4th ed. 2008), which also has sections listing African–American, Asian/Pacific Island, Hispanic, and Native American judges.

Sometimes information is needed about a judge involved in an older case or sitting on a particular court. If only the last name at the head of an opinion is known, the first step may be to determine a judge's full name. This can be found in tables in the front of most reporter volumes. Since 1882, for example, the *Federal Reporter* has listed the sitting federal judges, with footnotes indicating any deaths, retirements, or appointments since the previous volume. Similar listings appear in each of West's regional reporters and in most official state reports.

Biographical information on many appellate judges can be found in standard sources such as *American National Biography* (1999) or *Who Was Who in America* (1943–date). The Federal Judiciary Center maintains a Biographical Directory of Federal Judges <www.fjc.gov/public/home.nsf/hisj>, with information on all life-tenured federal judges since 1789. Entries include links to information about manuscript sources and lists of more extensive biographical sources, if available. A print version, *Biographical Directory of the Federal Judiciary, 1789–2000*, was published in 2001.

§ 9.6   Forms and Jury Instructions

Many basic transactions and court filings occur with regularity in the course of legal practice. Rather than redraft these documents each time, attorneys frequently work from sample versions of standard legal documents and instruments. Model forms are available from a variety of sources, in both printed collections and electronic products. Some sets of forms are annotated with discussion of the underlying laws, checklists of steps in completing the forms, and citations to cases in which the forms were in issue.

Several multi-volume compilations of forms are published. Some of these are comprehensive national works containing both procedural forms, such as complaints and motions, and transactional forms, such as contracts and wills. Most, however, are limited to particular jurisdictions or particular types of forms.

Two of the major national form sets are published as adjuncts to *American Jurisprudence 2d* and are linked to that encyclopedia by frequent cross-references. *American Jurisprudence Legal Forms 2d* (1971–date) provides forms of instruments such as contracts, leases, and wills, and *American Jurisprudence Pleading and Practice Forms* (rev ed., 1966–date) focuses on litigation and other practice before courts and administrative agencies. Both sets are divided into several hundred topical chapters mirroring the organization of *Am. Jur. 2d.*

Other comprehensive sets include Jacob Rabkin & Mark H. Johnson, *Current Legal Forms, with Tax Analysis* (1948–date), and *West's Legal Forms* (2d ed. 1981–date). Unlike the *Am. Jur.* sets, these are arranged by broad practice area such as estate planning or real estate. This makes them useful for developing an understanding of a wide range of related issues, as well as for finding forms on specific topics.

Three major sets devoted to forms used in federal practice are *Bender's Federal Practice Forms* (1951–date), *Federal Procedural Forms, Lawyers' Edition* (1975–date) and *West's Federal Forms* (1952–date). Each of these has a different structure. *Bender's Federal Practice Forms* is arranged by court rule. *Federal Procedural Forms, Lawyers' Edition* is a companion to West's encyclopedic *Federal Procedure, Lawyers' Edition*, and is organized similarly, with several dozen subject chapters. *West's Federal Forms* is arranged instead by court, with separate volumes covering forms needed in the Supreme Court, Courts of Appeals, District Courts, Bankruptcy Courts, and specialized national courts such as the Court of Federal Claims. *Federal Local Court Forms* (3d ed. 2002–date) contains forms for specific U.S. Courts of Appeals and District Courts.

Sets of forms, varying in complexity and size, are also published for most states and for particular subject areas. Some sets, such as *Bender's Forms of Discovery* (1963–date), are geared toward specific stages of litigation. Practice-oriented treatises and manuals frequently include appendices of sample forms, and compilations of official forms are published in some states.

Several sets of forms are available online and on CD–ROM, simplifying the drafting process by reducing the amount of text that needs to be entered. Lexis provides access to dozens of forms collections, including *Bender's Federal Practice Forms*, *Bender's Forms of Discovery*, and *Current Legal Forms*, as well as sets for several individual states. Westlaw has the two *Am. Jur.* form sets (AMJUR–LF and AMJUR–PP), *Federal Procedural Forms* (FED-PROF), and numerous state-specific collections, as well as two broad multi-jurisdictional databases, FORMS–ALL combining the various published sets and ALLFRMS with more than 45,000 official forms from federal and state courts and agencies. FORM-FINDER, accessible from a link at the top of every screen, covers a smaller number of titles but offers an extensive template on which you can choose one of four dozen topical areas and then specific subtopics, document types, and jurisdictions in which to search.

A more limited range of forms is available from free Internet sites, and some may be sufficient for simple transactions or court filings. Official forms from federal agencies are available through Forms.gov: The U.S. Government's Official Hub for Federal Forms <www.forms.gov>. LexisOne <www.lexisone.com> provides free access to more than 6,000 forms, listed topically and by jurisdiction. FindLaw <forms.lp.findlaw.com> has links to official sites for federal circuits and states, as well as an extensive list of sites providing free and fee-based legal forms. Before using any form, particularly one found at a free website, it is necessary to make sure that it conforms with the law of the jurisdiction.

Most jurisdictions have sets of *model* or *pattern jury instructions*, used by judges to explain the applicable law to jurors before they weigh the evidence and reach their decisions. Some of these are produced by state bar associations or judicial committees, while others are unofficial commercial publications. In some states model jury instructions are used by judges only as guides, but in others the instructions must be read verbatim if they are applicable.[38]

Model jury instructions are useful for researchers because they provide a concise summary of a jurisdiction's ruling law often accompanied by notes summarizing the leading cases. In a way, they can serve the same function as a *Restatement* or legal encyclopedia in outlining a state's basic legal doctrines.

Sets of jury instructions are published for every state, for several federal circuits, and for some specialized areas of litigation. The subject heading used by the Library of Congress and in most online catalogs for these sets is "Instructions to juries—[Jurisdiction]," and several states provide access to instructions on court or bar websites.[39] Most jurisdictions have separate publications for civil and criminal instructions.

---

38. Frederick D. (Rick) Williams, *Jury Instructions: A Primer for Young Lawyers*, For the Def., Jan. 1996, at 28, provides a brief, useful introduction to the use of instructions in litigation.

39. A pair of online articles by Margi Heinen & Jan Bissett provide convenient lists of state sources: *Reference from Coast to Coast—Revisiting Jury Instructions (Part 1)—Alabama Through Mississippi*, LLRX.com (June 17, 2002) <www.llrx.com/columns/reference38.htm>, and *Reference from Coast to Coast—Revisiting Jury Instructions (Part 2)—Missouri through Wyoming*, LLRX.com (July 15, 2002) <www.llrx.com/columns/reference39.htm>. For free online sources, Heinen and Bissett updated their links in *Reference from Coast to Coast: Jury Instructions Update*, LLRX.com (July 27, 2007) <www.llrx.com/columns/reference53.htm>.

Some sets of pattern instructions are available for the courts in individual federal circuits, but there is no general set of officially approved jury instructions for the federal courts. There are, however, two sets of commercially published, unofficial instructions covering both criminal and civil cases. Kevin F. O'Malley et al., *Federal Jury Practice and Instructions* (5th & 6th ed. 2000–date) is an extensive and respected collection with explanatory comments and notes of relevant cases. Leonard B. Sand et al., *Modern Federal Jury Instructions* (1984–date) is a similar work, consisting of sample instructions, comments, and case notes.

Both Westlaw and Lexis include instructions for federal courts and for several states. Westlaw has *Federal Jury Practice and Instructions* (FED–JI) and publications for about thirty states, while Lexis provides the competing *Modern Federal Jury Instructions* and instructions for about twenty states. Westlaw also has a combined JI–ALL database, and databases of actual jury instruction filings submitted in recent cases.

Chapter 10

SECONDARY SOURCES, PART 1: ENCYCLOPEDIAS, RESTATEMENTS, AND TEXTS

Table of Sections

While primary sources of law such as legislative enactments and judicial decisions determine legal rights and govern procedures, these can be notoriously difficult places to find answers. It is generally best to begin a research project by looking first for an overview and analysis written by a lawyer or legal scholar. This chapter and the next cover the major secondary source materials of American law—the encyclopedias, texts, and journal articles that provide background information and attempt to synthesize the mass of conflicting primary sources into a coherent body of doctrine.

Law reviews, to be discussed in Chapter 11, are where much of academic legal theory is published. The materials covered in this chapter serve the more straightforward purpose of explaining legal concepts, providing the context necessary to see how a particular issue relates to other concerns. They can serve as an introduction to a new area of law or refresh your recollection of a familiar area.

An important feature of most secondary sources is that they provide references to the primary sources which are the essential next step in most research. Texts and articles discuss the relevant cases and statutes, and contain extensive footnotes to these and other sources. These notes can provide a more coherent and sophisticated presentation of the primary sources than if you start with your own keyword search or a collection of headnotes in an annotated code or digest.

§ 10.1   Overviews and Interdisciplinary Encyclopedias

Even basic legal texts can be daunting to someone new to legal research generally or to a particular area of law. For a start in understanding and analyzing an issue, it may be helpful to begin with resources written for a more general audience.

Several works provide a broad outline of the American legal system, including *Fundamentals of American Law* (Alan B. Morrison ed., 1996) and E. Allan Farnsworth, *An Introduction to the Legal System of the United States* (3d ed. 1996). These explain common legal concepts and procedures, survey doctrinal areas such as contract law, corporations, and labor law, and provide references to major cases and other sources. Farnsworth's book is quite short, but it includes "Suggested Readings" of basic texts in each area it discusses.

Oxford Companion to American Law (Kermit L. Hall ed., 2002) is a one-volume work covering a broad range of major legal concepts, institutions, cases, and historical figures, with most articles accompanied by references for further reading. *The New Oxford Companion to Law* (Peter Cane & Joanne Conaghan eds., 2008) focuses on British institutions and legal history, but it also covers American and general topics and contains a great deal of useful information on legal history and our common law heritage.

Encyclopedic works for a general audience such as *Encyclopedia of American Law* (David Schultz ed., 2002) or *The U.S. Legal System* (Timothy L. Hall ed., 2004) provide a basic introduction to legal issues. Somewhat more comprehensive coverage is provided by *West's Encyclopedia of American Law* (2d ed. 2005, supplemented by an annual *American Law Yearbook*). *West's Encyclopedia* has some 5,000 entries, including articles on basic legal doctrines and terminology, major court decisions, government agencies, and influential jurists and lawyers. Its articles are a mix of legal theory, history, and politics. Volume 9, for example, includes biographies of Phyllis Schlafly and O.J. Simpson as well as overviews of Securities, Sex Discrimination, and Stare Decisis. Some articles cite one or two primary sources and include brief bibliographies, but generally they are rather short and provide too few research leads.

Greater depth is provided by interdisciplinary encyclopedias focusing on specific topics. These include several well-respected works with contributions from legal scholars as well as historians and political scientists. Works on constitutional law, such as *Encyclopedia of the American Constitution* (Leonard W. Levy & Kenneth

L. Karst eds., 2d ed. 2000) and *The Oxford Companion to the Supreme Court* (Kermit L. Hall ed., 2d ed. 2005), were discussed in Chapter 2, at page 32.

The fields of criminal law, criminology and criminal justice have several encyclopedic works with overlapping coverage. *Encyclopedia of Crime and Justice* (Joshua Dressler ed., 2d ed. 2002), is one of the most wide-ranging and highly respected of these works, with extensive articles on both legal and behavioral aspects of criminal and law enforcement activity.[1] Other titles include:

Encyclopedia of Crime and Punishment (David Levinson ed., 2002)

Encyclopedia of Criminology and Deviant Behavior (Clifton D. Bryant ed., 2001)

Encyclopedia of Forensic Sciences (Jay A. Siegel ed., 2000)

Encyclopedia of Law Enforcement (Larry E. Sullivan & Marie Simonetti Rosen eds., 2005)

Encyclopedia of Prisons and Correctional Facilities (Mary Bosworth ed., 2005)

Encyclopedia of White–Collar and Corporate Crime (Lawrence M. Salinger ed., 2005)

Several other interdisciplinary encyclopedias are expressly focused on law-related issues, while others provide more general perspectives of ethical or societal concerns. The following works all contain extensive coverage of legal topics:

Civil Rights in the United States (Waldo E. Martin Jr. & Patricia Sullivan eds., 2000)

Encyclopedia of American Civil Liberties (Paul Finkelman ed., 2006)

Encyclopedia of Applied Ethics (Ruth Chadwick ed., 1998)

Encyclopedia of Bioethics (Stephen G. Post ed., 3d ed. 2004)

Encyclopedia of Business Ethics and Society (Robert W. Kolb ed., 2008)

Encyclopedia of Civil Rights in America (David Bradley & Shelley Fisher Fishkin eds., 1998)

Encyclopedia of Disability (Gary L. Albrecht ed., 2005)

---

1. The current Chief Justice of the Wisconsin Supreme Court noted in a review of the first edition that she "expected to find the articles ... simplistic and unsatisfactory for the legal specialist," but ended up recommending the work to her clerks "for its value in providing an overview and a starting point for research." Shirley S. Abrahamson, *Some Enlightenment on Crime*, 83 MICH. L. REV. 1157, 1163 (1985) (reviewing ENCYCLOPEDIA OF CRIME AND JUSTICE (Sanford H. Kadish ed., 1983)).

Encyclopedia of Education Law (Charles J. Russo ed., 2008)

Encyclopedia of Environment and Society (Paul Robbins ed., 2007)

Encyclopedia of Ethics (Lawrence C. Becker & Charlotte B. Becker eds., 2d ed. 2001)

Encyclopedia of Law and Society (David S. Clark ed., 2007)

Encyclopedia of Legal and Forensic Medicine (Jason Payne–James et al. eds., 2005)

Encyclopedia of Marriage and the Family (David Levinson ed., 1995)

Encyclopedia of Psychology and Law (Brian L. Cutler ed., 2008)

Encyclopedia of Public Administration and Public Policy (Evan M. Berman ed., 2d ed. 2008)

Encyclopedia of Science, Technology, and Ethics (Carl Mitcham ed., 2005)

International Encyclopedia of the Social and Behavioral Sciences (Neil J. Smelser & Paul B. Baltes eds., 2001)

International Encyclopedia of the Social Sciences (William A. Darity, Jr. ed., 2d ed. 2008)

New Palgrave Dictionary of Economics and the Law (Peter Newman ed., 1998)

Religion and the Law in America: An Encyclopedia of Personal Belief and Public Policy (Scott A. Merriman ed., 2007)

Works such as these provide background information on legal issues, and can place these issues in a broader social or historical context. They generally will not, however, answer specific questions about particular legal situations, and they contain relatively few references to the primary sources needed for thorough research. For more detailed coverage, we must turn to works designed specifically for lawyers and law students.

§ 10.2 Legal Encyclopedias

"Legal encyclopedia" is a term with a very specific meaning. It is not simply a general encyclopedia about legal topics (such as *West's Encyclopedia of American Law*), but a work that attempts to describe systematically and exhaustively the entire body of a jurisdiction's legal doctrine. Two legal encyclopedias attempt to cover all of American law, while others focus on the jurisprudence of individual states.

Articles in a legal encyclopedia are arranged alphabetically, but they are generally not on topics as specific as DNA evidence or summary judgment. A typical legal encyclopedia has only about four hundred articles, roughly mirroring the number of topics of the West key number system. Some articles cover very broad doctrinal areas such as corporations or evidence and are subdivided into hundreds or thousands of numbered sections.

Legal encyclopedias are relatively easy to use and provide straightforward summaries of the law, but in most instances their perspective is quite limited. The articles tend to emphasize case law and neglect statutes and regulations, and they rarely examine the historical or public policy aspects of the rules they discuss. Unlike law review articles or scholarly treatises, they simply summarize legal doctrine without criticism or suggestions for improvement. Encyclopedias also tend to be relatively slow to reflect changes in the law or to cover significant trends in developing areas.

At one time legal encyclopedias were viewed as serious and reliable statements of law and were frequently cited by the courts. Today, however, they are generally not viewed as persuasive secondary authority but as introductory surveys and as sources for extensive citations to judicial decisions.

(a) *American Jurisprudence 2d* and *Corpus Juris Secundum*

Two national legal encyclopedias were once competing works but are now both published by Thomson West: *American Jurisprudence 2d (Am. Jur. 2d)* and *Corpus Juris Secundum (C.J.S.)*.[2] Each of these sets contains more than 140 volumes, with alphabetically arranged articles on topics from abandoned property to zoning. Each article is divided into numbered sections, and begins with a section-by-section outline of its contents and an explanation of its scope.

Both *Am. Jur. 2d* and *C.J.S.* explain doctrinal concepts and provide references to cases and other sources. The two works are quite similar, but there are some differences. In *C.J.S.*, but not *Am. Jur. 2d*, each section or subsection begins with a concise "black letter" statement of the general legal principle. The discussion in *Am. Jur. 2d* tends to focus a bit more on federal law, while *C.J.S.* seeks to provide an overall synthesis of state law. *Am. Jur. 2d* is generally viewed as more accessible, while *C.J.S.* is a bit more comprehensive. Until the 1980s, in fact, *C.J.S.* claimed to represent "the entire American law as developed by all reported cases";

---

2. *Am. Jur. 2d* began publication in 1962 and superseded *American Jurisprudence* (1936–60), which had in turn superseded *its* predecessor, *Ruling Case Law* (1914–31). *C.J.S.* began publication in 1936 and superseded *Corpus Juris* (1911–37). These older encyclopedias may still be of value in historical research, as may even earlier works such as *American and English Encyclopedia of Law* (1887–96). All of these older works are available online as part of Westlaw's Rise of American Law database.

recently published volumes are more selective and are instead "a contemporary statement of American law as derived from reported cases and legislation."

Am. Jur. 2d and *C.J.S.* include extensive footnotes to illustrative cases from around the country. A cited decision from your jurisdiction is obviously the most useful, but almost any case can be used as a springboard to further research. Both encyclopedias provide relevant West key numbers, before each section in most articles, which can also be used to find cases on Westlaw or in West digests. *Am. Jur. 2d* also includes references to *American Law Reports (ALR)* annotations, which describe and analyze cases on specific topics. (Key numbers, digests and *ALR* are discussed in Chapter 8 on case research.)

Illustrations 10–1 and 10–2 on pages 353–354 show pages from the *Am. Jur. 2d* and *C.J.S.* Trusts articles, discussing the application of the Statute of Frauds to trusts. While both encyclopedias list numerous cases to support their text, there is no overlap between the cases cited. Both works list relevant West key numbers, and *Am. Jur. 2d* also cites related material in other reference works.

Although both *Am. Jur. 2d* and *C.J.S.* provide copious footnotes to court decisions, neither work cites any state statutes. Even when expressly discussing state statutory provisions, the footnotes refer to cases that cite these statutes. The focus is squarely on case law, although both works do cite federal statutes and uniform laws.

Volumes in both sets are updated annually with pocket part supplements providing notes of new developments, and each encyclopedia publishes several revised volumes each year. In the instance of Illustrations 10–1 and 10–2, the *Am. Jur. 2d* volume was published in 2005 while the *C.J.S.* volume dates from 2002. Some volumes are several years older than these and may reflect outdated trends or cite cases that are no longer good law. As with any other source, updating is essential to ensure that you are relying on current information.

The basic means of access to the encyclopedias are the multivolume softcover indexes published annually for each set. The indexes are very detailed and extensive, but finding the right section can require patience and flexibility. You may need to rethink your search terms or to follow cross-references to other headings. Each encyclopedia also includes a tables volume listing the federal statutes, regulations, court rules, and uniform laws it discusses, and *C.J.S.* has a multi-volume table of cited cases.

Westlaw provides access to both encyclopedias in its AMJUR and CJS databases, while *Am. Jur. 2d* is also available through Lexis and on CD–ROM. The electronic versions include tables of contents and article outlines, making it possible to see how a particular section fits in a broader context. You can begin by browsing through the table of contents, use checkboxes to restrict a search to specific articles or sections, and link from a displayed section to its place in the outline for its article.

The online encyclopedias do not include the indexes, so restricting a keyword search to terms used in section headings may be the most productive way to focus in on relevant material. Westlaw uses the fields *pr* or *prelim* for the topic and subdivision headings, and *ti* or *title* for individual section headings. On Lexis, you can choose to search only the table of contents and then link from the list of headings to the full text. A natural language search, which ranks documents by relevance rather than age, can also be effective with resources such as encyclopedias in which all documents are updated annually.

The print version of *Am. Jur. 2d* is often shelved with several related publications. The *Am. Jur. Deskbook* provides a variety of reference information for lawyers, such as historical documents, government agency information, statistics, and financial tables. Several multi-volume adjunct sets to *Am. Jur. 2d* are also published, some focusing on trial preparation and practice (*Am. Jur. Trials* and *Am. Jur. Proof of Facts*) and others providing legal forms (*Am. Jur. Legal Forms 2d* and *Am. Jur. Pleading and Practice Forms*). These sets are also available on Westlaw and CD–ROM.

Am. Jur. 2d and *C.J.S.* are both included as citing sources in KeyCite, so any case or federal statute that is cited in the encyclopedia will include the title of the section in its KeyCite display. Shepard's on Lexis covers other secondary sources, but not these national encyclopedias.

(b) Jurisdictional Encyclopedias

Several states have multi-volume encyclopedias specifically focusing on the law of their jurisdictions. While not generally viewed as authoritative, state encyclopedias can provide both a good general overview of state law and extensive footnotes to primary sources. Unlike *Am. Jur. 2d* and *C.J.S.*, they include references to state statutes and often do a better job than the national encyclopedias of integrating treatment of statutory and case law. Their treatment of jurisdictionally specific concepts, such as community property or oil and gas law, can be particularly useful.

Only sixteen states have their own legal encyclopedias, but these are generally jurisdictions with the largest populations and the most lawyers. Depending on its publisher, each state encyclopedia is available through either Westlaw or Lexis as well as in print. The following list indicates Westlaw databases; Lexis encyclopedias can be found with other state materials or in the Secondary Legal / Jurisprudences, ALR & Encyclopedias folder:

California Jurisprudence 3d (West, CAJUR)

Florida Jurisprudence 2d (West, FLJUR)

Illinois Law and Practice (West, IL–LP)

Indiana Law Encyclopedia (West, IN–ENC)

Maryland Law and Practice (West, MD–ENC)

Michigan Civil Jurisprudence (West, MIJUR)

Michigan Law and Practice, 2d ed. (LexisNexis)

Dunnell Minnesota Digest (LexisNexis)

New York Jurisprudence 2d (West, NYJUR)

Strong's North Carolina Index 4th (West, NCINDEX)

Ohio Jurisprudence 3d (West, OHJUR)

Pennsylvania Law Encyclopedia (LexisNexis)

South Carolina Jurisprudence (West, SCJUR)

Tennessee Jurisprudence (LexisNexis)

Texas Jurisprudence 2d (West, TXJUR)

Michie's Jurisprudence of Virginia and West Virginia (Lexis-Nexis)

Some of these works are called *Encyclopedia*, while others are entitled *Jurisprudence*. To confuse matters further, Minnesota' encyclopedia is a *Digest* and North Carolina's is an *Index*. Despite these titles, each of these works is a comprehensive summary of its state's legal doctrine, organized like *Am. Jur. 2d* or *C.J.S.* into several hundred alphabetically arranged articles and regularly updated by annual supplements and revised volumes.

Many states have other reference works with extensive coverage of their law, although not necessarily made up of alphabetically arranged articles like the national encyclopedias. Sets such as *Kentucky Jurisprudence* and *New Jersey Practice*, for example, contain separate volumes for doctrinal areas such as criminal procedure, domestic relations, and evidence. They may not cover all legal topics comprehensively, but they do address most major areas. The state research guides listed in Chapter 12 on pages 392–398 can help you identify available resources.

West Group also publishes an encyclopedia focusing specifically on federal law, *Federal Procedure, Lawyers' Edition* (available on Westlaw as the FEDPROC database). It emphasizes procedural issues in civil, criminal and administrative proceedings, but many of its eighty chapters also discuss matters of substantive federal law. Because it deals exclusively with federal law rather than attempting to generalize about fifty state jurisdictions, it is often more precise and useful than *C.J.S.* or *Am. Jur. 2d* and includes helpful pointers for federal practice.

§ 10.3   *Restatements of the Law*

Encyclopedias seek to summarize and define American legal doctrine. A series produced by the American Law Institute (ALI) known as *Restatements of the Law* has a similar purpose, but it is produced by leading scholars and is more highly regarded by the courts.

The ALI was founded in 1923 and now has some 3,000 members, consisting of leading judges, lawyers and law teachers. The organization's purposes, according to its certificate of incorporation, are "to promote the clarification and simplification of the law and its better adaptation to social needs" and "to secure the better administration of justice."[3] The primary vehicles for achieving these goals are the *Restatements*, a series that attempts to articulate the basic doctrines governing American law. The *Restatements* are useful both for students learning legal rules and for lawyers seeking to apply those rules to issues arising in practice.

Each *Restatement* covers a distinct area of law. The first series of *Restatements* was published between 1932 and 1944, and covered nine areas of law: *Agency, Conflict of Laws, Contracts, Judgments, Property, Restitution, Security, Torts,* and *Trusts.* An updated series of *Restatements of the Law (Second)* was issued between 1958 and 1992 for all the original topics except restitution and security, as well as *Foreign Relations Law.* The ALI began working on *Restatement of the Law (Third)* in 1978, and has published several volumes in this series: *Agency* (2006), *Foreign Relations Law* (1987), *The Law Governing Lawyers* (2000), *Property–Mortgages* (1997), *Property–Servitudes* (2000), *Property–Wills and Other Donative Transfers* (vols. 1–2, 1999–2003), *Suretyship and Guaranty* (1996), *Torts–Apportionment of Liability* (2000), *Torts–Products Liability* (1998), *Trusts* (vols. 1–3, 2003–07), and *Unfair Competition* (1995),

The *Restatement* Format. A *Restatement* is divided into chapters, each examining a major aspect of the field. Most chapters are then divided into topics and titles, and finally into numbered sections, each of which deals with a general principle of law. A section contains a concise "black letter" statement of law, followed by explanatory comments and illustrations of particular examples of the general proposition. The comments and illustrations are in

---

3. American Law Institute, Certificate of Incorporation, Feb. 23, 1923   <www.ali.org/doc/charter.pdf>.

turn followed by Reporter's Notes with background information on the development of the section.[4]

The section numbering is continuous throughout each *Restatement*, so only the section number is included in a citation. Illustration 10–3 on page 355 shows *Restatement (Third) of Trusts* § 20 (2003) and its use of black-letter rule, comment, and illustration.

The *Restatement* Process. *Restatements* go through an elaborate drafting procedure. Once a project has been chosen and approved by the Council, the ALI's governing body, the first step is the appointment of a Reporter, a leading scholar in the subject area. The Reporter prepares a *preliminary draft*, which is reviewed by a committee of fifteen to twenty appointed Advisors, also specialists in the area. A revised text, called the *Council draft*, is then reviewed by the Council. The Council may decide that a draft is not yet ready for approval but would benefit from discussion at the ALI's annual meeting, and may circulate a *discussion draft* to the members. If the Council approves the draft, it is submitted as a *tentative draft* to all members of the ALI, considered, debated, and often further amended at the annual meeting.[5] The text may be returned to the Reporter for revision or redrafting and may go through several tentative drafts before a *proposed final draft* is submitted for approval by the Council and membership. Once approved, the final text is published as a *Restatement*.[6]

These various drafts are often treated as a form of legislative history of the *Restatements*, and are frequently cited to explain, support, or attack particular *Restatement* rules. Transcripts of ALI discussions of drafts are printed in the *Proceedings* of the Institute. Like the drafts themselves, these provide insights into the rationale for the formulation of a *Restatement* as adopted.

Finding *Restatements*. The final, approved *Restatements* are published in bound volumes and are available in most law libraries. The various drafts are distributed to ALI members in paperback pamphlets and are less widely available, although larger law libraries generally have copies.

The *Restatements* are also available on both Westlaw and Lexis. Lexis has only the most recent final version of each *Restatement*, while Westlaw has the complete first, second and third series as

---

4. In the three earliest *Restatements* in the second series (*Agency*, *Torts*, and *Trusts*), the Reporter's Notes are not printed after each section but appear in separate appendix volumes.

5. Current projects that have reached the tentative draft stage include *Restatements Third* covering *Employment Law*; *Restitution and Unjust*

Enrichment; and *Torts: Liability for Physical and Emotional Harm (Basic Principles)*.

6. *About the American Law Institute* <www.ali.org/ali/thisali.htm>; Harvey S. Perlman, *The Restatement Process*, 10 Kan. J.L. & Pub. Pol'y 2, 4–5 (2000).

well as recent discussion and tentative drafts. (Each *Restatement* can be searched individually, and the REST database combines all available *Restatements* and drafts.) HeinOnline <www.heinonline. org> offers an American Law Institute collection, which provides access to PDF versions of the *Restatements* along with other ALI materials such as annual reports and proceedings.

The American Law Institute website <www.ali.org> has information on publications and pending projects, but it does not provide free access to the full text of its *Restatements*.

The Influence of the *Restatements*. The *Restatements* are not law, but they are perhaps more persuasive in the courts than any other secondary material.[7] Numerous court decisions and law review articles have discussed or criticized *Restatement* doctrines and applied them to particular situations. These are very useful in determining the scope and value of *Restatement* principles.

The appendices for *Restatements* in the second and third series contain annotations of court decisions which have applied or interpreted each section. These appendices are kept up to date by annual pocket parts or supplementary pamphlets, and by revised or added volumes as necessary. Westlaw incorporates the case citations after each section, while Lexis has separate hyperlinked files for rules and case citations. Cases and law review articles citing *Restatements* can also be found through KeyCite or Shepard's (and in print in *Shepard's Restatement of the Law Citations*).

Other ALI Works. The ALI has produced several other influential publications. In the 1990s it launched a new series of works known as *Principles* rather than *Restatements*. The difference between the two forms is that a *Restatement* is "firmly grounded in the existing case law [and] an effort to restate the governing rules in a coherent and systematic way," while *Principles* "make no pretense of being bound by existing law [and] are explicitly recommendations for change."[8]

Completed *Principles* projects include *Principles of Corporate Governance: Analysis and Recommendations* (1994), *Principles of the Law of Family Dissolution: Analysis and Recommendations* (2002), and *Principles of the Law: Intellectual Property: Principles*

---

7. The *Restatements* have been expressly adopted by statute in the Virgin Islands and the Northern Marianas Islands. Both jurisdictions provide that the "rules of the common law as expressed in the restatements of the law approved by the American Law Institute ... shall be the rules of decision in the courts." V.I. CODE ANN. tit. 1, § 4 (1995); 7 N. MAR. I. CODE § 3401 (2004). On the influence of the *Restatements*, see, e.g.,

Kristen David Adams, *The Folly of Uniformity? Lessons from the Restatement Movement*, 33 HOFSTRA L. REV. 423 (2004); Harold G. Maier, *The Utilitarian Role of a Restatement of Conflicts in a Common Law System: How Much Judicial Deference Is Due to the Restaters or "Who Are These Guys, Anyway?"*, 75 IND. L.J. 541 (2000).

8. Perlman, supra note 6, at 4.

Governing Jurisdiction, Choice of Law, and Judgments in Transnational Disputes (2008). Several other projects are in the draft stages. *Principles* are published in a similar format to *Restatements.* Final versions are available through both Westlaw and Lexis, and Westlaw has several tentative and discussion drafts as well.

The ALI has also produced model legislation, including the Model Penal Code and the Uniform Commercial Code, as discussed in Chapter 3 at pages 88–90. A comprehensive list of ALI projects is available on its website.[9]

§ 10.4   Texts, Treatises and Monographs

Legal texts and treatises play a vital role in legal research. They analyze the developing common law and contribute their own influence to this development. By synthesizing decisions and statutes, these works help to impose order on the chaos of individual precedents. Although they lack legal authority and effect, some are written by scholars of outstanding reputation and are well respected by the courts.

(a) Types of Law Books

Thousands of texts and treatises written by legal scholars and practitioners address topics of substantive and procedural law. These range from multi-volume specialized treatises and detailed surveys to short monographs on specific issues or limited aspects of practice in particular jurisdictions. Some offer convenient practice checklists and sample forms. While there is considerable overlap between types of books, several major genres can be recognized.

— **Treatises.** These are scholarly surveys providing exhaustive coverage of particular fields of law. A treatise is similar to an encyclopedia in that it methodically outlines the basic aspects of legal doctrine, but its focus on a specific subject allows a treatise to provide greater depth and insight.

Illustration 10–4 on page 356 shows a page from *Scott and Ascher on Trusts,* a multi-volume treatise covering trust law in much greater detail than the encyclopedias or other more general sources. Unlike the encyclopedias, the treatise quotes from and cites the original text of the 1676 Statute of Frauds and provides historical background to help readers understand the development of trust doctrine.

The traditional treatise is a multi-volume work covering a broad area of legal doctrine such as contracts or trusts.[10] Modern

---

9. *Past and Present ALI Projects* <www.ali.org/doc/past_present_ ALIprojects.pdf>.

10. The history of treatise publication is described in A.W.B. Simpson, *The*

Rise and Fall of the Legal Treatise: Legal Principles and the Forms of Legal

treatises tend to focus on increasingly narrow areas of law, and many are just one or two volumes. Treatises are published in bound volumes or looseleaf binders, and are generally updated annually with either pocket parts or looseleaf supplements. Some are updated more frequently, on a quarterly or semiannual basis. When using a treatise in any format, print or online, you should be aware of the date of its most recent supplementation and check for more recent authority as necessary.

Many treatises were originally written by leading scholars, such as James William Moore (*Moore's Federal Practice*) or John H. Wigmore (*Wigmore on Evidence*), but a number of titles are now produced by editorial staffs at publishing companies. These provide extensive commentaries and numerous references to primary sources, but they are generally not accorded the same level of deference as the work of a respected scholar. Some treatises, in fact, are now little more than collections of case references, useful for its research value but not as analysis.[11]

Some looseleaf services (as distinguished from treatises published in binders) provide a treatise-type function, explaining the basic doctrines of a subject area along with their presentation of primary sources such as statutes, regulations, and cases. The discussion in looseleaf services is usually straightforward and concise, designed more for rapid assimilation by working attorneys than for lengthy consideration by academics. The excerpt from CCH's Food Drug Cosmetic Reports shown in Illustration 5–9 on page 213 is an example of a service's explanatory analysis.

Most treatises are national in scope and analyze laws from various jurisdictions. Some works, however, focus specifically on federal law or on the law of an individual state. Smaller jurisdictions have very few treatises, but some large states have several multi-volume treatises. California, for example, has several treatises written by the late B.E. Witkin and members of the Witkin Legal Institute <www.witkin.com>, including *California Criminal Law*

Literature, 48 U. Chi. L. Rev. 632 (1981). The literary quality of historical American treatises is succinctly summarized in Lawrence M. Friedman, A History of American Law 477, 543 (3d ed. 2005): "Most nineteenth-century treatises were barren enough reading when they first appeared and would be sheer torture for the reader today.... [The early twentieth century] was the age of huge, elephantine treatises. Samuel Williston built a monumental structure (1920–1922) out of the law of contracts, volume after volume, closely knit, richly footnoted, and fully armored against the intrusion of any ethical, economic, or social ideas whatsoever.... [E]ach branch or field of law had at least one example of an arid and exhaustive treatise."

11. Gary E. O'Connor, *Restatement (First) of Statutory Interpretation*, 7 N.Y.U. J. Legis. & Pub. Pol'y 333, 343 (2004), noted that one such work was "less a coherent treatise than a stringing together of older and more recent citations under the relevant sections. That is, the updates appear to be more of a gradual process of citation accretion, rather than an effort to present a comprehensive, coherent view" of its field.

(3d ed. 2000–date), *California Evidence* (4th ed. 2000–date), and *California Procedure* (5th ed. 2008–date).

— Hornbooks. These are straightforward one-volume statements of the law on a specific subject, such as *McCormick on Evidence* or *Wright on Federal Courts*. They are written primarily for law students but can be of value to anyone seeking an overview of a doctrinal area. There is no clear line distinguishing hornbooks from treatises, and some hornbooks (such as those by McCormick and Wright) have become influential sources of persuasive authority and are widely used by the bar. Some hornbooks are also published in two-or three-volume "practitioners' editions," further blurring the distinction between treatises and hornbooks.

Hornbooks are distinct from the *casebooks* designed as teaching tools, which reprint case excerpts for discussion and tend to provide a less straightforward summary of legal doctrine. Many casebooks consist primarily of reprinted material and questions for classroom discussion, but some include discussion and references that can be useful for research purposes.

— Practitioners' Handbooks and Manuals. These works are somewhat similar to treatises but they tend to address practical concerns, and many provide useful features designed to simplify routine aspects of law practice.[12] These are less useful for students but can be invaluable in real life. Handbooks and manuals are often published by organizations such as the Practising Law Institute (PLI) and bar associations, in many instances as course materials for continuing legal education programs. Some works provide a cohesive overview of an area of law, while others present chapters by practitioners on a variety of developing topics.

Works focusing on the law of a specific state can be particularly useful for quickly determining the laws in force and finding relevant primary sources. In smaller jurisdictions with few state-specific treatises, continuing legal education handbooks can be among the best available resources for summaries of state law.

— Scholarly Monographs. These cover relatively narrow topics and differ from treatises in that they tend to focus heavily on the historical background, underlying causes and policies, and trends in particular areas of the law. Works such as Gary L. Francione's *Animals as Persons* (2008) or Neil Netanel's *Copyright's Paradox* (2008) can help provide an understanding of the history or policy background of a particular area.

---

12. Practice-oriented legal materials have a long history in American legal publishing. "With some exceptions, American legal literature was (and is) rigorously practical. Books were written for the practicing lawyer. The goal was to help him earn a living, not to slake his intellectual curiosity." LAWRENCE M. FRIEDMAN, A HISTORY OF AMERICAN LAW 244 (3d ed. 2005).

Monographs tend to be more interdisciplinary in nature than other legal writings. They are often published by university presses or general-interest publishers, and are similar to scholarly works in other disciplines. Because they are generally not exhaustive in their coverage of doctrinal issues and are rarely updated on a regular basis, such works are usually not the best sources for current research leads.[13]

— **Self–Help Publications.** These are written for the general public and often provide clear introductions to areas of law. One of the major publishers is Nolo <www.nolo.com> (e.g., *Patent It Yourself* and *Your Rights in the Workplace*). Books for nonlawyers can be useful starting points but may oversimplify complex issues or fail to reflect variations in the law between jurisdictions. They also tend to provide fewer leads to primary sources than works designed specifically for lawyers, making them less useful as springboards for further research.

For any of these publications to be reliable for coverage of current legal issues, they must reflect changes in the law promptly and accurately. Some form of updating, whether by looseleaf inserts, pocket parts or periodic revision, is usually essential to preserve a legal text's research value. An outdated text may be of historical or intellectual interest, but it cannot be relied upon as a statement of current law.

Part of the process of using a text for the first time is deciding whether it will assist you in your research. Even without extensive use and expertise in a subject area, you can ask several questions when encountering a new work:

— What is its purpose and intended audience? Is it written for experienced specialists or a more general readership?

— How is it organized, and what is its scope? Does it cover too broad an area for your purposes, or does it focus on issues that don't concern you?

— What is the reputation of the author? Has she written other texts or articles in this area?

13. Doctoral dissertations are an extensive body of scholarly research that are often overlooked by law students and lawyers. A dissertation is usually the product of several years of research, and it often provides an extensive bibliography of published and manuscript sources. Reading a dissertation once required searching a *Dissertation Abstracts* database or publication and then borrowing or purchasing a print or micro-form copy. ProQuest Dissertations & Theses—Full Text <www.proquest. com> now provides online access to most dissertations since 1997 as well as selected earlier works. (It also indexes dissertations back to 1861, including abstracts beginning in 1980.) Digital access has transformed dissertations from esoteric and hard-to-find items to readily available research tools.

— How useful are such features as the work's footnotes, tables, bibliography, and index? Do they lead effectively to relevant passages in the work and to other resources?

— Is the work supplemented in an adequate and timely manner?

Ultimately the deciding factor in determining whether you will turn to a text a second time is: Did it help answer your question? Did it clarify matters and provide fruitful research leads? With growing familiarity in a particular area of law, you will develop a sense of which texts are useful for background information, for assistance in working through complicated legal issues, or for references to primary sources and other materials.

(b) Finding Books

There are several ways to find relevant and useful texts and treatises, from your local law library's online catalog to guides and bibliographies of published and online resources.

Library Collections. The basic starting place in looking for most law books is your law library's online catalog. A title keyword search can be used initially to find a few relevant works, but it is important to go beyond keywords and use the subject headings for more comprehensive research. If you search by keyword for "professional responsibility," you might miss relevant works using the phrase "legal ethics" in their titles. A subject search will catch relevant works regardless of their titles. In most online catalogs, each record's subject headings are hyperlinked to a list of other works on the same topic. The entry for one relevant text is a springboard to others.

Most online catalogs have "advanced search" or "expanded search" screens that allow you to search for a combination of terms in specific fields. You can use this to find a particular work by a prolific author, or to narrow your search to works assigned to two specified subject headings. The advanced screen usually permits you to limit a search to a specific library collection or location, or to find works from a specific date range. These options can be particularly useful if a general keyword search turns up an unmanageably large number of publications.

In most libraries, books are shelved by subject using a call number classification system. One advantage of this system is that you can browse nearby books once you have located one relevant text. Most libraries use the Library of Congress (LC) classification system, in which United States law is assigned to numbers within the KF classification. The list of major treatises and hornbooks in the Appendix on pages 449–479 includes the LC classification ranges for several dozen major subject areas within American law.

Online catalogs from other libraries may also be helpful in identifying resources available for purchase or interlibrary loan. The catalogs for major research libraries such as Harvard University <hollis.harvard.edu> or the Library of Congress <catalog.loc.gov> are available and can help in your research whether or not you plan to use these libraries' collections.

The American Bar Association's list of approved law schools <www.abanet.org/legaled/approvedlawschools/alpha.html> provides links to school websites, from which academic law library catalogs can be reached. FindLaw has a list of law schools by state <stu.findlaw.com/schools/usaschools/> with direct links to library websites and online catalogs for many of the law schools listed. Even more library catalogs are accessible through resources such as lib-web-cats <www.librarytechnology.org/libwebcats/>, a directory of libraries throughout the world. Searches can be limited by geographic location or by choosing "Law" from a Library Type pulldown menu.

No law library has every possible text, so research limited to one library's holdings may miss important works. WorldCat provides access to records for more than a billion items in more than 10,000 libraries worldwide. This database is available in two forms. One <www.worldcat.org> is free to the public, while the other <www.oclc.org/firstsearch/> is available through subscribing libraries and provides more sophisticated search capabilities. Both interfaces have "advanced search" screens allowing you to combine keywords with words in the author, title or subject fields and to limit results by date.

Online Databases. Many treatises and other texts are available electronically as well as in print. Electronic texts are not necessarily more current than their print counterparts, but full-text searching allows means of access beyond browsing and subject indexes.

Once you have found a relevant treatise section using a keyword search, unless you are very familiar with the subject area or looking only for very specific information you should link to the table of contents to explore related material. If you read only the individual retrieved sections, you'll learn little about the contours in that area of law.[14]

---

14. See Jasper L. Cummings, Jr., *Legal Research in Federal Taxation*, in TAX PLANNING FOR DOMESTIC & FOREIGN PARTNERSHIPS, LLCS, JOINT VENTURES & OTHER STRATEGIC ALLIANCES 2007, at 739, 761–62 (PLI Tax Law and Estate Planning Course Handbook Series, No. J–761, 2007), WL 761 PLI/Tax 739, 761–62

("Reading an online source like a book is of oxygen-level importance to thorough and thoughtful online research. The point of doing this is to free yourself from the yoke of the search term, and allow you to go where the book leads you and to use its table of contents as a guide.").

The Appendix in this volume, listing major treatises and hornbooks by subject, indicates which titles are available through one of the online systems. Westlaw provides access to several hundred treatises, including major works such as *Couch on Insurance*, *McCarthy on Trademarks and Unfair Competition*, Rotunda & Nowak's *Treatise on Constitutional Law*, and Wright & Miller's *Federal Practice and Procedure*. The TEXTS database combines access to all available texts and treatises, and specific works are listed by subject in the Westlaw directory. Westlaw's ResultsPlus also provides links to several major treatises.

Lexis has hundreds of Matthew Bender texts and treatises, including *Chisum on Patents*, *Collier on Bankruptcy*, *Immigration Law and Procedure*, and *Nimmer on Copyright*, as well as selected works from other publishers. These can be found by browsing in either "Secondary Legal" or "Area of Law—By Topic" directories.

Treatises available through the database systems can provide a solid start in research, but no system has comprehensive coverage of available resources. Each has works published by its own parent company and not others, and many major treatises are unavailable online. This is different from other areas such as case law and law reviews, where Westlaw and Lexis provide much broader coverage with access to many of the same resources.

Footnotes and Other References. Following research leads provided by other sources is usually a reliable way to find useful works. Treatises are often cited in cases and law review articles, and these references are likely to lead to works that are considered well-reasoned and reputable. You can identify highly esteemed treatises through searches in case or journal databases (e.g., "leading w/2 treatise w/5 contracts") or simply note the treatises that are cited repeatedly by judges or law professors.

Recommendations from lawyers, professors or reference librarians can also be effective in identifying the most reliable and influential sources. If you receive an assignment in an unfamiliar area from a supervising attorney, consider asking what secondary sources she would use to begin the research. When talking to a partner or professor in her office, notice which works she keeps handy on her desktop or nearby shelves.

Guides to Treatises. As has already been noted, the Appendix at pages 449–479 provides a brief list of major treatises and hornbooks in several dozen subject areas. Several other printed guides list legal publications by subject, but many of them do not differentiate between major, regularly updated treatises and obscure monographs.

One of the most reliable and thorough guides, updated annually, is found in Kendall Svengalis's *Legal Information Buyer's Guide and Reference Manual.* A chapter on treatises spans more than three hundred pages and provides annotated listings in about sixty subject areas. The annotations provide useful summaries of the scope of the works listed, as well as the annual cost of maintaining subscriptions.[15]

Treatises and practice materials focusing on the law of particular jurisdictions can be found in most state legal research guides, listed in Chapter 12 at pages 392–398. Multistate guides include *State Practice Materials: Annotated Bibliographies* (Frank Houdek ed., 2002–date), which provides descriptive listings of treatises by subject for more than half of the states, and Francis R. Doyle, *Searching the Law: The States* (4th ed. 2003), which has lengthy but unannotated lists.

IndexMaster <www.indexmaster.com> is a subscription database that provides searchable access to the tables of contents and indexes from more than 8,000 legal titles. Search results link to PDFs of the table of contents or index, helping you to gauge whether the title might be worth tracking down.

Historical Texts. Most approaches to finding books assume that you are looking for current materials, as legal research usually involves determining the law now in effect. You may also need information on legal developments occurring decades or centuries ago. The background of a court decision, statute, or constitutional provision can affect its current interpretation and is thus of more than historical or scholarly interest.

Classic texts such as William Blackstone's *Commentaries on the Laws of England* (1765–69) and Oliver Wendell Holmes's *The Common Law* (1881) are published in modern facsimile editions, and the original works may be found in rare book collections in both general and law libraries. Historical texts are also widely available in PDF in several subscription online databases.

At least three resources focus specifically on law books. The Making of Modern Law: Legal Treatises, 1800–1926 <www.gale.cengage.com/ModernLaw/> has more than 21,000 American and

---

15. A "Topical Guides" chapter in JULIUS J. MARKE ET AL., LEGAL RESEARCH AND LAW LIBRARY MANAGEMENT (rev. ed. 2006–date) has annotated listings in more than thirty subject areas of treatises and handbooks, as well as current awareness sources, looseleaf services, forms, periodicals, and Internet resources. FRANK S. BAE ET AL., SEARCHING THE LAW (3d ed. 2005) has more extensive but unannotated listings of treatis-

es and other works in more than one hundred subject fields, and AMBER HEWETTE & DIANE MURLEY, LAW FOR THE LAYPERSON: AN ANNOTATED BIBLIOGRAPHY OF SELF-HELP LAW BOOKS (3d ed. 2006) covers books for the general public. Older works that may still be of use include ENCYCLOPEDIA OF LEGAL INFORMATION SOURCES (Brian L. Baker & Patrick J. Petit eds., 2d ed. 2003) and RECOMMENDED LAW BOOKS (James A. McDermott ed., 2d ed. 1986). McDermott's slim vol-

British works from the nineteenth and early twentieth centuries, searchable by author, title, or subject as well as full text. HeinOnline's Legal Classics library <www.heinonline.org> has a more selective collection of over 1,300 titles, ranging in publication date from the early 17th century through the late 20th century, fully searchable or browsable by subject. West's Rise of American Law covers some 400 older encyclopedias and treatises from 1820 to 1970, and is available through Westlaw as an additional subscription (ROAL–ALL database).

Legal materials are also included in more general online book collections. Early American Imprints <www.readex.com> focuses on American works and has more than 70,000 books, pamphlets and broadsides, in two sets: Series I: Evans, 1639–1800; and Series II: Shaw–Shoemaker, 1801–1819. Works published before 1700 can be found in Early English Books Online (EEBO) <eebo.chadwyck.com>, and English books from the 1700s are in Eighteenth Century Collections Online (ECCO) <www.gale.cengage.com/EighteenthCentury/>. ECCO has some works published in the colonies, but it excludes many of the books covered in Early American Imprints.

Other more general digitization projects are also being undertaken. Google Book Search <books.google.com> is digitizing millions of books from several major research libraries. The full text is searchable, and PDF copies of books in the public domain (generally those published prior to 1923) are available.[16] Other projects include the Internet Archive's Text Archive <www.archive.org/details/texts>, which has digitized more than a million books.

Not all books have been digitized, of course, and bibliographies of historical publications can still be useful in identifying relevant works. Major guides to sources in English legal history are J. N. Adams & G. Averley, *A Bibliography of Eighteenth Century Legal Literature* (1982) and J. N. Adams & M. J. Davies, *A Bibliography of Nineteenth Century Legal Literature* (1992–96). Morris L. Cohen, *Bibliography of Early American Law* (1998–2003) provides a comprehensive record of American law publishing up to 1860. In seven volumes, this magisterial work provides a descriptive listing of monographs, treatises and other works by subject, with extensive indexing by author, title, jurisdiction and year.[17]

---

ume, while outdated, includes insightful comments from practicing lawyers and excerpts from book reviews.

16. Under a pending settlement between Google and copyright holders, more of in-copyright works will likely be available in the near future. See, e.g.,

Miguel Helft & Motoko Rich, *Google Strikes Deal to Allow Book Scans*, N.Y. TIMES, Oct. 29, 2008, at B1.

17. For more information on legal history resources, see Morris L. Cohen, *Researching Legal History in the Digital Age*, 99 LAW LIBR. J. 377 (2007).

TRUSTS   **§ 60**

    4. *Necessity of Writing; Conformance to Statutes of Wills and Frauds*

        a. In General

§ 60   Generally

Research References

West's Key Number Digest, Trusts ⟐17(1) to 29
Am. Jur. Pleading and Practice Forms, Complaint, petition, or declaration—
    Allegation—Creation of express trust—By declaration. Trusts § 19
Restatement Third, Trusts §§ 17, 20 to 24

    A valid, enforceable trust can be created orally, without a writing, in the absence of specific statutory provisions to the contrary,[1] such as provisions of a statute like the Statute of Frauds or Statute of Wills.[2] In some jurisdictions, however, no oral trusts are allowed and a writing is required.[3] Thus, for example, the rule has been stated as being that an express trust cannot be proved by parol evidence, but must be manifested and proved by some writing,[4] signed by the party declaring the trust;[5] or that an express trust can never be implied or arise by operation of law and can be proved only by some instrument in writing,[6] signed by the party enabled by law to declare the trust.[7]

    A valid testamentary trust can be created only where the purported will attempting to create it is within the statute of wills.[8] In addition,

---

Where there is no language in the applicable instrument from which an intent to create a new trust at the time of its execution could be inferred, and the only expression of intent is to extend the life of an existing trust, the requirement of an intent to create a trust is not met. Starling v. Taylor, 1 N.C. App. 287, 161 S.E.2d 204 (1968).

[Section 60]

[1]Cabaniss v. Cabaniss, 464 A.2d 87 (D.C. 1983).

    An express trust may be created orally or in writing. In re Marcus Trusts, 2 A.D.3d 640, 769 N.Y.S.2d 56 (App. Div. 2d Dep't 2003).

    Except as required by a statute other than the Uniform Trust Code, a trust need not be evidenced by a trust instrument, but the creation of an oral trust and its terms may be established only by clear and convincing evidence. Uniform Trust Code § 407.

    As to intent to create a trust as a ba-

sic requirement for creation of a valid trust, see §§ 57 et seq.

[2]Huff v. Byers, 209 Ky. 375, 272 S.W. 897 (1925).

[3]Welch v. Cooper, 11 Ark. App. 263, 670 S.W.2d 454 (1984); Lollis v. Lollis, 291 S.C. 525, 354 S.E.2d 559 (1987).

[4]Lollis v. Lollis, 291 S.C. 525, 354 S.E.2d 559 (1987).

[5]§ 63.

[6]Welch v. Cooper, 11 Ark. App. 263, 670 S.W.2d 454 (1984).

    An "express trust" shall be created or declared in writing. Hayes v. Clark, 242 Ga. App. 411, 530 S.E.2d 38 (2000).

    As to trusts by operation of law, generally, see §§ 128 et seq.

[7]§ 63.

[8]Atwood v. Rhode Island Hospital Trust Co., 275 F. 513, 24 A.L.R. 156 (C.C.A. 1st Cir. 1921); Cramer v. Hartford-Connecticut Trust Co., 110 Conn. 22, 147 A. 139, 73 A.L.R. 201

101

Illustration 10–1. 76 AM. JUR. 2D *Trusts* § 60 (2005).

§ 28

2. *Parol Trusts and Effect of Statute of Frauds*

§ 28 Generally

Whether an express trust is required to be in writing or may be created or proved by parol depends on the statutory provisions relating thereto, if any, in the jurisdiction.

Research References

West's Key Number Digest, Trusts ⬚17, 17(1)

Except as otherwise provided by statute an enforceable trust can be created without a writing.[1] While in many jurisdictions express trusts must be created or proved by a writing and cannot be created or proved by parol,[2] it is more accurate to state that in such jurisdictions, under statutes to that effect, an express trust in land cannot be created or proved by parol,[3] but that in most of such jurisdictions an express trust in personalty can be created or proved by parol.[4] A parol trust cannot be found in the absence of an agreement.[5]

§ 29 Trusts in or affecting land—Statutes relating specifically to trusts

In jurisdictions which have adopted some form of statute similar to the original statute of frauds relating to trusts, or recognize

such rule, express trusts in lands cannot be created or declared, or manifested or proved, by parol; nor can an express trust be engrafted by parol on a conveyance absolute in form.

Research References

West's Key Number Digest, Trusts ⬚17(3)

At common law a trust can be created by parol,[1] but in those states in which the English statute of frauds, requiring that all declarations or creations of trusts in lands, tenements or hereditaments be in writing, has been substantially reenacted, the rule of construction adopted is that the trust need not be created by writing, but the evidence of the existence of the trust must be in writing.[2] In at least one jurisdiction, though, it is the requirement that all express trusts must be created or declared in writing.[3]

While a parol trust in land is valid and enforceable at common law and general equity jurisprudence,[4] it is the rule, where the provisions of the statute of frauds, which are expressly applicable to trusts in lands, tenements, and hereditaments, have been enacted, that express trusts in lands cannot be created[5] or declared or cannot be manifested and proved, according to the particular wording of the statute invoked, by parol.[6] The operation of the rule is not affected by the fact that the

---

[Section 28]

[1]U.S.—Sherwin v. Oil City Nat. Bank, 229 F.2d 835 (3d Cir. 1956); Stone v. Stone, 330 F. Supp. 1026 (W.D. Va. 1971), aff'd in part, rev'd in part on other grounds, 460 F.2d 64 (4th Cir. 1972); Chandler v. U.S., 177 F. Supp. 565, 59-2 U.S. Tax Cas. (CCH) ¶ 11890, 4 A.F.T.R.2d 6047 (D.N.H. 1959), stating Massachusetts law.

Fla.—In re Craft's Estate, 320 So. 2d 874 (Fla. Dist. Ct. App. 4th Dist. 1975).

Or.—Smiley v. King, 278 Or. 555, 564 P.2d 1348 (1977).

[2]U.S.—Wallace v. District No. 2, Marine Engineers Benev. Ass'n AFL-CIO, 392 F. Supp. 899, 89 L.R.R.M. (BNA) 2947 (E.D. La. 1975).

Ark.—Horton v. Koner, 12 Ark. App. 38, 671 S.W.2d 235 (1984).

Pa.—McHenry v. Stapleton, 443 Pa. 186, 278 A.2d 892 (1971).

[3]§ 29.

[4]§ 32.

[5]Ky.—Hoheimer v. Hoheimer, 30 S.W.3d 176 (Ky. 2000).

[Section 29]

[1]U.S.—Bricklayers, Masons and Plasterers Intern. Union of America, Local Union No. 15, Orlando, Florida v. Stuart Plastering Co., Inc., 512 F.2d 1017, 89 L.R.R.M. (BNA) 2389, 77 Lab. Cas. (CCH) ¶ 10871 (5th Cir. 1975).

Ariz.—King v. Uhlmann, 103 Ariz. 136, 437 P.2d 928 (1968).

Fla.—Fraser v. Lewis, 187 So. 2d 684 (Fla. Dist. Ct. App. 3d Dist. 1966).

[2]Ariz.—Remele v. Hamilton, 78 Ariz. 45, 275 P.2d 403 (1954).

N.J.—Vreeland v. Dawson, 55 N.J. Super. 456, 151 A.2d 62 (Ch. Div. 1959).

[3]Ga.—Hancock v. Hancock, 205 Ga. 684, 54 S.E.2d 385 (1949).

[4]Ky.—Horn v. Horn, 562 S.W.2d 319 (Ky. Ct. App. 1978).

Okla.—Ellis v. Benbrook, 1962 OK 79, 370 P.2d 543 (Okla. 1962).

[5]Neb.—Schaneman v. Wright, 238 Neb. 309, 470 N.W.2d 566 (1991).

[6]Mich.—Children of Chippewa, Ottawa and Potawatomy Tribes v. Regents of University of Michigan, 104 Mich. App. 482, 305 N.W.2d 522 (1981).

Illustration 10–2. 90 C.J.S. *Trusts* §§ 28–29 (2002).

§ 20   TRUSTS   Ch. 5

§ 20.   Validity of Oral Inter Vivos Trusts

> **Except as required by a statute of frauds, a writing is not necessary to create an enforceable inter vivos trust, whether by declaration, by transfer to another as trustee, or by contract.**

Comment:

    a. Common-law and statutory rules. Most states have enacted statutory provisions like Section 7 of the English Statute of Frauds, specifically requiring a writing for the inter vivos creation of enforceable trusts of interests in land. In some of the remaining states, statutory provisions requiring a writing for certain contracts or conveyances affecting land have been held applicable to the creation of trusts of interests in land; and some state-court decisions have treated Section 7 of the Statute of Frauds as part of the common law.

    In a few states, statutes require a writing for the creation of enforceable inter vivos trusts of personal property.

    All of the foregoing requirements, however worded, whether expressly stated in a statute or judicially recognized by construction or as common law, are referred to in this Restatement as "statutes of frauds."

    Unless a statute of frauds requires a writing for the creation of an enforceable inter vivos trust, a property owner may declare a trust or transfer property during life to another in trust without a writing. Thus, in all but a few jurisdictions, during the settlor's lifetime, enforceable trusts of personal property may be created orally. Similarly, absent a statute-of-frauds requirement, enforceable trusts of personalty may be created by contract, or (as often occurs) by receipt of payments under contracts, without a writing even if the promisor's performance is expected to occur after the settlor's death.

    In addition, judicial decisions in several jurisdictions that have no express counterpart of Section 7 of the English Statute of Frauds allow enforceable inter vivos trusts of land to be declared or created by transfer without need of a writing.

Illustrations:

    1. S orally declares that she holds her diamond brooch and earrings in trust for B, to be turned over to B at age 20. In a state that has a typical statute of frauds, S has created an enforceable trust.

    2. S designates T as payee of the proceeds of a large insurance policy on S's life. At her request, T orally promises that

Illustration 10–3. RESTATEMENT (THIRD) OF TRUSTS § 20 (2003).

Frauds and the Wills Act that a "writing" acquired legal significance.[3] Moreover, modern law, having basically eliminated the concept of a seal, has magnified the importance of the distinction between transactions that are evidenced by written instruments and those that are not.

§ 6.2. The Statute of Frauds

The Statute of Frauds,[1] enacted in 1676, provided, in § 7, that

> all declarations or creations of trusts or confidences of any lands, tenements, or hereditaments, shall be manifested and proved by some writing signed by the party who is by law enabled to declare such trust, or by his last will in writing, or else they shall be utterly void and of none effect.

Section 8 provided, however, that "a trust or confidence shall or may arise or result by the implication or construction of law." Shortly after its enactment, the courts began to construe it, and they continue, to this day, in most states, to construe its successors. As a result, there is an immense body of case law. Although the decisions depend to some extent on the language of the particular statute, there has developed something like a common law with respect to the requirement of a writing, so that the exact wording of the statute at hand is sometimes less important than one might expect.[2] The English cases construing the original Statute of Frauds probably still have authority in England, although the statute itself has been superseded by the Law of Property Act, 1925, § 53,[3] which uses somewhat different language. So also, in the United States, courts sometimes still follow the early English decisions, even when the language of the relevant statute differs from that of the original English statute. As we shall see, the English courts held, notwithstanding the statute, that it was possible to

---

[3] *See* Restatement (Second) of Trusts § 39 (1959) (except as provided by statute, no writing necessary to create enforceable trust); Restatement (Third) of Trusts § 20 (2003) (same).

§ 6.2. [1] Stat. 29 Chas. II, c. 3 (1676).

[2] *See* Restatement (Second) of Trusts § 40 cmt. a (1959); Restatement (Third) of Trusts § 22 cmt. a (2003).

[3] Stat. 15 Geo. V, c. 20, § 53 (1925).

See generally Burgess, *Trusts, Equitable Interests and the New Zealand Statute of Frauds*, 6 Otago L. Rev. 95 (1985); Davies, *Informally Created Trusts of Land and Some Alternatives to Them*, 106 Law Q. Rev. 539 (1990).

Illustration 10–4. 1 Austin Wakeman Scott et al., Scott and Ascher on Trusts § 6.2 (2006).

Chapter 11

SECONDARY SOURCES, PART 2: PERIODICALS

Table of Sections

Legal periodicals appear in a wide range of forms, from scholarly law reviews to blogs covering the most recent breaking news, and they serve a variety of research functions. Some law review articles provide analyses and insights that merit study even decades after publication. Bar association journals tend to highlight current practice trends, and legal newspapers, newsletters and blogs provide current awareness of new developments. All of these resources can serve as springboards to further research by providing citations to primary sources and other secondary sources.

Most legal research requires access to nonlegal periodicals, such as scientific journal articles to underlie a tort claim, contemporary coverage of business developments, or historical newspaper coverage of political changes. These interdisciplinary and fact-finding resources can be just as valuable as the publications of lawyers and legal academics.

§ 11.1 Scholarly and Professional Journals

Journals play a central role in legal analysis. They often offer more intense and focused treatment of specific issues than treatises, and they cover new developments more quickly. Their extensive footnotes can lead to a wealth of primary sources and other research leads.

Academic Law Reviews. Some of the most important scholarly commentary in American law appears in the academic legal journals known as law reviews. Since the late 19th century, academic law reviews have been an important intellectual force with thorough discussion of legal developments and extensive analysis of important decisions and statutes.[1] A number of influential articles have led directly to major changes in legal doctrine. Thousands of law review articles are published every year, so effective research requires learning several means of access and evaluating articles carefully.[2]

The terms "law journal" and "law review" in periodical names do not have distinct meanings. Many legal newspapers are called "journals," as in the *National Law Journal* or the *New York Law Journal*, but the name is also used by prestigious academic law reviews such as the *Yale Law Journal*. Some journals, such as *Constitutional Commentary* or *Health Matrix*, use neither term in their titles but are nonetheless academic law reviews. It is a periodical's form and content that determine its nature, not its title.[3]

---

1. For historical background, see Michael I. Swygert & Jon W. Bruce, *The Historical Origins, Founding, and Early Development of Student–Edited Law Reviews*, 36 HASTINGS L.J. 739 (1985). There is a vast literature on law reviews. For works up to the mid–1990s, see Mary Beth Beazley & Linda H. Edwards, *The Process and the Product: A Bibliography of Scholarship about Legal Scholarship*, 49 MERCER L. REV. 741 (1998).

2. A recent study found that forty-three percent of law review articles are never cited at all, and about 79% get ten or fewer citations. Thomas A. Smith, *The Web of Law*, 44 SAN DIEGO L. REV. 309, 335–36 (2007). "The large majority of law review articles quickly and irreversibly become completely obscure or 'dead,' and ... are never or rarely cited." Id. at 346.

Several attempts have been made to rank the relative prestige of various law reviews. The most extensive ranking system is John Doyle's *Law Journals: Submissions and Ranking* <lawlib.wlu.edu/LJ/>, which is updated annually and provides several ways to rank more than 1,500 journals based on their citation in journal articles and cases. Articles ranking law reviews include Robert M. Jarvis & Phyllis Coleman, *Ranking Law Reviews: An Empirical Analysis Based on Author Prominence*, 39 ARIZ. L.

REV. 15 (1997); Robert M. Jarvis & Phyllis Coleman, *Ranking Law Reviews by Author Prominence—Ten Years Later*, 99 LAW LIBR. J. 573 (2007); Fred R. Shapiro, *The Most–Cited Law Reviews*, 29 J. LEG. STUD. 389 (2000). Topical law reviews have been ranked in Tracey E. George & Chris Guthrie, *An Empirical Evaluation of Specialized Law Reviews*, 26 FLA. ST. U. L. REV. 813 (1999). A law review's reputation is still important for authors deciding where to place their articles, but it has less significance for researchers than it did when it was necessary to decide which library volumes to examine. See Glenn Reynolds, *Little Things*, TCS DAILY (Feb. 20, 2002) <www.tcsdaily.com/article.aspx?id= 022002A> (noting that keyword searching has led legal scholars to cite more articles in comparatively obscure journals rather than consulting only prestigious leading law reviews).

3. *Contra* Sam Joyner, *Tulsa Law Journal Name Change*, TULSA L. MAG., Fall 2001, at 7, 7 ("The University of Tulsa College of Law is proud to announce that we have changed the name of our primary student-edited publication from the *Tulsa Law Journal* to the *Tulsa Law Review*, effective June 2001. The change occurred as a result of input from students, faculty, subscribers and alumni who recognized that the title

The law review is a form of scholarly publication unknown to most disciplines. It is usually edited by law students rather than established scholars, and serves as an educational tool for its editors as well as a forum for discussion of legal developments and theories. At most law reviews, law students exercise complete control over the acceptance and editing of articles submitted by established law professors and scholars.[4] This system remains the norm despite frequent criticism over the years. Law reviews have been criticized for other reasons as well, including their irrelevancy to legal practice and their sheer proliferation.[5]

Most law reviews follow a fairly standard format, containing lengthy *articles* and shorter *essays* by professors and lawyers, as well as *comments* or *notes* by students. Articles and essays by established scholars are more influential, but the student contributions can also be very useful in research. Like articles, they usually begin with an introductory section providing a summary of the relevant legal doctrine and citing the key literature. This introduction can provide an excellent overview and a starting point for research.[6] The entire text is usually accompanied by extensive footnotes containing citations to other sources as well as substantive information that can aid in research. An author and a team of law student editors may have worked months to gather citations

Tulsa Law Review more accurately reflects the type of multi-subject, general interest publication that we have become.")

4. James Lindgren, *An Author's Manifesto*, 61 U. CHI. L. REV. 527, 535 (1994) ("In some other parts of the academy, legal journals are considered a joke. Scholars elsewhere frequently can't believe that, for almost all our major academic journals, we let students without advanced degrees select manuscripts."). On the differences between student-edited law reviews and peer-reviewed journals in other disciplines, see also Lawrence M. Friedman, *Law Reviews and Legal Scholarship: Some Comments*, 75 DENV. U. L. REV. 661 (1998); Gerald N. Rosenberg, *Across the Great Divide (Between Law and Political Science)*, 3 GREEN BAG 2D 267, 270–71 (2000).

5. See, e.g., Harry T. Edwards, *The Growing Disjunction Between Legal Education and the Legal Profession*, 91 MICH. L. REV. 34 (1992); Kenneth Lasson, *Scholarship Amok: Excesses in the Pursuit of Truth and Tenure*, 103 HARV. L. REV. 926 (1990); Richard A. Posner, *Against the Law Reviews*, LEGAL AFF.,

Nov.–Dec. 2004, at 57, 58 ("[A]rticles that criticize judicial decisions or, more constructively, discern new directions in law by careful analysis of decisions ... are of great value to the profession, including its judicial branch, but they are becoming rare ... ").

The anti-law review literature has engendered a counter-literature in their defense. See, e.g., Howard Denemark, *How Valid Is the Often–Repeated Accusation That There Are Too Many Legal Articles and Too Many Law Reviews?*, 30 AKRON L. REV. 215, 232 (1996) ("If we cannot predict which ones will make a difference—and we cannot—we should be very circumspect about asserting that there are too many legal articles in too many law reviews."); Wendy J. Gordon, *Counter-Manifesto: Student–Edited Reviews and the Intellectual Properties of Scholarship*, 61 U. CHI. L. REV. 541 (1994); Cameron Stracher, *Reading, Writing, and Citing: In Praise of Law Reviews*, 52 N.Y.L. SCH. L. REV. 349 (2007/08).

6. See Gordon, supra note 5, at 548 ("If I want to learn about a new area, I can do so by picking up virtually any article.")

and verify their accuracy, and an article on point can provide extensive leads to primary and secondary sources.

The terms *comment* and *note* are not quite interchangeable, but they have different meanings depending on the journal. In some, *comments* are similar in form to articles and provide extended analysis of legal issues while *notes*, or *casenotes*, are shorter examinations of specific cases. Other journals reverse this and have lengthy *notes* and short *case comments*. Student work was traditionally published without author attribution or was identified only by the author's initials, but now almost every law review identifies the student authors of notes and comments. Student authors must be identified as such in citations to their work.[7] Student-written works are not less useful for research purposes than articles by professors, but to some they may be considered less persuasive authority.

Illustration 11–1 on page 377 shows a page from an article in a recent law review issue on the topic of legal scholarship. The page shown includes nine footnotes providing references to several other articles as well as a seventeenth-century French work.

Practically every law school approved by the American Bar Association has a general law review that publishes articles on a wide range of topics, and most schools also have additional journals on specialized subjects. Nearly three dozen law reviews are published on issues in environmental law, for example, and almost twenty on issues of gender, sexuality, or sexual orientation. Some larger law schools have multiple specialized journals.

A few subject-specialized academic journals are edited by faculty rather than students. These include several highly respected journals such as *Constitutional Commentary* at the University of Minnesota, *Journal of Empirical Legal Studies* at Cornell, *Journal of Law, Economics and Organization* at Yale, *Tax Law Review* at New York University, and three titles—*Journal of Law and Economics; Journal of Legal Studies;* and *Supreme Court Review*—at the University of Chicago.

Michael H. Hoffheimer's *On-Line Directory of Law Reviews and Scholarly Legal Publications* <www.lexisnexis.com/lawschool/prodev/lawreview/> is a useful source for identifying both general and specialized law reviews. It lists more than six hundred journals

---

7. THE BLUEBOOK: A UNIFORM SYSTEM OF CITATION R. 16.6.2, at 142–43 (18th ed. 2005); ALWD CITATION MANUAL: A PROFESSIONAL SYSTEM OF CITATION R. 23.1(a), at 217 (3d ed. 2006). *The Bluebook* flags student work by indicating the type of piece ("Note" or "Comment"), while the ALWD Manual instead adds the identification "Student Author" after the author's name. The ALWD approach, which has been adopted by only about two dozen journals, "may be a step backwards from the *Bluebook*'s innocuous designations." Alex Glashausser, *Citation and Representation*, 55 VAND. L. REV. 59, 87 (2002).

by subject, with separate listings of student-edited journals and non-student-edited peer review and trade journals. It is designed principally as a resource for authors and provides addresses and other contact information for each journal.

In recent years, law professors and other scholars have sought to escape the constraints of the law review system by finding new avenues for publishing their scholarship. Some authors post works on their own websites, and many use repositories of working papers and other current scholarship such as Berkeley Electronic Press <www.bepress.com>, NELLCO Legal Scholarship Repository <lsr.nellco.org>, and Social Science Research Network (SSRN) <www.ssrn.com>. Both the law review and the open access movement continue to flourish.[8]

Other Law Journals. Specialized journals are also issued by bar associations and commercial publishers. Articles in these journals tend to be shorter and more practical than those found in academic law reviews, often focusing on current developments of interest to practicing lawyers. They are also more likely to feature articles written by practitioners than the general-interest law reviews.[9]

Among the most respected of the specialized bar journals are several published by sections of the American Bar Association, such as *Administrative Law Review*, *Antitrust Law Journal*, and *Business Lawyer*. Some commercial publications such as *Tax Notes* or the *Journal of Passthrough Entities* are major vehicles for lawyers in specialized areas such as taxation to exchange ideas about current developments.

Most national and state bar associations also publish monthly or quarterly magazines with shorter articles and more emphasis on graphics and readability. Even a glossy magazine, however, may contain valuable articles on topics of current interest, particularly those focused on a specific jurisdiction. Because they are written for lawyers, even short articles generally have footnotes providing references to cases, code provisions, and other sources.

Journals in Other Disciplines. Effective legal research, whether academic or practical, is not limited to the insular world of law journals. Several major interdisciplinary legal journals, such as

---

8. The clarion call of the open access movement for legal scholarship was Bernard J. Hibbitts, *Last Writes? Re-Assessing the Law Review in the Age of Cyberspace*, 71 N.Y.U. L. REV. 615 (1996). See also Symposium, *Open Access Publishing and the Future of Legal Scholarship*, 10 LEWIS & CLARK L. REV. 733 (2006); Symposium, *Who Needs Law Reviews?: Legal Scholarship in the Age of Cyberspace*, 30 AKRON L. REV. 173 (1996).

9. See Robert M. Lawless & Ira David, *The General Role Played by Specialty Law Journals: Empirical Evidence from Bankruptcy Scholarship*, 80 AM. BANKR. L.J. 523, 542–43 (2006).

Law & Human Behavior and *Law & Society Review*, contain articles providing a broader perspective on legal issues, and journals in related disciplines such as economics, history, political science, and psychology can provide invaluable background and analysis. More than 20,000 scholarly journals are published, so a large pool of information is available if you know how to find it.[10]

§ 11.2 Finding Articles

You can find articles in periodicals and journals through a variety of means. The full-text databases in Lexis and Westlaw are among the most convenient and most frequently used resources, and PDF-based databases such as HeinOnline and JSTOR are particularly useful for historical and cross-disciplinary research. Indexes available online and in print can expand retrieval beyond full-text sources and focus it more accurately on a specific topic. You can also use tools such as KeyCite and Shepard's Citations to find articles discussing particular cases, statutes or other authorities.

(a) Full–Text Resources

Full-text searching has been the dominant means of finding journal articles for years, and increasing digitization has now made it a viable approach for both historical and current research. Several resources are available for this purpose.

Westlaw and Lexis. Both Westlaw and Lexis have databases containing articles from several hundred law reviews, with coverage for some reviews extending back to the early 1980s and many more beginning in the 1990s. You can search in a specific law review or in databases combining the hundreds of available titles. In Westlaw the JLR database covers U.S. and Canadian journals and law reviews, while TP–ALL combines these materials with treatises and other texts. Lexis law review coverage is available in the Secondary Legal folder on lexis.com (for most legal professionals and law students) and through LexisNexis Academic <web.lexis-nexis.com/universe/> (for university faculty and students).

Both natural language and terms and connectors search methods can be useful in law review research. A natural language search finds articles that use keywords most frequently and are therefore

---

10. Estimates of the number of scholarly journals vary. See, e.g., Stevan Harnad et al., *The Access/Impact Problem and the Green and Gold Roads to Open Access*, 30 SERIALS REV. 310 (2004) (estimating that 24,000 peer-reviewed journals publish about 2.5 million articles per year); Carol Tenopir, *Online Scholarly Journals: How Many?*, LIB. J., Feb. 1, 2004, at 32 (estimating almost 50,000 scholarly journals). The Elektronische Zeitschriftenbibliothek EZB (Electronic Journals Library) <rzblx1.uni-regensburg.de/ezeit/> provides links to the homepages for more than 40,000 titles, of which nearly half are available free online.

most likely to be relevant. Because it lists articles by relevance rather than date and limits retrieval to the number of documents you specify, you must be careful not to rely on outdated articles or miss any important contributions. A terms and connectors search can be used to pinpoint discussion or footnotes using any particular combination of words, including phrases, case names, or titles of other articles or books. Even an article that is not directly on point may provide references to more relevant sources, including treatises or journal volumes that are not themselves in the online database.

Because the databases contain thousands of lengthy articles, a search limited to the *ti* field (in Westlaw) or *title* segment (in Lexis) may lead to a smaller but more relevant group of documents. You can also focus retrieval in terms and connectors searches by using proximity connectors and the *atleast* or *term frequency* features. You can use the *au* field in Westlaw and the *name* segment in Lexis to find articles by particular authors. (The *author* segment on Lexis includes footnotes after authors' names, and therefore searches the names of everyone acknowledged for comments or research assistance.)

One difference in law review articles between Westlaw and Lexis is that Lexis includes a "Summary" before the text. This is not an abstract explaining the scope and purpose of the article, but a computer-generated selection of sentences from the text that may or may not be of assistance. Most articles and student notes and comments begin with an introductory section outlining the main themes and organization of the work, but relatively few law reviews provide real abstracts.

HeinOnline. In less than a decade since its launch in 2000, HeinOnline <www.heinonline.org> has become an essential tool in law review research. It provides digitized page images from the printed journals, allowing desktop access to be the equivalent of going to the library shelves. HeinOnline's coverage extends to the first volumes of most journals in its database, making it particularly valuable in legal history research. It includes more than 1,200 law reviews, and for most titles its coverage extends nearly (but not quite) to the most recent issues.

HeinOnline offers full-text searching of its journals, but its search mechanism is not as flexible or sophisticated as those of Westlaw and Lexis. A "Field Search" screen provides options to search for words or phrases in author, title or text fields and to limit a search to specific subjects, journals or dates. The Boolean connectors AND, OR and NOT can be used, but not proximity connectors. HeinOnline is most useful for historical research in articles not otherwise available online, or for retrieving PDF versions of articles identified through Westlaw or Lexis searches.

EbscoHost Legal Collection. Legal Collection <www.ebscohost.com> is a subscription database with the full text of more than three hundred law journals (but only about fifty U.S. academic law reviews). Its coverage generally begins in the mid–1990s but is frequently more current than HeinOnline. Search options are similar to those in HeinOnline, with field searches and basic Boolean connectors.

Legal Periodicals FullText and LegalTrac. These online subscription resources are primarily indexes (and will be discussed below), but they provide access to some full-text articles. Legal Periodicals FullText has full text for more than 300 journals and LegalTrac for about 150 titles. Coverage in each varies by journal, but generally begins in the mid- to late–1990s. In both databases, full text is searchable but is not included in the default search. In Legal Periodicals FullText, check an "Also search within the full text of the articles, for extra results" box. In LegalTrac, choose to search "Entire Document" rather than "Keyword."

Law Review Websites. Free Internet sites provide some access to recent law review literature. Some law review websites feature only tables of contents or abstracts or are not updated regularly, but a growing number make the full text of recent articles available. A few law reviews, such as the *Virginia Journal of Law and Technology* <www.vjolt.net>, are published only electronically.

The University of Southern California Law Library provides a convenient list of links to law review websites <law.usc.edu/library/resources/journals.cfm>, noting which sites provide the full text of articles, as well as which are limited to abstracts or tables of contents. FindLaw provides a similar listing, divided into more than forty subject categories <stu.findlaw.com/journals/>. Some articles on law review websites may be retrieved through general search engines, but generally these sites are useful for finding specific articles rather than searching by subject.

The standard law review is still published in print, but several reviews have launched online-only adjunct journals for shorter, more timely pieces. Examples include *Harvard Law Review Forum* <www.harvardlawreview.org> (2005–date), *Yale Law Journal Pocket Part* <yalelawjournal.org> (2005–date), *Michigan Law Review First Impressions* <www.michiganlawreview.org> (2006–date), and *Virginia Law Review In Brief* <virginialawreview.org> (2007–date). Articles in these online journals are generally included in Westlaw and Lexis law review databases.

General Scholarly Journal Sites. Legal periodicals are also available through more general scholarly literature websites. JSTOR <www.jstor.org> covers several dozen major law reviews, for example, along with hundreds of journals in other disciplines. It does not have recent issues (generally from the past three to five years), but like HeinOnline it has retrospective coverage and is full-text searchable.

Google Scholar <scholar.google.com> provides free full-text access to thousands of law review articles, found in many journal and working paper websites as well as some subscription sites. Notable among these is HeinOnline's law journal collection, for which Google Scholar can be a powerful, quick search tool. Its advanced search screen permits limiting a search to words or phrases in the titles of articles, and to specific publication dates. It also has a very useful feature showing how many articles in its database have cited each article listed, with direct links to those citing articles. Google Scholar can be a free and convenient place to begin research. A major drawback is that there is no way of learning the scope of its coverage, and therefore no way of knowing whether important articles are omitted.[11]

(b) Indexes and Citators

Full-text searching is a powerful tool, but it does have limitations. Searching for keywords can retrieve many extraneous articles that mention these words only in passing. An index is a way to narrow retrieval to articles more specifically on point. In addition, thousands of articles are not available electronically and might never be found through full-text online searches. Periodical indexes remain valuable resources, especially when you can follow links directly from index entries to the full text of articles.

ILP and LegalTrac. There are two general indexes to English-language legal periodical literature. Both are issued in printed

---

11. See Kathleen Bauer & Nisa Bakkalbasi, *An Examination of Citation Counts in a New Scholarly Communication Environment*, D-Lib Mag., Sept. 2005 <www.dlib.org/dlib/september05/bauer/09bauer.html> ("[U]ntil Google Scholar gives a full account of what material it is indexing and how often that index is updated, it cannot be considered a true scholarly resource ... An understanding of the material being covered is central to the validity of any search of scholarly material."); Péter Jacsó, *Google Scholar: The Pros and the Cons*, 29 Online Info. Rev. 208, 209 (2005) ("The underlying problem with Google Scholar is that Google is as secretive about its coverage as the North Korean government about the famine in the country. There is no information about the publishers whose archive Google is allowed to search, let alone about the specific journals and the host sites covered by Google Scholar."); Philipp Mayr & Anne–Kathrin Walter, *An Exploratory Study of Google Scholar*, 31 Online Info. Rev. 814, 828 (2007) ("It appears that the index is not updated regularly. The coverage and up-to-dateness of individual, specific web servers varies greatly.... Google Scholar does not offer the transparency and completeness to be expected from a scientific information resource.")

volumes with monthly updating pamphlets, but for most researchers the most convenient form of access is online. Index to Legal Periodicals and Books (ILP) is part of the WilsonWeb system, and is available through Lexis and Westlaw as well. LegalTrac is available as part of the Gale's InfoTrac system, and is known as Legal Resource Index (LRI) on Westlaw and Lexis.

Each of these indexes covers more than a thousand law reviews and periodicals, with nearly three decades of online coverage. The WilsonWeb and InfoTrac versions both offer basic and advanced search screens, with the advanced screen offering options to search specific fields such as author, title and subject, and to limit a search by date. In either system, lists of results can be sorted by relevance or date.

The two databases have slightly different approaches to indexing. LegalTrac uses Library of Congress subject headings with detailed subdivisions, while ILP generally has somewhat broader headings. Articles on the open access movement, for example, might be indexed under "Legal literature–Access" and "Open access journals—Laws, regulations and rules" in LegalTrac and "Open access (Internet)" in ILP. Neither approach is better for all purposes, but each has advantages. Sometimes your research may have a very specific focus, while at other times a broader survey is appropriate.

Depending on the database system used, the indexes may also offer direct links to the full text of articles listed. The most extensive access to full text is provided by Westlaw's versions of both ILP and LRI, in that every record for articles in Westlaw's JLR database is linked and noted "<<Full Text Available>>" in the results list. The WilsonWeb and InfoTrac versions also provide direct full-text access to some articles. Even if the index database doesn't include the full text, many library online systems provide a link resolver that automatically searches other subscribed and free databases for the full text of the article.

Illustration 11–2 on page 378 shows records for several articles found by searching for "open access" in LegalTrac. Links to the full text and a PDF image of one of the articles are included below its citation. Further results from bar journals and legal newspapers are available by clicking on the Magazines and News tabs. The full record for each article (not shown) includes links to its subject headings, making it easy to use one relevant work to find others.

Coverage in the online versions of ILP and LegalTrac/LRI extends to 1981 and 1980 respectively. Access to older articles from 1918 to 1981 is available through Legal Periodicals Retro, cumulating information from earlier *Index to Legal Periodicals* volumes. WilsonWeb allows the two databases to be combined, so that one search can find articles from a ninety-year span of legal scholarship. In many libraries, link resolvers lead from the older entries to full text in HeinOnline.

Printed versions of the indexes are still published, although they are used far less than their online counterparts. One possible advantage of the printed indexes is that they have separate sections listing cases and statutes that are the focus of articles, notes or comments. This may be a quicker way to identify works that discuss particular legal authorities in depth. *ILP* also has a section listing book reviews; *CLI* lists reviewed books by author and title in its author section.

The printed versions of the periodical indexes have some idiosyncracies of which users should be aware. *Index to Legal Periodicals and Books (ILP)* indexes articles by subject and author, but in printed volumes before 1983 full bibliographic information appeared *only* under subject entries. The author entries consisted merely of subject heading cross-references, each followed by the first letter of the article's title. If you were looking for work by a specific author, you needed to turn to the appropriate subject heading and then scan its listings to find the title and location of the article.

The printed counterpart to LegalTrac, known as the *Current Law Index (CLI)*, has been published since 1980. Each annual index consists of two volumes with separate author and subject sections. *CLI*'s scope is somewhat narrower than LegalTrac and LRI because it omits their coverage of legal newspapers and relevant articles in non-law periodicals.

KeyCite and Shepard's. KeyCite and Shepard's Citations serve two important purposes in periodical research. You can find articles that cite a primary source such as a case or statute, and you can track a law review article to find later sources in which *it* is cited. Almost every listing includes a link to the full text, although Shepard's on Lexis also includes citations to some articles back to 1957 that are not available in the database.

In print versions of *Shepard's Citations* (but not on Lexis), coverage is generally limited to nineteen national law reviews. References to federal statutes and cases are listed in *Shepard's Federal Law Citations in Selected Law Reviews*. References to state statutes and cases appear in individual state *Shepard's* volumes (not the regional reporter *Shepard's* editions), and add citations to law reviews published in the state. Sources citing law review articles are listed in *Shepard's Law Review Citations*.

You can also find references to a particular article in full-text databases on Westlaw, Lexis, or HeinOnline simply by using its title or citation as a search term. A full-text search can go beyond the scope of KeyCite or Shepard's and find references to *any* published work of interest—including articles in early or obscure law reviews, journal literature in other disciplines, treatises, or monographs.

Other Legal Indexes. While the major periodical indexes provide extensive coverage, several specialized indexes are also available. Some of these cover articles not found in the general indexes, such as articles from other countries or in specialized or interdisciplinary journals.

The National Criminal Justice Reference Service Abstracts Database <www.ncjrs.gov/abstractdb/> has summaries of selected articles from nearly 200 journals in criminology and related disciplines, as well as government reports and other research sources. The criminal justice literature is also covered by *Criminal Justice Abstracts* (1968–date, quarterly) and *Criminal Justice Periodicals Index* (1981–date, online by subscription through ProQuest <www.proquest.com>).

Taxation has two specialized indexes: CCH's *Federal Tax Articles* (1969–date, monthly), with abstracts of journal articles arranged by Internal Revenue Code section; and *Index to Federal Tax Articles* (1975–date, quarterly), a subject/author index with retrospective coverage back to 1913. *Environmental Law Reporter* includes a monthly "Journal Literature" feature listing new law review articles by subject.

For research in legal history, the predecessor to the *Index to Legal Periodicals*, entitled *Index to Legal Periodical Literature* (1888–1939), may be of use. The first volume provides retrospective coverage from 1770 to 1886.[12]

The *Index to Periodical Articles Related to Law* (1958–2005 in print; 1958–date on HeinOnline) covers a wide range of articles in magazines and scholarly journals on legal issues. The HeinOnline database (in the Law Journal Library) can be searched by title keyword, author, or subject.

General Periodical Indexes. Legal research is rarely confined to cases, statutes, and law review articles. You also need to be able to find information in a wide variety of disciplines. Several indexes to nonlegal periodical literature can supply valuable leads. Some of these are specialized indexes in particular disciplines, while

---

12. *Index to Legal Periodical Literature* is sometimes called the Jones–Chipman index after the names of its editors, Leonard A. Jones (vols. 1–2) and Frank E. Chipman (vols. 3–6). The development of legal periodical indexes is discussed in Richard A. Leiter, *A History of Legal Periodical Indexing*, LEGAL REF-ERENCE SERVICES Q., Spring 1987, at 35. KERMIT L. HALL, A COMPREHENSIVE BIBLIOGRAPHY OF AMERICAN CONSTITUTIONAL AND LEGAL HISTORY (1984–91) lists books and articles published between 1896 and 1987 and is another potentially useful source for legal historians.

others have comprehensive coverage of a wide range of sources (sometimes including legal journals). The online versions of many indexes link directly to full-text PDF versions of the articles listed.

Indexes from other disciplines such as ABI/INFORM (business and economics), America: History & Life (U.S. and Canadian history), EconLit (economics), PAIS International (public policy), PsycINFO (psychology and related disciplines), or Sociological Abstracts may offer background information or interdisciplinary perspectives. A few indexes are available free on the Internet, such as the National Library of Medicine's PubMed version of MEDLINE, the comprehensive index of biomedical journals <www.pubmed. gov>. Most index databases, however, are accessible by subscription only. A few are available through Westlaw or Lexis, and researchers in university or law school libraries usually have access to many others. Most of these databases include searchable abstracts, which can be invaluable both in finding articles and in identifying whether they would be of value.

Thomson Reuters (formerly Institute for Scientific Information) publishes ISI Web of Knowledge <www.isiwebofknowledge. com>, a very broad citation index covering more than 23,000 journals. It functions like KeyCite or Shepard's in that it can run a "Cited Reference Search" to find articles citing a particular author or source, and you can also search for articles by author or keyword. Web of Knowledge has three components which can be searched separately or together. The most useful in legal research is Social Sciences Citation Index (covering 1966–date), which includes extensive coverage of law journals. The others are Science Citation Index (1955–date) and Arts & Humanities Citation Index (1976–date).

Other major multidisciplinary indexes, one or more of which may be available by subscription at an academic library, include EBSCOhost Academic Search Complete <www.ebscohost.com>, InfoTrac OneFile <www.gale.cengage.com/onefile>, and ProQuest Central <proquest.com>. All of these databases serve as one-stop shops for a wide range of journal literature.

IngentaConnect <www.ingentaconnect.com> also has comprehensive coverage of current journal literature, with tables of contents information from more than 30,000 publications. One advantage of IngentaConnect is that searching is free to researchers unaffiliated with subscribing institutions. Most articles are available for fee-based download by nonsubscribers.

JSTOR <www.jstor.org> was mentioned earlier as a source for retrospective coverage of several dozen legal journals; it also has full-text comprehensive coverage of several hundred other non-law scholarly journals. Two other subscription web services with access to older journal articles from as far back 1665 are Periodicals Archive Online <pao.chadwyck.com> (full text of more than five hundred journals) and Periodical Index Online <pio.chadwyck.com> (indexing of more than five thousand other journals).

(c) Current Scholarship

The full-text databases and standard legal periodical indexes are valuable for subject searches, when you are trying to find articles on a particular topic. When you are looking for current scholarship in an area, you can use a different set of tools specifically designed to keep the scholarly community apprised of recent and forthcoming articles.

Social Science Research Network (SSRN) and Berkeley Electronic Press (bepress) were mentioned earlier as alternative to traditional law reviews for disseminating scholarship. SSRN's Legal Scholarship Network (LSN) and the bepress Legal Repository are both major repositories for working papers and pre-publication versions of law review articles, and much newer work is available here long before it appears in print.

You can search SSRN's electronic library <papers.ssrn.com> by author or by keywords in titles and abstracts. The default display is relevance, but you can focus on recent scholarship by sorting search results by date posted. Faculty and students at subscribing institutions can also sign up for weekly e-mail notification of abstracts of new articles in any of more than a hundred LSN subject-matter e-journals.

The bepress Legal Repository <law.bepress.com/repository/> can be searched by author or keyword, and articles in more than one hundred subject topics can be browsed to survey recent scholarship. The system includes an option to receive e-mail notifications of future documents that match a search request.

Several resources provide information about new issues of law reviews. The most extensive of these is Washington & Lee Law School's Current Law Journal Content (CJLC) <lawlib.wlu. edu/CLJC/>, which is available free and has tables of contents for more than 1,400 law journals. Article titles can be searched with Boolean connectors, root expansion, and phrase searching. CJLC also allows you to save searches and receive weekly e-mail alerts of search results in new tables of contents. Coverage for most journals is retrospective to 2000, so for recent law review literature CJLC can also serve as a free alternative to the subscription indexes.

Current Index to Legal Periodicals (*CILP*) <lib.law.washington.edu/cilp/cilp.html>, published weekly by the University of Washington's Marian Gould Gallagher Law Library, also provides tables of contents for new law review issues with the added value of subject indexing. It covers more than six hundred law reviews, indexing articles under approximately one hundred subject headings. Subscribers can receive customized weekly e-mail "Smart-CILP" updates limited to particular subjects and journal titles. Online access, limited to the most recent eight weeks, is also available through Westlaw as the CILP database.

The Tarlton Law Library at the University of Texas provides Contents Pages from Law Reviews and Other Scholarly Journals <tarlton.law.utexas.edu/tallons/content_search.html>. This covers more than 750 titles, and is available free and updated daily. Although it lacks subject indexing, it can be searched for authors' names or title keywords. Its scope is limited to the most recent three months. Like *CILP*, its purpose is to provide access to articles too new to be covered by the standard commercial indexes.

§ 11.3 Sources for News and Current Awareness

Practicing lawyers must keep aware of developments in their areas of practice.[13] They must maintain current knowledge of new court decisions, pending legislation, and agency announcements, as well as changes in the political, financial or business world.

Current awareness serves another purpose as well. Individual research assignments can build your expertise on specific questions, but they don't give you a broad overview of an area of law. Only by reading about new developments on a regular basis will you develop the confidence that you're seeing the big picture and that your knowledge has no significant gaps. If you are new to a practice area, find out what senior attorneys read on a daily or weekly basis and sign up to see these publications. If you will be working extensively with a particular industry, reading its trade or professional journals will help you communicate with your clients and anticipate their concerns.

There are several approaches to keeping on top of current activities and new developments in the law, including legal and general-interest newspapers, newsletters, and blogs. Using features

---

13. See MODEL RULES OF PROF'L CONDUCT R. 1.1 cmt. 6 (2008) ("To maintain the requisite knowledge and skill, a lawyer should keep abreast of changes in the law and its practice, engage in continuing study and education and comply with all continuing legal education requirements to which the lawyer is subject.")

Current awareness demands can undoubtedly be stressful. See Steven Keeva, *The Joy of Not Knowing*, LAW PRAC. MGMT., Jan./Feb. 2000, at 46, 46 ("The amount of law the average lawyer is required to know these days seems to proliferate like some mutant culture spilling from legislative and judicial petri dishes. And keeping up with clients' businesses in today's nanosecond environment demands constant vigilance. Each day there's more to know, and feeling responsible for knowing it all creates anxiety and a sense of depletion.")

like Westlaw's WestClip and Lexis Alerts, you can set up automated searches that will run at the frequency of your choice and notify you by e-mail if a search retrieves new documents matching your criteria. Similarly, you can use the free alerting features of major search engines like Google Alerts <www.google.com/alerts> and Yahoo! Alerts <alerts.yahoo.com> to automatically search the web for specific terms. Results can be delivered to you through e-mail or RSS ("Really Simple Syndication") feeds. RSS feeds use aggregator programs or sites such as Bloglines <www.bloglines.com> or News-Gator <www.newsgator.com> to display feed results. Browsers such as Internet Explorer version 7 have built-in RSS feed display capabilities. With RSS feeds, you to create custom news pages by bringing together news and blog headlines from multiple sources.

(a) Legal Newspapers

News on developments in the legal profession is available from a number of daily and weekly newspapers. Legal newspapers often cover developing topics and decisions of lower courts which may not be reported elsewhere. They also contain court calendars and legal announcements that are required by statute or court order to be published in local newspapers.

The articles and essays published in legal newspapers can be hard to track down, but many newspaper websites now have searchable archives, available free or by subscription. LegalTrac and LRI include indexing coverage of several legal newspapers. Seven newspapers (*Chicago Daily Law Bulletin, Legal Times, Los Angeles Daily Journal, National Law Journal, New Jersey Law Journal, New York Law Journal,* and *Pennsylvania Law Weekly*) have been covered since the early 1980s, and *Lawyers Weekly* publications from seven states (Massachusetts, Michigan, Missouri, North Carolina, Rhode Island, South Carolina, and Virginia) were added in 2002 or 2003. Complete coverage of these *Lawyers Weekly* newspapers is available in LegalTrac, but LRI on Lexis and Westlaw has only the most recent several months.

Westlaw provides access to several dozen daily and weekly newspapers, including every LegalTrac title except the *Los Angeles Daily Journal.* The LEGALNP database provides combined coverage of its legal newspapers. Lexis has a smaller collection of newspapers, but its Legal News Publications file includes the *Chicago Daily Law Bulletin* and the *Lawyers Weekly* newspapers.

One of the leading Internet sources for current legal news is law.com <www.law.com>, with stories from *Legal Times, National Law Journal,* and regional newspapers. Its website includes Quest, a legal search engine that indexes these and other newspapers as well as blogs and publications from law firm websites.

Other sources for current legal news, providing a variety of original and wire service material, include the *ABA Journal*'s Law News Now <abajournal.com/news>, the University of Pittsburgh School of Law's JURIST <jurist.law.pitt.edu>, and FindLaw Legal News <news.findlaw.com>.

Legal newspapers across the country are listed by state in two publications: "Legal Newspapers in the U.S.," in *Legal Research-er's Desk Reference* (Arlene L. Eis ed., biennial), and "Appendix D: State and Local Legal Newspapers," in Kendall F. Svengalis, *Legal Information Buyer's Guide & Reference Manual* (annual). Both lists indicate frequency of publication and provide contact information and URLs. Each includes a few titles omitted by the other.

(b) General Newspapers

Legal newspapers focus on law-related activity, but for a broad-er picture of developments in business, politics and society you'll need to monitor more general sources such as major newspapers or news websites. News stories can also be rich resources for factual research or background information.

Two of the most convenient news sources for law students are Westlaw and Lexis. Westlaw provides access to hundreds of newspa-pers, as well as wire services and business publications; and Lexis's news library has the text of newspapers, magazines, trade journals, newsletters, and wire services. The two systems have considerable overlap in coverage, but each has sources not found in the other; both, for example, have the *New York Times* and the *Washington Post*, while only Lexis has the full text of the *Wall Street Journal*. Each has files combining its news sources. Westlaw's ALLNEWS covers its newspapers, while ALLNEWSPLUS adds wire service stories as well. On Lexis, you can choose from files covering the most recent ninety days, the most recent two years, or all available news sources.

Other electronic sources of news include websites for individual newspapers, such as the New York Times <www.nyt.com> and the Washington Post <www.washingtonpost.com>, and multisource subscription databases such as Factiva <www.factiva.com>. Google News <news.google.com> provides free and very current coverage of a wide range of newspapers, magazines, and wire services. Websites for newspapers and other news sources can be found through search engines or directory sites such as NewsVoyager <www.newsvoyager.com>.

Back issues of major newspapers are usually available in large libraries on microfilm, and ProQuest Historical Newspapers <www.proquest.com> provides subscription-based web access to PDF im-ages of several major newspapers from as far back as 1764. Coverage, with varying dates for each source, includes the *Atlanta Constitution*, *Boston Globe*, *Chicago Tribune*, *Christian Science Monitor*, *Hartford Courant*, *Los Angeles Times*, *New York Times*, *New York Tribune*, *San Francisco Chronicle*, *Wall Street Journal*, and *Washington Post*.

Numerous other historical newspapers have been digitized in recent years, vastly increasing access to contemporary accounts of major legal developments. America's Historical Newspapers, 1690–1922 <www.newsbank.com/readex/?content=96> covers more than 2,000 historical newpapers from all fifty states. 19th Century U.S. Newspapers <www.gale.cengage.com/DigitalCollections/> has 500 titles from the 1800s, and NewspaperARCHIVE.com <newspaper archive.com> has newspapers from nearly 800 cities, with the broadest coverage in the twentieth century. Google News Archive <news.google.com/archivesearch> searches a variety of databases, including ProQuest, with a range of free, fee-based and subscription options for viewing the full text of articles.

(c) Newsletters and Looseleaf Services

In addition to newspapers and magazines covering legal developments generally, numerous more specific publications are available in topical areas. Many of these are available both in print and online, with e-mail or RSS notification of new developments.

Many newsletters are published as part of looseleaf services, which have already been discussed in other chapters for their publication of primary sources and summaries of legal doctrine. Some looseleaf services include pamphlets as part of their weekly updates, while others are in effect newsletters reporting on current developments. BNA's *The United States Law Week*, for example, reports every week not only on the Supreme Court, but also on new court decisions and legislative, regulatory and professional developments. BNA also publishes similar services in several specific areas, including *Antitrust & Trade Regulation Report*, *Criminal Law Reporter*, *Family Law Reporter*, and *Securities Regulation & Law Report*. These serve as major current awareness tools in their fields.

A large number of additional current awareness newsletters are published online and in print. Specialized newsletters often have a limited circulation and can be hard to find in academic or public law libraries, but they may be the best available sources for information about newly developing areas of law. Newsletters are often the forum through which practitioners in very specialized areas share information and documents. For example, a newsletter may include copies of pleadings or other trial court documents as well as articles on recent developments.

Several newsletter publishers make their products available through Westlaw or Lexis. Westlaw has more than fifty Andrews Publications reporters, some on very specific topics of litigation such as repetitive stress injury and others on broader areas such as antitrust or disability litigation. Westlaw also has some three hundred other newsletters, some focusing on specific states and others providing nationwide coverage, listed in the Law Reviews, Bar Journals & Legal Periodicals section of its directory. The LEGNEWSL database combines access to all of the newsletters on Westlaw.

Lexis provides access to dozens of Mealey's Litigation Reports files on specific litigation topics from antidepressant drugs to welding rods, and Mealey's Litigation News for specific jurisdictions. Lexis also has a Combined Legal Newsletters file, in its Secondary Legal folder, but it only covers about thirty publications and does not include the Mealey's titles.

In addition to its looseleaf services, BNA publishes about two dozen daily newsletters in areas such as environmental law, labor law, and taxation. Some of these are available in both print and online versions, but others are electronic-only publications.

Numerous law firms produce newsletters for their clients and other readers, often providing useful information about developing areas of law. They are generally available through law firm websites, and can be identified through topical browsing or keyword searches in resources such as Mondaq <www.mondaq.com>, a compendium of information from accountants, law firms, and consulting firms. Free registration is required to view the full text of articles.

You can identify available newsletters in a subject area in the annual *Legal Newsletters in Print*, which describes more than 2,200 newsletters and has information about subscription prices and Internet access. A subject index provides topical access to its listings. This publication is available to online subscribers, along with *Legal Looseleafs in Print* and *Directory of Law–Related CD–ROMs*, as part of the LawTRIO database <www.infosourcespub.com>.

(d) Blogs and Other Resources

In recent years, blogs have become a major vehicle for timely dissemination of information and opinion. Law blogs (sometimes called "blawgs") are written on a variety of topics, ranging from general ruminations on legal issues such as the University of Chicago Law School Faculty Blog <uchicagolaw.typepad.com> to very focused resources such as the Wisconsin Truck Accident Law Blog <www.wisconsintruckaccidentlawblog.com>. Some blogs have become leading sources of current information. SCOTUSblog <www.scotusblog.com>, for example, often is the first available source with breaking news about the Supreme Court. Others are major sources for the exchange of new ideas in legal scholarship.[14]

Several directories of legal blogs are available. Two of the most extensive, both in blogs covered and in subject categories, are the ABA Journal's Blawg Directory <www.abajournal.com/blawgs> and Justia Blawg Search <blawgsearch.justia.com>. Both sites provide samples of recent postings, links to the blog sites, and search engines for searching blog postings. More general resources that can be used to search for blog postings include Technorati <www.technorati.com> and Google Blog Search <blogsearch.google.com>.

E-mail listservs and discussion groups provide another effective way to keep on top of developments in a particular area, and can also be used to seek assistance with difficult research issues. Some lists disseminate information from organizations or government agencies, while others are designed for specialists in an area to share news and ideas. Posing questions to a list often yields results that would otherwise elude most researchers. Chances are that some list subscriber may be able to help with a thorny legal issue or can identify a source for an obscure document. Older messages to a list, if available in a searchable Internet archive, may form a valuable repository of information in the area.

More than seventy-five lists on legal topics are maintained by the Washburn University School of Law <www.washlaw.edu/listservs/>, and hundreds of others are available. L–Soft CataList <www.lsoft.com/lists/listref.html> is a catalog of more than 50,000 discussion groups. It does not have a subject directory, but its search feature can be used to find lists on legal and nonlegal topics of interest.

---

14. See Symposium, *Bloggership: How Blogs Are Transforming Legal Scholarship*, 84 WASH. U.L. REV. 1025 (2006); Margaret A. Schilt, *The Future of Legal Scholarship*, LEGAL TIMES, July 9, 2007, at 26.

1136   *University of California, Davis*   [Vol. 37:1135]

"There are various forms of curiosity: one, based on self-interest, makes us want to learn what may be useful, another, based on pride, comes from a desire to know what others don't."[1]

The student-run law review is a puzzling phenomenon. To the legal outsider, the practice of allowing second- and third-year law students to select and edit the research of established scholars seems preposterous.[2] How could students *possibly* know what constitutes a significant advance in a line of legal argument? And how *dare* students tell law professors what is and what is not good scholarship? The very idea of it sounds like the proverbial asylum where the inmates are in charge.[3]

But, ridiculous as it may be, this is the system of scholarship that legal academics and law students have inherited.[4] Ever since curmudgeon Fred Rodell identified the two fundamental problems with law reviews — their form and their content[5] — legal scholars have spilled a great deal of ink extolling the virtues and vices of law reviews.[6] Critics continue to excoriate the law review system[7] and apologists continue to defend it.[8]

Yet in spite of all this lively debate about the pros and cons of the law review system, there has been little discussion of why law students become involved with law reviews.[9] What attracts law students to the law review in the first place, and what holds them there?

---

[1] LA ROCHEFOUCAULD, MAXIMS 59 (Leonard Tancock ed., Penguin Books 1959) (1665).

[2] *See* James Lindgren, *An Author's Manifesto*, 61 U. CHI. L. REV. 527, 535 (1994) ("In some other parts of the academy, legal journals are considered a joke. Scholars elsewhere frequently can't believe that, for almost all our major academic journals, we let students without advanced degrees select manuscripts.").

[3] *See* John G. Kester, *Faculty Participation in the Student-Edited Law Review*, 36 J. LEGAL EDUC. 14, 14 (1986).

[4] *See generally* Bernard Hibbitts, *Last Writes? Reassessing the Law Review in the Age of Cyberspace*, 71 N.Y.U. L. REV. 615 (1996), *available at* http://www.law.pitt.edu/hibbitts /lastrev.htm (last visited Jan. 20, 2004) (analyzing history of law reviews and their future as technology and Internet continue to develop).

[5] Fred Rodell, *Goodbye to Law Reviews*, 23 VA. L. REV. 38, 38 (1937).

[6] *See, e.g.*, Symposium, *Law Review Conference*, 47 STAN. L. REV. 1117 (1995); Symposium, *Law Review Editing: The Struggle Between Author and Editor Over Control of the Text*, 70 CHI.-KENT L. REV. 71 (1994); Symposium, *Who Needs Law Reviews?: Legal Scholarship in the Age of Cyberspace*, 30 AKRON L. REV. 173 (1996).

[7] *See, e.g.*, James Lindgren, *Fear of Writing*, 78 CAL. L. REV. 1677 (1990).

[8] *See, e.g.*, Phil Nichols, Note, *A Student Defense of Student Edited Journals: In Response to Professor Roger Cramton*, 1987 DUKE L.J. 1122 (1987).

[9] *But see, e.g.*, Vincent E. Gunter, *The Moon, the Stars, and All the Planets*, 30 STETSON L. REV. 547 (2000) (discussing student's role as law review editor in chief); Nathan H. Saunders, Note, *Student-Edited Law Reviews: Reflections and Responses of an Inmate*, 49 DUKE L.J. 1663 (2000).

Illustration 11–1. J.C. Oleson, *You Make Me [Sic]: Confessions of a Sadistic Law Review Editor*, 37 U.C. DAVIS L. REV. 1135, 1136 (2004).

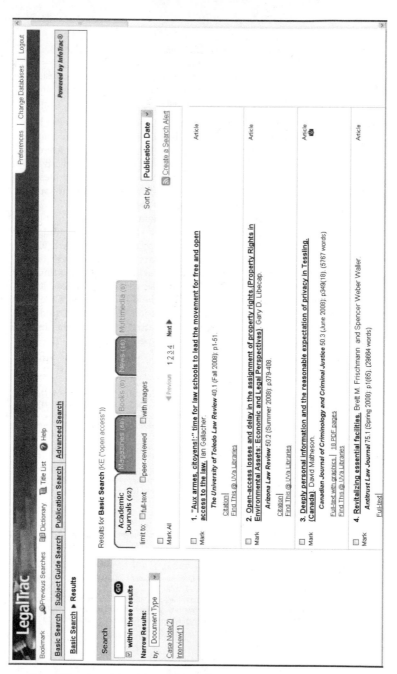

Illustration 11–2. Search results, LegalTrac
<infotrac.galegroup.com>.

Chapter 12

SECONDARY SOURCES, PART 3: REFERENCE RESOURCES

Table of Sections

This chapter looks at legal resources designed to provide answers to relatively simple questions. These resources generally do not contain primary source materials or analyze legal developments, but are instead sources for definitions, telephone numbers, addresses, facts, and statistics. Knowing how to find this information quickly can save valuable time.

§ 12.1 Dictionaries and Related Works

The law has developed its own means of expression over the centuries. Latin, law French, and the stylized language of legal documents have produced a terminology that can be difficult for the uninitiated to understand. Latin words and phrases are still prevalent, from the writs of *certiorari* or *habeas corpus* to doctrines such as *res ipsa loquitur*, and even everyday words such as *infant* or *issue* have specialized meanings in legal documents.

(a) Dictionaries

A good law dictionary is needed to understand the language of the law. The leading work, *Black's Law Dictionary* (Bryan A. Garner ed., 8th ed. 2004, available as the BLACKS database on Westlaw) provides definitions for more than 40,000 terms, and it includes pronunciations and nearly 3,000 quotations from scholarly works as well as tables of legal abbreviations and legal maxims. It can be used to find new legal terminology and to define older terms found in historical documents.[1] Illustration 12–1 on page 399 shows a page from *Black's* with definitions for terms from *duumviri* to *dysnomy*. A new 9th edition is being published in 2009.

Some lawyers continue to use *Ballentine's Law Dictionary* (William S. Anderson ed., 3d ed. 1969, available on Lexis). *Ballentine's* was once the major competitor to *Black's* and may still be useful for older terms, but it is now considerably out of date and lacks many modern legal terms and usages. A few lawyers swear by the even more outdated but scholarly three-volume set *Bouvier's Law Dictionary and Concise Encyclopedia* (Francis Rawle ed., 8th ed. 1914), which is available in HeinOnline's Legal Classics Library <www.heinonline.org>.[2]

Several other, shorter dictionaries can also be found in law libraries and bookstores. Among the best are Steven H. Gifis, *Law Dictionary* (5th ed. 2003), and Daniel Oran, *Oran's Dictionary of the Law* (4th ed. 2008). Two dictionaries that are available both in print and as free Internet resources are *Merriam-Webster's Dictionary of Law* (1996) <dictionary.lp.findlaw.com> and Gerald N. Hill & Kathleen Thompson Hill, *Real Life Dictionary of the Law* (1995) <dictionary.law.com>. Nolo, the self-help legal publisher, provides a plain-language law dictionary online, Everybody's Legal Glossary <www.nolo.com/glossary.cfm>.

Legal maxims sometimes found in court opinions, such as "Aliquis non debet esse Judex in propria causa,"[3] assume a knowledge of Latin and are thus impenetrable to many readers. *Black's* provides translations, definitions, and pronunciation aids for many maxims, and older dictionaries such as *Ballentine's* or *Bouvier's* include other phrases that are now obscure. *Latin Words & Phrases for Lawyers* (R. S. Vasan ed., 1980) provides extensive coverage of maxims and includes an index by subject. Russ ver Steeg, *Essential Latin for Lawyers* (1990) explains several dozen key phrases still in common use.

Attempts to transform legal writing from legalese jargon into plain English have made some headway in recent years.[4] Bryan A.

---

1. For a review of the 8th edition and background on earlier editions dating back to 1892, *see* Roy M. Mersky & Jeanne Price, *The Dictionary and the Man*, 9 GREEN BAG 2D 83 (2005). On the history of law dictionaries more generally, *see* D. S. Bland, *Some Notes on the Evolution of the Legal Dictionary*, 1 J. LEGAL HIST. 75 (1980); Gary L. McDowell, *The Politics of Meaning: Law Dictionaries and the Liberal Tradition of Interpretation*, 44 AM. J. LEGAL HIST. 257 (2000); Roy M. Mersky, *The Evolution*

and Impact of Legal Dictionaries, 23(1) LEGAL REFERENCE SERVICES Q. 19 (2004).

2. See Mary Whisner, *Bouvier's, Black's, and Tinkerbell*, 92 LAW LIBR. J. 99 (2000).

3. *Tellabs, Inc. v. Makor Issues & Rights, Ltd.*, 127 S.Ct. 2499, 2513 n. * (2007) (Scalia, J., concurring in the judgment) ("No man ought to be a judge of his own cause.").

4. RICHARD C. WYDICK, PLAIN ENGLISH FOR LAWYERS (5th ed. 2005) is the classic

Garner, *A Dictionary of Modern Legal Usage* (2d ed. 1995, 1st ed. 1987 available on Lexis) focuses on how words are used in legal contexts, with definitions and essays providing articulate advocacy for clear and simple writing. David Mellinkoff, *Mellinkoff's Dictionary of Legal Usage* (1992) is a complementary work that provides examples of usage and distinctions among related terms.

A thesaurus can be a handy tool when searching for an alternative to an overused or not-quite-correct word. William C. Burton, *Legal Thesaurus* (4th ed. 2007) focuses on words commonly used in legal writing and argument. Its first part lists main entries and their synonyms and alternatives, and its second part is an index with references from all listed words to the main entries in which they appear.

General dictionaries of the English language are used by courts even more frequently than legal dictionaries.[5] Major dictionaries include the *Random House Webster's Unabridged Dictionary* (2d ed. 2001), with over 315,000 entries, and *Webster's Third New International Dictionary of the English Language, Unabridged* (1993), with over 450,000 entries. The authoritative reference work on the history and development of the English language is the *Oxford English Dictionary*, which has representative quotations illustrating usage over the course of a word's lifespan. A twenty-volume second edition was published in 1989, and the third edition is underway as *OED Online* <dictionary.oed.com>.

Quotations are frequently used in legal writing, but they are not always cited to the volume and page of the sources in which they first appeared. The origins of many quotations are often less clear than they may seem, and famous politicians and jurists such as Abraham Lincoln and Oliver Wendell Holmes, Jr. are attributed with numerous expressions they probably never said.[6] A good quotation dictionary provides not only a list of quotations but also detailed information so that the original source can be confirmed

---

work on simplifying legal communication. Several other guides are available, including BRYAN A. GARNER, LEGAL WRITING IN PLAIN ENGLISH (2001). For a broader view of how things got so bad, see PETER TIERSMA, LEGAL LANGUAGE (1999). "Although some have suggested that legal English is a separate language, it seems best to regard it as a variety of English." Id. at 49.

5. On the Supreme Court's use of dictionaries, see, e.g., Ellen P. Aprill, *The Law of the Word: Dictionary Shopping in the Supreme Court*, 30 ARIZ. ST. L.J. 275 (1998); Craig Hoffman, *Parse the Sentence First: Curbing the Urge to Resort to the Dictionary When Interpreting Legal Texts*, 6 N.Y.U. J. LEGIS. & PUB. POL'Y 401 (2002); Samuel A. Thumma & Jeffrey L. Kirchmeier, *The Lexicon Has Become a Fortress: The United States Supreme Court's Use of Dictionaries*, 47 BUFF. L. REV. 227 (1999). In recent years, the Federal Circuit has also grappled with the role of dictionaries in construing patent claims. See, e.g., Joseph Scott Miller & James A. Hilsenteger, *The Proven Key: Roles and Rules for Dictionaries at the Patent Office and the Courts*, 54 AM. U. L. REV. 829 (2005).

6. See Fred R. Shapiro, *Quote . . . Misquote*, N.Y. TIMES MAG., July 27, 2008, at 16.

and the quotation read in context. The leading dictionary of legal quotations is Fred R. Shapiro, *Oxford Dictionary of American Legal Quotations* (1993), with over 3,500 quotations from American judges and legal commentators. Illustration 12–2 on page 400 shows a page from this dictionary with several quotations on the topic of legal research.

Shapiro has applied the same principled and thorough approach in editing the more general *Yale Book of Quotations* (2006). Other quotation books that may also be of use include *Quote It Completely!: World Reference Guide to More Than 5,500 Memorable Quotations from Law and Literature* (Eugene C. Gerhart ed., 1998, available online in HeinOnline's Legal Classics Library); and the general reference works *Bartlett's Familiar Quotations* (Justin Kaplan ed., 17th ed. 2002) and *The Oxford Dictionary of Quotations* (Elizabeth Knowles ed., 6th ed. 2004). The *Yale Book of Quotations* is arranged alphabetically by author, *Bartlett's* is chronological by author, and the others are arranged by subject. Each includes a word index for helping to identify and track down elusive quotations.

(b) Citation and Abbreviations Guides

One of the first hurdles encountered in understanding legal literature is the telegraphic citation form used in most sources. Legal citations are designed to provide in a very succinct manner the information necessary to find the source and to evaluate the scope of its precedential value.[7] All case citations, for example, identify not only where a case can be found but also the issuing court and the date of decision.

The citation form used in legal documents dates back centuries, but the standard guide to its present use is *The Bluebook: A Uniform System of Citation* (18th ed. 2005) <www.legalbluebook. com.>, which is compiled by the editors of the Columbia Law Review, Harvard Law Review, University of Pennsylvania Law Review, and Yale Law Journal.[8] The Association of Legal Writing

---

7. Judge Richard Posner has explained the reasons for standardized citation forms: "Let us consider what purposes are served by having a system of citation forms rather than a free-for-all. There are four. The first is to spare the writer or editor from having to think about citation form; he memorizes the book of forms, or uses its index.... The second purpose, which is self-evident, is to economize on space and the reader's time. The third, which is in tension with the second, is to provide information to the reader. The fourth is to minimize distraction." Richard A. Posner, *Goodbye to the Bluebook*, 53 U. CHI. L. REV. 1343, 1344 (1986). Other sources on the history and purpose of legal citation forms include Paul Axel–Lute, *Legal Citation Form: Theory and Practice*, 75 LAW LIBR. J. 148 (1982), and Byron D. Cooper, *Anglo-American Legal Citation: Historical Development and Library Implications*, 75 LAW LIBR. J. 3 (1982).

8. *The Bluebook* famously began life in 1926 as a 26–page pamphlet prepared by Erwin Griswold for his *Harvard Law Review* colleagues, although it was pre-

Directors' *ALWD Citation Manual* (Darby Dickerson ed., 3d ed. 2006) is preferred by numerous legal writing programs and a few journals as a more straightforward and easier-to-learn alternative to *The Bluebook*. Cornell Law School's Legal Information Institute publishes an online *Introduction to Basic Legal Citation* <www.law. cornell.edu/citation/>, a concise guide with examples using both *Bluebook* and *ALWD* rules.

There is a developing trend towards public domain citations that do not require reference to particular volumes and page numbers, as discussed in Chapter 6 on pages 219–220, but *The Bluebook* and other citation systems generally require citation to printed sources if the material is published in that form. Some electronic resources provide page images mirroring the printed version, while others (including Westlaw and Lexis) indicate the printed page numbers in the text of the electronic documents. In some instances, however, for a complete citation it may still be necessary to track down the original printed version in the library.

No matter what citation rules are followed, part of the puzzle is simply deciphering the abbreviations in order to identify sources. The online systems let you enter an unfamiliar citation using "Find" or "Get a Document," so recognizing a citation is not always necessary in order to obtain a document. This approach leads to a dead end, however, as often as it succeeds. Cases and law review articles contain numerous abbreviations and citations that are cryptic even to experienced researchers.

Reference works such as *Black's Law Dictionary* and *The Bluebook* contain tables listing the major abbreviations found in legal literature, but these are hardly comprehensive. The most convenient source for deciphering citations is probably the free online Cardiff Index to Legal Abbreviations <www.legalabbrevs. cardiff.ac.uk>. It has a British focus but includes many U.S. sources and can be searched by either abbreviation or title keyword. Specialized abbreviation dictionaries are also available. Mary Miles Prince, *Bieber's Dictionary of Legal Abbreviations* (5th ed. 2001, 4th

ceded by similar works used by *Yale Law Journal* editors. These pamphlets and subsequent *Bluebook* editions are available online in PDF <www. legalbluebook.com/Public/Introduction. aspx> and are reprinted in THE BLUE-BOOK: A SIXTY-FIVE YEAR RETROSPECTIVE (1998). Robert C. Berring's foreword notes that *The Bluebook* "has inflicted more pain on more law students than any other publication in legal history." 1 id. at v.

Over the years there has been an extensive law review literature on *The Bluebook*, much of it highly critical. For a review of this history and references to other articles, *see* Christine Hurt, *The Bluebook at Eighteen: Reflecting and Ratifying Current Trends in Legal Scholarship*, 82 IND. L.J. 49 (2007). One particularly intriguing analysis of *The Bluebook* is Aside, *Don't Cry Over Filled Milk: The Neglected Footnote Three to Carolene Products*, 136 U. PA. L. REV. 1553 (1988) (explaining that its rules are so mysterious that they could only have been produced by an advanced extraterrestrial race).

ed. 1993 available on Lexis) and Donald Raistrick, *Index to Legal Citations and Abbreviations* (3d ed. 2008) are the leading U.S. and British resources respectively. Their coverage overlaps, but each includes sources not found in the other.

§ 12.2 Directories

Earlier chapters discussed directories covering federal and state legislatures, administrative agencies, and courts. Numerous directories provide contact and biographical information for lawyers. Two of these provide national coverage of the U.S. legal profession, but neither includes every lawyer in the country.

The *Martindale-Hubbell Law Directory* is the more established source, dating to the nineteenth century.[9] Its electronic versions through Lexis, on CD, and on the Internet as the Martindale–Hubbell Lawyer Locator <www.martindale.com> have the most extensive coverage. Basic listings provide only mailing addresses, but most attorneys have more extensive entries with telephone numbers, e-mail addresses, and biographical information such as practice areas, education, bar admissions, professional affiliations, and areas of practice. Martindale–Hubbell has a Peer Review Rating system that evaluates lawyers on legal ability and ethical standards. Legal ability ratings range from A (Very High to Preeminent) to C (Good to High), and these are published only if accompanied by an ethical standards rating of V (Very High). Lawyers are generally rated only after five years of practice, and even then not all lawyers are rated.[10]

Martindale-Hubbell is also available in an annual printed edition consisting of eight volumes listing lawyers and law firms by state and city. The bulk of each volume contains "Professional Biographies," paid listings describing the practices of lawyers and law firms. Beginning with the 2009 edition, each volume begins with two alphabetical lists, "Index of Professional Biographical Listings" covering lawyers with paid listings and "Practice Profiles" listing other practicing lawyers. These lists have a one-line entry for each lawyer indicating date of birth, date of admission to practice, rating, college, and law school. The "Practice Profiles" section is now limited to lawyers with peer review ratings, so it

---

9. *Martindale-Hubbell Law Directory* was first published in 1931, and was preceded by *Martindale's American Law Directory* (1868–1930) and *Hubbell's Law Directory* (1870–1930). Law Library Microform Consortium publishes the volumes from 1868 through 1999 on microfiche. Its product catalog includes a brief feature, *The Martindale–Hubbell Story* <www.llmc.com/Historical_AARef. asp#page_18>, which tells the history of these directories.

10. A site designed for clients and the public, lawyers.com <www.lawyers. com>, has much of the same directory information as the other sources but omits the peer review ratings.

omits many people who were listed in previous editions. Even for lawyers listed, it omits addresses or other contact information.

West Legal Directory, the other nationwide directory of attorneys, is available as the WLD database on Westlaw. It has addresses and telephone numbers for practicing attorneys as well as lawyers working in areas such as business or legal education. For most attorneys included, it also has biographical information such as education, professional affiliations, and areas of practice. The PROFILER–WLD database is particularly useful for information on litigators, as it links the directory data with relevant cases, briefs, pleadings, other documents, and summaries of litigation history.

Two versions of WLD are available free on the Internet from FindLaw. The Thomson Legal Record <legalrecords.findlaw.com> is on FindLaw for Legal Professionals, and includes access to the litigation records from Westlaw but not the biographical data for most attorneys. Findlaw's site for the public has a simpler FindLaw Lawyer Directory <lawyers.findlaw.com> with basic contact information.

Several other national directories of lawyers and law firms are available in print or online, although none is as comprehensive as *Martindale-Hubbell* or WLD. *Who's Who in American Law* (biennial, online as part of Marquis Who's Who on the Web <www.marquiswhoswho.com>) is a source of biographical information on prominent judges, attorneys and legal scholars, covering about 25,000 people in each edition. Steven Naifeh & Gregory White Smith, *The Best Lawyers in America* (annual) is a guide to highly respected practicing attorneys, chosen for inclusion by their peers. For each state, lawyers are listed under about seventy specialties and then within each specialty by city. This topical arrangement allows potential clients to browse listings in nearby cities. A subscription-based Best Lawyers website <www.bestlawyers.com> has some free access, but listings are limited to lawyers who have purchased links to their law firm website biographies, or, if there are no paid listings for a particular city and specialty, to a single listed attorney chosen at random. Lawyers in some states are listed on Avvo <www.avvo.com>, a free directory that includes information on citations for professional misconduct and allows clients to add reviews.

The *Law Firms Yellow Book* (semiannual in print or online by subscription <www.leadershipdirectories.com/products/lyb.html>) has contact and brief biographical information on management and recruiting personnel for over 700 law firms. Vault <www.vault.com> is an online directory that profiles and ranks large and midsize law firms on measures such as salary, diversity and pro bono participation. Some of its information is available free. The

National Association for Law Placement's annual *Directory of Legal Employers* <www.nalpdirectory.com> is a free online resource designed primarily for job-seeking lawyers with basic data on some 1,700 firms and other legal employers.

Other directories focus on attorneys working outside of law firms. *Directory of Corporate Counsel* (annual) has biographical information on lawyers working for some 8,000 corporations and nonprofit organizations. The National Legal Aid and Defender Association <www.nlada.org> publishes *Directory of Legal Aid and Defender Offices in the United States*, and the National District Attorneys Association <www.ndaa.org> publishes the *National Directory of Prosecuting Attorneys*. Both are updated irregularly. The Association of American Law Schools <www.aals.org> publishes an annual *Directory of Law Teachers*, with biographies of faculty members of all accredited law schools in the United States.

State and regional directories often provide more thorough listings of local lawyers than national directories. Legal Directories Publishing Co. publishes directories for twenty-three states (Alabama, Arkansas, Georgia, Illinois, Indiana, Iowa, Kansas, Kentucky, Louisiana, Minnesota, Mississippi, Missouri, Nevada, North Carolina, Ohio, Oklahoma, Pennsylvania, South Carolina, Tennessee, Texas, Virginia & West Virginia, and Wisconsin). These provide simple alphabetical listings with addresses and telephone numbers, and very few biographical entries, but they are likely to include names missing from the national directories. Information from these directories is available online in a free Attorney and Firm Directory Search <www.legaldirectories.com/search.asp>.

Many state and local bar associations publish directories or offer attorney search features on their websites. Links to bar associations and other legal organizations are available from several websites including FindLaw <www.findlaw.com/06associations/> and WashLaw <www.washlaw.edu/bar/>.

Bar associations and other professional and trade organizations can also be invaluable sources of information in their areas of interest. Two directories are notable for their broad coverage of both legal and nonlegal organizations. *Encyclopedia of Associations* (annual, available online as Associations Unlimited <www.gale.cengage.com> and in Lexis) has descriptions and contact information for nearly 24,000 national organizations. *National Trade and Professional Associations of the United States* (annual, available online by subscription <www.associationexecs.com>) is less extensive but just as useful for basic information on major business-related organizations.

Companies are the subject of a number of print and electronic directories and databases. Several of these are available through either Westlaw or Lexis. The amount of available information depends in part on whether a company is publicly or privately held; because public companies must report to their shareholders and government regulators, far more information is available for them. Basic information on public corporations is available in sources such as *Standard & Poor's Register of Corporations, Directors & Executives*, available in Lexis, and more extensive background and financial information can be found in S & P's *Corporate Descriptions Plus News* database in Lexis or *Hoover's Company Profiles* in both Westlaw (HOOVCP) and Lexis. Parent and subsidiary companies can be identified in the *Directory of Corporate Affiliations*. *Ward's Business Directory of U.S. Private and Public Companies* includes information on more than 100,000 privately held companies. The broadest databases, such as *American Business Directory* and *Dun's Electronic Business Directory* (both available under some Westlaw subscriptions), cover millions of private businesses and provide basic contact information and employment data.

While most directories are somewhat specialized, a few try to answer a wider range of inquiries. *Law and Legal Information Directory* (annual) has information culled from a number of directories, listing legal organizations, consultants, research centers, law libraries, lawyer referral services, legal aid and defender offices, and a variety of federal and state government agencies. *The Legal Researcher's Desk Reference* (Arlene L. Eis ed., biennial, with a companion website for subscribers) is a handy paperback work with an array of directory information including government offices, courts, and bar associations, and other resources such as state court structure charts.

§ 12.3   Statistics

Legal researchers need demographic and statistical information for many purposes, from supporting a discrimination claim to preparing for the deposition of an expert witness. These statistics are available from an array of printed and online sources.

Statistics on the federal courts, such as the number of cases commenced and terminated by district and by subject, can be found in the Administrative Office of the U.S. Courts' annual *Judicial Business of the United States Courts* and on its website <www.uscourts.gov/judbususc/judbus.html>. The National Center for State Courts site has a Court Statistics Project page <www.ncsconline.org/D_Research/csp/CSP_Main_Page.html> that offers several ways to query its statistical database and examine state court business. It includes PDF versions of two annual publications, *Examining the Work of State Courts* and *State Court Caseload Statistics*.

The Lawyer Statistical Report, published periodically by the American Bar Foundation, is the leading source on the composition of the U.S. legal profession. The most recent report, published in 2004, provides data as of 2000. The American Bar Association's Market Research Department has links to various websites with statistics on the legal profession, including demographics, salaries, and quality of life surveys <www.abanet.org/marketresearch/resource.html>.

Criminal statistics are available in two major resources issued by the U.S. Department of Justice. The Federal Bureau of Investigation publishes the annual *Uniform Crime Reports* (also known as *Crime in the United States*) <www.fbi.gov/ucr/ucr.htm>, focusing on criminal activities. The Bureau of Justice Statistics (BJS) provides the *Sourcebook of Criminal Justice Statistics* <www.albany.edu/sourcebook/>, which has a broader survey of the social and economic impacts of crime. The current *Sourcebook* is updated weekly and is not available in print. The BJS website <www.ojp.usdoj.gov/bjs/> has links to a variety of other statistics and publications.

The U.S. Census Bureau <www.census.gov> prepares the Census of Population and Housing every ten years, and every census since 1790 is available on its website <www.census.gov/prod/www/abs/decennial/>. The Census Bureau also undertakes an extensive Economic Census every five years, and publishes a vast range of statistical information on business and industry. The key to finding relevant economic information about a particular industry is to determine its North American Industry Classification System (NAICS) code <www.census.gov/eos/www/naics/>. The NAICS page also has information on the older Standard Industrial Classification (SIC) system which is still used by several sources.

The *Statistical Abstract of the United States* is published annually by the Census Bureau in print and on the Internet <www.census.gov/compendia/statab/>. This general reference source covers a wide range of economic and demographic statistics, and is particularly useful because it gives source information for each table. It thus serves as a convenient lead to agencies and publications with more extensive coverage of specific areas. Illustration 12–3 on page 401 shows a table from the *Statistical Abstract*, providing information about the number of law degrees conferred per year, from 1970 to 2006. The table includes a source reference to the annual publication *Digest of Education Statistics*, where more detailed information may be available. The *Statistical Abstract* website includes PDF versions of the publication back to the first edition in 1878.

The *Statistical Abstract* is supplemented by two additional print and online publications with more detailed information for specific geographical areas, *State and Metropolitan Area Data Book* (6th ed. 2006) <http://www.census.gov/compendia/smadb/> and *County and City Data Book* (14th ed. 2007) <http://www.census.gov/statab/www/ccdb.html>. These are published in new editions every seven to nine years.

The FedStats website <www.fedstats.gov> has links to statistical sites from about a hundred federal government agencies. It overlaps with the *Statistical Abstract* in coverage, but may provide some leads not found there. Sources can be located by topic and by agency.

Historical Statistics of the United States: Earliest Times to the Present (Susan B. Carter et al. eds., 2006) is a comprehensive compendium of statistics from the *Statistical Abstract* and hundreds of other sources. It is available either in a five-volume printed set or in a subscription online version <hsus.cambridge.org>.

Even more extensive statistical information is available from LexisNexis Statistical <web.lexis-nexis.com/statuniv/>, a companion site of LexisNexis Academic and LexisNexis Congressional. This subscription product adds more than 100,000 tables each year, from federal agencies, state governments, and private sources, with links to PDF versions of statistical reports. The information is also available in the print indexes *American Statistics Index* (1973–date, covering U.S. government sources) and *Statistical Reference Index* (1980–date, covering state government and private sources), and their accompanying microfiche sets.

A third component of LexisNexis Statistical is *Index to International Statistics* (1983–date), which covers statistics from major intergovernmental organizations. Much of its data comes from the United Nations, which publishes several statistical compendia including a general *Statistical Yearbook* and more specific works such as *Demographic Yearbook, Energy Statistics Yearbook, International Trade Statistics Yearbook,* and *National Accounts Statistics. International Historical Statistics: 1750–2005* (B. R. Mitchell ed., 2007) is a three-volume compendium of demographic, industrial and social statistics. The U.S. Bureau of Labor Statistics maintains an extensive list of statistical agency websites around the world <www.bls.gov/bls/other.htm>.

Most statistical sources focus on facts rather than opinions, but public surveys can be important resources in many areas of the law from discrimination to trademark infringement. Polls and other sources of public opinion are available through a number of electronic sources. Gallup, Inc. <www.gallup.com> has free access to recent poll results and allows keyword searching of questionnaires and poll analyses on major topics such as the Supreme Court and election results. Two subscription resources, Polling the Nations and the iPoll Databank at the Roper Center for Public Opinion Research <http://www.ropercenter.uconn.edu/>, have access to polling and survey data from hundreds of organizations, accessible by keyword search or through subject indexes.[11]

§ 12.4 Public Records

Factual research can be vital in establishing a claim, locating a witness, or negotiating a settlement. News databases and Internet searches can provide a great deal of factual background information, and much more is available through public records databases. These are the resources to use for information such as the value of real property or the status of a professional license.

Public records are maintained by federal, state and local governments. They can often be obtained for free from official websites, but the most convenient starting points for many are extensive public record databases such as those on Westlaw and Lexis. Both systems have information including real property records, people locators, professional licenses, and motor vehicle records. The default search screen for most public records databases is a fill-in-the-blanks form. Terms-and-connectors searches can be used, but natural language is generally not an option. Some, but not all, of these databases are available to academic subscribers.

There is considerable variation in the amount of information that jurisdictions make available on their websites. In some instances, official sites may have more current or more extensive information than that available from Westlaw or Lexis. Some cities and counties have searchable online property databases, and others include information such as birth or marriage records. Several sites have links to free public record sites in all fifty states. Good places to start include BRB Publications Inc.'s Free Resource Center <www.brbpub.com/pubrecsites.asp>, NETR Public Records Online Directory <publicrecords.netronline.com>, and the searchsystems.net Public Record Locator <www.searchsystems.net>.

A great deal of public record information is not online but is available by other methods such as telephone or in-person inquiries. *The Sourcebook to Public Record Information: The Comprehensive Guide to County, State, & Federal Public Records Sources* (annual) is a thorough listing of local and state offices with instructions for obtaining records from each. The *Sourcebook*'s publisher, Michael Sankey, has also written *The Public Record Research Tips*

---

11. These and other electronic polling resources are compared in Stephen Woods, *Public Opinion Poll Question Databases: An Evaluation*, 33 J. Acad. Librarianship 41 (2007). On the early history of public opinion polling and the pioneering work of George Gallup and Elmo Roper, see Barry Cushman, *Mr. Dooley and Mr. Gallup: Public Opinion and Constitutional Change in the 1930s*, 50 Buff. L. Rev. 7, 77–101 (2002).

Book (2008), which has detailed information on the types of records available and ways to access them.

Business entities generate extensive public record filings. Publicly held corporations must file a wide range of documents with the Securities and Exchange Commission, including annual and quarterly financial reports, and these are available free through the SEC's IDEA system <idea.sec.gov>. SEC filings are also accessible through several subscription databases, including Westlaw and Lexis. Both public and private companies must register with secretaries of state or similar state offices. The National Association of Secretaries of State <www.nass.org> has links to state sites, most of which have searchable databases providing basic information such as addresses, officers and registered agents.

§ 12.5   Specialized Research Guides

This text examines legal research generally, but researchers should be aware that specialized areas of law and specific jurisdictions have many idiosyncrasies. Numerous guides to these topics are available. Many guides (sometimes called "pathfinders") have been published in legal bibliography journals such as *Law Library Journal*, *Legal Reference Services Quarterly*, and LLRX.com <www. llrx.com>. William S. Hein & Co. publishes a *Legal Research Guides* series of more than fifty monographs on specific topics such as grandparent visitation rights or identity theft.

Tax research is the focus of several published works, including Joni Larson & Dan Sheaffer, *Federal Tax Research* (2007) and Gail Levin Richmond, *Federal Tax Research: Guide to Materials and Techniques* (7th ed. 2007). *Specialized Legal Research* (Penny Hazelton ed., 1987–date) covers more than a dozen topics, with chapters on admiralty, banking law, copyright, customs, environmental law, government contracts, immigration, income tax, labor and employment law, military and veterans law, patents and trademarks, securities regulation, and the Uniform Commercial Code. The volume also includes a bibliography of other specialized legal research sources.

Legal materials can vary greatly from state to state, and law library websites often provide guidance on legal research issues in their home jurisdictions. A state-specific research guide can provide valuable details and information on sources. One of the most useful sources for identifying state materials is the looseleaf set, *State Practice Materials: Annotated Bibliographies* (Frank G. Houdek ed., 2002–date). Its chapters, to date covering twenty-six states and the District of Columbia, discuss major state primary sources, treatises, and research methods.

Following is a selective list of guides to state legal research resources and methods:

Alabama   Gary Orlando Lewis, *Legal Research in Ala-
                       bama: How to Find and Understand the
                       Law in Alabama* (2001).
                       Scott DeLeve, "Alabama Practice Materials: A
                       Selective Annotated Bibliography" (2005),
                       in *State Practice Materials: Annotated Bib-
                       liographies*.

Alaska   Catherine Lemann & Susan Falk, "Alaska
                       Practice Materials: A Selective Annotated
                       Bibliography" (2008), in *State Practice Ma-
                       terials: Annotated Bibliographies*.

Arizona   Tamara S. Herrera, *Arizona Legal Research*
                       (2008).
                       Kathy Shimpock–Vieweg & Marianne Sidorski
                       Alcorn, *Arizona Legal Research Guide*
                       (1992).

Arkansas   Coleen M. Barger, *Arkansas Legal Research*
                       (2007).
                       Kathryn C. Fitzhugh, "Arkansas Practice Mate-
                       rials II: A Selective Annotated Bibliogra-
                       phy," 21 *U. Ark. Little Rock L.J.* 363
                       (1999).

California   Larry D. Dershem, *California Legal Research
                       Handbook* (2d ed. 2008).
                       John K. Hanft, *Legal Research in California*
                       (6th ed. 2007).
                       Judy C. Janes, "California Practice Materials: A
                       Selective Annotated Bibliography" (2005),
                       in *State Practice Materials: Annotated Bib-
                       liographies*.
                       Hether C. Macfarlane & Suzanne E. Rowe, *Cal-
                       ifornia Legal Research* (2008).
                       Daniel W. Martin, ed., *Henke's California Law
                       Guide* (8th ed. 2006).

Colorado   Mitch Fontenot, "Colorado Practice Materials:
                       A Selective Annotated Bibliography"
                       (2004), in *State Practice Materials: Annotat-
                       ed Bibliographies*.

Connecticut   Shirley Bysiewicz, *Sources of Connecticut Law*
                       (1987).

Lawrence G. Cheeseman & Arlene C. Bielefeld, *The Connecticut Legal Research Handbook* (1992).

Jessica G. Hynes, *Connecticut Legal Research* (forthcoming 2009).

Jonathan Saxon, "Connecticut Practice Materials: A Selective Annotated Bibliography," 91 *Law Libr. J.* 139 (1999).

Delaware

Patrick J. Charles & David K. King, "Delaware Practice Materials: A Selective Annotated Bibliography," 89 *Law Libr. J.* 349 (1997).

District of Columbia

Leah F. Chanin, "Legal Research in the District of Columbia," in *Legal Research in the District of Columbia, Maryland and Virginia* (2d ed. 2000).

Michelle Wu, "District of Columbia Practice Materials: A Selective Annotated Bibliography" (2002), in *State Practice Materials: Annotated Bibliographies*.

Florida

Barbara J. Busharis & Suzanne E. Rowe, *Florida Legal Research: Sources, Process, and Analysis* (3d ed. 2007).

Nancy L. Strohmeyer, "Florida Practice Materials: A Selective Annotated Bibliography" (2007), in *State Practice Materials: Annotated Bibliographies*.

Betsy L. Stupski, *Guide to Florida Legal Research* (7th ed. 2008).

Georgia

Leah F. Chanin & Suzanne L. Cassidy, *Guide to Georgia Legal Research and Legal History* (1990).

Nancy P. Johnson, Elizabeth G. Adelman & Nancy J. Adams, *Georgia Legal Research* (2007).

Nancy P. Johnson, Kreig L. Kitts & Ronald E. Wheeler, Jr., "Georgia Practice Materials: A Selective Annotated Bibliography" (2007), in *State Practice Materials: Annotated Bibliographies*.

Hawai'i

Leina'ala R. Seeger, "Hawaii Practice Materials: A Selective Annotated Bibliography" (2004), in *State Practice Materials: Annotated Bibliographies*.

Idaho	Tenielle Fordyce–Ruff & Suzanne E. Rowe, *Idaho Legal Research* (2008). Leina'ala R. Seeger, "Idaho Practice Materials: A Selective Annotated Bibliography," 87 *Law Libr. J.* 534 (1995).
Illinois	Phill W. Johnson, "Illinois Practice Materials: A Selective Annotated Bibliography" (2006), in *State Practice Materials: Annotated Bibliographies*. Laurel Wendt, *Illinois Legal Research Guide* (2d ed. 2006). Mark E. Wojcik, *Illinois Legal Research* (2003).
Indiana	Richard E. Humphrey, "Indiana Practice Materials: A Selective Annotated Bibliography" (2004), in *State Practice Materials: Annotated Bibliographies*.
Iowa	John D. Edwards, *Iowa Legal Research Guide* (2003).
Kansas	Joseph A. Custer & Christopher L. Steadham, *Kansas Legal Research* (2008). Joseph A. Custer et al., *Kansas Legal Research and Reference Guide* (3d ed. 2003). Joseph A. Custer, "Kansas Practice Materials: A Selective Annotated Bibliography" (2002), in *State Practice Materials: Annotated Bibliographies*.
Kentucky	Kurt X. Metzmeier et al., *Kentucky Legal Research Manual* (3d ed. 2005).
Louisiana	Mary Garvey Algero, *Louisiana Legal Research* (forthcoming 2009). Win–Shin S. Chiang, *Louisiana Legal Research* (2d ed. 1990). Catherine Lemann, "Louisiana Practice Materials: A Selective Annotated Bibliography" (2006), in *State Practice Materials: Annotated Bibliographies*.
Maine	Christine I. Hepler & Maureen P. Quinlan, *Maine State Documents: A Bibliography of Legal Publications and Law–Related Materials* (2003). William W. Wells, *Maine Legal Research Guide* (1989).

Maryland	Pamela J. Gregory, "Legal Research in Maryland," in *Legal Research in the District of Columbia, Maryland and Virginia* (2d ed. 2000).
Massachusetts	Mary Ann Neary, ed., *Handbook of Legal Research in Massachusetts* (rev. ed. 2002).
Michigan	Richard L. Beer & Judith J. Field, *Michigan Legal Literature: An Annotated Guide* (2d ed. 1991). Pamela Lysaght, *Michigan Legal Research* (2006).
Minnesota	Vicente E. Garces, "Minnesota Practice Materials: A Selective Annotated Bibliography" (2002), in *State Practice Materials: Annotated Bibliographies*. John Tessner et al., *Minnesota Legal Research Guide* (2d ed. 2002).
Mississippi	Anne M. Klingen, "Mississippi Practice Materials: A Selective Annotated Bibliography" (2002), in *State Practice Materials: Annotated Bibliographies*.
Missouri	Wanda M. Temm & Julie M. Cheslik, *Missouri Legal Research* (2007).
Montana	Robert K. Whelan et al., *A Guide to Montana Legal Research* (8th ed. 2003) <www.montanacourts.org/library/guides/guide.pdf>.
Nebraska	Kay L. Andrus et al., *Research Guide to Nebraska Law* (2008 ed.). Beth Smith, "Nebraska Practice Materials: A Selective Annotated Bibliography" (2004), in *State Practice Materials: Annotated Bibliographies*.
Nevada	G. LeGrande Fletcher, "Nevada Practice Materials: A Selective Annotated Bibliography," 91 *Law Libr. J.* 313 (1999). Jennifer Larraguibel Gross et al., *Nevada Legal Research Guide* (2005).

New Jersey	Cameron Allen, *A Guide to New Jersey Legal Bibliography and Legal History* (1984). Paul Axel–Lute, *New Jersey Legal Research Handbook* (5th ed. 2008), with Web supplement <law-library.rutgers.edu/ilg/njlrhb5.php>. David A. Hollander, "New Jersey Practice Materials: A Selective Annotated Bibliography" (2008), in *State Practice Materials: Annotated Bibliographies*.
New Mexico	Mary A. Woodward, "New Mexico Practice Materials: A Selective Annotated Bibliography," 84 *Law Libr. J.* 93 (1992).
New York	Elizabeth G. Adelman & Suzanne E. Rowe, *New York Legal Research* (2008). William H. Manz, *Gibson's New York Legal Research Guide* (3d ed. 2004).
North Carolina	Miriam J. Baer & James C. Ray, *Legal Research in North Carolina* (2006). Jean Sinclair McKnight, *North Carolina Legal Research Guide* (1994).
Ohio	Katherine L. Hall & Sara A. Sampson, *Ohio Legal Research* (2009). Kenneth S. Kozlowski & Susan N. Elliott, "Ohio Practice Materials: A Selective Annotated Bibliography" (2005), in *State Practice Materials: Annotated Bibliographies*. Melanie K. Putnam & Susan Schaefgen, *Ohio Legal Research Guide* (1997).
Oklahoma	Ann Walsh Long, "Oklahoma Practice Materials: A Selective Annotated Bibliography" (2007), in *State Practice Materials: Annotated Bibliographies*.
Oregon	Mary Clayton & Stephanie Midkiff, "Oregon Practice Materials: A Selective Annotated Bibliography" (2005), in *State Practice Materials: Annotated Bibliographies*. Suzanne E. Rowe, *Oregon Legal Research* (2d ed. 2007).
Pennsylvania	Barbara J. Busharis & Bonny L. Tavares, *Pennsylvania Legal Research* (2007).

Joel Fishman & Marc Silverman, "Pennsylvania Practice Materials: A Selective Annotated Bibliography" (2003), in *State Practice Materials: Annotated Bibliographies*.
Frank Y. Liu et al., *Pennsylvania Legal Research Handbook* (2008 ed.).

Puerto Rico   Luis Muñiz Argüelles & Migdalia Fraticelli Torres, *La Investigación Jurídica en el Derecho Puertorriqueño: Fuentes Puertorriqueñas, Norteamericanas y Españolas* (4th ed. 2006).

Rhode Island   Daniel J. Donovan, *Legal Research in Rhode Island (including Federal and State Research Materials)* (4th ed. 2004).

South Carolina   Paula Gail Benson & Deborah Ann Davis, *A Guide to South Carolina Legal Research and Citation* (1991).
Pamela Rogers Melton & Christine Sellers, "South Carolina Practice Materials: A Selective Annotated Bibliography" (2008), in *State Practice Materials: Annotated Bibliographies*.

South Dakota   Matthew E. Braun & Kasia Solon, "South Dakota Practice Materials: A Selective Annotated Bibliography" (2008), in *State Practice Materials: Annotated Bibliographies*.
Delores A. Jorgensen, *South Dakota Legal Research Guide* (2d ed. 1999).

Tennessee   Toof Brown, III, "Tennessee Practice Materials: A Selective Annotated Bibliography" (2004), in *State Practice Materials: Annotated Bibliographies*.
Sibyl Marshall & Carol McCrehan Parker, *Tennessee Legal Research* (2007).

Texas   Matthew C. Cordon & Brandon D. Quarles, *Specialized Topics in Texas Legal Research* (2005).
Brandon D. Quarles & Matthew C. Cordon, *Researching Texas Law* (2d ed. 2008).
Brandon D. Quarles & Matthew C. Cordon, "Texas Practice Materials: A Selective An-

Practice Materials: Annotated Bibliographies.

Spencer L. Simons, *Texas Legal Research* (forthcoming 2009).

Utah   Kory D. Staheli, "Utah Practice Materials: A Selective Annotated Bibliography," 87 *Law Libr. J.* 28 (1995).

Vermont   Virginia Wise, *A Bibliographical Guide to the Vermont Legal System* (2d ed. 1991).

Virginia   John D. Eure & Gail F. Zwirner, eds., *A Guide to Legal Research in Virginia* (6th ed. 2008).

Leslie A. Lee, "Virginia Practice Materials: A Selective Annotated Bibliography" (2002), in *State Practice Materials: Annotated Bibliographies*.

Sarah K. Wiant, "Legal Research in Virginia," in *Legal Research in the District of Columbia, Maryland and Virginia* (2d ed. 2000).

Washington   Penny A. Hazelton et al., *Washington Legal Researcher's Deskbook 3d* (2002).

Julie Heintz-Cho et al., *Washington Legal Research* (2d ed. forthcoming 2009).

West Virginia   Ann Walsh Long, "Washington Practice Materials: A Selective Annotated Bibliography" (2004), in *State Practice Materials: Annotated Bibliographies*.

Wisconsin   Ellen J. Platt & Mary J. Koshollek, "Wisconsin Practice Materials: A Selective, Annotated Bibliography," 90 *Law Libr. J.* 219 (1998).

Theodore A. Potter & Jane Colwin, *Legal Research in Wisconsin* (2d ed. 2008).

Wyoming   Debora A. Person, *Wyoming State Documents: A Bibliography of State Publications and Related Materials* (2006).

384(1), 418(7). C.J.S. *Sales* §§ 363, 365–366, 391–393, 403.]

duumviri (d[y]oo-**əm**-və-rı), *n. pl.* [fr. Latin *due* "two" + *viri* "men"] **1.** *Roman law.* Magistrates elected or appointed in pairs to hold an office or perform a function.

duumviri municipales (d[y]oo-**əm**-və-rı myoo-nis-ə-**pay**-leez). [Latin] Two judicial magistrates annually elected in towns and colonies.

duumviri navales (d[y]oo-**əm**-və-rı nə-**vay**-leez). [Latin] Two officers appointed to man, equip, and refit the navy.

2. Two peers in authority. — Also termed *duoviri.*

dux (dəks), *n.* [fr. Latin *ducere* "to lead"] **1.** *Roman law.* An army commander. **2.** *Roman law.* A military governor of a province. • This term was eventually used also as a title of distinction. **3.** *Hist. (cap.)* Duke; a title of nobility. See DUKE.

DWAI. *abbr.* Driving while ability-impaired. See DRIVING UNDER THE INFLUENCE.

dwell, *vb.* **1.** To remain; to linger <the case dwelled in her memory>. **2.** To reside in a place permanently or for some period <he dwelled in California for nine years>.

dwelling defense. See CASTLE DOCTRINE.

dwelling house. 1. The house or other structure in which a person lives; a residence or abode. **2.** *Real estate.* The house and all buildings attached to or connected with the house. **3.** *Criminal law.* A building, a part of a building, a tent, a mobile home, or another enclosed space that is used or intended for use as a human habitation. • The term has referred to connected buildings in the same curtilage but now typically includes only the structures connected either directly with the house or by an enclosed passageway. — Often shortened to *dwelling.* — Also termed (archaically) *mansion house;* (more broadly) *dwelling place.* [Cases: Burglary 4. C.J.S. *Burglary* §§ 27–28, 30–37.]

"A 'dwelling house' or 'dwelling' has been defined in connection with the crime of arson as any house intended to be occupied as a residence, or an enclosed space, permanent or temporary, in which human beings usually stay, lodge, or reside. If a building is not used exclusively as a dwelling, it is characterized as a dwelling if there is internal communication between the two parts of the building. Dwellings include mobile homes and a boat, if the person resides on it." 5 Am. Jur. 2d *Arson and Related Offenses* § 13, at 789 (1995).

quasi-dwelling-house. *Hist.* Any outbuilding, such as a barn, that is in proximity to the building used as a residence. See BURGLARY (1).

DWI. *abbr.* DRIVING WHILE INTOXICATED.

DWOP (dee-wop). *abbr.* See *dismissal for want of prosecution* under DISMISSAL (1).

DWOP docket. See DOCKET (2).

dyarchy (dı-ahr-kee), *n.* [fr. Greek *dy* "two" + *archein* "rule"] See DIARCHY.

dyathanasia (dı-ath-ə-**nay**-zhə), *n.* The act of permitting death to occur naturally by withholding, terminating, or not offering life-prolonging treatments or intervention. — Also termed *passive mercy killing.* See EUTHANASIA.

Dyer Act. A federal law, originally enacted in 1919, making it unlawful either (1) to transport a stolen motor vehicle across state lines, knowing it to be stolen, or (2) to receive, conceal, or sell such a vehicle, knowing it to be stolen. 18 USCA §§ 2311–2313. — Also termed *National Motor Vehicle Theft Act.* [Cases: Automobiles 341. C.J.S. *Motor Vehicles* §§ 1528–1531, 1533–1540.]

dyet. See DIET.

dying declaration. See DECLARATION (6).

dying without issue. See FAILURE OF ISSUE.

dynamite charge. See ALLEN CHARGE.

dynamite instruction. See ALLEN CHARGE.

dynasty. 1. A powerful family line that continues for a long time <an Egyptian dynasty>. **2.** A powerful group of individuals who control a particular industry or field and who control their successors <a literary dynasty> <a banking dynasty>.

dynasty trust. See TRUST.

dysnomy (dis-nə-mee), *n.* [fr. Greek *dys* "bad" + *nomos* "law"] The enactment of bad legislation. Cf. EUNOMY.

Illustration 12–1. BLACK'S LAW DICTIONARY 546
(Bryan A. Garner ed., 8th ed. 2004)

LEGAL RESEARCH

of values. It is through the union of objective legal science and a critical theory of social values that our understanding of the human significance of law will be enriched.

> **Felix S. Cohen,** "Transcendental Nonsense and the Functional Approach," 35 *Columbia Law Review* 809, 849 (1935)

16 Interests, points of view, preferences, are the essence of living. Only death yields complete dispassionateness, for such dispassionateness signifies utter indifference.... The judge in our society owes a duty to act in accordance with those basic predilections inhering in our legal system (although, of course, he has the right, at times, to urge that some of them be modified or abandoned). The standard of dispassionateness obviously does not require the judge to rid himself of the unconscious influence of such social attitudes.

> **Jerome N. Frank,** *Courts on Trial* 413 (1949)

LEGAL RESEARCH

See also LAW BOOKS; LAW LIBRARIES

1 It is also to be borne in mind, that digests and elementary treatises are only the abstracts of adjudicated cases, and not always sure therefore of stating accurately the points decided. In fact, experienced counsel will never, in a case of importance, trust to a short sentence, which, the laborious compiler says, contains in an abbreviated form the principles of a question settled, when they have the original case itself within their reach; for they have learned by observation the errors and the imperfections of digests.

> **James Madison Porter,** Book Review, 27 *North American Review* 167, 182 (1828)

2 It is a great mistake to be frightened by the ever increasing number of reports. The reports of a given jurisdiction in the course of a generation take up pretty much the whole body of the law, and restate it from the present point of view. We could reconstruct the corpus from them if all that went before were burned.

> **Oliver Wendell Holmes, Jr.,** "The Path of the Law," 10 *Harvard Law Review* 457, 458 (1897)

3 There is another case bearing upon this proposition which neither counsel nor we

have been able to find; but it holds that there was no such defect in the ballot used as to defeat the election. The departure from the statute in that case was much greater than in this one.

> **Horace E. Deemer,** *Kinney v. Howard,* 133 Iowa 94, 103, 110 N.W. 282 (1907)

4 I do not feel that any one ever really masters the law, but it is not difficult to master the approaches to the law, so that given a certain state of facts it is possible to know how to marshal practically all the legal decisions which apply to them.

> **Calvin Coolidge,** *The Autobiography of Calvin Coolidge* 76 (1929)

5 I made no preparations for the trial. It is not my policy to look up law in advance of the trial of a lawsuit. I have learned from experience that no matter how strange and fantastic is my own notion of the law, it is safe to assume that somewhere in the reports there will be decision that will support it. And maybe I won't have to look it up at all. I really have, I must confess, a singular aversion to looking up law. At one time I seriously considered specializing exclusively in a certain class of cases dealing with what is commonly referred to as "the unwritten law," but I didn't seem able to work up that type of practice.

> **Robert T. Sloan,** "Daisy Whiffle v. The Twitter Bird Seed Company," in *The Judicial Humorist* 20, 22–23 (William L. Prosser ed. 1952)

6 Justice Robert H. Jackson liked to tell of the time when, as a young lawyer before an upstate New York judge, he cited in his support a case newly decided by the Supreme Court, and handed up the advance sheets to prove his point. The judge handed them back, glaring, and said, "I don't take no law from no magazines."

> **Martin Mayer,** *The Lawyers* 497 (1967)

LEGAL WRITING

See also LANGUAGE; LAW REVIEWS; QUOTATIONS; WORDS

1 I should apologize, perhaps, for the style of this bill. I dislike the verbose and intricate style of the English statutes, and in our revised code I endeavored to restore it to the

288

Table 293. First Professional Degrees Earned in Selected Professions: 1970 to 2006

[First professional degrees include degrees which require at least 6 years of college work for completion (including at least 2 years of preprofessional training). Based on survey; see Appendix III]

Type of degree and sex of recipient	1970	1975	1980	1985	1990	1995	2000	2004	2005	2006
Medicine (M.D.):										
Institutions conferring degrees	86	104	112	120	124	119	118	118	120	119
Degrees conferred, total	8,314	12,447	14,902	16,041	15,075	15,537	15,286	15,442	15,461	15,465
Percent to women	8.4	13.1	23.4	30.4	34.2	38.8	42.7	46.4	47.3	48.9
Dentistry (D.D.S. or D.M.D.):										
Institutions conferring degrees	48	52	58	59	57	53	54	53	53	54
Degrees conferred, total	3,718	4,773	5,258	5,339	4,100	3,897	4,250	4,335	4,454	4,389
Percent to women	0.9	3.1	13.3	20.7	30.9	38.4	40.1	41.8	43.8	44.5
Law (LL.B. or J.D.):										
Institutions conferring degrees	145	154	179	181	182	183	190	195	198	197
Degrees conferred, total	14,916	29,296	35,647	37,491	36,485	39,349	38,152	40,209	43,423	43,440
Percent to women	5.4	16.1	30.2	38.5	42.2	42.6	46.9	49.4	48.7	48.0
Theological (B.D., M.Div., M.H.L.):										
Institutions conferring degrees	(NA)	(NA)	(NA)	(NA)	(NA)	192	198	200	(NA)	(NA)
Degrees conferred, total	5,298	5,095	7,115	7,221	5,961	5,978	6,129	5,332	5,533	5,666
Percent to women	2.3	6.8	13.8	18.5	24.8	25.7	29.2	34.2	35.6	33.6

NA Not available.
Source: U.S. National Center for Education Statistics, *Digest of Education Statistics*, annual.

Illustration 12–3. U.S. CENSUS BUREAU, STATISTICAL ABSTRACT OF THE UNITED STATES 184 tbl. 293 (128th ed. 2009).

Chapter 13

INTERNATIONAL LAW

Table of Sections

The first twelve chapters of this book have focused on researching the law of the United States. In the final two chapters, we broaden our view and look at legal materials affecting our relations with other countries and at sources from outside this country. A modern legal practice often requires knowledge of international and foreign law. Lawyers representing an American firm investing in another country, for example, must be aware of treaties between the two nations as well as the investment and trade laws of both countries. This chapter focuses on international law, while research in the law of foreign countries is the subject of Chapter 14.

Public international law is the body of rules and procedures intended to govern relations between nation states.[1] Although its primary historical functions have been the preservation of peace and regulation of war, international law now governs an ever broader range of transnational activities. It regulates matters from copyright protection to the rights of refugees, and trade conven-

---

1. *Private* international law (or conflict of laws) determines where, and by whose law, controversies involving more than one jurisdiction are resolved, as well as how foreign judgments are enforced.

tions have made international law an inherent aspect of commercial activity.

The classic statement of the sources of international law is Article 38 of the Statute of the International Court of Justice, identifying the bases on which it decides disputes:

(a) international conventions, whether general or particular, establishing rules expressly recognized by the contesting States;

(b) international custom, as evidence of a general practice accepted as law;

(c) the general principles of law recognized by civilized nations;

(d) ... judicial decisions and the teachings of the most highly qualified publicists of the various nations, as subsidiary means for the determination of rules of law.[2]

Treaties and *international custom* are generally considered the two most important sources. If a treaty is relevant to a problem involving its signatories, it is the primary legal authority. International custom is the actual conduct of nations when it is consistent with the rule of law. Custom is not defined in specific legal sources but is established by evidence of state practices. *General principles of law* are the most amorphous of the sources but are usually considered to be basic principles articulated in the classic texts of international law. *Judicial decisions* and *scholarly writings* are less important than treaties and international custom. Cases are generally not considered binding precedents in subsequent disputes, but they can aid in interpreting treaties and in defining international custom.

The Internet has had a dramatic impact on international legal research. Many sources that were once difficult to identify and locate are now widely available online from the United Nations and other organizations. In researching international law in this increasingly global age, it is important for American lawyers *not* to limit their inquiry to U.S. sources. A facility with other languages assists greatly in broadening the scope of research, but there are many English-language resources available for serious international law study.

§ 13.1 Preliminary Research

The first step in approaching most research problems in international law is to turn to a reference work, a treatise, or a law review article for general information and for help in analyzing the issues involved.

---

2.   59 Stat. 1055, 1060.

Encyclopedias and Treatises. The *Encyclopedia of Public International Law* (Rudolf Bernhardt ed., 1992–2000), published under the auspices of the Max Planck Institute for Comparative Public Law and International Law, is a five-volume work providing a comprehensive view of international law issues. Its articles are written by respected authorities, are short but informative, and include brief bibliographies for further research. A revised edition is in progress, and completed articles are available electronically by subscription as the *Max Planck Encyclopedia of Public International Law* <www.mpepil.com>.

Edmund Jan Osmańczyk, *Encyclopedia of the United Nations and International Agreements* (Anthony Mango ed., 3d ed. 2003) is another multi-volume encyclopedia with wide coverage of international law issues, as well as excerpts from treaties and other major documents. Shorter reference works include Anthony Aust, *Handbook of International Law* (2005) and *Routledge Handbook of International Law* (David Armstrong ed., 2008).

Several general treatises provide overviews of international law doctrine. *Oppenheim's International Law* (Robert Jennings & Arthur Watts eds., 9th ed. 1992) is an updated version of a classic work. More modern treatises include Ian Brownlie, *Principles of Public International Law* (7th ed. 2008), Antonio Cassese, *International Law* (2d ed. 2005), and Malcolm N. Shaw, *International Law* (5th ed. 2003). The American Law Institute's *Restatement of the Law, Third, Foreign Relations Law of the United States* (1987) summarizes American law and practice in international law and foreign relations.

The historically acknowledged classic texts of international law, originally published between 1557 and 1866, were collected and published by the Carnegie Endowment for International Peace in a set of forty volumes, *The Classics of International Law* (James Brown Scott ed., 1911–50). Texts appear in their original versions and, if needed, in English translation. This series is available electronically in the Legal Classics Library on HeinOnline <www.heinonline.org>.

Journal Articles. International law has an extensive library of scholarly periodicals, including more than seventy specialized journals published at U.S. law schools. Among the more prestigious professional journals are the *American Journal of International Law* and *International and Comparative Law Quarterly. Recueil des Cours,* containing lectures presented at the Hague Academy of International Law, is a particularly valuable resource of international scope. Many national societies of international law produce annual publications such as the *British Yearbook of International Law* or the *Annuaire Français de Droit International,* which usually contain scholarly articles as well as reprints of selected major documents. *American Society of International Law Proceedings* (1907–date) provides shorter discussions of topics of current interest. A number of these yearbooks and other sources are available through HeinOnline's subscription-based Foreign and International Law Resources Database.

International law topics are also well represented in the standard law review literature discussed in Chapter 11, and articles can be found through any of the full-text and index resources discussed there. *Index to Foreign Legal Periodicals* (1960–date, quarterly, available through Westlaw and other database systems) principally covers journals published in countries outside the common law system, but it also indexes articles on international law in selected American law reviews. *Public International Law: A Current Bibliography of Books and Articles* (1975–date, semiannual) is a comprehensive index of the literature in the field.

Dictionaries. International law has its own specialized terminology, and a dictionary may be an essential tool in understanding key concepts. The leading work is *Parry and Grant Encyclopaedic Dictionary of International Law* (John P. Grant & J. Craig Barker eds., 2d ed. 2004), which has descriptive entries with citations to major sources. James R. Fox, *Dictionary of International and Comparative Law* (3d ed. 2003) has more concise definitions of terms. More specialized works, such as H. Victor Condé, *A Handbook of International Human Rights Terminology* (2d ed. 2004) and Walter Goode, *Dictionary of Trade Policy Terms* (5th ed. 2007), are also available.

§ 13.2   U.S. Practice in International Law

For American lawyers and law students, materials on United States practice in international law are the most frequently consulted research sources in this field. These include treaties and the materials needed to interpret them as well as documents dealing with issues in U.S. foreign relations.

(a) Treaties

Treaties are formal agreements between countries, and they have legal significance for both domestic and international purposes. Article VI of the U.S. Constitution provides that treaties are part of the supreme law of the land, giving them the same legal effect and status as federal statutes. Treaties and statutes can supersede each other as the controlling law within the United States, but a treaty that is no longer valid as U.S. law may still be binding in international law.

Treaty research generally involves several aspects: (1) finding its text in an authoritative source; (2) determining whether it is in force and with what parties and reservations; and (3) interpreting its provisions, with the aid of commentaries, judicial decisions, and legislative history. The resources available may depend in large part on whether the United States is a party to the treaty, so answering that question is an important first step in research.

Treaty Process. Treaties between two governments are called *bilateral*, and those entered into by more than two governments are called *multilateral*. Parties' initial signatures to a treaty establish their agreement that its text is authentic and definitive, but nations are not bound until they approve the treaty through ratification, accession, or some other procedure. Parties to multilateral treaties may add RUDs: *reservations* excluding certain provisions, or *understandings* or *declarations* providing their own interpretations of treaty terms. The texts of treaties usually identify the point at which they enter into force, often (in the case of multilateral conventions) when a specified number of nations have indicated their ratification or accession.

Treaties of the United States are negotiated and drafted by the executive branch but require approval by two-thirds of the Senate. After Senate approval, they are ratified and proclaimed by the President. For domestic purposes, a treaty generally becomes law when it is proclaimed by the President.

The President makes *executive agreements* with other countries under the Article II authority to conduct foreign affairs. These are similar in form and effect to treaties, but they do not require Senate approval and hence are often used to streamline the process and avoid controversy. The sources and research procedures discussed in this section generally apply to both treaties and executive agreements.

Sources. Treaties are published in a variety of forms—official and unofficial, national and international, current and retrospective. Until 1949, treaties were published in the *Statutes at Large* for each session of Congress. Compilations of early treaties entered into by the United States between 1778 and 1845 appear in volumes 7 and 8 of the *Statutes at Large*, and volume 64 includes a complete list of all treaties appearing in the set. These treaties were reprinted in *Treaties and Other International Agreements of the United States of America 1776–1949* (Charles I. Bevans comp., 1968–75, available on HeinOnline), which contains four volumes of multilateral treaties (arranged chronologically), eight volumes of bilateral treaties (arranged alphabetically by country), and indexes by country and subject.[3]

---

3. *Bevans* superseded two predecessors: *Treaties, Conventions, International Acts, Protocols, and Agreements Between the United States of America and*

Beginning in 1950, *United States Treaties and Other International Agreements* (*UST*) has been the official, permanent form of publication for treaties and executive agreements to which the United States is a party. *UST* volumes are published after a long delay, currently more than twenty years. Illustration 13–1 on page 425 shows the first page of a treaty between the United States and Iran, as published in *UST*.

Before they appear in *UST*, treaties and agreements are issued in a numbered series of separately paginated pamphlets, *Treaties and Other International Acts Series* (*TIAS*).[4] *TIAS* publication is more current than *UST*, but still involves a time lag of about ten years.

Because of the long delays in the publication of *TIAS* and *UST*, several commercial services are important sources for access to current treaties. Both Westlaw and Lexis have comprehensive treaty databases, with coverage from the 1770s through recent months. HeinOnline's Treaties and Agreements Library has PDF versions of treaties in *Statutes at Large*, *UST*, and *TIAS*, as well as more recent treaties not yet published in these sources. *Treaties and International Agreements Online* <www.oxfordonline.com/oceanalaw> is another extensive subscription site with thousands of treaties. Its index by title, subject, country and date is available free after registration.

Other sources for new treaties and agreements include *Hein's UST Current Service* (1990–date) on microfiche, and *Consolidated Treaties & International Agreements* (1990–date) in print. The American Society of International Law's bimonthly *International Legal Materials* (1962–date) contains the texts of treaties of major significance and sometimes provides drafts before final agreement. These documents are available in *ILM* databases on Westlaw, Lexis and HeinOnline.

Recent treaties and agreements are available on the Department of State website <www.state.gov/s/l/treaty/caseact/> within six months of the date they enter into force, under terms mandated by Congress in 2004.[5] Coverage extends to 1998. Other online government collections of treaties include trade agreements from

Other Powers (William M. Molloy comp., 1910–38), and *Treaties and Other International Acts of the U.S.A.* (Hunter Miller ed., 1931–48). Another source for treaties between the United States and Indian nations is volume two of *Indian Affairs: Laws and Treaties* (C.J. Kappler comp., 1904). All of these sets are available in HeinOnline's Treaties and Agreements Library, and Kappler is also online free <digital.library.okstate.edu/kappler/>.

4. *TIAS* succeeded two separate series, *Treaty Series* (1908–45) and *Executive Agreement Series* (1929–45).

5. Intelligence Reform and Terrorism Prevention Act of 2004, § 7121(a), Pub. L. No. 108–458, 118 Stat. 3638, 3807 (codified at 1 U.S.C. § 112a(d) (2006)).

the Office of the United States Trade Representative <www.ustr. gov> and tax treaties from the Internal Revenue Service <www.irs. gov/businesses/international/>. Some treaty collections on particular subjects are available from commercial publishers, including the CCH looseleaf service *Tax Treaties* and *Extradition Laws and Treaties* (I.I. Kavass & A. Sprudzs eds. 1979–date).

A citation to a treaty includes its name, the date of its signing, the parties (if there are three or fewer), and references to the main sources of publication. For example, the treaty in Illustration 13–1 is cited as: Treaty of Amity, Economic Relations, and Consular Rights, Aug. 15, 1955, U.S–Iran, 8 U.S.T. 899, 284 U.N.T.S. 93. The signing date is particularly important because it is the date that is used to identify treaties in most lists and indexes.

The Bluebook generally specifies citation of bilateral treaties to an official U.S. source (usually *Statutes at Large* or *UST*), if available, and of multilateral treaties to an official international source as well (usually the *United Nations Treaty Series*).[6] Because many recent treaties do not appear in these standard sources, they are often cited to journals, commercially published compilations, and electronic sources.

Indexes and Guides. Treaties are generally published chronologically rather than by subject, so you many need a guide or index to identify agreements on a particular topic. Many of these same resources also have information on treaty status.

Treaties in Force, an annual publication of the Department of State, is the official index to current United States treaties and agreements. It provides citations to all of the major treaty publications, including *Bevans, UST, TIAS*, and the *United Nations Treaty Series*. The first section of *Treaties in Force* lists bilateral treaties by country and, under each country, by subject; and the second section lists multilateral treaties by subject. Illustration 13–2 on page 426 shows the page from *Treaties in Force* that lists the bilateral treaty shown in Illustration 13–1. *Treaties in Force* is available on the Web <www.state.gov/s/l/treaty/treaties/> along with monthly lists of recent treaty actions. Westlaw (USTIF database) and Lexis have the current *Treaties in Force*, and HeinOnline has past editions back to 1929.

A commercially published *Guide to the United States Treaties in Force* is also issued annually in print and on HeinOnline, and has subject and country indexes to both bilateral and multilateral treaties. These can be useful because the official *Treaties in Force*

---

6. The Bluebook: A Uniform System of Citation R. 21.4, at 170 (18th ed. 2005). The ALWD uses the full treaty title to indicate the parties and requires citation to just one treaty source. ALWD Citation Manual: A Professional System of Citation R. 21.1, at 187–89 (3d ed. 2006).

doesn't index bilateral treaties by subject or list multilateral conventions by country.

The major collections and series of U.S. treaties and international agreements are indexed by subject, date, and country in *United States Treaty Index: 1776–2000 Consolidation* (Igor I. Kavass ed., 2001–date), which is updated semiannually by *Kavass' Current Treaty Index*, available in print and on HeinOnline.

Interpretation. Like statutes or constitutional provisions, most treaties contain ambiguities that can lead to controversies in interpretation and application. Several resources can assist in understanding treaty terms, including court decisions and documents produced during a treaty's drafting and consideration.

Decisions from the Supreme Court or the U.S. Courts of Appeals can be determinative in interpreting a treaty's meaning or effect, and other court decisions can provide useful guidance even if they are not binding. Neither KeyCite nor Shepard's covers citations to treaties, but you can use a treaty's name or citation in a full-text search and learn of cases from law review articles and other secondary sources.

The *United States Code Service* includes two volumes that can be useful starting points in finding cases. "International Agreements" contains the texts of about three dozen major conventions and treaties, accompanied by research references and case annotations, and "Annotations to Uncodified Laws and Treaties" has no treaty texts but provides broader coverage of decisions interpreting U.S. treaties.

For United States treaties, records of Senate deliberation are another valuable source of documentation on terms and meaning.[7] Most congressional documents have already been discussed in Chapter 4, but two series of Senate documents relate specifically to treaty consideration. *Treaty Documents* (until 1980, called *Senate Executive Documents*) contain the text of treaties as they are transmitted to the Senate for its consideration, and usually include messages from the President and the Secretary of State. The Senate Foreign Relations Committee analyzes treaties and issues *Senate Executive Reports* with its recommendations. Both Treaty Documents and Senate Executive Reports are issued in numbered series identifying the Congress and sequence in which they were issued.

---

7. The Senate website has a primer on treaty process <www.senate.gov/artandhistory/history/common/briefing/Treaties.htm>. For more detail, see CONGRESSIONAL RESEARCH SERVICE, TREATIES AND OTHER INTERNATIONAL AGREEMENTS: THE ROLE OF THE UNITED STATES SENATE, S. Prt. 106–71 (2001). The value of Senate materials in determining the intent of treaty parties has been the subject of dispute. See *United States v. Stuart*, 489 U.S. 353, 367 n.7 (1989).

LexisNexis Congressional includes coverage of Senate treaty materials from 1817, with the full text of documents and reports. This information is also available in the printed *CIS Index to US Senate Executive Documents & Reports* (1987, for documents before 1970) and *CIS/Index* (1970–date). Like other CIS indexes, these are accompanied by microfiche copies of all indexed documents and reports.

The Senate Foreign Relations Committee website has a list of pending treaties indicating actions taken <foreign.senate.gov/ treaties.pdf>. *Congressional Index*, CCH's weekly looseleaf service, also includes a table of treaties pending before the Senate, with references to Treaty Documents, Executive Reports, hearings, and ratifications.

(b) Foreign Relations Documents

State practice is the primary evidence of custom, one of the major sources of international law. To study state practice, it is best to turn to sources that explain how a particular nation has acted in the past.

Reference works such as *Encyclopedia of U.S. Foreign Relations* (Bruce W. Jentleson & Thomas G. Paterson eds., 1997) can provide a background understanding of U.S. practice. More detailed discussion can be found in a series of digests prepared by the Department of State. *Digest of United States Practice in International Law* compiles excerpts from treaties, decisions, diplomatic correspondence, and other documents reflecting the U.S. position on major issues of international law, accompanied by explanatory commentary. Recent volumes are published annually, but the years from 1981 to 1999 are covered by multiyear cumulations. The Department of State website <www.state.gov/s/l/c8183.htm> has links to the full text of documents excerpted in the digests since 1989.

The Department of State also published earlier encyclopedic digests of U.S. practice that may be of value for historical research. The last of these was Marjorie M. Whiteman, *Digest of International Law* (1963–73), focusing largely on the period from the 1940s to the 1960s. Its predecessors were compiled by Francis Wharton (1886; 2d ed. 1887); John Bassett Moore (1906) (covering the period 1776 to 1906 and effectively superseding Wharton); and G.H. Hackworth (1940–44) (covering the period 1906 to 1939). These digests have all been digitized as part of HeinOnline's Foreign and International Law Resources Database.

More extensive documentation of U.S. practice can be found in *Foreign Relations of the United States* (1861–date), a comprehensive record of material relating to such issues as treaty negotiation and international conflicts. There is a time lag of more than thirty years between the original (often confidential) issuance of these documents and their publication in this series. The set from 1861 to 1960 is available online through subscription databases and for free from the University of Wisconsin <digicoll.library.wisc.edu/FRUS/>, and selected volumes for the Truman through Ford administrations are available from the Department of State <www.state.gov/r/pa/ho/frus/>.[8]

§ 13.3   General Treaty Research

The United States is not a party to every major multilateral treaty. The International Covenant on Economic, Social and Cultural Rights (ICESCR), the Vienna Convention on the Law Treaties, and the United Nations Convention on the Law of the Sea are just three of the many agreements that the U.S. has not ratified.[9] Regional agreements in other parts of the world and bilateral treaties between other countries may also be important research sources. In addition to the U.S. treaty resources already discussed, more general resources are frequently needed as well.

General Sources. The most comprehensive source for modern treaties is the *United Nations Treaty Series* (*UNTS*), containing more than 2,300 volumes and available free online as the United Nations Treaty Collection <treaties.un.org>. Since 1946 this series has published all treaties registered with the U.N. by member nations in their original languages, as well as in English and French translations. Illustration 13–3 on page 427 shows the first page of the 1993 Chemical Weapons Convention, as published in *UNTS*. Footnote 1 identifies the ratifications that caused the convention to enter into force in 1997.

The United Nations Treaty Collection website includes summaries and information on ratification status as well as treaty texts, but its interface can be a bit daunting. Title searches must use exact phrases rather than keywords, for example, and you cannot retrieve treaties by citation. The *UNTS* is also available online by subscription in HeinOnline's United Nations Law Collec-

---

8. For more information on the use of foreign relations documents and related sources, see SOURCES OF STATE PRACTICE IN INTERNATIONAL LAW (Ralph Gaebler & Maria Smolka–Day eds., 2002), which covers the United States, Canada, and twelve European countries, and Silke Sahl, *Researching Customary International Law, State Practice and the Pronouncements of States Regarding International Law*, GlobaLex (June/July 2007), <www.nyulawglobal.org/globalex/Customary_International_Law.htm>.
NATIONAL TREATY LAW AND PRACTICE (Duncan B. Hollis et al. eds., 2005) analyzes the treaty practices of nineteen countries, including the United States.

9. On the ambivalent relationship between the United States and human rights conventions, see NATALIE HEVENER KAUFMAN, HUMAN RIGHTS TREATIES AND THE SENATE: A HISTORY OF OPPOSITION (1990).

tion, which may be a more convenient source if you want to retrieve documents by volume and page number.

Treaties predating the creation of the United Nations can be found in two older series. The *League of Nations Treaty Series (LNTS)* (1920–46) is similar in scope to the *UNTS*, and a retrospective collection, *Consolidated Treaty Series (CTS)* (1969–86) contains all treaties between nation states from 1648 to 1919. *CTS* prints treaties in the language of one of the signatories, usually accompanied by an English or French translation. There is no subject index, but the set includes a chronological list and an index to parties.

Both the Organization of American States (OAS) <www.oas.org/juridico/english/treaties.html> and the Council of Europe <conventions.coe.int> provide access to treaties among their members, in printed treaty series and online. The Hague Conference on Private International Law <www.hcch.net> has the text of several dozen conventions it has drafted on issues such as international civil procedure and recognition of judgments. Many foreign countries publish current treaties in their official gazettes and on government websites, and new treaties are often printed in international law yearbooks and journals.

The United Nations Audiovisual Library of International Law <www.un.org/law/avl/> includes a Research Library with links to sources for treaties, as well as jurisprudence, yearbooks, other official documents, and scholarly writings in international law. In addition to United Nations resources, it also has links to sites maintained by other organizations and nearly three dozen national treaty collections.

Subject Collections. Several resources reprint or provide links to major international treaties and other documents. The American Society of International Law's Electronic Information System for International Law (EISIL) <www.eisil.org> is designed to provide links to authoritative websites for primary and other materials in international law. It has thousands of links to treaties and other primary documents in thirteen major subject areas. In addition to links to the primary sources, each record also includes a "More Information" button with citations, dates, and brief descriptions.

The University of Minnesota Law School maintains a more selective list of about 75 frequently-cited treaties <local.law.umn.edu/library/pathfinders/most-cited.html>, with official citations and links to EISIL and other sources. Other free sources for the texts of major multilateral treaties and conventions include the Multilaterals Project at the Fletcher School <www.fletcher.tufts.edu/multilaterals.html> and the University of Minnesota Human Rights Library <www.umn.edu/humanrts/>.

Several collections reprint a variety of important international law documents, usually in specific areas. The most comprehensive of these collections is the nine-volume *International Law and World Order: Basic Documents* (Burns H. Weston & Jonathan C. Carlson eds., 1994–date). Others include *Basic Documents in International Law* (Ian Brownlie ed., 5th ed. 2002); *Basic Documents on Human Rights* (Ian Brownlie & Guy S. Goodwin–Gill eds., 4th ed. 2002); *Basic Documents on International Migration Law* (Richard Plender ed., 3d ed. 2007); *Basic Documents on International Trade Law* (Chia–Jui Cheng ed., 3d ed. 1999); *Documents in International Environmental Law* (Philippe Sands & Paolo Galizzi eds., 2d ed. 2004); and *International Criminal Law Deskbook* (John P. Grant & J. Craig Barker eds., 2006).

Indexes and Status Tables. The *United Nations Treaty Series* has indexes for every 50 or 100 volumes, but no cumulative official index. This is less significant now that the United Nations Treaty Collection is available free online, and it will become less so as its search interface becomes more user-friendly.

Other sources for finding treaties are available. Christian L. Wiktor, *Multilateral Treaty Calendar, 1648–1995* (1998) lists more than 6,000 agreements chronologically, identifies sources in more than 100 publications, and provides information on treaty status. M.J. Bowman & D.J. Harris, *Multilateral Treaties: Index and Current Status* (1984, with 11th cum. supp. 1995) covers more than 1,000 agreements with information on sources and parties, but it has not been updated in several years. Peter H. Rohn, *World Treaty Index* (2d ed. 1983–84) is growing increasingly dated, but it provides comprehensive coverage of some 44,000 bilateral and multilateral treaties from 1900 to 1980 and is available online <db.lib.washington.edu/wti/wtdb.htm>.

The source for determining the status of and identifying the parties to major conventions is *Multilateral Treaties Deposited with the Secretary–General*, published by the United Nations and available online <treaties.un.org>. This listing of several hundred treaties is arranged by subject, and provides citations, information on status, a list of parties with dates of signature and ratification, and the text of any reservations imposed by individual parties. Coverage is limited to treaties concluded under U.N. auspices or for which the Secretary–General acts as depository, so it excludes some major agreements such as the Geneva Conventions of 1949 <www.icrc.org/ihl> and the Convention on International Trade in Endangered Species (CITES) <www.cites.org>. Illustration 13–4 on page 428 shows the first page of the entry for the Chemical Weapons Convention, with 186 countries now parties to the convention. Individual countries' declarations, reservations, and objections are noted on pages following the list of parties. Information on the ratification of major human rights conventions is also available from the United Nations Office of the High Commissioner for Human Rights <www2.ohchr.org/english/bodies/ratification/>.

Interpretation. Scholarly commentary and judicial decisions are the standard sources of treaty interpretation. An additional source available for the interpretation of some multilateral conventions is the *travaux preparatoires* (documents created during the drafting process such as reports and debates). These are recognized under the 1969 Vienna Convention on the Law of Treaties as a source for clarifying ambiguous treaty terms.[10] *Travaux* for many treaties are difficult to find, but they have been compiled and published for several conventions, e.g. Jean Allain, *The Slavery Conventions: the Travaux Préparatoires of the 1926 League of Nations Convention and the 1956 United Nations Convention* (2008) or United Nations Office on Drugs and Crime, *Travaux Préparatoires of the Negotiations for the Elaboration of the United Nations Convention Against Transnational Organized Crime and the Protocols Thereto* (2006).[11]

§ 13.4 Cases and Arbitrations

Although most disputes between nations are resolved by direct negotiation between the parties, some are submitted to international tribunals, arbitral bodies, or temporary commissions convened for particular disputes. Courts established by regional organizations resolve disputes between nations and their citizens, developing a growing body of international human rights law. Decisions of domestic courts on matters of international law can also be important sources, particularly as evidence of international legal custom.

(a) International Court of Justice

The preeminent international tribunal is the International Court of Justice (ICJ), also known as the World Court, which settles legal disputes between nations. The ICJ was created in 1945 by the Charter of the United Nations as one of the organization's principal organs, succeeding the Permanent Court of International Justice (PCIJ) of the League of Nations. The Court meets at the Hague and consists of fifteen justices elected to nine-year terms.

---

10. Vienna Convention on the Law of Treaties, May 23, 1969, art. 32, 1155 U.N.T.S. 331, 340 ("Recourse may be had to supplementary means of interpretation, including the preparatory work of the treaty and the circumstances of its conclusion . . .").

11. For a guide to published sources and more information, see Jon-

athan Pratter, *À la Recherche des Travaux Préparatoires: An Approach to Researching the Drafting History of International Agreements*, GlobaLex (May/June 2008) <www.nyulawglobal. org/globalex/Travaux_Preparatoires1. htm>.

The ICJ issues only a handful of decisions each year. These decisions are published in *Reports of Judgments, Advisory Opinions and Orders* and are available on the ICJ website <www.icj-cij.org>. The site has material from every case the Court has heard since its inception and from cases heard by the PCIJ, as well as information on the current docket and basic documents such as the Statute of the Court and rules. Illustration 13–5 on page 429 shows the opening page of the Court's decision in *Liechtenstein v. Germany*, from the I.C.J. *Reports of Judgments*.

Decisions are also available through online databases such as HeinOnline and Westlaw (INT–ICJ database). *International Law Reports* (1956–date) and its predecessor *Annual Digest and Reports of Public International Law Cases* (1932–55) contain all PCIJ and ICJ decisions and English translations of selected decisions of regional and national courts on international law issues.

Among the most extensive works on the ICJ are Shabtai Rosenne, *The Law and Practice of the International Court, 1920–2005* (4th ed. 2006) and *The Statute of the International Court of Justice: A Commentary* (Andreas Zimmermann et al. eds., 2006). Shorter works include Terry D. Gill, *Rosenne's The World Court: What It Is and How It Works* (6th ed. 2003) and *La Cour internationale de Justice/International Court of Justice* (2006), an illustrated history published to celebrate the Court's sixtieth anniversary.

(b) Other Courts

The ICJ is not the only court of international scope. The Project on International Courts and Tribunals <www.pict-pcti. org> has information on dozens of global and regional tribunals of general and specialized jurisdiction, with links to basic documents and cases. Its website also has a chart <www.pict-pcti.org/ publications/synoptic_chart.html> describing each court and classifying it as existing, extinct, aborted, dormant, nascent, or proposed.

The World Legal Information Institute's International Courts & Tribunals Library <www.worldlii.org/int/cases/> allows searching across more than 20,000 decisions from about twenty of these tribunals.

International Courts. An International Criminal Court <www.icc-cpi.int> with jurisdiction over war crimes, genocide, and crimes against humanity had its first session in March 2003. Cases, documents, and background information are available on the court's website, and major secondary sources include William Schabas, *An Introduction to the International Criminal Court* (3d ed. 2007), *The Legislative History of the International Criminal Court* (M. Cherif Bassiouni ed., 2005), and *The Rome Statute of the International Criminal Court: A Commentary* (Antonio Cassese et al. eds., 2002). Cyril Laucci, *The Annotated Digest of the International Criminal Court* (2007–date) has abstracts of the ICC's developing case law, arranged by provisions of its statute, rules and regulations.

More focused international criminal courts have been convened to address specific violations of international humanitarian law. The International Criminal Tribunal for the former Yugoslavia (ICTY) <www.icty.org> was established in 1993, the International Criminal Tribunal for Rwanda (ICTR) <www.ictr.org> in 1994, and the Special Court for Sierra Leone <www.sc-sl.org> in 2002. Each of these courts has case documents and other information on its website. Their procedures and jurisprudence are discussed in William Schabas, *UN International Criminal Tribunals: The Former Yugoslavia, Rwanda, and Sierra Leone* (2006), and major cases can be found in print in *Annotated Leading Cases of International Criminal Tribunals* (André Klip & Göran Sluiter eds., 1999–date).[12]

More general works on international criminal law include *Archbold: International Criminal Courts: Practise, Procedure, and Evidence* (Karim A.A. Khan et al. eds., 2d ed. 2005), John R.W.D. Jones & Steven Powles, *International Criminal Practice* (3d ed. 2003), and *International Criminal Law* (M. Cherif Bassiouni ed., 3d ed. 2008).

The World War II war crimes trials held by the International Military Tribunals in Nuremberg and Tokyo are available in several printed sources including *The Trial of German Major War Criminals* (1946–51) and *The Tokyo War Crimes Trial* (R. John Pritchard & Sonia Magbanua Zaide eds., 1981–87). The U.S. government publication *Nazi Conspiracy and Aggression* (1946–47) is available in HeinOnline's Legal Classics Library.

Another court of worldwide scope, the International Tribunal for the Law of the Sea (ITLOS) <www.itlos.org>, was created by the United Nations Convention on the Law of the Sea and established in 1996. ITLOS rules and cases are available on its website, and publications include Gudmundur Eiriksson, *The International Tribunal for the Law of the Sea* (2000) and P. Chandrasekhara Rao & Ph. Gautier, *The Rules of the International Tribunal for the Law of the Sea: A Commentary* (2006).

Regional Courts. The decisions of the courts of regional organizations have assumed growing importance in international law as the range of disputes over which they exercise jurisdiction

---

12. For more information on resources about these courts, see Amy Burchfield, *International Criminal Courts for the Former Yugoslavia, Rwanda and Sierra Leone: A Guide to Online and Print Resources*, GlobaLex (Oct. 2005) <www.nyulawglobal.org/globalex/International_Criminal_Courts.htm>.

grows. Among the most important of these regional courts are the European Court of Justice, the European Court of Human Rights, and the Inter–American Court of Human Rights.

The European Court of Justice <curia.europa.eu>, an organ of the European Union, resolves disputes between EU institutions and member states over the interpretation and application of EU treaties and legislation. A subordinate Court of First Instance was established in 1988 to handle certain classes of cases and reduce the Court of Justice's workload. All decisions since the Court's inception are available on its website, as well as through Westlaw and Lexis. The official *Reports of Cases Before the Court of Justice and the Court of First Instance* includes decisions from both courts, and commercial print sources include CCH's *European Union Law Reporter* (1972–date) and *Common Market Law Reports* (1962–date). Commentaries include Anthony Arnull, *The European Union and Its Court of Justice* (2d ed. 2006) and L. Neville Brown & Tom Kennedy, *The Court of Justice of the European Communities* (5th ed. 2000).

The European Court of Human Rights <www.echr.coe.int> was created under the European Convention of Human Rights of 1950 for the international protection of the rights of individuals. The Court's website has basic texts and searchable case law. Decisions are published officially in *Reports of Judgments and Decisions*, and are also reported commercially in *European Human Rights Reports* (1979–date, available as Westlaw's EHR–RPTS database). Cases are summarized in *Human Rights Case Digest* (1990–date, bimonthly, available on HeinOnline), and a variety of documents and decisions appear in the annual *Yearbook of the European Convention on Human Rights* (1958–date). *Human Rights Practice* (Jessica Simor ed., 2000–date) is a detailed guide to the Convention's articles and court procedures. Other secondary sources include Clare Ovey & Robin White, *Jacobs and White, The European Convention on Human Rights* (3d ed. 2002) and *Theory and Practice of the European Convention on Human Rights* (Pieter van Dijk et al. eds., 2006).

The Inter–American Commission on Human Rights <www.cidh.oas.org> was created in 1959 and hears complaints of individuals and institutions alleging violations of human rights in the American countries. The Commission, or a member state, can refer matters to the Inter–American Court of Human Rights <www.corteidh.or.cr>, created in 1978. At least twenty-five countries (not including the United States) have accepted its jurisdiction. The Court's decisions are reported in two series of judgments (advisory opinions in Series A, *Judgments and Opinions*; and contentious cases in Series C, *Decisions and Judgments*), in its annual report, and on its website. The *Inter-American Yearbook on Human Rights* (1985–date) covers the work of both the Commission and the Court and includes selected decisions and other documents. Secondary sources include Jo M. Pasqualucci, *The Practice and Procedure of the Inter–American Court of Human Rights* (2003).

A third regional human rights court, the African Court on Human and Peoples' Rights, was created in 2002 but has not yet begun operations. The African International Courts and Tribunals site <www.aict-ctia.org> has information on its development.

National Courts. Domestic courts often address issues of international law, and their decisions can have international significance. As mentioned earlier, *International Law Reports* contains decisions of national courts on international law issues. The Hague Justice Portal <www.haguejusticeportal.net> has a DomCLIC (Domestic Case Law on International Crimes) project with documents from courts in three dozen countries. The American Society of International Law's i.lex: The Legal Research System for International Law in U.S. Courts <ilex.asil.org> is a searchable database of selected U.S. court cases, with summaries of each case's background and significance.

Cases from the U.S. and other countries under the Convention on Contracts for the International Sale of Goods are available through UNILEX <www.unilex.info> and Pace University's Institute of International Commercial Law <www.cisg.law.pace.edu>. Case Law on UNCITRAL Texts (CLOUT) <www.uncitral.org/uncitral/en/case_law.html> has international trade law cases, and ECOLEX <www.ecolex.org> is a gateway to environmental law decisions by national and international courts as well as treaties, legislation and other resources. Refworld <www.refworld.org>, from the Office of the U.N. High Commissioner for Refugees, has searchable judgments on human rights from domestic and regional courts, as well as thousands of other documents relating to the granting of refugee status.

(c) Arbitrations

Many disputes between nations and between commercial partners are settled by arbitration. Arbitrations between nations are published in the United Nations series, *Reports of International Arbitral Awards (RIAA)* (1948–date), which includes agreements reached by mediation or conciliation as well as awards resulting from contested arbitrations. RIAA is available online from the U.N. <www.un.org/law/riaa/> and from HeinOnline.[13]

---

13. For historical arbitrations, see REPERTORY OF INTERNATIONAL ARBITRAL JURISPRUDENCE (1989–91), arranging arbitral decisions from 1794 to 1987 by subject, and SURVEY OF INTERNATIONAL ARBITRATIONS, 1794–1989 (A. M. Stuyt ed., 3d. ed. 1990), digesting these early decisions. The Hague Peace Conferences of

Several sources cover international arbitrations between private parties, including *Mealey's International Arbitration Report* (1986–date, monthly, available in Lexis), *World Arbitration Reporter* (Hans Smit & Vratislav Pechota eds., 1986–date), and *Yearbook: Commercial Arbitration* (1975–date). Recent treatises in the area include Margaret L. Moses, *The Principles and Practice of International Commercial Arbitration* (2008) and Alan Redfern et al., *Law and Practice of International Commercial Arbitration* (4th ed. 2004). The subscription site Kluwer Arbitration <www.kluwer arbitration.com> has access to a variety of major sources, including conventions, rules, and case law.

§ 13.5   International Organizations

National governments are the major parties in international law, but worldwide and regional intergovernmental organizations (IGOs) play a vital role by establishing norms, promoting multilateral conventions, and providing mechanisms for the peaceful resolution of conflicts. Several IGOs have established adjudicatory bodies by whose decisions nations agree to be bound. Even when not acting as lawmaking bodies, international organizations compile and publish many of the most important research sources in international law.[14]

(a) United Nations and Related Agencies

The purposes of the United Nations are (1) to maintain international peace and security; (2) to develop friendly relations among nations based on respect for equal rights and self-determination; (3) to achieve international cooperation in solving international problems and in promoting respect for human rights and fundamental freedoms; and (4) to be a center for harmonizing the actions of nations in attaining these goals.[15]

The United Nations' six principal organs are the General Assembly, Security Council, Economic and Social Council, Trusteeship Council, Secretariat, and International Court of Justice (ICJ). Its website <www.un.org> provides a wealth of information on the

---

1899 and 1907 created the Permanent Court of Arbitration and the International Commission of Inquiry; their decisions were published in the HAGUE COURT REPORTS (James B. Scott ed., 1916–32, available on HeinOnline). THE PERMANENT COURT OF ARBITRATION: INTERNATIONAL ARBITRATION AND DISPUTE RESOLUTION (P. Hamilton et al. eds., 1999) summarizes its work.

14. Nongovernmental organizations (NGOs) such as Amnesty International

are major advocates for causes such as environmental protection, health care, and human rights, and many publish useful resources for the international legal researcher. See Duke University Libraries' NGO Research Guide <library. duke.edu/research/subject/guides/ngo_ guide/> for more information and links to NGO websites.

15. Charter of the United Nations, June 26, 1945, art. 1, 59 Stat. 1031, 1037.

organization, including news, descriptive overviews of its activities, and access to numerous documents. The best printed source for basic information on the U.N.'s structure and membership is *United Nations Handbook*, published annually by the New Zealand Ministry of External Relations and Trade.[16]

The *Yearbook of the United Nations* is one of the best starting points for historical research on U.N. activities. Although coverage is delayed three or four years, this publication summarizes major developments, reprints major documents, and provides references to other sources for the year covered. It is available free online <unyearbook.un.org>, with retrospective coverage from the first volume in 1946.

The *General Assembly Official Records* (GAOR) are among the most important documents for U.N. research. The records of the meetings of the assembly and its committees are accompanied by *Annexes* containing the more important documents produced during the session, and by *Supplements* containing annual reports submitted by the Secretary–General, Security Council, International Court of Justice, and various committees. The final supplement each year is a compilation of the resolutions passed by the General Assembly during the session.

Resolutions are also reprinted in the *Yearbook of the United Nations* and are available on the Internet. The UN Documentation Centre <www.un.org/documents/> has browsable access to General Assembly and Security Council resolutions since 1946, as well as recent meeting records and other major documents. The United Nations Official Document System <documents.un.org> is a search engine with the full text of all resolutions since 1946 and other documents beginning in 1993.

The United Nations also produces several specialized yearbooks. The *Yearbook of the International Law Commission* <untreaty.un.org/ilc/publications/yearbooks/yearbooks.htm> reports on efforts to develop and codify selected fields of international law; the *Juridical Yearbook* <www.un.org/law/UNJuridical Yearbook/> contains the texts of treaties and other documents relating to legal activities of the U.N. and related organizations. The United Nations Commission on International Trade Law's *UNCITRAL Yearbook* <www.uncitral.org/uncitral/en/publications/

---

16. More extensive commentaries include THE CHARTER OF THE UNITED NATIONS: A COMMENTARY (Bruno Simma ed., 2d ed. 2002); SIMON CHESTERMAN ET AL., LAW AND PRACTICE OF THE UNITED NATIONS: DOCUMENTS AND COMMENTARY (2008); BENEDETTO CONFORTI, THE LAW AND PRACTICE OF THE UNITED NATIONS (3d rev. ed. 2005); and THE UNITED NATIONS: LAW AND PRAC-

TICE (Franz Cede & Lilly Sucharipa–Behrmann eds., 2001). The *Max Planck Yearbook of United Nations Law* (1997– date) is a major source for current scholarly commentary; older volumes are available free online <www.mpil.de/ww/en/pub/research/details/publications/institute/mpyunl.cfm>.

yearbook.html> focuses on the modernization and harmonization of the rules of international business. Each of these yearbook websites has complete retrospective coverage of earlier volumes, and they are available as well in HeinOnline's United Nations Law Collection.

A broad range of other U.N. publications are available, and are indexed in UNBISNET <unbisnet.un.org>, the United Nations Bibliographic Information System. It covers materials since 1979, with older documents gradually being added. A commercial electronic service, *Access UN: Index to United Nations Documents and Publications* <infoweb.newsbank.com>, has comprehensive retrospective coverage.

United Nations Documentation: Research Guide <www.un.org/Depts/dhl/resguide/> is a concise introduction to U.N. resources, including an explanation of its document symbols, discussion of the major organizational units, and more in-depth coverage of some topics such as human rights and international law.[17]

The United Nations also coordinates the work of several "specialized agencies" in particular subject fields, such as the Food and Agriculture Organization, the International Labour Organisation, and the World Health Organization, several of which have extensive law-related activities. The United Nations System website locator <www.unsystem.org> provides access to sites for more than eighty specialized organizations.

(b) World Trade Organization

The World Trade Organization <www.wto.org> was established in 1995 as the principal international body administering trade agreements among member states, succeeding the General Agreement on Tariffs and Trade (GATT).[18] The WTO acts as a forum for negotiations, seeks to resolve disputes, and oversees national trade policies. It is governed by a Ministerial Conference, which meets every two years, while most operations are handled by its General Council. Basic documents governing WTO operations are available on its website, and an *Annual Report* (1996–date) provides trade statistics and a commentary on the organization's work every year.

---

17. Several more extensive guides are published, including INTERNATIONAL INFORMATION: DOCUMENTS, PUBLICATIONS, AND ELECTRONIC INFORMATION OF INTERNATIONAL GOVERNMENTAL ORGANIZATIONS (Peter I. Hajnal ed., 2d ed. 1997–2001). See also Maureen Ratynski Andersen, *Where to Begin . . . When You Don't Know How to Start: Tips for Researching U.N. Legal Materials*, 31 INT'L J. LEGAL INFO. 264 (2003), and Wiltrud Harms, *Selected U.N. Resources and Research Tools: Overview and Search Tips for Legal Research*, GlobaLex (Sept./Oct. 2007) <www.nyulawglobal.org/globalex/UN_Resources_Research_Tools.pdf>.

18. Pre-WTO documents are available from the GATT Digital Library: 1947–1994 <gatt.stanford.edu>.

WTO panel decisions and appellate body reports are available in the "Dispute Settlement" section of the WTO website as well as in several commercial series, including the looseleaf *International Trade Law Reports* (1996–date), the bound *World Trade Organization Dispute Settlement Decisions: Bernan's Annotated Reporter* (1998–date), and Westlaw and Lexis. The subscription website WorldTradeLaw.net <www.worldtradelaw.net> has summaries and texts of decisions as well as other WTO documents. *WTO Appellate Body Repertory of Reports and Awards, 1995–2006* (3d ed. 2007) provides subject access to its jurisprudence.

Commentaries on the WTO include Mitsuo Matsushita et al., *The World Trade Organization: Law, Practice, and Policy* (2d ed. 2006) and *The World Trade Organization: Legal, Economic and Political Analysis* (Patrick F. J. Macrory et al. eds., 2005).

(c) European Union and Other Regional Organizations

For American lawyers, the European Union <europa.eu> is probably the most frequently encountered of the world's many regional organizations. The EU was established in 1993 by the Treaty on European Union (the Maastricht Treaty) as the more ambitious successor to the European Communities (European Atomic Energy Community, European Coal and Steel Community, and European Economic Community). As economic and social developments have led to increasing European integration and the Treaty on European Union has been amended by the Treaty of Amsterdam (1997) and the Treaty of Nice (2001), the EU can be seen more as a supranational government than as a regional organization.

The major institutions of the EU are the European Commission, which proposes legislation, implements policies, and manages the Union; the European Parliament, a large elected body with legislative and advisory functions; the Council, which coordinates economic policies, concludes international agreements, and legislates in conjunction with the European Parliament; and the European Court of Justice (discussed in § 13.4 with other regional courts). The EU legislates through *regulations*, which are directly binding and don't require implementing legislation in member states, and *directives*, which must be implemented by member states to become effective.

Official sources of EU legal information include the *Official Journal of the European Union*, consisting of two series, *Legislation* (L) and *Information and Notices* (C), and the semiannual *Directory of Community Legislation in Force*, which provides subject access to treaties, regulations, directives and other legislative actions. Legislation and major documents are published in the EU's twenty official languages: Czech, Danish, Dutch, English, Estonian, Finnish, French, German, Greek, Hungarian, Italian, Latvian, Lithuanian, Maltese, Polish, Portuguese, Slovak, Slovene, Spanish and Swedish.

EUR–Lex <eur-lex.europa.eu> is a free website with access to the *Official Journal of the European Union* back to 1998, as well as the EU treaties, legislation, case law and legislative proposals. Westlaw and Lexis also have extensive EU databases. The EU–ALL database on Westlaw combines the treaties (EU–TREATIES), legislative acts (EU–LEG), case law, and other documents. In addition to primary sources, Lexis has the four-volume treatise *Smit & Herzog on the Law of the European Union* (2d ed. 2005–date).

Several other reference sources on EU law are published. *Encyclopedia of European Union Law: Constitutional Texts* (Neville March Hunnings ed., 1996–date) has annotated versions of the treaties and other major texts in seven large volumes. CCH's *European Union Law Reporter* (1972–date) is one of the most convenient starting points for many American lawyers, because of its familiar looseleaf format and frequent supplementation. One-volume works include Anthony Arnull et al., *Wyatt and Dashwood's European Union Law* (5th ed. 2006), P.S.R.F. Mathijsen, *A Guide to European Union Law* (9th ed. 2007), and Takis Tridimas, *The General Principles of EU Law* (2006).[19]

Other important regional organizations include the Organization of American States (OAS) <www.oas.org> and the Council of Europe <www.coe.int>, both of which draft and promote multilateral treaties among their member states. As discussed in § 13.4, they both have judicial systems designed to protect human rights in their regions.

Information on about two dozen major intergovernmental organizations can be found in *International Encyclopaedia of Laws: Intergovernmental Organizations* (1997–date). The biennial *Yearbook of International Organizations*, also available online by subscription <www.uia.be>, is a five-volume directory with profiles and contact information for thousands of international groups and associations. The University of Michigan Library maintains an extensive annotated collection of links to international organization websites <www.lib.umich.edu/govdocs/intl.html>.

---

19. For more information on EU resources, see Duncan E. Alford, *European Union Legal Materials: An Infrequent User's Guide*, GlobaLex (Oct. 2008) <www.nyulawglobal.org/globalex/European_Union1.htm> and Marylin J. Raisch, *European Union Law: An Integrated Guide to Electronic and Print Research*, LLRX.com (May 29, 2007) <www.llrx.com/features/eulaw2.htm>. The University of California Library maintains a lengthy list of links to EU resources <www.lib.berkeley.edu/doemoff/govinfo/intl/gov_eu.html>.

§ 13.6 Sources for Further Information

International law has a wide range of print and electronic resources beyond those mentioned in this brief survey, and bibliographies and research guides can be invaluable sources of leads and research tips. The American Society of International Law's *ASIL Electronic Resource Guide* <www.asil.org/erghome.cfm> is a particularly useful and frequently updated guide. Its twelve chapters have narrative descriptions of and links to resources in several specific areas, including treaties, international organizations (with separate chapters on the European Union and the United Nations), and several topical areas such as human rights, environmental law, and intellectual property.

Another major Internet source for international law information is GlobaLex <www.nyulawglobal.org/Globalex/>, which publishes several dozen research guides on specific topics, each accompanied by numerous links to resources. Several of its articles have already been cited in this chapter.

Marci Hoffman & Mary Rumsey, *International and Foreign Legal Research: A Coursebook* (2008) is a thorough examination of research methods in print and online, covering public international law, international organizations, and several specialized topics including human rights, international environmental law, and international trade law. George Washington University Journal of International Law and Economics, *Guide to International Legal Research* (annual) has annotated listings of published and online resources.

TREATY OF AMITY, ECONOMIC RELATIONS, AND CONSULAR RIGHTS BETWEEN THE UNITED STATES OF AMERICA AND IRAN

The United States of America and Iran, desirous of emphasizing the friendly relations which have long prevailed between their peoples, of reaffirming the high principles in the regulation of human affairs to which they are committed, of encouraging mutually beneficial trade and investments and closer economic intercourse generally between their peoples, and of regulating consular relations, have resolved to conclude, on the basis of reciprocal equality of treatment, a Treaty of Amity, Economic Relations, and Consular Rights, and have appointed as their Plenipotentiaries:

The President of the United States of America:

Mr. Selden Chapin, Ambassador Extraordinary and Plenipotentiary of the United States of America at Tehran; and

His Imperial Majesty, the Shah of Iran:

His Excellency Mr. Mostafa Samiy, Under Secretary of the Ministry of Foreign Affairs;

Who, having communicated to each other their full powers found to be in due form, have agreed upon the following articles:

Article I

There shall be firm and enduring peace and sincere friendship between the United States of America and Iran.

Article II

1. Nationals of either High Contracting Party shall be permitted, upon terms no less favorable than those accorded to nationals of any third country, to enter and remain in the territories of the other High Contracting Party for the purpose of carrying on trade between their own country and the territories of such other High Contracting Party and engaging in related commercial activities, and for the purpose of developing and directing the operations of an enterprise in which they have invested, or in which they are actively in the process of investing, a substantial amount of capital.

TIAS 3853

88465 O—57——58

Illustration 13–1. Treaty of Amity, Economic Relations, and Consular Rights, Aug, 15, 1955, U.S.-Iran, 8 U.S.T. 899, 901.

Bilateral Treaties in Force as of January 1, 2008

Agricultural commodities agreement, with exchange of notes.
Signed at Tehran December 20, 1966.
Entered into force December 20, 1966.
17 UST 2372; TIAS 6183; 681 UNTS 101.

AVIATION

Air transport agreement, with exchange of notes.
Signed at Tehran February 1, 1973.
Entered into force January 9, 1974.
26 UST 1929; TIAS 8149; 1027 UNTS 129.

Memorandum of agreement relating to the provision of technical assistance to the Iranian Civil Aviation Organization, with annex.
Signed at Washington and Tehran May 12 and June 9, 1977.
Entered into force June 9, 1977.
29 UST 5319; TIAS 9111.

CLAIMS

Declarations of the Government of the Democratic and Popular Republic of Algeria concerning commitments and settlement of claims by the United States and Iran with respect to resolution of the crisis arising out of the detention of 52 United States nationals in Iran, with Undertakings and Escrow Agreement.[1]
Initialed at Algiers January 19, 1981.
Entered into force January 19, 1981.
TIAS

Settlement agreement regarding certain claims before the Iran-U.S. Claims Tribunal, with annex.
Signed at The Hague February 9, 1996.
Entered into force February 9, 1996.
TIAS

Settlement agreement on the case concerning the aerial incident of July 3, 1988 before the International Court of Justice, with annexes.
Signed at The Hague February 9, 1996.
Entered into force February 9, 1996.
TIAS

General agreement on the settlement of certain I.C.J. and Tribunal cases, with related statement.
Signed at The Hague February 9, 1996.
Entered into force February 9, 1996.
TIAS

NOTE
1   For technical agreements concerning the security account, see NETHERLANDS — CLAIMS.

COMMERCE

Treaty of amity, economic relations, and consular rights.
Signed at Tehran August 15, 1955.
Entered into force June 16, 1957.
8 UST 899; TIAS 3853; 284 UNTS 93.

CONSULS
See COMMERCE

DEFENSE

Mutual defense assistance agreement.
Exchange of notes at Washington May 23, 1950.
Entered into force May 23, 1950.
1 UST 420; TIAS 2071; 81 UNTS 3.

Agreement relating to the continuation of military assistance to Iran.
Exchange of notes at Tehran April 24, 1952.
Entered into force April 24, 1952.
5 UST 788; TIAS 2967

Agreement relating to the disposition of equipment and materials no longer required in the furtherance of the mutual defense assistance program.
Exchange of notes at Tehran July 12 and October 31, 1957.
Entered into force October 31, 1957
8 UST 2369; TIAS 3952; 303 UNTS 320.

Agreement relating to the safeguarding of classified information, with annex.
Exchange of notes at Tehran May 28 and June 6, 1974.
Entered into force June 6, 1974.
25 UST 1266; TIAS 7857.

Agreement relating to the furnishing of certain federal catalog data and cataloging services to Iran.
Signed at Washington December 5, 1974, and at Tehran January 25, 1975.
Entered into force January 25, 1975.
26 UST 302; TIAS 8034; 991 UNTS 401.

Agreement concerning management, disposal, and utilization of funds derived from the sale of military assistance program property.
Signed at Tehran October 6, 1975.
Entered into force October 6, 1975.
TIAS

Agreement concerning management, disposal, and utilization of funds derived from sale of military assistance program property.
Signed at Tehran October 19, 1976
Entered into force October 19, 1976
TIAS

Memorandum of understanding concerning revisions of Foreign Military Sales letters of offer and acceptance in force between the United States and Iran.
Signed at Tehran February 3, 1979.
Entered into force February 3, 1979.
30 UST 3597; TIAS 9415.

DISASTER ASSISTANCE

Memorandum of understanding relating to the provision of advisory technical assistance to Iran in organizing its civil emergency preparedness capability
Signed January 26, 1977.
Entered into force January 26, 1977
30 UST 4354; TIAS 9461.

ECONOMIC AND TECHNICAL COOPERATION

General agreement for economic cooperation.
Signed at Tehran December 21, 1961.
Entered into force December 21, 1961.
12 UST 3229; TIAS 4930; 433 UNTS 269.

Joint communique concerning United States-Iran relations and establishment of a Joint Commission for cooperation in various fields.
Issued at Tehran November 2, 1974.
Entered into force November 2, 1974
25 UST 3073; TIAS 7967

Agreed minutes of the Joint Commission:
March 4, 1975 (26 UST 420; TIAS 8042).
August 7, 1976 (27 UST 4329; TIAS 8455).
February 28, 1978 (30 UST 1027; TIAS 9238; 1152 UNTS 183).

EDUCATION

Agreement for financing certain educational exchange programs.
Signed at Tehran October 24, 1963.
Entered into force October 24, 1963.
14 UST 1510; TIAS 5451; 489 UNTS 303.

FINANCE

Agreement relating to investment guaranties under section 413(b)(4) of the Mutual Security Act of 1954, as amended.
Exchange of notes at Tehran September 17 and 21, 1957.
Entered into force September 24, 1957.
8 UST 1599; TIAS 3913; 293 UNTS 287.

Agreement supplementing the agreement of September 17 and 21, 1957 relating to investment guaranties.
Exchange of notes at Tehran March 12, 1970.
Entered into force March 12, 1970
22 UST 1030; TIAS 7146; 797 UNTS 396.

HOSTAGES
See CLAIMS

JUDICIAL ASSISTANCE

Agreement on procedures for mutual assistance in connection with matters relating to the Lockheed Aircraft Corporation, Grumman Corporation and Northrop Corporation.
Signed at Washington June 14, 1977.
Entered into force June 14, 1977
28 UST 5205; TIAS 8621

METEOROLOGY

Agreement relating to a cooperative program to improve and modernize the Iranian meteorological services, with annexes.
Signed at Tehran November 26, 1977.
Entered into force November 26, 1977.
29 UST 5546; TIAS 9127; 1134 UNTS 359.

MISSIONS, MILITARY

Agreement relating to the privileges and immunities granted American military and non-military technicians assisting in the modernization program of the Imperial Iranian Armed Forces.
Exchange of notes at Tehran May 24 and 30, 1973.
Entered into force May 30, 1973.
25 UST 3048; TIAS 7963.

PEACE CORPS

Agreement relating to the establishment of a Peace Corps program in Iran.
Exchange of notes at Tehran September 5 and 16, 1962.
Entered into force September 16, 1962.
22 UST 434; TIAS 7078; 791 UNTS 19.

POSTAL MATTERS

Parcel post agreement with detailed regulations for execution.
Signed at Tehran July 15 and at Washington August 28, 1969.
Entered into force January 1, 1971.
21 UST 2605; TIAS 7002; 775 UNTS 17.

Illustration 13–2. U.S. Dep't of State, Treaties in Force: A List of Treaties and Other International Agreements of the United States in Force on January 1, 2008, at 130 (2008).

1997   United Nations — Treaty Series • Nations Unies — Recueil des Traités   317

CONVENTION[1] ON THE PROHIBITION OF THE DEVELOPMENT, PRODUCTION, STOCKPILING AND USE OF CHEMICAL WEAPONS AND ON THEIR DESTRUCTION

PREAMBLE

The States Parties to this Convention,

Determined to act with a view to achieving effective progress towards general and complete disarmament under strict and effective international control, including the prohibition and elimination of all types of weapons of mass destruction,

Desiring to contribute to the realization of the purposes and principles of the Charter of the United Nations,

Recalling that the General Assembly of the United Nations has repeatedly condemned all actions contrary to the principles and

[1] Came into force on 29 April 1997, in accordance with article XXI:

Participant	Date of deposit of the instrument of ratification		Participant	Date of deposit of the instrument of ratification	
Albania	11 May	1994	Latvia	23 July	1996
Algeria	14 August	1995	Lesotho	7 December	1994
Argentina	2 October	1995	Maldives	31 May	1994
Armenia	27 January	1995	Mauritius	9 February	1993
Australia	6 May	1994	Mexico	29 August	1994
Austria	17 August	1995	Monaco	1 June	1995
Belarus	11 July	1996	Mongolia	17 January	1995
Brazil	13 March	1996	Morocco	28 December	1995
Bulgaria	10 August	1994	Namibia	24 November	1995
Cameroon	16 September	1996	Netherlands	30 June	1995
Canada	26 September	1995	(For the Kingdom in Europe.)		
Chile	12 July	1996	New Zealand	15 July	1996
Cook Islands	15 July	1994	Norway	7 April	1994
Costa Rica	31 May	1996	Oman	8 February	1995
Côte d'Ivoire	18 December	1995	Papua New Guinea	17 April	1996
Croatia	23 May	1995	Paraguay	1 December	1994
Czech Republic	6 March	1996	Peru	20 July	1995
Denmark	13 July	1995	Poland	23 August	1995
Ecuador	6 September	1995	Portugal	10 September	1996
El Salvador	30 October	1995	(Confirming the declaration made upon signature*)		
Ethiopia	13 May	1996	Republic of Moldova	8 July	1996
Fiji	20 January	1993	Romania	15 February	1995
Finland	7 February	1995	Saudi Arabia	9 August	1996
France	2 March	1995	Seychelles	7 April	1993
Georgia	27 November	1995	Slovakia	27 October	1995
Germany	12 August	1994	South Africa	13 September	1995
(Confirming the declaration made upon signature*)			Spain	3 August	1994
Greece	22 December	1994	(Confirming the declaration made upon signature*)		
(Confirming the declaration made upon signature*)			Sri Lanka	19 August	1994
Hungary	31 October	1996	Sweden	17 June	1993
India	3 September	1996	Switzerland	10 March	1995
Ireland	24 June	1996	Tajikistan	11 January	1995
(Confirming the declaration made upon signature*)			Turkmenistan	29 September	1994
Italy	8 December	1995	United Kingdom of Great Britain and Northern Ireland	13 May	1996
(Confirming the declaration made upon signature*)			Uruguay	6 October	1994
Japan	15 September	1995	Uzbekistan	23 July	1996

(Continued on page 318)

Vol. 1974, I-33757

Illustration 13–3. Convention on Prohibition of the Development, Production, Stockpiling and Use of Chemical Weapons and on Their Destruction, Jan. 13, 1993, 1974 U.N.T.S. 317.

3. Convention on the Prohibition of the Development, Production, Stockpiling and Use of Chemical Weapons and on their Destruction

Geneva, 3 September 1992

ENTRY INTO FORCE:	29 April 1997, in accordance with article XXI(1).
REGISTRATION:	29 April 1997, No. 33757.
STATUS:	Signatories: 165. Parties: 186.
TEXT:	United Nations, *Treaty Series*, vol. 1974, p. 45; and depositary notifications C.N.246.1994.TREATIES-5 of 31 August 1994 (procès-verbal of rectification of the original of the Convention: Arabic, Chinese, English, French, Russian and Spanish texts); C.N.359.1994.TREATIES-8 of 27 January 1995 (procès-verbal of rectification of the original of the Convention: Spanish text); C.N.454.1995.TREATIES-12 of 2 February 1996 (procès-verbal of rectification of the original of the Convention: Arabic and Russian texts); C.N.916.1999.TREATIES-7 of 8 October 1999 [acceptance of amendment for a change to Section B of Part VI of the Annex on Implementation and Verification ("Verification Annex"), effective 31 October 1999] and C.N.610.2005.TREATIES-4 of 29 July 2005 [Approval of changes to Part V of the Annex on Implementation and Verification ("Verification Annex")]; and C.N.157.2000.TREATIES-1 of 13 March 2000 [acceptance of corrections to amendments, effective 9 March 2000].

Note: At its 635th plenary meeting on 3 September 1992 held in Geneva, the Conference on Disarmament adopted the "Report of the *Ad Hoc* Committee on Chemical Weapons to the Conference on Disarmament", including the Convention on the Prohibition of the Development, Production, Stockpiling and Use of Chemical Weapons and on Their Destruction, contained in the Appendix to the Report. At its 47th session held in New York, the General Assembly, by resolution A/RES/47/39[1] adopted on 30 November 1992, commended the Convention. In the same resolution, the General Assembly also welcomed the invitation of the President of the French Republic to participate in a ceremony to sign the Convention in Paris on 13 January 1993 and requested the Secretary-General, as Depositary of the Convention, to open it for signature in Paris on that date. The Convention was opened for signature in Paris, from 13 January to 15 January 1993. Thereafter, it remained open for signature at the Headquarters of the United Nations in New York, until its entry into force, in accordance with article XVIII.

Participant	Signature		Ratification, Accession(a), Acceptance(A), Succession(d)		Participant	Signature		Ratification, Accession(a), Acceptance(A), Succession(d)	
Afghanistan	14 Jan	1993	24 Sep	2003	Bosnia and Herzegovina	16 Jan	1997	25 Feb	1997
Albania	14 Jan	1993	11 May	1994	Botswana			31 Aug	1998 a
Algeria	13 Jan	1993	14 Aug	1995	Brazil	13 Jan	1993	13 Mar	1996
Andorra			27 Feb	2003 a	Brunei Darussalam	13 Jan	1993	28 Jul	1997
Antigua and Barbuda			29 Aug	2005 a	Bulgaria	13 Jan	1993	10 Aug	1994
Argentina	13 Jan	1993	2 Oct	1995	Burkina Faso	14 Jan	1993	8 Jul	1997
Armenia	19 Mar	1993	27 Jan	1995	Burundi	15 Jan	1993	4 Sep	1998
Australia	13 Jan	1993	6 May	1994	Cambodia	15 Jan	1993	19 Jul	2005
Austria	13 Jan	1993	17 Aug	1995	Cameroon	14 Jan	1993	16 Sep	1996
Azerbaijan	13 Jan	1993	29 Feb	2000	Canada	13 Jan	1993	26 Sep	1995
Bahamas	2 Mar	1994			Cape Verde	15 Jan	1993	10 Oct	2003
Bahrain	24 Feb	1993	28 Apr	1997	Central African Republic	14 Jan	1993	20 Sep	2006
Bangladesh	14 Jan	1993	25 Apr	1997	Chad	11 Oct	1994	13 Feb	2004
Barbados			7 Mar	2007 a	Chile	14 Jan	1993	12 Jul	1996
Belarus	14 Jan	1993	11 Jul	1996	China	13 Jan	1993	25 Apr	1997
Belgium	13 Jan	1993	27 Jan	1997	Colombia	13 Jan	1993	5 Apr	2000
Belize			1 Dec	2003 a	Comoros	13 Jan	1993	18 Aug	2006
Benin	14 Jan	1993	14 May	1998	Congo	15 Jan	1993	4 Dec	2007
Bhutan	24 Apr	1997	18 Aug	2005					
Bolivia	14 Jan	1993	14 Aug	1998					

XXVI 3. Disarmament   1

Illustration 13–4. 2 United Nations, Multilateral Treaties Deposited with the Secretary-General (2009), <treaties.un.org>.

6

INTERNATIONAL COURT OF JUSTICE

2005
10 February
General List
No. 123

YEAR 2005

10 February 2005

CASE CONCERNING
CERTAIN PROPERTY

(LIECHTENSTEIN *v.* GERMANY)

PRELIMINARY OBJECTIONS

Historical background — Confiscation by Czechoslovakia in 1945 under the Beneš Decrees of property belonging to Prince Franz Josef II of Liechtenstein — Special régime with regard to German external assets and other property seized in connection with the Second World War — Article 3, paragraphs 1 and 3, of Chapter Six of the Settlement Convention — Final Settlement with respect to Germany.
Pieter van Laer painting confiscated under the Beneš Decrees — Claim by Prince Hans-Adam II of Liechtenstein for the return of the painting dismissed by German courts in 1990s on the basis of Article 3, Chapter Six, of the Settlement Convention — Claim brought by Prince Hans-Adam II of Liechtenstein before the European Court of Human Rights dismissed.

* *

Jurisdiction of the Court based on Article 1 of the European Convention for the Peaceful Settlement of Disputes — Limitation ratione temporis *contained in Article 27 (a) of that Convention.*
Six preliminary objections to the jurisdiction of the Court and the admissibility of the Application raised by Germany.

*

Germany's first preliminary objection.
Contention by Germany that there is no dispute between the Parties — No "change of position" with regard to Germany's treatment of Liechtenstein property confiscated in connection with the Second World War said to have occurred — Germany has never accepted the validity of the Beneš confiscations — German courts have consistently held that they are barred by the Settlement Convention from adjudicating on the lawfulness of confiscation

4

Illustration 13–5. Certain Property (Liechtenstein v. Germany), 2005 I.C.J. 6 (Feb. 10).

Chapter 14

THE LAW OF OTHER COUNTRIES

Table of Sections

Globalization has made the laws of other countries increasingly significant to American social, economic and legal life. The law of a foreign country may be relevant in U.S. court proceedings involving international trade or family law, and scholars and lawmakers can study other legal systems to better understand and improve our own. A serious legal problem involving a foreign legal system requires consultation with a lawyer who is trained and licensed in that jurisdiction, but any American lawyer dealing with a transnational matter must be able to develop a basic understanding of the other country's law.[1]

Foreign law sources are also essential to the study of comparative law, in which differences among national legal systems are analyzed. The extent to which American courts should cite precedent from other countries is the subject of vigorous debate, involv-

---

1. *Hart v. Carro, Spanbock, Kaster & Cuiffo*, 211 A.D.2d 617, 619, 620 N.Y.S.2d 847, 849 (1995) ("When, as here, counsel is retained in a matter involving foreign law, it is counsel's responsibility to conduct the matter properly and to know, or learn, the law of the foreign jurisdiction."). On the increasingly global nature of legal practice, see Richard L. Abel, *Transnational Law Practice*, 44 CASE W. RES. L. REV. 737 (1994); Leonard Bierman & Michael A. Hitt, *The Globalization of Legal Practice in the Internet Age*, 14 IND. J. GLOBAL LEGAL STUD. 29 (2007); Peter Roorda, *The Internationalization of the Practice of Law*, 28 WAKE FOREST L. REV. 141 (1993). Business practice is not the only area of law affected by global change. See Scott L. Cummings, *The Internationalization of Public Interest Law*, 57 DUKE L.J. 891 (2008).

ing Supreme Court justices and members of Congress as well as legal scholars.[2] While the influence accorded to foreign law regarding constitutional issues such as capital punishment is controversial, there is no question that decisions from common law countries have had persuasive value in the development of American tort and contract doctrine. The resources discussed in this chapter provide starting points for the American researcher.

§ 14.1   Legal Systems of the World

The legal systems of most countries can be described as either *common law* or *civil law*. Each system has its own history, fundamental principles and procedures, and forms of publication for legal sources. As explained in Chapter 1, legal doctrine under the common law is traditionally developed over time through specific cases decided by judges rather than from broad, abstract codifications. Judicial decisions are traditionally the most important and vital source of new legal rules in a common law system.

The civil law system refers to the legal tradition, based on Roman law, that characterizes the countries of continental Europe, Latin America, and parts of Africa and Asia. Civil law has several distinctive characteristics, including the predominance of comprehensive and systematic codes governing large fields of law (civil, criminal, commercial, civil procedure, and criminal procedure), little weight for judicial decisions as legal authority, and great influence of legal scholars who interpret, criticize and develop the law through commentaries on the codes.[3]

Some jurisdictions do not fit clearly into either the civil law or common law systems. A few countries, such as Scotland and South Africa, have aspects of both civil law and common law. Others are strongly influenced by customary law or traditional religious systems, particularly Islamic or Talmudic law. The law of these countries may be a mixture of civil *or* common law and the customary or religious legal system. A few countries combine elements of three or more legal systems.

JuriGlobe: World Legal Systems <www.juriglobe.ca>, from the University of Ottawa Faculty of Law, is an online guide with maps, descriptions of the major systems, and lists of countries in each

---

2. See Austen L. Parrish, *Storm in a Teacup: The U.S. Supreme Court's Use of Foreign Law*, 2007 U. Ill. L. Rev. 637, 638–40 (citing numerous comments and articles by justices, legislators, and scholars, as well as proposed legislation to prohibit citation of foreign law sources).

3. For a brief introduction, see James Apple & Robert Deyling, A Primer

on the Civil Law System (2001) <www.fjc.gov/public/pdf.nsf/lookup/CivilLaw.pdf/$file/CivilLaw.pdf>. A more detailed explanation can be found in books such as John Henry Merryman & Rogelio Pérez-Perdorno, The Civil Law Tradition: An Introduction to the Legal Systems of Europe and Latin America (3d ed. 2007) and Alan Watson, The Making of the Civil Law (1981).

category. Texts discussing the history and concepts of the world's legal systems include René David & John E.C. Brierly, *Major Legal Systems in the World Today: An Introduction to the Comparative Study of Law* (3d ed. 1985), H. Patrick Glenn, *Legal Traditions of the World: Sustainable Diversity in Law* (3d ed. 2007), and Konrad Zweigert & Hein Kötz, *An Introduction to Comparative Law* (3d ed. 1998).

The differences between the common law and civil law systems have become less marked in recent years, as each system adopts features of the other. American jurisdictions have increasingly adopted comprehensive subject codifications, such as the Uniform Commercial Code, while judicial decisions are being given greater weight in some civil law countries.[4] Nonetheless, basic differences remain in how legal issues are perceived and research is conducted.

§ 14.2   Reference Sources in Foreign and Comparative Law

While thorough research on a foreign law issue can be under-taken only in original sources, print and online reference resources can provide a working knowledge of major legal issues. It is usually best to begin with an encyclopedia or treatise for a general intro-duction to a national legal system or a specific subject, and then to find translations or summaries of the primary sources. Foreign law research guides with descriptions and links for sources can help clarify the range of research options.

(a) Encyclopedias and Legal System Guides

Several encyclopedic works provide coverage of national legal systems and specific legal topics within those systems.

Legal Systems of the World: A Political, Social, and Cultural Encyclopedia (Herbert M. Kritzer ed., 2002) provides an introducto-ry overview by jurisdiction and subject. Articles on countries dis-cuss history, major legal concepts, and the structure of the legal system, with references for further reading. Subject articles gener-ally compare civil law and common law approaches.

The Oxford International Encyclopedia of Legal History (Stan-ley N. Katz ed., 2009) is a new six-volume set with more than 1,000 articles on a wide range of legal topics in ancient, medieval, and modern legal systems. Articles include cross-references and bibliog-raphies.

Surveys of the legal systems of more than 170 jurisdictions are included in *Modern Legal Systems Cyclopedia* (Kenneth Robert

---

4. See, e.g., Arthur T. Von Mehren, *Some Reflections on Codification and* *Case Law in the Twenty–First Century*, 31 U.C. DAVIS L. REV. 659 (1998).

Redden & Linda L. Schlueter eds., 1984–date). The entries range in length from three to more than a hundred pages, and vary considerably in quality. The publication dates of individual chapters are not indicated, but some are now clearly obsolete. The set has not ceased publication, but it has not been updated since 2005.

The United States government publishes several guides to the legal and business environments in foreign countries. The International Trade Administration's Export Portal <www.export.gov/mrktresearch/> has legal and commercial guides for specific countries and industries, and the State Department's Judicial Assistance site <travel.state.gov/law/info/judicial/judicial_702.html> covers topics such as enforcement of judgments and obtaining evidence abroad. The Central Intelligence Agency's *World Factbook* <https://www.cia.gov/library/publications/the-world-factbook/> has demographic and economic information about the countries of the world.

Basic country information, such as economic conditions, political developments, and statistics, can also be found in annual reference sources such as *Europa Year Book: A World Survey* and *The Statesman's Yearbook*. Both of these are available in online editions, as *Europa World Plus* <www.europaworld.com> and *Statesman's Yearbook Online* <www.statesmansyearbook.com>. *Law and Judicial Systems of Nations* (4th ed. 2002) has a concise overview of bar organization, legal education, and court systems of 193 countries, with a brief explanation of each legal system.

A number of guides to the legal systems of specific countries are published in English. These generally explain legal institutions, summarize major doctrines, and provide leads to research resources. A sample of recently published titles includes Catherine Elliott et al., *French Legal System* (2d ed. 2006); Charles M. Fombad & Emmanuel K. Quansah, *The Botswana Legal System* (2006); Elena Merino–Blanco, *Spanish Law and Legal System* (2d ed. 2006); and Richard Ward & Amanda Akhtar, *Walker & Walker's English Legal System* (10th ed. 2008). Some works cover the legal systems of a region, such as Rose–Marie Belle Antoine, *Commonwealth Caribbean Law and Legal Systems* (2d ed. 2008) or Chibli Mallat, *Introduction to Middle Eastern Law* (2007).

The *International Encyclopedia of Comparative Law* (1971–date) is the most comprehensive treatment of its subject, but it is still incomplete after nearly forty years. Of seventeen planned volumes, only four (Business and Professional Organizations, Persons and Family, Restitution/Unjust Enrichment, and Torts) have been published in their final bound format. Pamphlets on specific topics have been published in other areas. Volume 1 of the set consists of a series of "National Reports" pamphlets on individual countries, but most of these were published in the 1970s and may be of historical value only.

Two recent one-volume reference works have more current coverage of comparative law issues. Both *Elgar Encyclopedia of Comparative Law* (Jan Smits ed., 2006) and *The Oxford Handbook of Comparative Law* (Mathia Reimann & Reinhard Zimmermann eds., 2006) contain chapters by leading scholars analyzing the legal systems of specific countries or regions as well as studies of particular topics and subject areas.

International Encyclopaedia of Laws (IEL) consists of several sets focusing on specific subjects with separate monographic pamphlets for individual countries. The oldest and most extensive of these works, *International Encyclopaedia for Labour Law and Industrial Relations* (1977–date), covers more than sixty countries. Newer sets covering fewer countries are available in almost two dozen other subject areas, but the chances of finding a specific country covered for a specific subject are not always promising. European countries are more represented than others, but nearly a hundred countries can be found in at least one set.[5] The IEL website <www.ielaws.com> includes lists of which countries are covered in each set, under the heading "Published Monographs."

(b) Research Guides and Indexes

When starting research in the law of another country, you need a sense of the available publications and the sources in which you will need to conduct research. Several guides to foreign law research have broad coverage of many subjects and jurisdictions, while others are specialized bibliographic surveys of particular countries, regions, or subjects.

Foreign Law Guide <www.foreignlawguide.com>, a subscription site by Thomas H. Reynolds & Arturo A. Flores, is one of the best starting points. For almost every country in the world, it has a description of its legal system, notes on the major codifications and gazettes, sources for legislation and court decisions (including those available in English or on the Internet), and a detailed listing of codes and laws covering specific subject areas. If available, links are provided to online sources. Illustration 14–1 on page 446 shows an excerpt from the Albania section of Foreign Law Guide with infor-

---

5. The areas of focus of these encyclopedias, and the approximate number of countries each covers, are: Civil Procedure (33), Commercial and Economic Law (19), Constitutional Law (38), Contracts (32), Corporations and Partnerships (23), Criminal Law (21), Cyber Law (12), Energy Law (18), Environmental Law (42), Family and Succession Law (29), Insurance Law (16), Intellectual Property (35), Medical Law (26), Private International Law (16), Property and Trust Law (9), Social Security Law (28), Sports Law (9), Tort Law (16), and Transport Law (21). Some topics include documents and case law as well as national monographs.

mation about basic primary sources, including references to translations and online sources. An eight-volume print version, *Foreign Law: Current Sources of Codes and Basic Legislation in Jurisdictions of the World* (1989–2007), is no longer being updated.

GlobaLex <www.nyulawglobal.org/globalex/> has guides prepared by librarians or attorneys on researching the legal systems of nearly 120 countries. These guides generally summarize the legal system, describe available documentation, and provide extensive links to electronic resources. Some country-specific guides are also available from Law Library Resource Xchange (LLRX) <www.llrx.com/comparative_and_foreign_law.html>.

Other guides to research in foreign legal systems include Marci Hoffman & Mary Rumsey, *International and Foreign Legal Research: A Coursebook* (2008) and Claire M. Germain, *Germain's Transnational Law Research: A Guide for Attorneys* (1991–date), which includes chapters on about twenty European countries.

Articles on foreign legal issues can be found in the standard legal periodical databases and indexes discussed in Chapter 11. More specialized resources are also available. *Index to Foreign Legal Periodicals* (1960–date, quarterly; available through various database systems including Westlaw commercial subscriptions) covers more than 500 journals from seventy-five countries, as well as commemorative *festschriften* and other collections of essays. It indexes journals published outside the United States, the United Kingdom, and the Commonwealth, as well as articles in selected American and Commonwealth journals on international law, comparative law, or the domestic law of other countries. Westlaw has access to *Index to Canadian Legal Literature* (ICLL) and *Legal Journals Index* (LJI), which covers more than four hundred British and European publications. The Peace Palace Library in the Netherlands has a free database with searchable tables of contents from 450 journals beginning in 2003 <www.ppl.nl/toc/>[6]

(c) Summaries and Translations of Laws

If you are relying on English-language sources in your research, you can find many multinational summaries and digests on specific subjects as well as translations of some actual laws. While summaries and translations cannot substitute for the original

---

6. Older sources for literature on foreign legal systems include *Szladits' Bibliography on Foreign and Comparative Law* (Charles Szladits et al. eds., 1955–2001), covering books and articles in English from 1790 to 1998, and *Introduction bibliographique à l'histoire du droit et à l'ethnologie juridique/Biblio-* *graphical Introduction to Legal History and Ethnology* (John Gilissen ed., 1963–88). *A Legal Bibliography of the British Commonwealth of Nations* (W. Harold Maxwell & Leslie F. Maxwell eds., 1955–64) has extensive lists of materials from the United Kingdom, Canada, Australia, and other Commonwealth countries.

sources, they can provide some familiarity with the basic concepts and issues of a foreign law problem.[7]

The basic laws of government structure and individual liberties are found in national constitutions. Two works provide introductory overviews. *Encyclopedia of World Constitutions* (Gerhard Robbers ed., 2007) covers almost 200 countries and discusses matters such as constitutional history, lawmaking process, and protected fundamental rights. Robert L. Maddex, *Constitutions of the World* (3d ed. 2008) provides summaries of constitutions and brief constitutional histories for about 120 countries. Concourts.net <www.concourts.net> is a useful site with a chart and map indicating the types of constitutional courts and the nature of judicial review in most of the world's countries.

The most comprehensive printed collection of current constitutions in English translation is the looseleaf set, *Constitutions of the Countries of the World* (1971–date, online by subscription <www.oxfordonline.com/oceanalaw>). For some foreign-language countries, the original text of the constitution is included as well.[8] The University of Bern's International Constitutional Law <www.oefre.unibe.ch/law/icl/> has more than ninety constitutions in English, with introductory pages providing constitutional background and history. The University of Richmond's Constitution Finder <confinder.richmond.edu> has links to constitutions from more than two hundred nations and territories, some in more than one language.

Extensive collections of historic constitutions have been assembled by Professor Horst Dippel of the University of Kassel. *Constitutions of the World, 1850 to the Present* (2002–date) is a set of modern constitutions on microfiche, and *Constitutions of the World from the Late 18th Century to the Middle of the 19th Century* (2005–date) is a print compilation with a companion website, The Rise of Modern Constitutionalism, 1776–1849 <www.uni-kassel.de/?dippel/projekt/>.

Basic laws and procedures for about eighty countries are summarized in the Martindale-Hubbell International Law Digest, available either in Lexis or at Martindale.com <www.martindale.com>

---

7. But see Mary Rumsey, *Basic Guide to Researching Foreign Law*, GlobaLex (January 2008) <www.nyulawglobal.org/globalex/Foreign_Law_Research1.htm> ("CAUTION: Although the internet is an increasingly important source of foreign law, it is sometimes impossible to find current foreign law on a topic, particularly in translation. Very few foreign laws, and even fewer cases, are translated into English.").

8. *Constitutions of Dependencies and Territories* (Philip Raworth ed.,

1998–date) complements this collection. Amos J. Peaslee & Dorothy Peaslee Xydis, *Constitutions of Nations* (1st–4th eds. 1950–85) may be useful for older constitutions. The first edition of Peaslee's collection is available in HeinOnline's Legal Classics Library. For leads to other historical sources, see John Trone, *Print Sources of Historical Constitutions*, 34 INT'L J. LEGAL INFO. 539 (2006).

as part of the "Search Legal Topics" section. Topics covered include business regulation, foreign trade, family law, property, and taxation. Most national digests are prepared by lawyers in that country and include references to codes, laws, and other sources. The format is similar to that shown for a U.S. law digest in Illustration 3–15 on page 107.

Laws affecting international business are the most likely sources to be available in English. Several collections covering specific topics are published, including *Digest of Commercial Laws of the World* (N. Stephan Kinsella & Paul E. Comeaux eds., rev. ed. 1998–date), *Investment Laws of the World* (International Centre for Settlement of Investment Disputes comp., 1973–date), and *International Securities Regulation* (Robert C. Rosen ed., 1986–date). *International Labor and Employment Laws* (William L. Keller & Timothy J. Darby eds., 3d ed. 2008) summarizes employment laws in 41 countries.

Several online collections on national laws are available from international organizations. The International Labour Organization's NATLEX <natlex.ilo.org> has abstracts of national labor laws in English, French or Spanish, with links to the full text in many instances. UNESCO's Collection of National Copyright Laws <www.unesco.org/culture/copyrightlaws/> has PDF copies of the laws, most translated into English. The World Intellectual Property Organization's Collection of Laws for Electronic Access (CLEA) <clea.wipo.int> has English-language summaries of national intellectual property legislation.[9]

Commercial laws of some countries are available through Lexis, Westlaw, and other databases, but online access to civil law sources in English is not extensive. The official French site Legifrance <www.legifrance.gouv.fr> has searchable English translations of major French codes, and the German Law Archive <www.iuscomp. org/gla/> has numerous sources in English including statutes, court decisions, and secondary sources.

Relatively few judicial decisions in foreign languages are translated into English, but several resources provide access to some case law. *International Law Reports* (1919–date) contains cases from national courts on international law and human rights topics, and Foreign Law Translations at the University of Texas Institute for Transnational Law <www.utexas.edu/law/academics/centers/transnational/work_new/> has decisions from Austria, France, Germany, and Israel. Specialized sources include *Bulletin on Constitutional Case–Law* (1993–date, in print and online <codices.coe.int>),

9. Other sites can be found through resources such as Charlotte Bynum, *Foreign Law: Subject Law Collections on the*   *Web*, GlobaLex (Dec. 2007) <www.nyulawglobal.org/globalex/Foreign_ Collections1.htm>.

East European Case Reporter on Constitutional Law (1994–date), and *International Labour Law Reports* (1978–date).

While they cannot substitute for professional translation, automated translation systems such as Google Translate <translate.google.com> or Yahoo! Babel Fish <babelfish.yahoo.com> can give you at least a sense of the scope and subject of a document.[10] They may help you determine whether a more accurate translation would be needed.

(d) Dictionaries

Part of the difficulty of doing legal research in a foreign legal system stems from differences in language. Even legal systems sharing the same language can have different meanings for the same terms. Legal dictionaries can help somewhat, but they can provide only a superficial sense of the differences in meaning and usage.

Numerous bilingual dictionaries translate foreign terms into English, although many of these simply translate words without explaining the underlying legal concepts.[11] Henry Saint Dahl, *Dahl's Law Dictionary: Spanish–English/English–Spanish* (4th ed. 2006) and *Dahl's Law Dictionary: French to English/English to French* (2d ed. 2001) are also represented (in older editions) in Lexis. Several multilingual law dictionaries are also published. Robert Herbst & Alan G. Readett, *Dictionary of Commercial, Financial and Legal Terms* (3d–6th eds. 1998–2003) provides terminology in English, French and German, and D.C. van Hoof et al., *Elsevier's Legal Dictionary* (2001) adds Dutch and Spanish as well.

---

10. Sarah Yates, *Scaling the Tower of Babel Fish: An Analysis of the Machine Translation of Legal Information*, 98 Law Libr. J. 481, 500 (2006) (machine translation "can usually convey enough of the gist of a text to indicate what type of information the document contains"). See also Chunyu Kit & Tak Ming Wong, *Comparative Evaluation of Online Machine Translation Systems with Legal Texts*, 100 Law Libr. J. 299 (2008).

11. "Translators of legal terminology are obliged to practise comparative law." Gerard–René de Groot & Conrad J.P. van Laer, *The Dubious Quality of Legal Dictionaries*, 34 Int'l J. Legal Info. 65, 66 (2006). The authors of this article surveyed 170 bilingual legal dictionaries, and found that most of them were simply word lists translating terminology with no explanation of different contexts or meanings in different legal systems. The surveyed dictionaries are listed with comments in Gerard–René de Groot & Conrad J.P. van Laer, *The Quality of Legal Dictionaries: An Assessment*, Maastricht Faculty of Law Working Paper 2008–6 <arno.unimaas.nl/show.cgi?fid=13383>.

Another author reached a similar conclusion after surveying more than thirty English–Spanish legal dictionaries. Dennis C. Kim–Prieto, *En la Tierra del Ciego, El Tuerto Es Rey*, 100 Law Libr. J. 251 (2008). He recommended only *Dahl's Law Dictionary: Spanish–English/English–Spanish* (4th ed. 2006), which makes clear the doctrinal distinctions among Spanish-speaking nations, and Jorge Vargas, *Mexican Legal Dictionary and Desk Reference* (2003), which focuses on one specific jurisdiction. Both of these works include references to code provisions and other sources to help explain terminology.

Citation forms for foreign legal materials can be confusing for American lawyers. *The Bluebook* includes citation information for more than thirty countries, covering statutory, judicial, and other frequently cited sources. More extensive coverage is provided by *Guide to Foreign and International Legal Citations* (2006) (available free online <www.law.nyu.edu/journals/jilp/>), which has profiles and citation guides for forty-five countries. Guides to citation format in other countries include *OSCOLA: The Oxford Standard for Citation Of Legal Authorities* (2006) <denning.law.ox.ac.uk/published/oscola.shtml> and the McGill Law Journal's *Canadian Guide to Uniform Legal Citation* (6th ed. 2006).

World Dictionary of Legal Abbreviations (Igor I. Kavass & Mary Miles Prince eds., 1991–date) has extensive lists of foreign abbreviations, with separate sections for some two dozen countries, languages, regions, and subjects.

§ 14.3 Original Sources

The next step after consulting available reference materials is to investigate primary legal sources from the country. Understanding these sources may still require understanding a foreign language and another legal system, but finding them has become much easier much in the age of the Internet. Many countries have both free and subscription-based legal databases similar to those available in the United States. This section focuses on resources available to most American researchers.

(a) Links to Country Websites

Several resources provide links to law-related websites in countries around the world. These include sites discussed earlier, including *Foreign Law Guide* <www.foreignlawguide.com> and GlobaLex <www.nyuglobalaw.org/globalex/>, both of which combine descriptive summaries with links to sources.

Other resources also have extensive links to websites. Major sites with country pages and links to constitutions, legislation, government sites, laws by subject, legal guides, and other resources include the Harvard Law Library's Foreign & International Law Resources: An Annotated Guide to Web Sites Around the World <www.law.harvard.edu/library/research/guides/int_foreign/web-resources/>, the Library of Congress's Guide to Law Online <www.loc.gov/law/help/guide.php> and the World Legal Information Institute (WorldLII) <www.worldlii.org>.

The Yale Law Library's Foreign Law Research Guide (by Country) <www.law.yale.edu/library/countries.asp> is a useful place to begin because it links to the more detailed listings at Harvard, Library of Congress, and WorldLII as well as Foreign

Law Guide entries (for subscribers), and also indicates what resources are available on Westlaw and Lexis.

The World Bank's *Doing Business* site <www.doingbusiness. org/lawlibrary/> has links to national laws on business-related topics, including civil codes and constitutions, for over 180 countries. You select the countries and the topics you'd like to see, click on "Create Report," and retrieve a list of specific acts and regulations linked to government website sources. Many of the documents are translated into English.

(b) Common Law Jurisdictions

The resources and research methods for other common law countries are similar to those of the United States, making them the most accessible of foreign legal systems. This section looks briefly at two of our most closely related common law jurisdictions: England (which is part of the United Kingdom but has a separate body of law from Northern Ireland and Scotland) and Canada.

The United Kingdom has an "unwritten" constitution, meaning that its basic constitutional principles are not found in one specific document. One major difference between British and U.S. law is that the U.K. Parliament has unlimited power, and its acts cannot be held unconstitutional. Canada's Constitution, dating to 1867, is the source of powers for both the federal Parliament and the provincial legislatures. Unlike in the United States, areas such as criminal law and family law are matters of Canadian federal law rather than provincial law, and in general any powers not specifically delegated to the provinces are reserved to the federal government.

Just as U.S. law recognizes the persuasive value of another state's case law but not its statutes, judicial decisions from other common law countries can influence the development of U.S. common law doctrine.

England has one straightforward structure of trial and appellate courts, with the House of Lords as the court of last resort (until its judicial function is replaced by the new Supreme Court of the United Kingdom in late 2009).[12] Civil actions are tried either in one of the three divisions of the High Court (Queen's Bench, Chancery, or Family) or in lower courts of limited jurisdiction, with review by the Court of Appeal and from there by the House of Lords. Criminal trials are conducted in a Crown Court, with the same two-tier appeal system.

---

12. See, e.g., BUILDING THE UK's NEW SUPREME COURT: NATIONAL AND COMPARATIVE PERSPECTIVES (Andrew Le Sueur ed., 2004); Mark Ryan, *The House of Lords and the Shaping of the Supreme Court*, 56 N. IRE. L.Q. 135 (2005).

The Canadian court system is more like that of the United States, although fundamental differences exist. U.S. state supreme courts, for example, are the final arbiters on issues of state law, while the Supreme Court of Canada is the final court of appeal for both federal and provincial courts. The Federal Court of Canada was created in 1971 and consists of trial and appellate divisions, with jurisdiction over matters such as intellectual property, maritime law, and claims against the government.

As in the United States, new British and Canadian decisions are published in official or authorized series of reports and in unofficial commercial reporters and online services. Westlaw and Lexis both have extensive coverage of judicial decisions from the United Kingdom and Canada. Free Internet access to decisions is provided by the British and Irish Legal Information Institute (BAILII) <www.bailii.org> and the Canadian Legal Information Institute (CanLII) <www.canlii.org>.

English decisions before 1865 were discussed in Chapter 6, at pages 224–225. For decisions since 1865, the standard source is the semi-official *Law Reports*, which now consists of four series: *Appeal Cases* (House of Lords and the Judicial Committee of the Privy Council); *Queen's Bench Division*; *Chancery Division*; and *Family Division*. Before appearing in these four separate series, new cases are published in *Weekly Law Reports*, which also has some decisions that are unreported in the four *Law Reports* series.

All England Law Reports (1936–date) is a commercially published reporter with some decisions not published in the *Weekly Law Reports*, and numerous specialized subject reporters such as *Criminal Appeal Reports* and *Family Law Reports* are also available. Westlaw has access to the *Law Reports* from 1865 (LAW–RPTS), dozens of specialized reporters, and a comprehensive file combining these sources (UK–RPTS–ALL). Lexis also has the *Law Reports* from 1865, the complete *All England Law Reports*, and several specialized reporters.

Citations for modern English cases have two significant differences from the form usually used in this country. The United Kingdom has adopted a neutral citation policy for decisions after 2001, mandating the citation of an official slip opinion numbering system in addition to published reports.[13] Most of these reports are designated by year, and then by volume number for that year, instead of having one series of sequentially numbered volumes as is the U.S. norm. The year is thus an essential part of the citation because it identifies the volume. Illustration 14–2 on page 447

---

13. Practice Direction (Judgments: Form and Citation), [2001] 1 W.L.R. 194.

shows a recent House of Lords decision, *Mirvahedy v. Henley,* [2003] UKHL 16, [2003] 2 A.C. 491.

Canada has authorized reports for its federal courts (*Canada Supreme Court Reports* and *Federal Court Reports*), as well as reports for provincial and territorial courts, unofficial series such as *Dominion Law Reports*, and a variety of specialized topical reporters. Westlaw and Lexis have Canada Supreme Court decisions back to 1876, as well as less comprehensive coverage of other courts. Both have databases (CAN–ALLCASES on Westlaw) with nation-wide coverage of Canadian case law.

Much case research in other common law countries is done by keyword through free and commercial database systems, but online research is supplemented by many of the same types of resources found in the United States including treatises, encyclopedias, and digests.

Like *Am. Jur. 2d* and *C.J.S.*, legal encyclopedias in other nations contain concise statements of ruling law and extensive footnote references to primary sources. *Halsbury's Laws of England* (4th & 5th eds. 1973–date) is more definitive than the American legal encyclopedias, in part because it covers just one jurisdiction and can encompass statutes and administrative sources as well as case law. Access to the set is provided by a subject index and by tables of cases and statutes cited. *Halsbury's Laws* is available online in Britain, but most U.S. Lexis subscriptions include only its "Monthly Review" summarizing new developments.

Two regional encyclopedias include coverage of Canadian federal law: *Canadian Encyclopedic Digest (Ontario)* (3d ed. 1973–date), and *Canadian Encyclopedic Digest (Western)* (3d ed. 1979–date). The CED database on Westlaw provides access to both works. A new series, *Halsbury's Laws of Canada*, began publication in 2006 and consists of separate monographs for individual topics. It is about halfway to its projected completion in 65 volumes.

Both England and Canada have a major national digest, somewhat similar to the West digest system: *The Digest: Annotated British, Commonwealth and European Cases* (3d ed. 1971–date), and the *Canadian Abridgment* (3d ed. 2003–date, available on Westlaw). Each country has tools for finding later cases that have considered an earlier decision, such as *Current Law Case Citator* in England and *Canadian Case Citations*. KeyCite flags, history, and citing references are available for Canadian cases on Westlaw.

Statutes in other common law jurisdictions are published both in session laws and in compilations of statutes in force, and are available from government and commercial websites. One major difference from the U.S. model is that statutes are generally compiled alphabetically by name or chronologically, rather than by subject as in the *United States Code*. Statutes are not assigned code titles and sections, but instead are usually identified by their original name and date of enactment. Public General Acts are available online <www.opsi.gov.uk/acts.htm>, with selected acts since 1837 and comprehensive coverage beginning with 1988.

The standard historical collection of English statutes is the *Statutes of the Realm* (1810–28), covering 1235 to 1714. This set is part of HeinOnline's English Reports Library, and some volumes are available free through British History Online <www.british-history.ac.uk>. Several other chronological collections were published during the 19th century under the title *Statutes at Large*, extending coverage to the beginning of the modern *Public General Acts* in 1866.[14] Justis <www.justis.com> has subscription online coverage of statutes from 1235 to date.

The first step in identifying and finding an older English statute is deciphering its citation. Acts before 1963 are generally cited not by calendar year but by regnal year (the year of a monarch's rule). The act that changed the citation system, for example, was passed during the session of Parliament that spanned the tenth and eleventh years of the reign of Elizabeth II, and is cited as Acts of Parliament Numbering and Citation Act, 10 & 11 Eliz. 2, ch. 34 (1962). Tables to convert regnal years to calendar years are printed in reference works such as *Black's Law Dictionary*, and a regnal year calculator is available online <www.albion.edu/english/calendar/Regnal_Years.html>.

For modern statutes, the most frequently used printed source is the unofficial compilation *Halsbury's Statutes of England and Wales* (4th ed. 1985–date). This is somewhat similar to U.S. annotated codes, in that sections are followed by footnote annotations to judicial decisions. Current English statutes are also available free from the UK Statute Law Database <www.statutelaw.gov.uk/>, as well as through Westlaw and Lexis. On Westlaw, the UK Statutes database (UK–ST) contains acts of Parliament, while the UK Laws in Force database (UK–LIF) combines these with regulations (known as *statutory instruments*). Another way to find case references to British statutes is by using *Current Law Statute Citator*, which lists statutes chronologically followed by references to amendments and judicial decisions.

For Canadian statutes there is no annotated, regularly updated publication similar to *Halsbury's Statutes*. Consolidated Statutes of Canada are available from the Department of Justice Canada <laws.justice.gc.ca>, and CanLII <www.canlii.org> has links as

---

14. Acts passed during the Commonwealth are not included in these collections but can be found in *Acts and Ordinances of the Interregnum, 1642–1660* (1911) <www.british-history.ac.uk/source.aspx?pubid=606>.

well to provincial sources. Coverage of much of this material is also available from Lexis, Westlaw, and other commercial databases. Westlaw covers federal statutes (CANFED–ST) and all ten provinces and three territories, while Lexis has legislation from the Parliament of Canada and the four most populous provinces (Alberta, British Columbia, Ontario, and Quebec).

Further information on the British and Canadian legal systems and sources is available from websites for their parliaments (<www.parliament.uk>, <www.parl.gc.ca>) and their governments generally (<www.direct.gov.uk>, <www.gc.ca>.)

(c) Civil Law Jurisdictions

In theory, a code in the civil law tradition is designed to cover all legal situations that might occur. Instead of searching for precedents in factually similar judicial decisions, as a civil law researcher you would look first to the abstract provisions of the code for a logical and appropriate legal principle.[15]

Extensive article-by-article commentaries on the major codes are among the most important legal sources in civil law countries. The most scholarly and reputable of these commentaries have considerable persuasive authority, often greater weight than judicial decisions. Foreign legal encyclopedias, particularly the French *répertoires* published by Dalloz, are often of higher quality and reputation than those in this country. Their articles are frequently written by leading legal scholars. Civil law countries also have a multitude of legal periodicals covering legal developments and often printing primary sources.

After introductory study in an encyclopedia, treatise, or journal article, your next step is to consult the relevant code (preferably in an edition accompanied by extensive commentary) or other statutes applicable to the problem. Most countries in the civil law system have several separately published codes. These include the basic general codes (civil, criminal, commercial, civil procedure and criminal procedure), and minor codes compiling statutes on specific subjects such as taxation, labor law, and family law. Illustration 14–3 on page 448 shows a page from the Dalloz edition of the French

---

15. "When a true code enthusiast confronts a problem, he reaches first for the code, and later for doctrine and cases. His resort to the code must seem as natural as searching precedents would be for an English barrister. The center of a civilian's private law universe, the civil code must stand out in his intellectual armory. In this sense, when lawyers and judges search for an answer to a difficult problem, they view the code as a fountainhead of stability and prefer to extend the code's provisions to new circumstances rather than to construe the code restrictively and to solve new problems by analogical extension of judicial precedents." Shael Herman, *The Fate and the Future of Codification in America*, 40 Am. J. Legal Hist. 407, 413 (1996) (footnote omitted). On principles of codification generally, see, e.g., Jean Louis Bergel, *Principle Features and Methods of Codification*, 48 La. L. Rev. 1073 (1988).

civil code. After article 8 ("Every French person enjoys civil rights"), the text has references to several decrees, international conventions, and other sources.

Official websites in many countries provide access to their codes. Westlaw and Lexis cover a small number of jurisdictions in their original language. Westlaw has some Mexican laws, and Lexis has material from Argentina, France, Italy, and Mexico.

After studying the code and commentary, you should then find administrative orders and judicial decisions implementing or interpreting the legislative norms. Legislation, regulations, decrees and other laws are most often found in official gazettes, comparable to but usually broader in scope than the *Federal Register*. Foreign Law Guide lists these sources and provides links where available. The University of Michigan's Government Gazettes Online <www.lib.umich.edu/govdocs/gazettes/> also has links to gazettes from sixty countries, with summary information about their contents and searchability. *Guide to Official Publications of Foreign Countries* (2d ed. 1997) is an annotated listing of gazettes, statistical yearbooks, court reports, and other publications for more than 170 countries. It includes commercially published guides, bibliographies, and directories as well as official sources.

Court decisions in civil law countries are published, but they are generally of secondary importance. Most jurisdictions have fewer court reports and less developed means for finding cases by subject. In many countries, legal periodicals publish court decisions in addition to articles and other legal news. In France, for example, the leading legal periodicals, *Recueil Dalloz* (1808–date) and *La Semaine Juridique* (1927–date), provide both legislative texts and judicial decisions, as well as scholarly articles.

A last resort in trying to find the law of a jurisdiction may be to contact its embassy. The amount of assistance provided by embassies can vary widely, but some provide copies of legal materials or explain where they can be found. Embassy.org <www.embassy.org/embassies/> lists embassies in Washington, D.C. with contact information, including e-mail addresses and website URLs. The Department of State's "Foreign Embassy Information & Publications" site <www.state.gov/s/cpr/rls/> provides access to the *Diplomatic List* with contact information and key personnel for embassies, and *Foreign Consular Offices in the United States* with similar data for consulates in Washington and other cities.

MAJOR PUBLICATIONS

MAJOR CODIFICATIONS

1. Civil Code

A draft civil code was issued in 1993 and enacted by Ligji 7,850 of 29 Jul 1994 as Kodi civil in *Fletorja zyrtare* 1994 pg. 491. In force 1 Jan 1995 (the text extends over four issues of the *Fletorja zyrtare* nos. 11, 12, 13 and 14 of 1994). Replaces the 1981 code and is much closer to the 1928 code's origins, which had been closely based on the old Italian civil code, although the influence of the new, 1942 Italian civil code is evident. Some articles translated in *Internationales Erbrecht*. ◌ Full English translation of articles 1–683 (persons, property, inheritance and obligations), as of 2004, at http://www.lexadin.nl/wlg/legis/nofr/eur/lxwealb.htm ‡ and also at http://www.legislationline.org/. ‡ Translated fully, as of 2001, at http://www.icnl.org/knowledge/library/Index.php. ‡

2. Code of Civil Procedure

Code of Civil Procedure. Law 8,116 of 29 Mar 1996 as Kodi i procedures civile in *Fletorja zyrtare* 1996 nos. 9–11, pgs. 343–479. In force 1 Jun 1996. Replacing Law 6,341 of 1981. Very substantially amended by Law 8,812 of 17 May 2001 in *Fletorja zyrtare* 12 Jun 2001. Replacing Law 6,341 of 1981. See "A short introduction to the Albanian civil procedure code" by I. Alimena (2007?) on the Euralius website at http://www.euralius.org.al/ (click on Assistance and then Analysis and Studies).

3. Commercial Code

Ligji 7,632 of 4 Nov 1992 (general part) [Kodi tregtar] in *Fletorja zyrtare* 1992 no. 8. "Law on the introductory part of a commercial code." German translation in 3 *Wirtschaft und Recht in Osteuropa* 348 (1994). A special part has never been enacted. This is a modernized version of the Kodi tregtar published in *Fletorja zyrtare* 15 Mar 1932. Please note: This "General part of the Commercial Code" was repealed and replaced by Law 9,901 of 14 Apr 2008. English translation on the website of the Ministry of Economy, Trade and Industry at http://www.mete.gov.al/. In effect, this is now a "General part."

4. Criminal Code

Kodi penal. Ligji 7,895 of 27 Jan 1995 in *Fletorja zyrtare* 1995 no. 2. Amended by Ligji 7,942 of 31 May 1995. This new codification totally replaces the 1977 code and is in force 1 Jun 1995. English translation at http://pbosnia.kentlaw.edu/resources/legal/albania/crim_code.htm and, as of 1 Dec 2004, at https://www.imolin.org/amlid/index.html. ‡ German translation published as *Die Strafgesetze Albaniens: Strafgesetzbuch vom 27.1.1995; Militarstrafgesetzbuch vom 28.9.1995*. Tirana, K.&B. Vlg., 2003.

5. Code of Criminal Procedure

Kodi procedura penale. Ligji 7,905 of 21 Mar 1995 in *Fletorja zyrtare* 1995 nos. 5–7. Amended by Ligji of 1 Aug 1995 in *Fletorja zyrtare* 1995. Entirely replaces the 1979 codification. English translation at http://pbosnia.kentlaw.edu/resources/legal/albania/crim_code.htm and, as of 1 Dec 2004, at https://www.imolin.org/amlid/index.html. ‡

OFFICIAL GAZETTE

Fletorja zyrtare. 1922–1942. Tirana, 1922–1942. Succeeded by: *Gazeta zyrtare e RPS të Shqipërisë*. 1944–1991. Tiranë, 1944–1991 (cited herein as *Gazeta zyrtare*).

Succeeded by: *Fletorja zyrtare Republikës të Shqipërisë*. 1991– . Tiranë, 1991– (cited herein as *Fletorja zyrtare*).

Illustration 14–1. Albania, Foreign Law Guide (2009), <www.foreignlawguide.com>.

[2003] 2 AC   Mirvahedy v Henley (HL(E))

A

House of Lords

Mirvahedy *v* Henley and another

[2003] UKHL 16

2002 Dec 9, 10;   Lord Nicholls of Birkenhead, Lord Slynn of Hadley,
B   2003 March 20   Lord Hobhouse of Woodborough, Lord Scott of Foscote
                                      and Lord Walker of Gestingthorpe

Animal — Horse — Characteristics — Frightened horse escaping from field and colliding with car on highway causing injury to driver — Whether due to characteristic found in species in particular circumstances — Whether keepers liable — Animals Act 1971 (c 22), s 2(2)

C

The claimant suffered personal injuries when the car he was driving was in collision with the defendants' horse, which had panicked due to some unknown event and escaped with two others from its field. On his claim for damages the judge found that the field had been adequately fenced so that the defendants had not been negligent and concluded that, although the horse had displayed characteristics normal for its species in the particular circumstances within the second limb of section 2(2)(b) of the Animals Act 1971[1], those characteristics had not caused the
D   damage. The Court of Appeal allowed an appeal by the claimant.
On appeal by the defendants—
Held, dismissing the appeal (Lord Slynn of Hadley and Lord Scott of Foscote dissenting), that under section 2(2)(b) of the 1971 Act the keeper of a non-dangerous animal was strictly liable for damage or injury caused by it while it was behaving in a way that, although not normal behaviour generally for animals of that species, was nevertheless normal behaviour for the species in the particular circumstances, such as
E   a horse bolting when sufficiently alarmed; and that, since the accident to the claimant had been caused by the defendants' horses behaving in an unusual way caused by their panic, they were liable to him (post, paras 20, 21, 44–48, 61, 69, 71–73, 141, 155–157, 161–163).
Cummings v Granger [1977] QB 397, CA and *Curtis v Betts* [1990] 1 WLR 459, CA approved.
Decision of the Court of Appeal [2001] EWCA Civ 1749, [2002] QB 769; [2002]
F   2 WLR 566 affirmed.

The following cases are referred to in their Lordships' opinions:
Barnes v Lucille Ltd (1907) 96 LT 680, DC
Behrens v Bertram Mills Circus Ltd [1957] 2 QB 1; [1957] 2 WLR 404; [1957] 1 All ER 583
Breeden v Lampard (unreported) 21 March 1985; Court of Appeal (Civil Division)
G   Transcript No 1035 of 1985, CA
Buckle v Holmes [1926] 2 KB 125, CA
Carver v Duncan [1985] AC 1082; [1985] 2 WLR 1010; [1985] 2 All ER 645, HL(E)
Cummings v Granger [1977] QB 397; [1976] 3 WLR 842; [1977] 1 All ER 104, CA
Curtis v Betts [1990] 1 WLR 459; [1990] 1 All ER 769, CA
Fitzgerald v E D and A D Cooke Bourne (Farms) Ltd [1964] 1 QB 249; [1963] 3 WLR 522; [1963] 3 All ER 36, CA
H   *Gloster v Chief Constable of Greater Manchester Police* [2000] PIQR P114, CA
Jaundrill v Gillett The Times, 30 January 1996; Court of Appeal (Civil Division) Transcript No 73 of 1996, CA
Kite v Napp The Times, 1 June 1982

---

[1] Animals Act 1971, s 2(2): see post, para 14.

Illustration 14–2. *Mirvahedy v. Henley*, [2003]
UKHL 16, [2003] 2 A.C. 491.

◼ LIVRE PREMIER **DES PERSONNES**

⬤ TITRE PREMIER **DES DROITS CIVILS**
(*L. n° 94-653 du 29 juill. 1994*).

Les divisions du titre Ier en chapitres et sections ont été supprimées par la L. n° 93-933 du 22 juill. 1993, qui a institué le titre Ier bis, infra. — Par la suite, la I.. n° 94-653 du 29 juill. 1994 a rétabli dans le titre Ier des chapitres II et III, infra, mais sans y rétablir de chapitre Ier.

Art. 7 (*L. 26 juin 1889*) L'exercice des droits civils est indépendant de l'exercice des droits politiques, lesquels s'acquièrent et se conservent conformément aux lois constitutionnelles et électorales.

Art. 8 (*L. 26 juin 1889*) Tout Français jouira des droits civils.
Al. 2 s. abrogés par L. 10 août 1927, art. 13.

BIBL. ▶ Flauss (ss. la dir.), *Petites affiches 25 mai 2000, n° spécial* (la France et le Pacte de New York relatif aux droits civils et politiques).

V. *Convention européenne du 4 nov. 1950 de sauvegarde des droits de l'homme et libertés fondamentales, publiée par Décr. n° 74-360 du 3 mai 1974* (D. et BLD 1974. 181), *avec ses protocoles additionnels. — V. aussi Décr. n° 86-282 du 28 févr. 1986* (D, et ALD 1986. 271) *portant publication du protocole n° 6 à cette convention ; Décr. n° 89-37 du 24 janv. 1989* (D. et ALD 1989. 103) *portant publication du protocole n° 7 à cette convention ; Décr. n° 90-245 du 14 mars 1990 (D. et ALD 1990. 181) portant publication du protocole n° 8 à cette convention ; Décr. n° 98-1055 du 18 nov. 1998 (JO 25 nov.) portant publication du protocole n° 11 à cette convention. — Sur l'acceptation du droit de recours individuel, V. Décr. n° 81-917 du 9 oct. 1981* (D. et BLD 1981. 349), *Décr. n° 86-1314 du 23 déc. 1986* (D, et ALD 1987. 45), *Décr. n° 90-415 du 14 mai 1990* (D. et ALD 1990. 242). — *Sur les immunités accordées aux personnes participant aux procédures devant la CEDH, V. Décr. n° 99-60 du 25 janv. 1999 (JO 30 janv.) portant publication de l'Accord européen de Strasbourg du 5 mars 1996.*

V. *Pacte international de New York du 19 déc. 1966 relatif aux droits civils et politiques, publié par Décr. n° 81-76 du 29 janv. 1981* (D. et BLD 1981. 79). — *Sur la levée d'une réserve française, V. Décr. n° 88-818 du 13 juill. 1988* (D. et ALD 1988. 384).

V. *Convention de New York du 26 janv. 1990 relative aux droits de l'enfant, publiée par Décr. n° 90-917 du 8 oct. 1990* (D. et ALD 1990. 424) ; ... *Protocole facultatif à cette convention, fait à New York le 25 mai 2000, concernant la vente d'enfants, la prostitution des enfants et la pornographie mettant en scène des enfants, publié par Décr. n° 2003-372 du 15 avr. 2003 (JO 24 avr.) ; ... Protocole facultatif à cette convention, fait à New York le 25 mai 2000, concernant l'implication d'enfants dans les conflits armés, publié par Décr. n° 2003-373 du 15 avr. 2003 (JO 24 avr.). — V. aussi L. n° 99-478 du 9 juin 1999 (JO 10 juin) visant à inciter au respect des droits de l'enfant dans le monde, notamment lors de l'achat de fournitures scolaires. — Sur le droit de l'enfant à l'instruction, V. C. éduc.* (Ord. n° 2000-549 du 15 juin 2000, JO 22 juin), art. L. 111-2 et L. 122-1.

Loi n° 46-940 du 7 mai 1946, *tendant à proclamer citoyens tous les ressortissants des territoires d'outre-mer.* **Art. unique** A partir du 1er juin 1946, tous les ressortissants des territoires d'outre-mer (Algérie comprise) ont la qualité de citoyen, au même titre que les nationaux français de la métropole ou des territoires d'outre-mer. Des lois particulières établiront les conditions dans lesquelles ils exerceront leurs droits de citoyens.

Illustration 14–3. Code civil [C. civ.] arts.
7–8 (106th ed. Dalloz 2007) (Fr.).

Appendix

TREATISES AND SERVICES BY SUBJECT

Note: Availability of online resources may depend on your subscription agreement. Some materials (such as West hornbooks) are not available to academic subscribers, and others (such as services and CCH treatises) may require separate subscriptions. Most services are also available directly from their publishers.

ADMINISTRATIVE LAW (KF5401–KF5425)

Multi-Volume Treatises

Charles H. Koch, Jr., *Administrative Law and Practice* (2d ed. 1997–date), available in Westlaw (ADMLP)

Richard J. Pierce, Jr., *Administrative Law Treatise* (4th ed. 2002–date)

Jacob A. Stein et al., *Administrative Law* (1977–date), available in Lexis

Hornbooks

Alfred C. Aman & William T. Mayton, *Administrative Law* (2d ed. 2001), available in Westlaw (ADMINLAW–HB)

Richard J. Pierce et al., *Administrative Law and Process* (5th ed. 2009)

ADMIRALTY AND MARITIME LAW (KF1096–KF1137)

Multi-Volume Treatises

Robert Force & Martin J. Norris, *The Law of Maritime Personal Injuries* (5th ed. 2004–date), available in Westlaw (MARITIME)

Robert Force & Martin J. Norris, *The Law of Seamen* (5th ed. 2003–date), available in Westlaw (SEAMEN)

Elijah E. Jhirad et al., *Benedict on Admiralty* (7th ed. 1958–date), available in Lexis

Thomas J. Schoenbaum, *Admiralty and Maritime Law* (4th ed. 2004–date), available in Westlaw (ADMMARL)

Hornbook

Thomas J. Schoenbaum, *Admiralty and Maritime Law* (4th ed. 2004–date)

ADVERTISING (KF1614–KF1617)

Multi-Volume Treatise

George Eric Rosden & Peter Eric Rosden, *The Law of Advertising* (1973–date), available in Lexis

One-Volume Treatise

Steven G. Brody & Bruce E.H. Johnson, *Advertising and Commercial Speech: A First Amendment Guide* (2d ed. 2004–date), available in Westlaw (PLIREF–SPEECH)

Service

Advertising Law Guide (CCH)

ANTITRUST & TRADE REGULATION (KF1601–KF1668)

Multi-Volume Treatises

Louis Altman, *Callmann on Unfair Competition, Trademarks and Monopolies* (4th ed. 1981–date), available in Westlaw (CALLMANN)

Philip Areeda & Herbert Hovenkamp, *Antitrust Law: An Analysis of Antitrust Principles and Their Application* (2d & 3d eds. 2000–date), available in CCH

Earl W. Kintner, *Federal Antitrust Law* (1980–date), available in Lexis

Julian O. Von Kalinowski et al., *Antitrust Laws and Trade Regulation* (2d ed. 1996–date), available in Lexis

One-Volume Treatises and Hornbooks

Phillip E. Areeda & Herbert Hovenkamp, *Fundamentals of Antitrust Law* (3d ed. 2004–date)

Carolyn L. Carter & Jonathan Sheldon, *Unfair and Deceptive Acts and Practices* (7th ed. 2008–date)

William C. Holmes, *Antitrust Law Handbook* (annual), available in Westlaw (ANTITRHDBK)

Herbert Hovenkamp, *Federal Antitrust Policy: The Law of Competition and Its Practice* (3d ed. 2005), available in Westlaw (ANTITRPOL–HB)

Dee Pridgen, *Consumer Protection and the Law* (annual), available in Westlaw (CONPROT)

Lawrence A. Sullivan & Warren S. Grimes, *The Law of Antitrust: An Integrated Handbook* (2d ed. 2006), available in Westlaw (ANTITRUST–HB)

Thomas V. Vakerics, *Antitrust Basics* (1985–date), available in Westlaw (ANTITRBAS)

Services

Antitrust & Trade Regulation Report (BNA), available in Lexis and Westlaw (BNA–ATRR)

Trade Regulation Reports (CCH), available in Lexis

ART AND ENTERTAINMENT LAW (KF4288–KF4305)

Multi-Volume Treatises

Leonard D. DuBoff & Sally Holt Caplin, *The Deskbook of Art Law* (2d ed. 1993–date)

Ralph E. Lerner & Judith Bresler, *Art Law* (3d ed. 2005), available in Westlaw (PLIREF–ART)

Alexander Lindey & Michael Landau, *Lindey on Entertainment, Publishing, and the Arts* (3d ed. 2004–date), available in Westlaw (LINDEY3D)

Thomas D. Selz et al., *Entertainment Law* (3d ed. 2006–date), available in Westlaw (ENTERTAIN)

One-Volume Treatises

Jessica L. Darraby, *Art, Artifact, Architecture and Museum Law* (annual), available in Westlaw (ARTARCHLAW)

Robert Fremlin & Michael Landau, *Entertainment Law* (rev. ed. 2006–date)

BANKING AND CONSUMER FINANCE (KF966–KF1040)

Multi-Volume Treatises

Henry J. Bailey & Richard B. Hagedorn, *Brady on Bank Checks* (rev. ed. 1997–date), available in Westlaw (BRADY)

Barkley Clark & Barbara Clark, *The Law of Bank Deposits, Collections, and Credit Cards* (rev. ed. 1999–date), available in Westlaw (BDECPP)

Michael P. Malloy, *Banking Law and Regulation* (1994–date), available in CCH

Michie on Banks and Banking (1931–date)

William H. Schlichting et al., *Banking Law* (1981–date), available in Lexis

One-Volume Treatises and Hornbooks

Carolyn L. Carter, *Repossessions* (6th ed. 2005–date)

Robert J. Hobbs, *Fair Debt Collection* (6th ed. 2008–date)

Fred H. Miller & Alvin C. Harrell, *The Law of Modern Payment Systems* (2003), available in Westlaw (MODPAYSYS–HB)

Dee Pridgen, *Consumer Credit and the Law* (annual), available in Westlaw (CONCRED)

Elizabeth Renuart et al., *Truth in Lending* (6th ed. 2007–date)

Services

Banking Report (BNA), available in Lexis and Westlaw (BNA–BNK)

Federal Banking Law Reports (CCH), available in Lexis

State Banking Law Reports (CCH)

BANKRUPTCY (KF1501–KF1548)

Multi-Volume Treatises

Collier on Bankruptcy (Lawrence P. King ed., 15th ed. 1985–date), available in Lexis

Daniel R. Cowans, *Bankruptcy Law and Practice* (7th ed. 1998–date)

Robert E. Ginsberg & Robert D. Martin, *Ginsberg and Martin on Bankruptcy* (5th ed. 2008–date), available in Loislaw and Westlaw (GMBKR)

Norton Bankruptcy Law and Practice (William L. Norton, Jr. ed., 3d ed. 2008–date), available in Westlaw (NRTN–BLP)

Henry J. Sommer, *Consumer Bankruptcy Law and Practice* (8th ed. 2006–date)

Hornbook

David G. Epstein et al., *Bankruptcy* (2d ed. 1993)

Services

Bankruptcy Law Reporter (BNA), available in Lexis and Westlaw (BNA–BLR)

Bankruptcy Law Reports (CCH)

Bankruptcy Service (West), available in Westlaw (BKRSERVICE)

CIVIL RIGHTS (KF1307, KF1325, KF4741–KF4786)

Multi-Volume Treatises

Ivan E. Bodensteiner & Rosalie Berger Levinson, *State and Local Government Civil Rights Liability* (1987–date), available in Westlaw (STLOCCIVIL)

Joseph G. Cook & John L. Sobieski, *Civil Rights Actions* (1983–date), available in Lexis

Michael B. Mushlin, *Rights of Prisoners* (3d ed. 2002–date), available in Westlaw (RGTSPRISON)

Sheldon H. Nahmod, *Civil Rights and Civil Liberties Litigation: The Law of Section 1983* (4th ed. 1997–date)

Prisoners and the Law (Ira P. Robbins ed., 1985–date)

Martin A. Schwartz & John E. Kirklin, *Section 1983 Litigation* (3d/4th eds. 1997–date)

Sexual Orientation and the Law (Roberta Achtenberg ed., 1985–date), available in Westlaw (SEXORIENT)

Isidore Silver, *Police Civil Liability* (1986–date), available in Lexis

Rodney A. Smolla, *Federal Civil Rights Acts* (3d ed. 1994–date), available in Westlaw (FCIVRTACTS)

One-Volume Treatises and Hornbooks

Michael Avery et al., *Police Misconduct: Law and Litigation* (annual), available in Westlaw (POLICEMISC)

Harold S. Lewis & Elizabeth J. Norman, *Civil Rights Law and Practice* (2d ed. 2004), available in Westlaw (CIVRIGHT–HB)

John W. Palmer & Stephen E. Palmer, *Constitutional Rights of Prisoners* (7th ed. 2004), available in Lexis

Robert G. Schwemm, *Housing Discrimination: Law and Litigation* (1990–date), available in Westlaw (HDISLL)

COMMERCIAL LAW (KF871–KF890)

Multi-Volume Treatises

Peter F. Coogan et al., *Secured Transactions under the Uniform Commercial Code* (1963–date), available in Lexis

Debtor-Creditor Law (Theodore Eisenberg ed., 1982–date), available in Lexis

Richard W. Duesenberg & Lawrence P. King, *Sales and Bulk Transfers under the Uniform Commercial Code* (1966–date), available in Lexis

Larry E. Edmondson, *Domke on Commercial Arbitration* (3d ed. 2003–date), available in Westlaw (DCMLARB)

Patricia F. Fonseca & John R. Fonseca, *The Law of Modern Commercial Practices* (2d rev. ed. 1998–date)

William D. Hawkland, *Uniform Commercial Code Series* (1982–date), available in Westlaw (HAWKLAND)

Lary Lawrence, *Lawrence's Anderson on the Uniform Commercial Code* (3d ed. 1981–date), available in Westlaw (ANDR–UCC)

Deborah L. Nelson & Jennifer L. Howicz, *Williston on Sales* (5th ed. 1994–date)

Jeremiah J. Spires et al., *Doing Business in the United States* (1978–date), available in Lexis

James J. White & Robert S. Summers, *Uniform Commercial Code* (5th ed. 2002–date), available in Westlaw (WS–UCC)

Hornbook

James J. White & Robert S. Summers, *Uniform Commercial Code* (5th ed. 2000)

Services

Consumer Credit Guide (CCH), available in Lexis

Secured Transactions Guide (CCH)

COMMUNICATIONS LAW (KF2761–KF2849)

Multi-Volume Treatises

Charles D. Ferris et al., *Telecommunications Regulation: Cable, Broadcasting, Satellite, and the Internet* (1983–date), available in Lexis

Harvey L. Zuckman et al., *Modern Communications Law* (1999–date)

One-Volume Treatises and Hornbooks

Morton I. Hamburg & Stuart Brotman, *Communications Law and Practice* (1995–date)

Peter W. Huber et al. *Federal Telecommunications Law* (2d ed. 1999–date)

Harvey L. Zuckman et al., *Modern Communications Law* (1999), available in Westlaw (MODCOMML–HB)

Services

Communications Regulation (Pike & Fischer)

Media Law Reporter (BNA)

CONFLICT OF LAWS (KF410–KF418)

Hornbooks

Eugene F. Scoles et al. *Conflict of Laws* (4th ed. 2004), available in Westlaw (CONFLICTS–HB)

Russell J. Weintraub, *Commentary on the Conflict of Laws* (5th ed. 2006–date)

CONSTITUTIONAL LAW (KF4501–KF4558)

Multi-Volume Treatises

Chester J. Antieau & William J. Rich, *Modern Constitutional Law* (2d ed. 1997–date)

Jennifer Friesen, *State Constitutional Law: Litigating Individual Rights, Claims, and Defenses* (4th ed. 2006–date)

Ronald D. Rotunda & John E. Nowak, *Treatise on Constitutional Law: Substance and Procedure* (4th ed. 2007–date)

Rodney A. Smolla, *Smolla and Nimmer on Freedom of Speech* (3d ed. 1996–date), available in Westlaw (FREESPEECH)

One-Volume Treatises and Hornbooks

Erwin Chemerinsky, *Constitutional Law: Principles and Policies* (3d ed. 2006)

Louis Fisher & David Gray Adler, *American Constitutional Law* (7th ed. 2007)

John E. Nowak & Ronald D. Rotunda, *Constitutional Law* (7th ed. 2004)

Laurence H. Tribe, *American Constitutional Law* (2d/3d eds. 1988–2000)

CONSTRUCTION LAW (KF901–KF902)

Multi-Volume Treatises

Philip L. Bruner & Patrick J. O'Connor, *Bruner & O'Connor on Construction Law* (2002–date), available in Westlaw (BOCL)

Construction Law (Steven G. M. Stein ed. 1986–date), available in Lexis

James J. Myers & Robert F. Cushman, *Construction Law Handbook* (1999–date), available in CCH and Loislaw

CONTRACTS (KF801–KF839)

Multi-Volume Treatises

E. Allan Farnsworth, *Farnsworth on Contracts* (3d ed. 2004–date)

Richard A. Lord, *Williston on Contracts* (4th ed. 1990–date), available in Westlaw (WILLSTN–CN)

Corbin on Contracts (Joseph M. Perillo ed., rev. ed.1993–date), available in Lexis

One-Volume Treatises and Hornbooks

E. Allen Farnsworth, *Contracts* (4th ed. 2004)

Howard O. Hunter, *Modern Law of Contracts* (2d rev. ed. 1999–date), available in Westlaw (MODCON)

John Edward Murray, Jr., *Murray on Contracts* (4th ed. 2001), available in Lexis

Joseph M. Perillo, *Calamari and Perillo on Contracts* (5th ed. 2003), available in Westlaw (CONTRACTS–HB)

CORPORATIONS (KF1384–KF1480, KFD213)

Multi-Volume Treatises

R. Franklin Balotti & Jesse A. Finkelstein, *The Delaware Law of Corporations and Business Organizations* (3d ed. 1998–date), available in CCH and Westlaw (DELC-BO)

Philip J. Blumberg et al., *Blumberg on Corporate Groups* (2d ed. 2005–date), available in CCH

Zolman Cavitch et al., *Business Organizations* (1963–date), available in Lexis

James D. Cox & Thomas Lee Hazen, *Cox and Hazen on Corporations* (2d ed. 2003–date)

Fletcher Cyclopedia of the Law of Private Corporations (1931–date), available in Westlaw (FLTR–CYC)

Byron E. Fox & Eleanor M. Fox, *Corporate Acquisitions and Mergers* (1968–date), available in Lexis

Martin D. Ginsburg & Jack S. Levin, *Mergers, Acquisitions, and Buyouts* (semiannual), available in CCH

Gladys Glickman, *Franchising* (1969–date), available in Lexis

William E. Knepper & Dan A. Bailey, *Liability of Corporate Officers and Directors* (7th ed. 2002–date), available in Lexis

Jonathan R. Macey, *Macey on Corporation Laws* (1998–date), available in CCH

F. Hodge O'Neal & Robert B. Thompson, *O'Neal and Thompson's Close Corporations and LLCs: Law and Practice* (rev. 3d ed. 1997–date), available in Westlaw (CCORPLLC)

Edward P. Welch et al., *Folk on the Delaware General Corporation Law* (5th ed. 2006–date), available in CCH

One-Volume Treatises and Hornbooks

James D. Cox & Thomas Lee Hazen, *Corporations* (2003)

Franklin A. Gevurtz, *Corporation Law* (2000), available in Westlaw (CORPS–HB)

Donald W. Glazer et al., *Glazer and FitzGibbon on Legal Opinions: Drafting, Interpreting, and Supporting Closing Opinions in Business Transactions* (3d ed. 2008–date)

Services

Business Franchise Guide (CCH), available in Lexis

Corporate Practice Series (BNA), available in Lexis and Westlaw (BNA–CORP)

Corporate Secretary's Guide (CCH)

Corporation (Aspen Publishers), available in CCH

Mergers & Acquisitions Law Report (BNA), available in Lexis and Westlaw (BNA–MALR)

CRIMINAL LAW AND PROCEDURE (KF9201–KF9479, KF9601–KF9763)

Multi-Volume Treatises

Joel M. Androphy, *White Collar Crime* (2d ed. 2001–date), available in Westlaw (WCCR)

Sara Sun Beale et al., *Grand Jury Law and Practice* (2d ed. 1997–date), available in Westlaw (GRJURLAW)

Susan W. Brenner & Lori E. Shaw, *Federal Grand Jury: A Guide to Law and Practice* (2d ed. 2006–date), available in Westlaw (FEDGRJURY)

James G. Carr & Patricia L. Bellia, *The Law of Electronic Surveillance* (2d ed. 1986–date), available in Westlaw (ELECTRSURV)

Joseph G. Cook, *Constitutional Rights of the Accused* (3d ed. 1996–date), available in Westlaw (CONRTACC)

Justin D. Franklin & Steven C. Bell, *Searches and Seizures, Arrests and Confessions* (2d ed. 1979–date), available in Westlaw (SSAC)

Randy Hertz & James S. Liebman, *Federal Habeas Corpus Practice and Procedure* (5th ed. 2005–date), available in Lexis

Nancy Hollander et al., *Wharton's Criminal Procedure* (14th ed. 2002–date)

Wayne R. LaFave et al., *Criminal Procedure* (3d ed. 2007–date), available in Westlaw (CRIMPROC)

Wayne R. LaFave, *Search and Seizure: A Treatise on the Fourth Amendment* (4th ed. 2004–date), available in Westlaw (SEARCHSZR)

Wayne R. LaFave, *Substantive Criminal Law* (2d ed. 2003–date), available in Westlaw (SUBCRL)

Mark S. Rhodes, *Orfield's Criminal Procedure Under the Federal Rules* (2d ed. 1985–date), available in Westlaw (ORFIELDS)

Paul H. Robinson, *Criminal Law Defenses* (1984–date), available in Westlaw (CRLDEF)

David S. Rudstein et al., *Criminal Constitutional Law* (1990–date), available in Lexis

Mark I. Soler et al., *Representing the Child Client* (1987–date), available in Lexis

Charles E. Torcia, *Wharton's Criminal Law* (15th ed. 1993–date), available in Westlaw (CRIMLAW)

One-Volume Treatises and Hornbooks

Thomas W. Hutchison et al., *Federal Sentencing Law and Practice* (annual), available in Westlaw (FLSP)

Wayne R. LaFave, *Criminal Law* (4th ed. 2003)

Wayne R. LaFave et al., *Criminal Procedure* (4th ed. 2004–date)

Charles H. Whitebread & Christopher Slobogin, *Criminal Procedure: An Analysis of Cases and Concepts* (5th ed. 2008)

Service

Criminal Law Reporter (BNA), available in Lexis and Westlaw (BNA–CRIMLR)

DISABILITIES (KF480, KF3469)

Multi-Volume Treatises

Americans with Disabilities Act: Employee Rights & Employer Obligations (Jonathan R. Mook ed., 1992–date), available in Lexis

Michael L. Perlin, *Mental Disability Law: Civil and Criminal* (2d ed. 1998–date)

Henry H. Perritt, Jr., *Americans with Disabilities Act Handbook* (4th ed. 2003–date), available in CCH and Loislaw

Gary E. Phelan & Janet Bond Atherton, *Disability Discrimination in the Workplace* (1992–date), available in Westlaw (DISDW)

One-Volume Treatises and Hornbooks

Peter Blanck et al., *Disability, Civil Rights Law, and Policy* (2004), available in Westlaw (DISCIVRT–HB)

John J. Coleman III, *Disability Discrimination in Employment* (1991–date), available in Westlaw (DISDE)

Laura F. Rothstein & Julia Rothstein, *Disabilities and the Law* (3d ed. 2006–date)

Peter Susser, *Disability Discrimination and the Workplace* (2005)

Services

Accommodating Disabilities: Business Management Guide (CCH), available in Lexis

National Disability Law Reporter (LRP Publications), available in Lexis and Westlaw (NDLRPTR)

EDUCATION LAW (KF4101–KF4257)

Multi-Volume Treatises

Education Law (James A. Rapp ed., 1984–date), available in Lexis

William A. Kaplin & Barbara A. Lee, *The Law of Higher Education* (4th ed. 2006)

Ronna Greff Schneider, *Education Law: First Amendment, Due Process and Discrimination Litigation* (2004–date), available in Westlaw (EDULAW)

One-Volume Treatise

Mark C. Weber, *Special Education Law and Litigation Treatise* (3d ed. 2008–date)

Service

Individuals with Disabilities Education Law Report (LRP Publications)

EMPLOYMENT AND LABOR LAW (KF3301–KF3580)

Multi-Volume Treatises

The Developing Labor Law: The Boards, the Courts, and the National Labor Relations Act (John C. Higgins ed., 5th ed. 2006–date)

Howard C. Eglit, *Age Discrimination* (2d ed. 1994–date)

R. Ben Hogan III & Robert D. Moran, *Occupational Safety and Health Act* (1977–date), available in Lexis

N. Peter Lareau et al., *Labor and Employment Law* (2003–date), available in Lexis

Lex K. Larson, *Employment Discrimination* (2d ed. 1994–date), available in Lexis

Barbara Lindemann & Paul Grossman, *Employment Discrimination Law* (4th ed. 2007–date)

Susan M. Omilian & Jean P. Kamp, *Sex-Based Employment Discrimination* (1990–date), available in Westlaw (SBEDIS)

Mark A. Rothstein et al., *Employment Law* (3d ed. 2004–date)

Charles A. Sullivan & Lauren M. Walter, *Employment Discrimination: Law and Practice* (4th ed. 2009–date), available in Loislaw

One-Volume Treatises and Hornbooks

Frank Elkouri & Edna Asper Elkouri, *How Arbitration Works* (6th ed. 2003)

Employee Benefits Law (Terese M. Connerton ed., 2d ed. 2000–date), available in Westlaw (ABA–BNA–EBL)

The Fair Labor Standards Act (Ellen C. Kearns ed., 1999–date)

The Family and Medical Leave Act (Michael J. Ossip & Robert M. Hale eds., 2006–date)

Robert A. Gorman & Matthew W. Finkin, *Basic Text on Labor Law: Unionization and Collective Bargaining* (2d ed. 2004), available in Westlaw (UNIONCB–HB)

William J. Holloway & Michael J. Leech, *Employment Termination: Rights and Remedies* (2d ed. 1993–date)

Labor Union Law and Regulation (William W. Osborne, Jr. ed., 2003–date)

Barbara T. Lindemann & David D. Kadue, *Age Discrimination in Employment Law* (2003–date)

Harold S. Lewis, Jr. & Elizabeth J. Norman, *Employment Discrimination Law and Practice* (2d ed. 2004), available in Westlaw (EMPDISCR–HB)

Henry H. Perritt, *Employee Dismissal Law and Practice* (5th ed. 2006–date), available in CCH and Loislaw

Randy Rabinowitz, *Occupational Safety and Health Law* (2d ed. 2002)

Mark A. Rothstein et al., *Employment Law* (3d ed. 2005)

Mark A. Rothstein, *Occupational Safety and Health Law* (annual), available in Westlaw (OSHL)

Services

Benefits Coordinator (RIA)

Collective Bargaining Negotiations and Contracts (BNA), available in Lexis and Westlaw (BNA–CBNC)

Employee Benefits Management (CCH), available in Lexis

Employment Coordinator (West), available in Westlaw (EMPC)

Employment Discrimination Coordinator (West), available in Westlaw (EDC)

Employment Discrimination Report (BNA), available in Lexis and Westlaw (BNA–EDR)

Employment Practices Guide (CCH), available in Lexis

Employment Safety and Health Guide (CCH), available in Lexis

Labor Relations Reporter (BNA), available in Lexis and Westlaw (LRR–ALL)

Occupational Safety & Health Reporter (BNA), available in Lexis and Westlaw (BNA–OSHR)

Pension & Benefits Reporter (BNA), available in Lexis and Westlaw (BNA–PEN)

Pension Coordinator (RIA)

Pension Plan Guide (CCH), available in Lexis

Wages/Hours Reports (CCH), available in Lexis

ENERGY AND NATURAL RESOURCES (KF1801–KF1873, KF5500–KF5510)

Multi-Volume Treatises

American Law of Mining (Cheryl Outerbridge ed., 2d ed. 1984–date), available in Lexis

George Cameron Coggins & Robert L. Glicksman, *Public Natural Resources Law* (1990–date)

Energy Law and Transactions (David J. Muchow & William A. Mogel eds., 1990–date), available in Lexis

Neil E. Harl, *Agricultural Law* (1980–date), available in Lexis

Eugene Kuntz, *A Treatise on the Law of Oil and Gas* (1962–date), available in Lexis

W.L. Summers, *The Law of Oil and Gas* (3d ed. 2004–date)

Howard R. Williams & Charles J. Meyers, *Oil and Gas Law* (1959–date), available in Lexis

One-Volume Treatises and Hornbooks

Owen L. Anderson et al., *Hemingway Oil and Gas Law and Taxation* (4th ed. 2004), available in Westlaw (OILGASLAW)

Jan Laitos, *Natural Resources Law* (2002), available in Westlaw (NATRSRC–HB)

Services

Energy Management and Federal Energy Guidelines (CCH)

Nuclear Regulation Reports (CCH)

Utilities Law Reports (CCH)

ENVIRONMENTAL LAW (KF3775–KF3816)

Multi-Volume Treatises

Frank P. Grad, *Treatise on Environmental Law* (1973–date), available in Lexis

Law of Environmental Protection (Sheldon M. Novick et al. eds., 1987–date)

The Law of Hazardous Waste (Susan M. Cooke ed., 1987–date), available in Lexis

James T. O'Reilly, *Superfund and Brownfields Cleanup* (annual), available in Westlaw (SUPERFUND)

William H. Rodgers, Jr., *Environmental Law* (1986–date)

Donald W. Stever, *Law of Chemical Regulation and Hazardous Waste* (1986–date)

Water and Water Rights (Robert E. Beck ed., 1991–date)

One-Volume Treatises and Hornbooks

Eric Pearson, *Environmental and Natural Resources Law* (3d ed. 2008)

William H. Rodgers, Jr., *Environmental Law* (2d ed. 1994)

A. Dan Tarlock, *Law of Water Rights and Resources* (1988–date), available in Westlaw (LWATRR)

William L. Want, *Law of Wetlands Regulation* (1989–date), available in Westlaw (LWETR)

Services

Chemical Regulation Reporter (BNA), available in Lexis and Westlaw (BNA–CHEM)

Environment Reporter (BNA), available in Lexis and Westlaw (BNA–ER)

Environmental Law Reporter (Environmental Law Institute), available in Lexis and Westlaw (ENVLRNA)

EVIDENCE (KF8931–KF8969, KF9660–KF9678)

Multi-Volume Treatises

Barbara E. Bergman & Nancy Hollander, *Wharton's Criminal Evidence* (15th ed. 1997–date), available in Westlaw (CRIMEVID)

David L. Faigman et al., *Modern Scientific Evidence* (annual)

Clifford S. Fischman, *Jones on Evidence: Civil & Criminal* (7th ed. 1992–date)

Paul C. Giannelli & Edward J. Imwinkelried, *Scientific Evidence* (4th ed. 2007–date), available in Lexis

Michael H. Graham, *Handbook of Federal Evidence* (6th ed. 2006–date), available in Westlaw (FEDEVID)

Edward J. Imwinkelried et al., *Courtroom Criminal Evidence* (4th ed. 2005–date), available in Lexis

McCormick on Evidence (Kenneth S. Broun ed., 6th ed. 2006), available in Westlaw (MCMK–EVID)

Christopher B. Mueller & Laird C. Kirkpatrick, *Evidence: Practice Under the Rules* (2d ed. 1999–date), available in CCH and Loislaw

Christopher B. Mueller & Laird C. Kirkpatrick, *Federal Evidence* (3d ed. 2007–date), available in Westlaw (FEDEV)

The New Wigmore: A Treatise on Evidence (Richard D. Friedman ed., 1996–date), available in CCH

Stephen A. Saltzburg et al., *Federal Rules of Evidence Manual* (9th ed. 2006–date), available in Lexis

Weinstein's Federal Evidence (Joseph M. McLaughlin ed., 1997–date), available in Lexis

John Henry Wigmore et al., *Evidence in Trials at Common Law* (4th ed. 1961–date), available in CCH and Loislaw

One-Volume Treatises and Hornbooks

McCormick on Evidence (Kenneth S. Broun ed., 6th ed. 2006)

Roger Park et al., *Evidence Law* (2d ed. 2004), available in Westlaw (EVIDENCE–HB)

Jack B. Weinstein & Margaret A. Berger, *Weinstein's Evidence Manual* (1987–date), available in Lexis

Glen Weissenberger & James J. Duane, *Weissenberger's Federal Evidence* (5th ed. 2006), available in Lexis

FAMILY LAW (KF501–KF553)

Multi-Volume Treatises

Adoption Law and Practice (Joan H. Hollinger ed., 1988–date), available in Lexis

Jeff Atkinson, *Modern Child Custody Practice* (2d ed. 2000–date), available in Lexis

Ann M. Haralambie, *Handling Child Custody, Abuse and Adoption Cases* (1993–date)

Family Law and Practice (Arnold H. Rutkin ed., 1985–date), available in Lexis

Thomas A. Jacobs, *Children and the Law: Rights and Obligations* (1995–date), available in Westlaw (CALRO)

Donald T. Kramer, *Legal Rights of Children* (2d ed. 2005–date)

John P. McCahey et al., *Child Custody and Visitation Law and Practice* (1983–date), available in Lexis

Brett R. Turner, *Equitable Distribution of Property* (3d ed. 2005–date), available in Westlaw (EQDP)

Valuation and Distribution of Marital Property (John P. McCahey ed., 1984–date), available in Lexis

One-Volume Treatise

Laura W. Morgan, *Child Support Guidelines: Interpretation and Application* (1996–date), available in Westlaw (CSGIA)

Services

Family Law Reporter (BNA), available in Lexis and Westlaw (BNA–FAMLR)

Family Law Tax Guide (CCH)

FEDERAL PRACTICE (KF8820–KF9058, KF9650)

Multi-Volume Treatises

Business and Commercial Litigation in Federal Courts (Robert L. Haig ed., 2d ed. 2005–date), available in Westlaw (BUSCOMLIT)

Steven Alan Childress & Martha S. Davis, *Federal Standards of Review* (3d ed. 1999–date), available in Lexis

Alba Conte & Herbert B. Newberg, *Newberg on Class Actions* (4th ed. 2002–date), available in Westlaw (CLASSACT)

Moore's Federal Practice (Daniel R. Coquillette et al. eds., 3d ed. 1997–date), available in Lexis

Kent Sinclair, *Sinclair on Federal Civil Practice* (4th ed. 2004–date), available in Westlaw (PLIREF–FEDPRAC)

Charles Alan Wright et al., *Federal Practice and Procedure* (1st–4th eds. 1969–date), available in Westlaw (FPP)

One-Volume Treatises and Hornbooks

Erwin Chemerinsky, *Federal Jurisdiction* (5th ed. 2007)

Eugene Gressman et al., *Supreme Court Practice* (9th ed. 2007)

Federal Appellate Practice (Philip Allen Lacovara ed., 2008)

Gregory P. Joseph, *Sanctions: The Federal Law of Litigation Abuse* (4th ed. 2008), available in Lexis

Stuart T. Rossman & Charles Delbaum, *Consumer Class Actions* (6th ed. 2006–date)

Michael E. Tigar & Jane B. Tigar, *Federal Appeals: Jurisdiction and Practice* (3d ed. 1999–date), available in Westlaw (FEDAPJP)

Charles Alan Wright & Mary Kay Kane, *Law of Federal Courts* (6th ed. 2002), available in Westlaw (LAWFEDCTS–HB)

Service

The United States Law Week (BNA), available in Lexis and Westlaw (BNA–USLW)

FOOD AND DRUG LAW (KF3861–KF3896)

Multi-Volume Treatises

Marden G. Dixon, *Drug Product Liability* (1974–date), available in Lexis

James T. O'Reilly, *Food and Drug Administration* (3d ed. 2007–date)

One-Volume Treatise

Pharmaceutical Law: Regulation of Research, Development, and Marketing (Michael E. Clark ed., 2007–date)

Services

Food Drug Cosmetic Law Reports (CCH), available in Lexis

Medical Devices Reports (CCH), available in Lexis

GOVERNMENT BENEFITS (KF3600–KF3750)

Multi-Volume Treatises

Arthur Larson & Lex K. Larson, *Larson's Workers' Compensation Law* (1952–date), available in Lexis

Harvey L. McCormick, *Medicare and Medicaid Claims and Procedures* (4th ed. 2005–date), available in Westlaw (MEDCLAIMS)

Harvey L. McCormick, *Social Security Claims and Procedures* (5th ed. 1998–date), available in Westlaw (SSCLP)

National Organization of Social Security Claimants' Representatives, *Social Security Practice Guide* (1984–date), available in Lexis

Barbara Samuels, *Social Security Disability Claims: Practice and Procedure* (2d ed. 1994–date), available in Westlaw (SSDCPP)

Social Security Law and Practice (Michael A. Rosenhouse ed., 1983–date), available in Westlaw (SSLP)

One-Volume Treatise

Barton F. Stichman & Ronald B. Abrams, *Veterans Benefits Manual* (annual)

Services

Medicare–Medicaid Guide (CCH), available in Lexis

Medicare Report (BNA), available in Lexis and Westlaw (BNA–MED)

Social Security Reporter (CCH), available in Lexis

Unemployment Insurance Reporter (CCH)

GOVERNMENT CONTRACTS (KF841–KF869.5)

Multi-Volume Treatises

John T. Boese, *Civil False Claims and Qui Tam Actions* (3d ed. 2006–date)

John Cosgrove McBride, *Government Contracts: Law, Administration, Procedure* (1962–date), available in Lexis

One-Volume Treatises and Hornbooks

John Cibinic, Jr. et al., *Administration of Government Contracts* (4th ed. 2006), available in CCH

John Cibinic & Ralph C. Nash, *Formation of Government Contracts* (3d ed. 1998), available in CCH

Steven W. Feldman, *Government Contract Guidebook* (4th ed. 2007), available in Westlaw (GCGUIDE)

W. Noel Keyes, *Government Contracts Under the Federal Acquisition Regulation* (3d ed. 2003–date), available in Westlaw (GCFAR)

Services

Federal Contracts Report (BNA), available in Lexis and Westlaw (BNA–FCR)

Government Contracts Reporter (CCH), available in Lexis

HEALTH CARE (KF3821–KF3838)

Multi-Volume Treatises

Steven E. Pegalis, *American Law of Medical Malpractice* (3d ed. 2005–date)

David W. Louisell et al., *Medical Malpractice* (1960–date), available in Lexis

Barry R. Furrow et al., *Health Law* (2000)

Health Law Practice Guide (Alice G. Gosfield ed., 1993–date)

Treatise on Health Care Law (Michael G. Macdonald ed., 1991–date), available in Lexis

One-Volume Treatises and Hornbooks

Scott Becker, *Health Care Law: A Practical Guide* (2d ed. 1998–date), available in Lexis

Barry R. Furrow et al., *Health Law* (2000), available in Westlaw (HEALTHLAW–HB)

Fay A. Rozovsky, *Consent to Treatment: A Practical Guide* (4th ed. 2007–date)

Services

Health Care Policy Report (BNA), available in Lexis and Westlaw (BNA–HCP)

Health Law Reporter (BNA), available in Lexis and Westlaw (BNA–HLR)

Health Care Compliance Reporter (CCH), available in Lexis

IMMIGRATION (KF4800–KF4848)

Multi-Volume Treatises

Austin T. Fragomen, Jr. et al., *Immigration Law and Business* (1983–date), available in Westlaw (IMLB)

Austin T. Fragomen, Jr. et al., *Immigration Procedures Handbook* (annual), available in Westlaw (IMPH)

Charles Gordon et al., *Immigration Law and Procedure* (rev. ed. 1966–date), available in Lexis

National Immigration Project of the National Lawyers Guild, *Immigration Law and Defense* (3d ed. 1988–date), available in Westlaw (IMLD)

One-Volume Treatises

Robert C. Divine, *Immigration Practice* (annual)

Austin T. Fragomen & Steven C. Bell, *Immigration Fundamentals: A Guide to Law and Practice* (4th ed. 1996–date), available in Westlaw (PLIREF–IMMIG)

Sarah B. Ignatius et al., *Immigration Law and the Family* (1995–date), available in Westlaw (IMLF)

Dan Kesselbrenner and Lory D. Rosenberg, *Immigration Law and Crimes* (1984–date), available in Westlaw (IMLC)

Richard D. Steel, *Steel on Immigration Law* (2d ed. 1992–date), available in Westlaw (STEEL)

Service

Immigration Law Service 2d (West), available in Westlaw (IMMLS2D)

INSURANCE (KF1146–KF1238)

Multi-Volume Treatises

Eric Mills Holmes, *Holmes's Appleman on Insurance, 2d* (1996–date), available in Lexis

Barry R. Ostrager & Thomas R. Newman, *Handbook on Insurance Coverage Disputes* (14th ed. 2008–date), available in CCH

Lee R. Russ & Thomas F. Segalla, *Couch on Insurance 3d* (1995–date), available in Westlaw (COUCH)

Rowland H. Long & Mark S. Rhodes, *The Law of Liability Insurance* (1966–date), available in Lexis

One-Volume Treatises

Barlow Burke, *Law of Title Insurance* (3d ed. 2000–date)

Graydon S. Staring, *Law of Reinsurance* (1993–date), available in Westlaw (REINSUR)

INTELLECTUAL PROPERTY (KF2971–KF3193)

Multi-Volume Treatises

Howard B. Abrams, *The Law of Copyright* (1991–date), available in Westlaw (COPYLAW)

Donald S. Chisum, *Chisum on Patents* (1978–date), available in Lexis

Jay Dratler, Jr., *Intellectual Property Law: Commercial, Creative, and Industrial Property* (1991–date), available in Westlaw (IPLCCIP)

Jay Dratler, Jr., *Licensing of Intellectual Property* (1994–date), available in Westlaw (LICENSIP)

Jerome Gilson & Anne Gilson LaLonde, *Gilson on Trademarks* (1974–date), available in Lexis

Paul Goldstein, *Goldstein on Copyright* (3d ed. 2005–date), available in CCH

Melvin F. Jager, *Trade Secrets Law* (2002–date), available in Westlaw (TRDSECRT)

J. Thomas McCarthy, *McCarthy on Trademarks and Unfair Competition* (4th ed. 1996–date), available in Westlaw (MCCARTHY)

Roger M. Milgrim, *Milgrim on Licensing* (1990–date), available in Lexis

Roger M. Milgrim, *Milgrim on Trade Secrets* (1967–date), available in Lexis

R. Carl Moy, *Moy's Walker on Patents* (4th ed. 2003–date), available in Westlaw (MOY–PAT)

Melville B. Nimmer & David Nimmer, *Nimmer on Copyright* (1963–date), available in Lexis

William F. Patry, *Patry on Copyright* (2006–date), available in Westlaw (PATRYCOPY)

Peter D. Rosenberg, *Patent Law Fundamentals* (2d ed. 1980–date), available in Westlaw (PATLAWF)

One-Volume Treatises and Hornbooks

Michael A. Epstein, *Epstein on Intellectual Property* (5th ed. 2005–date)

Jay Dratler, Jr., *Cyberlaw: Intellectual Property in the Digital Millenium* (2000–date), available in Westlaw (CIPDM)

Robert L. Harmon, *Harmon on Patents: Black–Letter Law and Commentary* (2007)

Robert L. Harmon, *Patents and the Federal Circuit* (8th ed. 2007–date)

Ronald B. Hildreth, *Patent Law: A Practitioner's Guide* (3d ed. 1998–date), available in Lexis

Siegrun D. Kane, *Kane on Trademark Law: A Practitioner's Guide* (5th ed. 2007–date), available in Lexis

Henry H. Perritt, Jr., *Trade Secrets: A Practitioner's Guide* (2d ed. 2005–date), available in Lexis

Roger E. Schechter & John R. Thomas, *Intellectual Property: The Law of Copyrights, Patents and Trademarks* (2003), available in Westlaw (IPCPTM–HB)

Services

Copyright Law Reports (CCH)

Patent, Trademark & Copyright Journal (BNA), available in Lexis and Westlaw (BNA–PTCJ)

INTERNET (KF390.5 .C6)

Multi-Volume Treatises

George B. Delta & Jeffrey H. Matsuura, *Law of the Internet* (3d ed. 2009–date), available in CCH and Westlaw (LOTIN)

Raymond T. Nimmer, *Information Law* (2002–date), available in Westlaw (INFOLAW)

One-Volume Treatises and Hornbooks

Internet and Online Law (Kent D. Stuckey ed., 1996–date), available in Westlaw (IOLAW)

F. Lawrence Street & Mark P. Grant, *Law of the Internet* (3d ed. 2001–date)

Jane K. Winn & Benjamin Wright, *The Law of Electronic Commerce* (4th ed. 2001–date), available in CCH

Services

Electronic Commerce & Law Report (BNA), available in Lexis and Westlaw (BNA–ECLR)

Guide to Computer Law (CCH)

Internet Law & Regulation (Pike & Fischer)

LEGAL ETHICS (KF305–KF314)

Multi-Volume Treatises

Geoffrey C. Hazard, Jr. & W. William Hodes, *The Law of Lawyering* (3d ed. 2001–date)

Ronald E. Mallen & Jeffrey M. Smith, *Legal Malpractice* (annual), available in Westlaw (LMAL)

One-Volume Treatises

James J. Alfini et al., *Judicial Conduct and Ethics* (4th ed. 2007–date)

Ronald D. Rotunda & John S. Dzienkowski, *Legal Ethics: The Lawyer's Deskbook on Professional Responsibility* (annual), available in Westlaw (LEGETH)

Services

ABA/BNA Lawyer's Manual on Professional Conduct (BNA), available in Lexis and Westlaw (ABA–BNA)

National Reporter on Legal Ethics and Professional Responsibility (LexisNexis)

LOCAL GOVERNMENT (KF5300–KF5332)

Multi-Volume Treatises

Sandra M. Stevenson, *Antieau on Local Government Law* (2d ed. 1998–date), available in Lexis

John Martinez et al., *Local Government Law* (1981–date)

Eugene McQuillin et al., *The Law of Municipal Corporations* (3d ed. 1949–date), available in Westlaw (MUNICORP)

Hornbook

Osborne M. Reynolds, Jr., *Handbook of Local Government Law* (2d ed. 2001)

MILITARY LAW (KF7201–KF7695)

Multi-Volume Treatises

Francis A. Gilligan & Frederic I. Lederer, *Court-Martial Procedure* (3d ed. 2006–date), available in Lexis

Stephen A. Saltzburg et al., *Military Rules of Evidence Manual* (6th ed. 2006–date), available in Lexis

One-Volume Treatise

David A. Schlueter, *Military Criminal Justice: Practice and Procedure* (7th ed. 2008–date), available in Lexis

PARTNERSHIPS AND LIMITED LIABILITY COMPANIES (KF1371–KF1381)

Multi-Volume Treatises

Alan R. Bromberg & Larry E. Ribstein, *Bromberg and Ribstein on Partnership* (1988–date), available in CCH

Larry E. Ribstein & Robert R. Keatinge, *Ribstein and Keatinge on Limited Liability Companies* (2d ed. 2004–date)

One-Volume Treatises and Hornbooks

Carter G. Bishop & Daniel S. Kleinberger, *Limited Liability Companies: Tax and Business Law* (1994–date), available in Westlaw (WGL–LLC)

Alan R. Bromberg & Larry E. Ribstein, *Bromberg and Ribstein on Limited Liability Partnerships and the Revised Uniform Partnership Act* (annual), available in CCH

William A. Gregory, *The Law of Agency and Partnership* (3d ed. 2001), available in Westlaw (AGENCY–HB)

PRODUCTS LIABILITY (KF1296–KF1297)

Multi-Volume Treatises

American Law of Products Liability 3d (Russell J. Davis et al. eds., 1987–date)

Louis R. Frumer & Melvin I. Friedman, *Products Liability* (1960–date), available in Lexis

David G. Owen et al., *Madden & Owen on Products Liability* (3d ed. 2000–date), available in Westlaw (MOPL)

Hornbook

David G. Owen, *Products Liability Law* (2d ed. 2008), available in Westlaw (PRODLB–HB)

Services

Consumer Product Safety Guide (CCH)

Product Safety & Liability Reporter (BNA), available in Lexis and Westlaw (BNA–PSLR)

Products Liability Reports (CCH)

PROPERTY (KF560–KF720, KF5599)

Multi-Volume Treatises

John A. Borron, Jr., *The Law of Future Interests* (3d ed. 2002–date)

Friedman on Contracts and Conveyances of Real Property (James Charles Smith ed., 7th ed. 2005–date), available in Westlaw (PLIREF–CONREL)

Friedman on Leases (Patrick A. Randolph, Jr. ed., 5th ed. 2004–date), available in Westlaw (PLIREF–LEASES)

Michael T. Madison & Jeffry R. Dwyer, *The Law of Real Estate Financing* (rev. ed. 1994–date), available in Westlaw (REFINLAW)

Grant S. Nelson & Dale A. Whitman, *Real Estate Finance Law* (5th ed. 2007), available in Westlaw (REALFNLAW)

Powell on Real Property (Patrick J. Rohan ed., 1949–date), available in Lexis

Julius L. Sackman et al., *Nichols on Eminent Domain* (3d ed. 1964–date), available in Lexis

Thompson on Real Property (David A. Thomas ed., 1st/2d eds. 1994–date), available in Lexis

One-Volume Treatises and Hornbooks

Steven J. Eagle, *Regulatory Takings* (3d ed. 2005), available in Lexis

Grant S. Nelson & Dale A. Whitman, *Real Estate Finance Law* (5th ed. 2007)

John Rao et al., *Foreclosures: Defenses, Workouts, and Mortgage Servicing* (2d ed. 2007–date)

Walter G. Robillard & Lane J. Bouman, *Clark on Surveying and Boundaries* (7th ed. 1997–date), available in Lexis

Robert S. Schoshinski, *American Law of Landlord and Tenant* (1980–date)

William B. Stoebuck & Dale A. Whitman, *The Law of Property* (3d ed. 2000), available in Westlaw (PROPLAW–HB)

REMEDIES (KF9010–KF9039)

Multi-Volume Treatises

Dan B. Dobbs, *Dobbs Law of Remedies: Damages, Equity, Restitution* (2d ed. 1993)

George E. Palmer, *The Law of Restitution* (1978–date)

Linda L. Schlueter, *Punitive Damages* (5th ed. 2005–date), available in Lexis

Hornbook

Dan B. Dobbs, *Law of Remedies: Damages, Equity, Restitution* (2d ed. 1993)

SECURITIES (KF1066–KF1084, KF1428–KF1457)

Multi-Volume Treatises

Harold S. Bloomenthal, *Securities Law Handbook* (annual), available in Westlaw (SECLAW–HB)

Harold S. Bloomenthal & Samuel Wolff, *Securities and Federal Corporate Law* (2d ed. 1998–date), available in Westlaw (SECFEDCORP)

John T. Bostelman, *The Sarbanes–Oxley Deskbook* (2003–date), available in Westlaw (PLIREF–SAROX)

Alan R. Bromberg & Lewis D. Lowenfels, *Bromberg & Lowenfels on Securities Fraud and Commodities Fraud* (2d ed. 1994–date), available in Westlaw (SECBROMLOW)

Thomas Lee Hazen, *Treatise on the Law of Securities Regulation* (6th ed. 2009–date), available in Westlaw (LAWSECREG)

Philip McBride Johnson & Thomas Lee Hazen, *Derivatives Regulation* (2004–date), available in CCH

Joseph C. Long, *Blue Sky Law* (1985–date), available in Westlaw (SECBLUE)

Louis Loss et al., *Securities Regulation* (3d/4th eds. 1989–date), available in CCH

The Practitioner's Guide to the Sarbanes–Oxley Act (John J. Huber et al. eds., 2004–date)

One-Volume Treatises and Hornbooks

Gary M. Brown, *Soderquist on the Securities Laws* (5th ed. 2006–date), available in Westlaw (PLIREF–SECLAW)

Thomas Lee Hazen, *The Law of Securities Regulation* (5th ed. 2006)

Charles J. Johnson, Jr. & Joseph McLaughlin, *Corporate Finance and the Securities Laws* (4th ed. 2006–date), available in CCH

Louis Loss & Joel Seligman, *Fundamentals of Securities Regulation* (5th ed. 2004–date), available in CCH

Services

Blue Sky Law Reports (CCH), available in Lexis

Commodity Futures Law Reports (CCH), available in Lexis

Federal Securities Law Reports (CCH), available in Lexis

Securities Regulation & Law Report (BNA), available in Lexis and Westlaw (BNA–SRLR)

SPORTS (KF3989)

Multi-Volume Treatises

Martin J. Greenberg & James T. Gray, *Sports Law Practice* (2d ed. 1998–date)

Law of Professional and Amateur Sports (Gary A. Uberstine ed., 1988–date)

Hornbook

Walter T. Champion, Jr., *Fundamentals of Sports Law* (2d ed. 2004), available in Westlaw (SPORTSLAW)

TAXATION (KF6271–KF6645)

Multi-Volume Treatises

Boris I. Bittker & Lawrence Lokken, *Federal Taxation of Income, Estates, and Gifts* (2d/3d eds. 1989–date), available in Westlaw (WGL–IEG)

Ian M. Comisky et al., *Tax Fraud & Evasion* (1994–date), available in Westlaw (WGL–FRAUD)

Jerome R. Hellerstein & Walter Hellerstein, *State Taxation* (3d ed. 1998–date), available in Westlaw (WGL–STATE)

Joseph Isenbergh, *International Taxation: U.S. Taxation of Foreign Persons and Foreign Income* (4th ed. 2006–date)

Philip F. Postlewaite & Samuel A. Donaldson, *International Taxation: Corporate and Individual* (4th ed. 2003)

William S. McKee et al., *Federal Taxation of Partnerships and Partners* (4th ed. 2007–date), available in Westlaw (WGL–PARTNER)

Jacob Mertens, Jr., *The Law of Federal Income Taxation* (1942–date), available in Westlaw (MERTENS)

Boris I. Bittker & James Eustice, *Federal Taxation of Corporations and Shareholders* (7th ed. 2000–date), available in Westlaw (WGL–CORP)

Jacob Rabkin & Mark H. Johnson, *Federal Income, Gift and Estate Taxation* (1942–date), available in Lexis

Arthur B. Willis et al., *Partnership Taxation* (6th ed. 1997–date), available in Westlaw (WGL–PARTTAX)

One-Volume Treatises and Hornbooks

Boris I. Bittker et al., *Federal Income Taxation of Individuals* (3d ed. 2002–date), available in Westlaw (WGL–INDV)

James S. Eustice & Joel D. Kuntz, *Federal Income Taxation of S Corporations* (4th ed. 2001–date), available in Westlaw (WGL–SCORP)

Douglas A. Kahn & Jeffrey S. Lehman, *Corporate Income Taxation* (5th ed. 2001)

Michael I. Saltzman, *IRS Practice and Procedure* (rev. 2d ed. 2002–date), available in Westlaw (WGL–IRSPRAC)

Richard B. Stephens et al., *Federal Estate and Gift Taxation* (8th ed. 2002–date), available in Westlaw (WGL–GIFTAX)

Joshua D. Rosenberg & Dominic L. Daher, *The Law of Federal Income Taxation* (2008), available in Westlaw (FEDTAX–HB)

Services

All States Tax Guide (RIA)

Federal Estate and Gift Tax Reports (CCH), available in Lexis

Federal Excise Tax Reports (CCH), available in Lexis

Federal Tax Coordinator 2d (RIA)

Inheritance, Estate and Gift Tax Reports (CCH)

Standard Federal Tax Reports (CCH), available in Lexis

State Tax Guide (CCH), available in Lexis

Tax Management Portfolios (BNA), available in Lexis and Westlaw (BNA–TMALL)

United States Tax Reporter (RIA)

TORTS (KF1246–KF1327)

Multi-Volume Treatises

Dan B. Dobbs, *The Law of Torts* (2001–date)

Michael Dore, *The Law of Toxic Torts* (1987–date)

Louis R. Frumer et al., *Personal Injury: Actions, Defenses, Damages* (1957–date), available in Lexis

Oscar S. Gray, *Harper, James and Gray on Torts* (3d rev. ed. 2006–date)

J. D. Lee & Barry A. Lindahl, *Modern Tort Law: Liability and Litigation* (2d ed. 1990–date), available in Westlaw (MTLLL)

Marilyn K. Minzer et al., *Damages in Tort Actions* (1982–date), available in Lexis

Robert D. Sack, *Sack on Defamation: Libel, Slander, and Related Problems* (3d ed. 1999–date), available in Westlaw (PLIREF–DEFAM)

Rodney A. Smolla, *Law of Defamation* (2d ed. 1999–date), available in Westlaw (LDEF)

Stuart M. Speiser et al., *The American Law of Torts* (1983–date)

Jacob A. Stein, *Stein on Personal Injury Damages* (3d ed. 1997–date), available in Westlaw (STEIN)

Hornbook

Dan B. Dobbs, *The Law of Torts* (2000)

Service

Toxics Law Reporter (BNA), available in Lexis and Westlaw (BNA–TLR)

TRANSPORTATION (KF2181–KF2654)

Multi-Volume Treatises

Patrick D. Kelly, *Blashfield Automobile Law and Practice* (3d/4th eds. 1977–date)

Charles F. Krause & Kent C. Krause, *Aviation Tort and Regulatory Law* (2002–date), available in Westlaw (AVIATION)

Services

Aviation Law Reports (CCH)

Federal Carriers Reports (CCH)

Shipping Regulation (Pike & Fischer)

TRUSTS AND ESTATES (KF726–KF780)

Multi-Volume Treatises

George G. Bogert & George T. Bogert, *The Law of Trusts and Trustees* (2d/3d eds. 1977–date), available in Westlaw (BOGERT)

William J. Bowe & Douglas H. Parker, *Page on the Law of Wills* (1960–date), available in Lexis

A. James Casner & Jeffrey N. Pennell, *Estate Planning* (6th ed. 1995–date)

Austin Wakeman Scott et al., *Scott and Ascher on Trusts* (4th/5th eds. 1987–date)

One-Volume Treatises and Hornbooks

Jerome A. Manning et al., *Manning on Estate Planning* (6th ed. 2004–date), available in Lexis

William M. McGovern & Sheldon F. Kurtz, *Wills, Trusts and Estates* (3d ed. 2004), available in Westlaw (WILLS–HB)

David Westfall & George P. Mair, *Estate Planning Law & Taxation* (4th ed. 2001–date), available in Westlaw (WGL–EPTAX)

Services

Estate Planning and Taxation Coordinator (RIA)

Financial and Estate Planning (CCH), available in Lexis

ZONING AND LAND USE (KF5691–KF5710)

Multi-Volume Treatises

Arden H. Rathkopf & Daren A. Rathkopf, *Rathkopf's The Law of Zoning and Planning* (1975–date), available in Westlaw (RLZPN)

Patrick J. Rohan, *Zoning and Land Use Controls* (1977–date), available in Lexis

Patricia E. Salkin, *American Law of Zoning* (5th ed. 2008–date), available in Westlaw (AMLZONING)

Norman Williams, Jr. & John M. Taylor, *American Land Planning Law* (rev. ed. 2003–date), available in Westlaw (ALPLAW)

E. C. Yokley, *Zoning Law and Practice* (4th ed. 1978–date), available in Lexis

One-Volume Treatises and Hornbooks

Daniel R. Mandelker, *Land Use Law* (5th ed. 2003–date), available in Lexis

Julian Conrad Juergensmeyer & Thomas E. Roberts, *Land Use Planning and Development Regulation Law* (2d ed. 2007)

*

Table of Cases

A

Acker v. Acker, 821 So.2d 1088 (Fla.App. 3 Dist.2002)—§ **6.2, n. 8.**

Anastasoff v. United States, 223 F.3d 898 (8th Cir.2000)—§ **7.2, n. 32.**

Andreshak v. Service Heat Treating, Inc., 439 F.Supp.2d 898 (E.D.Wis. 2006)—§ **8.5, n. 16.**

Appalachian Power Co. v. E.P.A., 208 F.3d 1015, 341 U.S.App.D.C. 46 (D.C.Cir.2000)—§ **5.2, n. 68.**

B

Bank One Chicago, N.A. v. Midwest Bank & Trust Co., 516 U.S. 264, 116 S.Ct. 637, 133 L.Ed.2d 635 (1996)— § **4, n. 1.**

Blanchard v. Bergeron, 489 U.S. 87, 109 S.Ct. 939, 103 L.Ed.2d 67 (1989)— § **4.1, n. 10.**

Brown v. Allen, 344 U.S. 443, 73 S.Ct. 437, 97 L.Ed. 469 (1953)—§ **6.1, n. 2.**

C

California v. Cabazon Band of Mission Indians, 480 U.S. 202, 107 S.Ct. 1083, 94 L.Ed.2d 244 (1987)—§ **1.1, n. 4.**

Campbell ex rel. Campbell v. Secretary of Health and Human Services, 69 Fed. Cl. 775 (2006)—§ **1.3, n. 16.**

Carroll, United States v., 105 F.3d 740 (1st Cir.1997)—§ **3.4, n. 39.**

Case Concerning Certain Property (Liechtenstein v. Germany), 2005 I.C.J. 6 (Feb. 10)—§ **13.6.**

Cass v. United States, 417 U.S. 72, 94 S.Ct. 2167, 40 L.Ed.2d 668 (1974)— § **3.4, n. 31.**

Cervase v. Office of the Federal Register, 580 F.2d 1166 (3rd Cir.1978)—§ **5.2, n. 61.**

D

Detroit Timber & Lumber Co., United States v., 200 U.S. 321, 26 S.Ct. 282, 50 L.Ed. 499 (1906)—§ **6.3, n. 10.**

Diffenderfer v. Diffenderfer, 491 So.2d 265 (Fla.1986)—§ **6.2, n. 8.**

E

Ellison v. Brady, 924 F.2d 872 (9th Cir. 1991)—§ **4.1, n. 18.**

F

Federal Crop Ins. Corp. v. Merrill, 332 U.S. 380, 68 S.Ct. 1, 92 L.Ed. 10 (1947)—§ **5.2, n. 39.**

Fourco Glass Co. v. Transmirra Products Corp., 353 U.S. 222, 77 S.Ct. 787, 1 L.Ed.2d 786 (1957)—§ **3.4, n. 31.**

Frigaliment Importing Co. v. B.N.S. Intern. Sales Corp., 190 F.Supp. 116 (S.D.N.Y.1960)—§ **3.2, n. 8.**

G

Garcia, People v., 29 A.D.3d 255, 812 N.Y.S.2d 66 (N.Y.A.D. 1 Dept. 2006)—§ **8.1.**

Glover v. Johnson, 931 F.Supp. 1360 (E.D.Mich.1996)—§ **1.4, n. 24.**

Goree v. State, 163 P.3d 583 (Okla.Crim. App.2007)—§ **6.2.**

Gozlon–Peretz v. United States, 498 U.S. 395, 111 S.Ct. 840, 112 L.Ed.2d 919 (1991)—§ **4.1, n. 24.**

H

Hamdan v. Rumsfeld, 548 U.S. 557, 126 S.Ct. 2749, 165 L.Ed.2d 723 (2006)— § **4.1, n. 19.**

*

Resource Index

References are to Pages
Boldface references are to Illustrations
See also Subject Index

Subject Index

References are to Pages
Boldface references are to Illustrations
See also Resource Index

†